Third International Conference on Dependency Linguistics

(Depling 2015)

Uppsala, Sweden
24 – 26 August 2015

ISBN: 978-1-5108-0816-4

Printed from e-media with permission by:

Curran Associates, Inc.
57 Morehouse Lane
Red Hook, NY 12571

Some format issues inherent in the e-media version may also appear in this print version.

Printed by Curran Associates, Inc. (2015)

For permission requests, please contact the Association for Computational Linguistics at the address below.

Association for Computational Linguistics
209 N. Eighth Street
Stroudsburg, Pennsylvania 18360

Phone: 1-570-476-8006
Fax: 1-570-476-0860

acl@aclweb.org

Additional copies of this publication are available from:

Curran Associates, Inc.
57 Morehouse Lane
Red Hook, NY 12571 USA
Phone: 845-758-0400
Fax: 845-758-2634
Email: curran@proceedings.com
Web: www.proceedings.com

Depling 2015

Third International Conference on Dependency Linguistics

Proceedings of the Conference

August 24–26 2015
Uppsala University
Uppsala, Sweden

Preface

The Depling 2015 conference in Uppsala is the third meeting in the newly established series of international conferences on dependency linguistics started in Barcelona 2011 and continued in Prague in 2013. The initiative to organize special meetings devoted to dependency linguistics, which is currently at the forefront of both theoretical and computational linguistics, has received great support from the community. We do hope that the present conference will manage to keep up the high standards set by the meetings in Barcelona and Prague.

This year we received a record number of 48 submissions, 37 of which were accepted for an acceptance rate of 77%. One paper was later withdrawn, making the total number of papers appearing in this proceedings volume 36. The 2015 edition of Depling has two special themes. The first is the status of function words, which attracted a large number of submissions. The second is translation and parallel corpora, which also saw a number of good papers. All in all, the proceedings contain a wide range of contributions to dependency linguistics, ranging from papers advancing new theoretical models, through empirical studies of one or more languages, to experimental investigations of computational systems – and many others topics in between. In addition to the contributed papers, this volume also introduces our two distinguished keynote speakers: Christopher Manning and Alain Polguère.

Our sincere thanks go to the members of the program committee, listed elsewhere in this volume, who thoroughly reviewed all the submissions to the conference and ensured the quality of the published papers. Thanks also to Nils Blomqvist who did a great job in putting the proceedings together and to Bengt Dahlqvist for keeping the conference website in great shape. Thanks finally to everyone who chose to submit their work to Depling 2015, without whom this volume literally would not exist. We welcome you all to Depling 2015 in Uppsala and wish you an enjoyable conference!

Eva Hajičová and Joakim Nivre
Program Co-Chairs, Depling 2015

Organizers

Local Arrangements Chair:

Joakim Nivre, Uppsala University

Program Co-Chairs:

Eva Hajičová, Charles University in Prague
Joakim Nivre, Uppsala University

Invited Speakers:

Christopher Manning, Stanford University
Alain Polguère, Université de Lorraine ATILF CNRS

Program Committee:

Margarita Alonso-Ramos, Universidade da Coruña
Miguel Ballesteros, Pompeu Fabra University
David Beck, University of Alberta
Xavier Blanco, Universitat Autònoma de Barcelona
Igor Boguslavsky, Universidad Politecnica de Madrid and Russian Academy of Sciences
Bernd Bohnet, Google
Marie Candito, Université Paris Diderot / INRIA
Jinho Choi, University of Colorado at Boulder
Benoit Crabbé, Université Paris 7 and INRIA
Eric De La Clergerie, INRIA
Marie-Catherine de Marneffe, The Ohio State University
Denys Duchier, Université d'Orléans
Dina El Kassas, Minya University
Gülsen Eryigit, Istanbul Technical University
Kim Gerdes, Sorbonne Nouvelle
Filip Ginter, University of Turku
Koldo Gojenola, University of the Basque Country UPV/EHU
Yoav Goldberg, Bar-Ilan University
Carlos Gómez-Rodríguez, Universidade da Coruña
Thomas Gross, Aichi University
Jan Hajič, Charles University in Prague
Hans Jürgen Heringer, University of Augsburg
Richard Hudson, University College London
Leonid Iomdin, Russian Academy of Sciences
Aravind Joshi, University of Pennsylvania
Sylvain Kahane, Université Paris Ouest Nanterre
Marco Kuhlmann, Linköping University
François Lareau, Université de Montréal
Haitao Liu, Zhejiang University

Table of Contents

The Case for Universal Dependencies

Christopher Manning
Stanford University
Department of Computer Science
manning@cs.stanford.edu

Universal Dependencies is a recent initiative to develop a linguistically informed, cross-linguistically consistent dependency grammar analysis and treebanks for many languages, with the goal of enabling multilingual natural language processing applications of parsing and natural language understanding. I outline the needs behind the initiative and how some of the design principles follow from these requirements. I suggest that the design of Universal Dependencies tries to optimize a quite subtle trade-off between a number of goals: an analysis which is reasonably satisfactory on linguistic grounds, an analysis that is reasonably comprehensible to non-linguist users, an analysis which can be automatically applied with good accuracy, and an analysis which supports language understanding tasks, such as relation extraction. I suggest that this is best achieved by a simple, fairly spartan lexicalist approach, which focuses on capturing a level of analysis of (syntactic) grammatical relations, something that can be found similarly defined in many theories of syntax. We take hope from the fact that already many people, coming from quite different syntactic traditions, have felt that Universal Dependencies is near enough to right that they can join the effort and contribute. However, the current proposal is certainly not perfect, and I will also touch on some of the thorny issues and how the current standard might yet be improved.

Proceedings of the Third International Conference on Dependency Linguistics (Depling 2015), page 1,
Uppsala, Sweden, August 24–26 2015.

Lexicon Embedded Syntax

Alain Polguère
ATILF UMR 7118, CNRS-Université de Lorraine
44 avenue de la Libération, BP 30687
54063 Nancy cedex, France
alain.polguere@univ-lorraine.fr

Abstract

This paper explores the notion of lexicon embedded syntax: syntactic structures that are preassembled in natural language lexicons. Section 1 proposes a lexicological perspective on (dependency) syntax: first, it deals with the well-known problem of lexicon-grammar dichotomy, then introduces the notion of lexicon embedded syntax and, finally, presents the lexical models this discussion is based on: lexical systems, as implemented in the English and French Lexical Networks. Two cases of lexicon embedded syntax are then treated: the syntax of idioms, section 2, and the syntax of collocations, section 3. Section 4 concludes on the possible exploitation of syntactic structures that can be extracted from lexical systems.

1 Lexicological Perspective on Syntax

1.1 Lexicon-Grammar Dichotomy

The task of modeling languages is often equated with a task of writing so-called *grammars*. This is clearly demonstrated by the fact that most theoretical proposals in modern linguistics are designated as specific types of grammars: Generative Grammar, Case Grammar, Lexical Functional Grammar, Word Grammar, Generalized Phrase Structure Grammar, Construction Grammar(s), Role and Reference Grammar, Functional Discourse Grammar, etc. (Polguère, 2011, pp 82–83). It should be noted that this focalization on an all-encompassing notion of grammar runs deep. For instance, the 1795 law that created the school of oriental language studies in France (INALCO[1]) specified as follows the linguistic descriptive task assigned to its professors:

> "Lesdits professeurs composeront en français la grammaire des langues qu'ils enseigneront: ces divers ouvrages seront remis au comité d'instruction publique."[2]

No mention of a need to compile **dictionaries** for oriental languages, as if it were natural to designate with the term *grammar* the main tool to be used by XVIIIth century officials and merchants for communicating with "locals". It should be stressed that this rather confusing notion of Grammar – with a capital *G* – is extremely broad and encompasses the set of **all** linguistic rules that make up a natural language. It is distinct from the grammar as a language module that stands in opposition with its functional counterpart: the lexicon. Both linguistic modules have been loosely characterized as follows by O. Jespersen – in terms of their corresponding fields of study:

> "[g]rammar deals with the general facts of language, and lexicology with special facts" (Jespersen, 1924, p 32).

In the present discussion, we will strictly abide by the above characterization and consider the grammar of a language as being the system of all general rules of that language – i.e. rules that are not properties assigned to given words – and the lexicon of that language as being the system of all its word-specific rules.

It is a well-established fact that there exists a blurry demarcation between grammar and lexicon (Keizer, 2007). Rules that are specific to linguistic entities that present analogies with "words" but are not strictly speaking lexical units are less lexical in nature and possess a certain grammatical flavor. For instance, rules that account for the properties

[1] http://www.inalco.fr

[2] 'Said professors will elaborate in French the grammar of languages they will be teaching: these various books will be submitted to the public instruction committee.'

Proceedings of the Third International Conference on Dependency Linguistics (Depling 2015), pages 2–9,
Uppsala, Sweden, August 24–26 2015.

of bound morphemes (the English derivative suffix *-ly*, the prefix *poly-*, etc.) belong to the lexicon because they are specific to a linguistic sign, hence not general, but they are borderline due to the morphological nature of the sign in question. In what follows, quite a few linguistic entities will be presented as belonging to lexical models based on this preliminary characterization of the respective scope of grammar and lexicon and in spite of widespread practices that may tend to view lexicons strictly as repositories of lexical units.

1.2 Focus on Lexicon Embedded Syntax

Another factor that blurs the lexicon-grammar partition is the very fact that, in any natural language, a considerable number of syntactic structures are preassembled in the lexicon. Valency-controlled dependencies – whose modeling is directly relevant to lexicological studies – are the most obvious manifestation of this phenomenon. A valency dictionary or lexical database (Fillmore et al., 2003; Mertens, 2010) is nothing but a lexicographic description of a significant part of lexicon embedded syntax. This fact is now widely acknowledged. What is much less known and/or taken into account, specially in Natural Language Processing, is the extent to which syntactic structures of natural languages find their origins in lexicons, thanks to the omnipresence of phraseology (Becker, 1975).

In what follows, we will focus of two types of lexicon embedded syntactic structures:

- lexico-syntactic structures of idioms (section 2);
- collocational syntactic structures (section 3).

We are particularly interested in showing how a rich formal lexical model (see 1.3 below) can account for lexicon embedded syntax and serve as repository of "canned" syntactic structures that are directly extractable from lexical data.

1.3 Lexical Systems

In order to provide data for the proper treatment of lexicon embedded syntax, lexical models need to have "phraseological genes": they have to be based on theoretical and descriptive principles that fully take into consideration the omnipresence of phraseology in natural languages. Such is the case of Explanatory Combinatorial Lexicology (Mel'čuk et al., 1995; Mel'čuk, 2006), that is being used as theoretical background in the present discussion. More specifically, we will refer to a new type of lexical model built within this framework – lexical systems (Polguère, 2009) –, using two specific instances of such models: the *English* and *French Lexical Networks* – hereafter, *en-* and *fr-LNs*.

Lexical systems are huge graphs of interconnected lexical entities. Polguère (2014) discusses the rationale behind the choice of this particular type of structure, formally characterized by four main properties.

Property 1. The lexical system of a language $\mathscr{L}$ is mathematically defined as an oriented graph: a set of nodes and a set of oriented edges (= ordered pairs of nodes).

- Nodes correspond, first, to lexical units of $\mathscr{L}$ (lexemes and idioms) and, second, to quasi-lexical units (linguistic clichés, proverbial clauses, etc.).
- Edges correspond primarily to Meaning-Text lexical function relations (Mel'čuk, 1996).[3]

Property 2. Nodes of the graph are non-atomic entities. They are "containers" for a rich variety of semantic and combinatorial information about the corresponding unit (grammatical characteristics, definition, etc.); they also contain pointers to lexicographic examples (sense illustrations), their content being informationally analogous to that of dictionary articles (Polguère, 2014, pp 15–16).

Property 3. Lexical systems possess a non-ontological graph structure that belongs to the family of so-called *small-world networks*. As such, they display remarkable mathematical properties (Gader et al., 2014, §3) that can be used to extract node clusters corresponding to *semantic spaces* (Polguère, 2014, §2.2.2).

Property 4. Each important piece of information in lexical systems (existence of a lexical unit, assignment of a grammatical characteristic, lexical link, etc.) possesses an associated measure of

[3]Other relations are, at the moment: copolysemy links (FOREST**1** [*of oak trees*] and FOREST**2** [*of antennas*] belong to the same polysemic vocable and are connected by a relation of metaphor), definitional inclusions (the meaning of DOG is included in the definition of [to] BARK) and formal inclusions (the lexeme BULLET is formally included in the lexico-syntactic structure of the idiom BITE THE BULLET) – we will examine this latter type of relation in section 2 below.

confidence that can be used to perform probabilistic computing on the graph. Measurement of confidence is particularly relevant for the implementation of *analogical reasoning* on lexical models.

Figure 1 illustrates the graph structure of lexical systems. It visualizes a semantic space controlled by the French lexeme FORÊT I 'forest' in the fr-LN. In this figure, spatialization and coloring of nodes visualize the result of an automatic semantic clustering performed on the lexical graph; this mode of visualization reflects semantic proximity inferred from the topology of the graph (Chudy et al., 2013).

Work on lexical systems started with experiments on the mechanical compilation of traditional Explanatory and Combinatorial models (Polguère, 2009), then evolved into full-scale lexicography with the construction of the fr-LN, the first manually-built lexical system (Lux-Pogodalla and Polguère, 2011; Gader et al., 2012). While lexicographically developing the fr-LN, a first version of a lexical system for the English language – the en-LN – has been automatically compiled from the Princeton WordNet (Gader et al., 2014). This latter lexical system offers a large-scale coverage of English in terms of wordlist. It is however essentially based on synonymy-like relations, inherited from WordNet; only the fr-LN fully reflects the amplitude of both paradigmatic and syntagmatic lexical function relations. Additionally, it is only in the fr-LN that the actual Explanatory Combinatorial approach to phraseology is fully implemented at present. For this reason, we will need to use both French and English illustrations in the following discussion, depending on the availability of data in the current language models.

Table 1 gives statistics on the en- and fr-LNs in their present state.

Graph characteriscs	**en-LN**	**fr-LN**
Num. lexical units = senses (LU)	206 995	26 020
Num. vocables = dict. entries (V)	156 587	16 981
Polysemy rate (LU/V)	1.32	1.53
Num. lexical functions links (LFL)	945 971	49 539
Num. other links (OL)	46	13 672
Connectivity rate ((LFL+OL)/LU)	4.57	2.43

Table 1: Current statistics on the en- and fr-LNs

2 Syntax of Idioms

We can now proceed with the examination of the first type of lexicon embedded syntax: the syntax of idioms. By this we mean lexico-syntactic structures that are associated with idioms in the fr-LN.[4]

Because they are semantically non-compositional, idioms are considered as full-fledged lexical units in Explanatory Combinatorial Lexicology. For this reason, they possess, just like lexemes, their own individual description in the fr-LN.

On the one hand, the behavior of idioms is known to be highly irregular (for instance, some idioms allow syntactic modification on some of their lexical constituents and other do not); on the other hand, it can be expected that general rules could be identified that condition part of idioms' behaviors, based on their lexico-syntactic structure. For this reason, it has been decided to specify, for each individual idiom in the fr-LN wordlist, its constitutive lexemes and its basic syntactic structure (Pausé, to appear). This is implemented as follows.

First, each phrasal part of speech – nominal idiom, verbal idiom, etc. – is linked to a set of syntactic templates that identify possible syntactic structures for idioms belonging to this part of speech. For instance, the *verbal idiom* part of speech (Fr. *locution verbale*) is associated, among others, with a syntactic template named `V Art NC` ('Verb + Article + Common noun') that designates the syntactic structure shown in Figure 2.

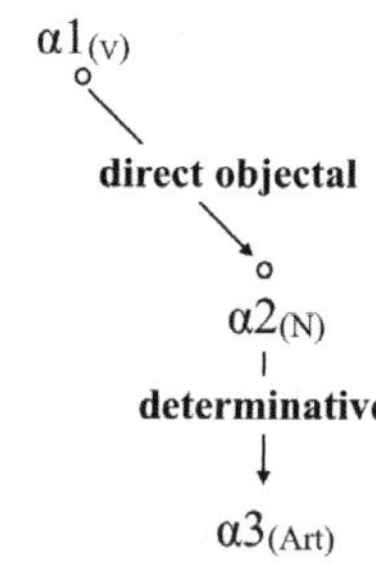

Figure 2: Syntactic structure of the `V Art NC` idiom template.

Second, each time an idiom is created in the fr-LN, two operations are performed:

1. the newly created idiom is linked to one of the syntactic templates associated to its part of speech;

[4]Work on assigning lexico-syntactic structures to idioms in the en-LN has not started yet and all our examples in this section will therefore be borrowed from French.

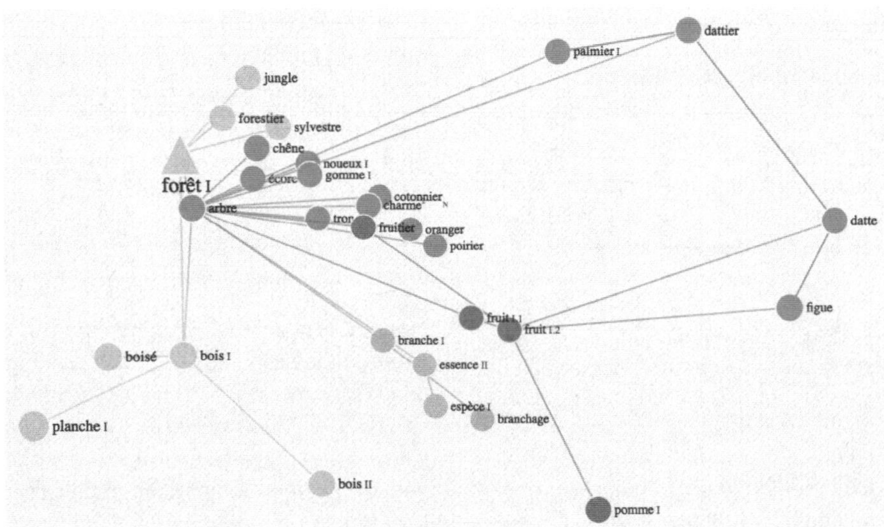

Figure 1: Semantic space controlled by Fr. FORÊT I 'forest' in the French Lexical Network (fr-LN)

2. lexical nodes in this syntactic template are linked to actual lexical units that make up the idiom.

For instance, Figure 3 shows how the lexico-syntactic structure of the idiom ⌜SUCRER LES FRAISES I⌝ 'to tremble because of advanced age' (lit. 'to sugar.the.strawberries')[5] is specified on the `V Art NC` template using the fr-LN lexicographic editor. In this figure, names appearing in the `Sense` column correspond to actual pointers to lexemes (senses) of the fr-LN; names in the `Form` column are only wordforms that will be used when displaying the instantiated syntactic template. (If nothing is specified, the name in the corresponding `Sense` cell will be displayed.)

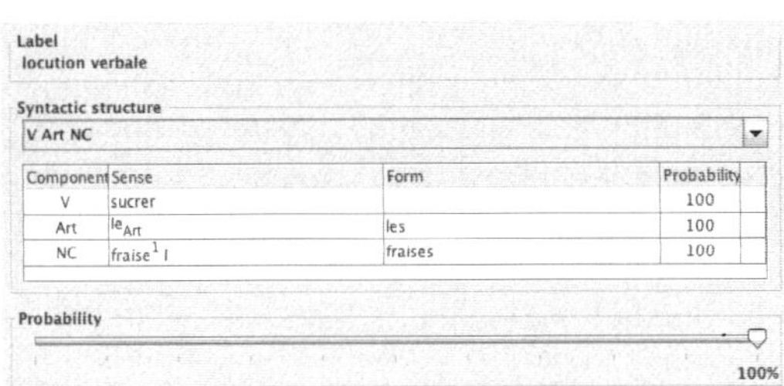

Figure 3: Specifying a lexico-syntactic structure.

Once the lexico-syntactic structure of ⌜SUCRER LES FRAISES I⌝ has been fully instanciated (Figure 3), in can be interpreted by the general – hence, grammatical – syntactic template of Figure 2 in order to derive the fully lexicalized syntactic structure shown in Figure 4.[6]

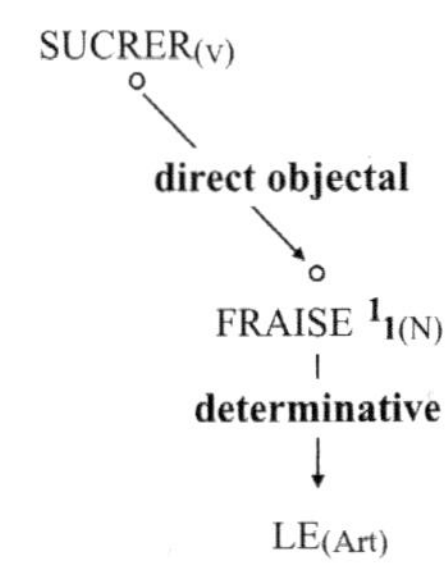

Figure 4: Syntax of ⌜SUCRER LES FRAISES I⌝.

To our knowledge, the fr-LN is the first lexical database that systematically accounts for the lexico-syntactic structure of idioms it contains – in point of fact, current lexical resources seldom provide individual descriptions for idioms. At present, it is possible to derive from fr-LN data 3,018 syntactic structures of individual idioms (such as that in Figure 4), which is only a small portion of the syntax of idioms embedded in the French lexicon.

[5]There is another sense ⌜SUCRER LES FRAISES II⌝, derived from the first one, that means 'to be senile'.

[6]An important piece of information is missing in this structure: the fact that the lexeme FRAISE $^{1}{}_{1}$ has to carry the grammeme 'plural' (⌜*sucrer les fraises*⌝ and not *⌜*sucrer la fraise*⌝). The fr-LN does not support yet the specification of grammemes in idiom syntactic structures.

3 Syntax of Collocations

3.1 Functional notion of collocation

We now examined a second case of lexicon embedded syntax: the syntax of collocations. *Collocation* is understood here as designating a functional rather than statistical notion (Hausmann, 1979); it can be defined as follows.

> A collocation, e.g. *to run a fever*, is a phraseological **but** compositional phrase made up of two main elements:
>
> 1. a semantically autonomous element – *fever* – called *base* of the collocation;
> 2. a bound element – *to run* – called *collocate* of the base; the collocate is said to be bound, or not "free", because its selection by the Speaker in order to express a given meaning depends on the prior selection of the base.

As collocations are modeled in lexical systems by means of standard syntagmatic lexical functions, we will start with a brief presentation of the notion of lexical functions (3.2). We will then proceed with the interpretation of syntagmatic lexical functions as a special type of grammar rules (3.3). Finally (3.4), we will show how such rules can be used to derive a considerable amount syntactic structures embedded in natural language lexicons.

3.2 Standard Lexical Functions

A given standard lexical function is a generalization of a lexical link that possesses the following properties:

- it is either paradigmatic (synonyms, antonyms, nominalizations, verbalizations, actant names, etc.) or syntagmatic (collocates that are intensifiers [***driving*** *rain*], light verbs [***to run*** *a fever*], etc.);
- it is recurrent and universally present in natural languages;
- it is often (though not necessarily) expressed by morphological means (*drive* → ***driver*** [actant name], *store* → ***megastore*** [intensifier], etc.).

For instance, **Magn** is the standard lexical function that denotes collocational intensifiers; it can be applied to any full lexical unit in order to return the set of all typical intensifiers for that unit.[7] This is illustrated in (1), with the two semantically related units FEVER and HEADACHE as arguments of **Magn**.

(1) a. **Magn**(*fever*) = *high* < *raging*
  b. **Magn**(*headache*) = *bad, severe* < *terrible, violent* < *pounding, splitting*

Note that collocative meanings can sometimes be expressed synthetically (within a paradigmatically related term) rather than analytically (as collocates). This phenomenon is call *fusion* and fused values of syntagmatic lexical functions are flagged with the "//" symbol in lexicographic descriptions; for instance:

(2) **Magn**($rain_V$) = *hard, heavily, //pour down*

Years of lexical studies on a wide spectrum of natural languages have allowed for the identification of a now stable set of approximately 65 *simple lexical functions*;[8] additionally, these functions can be combined to form *complex lexical functions* (Kahane and Polguère, 2001).

The system of lexical functions is a descriptive tool that allows for a rationalization and formalization of the web of paradigmatic and syntagmatic links that connect lexical units in natural languages. This explains why we have adopted lexical functions as the main structuring principle for lexical systems.

3.3 Standard Syntagmatic Lexical Functions as Grammar Rules

We will now focus on standard syntagmatic lexical functions in order to examine how they offer an original treatment of the syntax of collocations. For this, we will use as illustration one specific standard syntagmatic lexical function: $\textbf{Real}_1$. It is commonly characterized as follows.

> The lexical function application $\textbf{Real}_1$(L) stands for a full verb:
>
> - that expresses such meanings as 'to realize L', 'to do what is supposed to be done as regards to L' . . . ;

[7] A lexical function is thus quite similar to an algebraic function **f**, that can be applied to a given number x in order to return a given value y: $\mathbf{f}(x) = y$.

[8] The exact number of lexical functions varies according to the descriptive granularity one wants to adopt.

- that takes L as second deep-syntactic actant (i.e. first complement) and the first deep-syntactic actant of L as its first deep-syntactic actant (i.e. grammatical subject).[9]

In case of fusion, the meaning 'L' is encapsulated in the meaning of the lexical function application, together with the sense of realization, and therefore //**Real**$_1$(L) doesn't take L as second syntactic actant.

As an illustration, Figure 5 gives the so-called *article-view* of **Real**$_1$ values for BALLOON$_N$ **2** [*We could get there by balloon.*] in the en-LN.[10]

[X] uses a ~
Real$_1$: **fly**$_V$ 3 [ART ~], **pilot**$_V$ 1 [ART ~], **//balloon**$_V$ 1

Figure 5: **Real**$_1$(*balloon*$_N$ **2**) in the en-LN.

Standard lexical functions such as **Real**$_1$ can be conceptualized from at least two perspectives.

- From the viewpoint of the structure of lexical knowledge, they are universal relations that paradigmatically and syntagmatically connect lexical units within lexical systems.
- From the viewpoint of the universal system of deep-syntactic paraphrasing (Mel'čuk, 2013, Chap. 9), they are "meta lexical units" whose application to a given lexical unit (argument of the lexical function) stands for a set possible lexicalizations in a deep-syntactic structure.

In this latter case, it is important to note that each standard syntagmatic lexical function actually denotes two dependency structures: one for "normal" values of the lexical function application and one for "fused" values. Therefore, the two deep-syntactic trees[11] in Figure 6 are inherently associated to **Real**$_1$.

If we refer to what was said earlier about the lexicon-grammar dichotomy (section 1.1), we are entitled to consider that trees in Figure 6, because they correspond to general (in this case, universal) linguistic rules about syntactic structuring, are in essence grammatical: they designate syntactic potential that can be run on any lexical rules of the type illustrated in Figure 5 in order to participate in the generation of actual surface-syntactic structures.

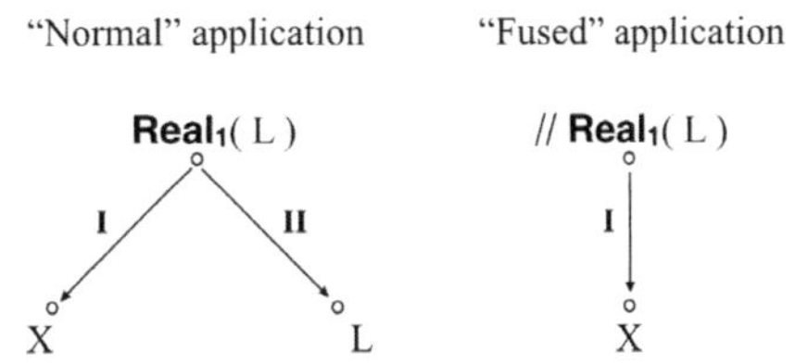

Figure 6: **Real**$_1$'s Deep-syntactic structures.

3.4 Deriving surface-syntactic structures

In this particular case, rules in Figures 5 and 6 allow for the generation of the three surface-syntactic structures in Figure 7.

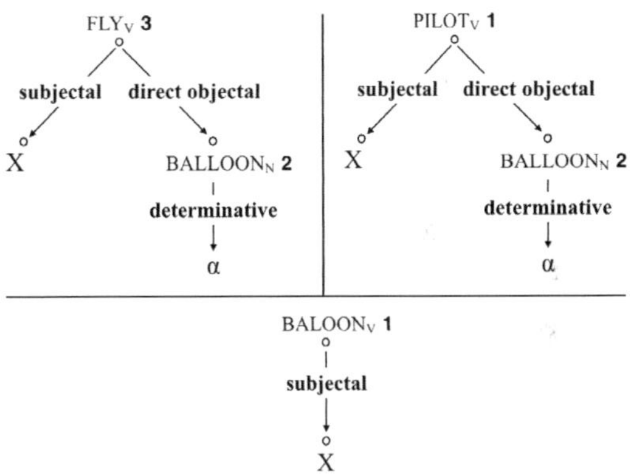

Figure 7: Derived surface-syntactic structures.

If we consider the prospect of such derivation throughout a full lexical system for a given language, we see that a considerable amount of lexicon embedded syntactic structures are extractable from these models. At present, a total number of 7,739 surface-syntactic micro-structures of the type given in Figure 7 can be extracted from the fr-LN.[12] This is of course only a small portion of what is available in the actual French lexicon.

[9] On the notions of semantic and deep-/surface-syntactic actants, see Mel'čuk (2015, Chap. 12).

[10] An article-view, in the lexicographic editor used for building the en- and fr-LNs, is a textual rendering of lexical data associated with a given headword. For details on how lexical function applications are computationally encoded in the en- and fr-LNs, see Gader et al. (2012).

[11] For a concise presentation of Meaning-Text levels of sentence representation and the deep- *vs.* surface-syntax dichotomy, see Kahane (2003).

[12] This corresponds to the number of syntagmatic lexical function relations already woven in the fr-LN.

4 Conclusion: Lexicalized Grammars the Other Way Round

By presenting the syntax of idioms and collocations, we hope to have shown that syntactic information embedded in natural language lexicons goes far beyond phenomena associated to active valency (subcategorization frames). Lexicon embedded syntax is conceptually **and quantitatively** an essential element of lexical knowledge.

It was also our goal to demonstrate that lexical systems such as the fr-LN are particularly suited to the modeling of embedded syntax. In our view, one very promising exploitation of such models for Natural Language Processing (NLP) is the use of large collections of extracted syntactic structures by NLP parsers, for such tasks as disambiguation or processing of phraseological expressions found in corpora.

Collections of syntactic structures extractable from lexical systems bear some conceptual resemblance with *lexicalized grammars* (Schabes et al., 1988), except for the fact that the perspective is totally inverted: rather than lexicalizing grammars, we propose to extract from lexical systems everything actual grammars do not know about syntax.

Acknowledgments

Lexicographic work on the French Lexical Network (fr-LN) originally started at the ATILF CNRS laboratory (Nancy, France) in the context of the RELIEF project funded by the Agence de Mobilisation Économique de Lorraine (AMEL) and the European Regional Development Fund (ERDF).

References

Joseph D. Becker. 1975. The Phrasal Lexicon. In: *Proceedings of the 1975 Workshop on Theoretical Issues in Natural Language Processing (TINLAP'75)*. Association for Computational Linguistics, Cambridge, Mass., 60–63.

Yannick Chudy, Yann Desalle, Benoıt Gaillard, Bruno Gaume, Pierre Magistry and Emmanuel Navarro. 2013. Tmuse: Lexical Network Exploration. In: *The Companion Volume of the Proceedings of IJCNLP 2013: System Demonstrations*. Asian Federation of NLP, Nagoya, 41–44.

Charles J. Fillmore, Christopher R. Johnson and Miriam R. L. Petruck. 2003. Background to FrameNet. *International Journal of Lexicography*, 16(3):235–250.

Nabil Gader, Veronika Lux-Pogodalla and Alain Polguère. 2012. Hand-Crafting a Lexical Network With a Knowledge-Based Graph Editor. In: *Proceedings of the Third Workshop on Cognitive Aspects of the Lexicon (CogALex III)*. The COLING 2012 Organizing Committee, Mumbai, 109–125.

Nabil Gader, Sandrine Ollinger and Alain Polguère. 2014. One Lexicon, Two Structures: So What Gives? In Heili Orav, Christiane Fellbaum and Piek Vossen (eds.): *Proceedings of the Seventh Global Wordnet Conference (GWC2014)*. Global WordNet Association, Tartu, 163–171.

Franz Josef Hausmann. 1979. Un dictionnaire des collocations est-il possible? *Travaux de littérature et de linguistique de l'Université de Strasbourg*, XVII(1):187–195.

Otto Jespersen. 1924. *The Philosophy of Grammar*. George Allen & Unwin, London.

Sylvain Kahane. 2003. The Meaning-Text Theory. In Vilmos Ágel, Ludwig M. Eichinger, Hans Werner Eroms, Peter Hellwig, Hans Jürgen Heringer and Henning Lobin (eds.): *Dependency and Valency. An International Handbook of Contemporary Research*. Handbücher zur Sprach- und Kommunikationswissenschaft / Handbooks of Linguistics and Communication Science, de Gruyter, Berlin & New York, 546–569.

Sylvain Kahane and Alain Polguère. 2001. Formal Foundation of Lexical Functions. In: *Proceedings of "COLLOCATION: Computational Extraction, Analysis and Exploitation"*. 39th Annual Meeting and 10th Conference of the European Chapter of the Association for Computational Linguistics, Toulouse, 8–15.

Evelien Keizer. 2007. The lexical-grammatical dichotomy in Functional Discourse Grammar. *Alfa – Revista de Lingüística*, 51(2):35–56.

Veronika Lux-Pogodalla and Alain Polguère. 2011. Construction of a French Lexical Network: Methodological Issues. In: *Proceedings of the First International Workshop on Lexical Resources, WoLeR 2011. An ESSLLI 2011 Workshop*. Ljubljana, 54–61.

Igor Mel'čuk. 1996. Lexical Functions: A Tool for the Description of Lexical Relations in the Lexicon. In Leo Wanner (ed.): *Lexical Functions in Lexicography and Natural Language Processing*. Studies in Language Companion Series 31, John Benjamins, Amsterdam/Philadelphia, 37–102.

Igor Mel'čuk. 2006. Explanatory Combinatorial Dictionary. In Giandomenico Sica (ed.): *Open Problems in Linguistics and Lexicography*. Polimetrica, Monza, 225–355.

Igor Mel'čuk. 2013. *Semantics: From meaning to text*, volume 2. Studies in Language Companion Series 135, John Benjamins, Amsterdam/Philadelphia.

Igor Mel'čuk. 2015. *Semantics: From meaning to text*, volume 3. Studies in Language Companion Series 168, John Benjamins, Amsterdam/Philadelphia.

Igor Mel'čuk, André Clas and Alain Polguère. 1995. *Introduction à la lexicologie explicative et combinatoire*. Duculot, Paris/Louvain-la-Neuve.

Piet Mertens. 2010. Restrictions de sélection et réalisations syntagmatiques dans DICOVALENCE. Conversion vers un format utilisable en TAL. In: *Proceedings of TALN 2010*. Montréal.

Marie-Sophie Pausé. To appear. Modélisation de la structure lexico-syntaxique des locutions au sein d'un réseau lexical. In Maurice Kauffer (ed.): *Actes du colloque international "Approches théoriques et empiriques en phraséologie"*. Eurogermanistik Series, Stauffenburg Verlag, Tübingen.

Alain Polguère. 2009. Lexical systems: graph models of natural language lexicons. *Language Resources and Evaluation*, 43(1):41–55.

Alain Polguère. 2011. Perspective épistémologique sur l'approche linguistique Sens-Texte. *Mémoires de la Société de Linguistique de Paris*, XX:79–114.

Alain Polguère. 2014. From Writing Dictionaries to Weaving Lexical Networks. *International Journal of Lexicography*, 27(4):396–418.

Yves Schabes, Anne Abeillé and Aravind K. Joshi. 1988. Parsing Strategies with 'Lexicalized' Grammars: Application to Tree Adjoining Grammars. In: *Proceedings of the 12th Conference on Computational Linguistics – Volume 2 (COLING'88)*. Association for Computational Linguistics, Budapest, 578–583.

Converting an English-Swedish Parallel Treebank to Universal Dependencies

Lars Ahrenberg
Linköping University
Department of Computer and Information Science
lars.ahrenberg@liu.se

Abstract

The paper reports experiences of automatically converting the dependency analysis of the LinES English-Swedish parallel treebank to universal dependencies (UD). The most tangible result is a version of the treebank that actually employs the relations and parts-of-speech categories required by UD, and no other. It is also more complete in that punctuation marks have received dependencies, which is not the case in the original version. We discuss our method in the light of problems that arise from the desire to keep the syntactic analyses of a parallel treebank internally consistent, while available monolingual UD treebanks for English and Swedish diverge somewhat in their use of UD annotations. Finally, we compare the output from the conversion program with the existing UD treebanks.

1 Introduction

Universal Dependency Annotation (UD) is an initiative taken to increase returns for investments in multilingual language technology (McDonald et al., 2013). The idea is that a common set of dependency relations, and a common set of definitions and guidelines for their application, will better support the development of a common cross-lingual infrastructure for the building of language technology tools such as parsers and translation systems.

UD actually comprises more than just dependency relations. To be compatible and possible to merge in a common collection, the resources for a language should use the same principles of tokenization, and common inventories of part-of-speech tags and morphological features. UD advocates a conservative approach to tokenization, which treats punctuation marks and some clitics as separate tokens, but treats all spaces as token separators. Thus, multiword expressions are not recognized as such until the dependency layer.

For parts-of-speech a tag set comprising 17 different tags only is recommended with a basis in the twelve categories proposed by (Petrov et al., 2012). For an overview, see Table 2 in section 3.

LinES (Ahrenberg, 2007) is a parallel treebank currently comprising seven sub-corpora (see Table 1). Future plans for LinES include a substantial increase in the amount of data included. This would also entail that new contents would not, as a rule, be manually reviewed. Harmonizing its markup with that of other treebanks would make it possible to develop more accurate taggers and parsers for it, and thus increase its usefulness as a resource. Conversely, the monolingual treebanks can be used to augment other treebanks for English or Swedish as training data for parsers and taggers.

Source	Segments	EN tkns	SE tkns
Access help	595	10451	8898
Auster	788	13512	13337
Bellow	604	10310	9964
Conrad	622	13063	12092
Europarl	594	9334	8715
Gordimer	756	15181	15778
Rowlings	605	10299	10635
Total	4564	82150	79419

Table 1: LinES corpora before conversion.

The primary aim of this work is the creation of a UD-compatible version of LinES, LinES-UD. As far as possible this should happen through automatic conversion. The hypothesis is that LinES markup is sufficient to support automatic conversion to universal dependencies for both languages by the same process.

Proceedings of the Third International Conference on Dependency Linguistics (Depling 2015), pages 10–19,
Uppsala, Sweden, August 24–26 2015.

The paper is organised as follows. The next section reports related work. Section 3 presents the primary differences between the design of the LinES treebank and the UD framework. In section 4 we describe our approach to develop the conversion program, and in section 5 we present and discuss the results. Section 6, finally, states the conclusions.

2 Related work

Universal Dependencies is a project involving several research groups around the world with a common interest in treebank development, multilingual parsing and cross-lingual learning (Universal dependencies, 2015). The annotation scheme for dependency relations has its roots in universal Stanford dependencies (de Marneffe and Manning, 2008; de Marneffe et al., 2014) and the project also embraces a slightly extended version of the Google universal tag set for parts-of-speech (Petrov et al., 2012). At the time of writing treebanks using UD are available for download from the LINDAT/CLARIN Repository Home for 18 different languages (Agić et al., 2015).

The first release of UD treebanks included six languages. Two of these, the ones for English and Swedish, were created by automatic conversion (McDonald et al., 2013). The English treebank used the Stanford parser (v1.6.8) on the WSJ section of the Penn treebank for this purpose. The Swedish Talbanken treebank was converted by a set of deterministic rules, and the outcome is claimed to have a high precision "due to the fine-grained label set used in the Swedish Treebank" (p. 93). The treebanks are divided into three sections for the purposes of parser development, a training part, a development part, and a test part. We refer to them in the sequel as the English UD Treebank (EUD) and the Swedish UD Treebank (SUD), respectively, using suffixes 1.0 and 1.1 to differentiate the versions. They have been used extensively in the current project for comparisons. In the most recent release (1.1) some corrections have been made to both treebanks. As far as the syntactic annotation is concerned, the corrections affect less than 1% of the tokens in EUD, and about 4% of the tokens in SUD. Most of the development work on LinES-UD was made with the previous versions as targets, but the comparisons reported in section 5 refers to the versions 1.1.

Several other UD treebanks have been developed as a result of automatic conversion, e.g. for Italian (Bosco et al., 2013), Russian (Lipenkova and Souček, 2014), and Finnish (Pyysalo et al., 2015). The process used here for LinES is quite similar to these works with the special twist that here two parallel treebanks are converted simultaneously. Thus, the approach is rule-based, although the rules are not available in an external rule format, but implemented as conditions and actions in a Perl script. Also, unlike these works no new language-specific UD-scheme is developed as part of this work, as such schemes exist for English and Swedish already.

3 Differences in design

The original LinES design has several differences from the UD treebanks. The differences pertaining to parts of speech are fairly small, while differences in sentence segmentation, tokenization and dependency analysis are larger.

We first observe that parallel treebanks are often created for different purposes than mono-lingual treebanks. UD treebanks have parser development as a primary goal, while the most important purpose of the LinES treebank is as a resource for studying the strategies of human translators and for testing properties that are sometimes claimed to be typical for translated texts. One way to describe the relation between a translation and its source text is by trying to quantify the amount of structural changes, or shifts, that have been performed. Such a task is obviously helped by using the same annotation scheme for both languages and the demands on consistency in application of the categories are high. A measure of structural change should reflect real differences; if they instead are introduced by alternative schemes of tokenization or by the use of different categories or definitions, the value of the measure is reduced.

Some of the differences in the available English and Swedish UD treebanks will be detailed in section 4. Here we only note that they pose problems for a developer of parallel English-Swedish treebanks. As just said, in a parallel treebank we would like to see parallel constructions be annotated in the same way for both languages, but if they are not annotated this way in the (usually much larger) available monolingual treebanks, the increase in parsing consistency that we expect from training the parser on a union of UD-treebanks, will not be as large as it could be.

3.1 Sentence segmentation

The largest syntactic unit in LinES is a translation unit. This means that it should correspond under translation to a similar unit in the other language. When the translator has chosen to translate one English sentence by two Swedish sentences, or two English sentences by one Swedish sentence, LinES treats the two sentences as a single sentential unit sharing a single root token. From the monolingual perspective there are two sentences, each with its own root, but from the bilingual perspective there is a single unit and a single root. The two sentences can be analysed as either being coordinated or one being subordinated to the other; in the first case one token that would be taken as the root from the monolingual perspective is assigned a conjoining relation to the other root, while in the second case the dependency would be adverbial. An example of a 1-2 alignment is given below, where the root verb of the second Swedish sentence, *skedde* corresponding to 'was' is seen as conjoined to the root verb of the first sentence, *varit*, corresponding to 'been'.

EN: *As Olivia said, it ought to have been a sad-feeling place but it wasn't; there was instead a renewal: ...*
SE: *Det borde, som Olivia brukade säga, ha varit ett dystert ställe men var det inte. Tvärtom skedde en förnyelse: ...*[1]

We note also that some punctuation marks such as the colon or the semi-colon are sometimes treated as sentence delimiters and sometimes not, even in monolingual treebanks. For example, in the English UD corpus the colon sometimes occur in mid-sentence and at other times at the end of sentences.

3.2 Tokenization

LinES treats a number of fixed multiword expressions from closed parts-of-speech categories as single tokens. English examples are mostly complex prepositions and adverbs such as *because of, after all, instead of, in spite of* while Swedish also has multiword determiners such as *den här* (this) and *den där* (that). Although they are not very numerous, some 10% of all sentences would contain a multiword token. As the tokenization principles for UD favours a strict adherence to spaces as separators, instead signalling multiword expressions in the dependency annotation, the conversion to UD must retokenize the data.

The treatment of clitics in LinES are largely the same as in UD with one exception, the English s-genitive. This is treated as a separate token in the English UD treebank, but in LinES it is taken as a morpheme, both for English and Swedish. While arguments can be given to treat the s-genitive as a phrasal clitic also in Swedish, it is usually not done, because it is harder to detect in Swedish than in English.

In LinES hyphens are regarded as token-internal characters. This is not the case in English UD, where many hyphens are treated as separate tokens.

3.3 Parts of speech

The inventory of parts-of-speech in LinES comprises 23 categories. Many of them correspond more or less directly to those used in UD, but there are a few differences. See Table 2 for an alignment of LinES part-of-speech labels to UD labels. The most problematic difference is that LinES makes a differentiation between verbs and participles, whereas UD distributes participles on the categories VERB, ADJ and NOUN. For the current conversion program we have chosen a simple mapping that does not consider all possible variation to determine what it should be converted to. When used as an attribute it is interpreted as an adjective, but in all other cases it is categorized as a verb.

Auxiliaries, including forms of the verbs *be* and its Swedish counterpart *vara*, are another issue. In LinES there is no distinct part-of-speech for auxiliaries; instead the distinction between auxiliaries and ordinary verbs is made on the basis of whether they participate in a verbal chain or not.

A third issue is the distinction between determiners and pronouns. In LinES a word is classified as a determiner only when it introduces a noun phrase. In UD, however, the distinction is not made in the same way. Rather than identifying the individual words that need re-categorization, we have kept the distinctions as in LinES.

[1]The source text is 'A Guest of Honor' by Nadine Gordimer, translation into Swedish by Magnus K:son Lindberg.

POS	EUD	SUD	LinES
ADJ	Yes	Yes	A, PCP
ADP	Yes	Yes	PREP, POSP
ADV	Yes	Yes	ADV
AUX	Yes	No	V
CONJ	Yes	Yes	CC, CCI
DET	Yes	Yes	DET, A, PRON
INTJ	Yes	Yes	IJ
NOUN	Yes	Yes	N, PCP
NUM	Yes	Yes	NUM, ORD
PART	Yes	Yes	ADV, INFM
PRON	Yes	Yes	PRON, POSS
PROPN	Yes	Yes	PN
PUNCT	Yes	Yes	FE, FI, FP
SCONJ	Yes	Yes	CS
SYM	Yes	No	SYM
VERB	Yes	Yes	V, PCP
X	Yes	Yes	No

Table 2: UD Part-of-speech tags, their application in EUD and SUD and their counterparts in LinES.

3.4 Dependency relations

The set of dependency relations in UD currently includes 40 relations; the exact number seem to change every now and then. For example, (de Marneffe et al., 2014) lists 42.

LinES uses 24 dependency relations which are largely based on those used in FDG or Functional Dependency Grammar (Tapanainen and Järvinen, 1997), but with some additions required by LinES corpora and some amendments. As in UD the dependencies largely favour content words to be governors, but not to the same extent. In LinES prepositions are heads, not just case markers, and in constructions with a copula + predicative, the copula is taken to be the head rather than the head of the predicative. For conversion to UD, then, these relations must be reversed, not just relabelled, which in turn may cause structural changes of other kinds. A reversal implies that dependents of the previous governor must be reanalyzed and a decision be made whether they should keep with the previous governor or become dependents of the new governor. For instance, in LinES annotation a copula can have both a subject dependent and adverbial dependents, while in UD all of these dependencies should be transferred to the predicative head.

One reversal may also affect the outcome of another reversal as when the object of the preposition is a clause with a copula, as in *Kim wanted to talk about how stupid I was*. Here, the mapping introduces a direct dependency between two tokens that previously only were indirectly related (see Figure 1).

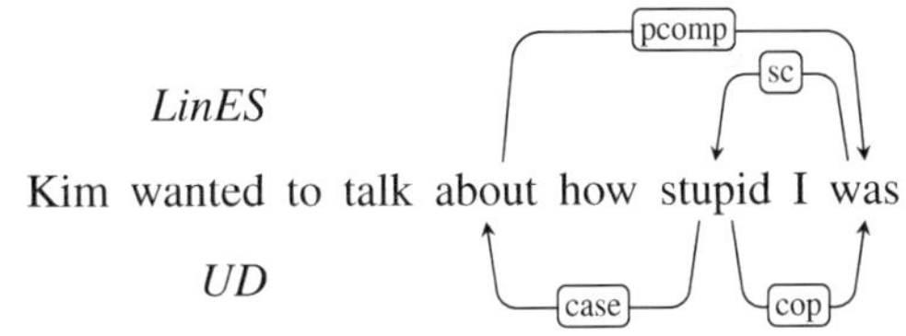

Figure 1: A reversal of governance affecting another. LinES relations above the sentence and UD relations below.

UD largely employs different dependency relations for different parts of speech, whereas LinES prefers to treat dependency relations as orthogonal to parts-of-speech. For example, in LinES there is a single subject dependency which applies to nominals as well as clauses or verb phrases, and a single object dependency applying to nominal as well as clausal dependents. In UD, on the other hand, nominal dependents are consistently assigned different relations than clausal dependendants, whether they are in a subject, complement, or modifier position. Similarly, modifiers are analysed differently as nominal (nmod), adjectival (amod), adverbial (advmod) or numerical (nummod).

LinES shares with UD the assumption that the first conjunct of a coordinated constructions should be the head. In UD all other conjuncts are then taken to be dependents of this first one, whereas in LinES they are (as in FDG) chained so that the next one in the chain is taken to be a dependent of the previous one rather than the first one. Chains of auxiliaries are treated similarly; the first one in a chain of auxiliaries becomes a dependent of the next one, rather than on the main verb, i.e., the head of the last auxiliary, as is the case in UD. Also in agreement with FDG, the subject is a dependent of the first (finite) auxiliary in LinES whereas it is a dependent of the main verb in UD.

LinES provides no dependency information for punctuation marks. The part-of-speech information is however more specific than the single category PUNCT used by UD.

LinES dependency graphs are strictly projective. There are special relations signalling that the dependency should actually not be with the head assigned, but with some other token, usually a (direct or indirect) dependent of the assigned head. There is one relation for fronted elements, one for postposed elements and one for noun-phrase-internal relations. The situation in UD is not quite clear; on the one hand there seem to be a desire to avoid non-projective relations as the relation 'dislocated' seems to relate a fronted or postposed element to the head of the clause. The relation 'remnant' as used by (de Marneffe et al., 2014) to handle ellipsis, is clearly non-projective, though.

The structural differences provide more or less of a challenge to conversion. Luckily, not all differences involve changes to the dependency structure. Many relations are apparently the same except possibly for the label. In other cases, and unlike the situation with subjects and objects, LinES actually has more specific relations than UD. For example, in LinES a difference is made between prepositions that introduce an adjunct and those introducing a complement (i.e., oblique objects), which is not made in UD. In the same vein, LinES separates adverbial modifiers of verbs from those modifying adjectives, and adjectival modifiers appearing before and after a head noun. For these cases conversion basically means relabelling.

4 Method

The descriptions and examples provided on (Universal dependencies, 2015) have been used to learn the intended meaning and use of the relations. Both English and Swedish pages have been consulted. Although this information is indicative rather than complete, and leaves a lot to the reader's interpretation, we decided that it would be sufficient for a first version of a conversion program. In addition we used the English and Swedish UD treebanks, EUD and SUD, made available by the UD consortium as references for comparing the output of our conversion program.

As we noted above it is important that the two halves of a parallel treebank are internally consistent in their annotation. Now, while both EUD and SUD are UD-conformant, there are differences in how they have applied UD. Thus, it was not possible to make LinES-UD internally consistent and at the same time make its English half consistent with EUD and its Swedish half consistent with SUD. In each case where there is a difference, we had to make a decision which one to follow.

Some of the differences between EUD and SUD are listed in Table 3. First we note that EUD employs a few more dependency labels than SUD. The following labels used in EUD are not found in SUD1.1: *conj:preconj, det:predet, goeswith, list, nmod:npmod, nmod:tmod, remnant*, and *reparandum*. On the other hand, SUD has one label, *nmod:agent*, not used in EUD. We decided to use the dependency labels found in SUD, including *nmod:agent*, as LinES has a special relation for agents in passive clauses.

Aspect	EUD	SUD
No. of pos tags	17	15
No. of dep. labels	45	38
Hyphens can be tokens	Yes	No
Negation as PART	Yes	No
's as own token	Yes	No
subj/dobj determiners	Yes	No

Table 3: Major differences relating to application of UD in the English and Swedish UD treebanks.

As for parts-of-speech we used the 17 categories found in EUD, although symbols (SYM) and unassigned (X) are quite rare in the corpus. For each language a small set of auxiliary verbs are assigned the category AUX. We also followed EUD in classifying the negation as PART(icle) and possessives as PRON(ouns) for both languages. However, in other aspects LinES UD is closer to SUD: hyphens are not separate tokens and determiners can not be subjects or objects. In the case of genitive -s, we decided to follow EUD for English, making it a separate token, but SUD for Swedish where it is taken to be a morpheme. This actually contradicts our desire to be internally consistent, but was made nevertheless.

4.1 Development phases

The conversion program has been developed iteratively in three phases. The goal of the first phase was to create UD-conformant annotations for all dependencies appearing in the LinES data. A first version was developed for one of the seven sub-corpora, and when the result appeared to be fairly complete, it was tested on the other six. The output was checked for remaining LinES-annotations. When this happened, the cause was quite often an annotation error in the LinES input file, which could be corrected. At other times defaults were introduced.

In the second phase the full LinES treebank was

used. To check for progress frequency statistics were collected on part-of-speech tags, dependency labels and their associations. Agreement with the EUD and SUD was checked by counting triplets of dependency label, dependent part-of-speech and head part-of-speech. A surprising observation was the large number of labels assigned to any given part-of-speech pair. As an example, see Table 4, where frequencies for dependency relations relating an adjective to a head noun are given. At least 18 dependency relations have instances for this pair in either EUD1.0 or LinES-UD. Where frequencies are low one can suspect that we are actually dealing with errors, either in the source data or in the conversion process.

Dependency	**EUD1.0 Frequency**	**LinES-UD Frequency**
amod	3198	3334
acl:relcl	31	0
conj	22	37
nmod	18	34
acl	9	108
case	8	1
appos	5	10
nsubj	5	2
compound	3	0
nmod:npmod	3	0
parataxis	3	0
advmod	2	6
det	1	214
advcl	1	2
nmod:poss	1	0
nummod	1	0
root	0	1
compound:prt	0	1

Table 4: Distribution of dependencies involving an ADJ(ective) as dependent and a NOUN as head in the English UD Treebank and the English half of Lines-UD after conversion. A subset of EUD1.0, selected so as to produce the same total number of dependencies as LinES-UD, was compared with the output of the conversion program.

When differences were striking, the reason was investigated by looking at a sample of instances, and a decision was made whether to change the program in some respect, or leaving it in that stage, usually for the reason that internal consistency between the English and Swedish parts of LinES were judged to be more important than agreement with the UD treebanks. The most striking difference in Table 4 concerns the relation *det*, where LinES-UD have 214 instances and EUD 1. This is explained by the fact that a number of common words that can be termed adjectival pronouns, such as *another, many, other, same, such* are treated differently in the two treebanks, either at the part-of-speech classification (e.g. *another* is DET in EUD, ADJ in LinES) or at the dependency classification: adjectives are regularly analysed as *amod* in EUD, while they can have a *det*-dependency in LinES.

Another difference is the number of 'acl:relcl'-relations for the pair ADJ - NOUN which is non-existing in the output from the conversion program. This turned out to be a miss in the program: relative clauses without relative pronouns or complementizers were not recognized.

When frequency statistics seemed to be fairly reasonable a manual review (by the author) was performed on 50 English and 50 Swedish segments. The results, all around 90%, are shown in Table 5. Apart from a rough quantitative measure of accuracy the review revealed several types of recurring errors in the output, necessitating a third phase of improving the conversion program.

4.2 The conversion program

The program takes three arguments: source and target files in XML-format and their associated alignment file. It returns monolingual files in conllu-format and a new alignment file.

Structure is as a rule handled before labels. The first structural change concerns tokenization. All multiword tokens in LinES have been split into their parts and the word alignment files have been updated accordingly. At the same time, the new tokens are assigned a new part-of-speech (from a specially designed word list) and an appropriate dependency relation, usually 'mwe' except for some multiword proper names, where 'name' is used. The new tokenization requires a renumbering of the tokens of the treebank, and consequently, a renumbering of the links. The total increase in number of tokens is about 0.9%.

Before the changes in the dependency structure are tackled, the part-of-speech mapping is performed. This is motivated by the fact that tagging usually precedes parsing and that it involves no loss of information, as all information pertaining to parts-of-speech or morphosyntactic features

Corpus	Tokens	UAS	LAS
LinES-UD SE	891	0.93	0.90
LinES-UD EN	959	0.91	0.88

Table 5: Accuracy (unlabelled and labelled) of the generated annotations for a small random sample of output from the conversion program.

Type of change	EN	SE
Relabelling	57891	54781
Reversal	9113	9511
Swap	5718	6726
Combination	61	84
Addition	10026	8662
Total	82809	79764

Table 6: Structural mappings and their frequencies in the conversions to LinES-UD. A change of governor is a Reversal if the new governor was previously a direct dependent, a Swap if it was not, and a Combination if it involves two reversals, as in Figure 1. Additions apply only to punctuation marks.

in LinES-corpora can still be accessed by the program. Most of the mapping is just relabelling, either one-to-one or many-to-one, but, as noted above, the category PCP (for participle) is mapped onto three UD tags using contextual information and the verbs are divided on the two categories AUX and VERB depending on whether they are part of a verbal chain or not.

The final step deals with the dependency tree. A new tree is generated from the existing one on the basis of rules that refer to dependency labels, local structure and properties of the two tokens related in the dependency. The more complex structural changes, i.e., reversals and swaps (head changes), are handled first. The given sentence is read three times, first to look for structural changes, then to handle relabellings, and finally to handle punctuation marks.

(Bosco et al., 2013) makes a distinction between 1:1 and 1:n dependency mappings; both of these types are handled as relabellings. The difference is that 1:n mappings, such as the splitting up the LinES object relation on the various corresponding UD dependencies (dobj, iobj, ccomp, xcomp), require inspection of the available morphosyntactic information and local properties of the tree to be performed correctly. In the final pass punctuation marks are assigned the relation 'punct' and a head. The UD recommendations have been followed as far as possible, but it is generally quite problematic to identify a proper head, especially for many of the internal punctuation marks that some authors of novels like to employ.

5 Results and evaluation

The conversion program has been applied to the full corpus and as a result a UD-version of the parallel treebank now exists. In fact, several versions have been generated, as the program is still being worked upon. Here we report on stable properties of the output.

The output has been checked for completeness and for the occurrence of dependency relations not belonging to UD. Although a few tokens, usually less than ten for each language, do not receive any dependency relation or a non-UD label, we can claim that the conversion program is successful in producing a parallel UD treebank. Such errors can be detected and fixed in a manual review.

Frequencies of structural mappings of different types are summarized in Table 6. The number of structural changes (reversals or swaps) is quite high, around 20% for both languages, a bit less for English and a bit higher for Swedish.

While the output is formally in agreement with UD relations and part-of-speech categories, there is no guarantee that they have been applied in agreement with their intended definitions. To check for this frequency statistics have been computed for parts-of-speech and dependency labels, and for dependency triplets.

Table 7 shows total number of instances for the most common dependencies for English and Swedish. We have omitted some, such as *list*, *goeswith*, and *compound*, that are used only for one language or have a low frequency for one language. For most relations the numbers are quite similar, but there are also exceptions. As the four underlying corpora are different, and we don't have a gold standard for either of them, we cannot determine with any certainty whether the differences are due to text properties, language-specific interpretations of the UD labels, or conversion errors.

More detail can be had by looking at frequencies for dependency triplets. Space is not sufficient to discuss all variation in this data, but we will look at a few pertinent cases. First, we can observe (as

Dependency	EUD1.1	EN LinES-UD	SUD1.1	SE LinES-UD
All	82809	82809	79764	79764
punct	10028	10025	8663	8662
case	7638	8157	8448	8284
nmod	6965	7537	7853	7824
det	6282	**8028**	5680	5145
nsubj	5864	**7215**	6234	6992
dobj	3762	3797	3535	4230
amod	3750	3620	3715	3503
mark	3063	2707	2571	**3631**
advmod	2923	**4692**	5165	5969
conj	2633	3276	3439	3603
aux	2627	2492	1996	1934
cc	2372	2529	2831	2981
cop	1456	1250	1294	1246
advcl	1352	1335	1478	1015
nmod:poss	1279	1535	1424	1562
ccomp	**1126**	**549**	436	560
xcomp	1104	1183	876	1204
nummod	1122	296	1172	225
appos	754	564	424	572
acl:relcl	**708**	**253**	1095	853
acl	707	**1598**	571	**966**
auxpass	650	642	39	167
nsubjpass	561	**70**	1121	**354**
mwe	207	382	**1562**	343

Table 7: Absolute frequencies for the most common dependency relations in each treebank. For both EUD and SUD subsets have been used that are of the same size in terms of number of tokens as the LinES treebank. Bold face is used for relations where differences are noteworthy.

in Figure 4) that the association between dependency labels and pairs of parts-of-speech is n-to-m with sometimes very high values on n and m. For instance, looking at all four treebanks there are no less than 93 pairs of part-of-speech with at least one instance of *nmod*. Similarly, there are 62 pairs with at least one instance of *nsubj*. Of course, often only a few pairs contribute to the vast majority of the instances, but there is almost always a long tail of other pairs.

Some differences can be explained with reference to the texts which are taken from different genres. EUD has newspaper (Wall Street Journal) prose, SUD 'professional prose', while LinES has a great share of literary prose. To illustrate, both EUD and SUD have more than three times as many numerals as the LinES corpus, which largely explains the frequency differences relating to *nummod*. Conversely, LinES_SE has ten times as many occurrences of the pronoun *han*, 'he' than SUD.

The *det*-relation is more frequent in LinES-UD_EN than in EUD1.1 for the reasons explained above, namely that it is used for many common words categorized as ADJ, where EUD uses *amod*. Thus, EUD has more instances of *amod*-relations in spite of having a lower relative frequency of adjectives.

LinES_EN has more *nsubj* instances than EUD. This is largely explained by the frequencies of third person singular pronouns as subjects, especially the pronouns *he* and *she* which are used to refer to the characters of the narrative. Together they account for more than 1000 instances of the difference. And to this can be added the pronouns tagged as PRON in LinES but as DET in EUD.

On the Swedish side, SUD has many more instances of NOUN as subject, while the Swedish LinES-UD again has more pronouns. 23.8% of all tokens in SUD are nouns, while the corresponding figure for Swedish LinES-UD is 17.4%. Conversely, SUD has only 6.2% pronouns, whereas Swedish LinES-UD has 11.1%.

The higher frequency of *advmod* in English LinES is partly explained by the higher relative frequency of adverbs, 5.5% as compared to 4.1%. In a corpus of 82000 tokens this is a difference of 1200 instances. The number of adverbs in the Swedish translations is even greater, 7.4%.

The difference in frequencies for *ccomp* in the English treebanks could also be explained by the differences in genres. However, while some verbs that take clausal complements, such as *announce* don't occur in LinES, there are no large differences in frequencies for common verbs taking clausal complements such as *say*, *think*, or *know*. Browsing the LinES file for occurrences of these words, no errors are detected, so the tentative conclusion is that they are used differently.

The conversion program identifies fewer relative clauses than it should, judging from the differences in frequency for the relations *acl* and *acl:relcl*. In particular it misses some that are not introduced by a relative pronoun or subjunction.

The very low figures for *nsubjpass* is partly due to the rules creating this dependency, which are too restrictive, for example missing instances where an auxiliary appears between the subject and the passive form. Another contributing factor is the Swedish word *som*, 'that', 'who', which introduces relative clauses. In SUD it is categorized as a PRON(oun) and assigned a core dependency, whereas in LinES it is categorized as a subjunction carrying the *mark*-dependency. Other words that are analyzed as *mark* much more often in Swedish LinES than in SUD1.1 are *när*, 'when', *då*, 'when, as' and *medan*, 'while'.

SUD1.1 has many more instances of the *mwe*-relation than the other treebanks. While EUD and LinES-UD_EN agree on mwe:s, SUD1.1 employs *mwe* for many word sequences that LinES regards as compositional, such as *när det gäller*, 'as regards', *mer än*, 'more than', *i samband med*, 'in connection with'.

While the most common dependency triplets such as <amod, ADJ, NOUN> and <nsubj, NOUN, VERB> appear in the same numbers, there are thus other triplets occurring in one treebank that don't occur at all in the other treebank of the same language. This indicates (i) that a parser trained on one of them might not perform very well on the sentences of the other, and (ii) that merging the treebanks may not be so helpful either. To test these hypotheses we trained Malt parsers on the two Swedish treebanks and tested various models. The LinES data was randomly divided into distinct sets for training, development and test and parsing models were then developed on the training data for both treebanks as well as for the merged treebank. As both Swedish treebanks are small with many tokens occurring in only one of them, the nouns, proper names, verbs and adjectives were de-lexified into combinations of part-of-speech tags and (LinES) morphological tags. The best results, obtained with the standard settings and finegrained de-lexification are shown in Table 8. No combo model from the merged treebank was able to improve performance on both test sets.

Model	Test data	UAS	LAS
LinES	LinES	0.751	0.701
Combo	LinES	0.739	0.687
SUD1.0	SUD1.0	0.738	0.697
Combo	SUD1.0	0.739	0.696

Table 8: Parsing results.

6 Conclusions

We have shown that the information in the LinES parallel treebank is sufficient to produce a treebank by automatic means, which, with a minimum of manual effort, is formally compliant with the UD inventory of dependency labels and part-of-speech categories, and its principles for tokenization. The program generates English and Swedish data, as well as the new alignment, in one go.

The current version is relatively stable, but there is still room for improvements. Even so, a manual review process will increase the quality of the annotation substantially. The conversion programme will facilitate the review process, however, as we can see from the comparisons with the EUD and SUD treebanks, where the problems seem to reside.

We have also shown that EUD and SUD, while UD-compatible, do not treat all phenomena in the same way. Thus, it is likely that future UD treebanks, whether developments of EUD and SUD, or created from other sources, will be more consistent with one another. In such a future scenario, LinES-UD is likely to follow suit and, rather than having to manually review the data once more, tweaking an automatic conversion program to the new developments will be more efficient.

We have pointed out that a parallell treebank developed for the study of human translation must be internally consistent to a maximal degree. Presently, this can only be achieved to the expense of deviating in many aspects from the available UD treebanks, some of which have been detailed in section 4. A possibility, of course is to maintain two versions of the data. As part of the parallel treebank, the two halves are maximally consistent with each other, but they both have alternative versions where the segmentation and annotation is more similar to the existing monolingual UD treebanks for each language.

References

Lars Ahrenberg 2007. LinES: An English-Swedish Parallel Treebank. *Proceedings of the 16th Nordic Conference of Computational Linguistics (NODALIDA, 2007).*

Cristina Bosco, Simonetta Magni, Maria Simi 2013. Converting Italian treebanks: Towards an Italian Stanford dependency treebank *7th Linguistic Annotation Workshop and Interoperability with Discourse.*

Janna Lipenkova and Milan Souček 2014. Converting Russian Dependency Treebank to Stanford Typed Dependencies Representation. Proceedings of the 14th Conference of the European Chapter of the Association for Computational Linguistics. pages 143-147.

Marie-Catherine de Marneffe and Christopher D. Manning 2008 The Stanford typed dependencies representation. Workshop on Cross-framework and Cross-domain Parser Evaluation.

Marie-Catherine de Marneffe, Timothy Dozat, Natalia Silveira, Katri Haverinen, Filip Ginter, Joakim Nivre, and Christopher D. Manning 2014 Universal Stanford Dependencies: A cross-linguistic typology Proceedings of the Ninth International Conference on Language Resources and Evaluation (LREC'14).

Ryan McDonald, Joakim Nivre, Yvonne Quimbach-Brundage, Yoav Goldberg, Dipanjan Das, Kuzman Ganchev, Keith Hall, Slav Petrov, Hao Zhang, Oscar Täckström, Claudia Bedini, Núria Bertomeu Castelló, and Jungmee Lee. 2013. Universal Dependency Annotation for Multilingual Parsing. *Proceedings of the 51st Annual Meeting of the ACL*, Sofia, Bulgaria, August 4-9 2013, pages 92-97.

Slav Petrov, Dipanjan Das, and Ryan McDonald. 2012. A universal part-of-speech tagset. *Proceedings of the Eight International Conference on Language Resources and Evaluation, LREC'12*, Istanbul, Turkey, May 23-25 2012.

Sampo Pyysalo, Jenna Kanerva, Anna Missilä, Veronika Laippala, and Filip Ginter 2015. Universal Dependencies for Finnish. *Proceedings of the 20th Nordic Conference on Computational Linguistics*, Vilnius, Lithuania, May 12-13, 2015.

Pasi Tapanainen and Timo Järvinen 1997. A non-projective dependency parser. *Proceedings of the fifth conference on Applied Natural Language Processing*, pages 64-71.

Agić, Željko and Aranzabe, Maria Jesus and Atutxa, Aitziber and Bosco, Cristina and Choi, Jinho and de Marneffe, Marie-Catherine and Dozat, Timothy and Farkas, Richárd and Foster, Jennifer and Ginter, Filip and Goenaga, Iakes and Gojenola, Koldo and Goldberg, Yoav and Hajič, Jan and Johannsen, Anders Trærup and Kanerva, Jenna and Kuokkala, Juha and Laippala, Veronika and Lenci, Alessandro and Lindén, Krister and Ljubešić, Nikola and Lynn, Teresa and Manning, Christopher and Martínez, Héctor Alonso and McDonald, Ryan and Missilä, Anna and Montemagni, Simonetta and Nivre, Joakim and Nurmi, Hanna and Osenova, Petya and Petrov, Slav and Piitulainen, Jussi and Plank, Barbara and Prokopidis, Prokopis and Pyysalo, Sampo and Seeker, Wolfgang and Seraji, Mojgan and Silveira, Natalia and Simi, Maria and Simov, Kiril and Smith, Aaron and Tsarfaty, Reut and Vincze, Veronika and Zeman, Daniel Universal Dependencies 1.1. 2015. https://lindat.mff.cuni.cz/repository/xmlui/handle/11234/LRT-1478

Universal Dependencies Universal Dependencies home page. 2015. http://universaldependencies.github.io/docs/

Targeted Paraphrasing on Deep Syntactic Layer for MT Evaluation

Petra Barančíková and **Rudolf Rosa**
Charles University in Prague
Faculty of Mathematics and Physics
Institute of Formal and Applied Linguistics
Czech Republic
{barancikova,rosa}@ufal.mff.cuni.cz

Abstract

In this paper, we present a method of improving quality of machine translation (MT) evaluation of Czech sentences via targeted paraphrasing of reference sentences on a deep syntactic layer. For this purpose, we employ NLP framework Treex and extend it with modules for targeted paraphrasing and word order changes. Automatic scores computed using these paraphrased reference sentences show higher correlation with human judgment than scores computed on the original reference sentences.

1 Introduction

Since the very first appearance of machine translation (MT) systems, a necessity for their objective evaluation and comparison has emerged. The traditional human evaluation is slow and unreproducible; thus, it cannot be used for tasks like tuning and development of MT systems. Well-performing automatic MT evaluation metrics are essential precisely for these tasks.

The pioneer metrics correlating well with human judgment were BLEU (Papineni et al., 2002) and NIST (Doddington, 2002). They are computed from an n-gram overlap between the translated sentence (hypothesis) and one or more corresponding reference sentences, i.e., translations made by a human translator.

Due to its simplicity and language independence, BLEU still remains the de facto standard metric for MT evaluation and tuning, even though other, better-performing metrics exist (Macháček and Bojar (2013), Bojar et al. (2014)).

Furthermore, the standard practice is using only one reference sentence and BLEU then tends to perform badly. There are many translations of a single sentence and even a perfectly correct translation might get a low score as BLEU disregards synonymous expressions and word order variants (see Figure 1). This is especially valid for morphologically rich languages with free word order like the Czech language (Bojar et al., 2010).

In this paper, we use deep syntactic layer for targeted paraphrasing of reference sentences. For every hypothesis, we create its own reference sentence that is more similar in wording but keeps the meaning and grammatical correctness of the original reference sentence. Using these new paraphrased references makes the MT evaluation metrics more reliable. In addition, correct paraphrases have additional application in many other NLP tasks.

As far as we know, this is the first rule-based model specifically designed for targeted paraphrased reference sentence generation to improve MT evaluation quality.

2 Related Work

Second generation metrics Meteor (Denkowski and Lavie, 2014), TERp (Snover et al., 2009) and ParaEval (Zhou et al., 2006) still largely focus on an n-gram overlap while including other linguistically motivated resources. They utilize paraphrase support in form of their own paraphrase tables (i.e. collection of synonymous expressions) and show higher correlation with human judgment than BLEU.

Meteor supports several languages including Czech. However, its Czech paraphrase tables are so noisy (i.e. they contain pairs of non-paraphrastic expressions) that they actually harm the performance of the metric, as it can reward mistranslated and even untranslated words (Barančíková, 2014).

String matching is hardly discriminative enough to reflect the human perception and there is growing number of metrics that compute their score based on rich linguistic features and matching based on parse trees, POS tagging or textual entail-

Proceedings of the Third International Conference on Dependency Linguistics (Depling 2015), pages 20–27,
Uppsala, Sweden, August 24–26 2015.

Original sentence	*Banks are testing payment by mobile telephone*					
Hypothesis	*Banky*	*zkoušejí*	*platbu*	*pomocí*	*mobilního*	*telefonu*
	Banks	are testing	payment	with help	mobile	phone
	Banks are testing payment by mobile phone					
Reference sentence	*Banky*	*testují*	*placení*	*mobilem*		
	Banks	are testing	paying	by mobile phone		
	Banks are testing paying by mobile phone					

Figure 1: Example from WMT12 - Even though the hypothesis is grammatically correct and the meaning of both sentences is the same, it doesn't contribute to the BLEU score. There is only one unigram overlapping.

ment (e.g. Liu and Gildea (2005), Owczarzak et al. (2007), Amigó et al. (2009), Padó et al. (2009), Macháček and Bojar (2011)).

These metrics shows better correlation with human judgment, but their wide usage is limited by being complex and language-dependent. As a result, there is a trade-off between linguistic-rich strategy for better performance and applicability of simple string level matching.

Our approach makes use of linguistic tools for creating new reference sentences. The advantage of this method is that we can choose among many traditional metrics for evaluation on our new references while eliminating some shortcomings of these metrics.

Targeted paraphrasing for MT evaluation was introduced by Kauchak and Barzilay (2006). Their algorithm creates new reference sentences by one-word substitution based on WordNet (Miller, 1995) synonymy and contextual evaluation. This solution is not readily applicable to the Czech language – a Czech word has typically many forms and the correct form depends heavily on its context, e.g., morphological cases of nouns depend on verb valency frames. Changing a single word may result in an ungrammatical sentence. Therefore, we do not attempt to change a single word in a reference sentence but we focus on creating one single correct reference sentence.

In Barančíková and Tamchyna (2014), we experimented with targeted paraphrasing using the freely available SMT system Moses (Koehn et al., 2007). We adapted Moses for targeted monolingual phrase-based translation. However, results of this method was inconclusive. It was mainly due to a high amount of noise in the translation tables and unbalanced targeting feature.

As a result, we rather chose to employ rule-based translation system. This approach has many advantages, e.g. there is no need for creating a targeting feature and we can change only parts of a sentence and thus create more conservative paraphrases. We utilize Treex (Popel and Žabokrtský, 2010), highly modular NLP software system developed for machine translation system TectoMT (Žabokrtský et al., 2008) that translates on a deep syntactic layer. We performed our experiment on the Czech language, however, we plan to extend it to more languages, including English and Spanish.

Treex is open-source and is available on GitHub,[1] including the two blocks that we contributed. In the rest of the paper, we describe the implementation of our approach.

3 Treex

Treex implements a stratificational approach to language, adopted from the Functional Generative Description theory (Sgall, 1967) and its later extension by the Prague Dependency Treebank (Bejček et al., 2013). It represents sentences at four layers:

- **w-layer:** word layer; no linguistic annotation
- **m-layer:** morphological layer; sequence of tagged and lemmatized tokens
- **a-layer:** shallow-syntax/analytical layer; sentence is represented as a surface syntactic dependency tree
- **t-layer:** deep-syntax/tectogrammatical layer; sentence is represented as a deep-syntactic dependency tree, where autosemantic words (i.e. semantically full lexical units) only have their own nodes; t-nodes consist of a t-lemma and a set of attributes – a *formeme* (information about the original syntactic form) and a

[1] `https://github.com/ufal/treex`

Source	*The Internet has caused a boom in these speculations.*
Hypothesis	Internet vyvolal boom v těchto spekulacích .
	Internet caused boom in these speculations .
	The Internet has caused a boom in these speculations.
Reference	Rozkvět těchto spekulací způsobil internet .
	Boom these speculations caused internet .
	A boom of these speculation was caused by the Internet.

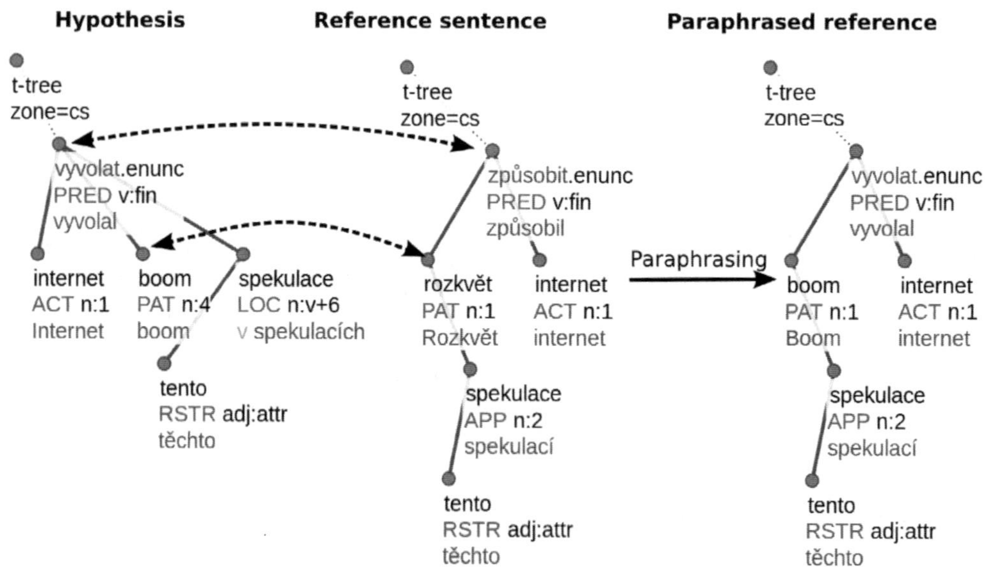

Figure 2: Example of the paraphrasing. The hypothesis is grammatically correct and has the same meaning as the reference sentence. We analyse both sentences to t-layer, where we create a new reference sentence by substituting synonyms from hypothesis to the reference. In the next step, we will change also the word order to better reflect the hypothesis.

set of *grammatemes* (essential morphological features).

We take the analysis and generation pipeline from the TectoTM system. We transfer both a hypothesis and its corresponding reference sentence to the t-layer, where we integrate a module for t-lemma paraphrasing. After paraphrasing, we perform synthesis to a-layer, where we plug in a reordering module and continue with synthesis to the w-layer.

3.1 Analysis from w-layer to t-layer

The analysis from the w-layer the to a-layer includes tokenization, POS-tagging and lemmatization using MorphoDiTa (Straková et al., 2014), dependency parsing using the MSTParser (McDonald et al., 2005) adapted by Novák and Žabokrtský (2007), trained on PDT.

In the next step, a surface-syntax a-tree is converted into a deep-syntax t-tree. Auxiliary words are removed, with their function now represented using t-node attributes (grammatemes and formemes) of autosemantic words that they belong to (e.g. two a-nodes of the verb form *spal jsem* ("I slept") would be collapsed into one t-node *spát* ("sleep") with the tense grammateme set to past; *v květnu* ("in May") would be collapsed into *květen* ("May") with the formeme *v+X* ("in+X").

We choose the t-layer for paraphrasing, because the words from the sentence are lemmatized and free of syntactical information. Furthermore, functional words, which we do not want to paraphrase and that cause a lot of noise in our paraphrase tables, do not appear here.

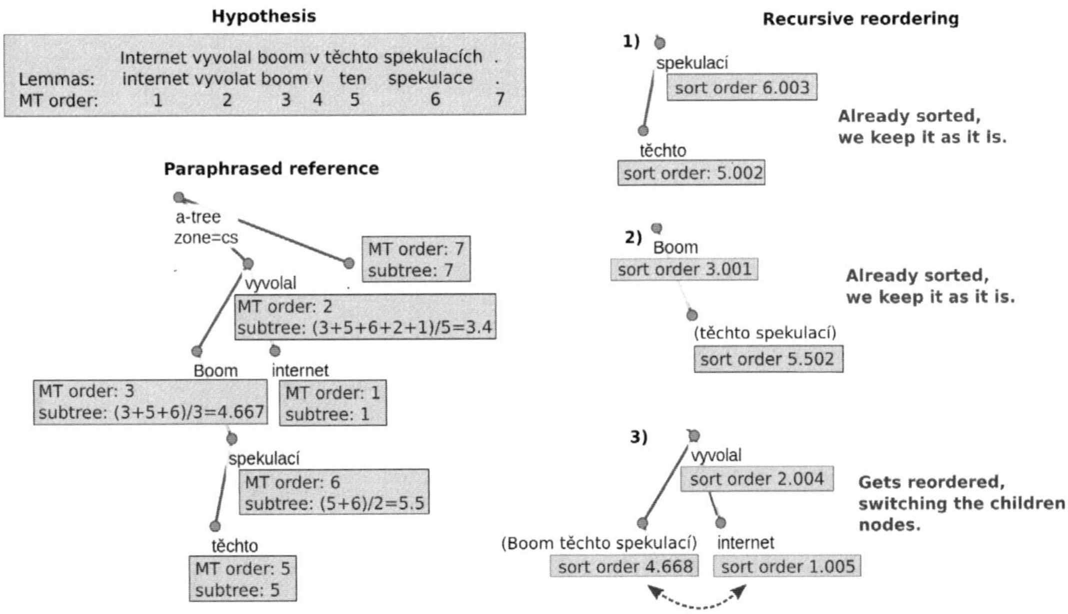

Figure 3: Continuation of Figure 2, reordering of the paraphrased reference sentence.

3.2 Paraphrasing

The paraphrasing module T2T::ParaphraseSimple is freely available at GitHub.[2]

T-lemma of a reference t-node R is changed from A to B if and only if:

1. there is a hypothesis t-node with lemma B
2. there is no hypothesis t-node with lemma A
3. there is no reference t-node with lemma B
4. A and B are paraphrases according to our paraphrase tables

The other attributes of the t-node are kept unchanged based on the assumption that semantic properties are independent of the t-lemma. However, in practice, there is at least one case where this is not true: t-nodes corresponding to nouns are marked for grammatical gender, which is very often a grammatical property of the given lemma with no effect on the meaning (for example, "a house" can be translated either as a masculine noun *dům* or as feminine noun *budova*),

Therefore, when paraphrasing a t-node that corresponds to a noun, we delete the value of the gender grammateme, and let the subsequent synthesis pipeline generate the correct value of the morphological gender feature value (which is necessary to ensure correct morphological agreement of the noun's dependents, such as adjectives and verbs).

3.3 Synthesis from t-layer to a-layer

In this phase, a-nodes corresponding to auxiliary words and punctuation are generated, morphological feature values on a-nodes are initialized and set to enforce morphological agreement among the nodes. Correct inflectional forms based on lemma and POS, and morphological features are generated using MorphoDiTa.

3.4 Tree-based reordering

The reordering block A2A::ReorderByLemmas is freely available at GitHub.[3]

The idea behind the block is to make the word order of the new reference as similar to the word order of the translation, but with some tree-based constraints to avoid ungrammatical sentences.

The general approach is to reorder the subtrees rooted at modifier nodes of a given head node so that they appear in an order that is on average similar to their order in the translation. Figure 3 shows the reordering process of the a-tree from Figure 2.

[2] `https://github.com/ufal/treex/blob/master/lib/Treex/Block/T2T/ParaphraseSimple.pm`

[3] `https://github.com/ufal/treex/blob/master/lib/Treex/Block/A2A/ReorderByLemmas.pm`

Our reordering proceeds in several steps. Each a-node has an order, i.e. a position in the sentence. We define the *MT order* of a reference a-node as the order of its corresponding hypothesis a-node, i.e. a node with the same lemma.

We set the MT order only if there is exactly one a-node with the given lemma in both the hypothesis and the reference. Therefore, the MT order might be undefined for some nodes.

In the next step, we compute the *subtree MT order* of each reference a-node R as the average MT order of all a-nodes in the subtree rooted at the a-node R (including the MT order of R itself). Only nodes with a defined MT order are taken into account, so the subtree MT order can be undefined for some nodes.

Finally, we iterate over all a-nodes recursively starting from the bottom. Head a-node H and its dependent a-nodes D_i are reordered if they violate the *sorting order*. If D_i is a root of a subtree, the whole subtree is moved and its internal ordering is kept.

The sorting order of H is defined as its MT order; the sorting order of each dependent node D_i is defined as its subtree MT order. If a sorting order of a node is undefined, it is set to the sorting order of the node that precedes it, thus favouring neighbouring nodes (or subtrees) to be reordered together in case there is no evidence that they should be brought apart from each other. Additionally, each sorting order is added 1/1000th of the original order of the node – in case of a tie, the original ordering of the nodes is preferred to reordering.

We do not handle non-projective edges in any special way, so they always get projectivized if they take part in a reordering process, or kept in their original order otherwise. However, no new non-projective edges are created in the process – this is ensured by always moving the subtrees at once.

Please note that each node can take part in at most two reorderings – once as the H node and once as a D_i node. Moreover, the nodes can be processed in any order, as a reordering does not influence any other reordering.

3.5 Synthesis from a-layer to w-layer

The word forms are already generated on the a-layer, so there is little to be done. Superfluous tokens are deleted (e.g. duplicated commas)the first letter in a sentence is capitalized, and the tokens are concatenated (a set of rules is used to decide which tokens should be space-delimited and which should not). The example in Figure 3) results in the following sentence: *Internet vyvolal boom těchto spekulací* ("The Internet has caused a boom of these speculations."), which has the same meaning as the original reference sentence, is grammatically correst and, most importantly, is much more similar in wording to the hypothesis.

4 Data

We perform our experiments on data sets from the English-to-Czech translation task of WMT12 (Callison-Burch et al., 2012), WMT13 (Bojar et al., 2013a). The data sets contain 13/14[4] files with Czech outputs of MT systems. Each data set also contains one file with corresponding reference sentences.

Our database of t-lemma paraphrases was created from two existing sources of Czech paraphrases – the Czech WordNet 1.9 PDT (Pala and Smrž, 2004) and the Meteor Paraphrase Tables (Denkowski and Lavie, 2010). Czech WordNet 1.9 PDT is already lemmatized, lemmatization of the Meteor Paraphrase tables was performed using MorphoDiTa (Straková et al., 2014).

We also performed fitering of the lemmatized Meteor Paraphrase tables based on coarse POS, as they contained a lot of noise due to being constructed automatically.

5 Results

The performance of an evaluation metric in MT is usually computed as the Pearson correlation between the automatic metric and human judgment (Papineni et al., 2002). The correlation estimates the linear dependency between two sets of values. It ranges from -1 (perfect negative linear relationship) to 1 (perfect linear correlation).

The official manual evaluation metric of WMT12 and WMT13 provides just a relative ranking: a human judge always compares the performance of five systems on a particular sentence. From these relative rankings, we compute the absolute performance of every system using the "> others" method (Bojar et al., 2011). It is computed as $\frac{wins}{wins+loses}$.

Our method of paraphrasing is independent of an evaluation metric used. We employ three dif-

[4] We use only 12 of them because two of them (FDA.2878 and online-G) have no human judgments.

	WMT12			WMT13		
references	original	paraphrased	reordered	original	paraphrased	paraphrased
BLEU	0.751	0.783	0.804	0.834	0.850	0.878
Meteor	0.833	0.864	0.868	0.817	0.871	0.870
Ex.Meteor	0.861	0.900	**0.903**	0.848	**0.893**	**0.893**

Table 1: Pearson correlation of a metric and human judgment on original references, paraphrased references and paraphrased reordered references. Ex.Meteor represents Meteor metric with exact match only (i.e. no paraphrase support).

ferent metrics - BLEU score, Meteor metric and Meteor metric without the paraphrase support (as it seem redundant to use paraphrases on already paraphrased sentences).

The results are presented in Table 1 as a Pearson correlation of a metric with human judgment. Paraphrasing clearly helps to reflect the human perception better. Even the Meteor metric that already contains paraphrases is performing better using paraphrased references created from its own paraphrase table. This is again due to the noise in the paraphrase table, which blurs the difference between the hypotheses of different MT systems.

The reordering clearly helps when we evaluate via the BLEU metric, which punishes any word order changes to the reference sentence. Meteor is more tolerant to word order changes and the reordering has practically no effect on his scores.

However, manual examination showed that our constraints are not strong enough to prevent creating ungrammatical sentences. The algorithm tends to copy the word order of the hypothesis, even if it is not correct. Most errors were caused by changes of a word order of punctuation.

6 Future Work

In our future work, we plan to extend the paraphrasing module for more complex paraphrases including syntactical paraphrases, longer phrases, diatheses. We will also change only parts of sentences that are dependent on paraphrased words, thus keeping the rest of the sentence correct and creating more conservative reference sentences.

We also intend to adjust the reordering function by adding rule-based constrains. Furthermore, we'd like to learn automatically possible word order changes from Deprefset (Bojar et al., 2013b), which contains an excessive number of manually created reference translations for 50 Czech sentences.

We performed our experiment on Czech language, but the procedure is generally language independent, as long as there is analysis and synthesis support for particular language in Treex. Currently there is full support for Czech, English, Portuguese and Dutch, but there is ongoing work on many more languages within the QTLeap[5] project.

Acknowledgments

This research was supported by the following grants: SVV project number 260 224 and GAUK 1572314. This work has been using language resources developed and/or stored and/or distributed by the LINDAT/CLARIN project of the Ministry of Education, Youth and Sports of the Czech Republic (project LM2010013).

References

Enrique Amigó, Jesús Giménez, Julio Gonzalo, and Felisa Verdejo. 2009. The Contribution of Linguistic Features to Automatic Machine Translation Evaluation. In *Proceedings of the Joint Conference of the 47th Annual Meeting of the ACL and the 4th International Joint Conference on Natural Language Processing of the AFNLP: Volume 1 - Volume 1*, ACL '09, pages 306–314.

Petra Barančíková. 2014. Parmesan: Meteor without Paraphrases with Paraphrased References. In *Proceedings of the Ninth Workshop on Statistical Machine Translation*, pages 355–361, Baltimore, MD, USA. Association for Computational Linguistics.

Petra Barančíková and Aleš Tamchyna. 2014. Machine Translation within One Language as a Paraphrasing Technique. In *Proceedings of the main track of the 14th Conference on Information Technologies - Applications and Theory (ITAT 2014)*, pages 1–6.

Eduard Bejček, Eva Hajičová, Jan Hajič, Pavlína Jínová, Václava Kettnerová, Veronika Kolářová, Marie Mikulová, Jiří Mírovský, Anna Nedoluzhko, Jarmila Panevová, Lucie Poláková, Magda

[5]http://qtleap.eu/

Ševčíková, Jan Štěpánek, and Šárka Zikánová. 2013. Prague Dependency Treebank 3.0.

Ondřej Bojar, Kamil Kos, and David Mareček. 2010. Tackling Sparse Data Issue in Machine Translation Evaluation. In *Proceedings of the ACL 2010 Conference Short Papers*, ACLShort '10, pages 86–91, Stroudsburg, PA, USA. Association for Computational Linguistics.

Ondřej Bojar, Miloš Ercegovčević, Martin Popel, and Omar F. Zaidan. 2011. A Grain of Salt for the WMT Manual Evaluation. In *Proceedings of the Sixth Workshop on Statistical Machine Translation*, WMT '11, pages 1–11, Stroudsburg, PA, USA. Association for Computational Linguistics.

Ondřej Bojar, Christian Buck, Chris Callison-Burch, Christian Federmann, Barry Haddow, Philipp Koehn, Christof Monz, Matt Post, Radu Soricut, and Lucia Specia. 2013a. Findings of the 2013 Workshop on Statistical Machine Translation. In *Proceedings of the Eighth Workshop on Statistical Machine Translation*, pages 1–44, Sofia, Bulgaria, August. Association for Computational Linguistics.

Ondřej Bojar, Matouš Macháček, Aleš Tamchyna, and Daniel Zeman. 2013b. Scratching the Surface of Possible Translations. In *Text, Speech and Dialogue: 16th International Conference, TSD 2013. Proceedings*, pages 465–474, Berlin / Heidelberg. Springer Verlag.

Ondřej Bojar, Christian Buck, Christian Federmann, Barry Haddow, Philipp Koehn, Matouš Macháček, Christof Monz, Pavel Pecina, Matt Post, Herve Saint-Amand, Radu Soricut, and Lucia Specia. 2014. Findings of the 2014 Workshop on Statistical Machine Translation. In *Proceedings of the Ninth Workshop on Statistical Machine Translation*, Baltimore, USA, June. Association for Computational Linguistics.

Chris Callison-Burch, Philipp Koehn, Christof Monz, Matt Post, Radu Soricut, and Lucia Specia. 2012. Findings of the 2012 Workshop on Statistical Machine Translation. In *Seventh Workshop on Statistical Machine Translation*, pages 10–51, Montréal, Canada.

Michael Denkowski and Alon Lavie. 2010. METEOR-NEXT and the METEOR Paraphrase Tables: Improved Evaluation Support For Five Target Languages. In *Proceedings of the ACL 2010 Joint Workshop on Statistical Machine Translation and Metrics MATR*.

Michael Denkowski and Alon Lavie. 2014. Meteor Universal: Language Specific Translation Evaluation for Any Target Language. In *Proceedings of the EACL 2014 Workshop on Statistical Machine Translation*.

George Doddington. 2002. Automatic Evaluation of Machine Translation Quality Using N-gram Co-occurrence Statistics. In *Proceedings of the Second International Conference on Human Language Technology Research*, HLT '02, pages 138–145, San Francisco, CA, USA. Morgan Kaufmann Publishers Inc.

David Kauchak and Regina Barzilay. 2006. Paraphrasing for Automatic Evaluation. In *Proceedings of the main conference on Human Language Technology Conference of the North American Chapter of the Association of Computational Linguistics*, HLT-NAACL '06, pages 455–462, Stroudsburg, PA, USA. Association for Computational Linguistics.

Philipp Koehn, Hieu Hoang, Alexandra Birch, Chris Callison-Burch, Marcello Federico, Nicola Bertoldi, Brooke Cowan, Wade Shen, Christine Moran, Richard Zens, Chris Dyer, Ondřej Bojar, Alexandra Constantin, and Evan Herbst. 2007. Moses: Open Source Toolkit for Statistical Machine Translation. In *Proceedings of the 45th Annual Meeting of the ACL on Interactive Poster and Demonstration Sessions*, ACL '07, pages 177–180, Stroudsburg, PA, USA. Association for Computational Linguistics.

Ding Liu and Daniel Gildea. 2005. Proceedings of the acl workshop on intrinsic and extrinsic evaluation measures for machine translation and/or summarization. pages 25–32. Association for Computational Linguistics.

Matouš Macháček and Ondřej Bojar. 2011. Approximating a Deep-syntactic Metric for MT Evaluation and Tuning. In *Proceedings of the Sixth Workshop on Statistical Machine Translation*, WMT '11, pages 92–98, Stroudsburg, PA, USA. Association for Computational Linguistics.

Matouš Macháček and Ondřej Bojar. 2013. Results of the WMT13 Metrics Shared Task. In *Proceedings of the Eighth Workshop on Statistical Machine Translation*, pages 45–51, Sofia, Bulgaria, August. Association for Computational Linguistics.

Ryan McDonald, Fernando Pereira, Kiril Ribarov, and Jan Hajič. 2005. Non-projective Dependency Parsing Using Spanning Tree Algorithms. In *Proceedings of the Conference on Human Language Technology and Empirical Methods in Natural Language Processing*, HLT '05, pages 523–530.

George A. Miller. 1995. WordNet: A Lexical Database for English. *COMMUNICATIONS OF THE ACM*, 38:39–41.

Václav Novák and Zdeněk Žabokrtský. 2007. Feature Engineering in Maximum Spanning Tree Dependency Parser. In Václav Matousek and Pavel Mautner, editors, *TSD*, Lecture Notes in Computer Science, pages 92–98. Springer.

Karolina Owczarzak, Josef van Genabith, and Andy Way. 2007. Labelled Dependencies in Machine Translation Evaluation. In *Proceedings of the Second Workshop on Statistical Machine Translation*, StatMT '07, pages 104–111, Stroudsburg, PA, USA. Association for Computational Linguistics.

Sebastian Padó, Daniel Cer, Michel Galley, Dan Jurafsky, and Christopher D. Manning. 2009. Measuring Machine Translation Quality as Semantic Equivalence: a Metric Based on Entailment Features. *Machine Translation*, 23(2-3):181–193, September.

Karel Pala and Pavel Smrž. 2004. Building Czech WordNet. *In Romanian Journal of Information Science and Technology*, 7:79–88.

Kishore Papineni, Salim Roukos, Todd Ward, and Wei-Jing Zhu. 2002. BLEU: A Method for Automatic Evaluation of Machine Translation. In *Proceedings of the 40th Annual Meeting on Association for Computational Linguistics*, ACL '02, pages 311–318, Stroudsburg, PA, USA. Association for Computational Linguistics.

Martin Popel and Zdeněk Žabokrtský. 2010. TectoMT: Modular NLP Framework. In *Proceedings of the 7th International Conference on Advances in Natural Language Processing*, IceTAL'10, pages 293–304, Berlin, Heidelberg. Springer-Verlag.

Petr Sgall. 1967. *Generativní popis jazyka a česká deklinace*. Number v. 6 in Generativní popis jazyka a česká deklinace. Academia.

Matthew G. Snover, Nitin Madnani, Bonnie Dorr, and Richard Schwartz. 2009. TER-Plus: Paraphrase, Semantic, and Alignment Enhancements to Translation Edit Rate. *Machine Translation*, 23(2-3):117–127, September.

Jana Straková, Milan Straka, and Jan Hajič. 2014. Open-Source Tools for Morphology, Lemmatization, POS Tagging and Named Entity Recognition. In *Proceedings of 52nd Annual Meeting of the Association for Computational Linguistics: System Demonstrations*, pages 13–18, Baltimore, Maryland, June. Association for Computational Linguistics.

Zdeněk Žabokrtský, Jan Ptáček, and Petr Pajas. 2008. Tectomt: Highly modular mt system with tectogrammatics used as transfer layer. In *Proceedings of the Third Workshop on Statistical Machine Translation*, StatMT '08, pages 167–170.

Liang Zhou, Chin yew Lin, and Eduard Hovy. 2006. Reevaluating machine translation results with paraphrase support. In *In Proceedings of EMNLP*.

Universal and Language-specific Dependency Relations for Analysing Romanian

Verginica Barbu Mititelu
Research Institute for Artificial Intelligence "Mihai Drăgănescu"
Romanian Academy
Romania
vergi@racai.ro

Cătălina Mărănduc
Faculty of Computer Science,
"Al. I Cuza" University,
Romania
catalina.maranduc@info.uaic.ro

Elena Irimia
Research Institute for Artificial Intelligence "Mihai Drăgănescu"
Romanian Academy
Romania
elena@racai.ro

Abstract

This paper is meant as a brief description of the Romanian syntax within the dependency framework, more specifically within the Universal Dependency (UD) framework, and is the result of a volunteer activity of mapping two independently created Romanian dependency treebanks to the UD specifications. This mapping process is not trivial, as concessions have to be made and solutions need to be found for various language specific phenomena. We highlight the specific characteristics of the UD relations in Romanian and argument the need for other relations. If they have already been defined for (an)other language(s) in the UD project, we adopt them.

1 Introduction

The context of the work presented below is the creation of various language resources for Romanian. Throughout time, several resources have been created, which are available on the Meta-Share platform (http://ws.racai.ro:9191/). Nevertheless, the need for a syntactically annotated corpus was underlined in (Trandabăţ et al., 2012). In the last years, two treebanks for Romanian were created. Although using different sets of relations, they both adopted the dependency grammar formalism and were created in complete awareness of each other.

Perez (2014) and Mărănduc and Perez (2015) reported on a treebank of (now) 5800 sentences, with 121 657 words and an average of 21 words per sentence. The sentences belong to all functional styles and cover different historical periods (the translated English FrameNet, Orwell's "1984", some Romanian belletristic texts, Wikipedia and Acquis Communautaire documents, political texts, etc.). They are annotated with dependency relations, but using a set of Romanian traditional grammar labels for the syntactic relations (such as prepositional attribute, adjectival attribute, direct complement, secondary complement, etc.). We refer to this corpus as UAIC-RoTb (the Romanian treebank created at "Al. I. Cuza" University of Iaşi).

Irimia and Barbu Mititelu (2015) report on a treebank (created at RACAI and further referred to as RACAI-RoTb) of (now) 5000 sentences. This corpus contains 5 sub-sections, covering the following genres: journalistic (news and editorials), pharmaceutical and medical short texts, legalese, biographies and critical reviews, fiction. From each such subsection of the Romanian balanced corpus (ROMBAC, Ion et al., 2012), the most frequent 500 verbs were selected and 2 sentences (with length varying from 10 to 30 words), illustrating the usage of each verb (so a total of 10 sentences per verb), were designated to be part of the treebank. They are annotated with dependency relations, but using a reduced set of labels, created with an eye to the UD set, but treating functional words as heads, differentiating among more types of objects (direct, indirect, secondary and prepositional) and disregarding the morpho-syntactic realizations of subjects and objects (so making no distinction between subjects or objects realized as nouns and subjects or objects realized as subordinate clauses, nor between subjects in active or in passive sentences).

Our effort now is to create a reference dependency Romanian treebank following the principles of the UD project by converting the annotation of these two treebanks into the UD style. The conversion process has not started yet, so we cannot report on any data about its performance. However, each team (the UAIC

Proceedings of the Third International Conference on Dependency Linguistics (Depling 2015), pages 28–37,
Uppsala, Sweden, August 24–26 2015.

and the RACAI one) has mapped the set of relations in their treebank to the UD set. For most of the situations, the two teams agree on the UD relations meant to describe various syntactic phenomena. However, there are cases when different solutions were given, as will be signalled below.

On the one hand, we will discuss below the UD relations from the perspective of their morpho-syntactic realization in Romanian, thus emphasizing language characteristics (section 3). On the other hand, we will describe language-specific constructions and bring arguments in favour of the treatment we propose (section 4). What we consider language-specific constructions are not necessarily constructions occurring only in Romanian. When they have been described for other languages as well, we will, in fact, add one more language argument supporting the respective relation.

2 Related work

Our effort of converting the treebanks in the UD annotation style is not singular. On the contrary, it aligns with the increasing number of such volunteer initiatives meant to offer treebanks for different languages consistently annotated, that could further help the development of multilingual parsers.

The 28 languages involved in this project now are Amharic, Ancient Greek, Basque, Bulgarian, Catalan, Chinese, Croatian, Czech, Danish, English, Finish, French, German, Greek, Hebrew, Hindi, Hungarian, Indonesian, Irish, Italian, Latin, Japanese, Korean, Persian, Romanian, Slovenian, Spanish, and Sweden. We can notice the world wide interest for this topic, both for spoken and for dead languages.

The desideratum in the UD project is to have consistent annotations of treebanks for different languages. Consequently, all teams adopt the same relations for syntactic analysis. Nevertheless, language specific phenomena benefit of close attention and, besides the universal set of relations, extensions are also possible in order to accommodate all linguistic phenomena. For example, the Czech, English, Finnish, Greek, Irish, and Swedish teams have already proposed some extensions, for a correct annotation of the reflexive marker of passive voice (Czech), of the possessive nominal constructions (English, Finnish, Irish, Swedish), of relative clauses (English, Finnish, Greek, Irish, Swedish), etc.

3 Universal dependency relations in Romanian

Our intention of automatically converting the two treebanks (UAIC-RoTb and RACAI-RoTb) to the UD annotation style was motivated by the need for a bigger, unified, harmonious, conformant to international standards resource. In the conversion process, we confronted various problems connected to the representation of language phenomena within the new formalism. The way we decided to deal with them is described below.

For marking the syntactic relations between parts of speech in Romanian, we have used the inventory of relations from the UD project (http://universaldependencies.github.io/docs/u/dep/index.html, an adapted version of the relations described in de Marneffe, 2014):

Relation label	**Description**
`root`	the head of a sentence
`nsubj`	nominal subject
`nsubjpass`	passive nominal subject
`csubj`	clausal subject
`csubjpass`	clausal passive subject
`dobj`	direct object
`iobj`	indirect object
`ccomp`	clausal complement
`xcomp`	open clausal complement
`nmod`	nominal modifier
`advmod`	adverbial modifier
`advcl`	adverbial clause modifier
`neg`	negation
`appos`	apposition
`amod`	adjectival modifier
`acl`	clausal modifier of a noun (adjectival clause)
`det`	determiner
`case`	case marking
`vocative`	addressee
`aux`	auxiliary verb
`auxpass`	passive auxiliary
`cop`	copula verb
`mark`	subordinating conjunction
`expl`	expletive
`conj`	conjunct
`cc`	coordinating conjunction
`discourse`	discourse element
`compound`	relation for marking

	compound words
name	names
mwe	multiword expressions that are not names
foreign	text in a foreign language
goeswith	two parts of a word that are separated in text
list	used for chains of comparable elements
dislocated	dislocated elements
parataxis	parataxis
remnant	remnant in ellipsis
reparandum	overridden disfluency
punct	punctuation
dep	unspecified dependency

Table 1. UD relations used for annotating the Romanian treebank.

We do not use the `nummod` relation, as we treat numerals as either nouns or adjectives.
We will highlight below the specific characteristics of some of these relations in the analysis of Romanian and what decision regarding annotation they involved.

3.1. Root

In our treebank the predicate of a sentence can be a verb, an adverb (what Romanian traditional grammar calls a predicative adverb) (1, 2), an interjection (3), a noun (4) or an adjective (5). When such a predicate is the head of a sentence, it is marked as `root`. Although cases when an adverb or an interjection is the root of a sentence are not mentioned on the UD website, we consider them possible in sentences similar to the ones exemplified for Romanian.

(1) **Jos** mafia!
Down mafia!
"Down with the mafia!"

(2) **Poate** că întârzie.
Maybe that is_late
"He may be late."

(3) **Marş** afară!
Shoo out!
"Get out!"

(4) Maria este **sora** mea.
Mary is sister-the my
"Mary is my sister."

(5) Maria este **înaltă**.
"Mary is tall."

If verbs, adverbs and interjections are commonly treated as predicates in Romanian linguistics, the last two are the result of adopting from UD the analysis of the copula *fi* "be" as being in `cop` relation with what traditional grammar analyses as a predicative.

Another situation when the root is not a predicate is represented by elliptical sentences, which lack a predicate, and thus their root is the head of the phrase they contain: in the Bi sentence below it is the noun *parc*. In case more than one argument or adjunct of the missing root are present, the head of the first one (in linear order) is the root of the sentence and all the others are attached to it by the relation they would have been attached to the verbal root if it had been present:

(6) A: Unde pleci?
Where leave-you?
"Where are you going?"
B: i) În **parc**.
In park
"To the park."
ii) În **parc**, cu Dan.
In park, with Dan
"To the park, with Dan."

3.2. Cop

In UD the copula *be* is linked by means of the relation *cop* to the predicative noun or adjective functioning as the root of the sentence. However, when the predicative is a clause, *be* is the root of the sentence and the clause predicative is `ccomp`. We adopted the same analysis for its Romanian equivalent, *fi*, in spite of the inconsistency in the analysis of this verb.

On the other hand, we can notice an inconsistent treatment of copular verbs in UD. Thus, the verb *be* is in `cop` relation to the root, whereas other copular verbs are analysed as roots: here is an example with *become* from the English treebank in its first release on the UD website (file en-ud-dev.conllu):

(7) John has **become** an engineer.
`root (become)`
`xcomp (become, engineer)`

In Romanian, the verb *deveni* "become" is always traditionally analysed as copular, whereas all the other copular verbs can also be predicative for some of their meanings. We illustrate this with *însemna*, which is predicative in (8a) and copular in (8b), according to the traditional grammar analysis:

(8) a) Copilul **a însemnat** tema.
Child-the has marked homework-the
"The child marked the homework."
b) Răspunsul lui **a însemnat** diplomație.
Answer-the his has meant diplomacy
"His answer meant/was_a_proof_of diplomacy."

In (8a) *tema* is the direct object and in (8b) *diplomație* is the predicative, not a direct object, as it does not pass the test specific to direct objects: substitution with an Accusative personal pronoun. Although the sentences may seem syntactically similar, they are different and traditional syntactic analysis captures the difference by assigning a distinct syntactic function to the two nouns following the verb.

Our solution for copular verbs (except *fi*, whose analysis is presented above), in line with other languages in the project, is to mark them as roots and treat them as regular raising verbs, so they take (i.e., their predicative is analysed as) an `xcomp` dependent. Consequently, the distinction between the two morphological values of such verbs (predicative and copular) is reflected in the different types of relation linking its second argument.

3.3. Subject

Subject is the only relation for which subtypes were created in UD in order to differentiate between active and passive sentences, on the one hand, and phrasal and clausal realization, on the other. Thus, four subtypes are used: `nsubj`, `nsubjpass`, `csubj`, `csubjpass`, which we adopted.

In Romanian, the nominal subject is sometimes doubled by a pronominal one, marking a certain illocutionary attitude of the speaker: threat, promise, and reassurance (see 9). As Romanian is a pro-drop language, the nominal subject may be omitted (10). Irrespective of the presence or absence of the nominal subject, the pronoun has a clitic behaviour in such examples (Barbu, 2003).

The analysis we propose within UD is the following: the nominal, when present, is marked as `nsubj`, while the pronoun in Nominative case is marked as `expl`, with *și* as `advmod`. The analysis of the pronominal doubling subject does not depend on the presence or absence of the nominal subject.

(9) Tata vine și **el** imediat.
Father-the comes and he immediately
"Father will also come immediately."

(10) Vine și **el** imediat.
Comes and he immediately
"He will also come immediately."

3.4. Objects

Direct, indirect, secondary objects. The Grammar of Romanian Language (GRL) describes three types of objects: direct, indirect and secondary. The last one is an object in the Accusative case, co-occurring with a direct object, also in Accusative. When only one Accusative object occurs with a verb, that object is always a direct one (see 12b). While the direct object may co-occur with either the indirect or the secondary object, the other two can never co-occur:

(11) Fata a dat nume păpușilor.
Girl-the has given names dolls-the-to
"The girl gave names to the dolls."

(12) a) Bunica i-a învățat pe copii o poezie.
Grandmother-the them-has taught PE children a poem
"Grandmother taught the children a poem."
b) Bunica a învățat o poezie.
Grandmother-the has learned a poem
"Grandmother has learned a poem."

Within UD, we analyse the direct object in (11) (*nume*) as `dobj` and the indirect object (*păpușilor*) as `iobj`. As in UD there is no label for the secondary object, in (12a) the direct object (*copii*) is analyzed as `iobj` and the secondary object (*poezie*) as `dobj`, adopting the Czech convention, supported by the semantic roles distribution in the sentence: the animate object is the addressee, and the non-animate is the patient.

Thus, unlike traditional grammar, when it is not the only object of the verb, the Accusative object is either direct or indirect, depending on the co-occurring object: when there is a Dative and an Accusative object, the Dative is `iobj`, and the Accusative is `dobj`; when two Accusatives co-occur, the [+Animate] one is `iobj`, and the [-Animate] one is `dobj`. So, an automatic analysis needs access to a word sense disambiguation tool or to a dictionary.

Object doubling. A characteristic of Romanian direct and indirect objects is their obligatory doubling by a clitic, when certain characteristics hold: for the direct object: definiteness, pre-verbal occurrence, co-occurrence with the preposition *pe*, pronominal realization; for the indirect object: [+Human], preverbal occurrence.

Thus, the direct object can have the types of realizations presented under (13), while the indirect object those under (14):

(13) a) Ascult **muzică**.
Listen-I music.
"I am listening to music."
b) **Îl** ascult pe **Ion/el**.
Cl.3.sg.masc.Acc. listen-I PE John/him.
"I am listening to John/him."
c) **Îl** ascult.
Him listen-I
"I am listening to him."

(14) a) Dau de mâncare **pisicii**.
Give-I of food cat-the-to
"I give food to the cat."
b) **Le** dau de mâncare **copiilor/lor**.
Cl.3.pl.Dat. give-I of food children-the-to/to-them
"I give the children/them food."
c) **Le** dau de mâncare.
To-them give-I of food
"I give them food."

When the direct or indirect object is not doubled, it is analysed as `dobj` and `iobj`, respectively, no matter if it is realised by a noun or a pronoun (see examples a) and c) under (13) and (14)). In the b) examples, the clitic is analysed as `expl` and it doubles a `dobj` or `iobj`, respectively.

3.5. Adverb modifiers

Adverbs can modify nouns (15), verbs (16), adjectives (17) and other adverbs (18) in Romanian and for all these cases we use the label `advmod`.

(15) Cititul **noaptea** nu este sănătos.
Reading-the at-night not is healthy
"Reading at night is not healthy."

(16) Citesc **noaptea**.
Read-I at-night
"I read at night."

(17) o casă **chiar** frumoasă
a house really beautiful
"a really beautiful house"

(18) Scrie **chiar** ordonat.
Writes really neatly
"He writes really neatly."

However, with some verbs, the adverb represents an obligatory dependent, without which the sentence is ungrammatical:

(19) Copilul se poartă *(**frumos**).
Child-the refl.cl.3.sg. behaves beautifully
"The child behaves himself."

As a consequence, in Romanian we use the `advmod` label both for non-core dependents and for core ones.

3.6. Subordinate clauses

Subordinate clauses are introduced by relative elements (and indefinites formed from relatives) or subordinating conjunctions. The relative elements are pronouns, adjectives or adverbs. The major difference between relatives (and indefinites) and conjunctions concerns their syntactic role within the clause they introduce: the former have a syntactic function in the subordinated clause, whereas the conjunctions lack it. As a consequence, we adopted the UD solution of treating them in different ways: relatives (and indefinites) establish a relation of whatever kind (`nsubj`, `dobj`, `iobj`, `advmod`, `amod`, etc.) with the head of the subordinated clause (20); the subordinating conjunction is only a marker of the syntactic subordination and establishes the relation `mark` with the head of the subordinated clause (21).

(20) Știu **cine** a venit.
Know-I who has come
"I know who has come."
`nsubj(venit, cine)`
`ccomp(Știu, venit)`

(21) Știu **că** vine târziu.
Know-I that comes late
"I know that (s)he comes late."
`mark(vine, că)`
`ccomp(Știu, vine)`

This way, we ensure, in fact, a consistent way of choosing the element in the subordinated clause meant to participate to the subordinating relation: the head of the subordinate clause.

A consistent annotation is ensured also for the relative elements, which can also function as interrogative elements in questions: they always establish a syntactic relation with the head of the clause:

(22) **Cine** a venit?
"Who has come?"

The conjunctive mood is formed with the conjunction *să*. It can occur both in main clauses (23) and in subordinate ones (24).

(23) **Să** mergem!
SĂ go-we
"Let's go!"
(24) Vreau **să** mergem.
Want-I SĂ go-we.
"I want us to go."

Our solution is to analyse both such occurrences in the same way, i.e. *să* is `mark` for the verb, in spite of the UD definition of the marker as a "word introducing a finite clause subordinate to another clause" (cf. http://universaldependencies.github.io/docs/u/dep/mark.html).

4 Language-specific constructions

In this section we describe constructions from Romanian for which the UD relations are not appropriate.

4.1. Agent complement

An agent complement may occur in constructions with the verb in the passive voice (25) or with non-finite verbs (26) or adjectives (27) with a passive meaning:

(25) Cartea a fost cumpărată **de Ion**.
Book-the has been bought by John
"The book was bought by John."
(26) Aceasta este calea de urmat **de_către** orice **om** integru.
This is way-the of followed by any man honest
"This is the way to follow for any honest man."
(27) Avea un comportament inacceptabil **de_către colegii** săi.
Had-he a behaviour unacceptable by colleagues-the his
"He had an unacceptable behaviour by his colleagues."

Besides the prepositional phrase (headed by the simple preposition *de* or by the compound preposition *de_către*[1]), the agent complement may also be realized by a subordinate relative clause:

(28) A fost angajat **de cine a avut încredere în el**.
Has been hired by who has had trust in him.
"He was hired by who trusted him."

In line with other languages displaying this syntactic specificity in the UD project (Swedish), we support the proposal of creating a subtype of the `nmod` relation: `nmod:agent`. We highlight the fact that in such cases `nmod` is also a core dependent of the head. For the last example, when the agent is realized as a subordinate clause (28), we propose `ccomp:agent`.

4.2. Prepositional object

This is a verb argument (i.e., it is part of the verb subcategorization frame) introduced by a preposition selected by the verb:

(29) Mă gândesc **la Maria**.
Refl.cl.1.sg.Acc. think of Mary
"I am thinking of Mary."

Prepositions are not heads in UD. So, the nominal is annotated as `nmod` on the verb and the preposition as `case` on the noun. However, `nmods` are defined as non-core dependents of a predicate in UD. Thus, annotating the prepositional objects as `nmod` implies treating them in exactly the same way as we treat adverbials realized by a prepositional phrase. In the following example, *la problemă* is the prepositional object and *la masa* is the time adverbial, in traditional grammar terms.

(30) Mă gândesc **la problemă la masa** de prânz.
Refl.cl.1.sg.Acc. think of problem at meal-the of noon
"I am thinking at the problem at lunch."

However, if `nmods` functioning as adverbials are optional, prepositional objects are obligato-

[1] In the pre-processing phase, compound prepositions are recognised (given their presence in our electronic lexicon) and marked as one token (using the underscore).

ry for the grammatical correctness of the sentence:

(31) Mă bazez *(**pe voi**).
Refl.cl.1.sg.Acc. count-I *(on you)
"I count *(on you)."

That is why we are not satisfied with this analysis of prepositional objects in which they are not distinguished from dependents which are not obligatory and we propose to redefine the `nmod` relation so that it covers both core and non-core dependents. In line with this redefinition, in RACAI-RoTb we introduce the `nmod:pmod` subtype of `nmod` to account for the obligatory prepositional objects of predicates, a phenomenon present in other languages, as well. However, in UAIC-RoTb such cases are analysed as `iobj`, given the occurrence in language of two parallel structures for indirect object: one with the noun in Dative case and another with the preposition *la* and the noun in Accusative. The latter structure is the norm for phrases containing a quantifier or a numeral in the standard language (32), but it witnesses an extension to all kinds of nouns in colloquial speech (33):

(32) Le spun o poveste *la trei copii.*
"I tell a story to three children."
(33) Le spun o poveste *la copii.*
"I tell a story to the children."

4.3. Possession

There are several ways of expressing possession in Romanian: sentences with the verb *avea* "to have" or its synonyms, genitive nouns or personal pronouns, possessive adjective (which we link by means of the `amod:poss` relation to the head nominal, see (4) above, where *mea* is in `amod:poss` relation with its head, *sora*) and pronouns and dative personal pronouns. We focus here on genitive and dative constructions, as the others do not raise any special problems.

The genitive constructions (involving nouns or personal pronouns) may have a possessive meaning (34) or not (35):

(34) Trecutul **castelului** este necunoscut.
Past-the of-castle-the is unknown
"The past of the castle is unknown."
(35) Reconstrucția **castelului** a început.
Rebuilding of-castle-the has started
"The rebuilding of the castle has started."

And this is the case in other languages as well: see Finish (http://universaldependencies.github.io/docs/fi/dep/nmod-poss.html, accessed on April 7). The subtype `nmod:poss` is used to annotate all these constructions, in spite of the semantic differences between them. And this is the way in which such cases are dealt with in UAIC-RoTb, as well. However, the RACAI-RoTB team uses only the label `nmod`, leaving the possessive value of genitives not specified.

As far as the possessive dative is concerned, it is always realised by a pronominal clitic on the verb:

(36) **Mi**-am pierdut fularul (*meu).
Cl.1.sg.Dat-have-I lost scraf-the (*my)
"I have lost my scarf."

The co-occurrence of the possessive adjective (*meu*) in such constructions makes them pleonastic.

For the clitic analysis the RACAI-RoTb team decided to use the `nmod:poss` relation to link it to the verb. The UAIC-RoTb team opted for the `iobj` relation for such cases.

4.4. Reflexive pronouns

Reflexive pronouns can have various semantic values:

- reflexive value: see examples (29), (30) and (31) above;
- reciprocal value:

(37) Doi copii **se** bat.
Two children SE fight
"Two children are fighting."

- passive value:

(38) **Se** bat albușurile cu zahăr.
SE beat whites with sugar
"Egg whites are beaten with sugar."

- pronominal value:

(39) Ion **se** spală.
John SE washes
"John is washing himself."

- impersonal value:

(40) **Se** înnoptează.
SE gets_dark
"It is getting dark."

For the reflexive, reciprocal and impersonal value, when the reflexive pronoun (either in Accusative or in Dative case) has no syntactic function and is a mere marker of the reflexive, reciprocal or impersonal voice of the verb, according to traditional grammar, we adopt the relation `compound:reflex`, a subtype of the `compound` relation, to link the pronoun to the verb, as proposed for Czech.

For the passive value, when the occurrence of the pronoun blocks the occurrence of the passive auxiliary (*fi*), we propose the relation `auxpass:reflex`, a subtype of the `auxpass` relation, to link the pronoun to the verb.

For the pronominal value, we need no other relation, as the pronoun has a syntactic function: `dobj` or `iobj` (in (37) it is a `dobj`).

4.5. Participles

The Romanian participle has some characteristics that make it similar to adjectives (it inflects for number, for gender and for case and can modify a noun) and others that prove its verbal nature (it can take arguments):

(41) poezii **recitate** de meseni la comanda lui Charles
poems recited by diners at order-the def.art.masc.sg.Genit. Charles
"poems recited by diners at Charles' order"

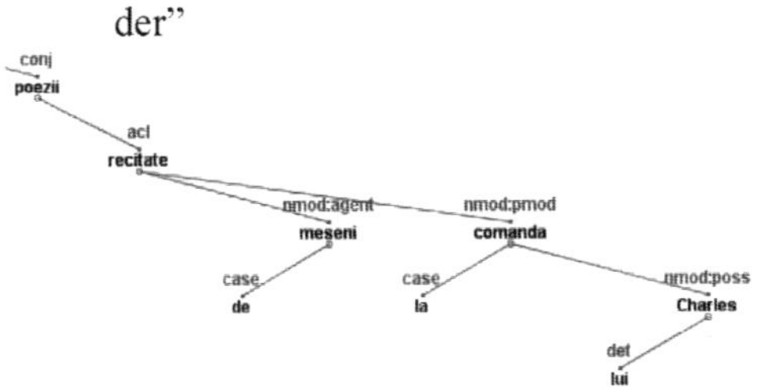

Fig. 1. The arguments of the participle *recitate*.

Given the participle possibility of having arguments, we decided to analyse the participles that determine a noun as establishing the `acl` relation to that noun.

4.6. Putting semantics into adverbials

UAIC-RoTb contains semantic information about the adjuncts occurring therein: they express time, place, manner, instrument, exception, purpose, cause, etc. They are morphologically realised as adverbs, noun phrases, prepositional phrases (containing a noun) or subordinate clauses. Considering potential further processing of the treebank for various applications, a part of the semantic information was preserved, namely the time adjuncts. They are annotated as `advmod:time`, `nmod:time` or `advcl:time`, respectively.

4.7. Infinitive or conjunctive?

A specific syntactic feature is the verb mood selected for expressing the clausal argument of a verb. UAIC-RoTb has an incipient parallel treebank containing 250 sentences of the novel "1984" by G. Orwell, annotated in English, French and Romanian, which allows us to compare the syntax of the three languages. In English and in French the second verb is an infinitive directly related to the first one or related by means of a preposition:

(42) Il cesse **de** parler / He ceases **to** speak / El încetează **să** vorbească.

In Romanian the conjunctive mood is selected, which has the conjunction *să* as a marker. The structure with the second verb in the infinitive with preposition is possible in Romanian but less frequent and either obsolete or formal.

(43) Noi încetăm (de) **a vorbi**.

The Romanian subjunctive has inflexion for person and number:

(44) Nous cessons de parler. / We cease to speak. / Noi încetăm să **vorbim.**

Thus, in Romanian we can have either two clauses (when the second verb is in the conjunctive mood) or only one (when the second verb is in the infinitive mood), in traditional grammar terms. Both cases correspond to English and French structures with a non-finite verb. However, this issue disappears as the dependency grammar treats all verbs identically, i.e. as heads of clauses, irrespective of their finite or non-finite form.

4.8. The verb *a putea* "can"

The problem of the mood of the second verb in Romanian gets more complicated if we compare the structures containing modal verbs in the three languages.

(45) We **must** eat. /Il **faut** manger. /**Trebuie** să mâncăm.

In the languages that have modal verbs, they take short infinitive. In Romanian, among the potential modal verbs, only *a putea* "can" displays this syntactic behaviour, as well as the usual one, with the second verb at the subjunctive mood.

(46) Putem **scrie.** / Putem **să scriem.**
"We can write".

Romanian does not have modal verbs. However, there are a number of syntactic phenomena that make us conclude that *a putea* is the only verb in the process of transition to the status of modal verb.

The constructions with the verb *a putea* followed by a short infinitive are synonymous and commutable with those where it is followed by a conjunctive (see 46). Statistically, the infinitive is more frequent than the conjunctive: out of 150 examples containing this verb in UAIC-RoTb, 33% contain a conjunctive, 24% contain no following verb (so, they are statistically irrelevant), and 43% contain a short infinitive without any preposition.

There are a lot of dependents of the verb *a putea* that are advanced one level up in the tree: originally, they are arguments of the infinitive verb occurring after *a putea*:

(47) Problema ţărănească nu se poate rezolva.
Problem-the rustic not SE can solve
"The peasants' problem cannot be solved".

The subject *problema* belongs to the subcategorization frame of the verb *rezolva*. However, its number agreement with the verb *poate* proves its new syntactic status, that of subject of *poate*. *Se* is the passive maker of the verb *rezolva*, although raised on *poate*.

Other core-dependents are also raised on the verb *a putea*: here is an example with an indirect object:

(48) Nu-**mi** putea da o cameră.
Not-to-me could-he give a room
"He could not give me a room."

We consider that *a putea* should be analysed as `aux` when followed by an infinitive, and as a root when followed by a subjunctive.

5 Conclusion

The Universal Dependency grammar project offers the material for a comparative and contrastive study of the languages involved in it. The same phenomenon can be studied in various languages and similarities, as well as differences highlighted.

During our process of automatically converting the annotation of the two Romanian treebanks into UD annotation, we had to find solutions for various language phenomena and they were either of the type "use a UD label to cover more situations than those presented within the UD project" or of the type "postulate a new label, a subtype of a relation existing in UD".

One of the results of our working methodology is the heterogeneity of the syntactic relations covered by a UD label: see the case of `nmod` presented above. Another result is the blurring of the very clear border between some syntactic functions: see the case of direct object, indirect object and secondary object.

References

Blanca Arias, Núria Bel, Mercè Lorente, Montserrat Marimón, Alba Milà, Jorge Vivaldi, Muntsa Padró, Marina Fomicheva, Imanol Larrea. 2014. Boosting the Creation of a Treebank. In Calzolari, Nicoletta, Choukri, Khalid; Declerck, Thierry (et al.) (eds.) *Proceedings of the Ninth International Conference on Language Resources and Evaluation (LREC'14): May 26-31, 2014 Reykjavik, Iceland.* [s.l.]: ELRA. p. 775-781.

Verginica Barbu. 2003. Construcţii cu subiect dublu în limba română actuală. O perspectivă HPSG. In G. Pană Dindelegan, *Aspecte ale dinamicii limbii române actuale*. Editura Universităţii din Bucureşti, p. 73-79.

GRL – V. Guţu Romalo (ed.). 2005. *The Grammar of Romanian Language*. Romanian Academy Publishing House, second volume.

Radu Ion, Elena Irimia, Dan Ştefănescu, Dan Tufiş 2012. ROMBAC: The Romanian Balanced Annotated Corpus. In *Proc. LREC'12* Istanbul, Turkey.

Elena Irimia and Verginica Barbu Mititelu. 2015. *Building a Romanian Dependency Treebank.* Corpus Linguistics 2015, Lancaster, UK, 21-24 July 2015.

Igor Mel'čuk. 1988. *Dependency Syntax: Theory and Practice.* The SUNY Press, Albany, N.Y.

Joakim Nivre, Johan Hall, Jens Nilsson, Atanas Chanev, Gül¸sen Eryigit, Sandra Kübler, Svetoslav Marinov, and Erwin Marsi. 2007. Maltparser: A languageindependent system for data-driven dependency parsing. *Natural Language Engineering*, 13:95–135.

Montserrat Marimon and Nuria Bel. 2014. Dependency structure annotation in the IULA Spanish LSP Treebank. *Language Resources and Evaluation*. Amsterdam: Springer Netherlands.

Marie-Catherine de Marneffe, Timothy Dozat, Natalia Silveira, Katri Haverinen, Filip Ginter, Joakim Nivre, Christopher D. Manning. 2014. Universal Stanford Dependencies: A cross-lingustic typology, *Proceedings of LREC 2014*: 4585-4592.

Cătălina Mărănduc and Augusto-Cenel Perez. 2015. *A Romanian dependency treebank*, CICLing 2015, Cairo, 14-20 April.

Augusto-Cenel Perez. 2014. *Resurse lingvistice pentru prelucrarea limbajului natural*. PhD thesis, "Al. I Cuza" University, Iasi.

Randolph Quirk, Sidney Greenbaum, Geoffrey Leech, Jan Svartvik. 1985. A Comprehensive Grammar of the English Language. Longman.

Lucien Tesnière. 1959. *Éléments de syntaxe structurale*. Klincksieck, Paris.

Diana Trandabăţ, Elena Irimia, Verginica Barbu Mititelu, Dan Cristea, Dan Tufiş. 2012. *The Romanian Language in the Digital Age. Limba română în era digitală*. In White Papers Series (Rehm, Georg and Uszkoreit, Hans). Springer-Verlag, Berlin, Heidelberg.

Emotion and Inner State Adverbials in Russian

Olga Boguslavskaya
Russian Language Institute,
Russian Academy of Sciences
Russia
Boguslavskaya.Olga@gmail.com

Igor Boguslavsky
Universidad Politécnica de Madrid / Institute for Information Transmission Problems
Spain / Russia
Igor.M.Boguslavsky@gmail.com

Abstract

We study a group of adverbials that are composed of a preposition and a noun denoting an emotion or an inner state, such as *v jarosti* 'in a rage', *s udovol'stviem* 'with pleasure', *ot radosti* 'out of joy', *s gorja* 'out of grief', *na udivlenie* 'to the surprise of', *k dosade* 'to one's disappointment' etc. Being collocations, they occupy an intermediate position between free phrases and idioms. On the one hand, some of them are simple adverbial derivatives of nouns and therefore inherit some of their properties. On the other hand, they may have specific properties of their own. Two types of properties of the adverbials are studied: the actantial properties in their correlation with the properties of the source nouns, and the semantics proper. At the end a case study of the adverbials of the gratitude field is given. We show that adverbial derivatives can be shifted in the dependency structure from the subordinate clause to the main one.

1. Introduction

We proceed from the obvious assumption that adverbial derivatives refer to the same situation as the source lexical unit (LU). This implies that, given the semantic structure with predicate P, our linguistic description should be able to produce a syntactic structure in which P is realized by means of an adverbial derivative of P and determine possible syntactic positions for LUs that correspond to semantic actants of P. And, the other way round, given sentences such as *John replied by a nod* and *John nodded in reply*, we should be able to discover that in both cases the semantic actants of 'reply' are 'John' and 'his nod'. Thus, our aim consists in describing semantic and syntactic properties of adverbial derivatives in their correlation with the source LU. For each predicate, we need to know its possible syntactic realizations (e.g. 'reply' --> *to reply – in reply*) along with semantic modifications associated with them. For each syntactic realization, we should specify possible ways of valency filling of the LU. The main difference between this approach and traditional valency dictionaries is that we concentrate on adverbial derivatives of predicates in their correlation with the source LU unit and take into consideration a much larger range of possible realizations of their semantic actants.

We study a group of nouns that denote emotions and inner states (EIS nouns). They are often used in specific adverbial prepositional phrases – *v jarosti* 'in a rage', *s udovol'stviem* 'with pleasure', *ot radosti* 'out of joy', *s gorja* 'out of grief', *na udivlenie* 'to the surprise of', *k dosade* 'to one's disappointment' etc. The phrases usually mean that a person is in this state or that this state is the cause or a consequence of some other state or event. For brevity, we will call such phrases EIS adverbials.

Russian explanatory dictionaries usually treat EIS adverbials as free phrases and attribute all their peculiarities, if any, to specific properties of corresponding prepositions. For example, the recent Active dictionary of Russian (ADR 2014), which provides deeply elaborated semantic definitions, lists among the senses of preposition *v* 'in', sense *v 4.1* which «is used to denote the state A2 of a person A1 or his relationship A2 with other people»: *On byl v sil'nom razdraženii (v polnom izumlenii, v upoenii, v ekstaze). V jarosti pnul sobačonku.* 'He was in a temper (in utter surprise, in ecstasy). In a rage, he kicked the dog'. Other detailed descriptions of semantics of Russian prepositions used in EIS adverbials can be found in Iomdin 1990-91, Iordanskaja-Mel'čuk 1996, Levontina 2004. However, even the most precise and detailed description of prepositions does not fully account for all peculiarities of adverbials. We intend to show that EIS adverbials manifest a number of features that are not derivable from the properties of prepo-

Proceedings of the Third International Conference on Dependency Linguistics (Depling 2015), pages 38–47,
Uppsala, Sweden, August 24–26 2015.

sitions or nouns alone but appear only in their combination. Special attention will be paid to semantic and syntactic properties of the adverbials.

In section 2 we will explain what we basically mean by adverbial derivatives and describe their certain properties relevant for our study. Section 3 will characterize EIS adverbials of different types. In section 4 we demonstrate a case study related to adverbials of the field of gratitude. We will conclude in 5.

2. Adverbial derivatives.

We consider EIS adverbials as adverbial derivatives of corresponding nouns. An adverbial derivative of lexical unit (LU) L is a LU or a phrase that has the same or a similar meaning to L and has an adverbial syntactic function, which means that it is primarily used as a verb modifier. For more details on syntactic derivatives in general and adverbial derivatives in particular we refer the reader to Boguslavsky 2014.

In Russian, there are three major types of adverbial derivatives: a) grammatical derivatives that can be derived from virtually any verb (deverbal adverbs, *deepričastija*); cf. (1a), b) lexico-syntactic derivatives (prepositional phrases) derived from nouns; cf. (1b), and c) lexical derivatives (adverbs); cf. (1c). The last two cases can be described as values of the lexical function Adv_i.

(1a) *Oni razgljadyvali kartinki, radujas' kak deti.*
'they were examining the pictures rejoicing like children'.
(1b) *Ja s bolšoj radostju prinimaju vaše priglašenie.*
'I accept your invitation with great joy'.
(1c) *Deti radostno prinjalis' narjažat' jolku.*
'the kids merrily began to decorate the Christmas tree'.

Deverbal adverbs retain the lexical meaning and syntactic properties of the source LU to a greater extent than other types of adverbial derivatives. They serve to express a secondary predication attached to the main one. Their most salient feature is that their subject is always coreferential with the subject of the main clause and is elided from the syntactic structure. As a rule, prepositional phrases and adverbs also retain the lexical meaning of the source word, but they can manifest noticeable semantic modifications.

As far as the actantial structure of adverbials is concerned, it is necessary to distinguish between three types of valency slots in the semantic definition of a LU depending on the syntactic position of the argument with respect to its predicate (Boguslavsky 2003)[1]. We call a valency slot of lexeme *L* ACTIVE if in the syntactic structure of the sentence it is filled by a word syntactically subordinated to *L*. Active valency slots are instantiated with syntactic actants. We call a valency slot PASSIVE if it is filled by a lexeme that syntactically subordinates *L*. Finally, we call it DISCONTINUOUS if there is no direct syntactic link between *L* and the word filling this slot.

To give an example, the valency slots of the verb *to precede* are active because in the prototypical sentence
(2a) *The conference preceded the workshop*
its actants syntactically depend on the verb. However, if one compares (2a) with the sentence
(2b) *The conference was before the workshop*
we will see that, from the purely semantic point of view, the preposition *before* denotes the same situation as the verb *to precede* - the situation of the temporal precedence of one event with respect to the other. This situation has at least two participants: an event that takes place earlier and another one that takes place later. These participants can be systematically expressed in a sentence with the given word and therefore the preposition *before* has the same semantic rights to have valency slots as the verb *to precede*. The only difference between these slots concerns their syntactic realization. In case of the verb, both slots are filled with phrases which are syntactically subordinated to the verb in the dependency tree (i.e. with the subject and with the direct object) and therefore they are active. With the preposition it is different: one of the slots is also filled with a subordinated NP (*before the workshop*) whereas the other is filled with a phrase which syntactically subordinates the preposition (*the conference was before*), which makes this slot passive.

Discontinous valency filling can be illustrated by quantifiers, cf. (3):
(3) *All the papers* [Q] *were revised* [P].

[1] When we speak of syntactic positions of arguments with respect to predicates, we refer to syntactic positions of LUs that correspond to these arguments and predicates.

All has two valency slots, one of which (Q) is filled by the NP it modifies, and another one (P) – by a VP. Using the terms introduced above, Q is filled in a passive way (since *papers* subordinates *all* in the dependency structure) while P is filled in a discontinous way (while there is no direct dependency link between *all* and *were revised*).

As we will show below, EIS adverbial valencies can be filled in all three ways – actively, passively, and discontinously.

It is noteworthy that the passive valencies of adverbial derivatives can have two sources. If we denote an adverbial derivative as Adv(L), where L is the source lexeme of the derivation, then a passive valency may be determined, on the one hand, by the Adv component of this formula, and on the other hand – by the L part. The first case can be illustrated by the adverbial *vo sne* 'in one's sleep' (cf. (4).

(4) *Vo sne on gromko stonal.*
lit. in sleep he loudly groaned.
'he groaned loudly while sleeping'.

As any adverbial, it is a modifier, and hence the modified word (*stonal* 'groaned ') is its passive argument.

In the second case, a passive valency of an adverbial derivative corresponds to one of the valency slots of L. For example, in (5) *v nakazanie* 'as a punishment' is subordinated to (= is a modifier of) a VP which denotes the punishment itself:

(5) *V nakazanie ego lišili slova.*
lit. in punishment him they.deprived of.word
'he was denied the right to speak as a punishment'.

While in (5) the syntactic governor (*lišili* 'they.denied') of the adverbial is an argument of L (*nakazanie* 'punishment'), in (4) the governor (*stonal* 'groaned') has nothing to do with the argument frame of L (*son* 'sleep').

3. Syntax and semantics of EIS adverbials.

The range of prepositions used for constructing EIS adverbials is rather wide: *s* (+Instr, +Gen, +Gen2[2]), *ot* (+Gen), *iz* (+Gen), *v* (+Loc), *na* (+Loc, Pl), *na* (+Acc), *k* (+Dat), *po* (+Dat). What strikes the eye is that the co-occurence of EIS nouns with prepositions is very selective. As is normal for collocations, even semantically similar nouns co-occur with different prepositions. The noun *strax* 'fear' combines with four causal prepositions – *ot, iz-za, iz* and *s* (+Gen or Gen2): *posedet' ot straxa* 'turn grey out of fear', *skryt'sja iz-za straxa nakazanija* 'escape for fear of punishment', *soglasit'sja iz straxa pered oglaskoj* 'agree for fear of publicity', *ubežat' so straxa (so straxu)* 'run away out of fear'. Of these four prepositions, *bojazn'* 'fear' does not co-occur with *s (*s bojazni).* *Užas* 'horror' mostly co-occurs with *ot* (*drožat' ot užasa* 'tremble with horror' (lit. 'from horror')). The main causal preposition *iz-za* 'because of' occurred together with *užas* only twice in the 230 million-strong Russian National Corpus, although *užas* itself occurred more than 25,000 times. *Panika* 'panic' rarely co-occurs with *ot* (only 10 examples in the corpus), even rarer with *iz-za* (2 examples), and never with *iz.* What is typical for *panika* is an adverbial with *v* 'in' – *v panike* 'in panic' (600 examples among the 3,500 occurrences of *panika* in the corpus).

Below, we will first discuss the actantial structure of EIS adverbials (Section 3.1) and then we will make some remarks about their semantic properties (Section 3.2).

3.1 Actantial structure

Most EIS predicates have two valency slots: Experiencer, who feels an emotion or is in a certain state, and Cause of the emotion or state: *father's rage*, *fear of spiders.* The Experiencer slot is instantiated with a genitive NP (*jarost' otca*), a possessive adjective (*naše gore*) or certain adjectives with the quantifier meaning (*vseobščee vosxiščenie* 'general admiration; = everybody felt admiration'). The Cause slot is instantiated by a larger range of elements: different prepositions (*ot, s, pered, na* and others), the infinitive (*strax byt' ubitym* 'fear of being killed'), the genitive case (*strax temnoty* 'fear of darkness'), the instrumental case (*vozmuščenie ego postupkom* 'indignation at his behaviour', *vosxiščenie ee krasotoj* 'admirarion for her beauty'). There are some EIS nouns that have more valency slots, e.g. *blagodarnost'* 'gratitude' (who is grateful, to whom and for what)[3], *obida* 'resentment' (who feels resentment, towards whom it is felt, and what caused this feeling).

[2] Gen2 is a special case form proper for certain classes of nouns and opposed to Gen: cf. *so straxa* (Gen) – *so straxu* (Gen2)

[3] More on the actantial structure of *blagodarnost'* in Section 4.

Now we will comment on the actantial structure of EIS adverbials.

Experiencer: The Experiencer slot of EIS adverbials is instantiated either in an active or discontinuous way. The active instantiation of the Experiencer slot has two variants:

(a) the form of the Experiencer is directly inherited from the source noun. Cf. *ego (naš, vseobščij) vostorg* 'his (our, universal) delight' – *k ego (našemu, vseobščemu) vostorgu* 'to his (our, universal) delight'; *razočarovanie roditelej*$_{Gen}$ 'disappointment of the parents' – *k razočarovaniju roditelej*$_{Gen}$ 'to the disappointment of the parents'.

(b) the form of the Experiencer is specific for the adverbial. Cf. *strax vragov*$_{Gen}$ 'fear of the enemies' – *na strax vragam*$_{Dat}$ 'so that the enemies tremble with fear'. The adverbial requires Dat, while the source noun only takes Gen.

For some adverbials, the active filling of the Experiencer slot is obligatory: *k radosti <užasu, vozmuščeniju, zavisti> Ivana* 'to Ivan's joy <horror, indignation, envy>'- **k radosti <užasu, vozmuščeniju, zavisti>* 'to the joy <horror, indignation, envy>'.

Very often, the Experiencer is not connected to the adverbial by a direct syntactic link. In (6), the one who feels astonishment is the subject of the subordinating verb and therefore instantiates both the slot of the verb (*perestal* 'stopped') and of the adverbial. In the first case, the instantiation is active, and in the second – discontinuous.

(6) *Ot udivlenija on perestal est'.*
'he stopped eating from astonishment'

Cause: The Cause slot of EIS adverbials is instantiated either in an active or a passive way. When the filling is active, the same prepositions and cases are used as the ones governed by the source nouns: *v otčajanii ot poraženija* 'in despair from defeat', *v užase pered pytkami* 'in horror of tortures', *v straxe byt' ubitym* 'in fear of being killed', *s vooduševleniem ot otkryvajuščixsja vozmožnostej* 'with enthusiasm for opening opportunities', *s obidoj za to, čto on ne pomog* 'with resentment for his failure to help'.

The passive instantiation of the Cause slot can be illustrated by example (7):

(7) *K našemu razočarovaniju, predstavlenie otmenili.*
'to our disappointment, the performance was cancelled'

Here, our disappointment was caused by the cancellation of the performance, which means that the Cause slot is filled by the subordinating verb (*otmenjat'* 'to cancel').

It is important to emphasize that the adverbials derived from different nouns, even if they are constructed with the same prepositions, may have different actantial properties. Cf. adverbials *s jarostju* 'with rage' and *s naslaždeniem* 'with relish'.

(8) *Otec s jarostju vyrval iz ruk Meri pis'mo.*
'Father tore the letter out of Mary's hand with rage'

(9) *Otec s naslaždeniem vykuril sigaru.*
'Father smoke a cigar with relish'.

In (8) only the Experiencer of the emotional state is expressed and nothing is known about its cause. The father's rage had obviously been caused by prior events, and this emotion manifested itself in the way in which he tore the letter out of Mary's hand. In (9) the idea of manifestation is also present. Judging by the way father was smoking a cigar one could see that he was enjoying it. But on top of that, the source of the emotion is also explicitly expressed: the relish is caused by the process of smoking.

3.2 Some observations on the semantics of EIS adverbials

EIS adverbials belong to three semantic groups: concomitant state, effect and cause.

Concomitant state adverbials are constructed with three prepositions – *v* 'in' (+Loc), *s* 'with' (+Instr) and *bez* 'without' (+Gen): *v otčajanii* 'in despair', *s vooduševleniem* 'enthusiastically, lit. with enthusiasm', *bez otvraščenija* 'without disgust'.

Let us compare two very close prepositions that form concomitant state adverbials with EIS - *v* 'in' as *v jarosti* 'in rage' and *s* 'with' as *s jarostju* 'with rage'. First, only one of them allows the cause of emotion to be expressed explicitly:

(10a) *V jarosti ot neudači on vybežal iz komnaty.*
lit. in rage from the failure he ran out of the room.

(10b) **S jarostju ot neudači on vybežal iz komnaty.*
lit. with rage from the failure he ran out of the room.

Second, the phrases in which the Cause is unexpressed are not entirely synonymous. While phrases with *s* emphasize the external manifestation of the emotion, phrases with *v* only indicate that the Experiencer is in a certain emotional state, disregarding its external manifestation. This opposition between *v* 'in' and *s* 'with' is incidental to a large group of phrases in which the noun denotes a state that can be manifested externally, such as *gnev* 'anger', *radost'* 'joy', *pečal'* 'grief', *vostorg* 'delight' etc. (ECD 1984: 208). It is noteworthy that the *s* 'with' phrases point at the manifestation of the emotion only when the action they modify itself has external manifestation. If the action is purely mental, the *s*-phrases lose the manifestation component and denote simple concomitance.

(11a) *Ona s blagodarnostju <negodovaniem> posmotrela na nego* [+ manifestation].
'she looked at him with gratitude <indignation>'

(11b) *On s blagodarnostju <negodovaniem> dumaet o svoix kollegax* [- manifestation].
'he thinks about his colleagues with gratitude <indignation>'

(12a) *Ona s otvraščeniem otvernulas'* [+ manifestation].
'she turned away with revulsion'

(12b) *Ja s otvraščeniem vspominaju etu scenu* [- manifestation].
'I recall this scene with revulsion'

Effect adverbials: There are three prepositions that combine with EIS nouns to convey the idea that a certain emotion or a mental state of person A1 is a result of some situation A2. These are *v* (+Acc), *k* (+Dat) and *na* (+Acc).

The first preposition is used in the predicate position only and combines with a very limited number of nouns. We know of three such nouns – *radost'* 'joy, happiness', *udovol'stvie* 'pleasure', and *tjagost'* 'burden, hard feeling'. Maybe there are some more, but hardly many more. The propositional form that serves as the left part of the lexicographic definition is (13a), and the definition itself is given in (13b). Examples are in (13c,d):

(13a) *A2 (jest') A1*$_{Dat}$ *v radost' (v udovol'stvie, v tjagost')*
lit. A2 (is) A1$_{Dat}$ in happiness (pleasure, hard feeling)

(13b) 'person A1 feels happiness (pleasure, hard feeling) caused by situation A2'

(13c) *Tjaželye trenirovki byli emu v radost'.*
lit. hard training-sessions were to.him in happiness
'hard training sessions made him happy'.

(13d) *Rabota byla ej ne v tjagost'.*
lit. work was to.her not in hard.feeling
'it was not hard for her to work'.

This construction requires that A2 be some lasting or repeated process or activity. It cannot be just a momentary action; cf. perfectly correct (14a) and dubious (14b):

(14a) *Postreljat' v tire bylo ej v udovol'stvie.*
'shooting (=giving a series of shots) in a shooting gallery gave her pleasure'

(14b) *??Vystrelit' bylo ej v udovol'stvie.*
'firing a shot gave her pleasure'

Another feature of this construction worth mentioning is that it is often used with the negation – cf. (13d) above.

Two other prepositions that make up effect adverbials are *k* and *na:*

(15a) *K razočarovaniju poeta ego nikto ne uznaval.*
'to the poet's disappointment nobody recognized him'

(15b) *Na radost' roditeljam Ivan blagopolučno zakončil školu.*
lit. to the happiness of the parents Ivan successfully graduated from school
'the parents were happy that Ivan graduated from school successfully'

Although these constructions convey largely similar meanings, there are several aspects that differentiate them.

1. Both prepositions take A1, the Experiencer of EIS, in the form of the possessive pronoun, but if it is expressed by a noun, preposition *na* requires the dative case, while *k* combines with the genitive.

2. Both constructions are largely lexicalized. One can say *na strax vragam* 'to the fear of the enemies', but not **na užas vragam* 'to the horror of the enemies' or **na ispug vragam* 'to the fright of the enemies'. One can say *k našemu užasu* 'to our horror', but not **k našemu straxu* 'to our fear' or **k našemu ispugu* 'to our fright'. The range of EIS nouns accepted by these prepositions is largely different, although there are some nouns in common. In general, *k* co-occurs with a larger set of nouns than *na*. Preposition *k* combines freely with: *radost'* 'happiness', *sčastje* 'happiness', *nesčastje* 'unhappiness', *užas* 'horror', *udovol'stvie* 'pleasure', *neudovol'stvie* 'displeasure', *vostorg* 'delight', *vosxiščenie* 'admiration' etc. Preposition *na* often co-occurs with: *radost'* 'happiness', *sčastje* 'happiness', *nesčastje* 'unhappiness', *strax* 'fear' etc. One can say *k našemu vosxiščeniju (vostorgu, udovol'stviju, udovletvoreniju)* 'to our admiration (delight,

pleasure, satisfaction)', but one cannot use preposition *na* with these nouns.

3. *Na*- and *k*-phrases differ with respect to the temporal correlation between the EIS and the motivating situation A2. In case of *k,* the EIS is simultaneous with A2. Cf.:

(16a) *Poet vypustil novuju knigu k radosti svoix počitatelej*

'the poet published a new book to the joy of his admirers'.

The joy of the admirers may be caused by the mere fact of publication. For example, the poet was not publishing anything for a long time, and now a new book appeared, and the admirers are happy about that. No information is implied as to whether this mental state will last for a longer period. Phrases with preposition *na* are different. They are usually oriented towards the future and imply that the mental state, once appeared, will last for a certain amount of time. Sentence (16b)

(16b) *Poet vypustil novuju knigu na radost' svoim počitateljam*

rather suggests another reason for joy: the admirers will be reading the new book and enjoy it. Let us give more examples to support this point. Sentence (17a)

(17a) *Na vysokom beregu my postroili krepost' na strax vragam*

'on a high riverbank we built a fortress for the enemies to fear us'

means that the fortress was built with the aim of producing durable fear on the part of the enemies and not just to give them a single fright. This is confirmed by verbal paraphrases. An adequate paraphrase requires a verb in the imperfective aspect (as in (17b)) and not in the perfective (as in (17c)):

(17b) *My postroili krepost', čtoby vragi bojalis'*$_{\text{Imperf}}$ (stative verb).

'we built a fortress for the enemies to fear us'

(17c) *My postroili krepost', čtoby vragi ispugalis'*$_{\text{Perf.}}$

'we built a fortress to frighten the enemies'.

In the same way, sentence (18) does not mean that the daughter did not rejoice at her mother's arrival, but rather that the consequences of this arrival would be sorrowful to the daughter.

(18) *Ne na radost' dočeri priexala ona v Peterburg.*

'it is not for her daughter's joy that she came to St. Petersburg'

Causative adverbials: Causative EIS adverbials are constructed with four prepositions: *ot* (+Gen), *iz-za* (+Gen), *iz* (+Gen), and *s* (+Gen): *pokrasnet' ot styda* 'turn red from shame', *mstit' iz-za revnosti* 'take revenge out of jealousy', *otkazat'sja iz otvraščenija* 'refuse out of disgust', *pljunut' s dosady* 'spit in annoyance'.

Semantic differences between causal prepositions are described in great detail in Iordanskaya-Mel'čuk 1996 and Levontina 2004. These differences are valid for EIS adverbials as well, and we will not repeat them here. We will only make several additional remarks.

As is known, there are several linguistically relevant varieties of cause. In particular, one distinguishes objective and subjective cause, on the one hand, and external and internal cause, on the other[4]. All causal EIS adverbials refer to internal subjective cause due to semantics of EIS nouns.

The causative preposition most widely used with EIS nouns is *ot* 'out of'. It combines freely with all the nouns of this class. However, the use of the main causal preposition *iz-za* 'because of' is rather restricted. It is not appropriate with a single noun. It requires that its group be extended. Cf.:

(19a) **Iz-za radosti ona zabyla svoe ogorčenie.*

lit. because of joy she forgot her grief

(19b) *Iz-za radosti, vnezapno oxvativšej ee, ona zabyla svoe ogorčenie.*

'because of joy that suddenly gripped her she forgot her grief'

(20a) ??*On stal agentom oxranki iz-za straxa.*

'he became a secret police agent because of fear'

(20b) *On stal agentom oxranki iz-za straxa pered arestom.*

lit. he became a secret police agent because of fear for arrest.

Other causal prepositions do not have this restriction, cf. preposition *iz:*

(20c) *On stal agentom oxranki iz straxa.*

'he became a secret police agent out of fear'

Another peculiarity of preposition *iz-za* is that it is not compatible with the second form of the genitive case of EIS (the form ending in *–u*), which freely accepts other causal prepositions: *ot straxu, iz straxu, so straxu,* but **iz-za straxu.*

4. Case study: gratitude

[4] For details, cf. Boguslavskaya 2003, Boguslavskaya and Levontina 2003.

The semantic field of gratitude is represented in Russian by several lexemes, among which there are verbs (*blagodarit'* 'to thank', *otblagodarit'* ≈'to do something in return showing one's gratitude'), nouns (*blagodarnost'* 'gratitude', *priznatelnost'* 'appreciation'), adjectives (*blagodarnyj* 'grateful', *priznatel'nyj 'appreciative'*) and adverbs (*blagodarno* 'gratefully', *priznatel'no* 'appreciatively'- the latter is somewhat obsolescent). All these lexemes (except the adverb *blagodarno* 'gratefully') can take three semantic arguments: "someone who feels gratitude", "someone to whom one is grateful", and "something for what one is grateful". Semantically, the primary lexeme of this group is the noun *blagodarnost'*^{1}, which is defined in the Active dictionary of Russian (ADR 2014) as 'a good feeling of person A1 towards person A2, who did a good A3 for A1'. Contrary to what one could expect, the propositional form of this meaning is not represented by a verb, but by an adjective (in a short form): *Ja blagodaren <priznatelen> emu za pomošč'* 'I am grateful to him for his help'.

As opposed to these adjectives, the verb *blagodarit'* 'to thank' does not convey the idea that person A1 feels gratitude. Instead, it means that person A1 desires to show person A2 that he appreciates good A3 that A2 has done for him and expresses it in a verbal way appropriate for such cases. These are quite different things. One can thank somebody without feeling grateful. And the other way round, one can feel grateful without saying it to person A2; cf.:

(21) *Ja blagodaren emu za pomošč', no ne imeju vozmožnosti poblagodarit' ego.*
'I am grateful for his help but have no opportunity to thank him'

The verb *blagodarit'* 'to thank', as is well-known, is performative. When uttering *Thank you* we are not informing the interlocutor of what we are doing, but performing an illocutionary act of gratitude. It is noteworthy that the adjectives *blagodarnyj* and *priznatel'nyj* 'grateful' (in the short form) are also performative. The utterance *Ja očen' blagodaren <priznatelen> vam za pomošč'* 'I am very grateful to you for your help' is a voiced compensation for a good deed, just like the a verbal phrase *Blagodarju vas* 'thank you' or a performative formula *Spasibo* 'thanks'.

The verb *blagodarit'* 'to thank' is nominalized by means of another sense of the noun *blagodarnost' – blagodarnost'*^{2} 'the act of expressing gratitude ':

(22) *Prezident načal svoju reč' s blagodarnosti Vnutrennim vojskam.*
'the president began his speech by thanks to the Internal security troops' (= 'began the speech with thanking')

The difference between the two wordsenses of the noun *blagodarnost'* is clearly seen in the pair (23a-b):

(23a) *On poblagodaril ee, no blagodarnosti ne oščushčal* (*blagodarnost'*^{1} – a feeling).
'he thanked her but did not feel any gratitude'

(23b) *Ego blagodarnost' prozvučala neiskrenne* (*blagodarnost'*^{2} – an act of expressing gratitude).
'his (expression of) gratitude sounded insincere'

While the verb *blagodarit'* 'to thank' is shifted from the basic concept of a feeling towards deliberately expressing this feeling, the adjective *blagodarnyj* 'grateful' (in the full form) and the adverb *blagodarno* 'gratefully' move towards expressing manifestation: phrases *blagodarnyj vzgljad* 'a grateful look' and *blagodarno posmotrel na nee* 'looked at her gratefully' describe a look in which the gratitude is manifested.

Adverbial phrases of gratitude are composed mostly with the following four prepositions – *s* 'with', *ot* 'out of', *iz* 'from' and *v* 'in':

(24a) *Ja s blagodarnostju prinimaju vaše priglashenie.*
lit. I with gratitude accept your invitation
'I am happy to accept your invitation'

(24b) *Ot blagodarnosti on daže proslezilsja.*
'feeling grateful (lit. from gratitude) he even shed a tear' (the action of shedding a tear is uncontrolled)

(24c) *Bol'noj prineset iz blagodarnosti to jaiček, to rybki, to medku.*
'out of gratitude the patients bring (to the doctors) sometimes some eggs, sometimes some fish, sometimes some honey'

(24d) *V blagodarnost' za konsul'taciju ona podarila vraču korobku konfet.*
'in gratitude for the consultation she gave the doctor a box of chocolate'

The adverbials represented in (24a-c) have been commented upon above (section 3.2). In (24a) the adverbial expresses the meaning of concomitance ('feeling grateful for some actions related to this situation'). Examples (24b,c) express causation. Example (24d) is more complicated and we will discuss it below.

The phrase *v blagodarnost'* 'in gratitude for' is close to two other adverbial phrases – *v znak blagodarnosti* lit. 'in sign of gratitude' and *v kačestve blagodarnosti* 'by way of gratitude'. The three expressions are often translated in the same way. However, the two latter expressions seem to be derived from two different senses of *blagodarnost': P v znak blagodarnosti* means that P is a sign of the fact that the Experiencer feels gratitude (*blagodarnost'*^{1}). *P v kačestve blagodarnosti* has a slightly different meaning: P serves as an expression of gratitude' (*blagodarnost'*^{2}). This observation is confirmed by the fact that pure feelings do not combine with *v kačestve* 'by way of': one cannot say **v kačestve ljubvi <družby>* 'by way of love <friendship>', while *v znak ljubvi <družby>* 'as a sign of love <friendship>' is perfect.

The idea of gratitude implies that person A1 is doing or is willing to do something for A2 to show that he appreciates the good that A2 has done for A1. Usually, this action consists in uttering certain conventional expressions. However, to express the gratitude one can perform any other action that would be pleasant to A2. For example, one can give A2 a bunch of flowers or dedicate him/her a poem. Nevertheless, a phrase denoting such a return action can hardly be attached to a gratitude word. One cannot say **On poblagodaril ee buketom cvetov <posvjashčeniem stixotvorenija>* 'he thanked her with a bunch of flowers < by dedicating a poem>'; **blagodarnost' buketom cetov <posvjaščeniem stixotvorenija>* 'gratitude with a bunch of flowers < by dedicating a poem>'.

A common wisdom is that one can only postulate a semantic valency slot for word L if it is instantiated by a LU directly connected to L in the dependency structure. For this reason, the action performed by A1 is not considered an argument of the verb *blagodarit'*, and still less so of the noun *blagodarnost'*. Nevertheless, this valency slot should be postulated. We can offer the following arguments in favour of this.

First, as mentioned above, a prototypical expression of gratitude consists in pronouncing certain verbal formulae, which cannot be governed by the verb *blagodarit': *poblagodaril spasibo* 'thanked with a thank you'. However, there exist non-verbal symbolic ways of expressing gratitude – by means of gestures, and they can be easily attached to *blagodarit': poblagodaril ulybkoj <kivkom, poklonom>* 'thanked with a smile <a nod, a bow>. Non-gesture actions can scarcely be used that way, although occasional examples can be found in the Russian National Corpus:

(25) *Doma on rasskazal otcu, kak on spas zjablika i kak zjablik poblagodaril ego zvonkoj pesenkoj.*

lit. at home he told his father how he saved a chaffinch and how the chaffinch thanked him with a ringing song.

Second, as shown in Mel'čuk 2014:18 (definition 12.2), to recognize a participant of a situation a semantic actant of LU L, it is not obligatory that this participant be directly linked to L in the syntactic structure. What is essential is that it should be expressible alongside L. An immediate syntactic link is not the only way a participant can be expressed alongside L. It may be linked to a LU that is a particular lexical function of L (these include support verbs $Oper_i$, $Func_{0/i}$, $Labor_{ij}$ and realization verbs $Real_i$, $Fact_{0/i}$, $Labreal_{ij}$, as well as complex lexical functions having these verbs as their last component). Here is one of the examples of Mel'čuk: the noun *danger* ('something dangerous') has two arguments: 'X is a danger for Y'. The dangerous element X cannot be an immediate syntactic dependent of *danger*. If John is dangerous for someone, we cannot say **John's danger or *danger by <from> John*. However, some of the lexical functions of *danger* (support verbs) can link the name of such an element to the noun: *John represents an enormous danger for our plans* [*represent* = $Oper_1$(*danger*)]. *The main danger for our plans comes from John* [*come from* =$Func_1$(*danger*)].

This is exactly what we see in (24d). The action carried out as a "realization" of the gratitude is expressed alongside the adverbial *v blagodarnost'* by means of the subordinating verb. At the same time, *v blagodarnost'* is the value of the lexical function Adv_1Real_1-M[5] of *blagodarnost'*. In (24d), giving a box of chocolate is the action that the Experiencer carries out paying his debt of gratitude.

---

[5] Lexical functions of $Real_i$-M and $Fact_i$-M group, which supplement $Real_i$ and $Fact_i$, were introduced in the inventory of lexical functions to denote realization of predicates with modal components (Apresjan 2001). Cf. Real1-M(*desire*) = *satisfy*, Real2-M(*challenge*)= *meet*, Real3-M(*advice*)=*follow*.

In this respect, the adverbial *v blagodarnost'* is similar to phrases *v otvet* 'in response', *po prikazu* 'by order of ', *po privyčke* 'by habit', *po tradicii* 'according to tradition' etc. that are also values of the same lexical function of the nouns *otvet* 'response', *prikaz* 'order', *privyčka* 'habit', and *tradicija* 'tradition'. With all these adverbials, the subordinating verb obviously instantiates the valency slot of the corresponding predicate, which is clearly seen in pairs (a)-(b) below.

(26a) *V otvet on požal plečami.*
'in response, he shrugged his shoulders'
(26b) *On otvetil požatiem pleč.*
'he responded by shrugging his shoulders'
(27a) *Marija Stjuart byla arestovana po prikazu korolevy.*
'Maria Stuart was arrested at the Queen's order'
(27b) *prikaz korolevy arestovat' Mariju Stjuart*
'the Queen's order to arrest Maria Stuart'
(28a) *Po privyčke on vo vsem obvinil amerikancev.*
'by habit, he accused Americans of everything'
(28b) *privyčka vo vsem obvinjat' amerikancev*
'the habit of accusing Americans of everything'
(29a) *Po tradicii oni legli spat' rano.*
'according to tradition, they went to bed early'
(29b) *tradicija ložit'sja spat' rano*
'the tradition of going to bed early'

The specific feature of the adverbial *v blagodarnost'* is that unlike these adverbials, its source predicate (*blagodarit'* 'to thank', *blagodarnost'* 'gratitude') cannot attach the actant, expressible alongside the adverbial.

Another derivative of *blagodarit'* 'to thank' that has a slot of the return action is the verb *otblagodarit'* 'to repay somebody's kindness; to show one's gratitude', which expresses the idea of compensation quite clearly:

(30a) *otblagodarit'* (perfective aspect only) = 'person A1 has done good A3 for person A2 as a compensation for good A4, which A2 did for A1'
(30b) *Škol'niki otblagodarili šefov za remont školy prazdničnym koncertom.*
'the schoolchildren expressed their gratitude to the sponsors by a festive concert'.

Some adverbials including *v blagodarnost'* can undergo an interesting syntactic process called *shifting* («smeščenie», in Russian). It consists in moving a certain element of the dependency structure from its natural position that directly corresponds to its semantic links to a higher position in the dependency tree. This phenomenon was described in Paducheva 1974 for negation and was later generalized in Boguslavsky 1978 and 1985. For example, in both sentences (31a) and (31b) the negative particle *ne* is linked to the preposition *v:*

(31a) *Ivan položil sumku ne v mašinu.*
lit. Ivan put his bag not in the car
'Ivan did not put his bag in the car'
(31b) *Ivan položil sumku ne v svoju mašinu.*
lit. Ivan put his bag not into his car
'Ivan put his bag into the car of another person'

However, in (31a) this is a proper syntactic position for negation, since what is negated is the phrase *v mašinu* 'in the car', while in (31b) this is the position of shifting, because what is negated is not the preposition but pronoun *svoju* 'his': (31b) = 'Ivan put his bag into not-his car'.

Now, let us look at sentences (32a-b):

(32a) *Xozjain trebuet, čtoby v blagodarnost' za učenie ja celyj god besplatno na nego rabotal.*
lit. the master demands that in gratitude for apprenticeship I for a whole year without payment for him worked
'the master demands that in gratitude for apprenticeship, I worked for him for a whole year without being paid'

Here, the adverbial *v blagodarnost'* makes part of the subordinate clause and, according to what we showed above, its syntactic governor (*rabotal* 'worked') fills its valency slot. Sentence (32b) shows that *v blagodarnost'* can be moved to the main clause without reinterpretation of its semantic links.

(32b) *Xozjain trebuet v blagodarnost' za učenie, čtoby ja celyj god besplatno na nego rabotal.*
lit. the master demands in gratitude for apprenticeship that I for a whole year without payment for him worked
'in gratitude for apprenticeship, the master demands that I worked for him for a whole year without being paid'

In (32b), just as in (32a), the in-return valency slot of *v blagodarnost'* is filled by the verb *rabotal* 'worked', although this verb is located in the subordinate clause and as such has no syntactic link with the adverbial.

Shifting of an adverbial from the subordinate clause into the main clause, exemplified by (32b), is possible if the predicate of the main clause has a modal meaning (cf. 'demand' in (32b)). Here are examples of the same phenomenon with other adverbials.

(33a) *V otmestku za prigovor «čubarovcam» «Sojuz» ugrožal, čto ubijstva i podžogi oxvatjat ves' gorod.*

'in retaliation for the sentence passed upon the members of the Čubarov band, "Sojuz" threatened that assassinations and arsons would spread all over the city'

(33b) '«Sojuz» threatened to retaliate... by organizing assassinations and arsons...'.

(34a) *On predložil v dokazatel'stvo svoej ljubvi, čto otdast vse svoe sostojanie na ustrojstvo škol dlja bednyx.*

'he suggested as a proof of his love that he would give all his fortune for establishing schools for the poor'

(34b) 'he will prove his love by giving all his fortune for establishing schools for the poor'

5. Conclusion

We have described semantic and syntactic properties of EIS adverbials in their correlation with the corresponding source LUs. This perspective makes it possible to treat different syntactic realizations of predicates along the same lines and offer a uniform description of semantic actants of both source LUs and their adverbial derivatives.

Acknowledgements

The work reported here was partially supported by the RFH grant (13-04-00343), the President's Grant for the Support of Leading Scientific Schools (НШ-3899.2014.6), and the "Historical memory and Rusian identity" grant.

References

ADR 2014 – *Активный словарь русского языка.* / Отв. ред. акад. Ю. Д. Апресян. — М.: Языки славянской культуры, 2014. — Т. 1.А– Б. — 408 с ; Т 2. В – Г. — 736 с.

Apresjan 2001 – Апресян Ю.Д. 2001. *О лексических функциях семейства REAL – FACT.* Nie bez znaczenia ... Prace ofiarowane Profesorowi Zygmuntowi Saloniemu z okazii jubileuszu 15000 dni praci naukowej. Białystok, 23-40.

Boguslavskaya 2003 – Богуславская О.Ю. 2003. *Структура значения прилагательного причина.* Русистика на пороге XXI века: проблемы и перспективы. Материалы международной научной конференции. М. С. 102 – 105.

Boguslavskaya 2004 – Богуславская О.Ю. *Причина 2, Основание 5, Резон 1.* Новый объяснительный словарь синонимов русского языка. Отв. ред. акад. Ю. Д. Апресян. — М.: Языки славянской культуры, Wiener Slavistisher Almanach 2004. Pp. 877-882.

Boguslavskaya, Levontina 2004 – Богуславская О.Ю., Левонтина И.Б. 2004. *Смыслы 'причина' и 'цель'' в естественном языке.* Вопросы языкознания. С. 68 – 88.

Boguslavsky 1985 – Богуславский И.М. 1985. *Исследования по синтаксической семантике.* М. Наука.

Boguslavsky I. 2003. *On the Passive and Discontinuous Valency Slots.* Proceedings of the 1st International Conference on Meaning-Text Theory. Paris, Ecole Normale Supérieure, June 16–18.

Boguslavsky I. 2014. *Argument structure of adverbial derivatives in Russian.* In: Proceedings of COLING 2014, the 25th International Conference on Computational Linguistics: Technical Papers, pp. 1071–1080, Dublin, Ireland, August 23-29 2014.

ECD 1984 – *Толково-комбинаторный словарь современного русского языка* (под ред. И.А.Мельчука и А.К.Жолковского). Wiener slawistischer Almanach. Sonderband 14, Wien, 1984.

I. Mel'čuk, Iordanskaja, L. 1996. *K semantike russkix pričinnyx predlogov (IZ-ZA ljubvi ~ OT ljubvi ~ IZ ljubvi ~ S ljubvi ~ PO ljubvi).* The Moscow Linguistic Journal, 2, 162-211.

I. Mel'čuk. 2014. *Semantics. From Meaning to Text.* v.3, John Benjamins Publishing Company.

Iomdin 1990 – Иомдин Л.Л. 1990. *Русский предлог ПО: этюд к лексикографическому портрету.* Metody formalne w opisie języków slowiańskich. Z. Saloni (ed.). Dzial wydawnictw Filii UW w Białymstoku. С. 241-260.

Iomdin 1991 – Иомдин Л.Л. 1991. *Словарная статья предлога ПО.* Семиотика и информатика. М. Вып. 32. С. 33-60.

Levontina 2004 – Левонтина И.Б. *Из-за 4, из 8.1....* Новый объяснительный словарь синонимов русского языка. Отв. ред. акад. Ю. Д. Апресян. — М.: Языки славянской культуры, Wiener Slavistisher Almanach 2004. Pp. 430-437.

Paducheva 1974 – Падучева Е.В. 1974. *О семантике синтаксиса.* Материалы к трансформационной грамматике русского языка. М.: Наука, 291 с.

Towards a multi-layered dependency annotation of Finnish

Alicia Burga[1], **Simon Mille**[1], **Anton Granvik**[3], **and Leo Wanner**[1,2]
[1] Natural Language Processing Group, Pompeu Fabra University, Barcelona, Spain
[2] Institució Catalana de Recerca i Estudis Avançats (ICREA)
[3] HANKEN School of Economics, Centre for Languages and Business Communication
firstname.lastname@upf.edu, anton.granvik@hanken.fi

Abstract

We present a dependency annotation scheme for Finnish which aims at respecting the multilayered nature of language. We first tackle the annotation of surface-syntactic structures (SSyntS) as inspired by the Meaning-Text framework. Exclusively syntactic criteria are used when defining the surface-syntactic relations tagset. Our annotation scheme allows for a direct mapping between surface-syntax and a more semantics-oriented representation, in particular predicate-argument structures. It has been applied to a corpus of Finnish, composed of 2,025 sentences related to weather conditions.

1 Introduction

The increasing prominence of statistical NLP applications calls for creation of syntactic dependency treebanks, i.e., corpora that are annotated with syntactic dependency structures. However, creating a syntactic treebank is an expensive and laborious task—not only because of the annotation itself, but also because a well-defined annotation schema is required. The schema must accurately reflect all syntactic phenomena of the annotated language, and, if the application for which the annotation is made is "deep" (as deep parsing or deep sentence generation), also foresee how each of the syntactic phenomena is reflected at the deeper levels of the linguistic description.

For Finnish, there are two well-known syntactic dependency-based treebanks: the Turku Dependency Treebank (TDT), and the FinnTreeBank. TDT, the most referenced corpus in Finnish (Haverinen et al., 2014), contains 15,126 sentences (204,399 tokens) from general discourse and uses a tagset of 53 relations (although just 46 are used at the syntactic layer), which is an adaptation of the Stanford Dependency (SD) schema for English (de Marneffe and Manning, 2008). The FinnTreeBank (Voutilainen et al., 2012) contains 19,764 sentences (169,450 tokens), mostly extracted from a descriptive Finnish grammar, which are annotated using a reduced tagset of only 15 relations.[1]

In what follows, we present an alternative annotation schema that is embedded in the framework of the Meaning-to-Text Theory (MTT) (Mel'čuk, 1988). This schema is based on the separation of linguistic representations in accordance with their level of abstraction. Subsequently, we distinguish between surface-syntactic (SSynt) and deep-syntactic (DSynt) annotations, and argue that this schema more adequately captures the syntactic annotation of Finnish. We designed our annotation scheme empirically, through various iterations over an air quality-related corpus of 2,025 sentences (35,830 tokens), which we make publicly available. However, since this paper focuses on the principles which underlie our annotation schema, rather than on the quality of the annotated resource itself, we do not provide an evaluation of the annotation quality.

The next section outlines our annotation scheme for Finnish and discusses the main syntactic criteria for the identification of the individual relation tags. Section 3 shows how the presented annotation can be projected onto a deep-syntactic annotation, while Section 4 details the principal differences between the TDT annotation schema and ours, before some conclusions are presented in Section 5.

2 A surface-syntactic annotation of Finnish

Our annotation schema for Finnish follows the methodology adopted for the elaboration of the

[1] According to KORP -https://korp.csc.fi- the FTB with all its versions joined contains 4,386,152 sentences (76,532,636 tokens). However, the limited number of relations makes an in-depth analysis and/or comparison difficult.

Proceedings of the Third International Conference on Dependency Linguistics (Depling 2015), pages 48–57,
Uppsala, Sweden, August 24–26 2015.

schema of the Spanish AnCora-UPF treebank (Mille et al., 2013). Taking into account a series of clearly cut syntactically-motivated criteria, a tagset of Finnish syntactic dependencies has been established. In what follows, we first present the SSynt relation tagset, and then discuss some of the main criteria applied for the identification of selected tags.

2.1 The SSynt dependency tagset

The SSynt annotation layer is language-dependent, and thus captures the idiosyncrasies of a specific language. An example of a Finnish surface-syntactic structure (SSyntS) is shown in Figure 1.

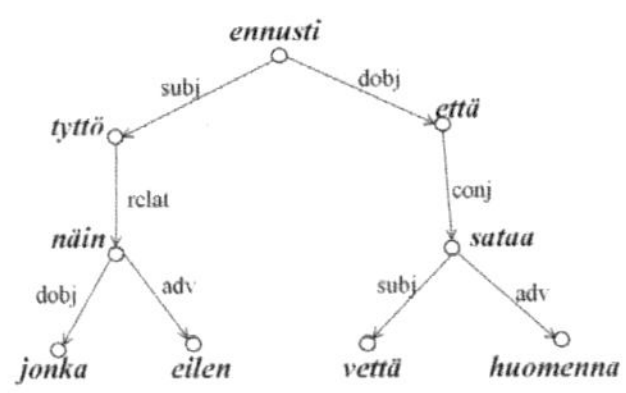

Figure 1: SSyntS of the sentence *Tyttö jonka näin eilen ennusti, että huomenna sataa vettä.* 'The girl whom I saw yesterday predicted that tomorrow it will rain'.

The Finnish SSynt tagset contains 36 relations, which are presented and described in Table 1 along with their distinctive syntactic properties. For comparison, consider the Spanish tagset, shown in Table 2.

As can be observed, many labels in the Finnish and Spanish tagsets are identical (e.g., *clitic, modif, relat*). This uniformity of labels across languages is one of the major motivations behind the Universal Stanford Dependencies (de Marneffe et al., 2014). We also think that using the same labels across languages facilitates the understanding of the annotations but, unlike in the USD proposal, we make the different syntactic characteristics encoded by identical relations in different languages explicit. Some prominent examples of relations with the same label in both tagsets, but with different definitions are *subj*, *obl_obj* and *copul*. The relation *subj* refers in both tagsets to the element that agrees with the verb in person and number, but in Finnish the relation is also defined with respect to the case: the dependent of this relation takes the case assigned by the verb. In Spanish, given that nominal phrases do not carry case (or, at least, they do not show any case marker), the case assignment is not used for the definition of the relation.

DepRel	Distinctive properties
adjunct	mobile sentential adverbial
adv	mobile verbal adverbial
appos	right-sided apposed element
attr	genitive complement of nouns
aux	non finite V governed by auxiliary verbs
aux_phras	multi-word marker
bin_junct	relates binary constructions
clitic	non-independent adjacent morpheme attached to its syntactic governor
compar	complement of a comparative element
conj	complement of a non-coordinating Conj (right-sided)
compl	non-removable adjectival object agreeing with another verbal actant
compos	relates a nominal head with prefixed modifiers in compound nouns
copul	non-locative complement of the copula *olla*; agrees with subject in number; its canonical order is to the right
coord	relates the first element of a coordination with the coord. conjunction (recursive)
coord_conj	complement of a coordinating Conj (right-sided)
det	non-repeatable first left-side modifier of noun
dobj	verbal dependent with case partitive, genitive, nominative or accusative (for pronouns); no agreement with verb
hyphen	reflects the orthographic necessity of hyphenating compounds
juxtapos	for linking two unrelated groups
modal	relates modal auxiliaries (which require genitive subjects) and main verb
modif	element modifying a noun; agrees in case and number
noun_compl	non-genitive complement of nouns
obj_copred	relates the main verb with a predicative adjective that modifies an object
obl_obj	verbal dependent with locative case (adessive, ablative, elative, illative, allative)
postpos	left-sided complement of an adposition or of an adverb acting as such
prepos	right-sided complement of an adposition or of an adverb acting as such
punc	for punctuation signs
quasi_coord	for coordinated elements with no connector; (e.g. specifications)
relat	right-sided finite verb modifying a noun
relat_expl	adjunct-like finite clause
restr	invariable & non-mobile adverbial unit
sequent	for numerical or formulaic elements belonging together (right-side)
subj	verbal dependent that controls number agreement on its governing verb; acquires the case assigned by the verb
subj_obj	subject-like element governed by passive, existential-possessive and impersonal verbs, with some object properties
subj_copred	relates the main verb with a predicative adjective that modifies the subject
verb_junct	right-sided verbal particle that gives the expression a particular meaning

Table 1: Dependency relations used at the Finnish surface-syntactic layer.

DepRel	Distinctive properties
abbrev	abbreviated apposition
abs_pred	non-removable dependent of an N making the latter act as an adverb
adv	mobile adverbial
agent	promotable dependent of a participle
analyt_fut	Prep *a* governed by future Aux
analyt_pass	non-finite V governed by passive Aux
analyt_perf	non-finite V governed by perfect Aux
analyt_progr	non-finite V governed by progressive Aux
appos	right-sided apposed element
attr	right-side modifier of an N
aux_phras	multi-word marker
aux_refl	reflexive Pro depending on a V
bin_junct	for binary constructions
compar	complement of a comparative Adj/Adv
compl1	non-removable adjectival object agreeing with subject
compl2	non-removable adjectival object agreeing with direct object
compl_adnom	prepositional dependent of a stranded Det
conj	complement of a non-coordinating Conj
coord	between a conjunct and the element acting as coordination conjunction
coord_conj	complement of a coordinating Conj
copul	cliticizable dependent of a copula agrees with subject in number and gender
copul_clitic	cliticized dependent of a copula;
det	non-repeatable left-side modifier of an N
dobj	verbal dependent that can be promoted or cliticized with an accusative Pro
dobj_clitic	accusative clitic Pro depending on a V
elect	non-argumental right-side dependent of a comparative Adj/Adv or a number
iobj	dependent replaceable by a dative Pro
iobj_clitic	dative clitic Pro depending on a V
juxtapos	for linking two unrelated groups
modal	non-removable, non-cliticizable infinitive verbal dependent
modif	for Adj agreeing with their governing N
num_junct	numerical dependent of another number
obj_copred	adverbial dependent of a V, which agrees with the direct object
obl_compl	right-side dependent of a non-V element introduced by a governed Prep
obl_obj	prepositional object that cannot be demoted, promoted or cliticized
prepos	complement of a preposition
prolep	for clause-initial accumulation of elements with no connectors
punc	for non-sentence-initial punctuations
punc_init	for sentence-initial punctuation
quant	numerical dependent which controls the number of its governing N
quasi_coord	for coordinated elements with the no connector
quasi_subj	a subject next to a grammatical subject
relat	right-sided finite V that modifies an N
relat_expl	adverbial finite clause
sequent	right-side coordinated adjacent element
subj	dependent that controls agreement on its governing V
subj_copred	adverbial dependent of a V agreeing with the subject

Table 2: Dependency relations used at the Spanish surface-syntactic layer.

obl_obj refers in Spanish to those verbal objects that are introduced by a preposition and cannot be demoted, promoted or cliticized. In Finnish, due to its case-inflected nouns, *obl_obj* is defined as the relation that links verbs with objects containing locative cases. Finally, *copul* is defined in both tagsets as the complement of copular verbs, which agrees with the subject in number. However, in the case of Spanish this element can cliticize, but in Finnish it cannot.

In contrast, such relation labels as *appos*, *coord* or *relat* share exactly the same properties across the two languages.

2.2 Syntactic criteria

The syntactically-motivated criteria described in (Burga et al., 2014) were used for creating the Finnish SSynt tagset. In this section, some remarks about Finnish idiosyncrasies related to these criteria are detailed.

• **Agreement**: Two elements are involved in agreement if they share some morphological features, such as number, person or case. If such agreement arises because one element transmits those features to the other, we conclude that those elements are syntactically related. On the other hand, if an element that admits morphological variation does not vary according to its governor/dependent, we can conclude that no agreement is involved in the dependency relation between the two. However, as already pointed out for Spanish (Burga et al., 2014), one has to be careful when analyzing agreement, because it depends not only on the licensing from the syntactic relation, but also on the Part-of-Speech (PoS) of each element. Thus, if the element to which the morphological feature(s) is (are) transmitted from another has a PoS that does not allow any morphological variation –or is lexically invariable, despite having a PoS that admits variability– , the agreement will not be visible. Then, to evaluate if agreement actually exists, one needs to use the prototypical head and dependent for each relation.[2] When applying this criterion, it is also important to keep in mind that different syntactic relations allow different types of agreement, namely: i) head transmits features to dependent (e.g., *modif*) (1a); ii) dependent transmits features to head (e.g., *subj*) (1b); and iii) dependent transmits features to a sibling

[2]This point is important because the non-visibility of agreement can cause a wrong division of relations, as happens in the TDT annotation scheme (see Section 4).

(e.g., *copul*) (1c).

(1) Possible agreement transmissions:

a. from head to dependent:

modif

märät | *kädet*
wet (NOM,PL) | hand (NOM, PL)

b. from dependent to head:

subj

He | *laulavat.*
They (3,PL) | sing (3,PL)

c. between two siblings:

subj, copul

Pojat ovat *väsyneitä.*
The_boys (PL) are tired (PL)

• **Governed Adposition / Conjunction / Grammeme**: Some relations require the presence of a preposition, a subordinating conjunction, or a grammeme (as, e.g., verbal finiteness or case). In Finnish, differently from English or Spanish, adpositions and inflected nouns are both admitted as alternative ways of expressing the same meaning.[3] However, beyond the way the meaning is conveyed at the surface, some units (namely the functional elements) are governed and some units (namely the content elements) are not. The governed elements in Finnish are mostly grammemes (case features), although it is also possible to find specific examples with governed adpositions. In the annotation scheme presented in this paper, this criterion is used for establishing the tagset (e.g., the relation *subj* does not require a particular case – the acquired case depends on the verbal head – whereas the relation *attr* requires genitive in the dependent), but does not imply a different analysis of configurations with governed and non-governed elements.

(2) Governed grammeme:

subj_obj, obl_obj

pitoisuuksia *verrataan* *raja-arvoihin.*
concentrations compare thresholds
(PAR) (PASS) (ILL)
Concentrations are compared to the threshold values.

(3) Governed adposition:

subj, dobj, noun_compl, postpos

HY tekee yhteistyötä Aalto-yliopiston kanssa.
HY makes collaboration U.Aalto with
(PAR) (GEN)
U.Helsinki collaborates with U.Aalto.

[3]This is the reason behind the TDT treating both kinds of configurations in the same way (see Section 4).

(4) Non-governed grammeme:

subj, adv

Mies käveli rannalla.
man (NOM) walked beach (ADE)
The man walked on the beach.

(5) Non-governed adposition:

subj, adv, postpos

Mies käveli rantaa pitkin.
man (NOM) walked beach (PAR) along
The man walked along the beach.

In (2–5), we display examples that illustrate governed and non-governed cases and adpositions. In (2), the case ILL of *raja-arvo* 'threshold values' is governed by the verb *vertaa* 'compare', and this requirement is what defines the type of relation holding between the verb and the inflected noun (*obl_obj*). In (3), the postposition *kanssa* is required by the predicate *tehdä yhteistyötä* 'collaborate', which motivates the relation *noun_compl*.[4] On the other hand, the adessive case in *ranta* 'beach' in (4) and the adposition *pitkin* 'along' in (5) are not required by any element. As a consequence, they contribute by themselves to the semantics of the sentences – which should be reflected at the deep-syntactic layer.

• **Linearization / Canonical order**:[5] By linearization/canonical order we make reference to the required (or preferred) direction between governor and dependent within a specific dependency relation. Although Finnish is a language with a quite flexible word order, there are certain syntactic relations that require a rigid linearization (e.g., *appos*) or, at least, prefer a certain order between head and dependent (e.g., *dobj, copul*).

As these criteria contribute to the definition of SSynt relations, they also serve, along with some features of the elements involved, to distinguish different syntactic configurations. For instance, the verb *olla* 'to be' is used in copulative, locative, and existential configurations. Therefore, we need some criteria to identify each of these uses.

In a copulative sentence, the subject is the element that agrees in person and number with the

[4]As the predicate comprises two elements, and the predicate itself is a noun, the relation is *noun_compl*. However, if the predicate were composed by just one verbal element, the relation received by the adposition would be the same as in (2), *obl_obj*.

[5]Thanks to a reviewer for providing some important Finnish judgments that have contributed to clarify this section.

verb and carries nominative case. The complement of the copula, on the other hand, is "the element that says something about the subject". It can be of four different types: i) a non-nominal element (such as an adjective), ii) a nominal element in a case different from nominative, iii) a nominal element in nominative that does not agree with the verb in person and/or number, and iv) a nominal element in nominative that also agrees with the verb in person and/or number.

In cases i–iii), the two previous criteria – agreement and governed grammeme – are enough for detecting subjects and complements of the copula. However, in cases where the two elements related to the verb are nominal elements that agree with the copula and are in nominative case, as in (6), linearization helps to determine which element is the subject (i.e., the element appearing before the copula) and which one is the complement of the copula (i.e., the element appearing after the copula). [6] Thus, as observed, (6a) and (6b) do not carry the same meaning: they are not exchangeable and (6b) is not the result of exchanging directions over the relations of (6a).

(6) Copulative:

a. subj, copul

Poika	*on*	*Hannes.*
boy (NOM)	is	Hannes (NOM)
The boy	*is*	*Hannes.*

b. subj, copul

Hannes	on	*poika.*
Hannes (NOM)	is	boy (NOM)
Hannes	is	a boy.

The *copul* relation, thus, conveys a rigid linearization when combined with certain morphological features, and therefore this criterion should explicitly intervene in the definition of the relation.

In the same way, locative sentences containing *olla* require the relation *adv* to be right-sided (7), opposite to existential sentences, which require it to be left-sided (8). Again, this distinction only applies in cases where the non-locative element is non-definite. If it is definite (e.g., a definite modifier is explicitly added), no existential interpretation is possible and therefore the distinction between locative and existential vanishes.

[6] Even if it is possible to find sentences with the two nominal elements at the same side of the copula, they are not interpreted as neutral copulative sentences, but are communicatively marked.

(7) Locative:

subj, adv

Pallo	*on*	*pöydällä.*
ball (NOM)	is	table (ADE)
The ball	is	on the table.

(8) Existential:

adv, subj_obj

Pöydällä	*on*	*pallo.*
table (ADE)	is	ball (NOM)
There is	a ball	on the table.

3 Towards a deep-syntactic annotation

Since we approach linguistic description in a multilayered way, our annotation scheme aims at obtaining not only the Surface-Syntactic layer, but also a shallow semantics-oriented layer, referred to as *Deep-Syntactic* (DSynt) layer in the Meaning-Text Theory. An example of a DSynt structure for Finnish is shown in Figure 2.

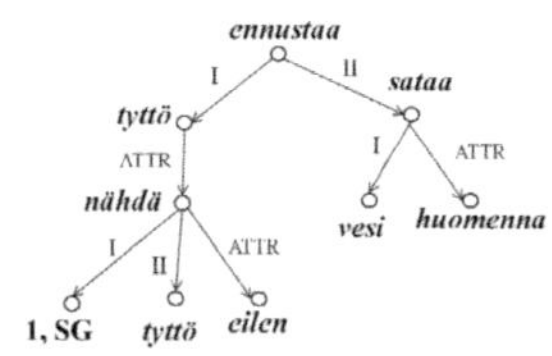

Figure 2: DSyntS of the sentence *Tyttö jonka näin eilen ennusti, että huomenna sataa vettä.* 'The girl whom I saw yesterday predicted that tomorrow it will rain'.

The main differences between a Surface-Syntactic structure (SSyntS) and a Deep-Syntactic structure (DSyntS) are the following:

(i) a SSyntS contains all the words of a sentence, while in a DSyntS all functional elements (such as governed adpositions or auxiliaries) are removed, so that only meaning-bearing (content) elements are left; Figure 2, for instance, does not contain the subordinating conjunction *että* present in Figure 1;

(ii) the SSynt tagset is language-idiosyncratic whereas in the DSyntS relations between the content elements are generic and predicate-argument oriented (thus, language-independent); for instance, *subj* and *dobj* in Figure 1 map to argumental relations in Figure 2 (respectively *I* and *II*), while *relat* and *adv* are mapped to the non-argumental relation *ATTR*.

In other words, during the mapping between surface- and deep-syntax, functional elements and predicate-argument relations have to be identified. Thanks to the existence of dedicated tools such as the graph-transducer MATE (Bohnet et al., 2000), the mapping of the SSynt-annotation onto the DSynt-annotation is facilitated. For instance, Mille et al. (2013) describe how they obtain the DSynt annotation of a Spanish treebank. To make the mapping straightforward, predicate-argument information is included in the tags of surface-syntactic annotation, enriching surface-syntactic relations with semantic information. Thus, for instance, instead of simply annotating the relation *obl_obj* when this relation is identified, specifying the argument number in the label is also required: *obl_obj0* corresponds to the first argument, *obl_obj1* to the second argument, *obl_obj2* to the third argument, etc. Then, their mapping grammar simply converted the labels and removed functional elements, before removing the predicate-argument information from the superficial annotation. For Finnish, instead, we followed another approach: we included a valency dictionary in which we store subcategorization information, i.e., the distribution of the arguments of a lemma and required functional elements associated with each of the arguments[7]. For illustration, see a sample entry of such a lexicon in Figure 3.

```
ennustaa {
  PoS = V
  gp = {
    I = {rel= subj|dpos = N|case = NOM}
    II = {rel =dobj|dpos = N|case = GEN}
    III = {rel = compl|dpos = A|case = GEN}
  }
  gp = {
    I = {rel= subj|dpos = N|case = NOM}
    II = {rel =dobj|dpos = V|case = GEN
         conj = että|finiteness = FIN}
  }}}
```

Figure 3: Sample lexicon entry for *ennustaa* 'to predict'.

The entry for *ennustaa* 'to predict' states that this word is a verb (*PoS = V*) and that it has two possible government patterns (*gp*): one with three arguments and one with two arguments. Consider *HSY ennustaa pölyämisen jatkuvan* 'HSY predicts the dust to continue' for the first and *Metla ennustaa, että koivu kukkii ...* 'Metla predicts that the birch will be in bloom ...' for the latter.

Thanks to this lexicon, rules can check in the input SSyntS if a word has a dependent of the type described in its entry, and perform the adequate mapping. For instance, if a dependent of *ennustaa* is a noun in the nominative case with the dependency *subj*, the latter will be mapped to *I* in the DSyntS. A nominal dependent in the genitive case with a dependency *dobj* would be mapped to the second argument (*II*), while a nominalized verb in genitive receiving the dependency *compl* would be mapped to its third argument (*III*). In the lexicon, governed conjunctions are also described, as in the description of the second argument of the second governed pattern: in this case, if *ennustaa* has a dependent *dobj* which is the conjunction *että*, which itself introduces a finite verb, not only will *dobj* be mapped to second argument (*II*), but the governed (functional) element will be removed, so that *II* will link both content words of the substructure, i.e., *ennustaa* and the dependent verb.

The lexicon currently contains more than 1400 entries, including about 300 verbs, 750 nouns, 220 adjectives, 50 adverbs and 100 prepositions, postpositions and conjunctions.[8]

One great advantage of this method is that this resource is not only useful for obtaining lexical valency information from syntactic structures, but also in the framework of rule-based text generation, that is, for the exact opposite mapping (producing syntactic relations and functional elements from abstract predicate-argument structures (Wanner et al., 2014)).[9]

4 Comparison with the TDT annotation scheme

In this section, we present a contrastive analysis of the TDT annotation scheme, the most referenced scheme for Finnish, with respect to its treatment of certain phenomena.

The last version of TDT (Haverinen et al., 2014) contains two layers of annotation. The first layer (the base-syntactic layer) contains 46 relations and

[7] As, e.g., in (Gross, 1984), and the *Explanatory Combinatorial Dictionary* (Mel'čuk, 1988).

[8] The lexicon furthermore contains additional information about the entries which is not related to subcategorization, such as morphological invariability, as well as the values for some lexical functions.

[9] A number of other annotations have resemblance with DSyntSs; cf. (Ivanova et al., 2012) for an overview of deep dependency structures. In particular, DSyntSs show some resemblance, but also some important differences, with PropBank structures, mainly due to the fact that the latter concern phrasal chunks and not individual nodes. The degree of "semanticity" of DSyntSs can be directly compared to Prague's tectogrammatical structures (Hajič et al., 2006), which contain *autosemantic* words only, leaving out *synsemantic* elements such as determiners, auxiliaries, (all) prepositions and conjunctions. Collapsed SDs (de Marneffe et al., 2006) differ from the DSyntSs in that they collapse only (but all) prepositions, conjunctions and possessive clitics, they do not involve any removal of (syntactic) information, and they do not add semantic information compared to the surface annotation.

uses the SD scheme adapted to Finnish. The second layer inserts additional dependencies over the first layer. This second layer tries, on the one hand, to cover more semantic phenomena (conjunct propagation for coordinations, and external subjects), but, on the other hand, it aims at covering some syntactic phenomena–gaps resulting from the first layer annotation–such as describing the function of relative pronouns.[10]

In the following, we present the principal characteristics of the pure-syntactic first layer annotation of TDT, focusing on the most relevant differences between TDT and the annotation scheme presented in this paper.

- Many relations in the TDT annotation scheme are based on the PoS and internal morphological processes of the dependent and/or the governor, rather than on particular syntactic properties of the relations themselves. Even if it cannot be denied that some PoS carry restrictions that others do not, it is important to recognize when those restrictions are imposed by morpho-syntactic factors and, therefore, should not be confused with pure syntactic restrictions. Thus, the TDT annotation scheme distinguishes between two different relations *advmod* and *nommod* for verbal modifiers (9), but the distinction is based only on the PoS of the dependent.[11]

  (9) Distinguishing relations using PoS:
  a. The dependent is an adverb:
  advmod
  Hän käveli kotiin hitaasti.
  He walked home slowly.
  b. The dependent is a noun:
  nommod
  Maljiakko oli pöydällä.
  The_vase was on_the_table.

  Not only is the PoS information duplicated in the annotation, but in those cases in which it is difficult to decide if a word is a noun or an adverb (e.g., *pääasiassa* 'mainly' (adverb) / 'main thing' (noun)), if a wrong PoS tag is chosen, the annotation error directly propagates to the syntactic annotation, as Haverinen et al. (2013) point out. If the syntactic behavior is not different when a dependent is an adverb or a noun, only one syntactic relation should be needed.

  Given that the TDT tagset sub-specifies some dependency tags according to the PoS of the elements involved, it is perfectly possible to choose an annotation that links heads and dependents that belong to different clauses (without being a relative configuration), as in (10). Such analysis is not syntactically accurate, given that it completely ignores the syntactic independence of each clause.

  (10) Edge between independent clauses:
  advmod
  Tulen heti, kun pääsen.
  I_will_come right_away, when I_can.

  In contrast, we keep the syntactic independence of each clause, and relate one to each other through the relation *adv* (11).[12]

  (11) Clause independence respected:
  adv adv conj
  Tulen heti, kun pääsen.
  I_will_come right_away, when I_can.

- When adapting the SD scheme to Finnish, some relations in the TDT annotation were ruled out for being considered "semantic in nature" (Haverinen et al., 2014, p.504). Nevertheless, the analysis of some other phenomena – and the consequent definition of dependencies related to them – still has a more semantic justification than a syntactic one. A first example of this observation, also related to the previous point, is the division of the genitive modifiers of nouns into three different relations: *poss* (12a), *gsubj* (12b) and *gobj* (12c). Although it is argued that such a division responds to the desire of obtaining a higher granularity of the scheme (Haverinen et al., 2014, p.507), the relation division actually depends on the semantics of the governor and not on the syntactic properties of these constructions. Thus, in (12a), *Matin* is a genitive modifier of the noun *penaali* 'pencilcase'; in (12b), due to the semantics of the head, *maljakon* 'vase' is considered a "subject-like" modifier of *särkyminen*

[10]The authors explain that this information is omitted in the first layer because of treeness restriction (Haverinen et al., 2014, p.505).

[11]In this section, we have tried to use the examples presented in (Haverinen, 2012), but in some cases these examples have been shortened/adapted according to format restrictions.

[12]Another way to analyze this sentence is considering a relative configuration, the subordinating clause being a specification of *heti* 'right away' / 'this moment'.

'breaking'; and in (12c), *perunan* 'potato' is considered a nominal modifier of *viljely* 'growing', but it is actually analyzed as a genitive object of the verb *viljellä* 'to grow'. The annotation scheme assumes, as (12b) and (12c) show, that the nominalization process undergone by the verb makes it transmit not only its semantics, but also its syntactic properties. As expected, when the annotation concerns genitive modifiers of nouns, the annotation errors propagate (Haverinen et al., 2013).

(12) Distinguishing modifiers of nouns:

a.

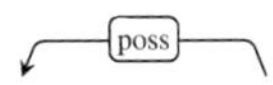

Matin *penaali*
Matti's pencilcase

b.

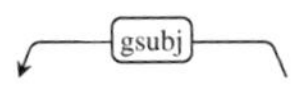

maljakon *särkyminen*
vase (GEN) breaking

c.

perunan *viljely*
potato (GEN) growing (N)

In the annotation schema presented in this paper, the three constructions are parallel and use the relation *attr*.

Another clear example of the prevalence of semantics over syntax in TDT is the treatment of copular verbs. They are treated in a specific way (13), different from any other verb (14), due to the semantic link between the subject and the complement of the copular verb. [13]

(13) TDT analysis, copulative sentences:

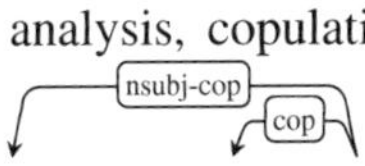

Huivi *on* *punainen.*
the_scarf (3,SG) is (3,SG) red
The scarf is red.

(14) TDT analysis of non-copulative:

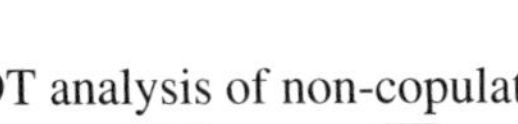

Poika *potkaisee* *palloa.*
the_guy (3,SG) kicks (3,SG) the_ball
The guy kicks the ball.

[13]The TDT annotation faces a problem of not resulting in a tree when, instead of a subject noun, a participial modifier appears. Thus, in those cases, they treat a copulative configuration as any other verbal construction, which weakens their original analysis (Haverinen, 2012, Section 5.13).

In both sentences, the verb agrees with the preverbal element in person and number, which is the morphological marker of the syntactic phenomenon of being a subject. However, the analysis assigned to each sentence does not capture such parallelism. The difference between both sentences concerns the second verbal complement: in copulative sentences, if its PoS licenses agreement, this element agrees with the subject in number; in non-copulative sentences, such an agreement does not happen. Therefore, two different relations hold between the verb and this complement, as (15) and (16) show.

(15) Our analysis of copulative sentences:

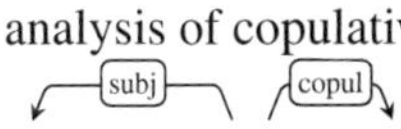

Huivi *on* *punainen.*
the_scarf (3,SG) is (3,SG) red
The scarf is red.

(16) Our analysis of non-copulative:

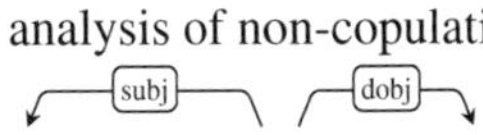

Poika *potkaisee* *palloa.*
the_guy (3,SG) kicks (3,SG) the_ball
The guy kicks the ball.

Finally, the prevalence of semantics over syntax in TDT is exemplified through the treatment of subjects, auxiliaries and content verbs. The TDT annotation schema takes the content verb as head of the sentence, and makes the subject hold on it (17).

(17) TDT treatment of auxiliaries:

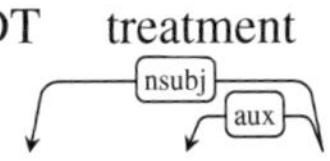

Hän *saattoi* *lähteä* *jo.*
he may (impf.) leave already
He may have left already.

If syntactic properties are prioritized in the course of the definition of the annotation schema, the subject relation should link the subject and the auxiliary (18), given that agreement holds between these two elements. Consequently, the auxiliary should head the relation between the two verbs. In the same way, the negative auxiliary should be also treated as the element heading the subject and the content verb.

(18) Our treatment of auxiliaries:

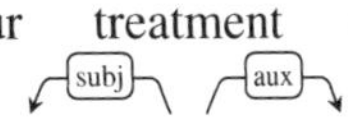

Hän *saattoi* *lähteä* *jo.*
he may (impf.) leave already
He may have left already.

- Given the semantic motivation for annotating differently similar syntactic phenomena (or vice versa), we would expect the TDT annotation schema to allow for a direct mapping from surface-syntax to deeper linguistic levels (or, in more concrete terms, to a predicate-argument structure, which we refer to as "semantics"). However, this is not the case.

  As detailed in Section 2.2, case markers and adpositions can be either functional or meaning-bearing, and each of them should be treated differently. TDT, however, treats as the same, on one hand, case markers and adpositions (Haverinen, 2012, p.2) and, on the other hand, elements that are purely functional and those ones that do convey a content. The examples in (19) show TDT's parallel treatment of case markers and adpositions (compare (19a) to (19b)), and of governed and non-governed elements (compare (19b) to (19c)). As can be observed, the same syntactic analysis is offered to sentences that differ in syntax: in (19a), the adessive case of *pöytä* 'table' is required for expressing a locative meaning with the verb *olla*, whereas in (19b), the genitive case is required by the adposition and not by the verb or the configuration itself. On the other hand, non-governed elements (such as *päällä* 'on_top_of' in (19b)) are treated in the same way as governed elements (such as *kanssa* 'with' in (19c)).

(19) TDT treatment of adpositions:

a.

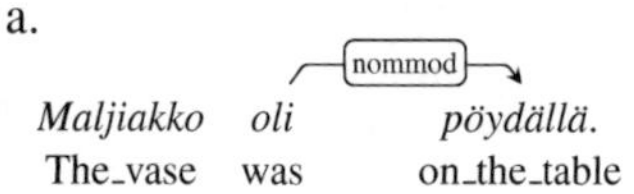

b.

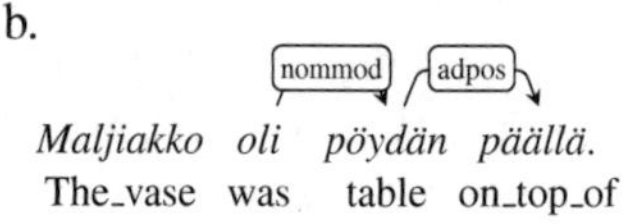

c.

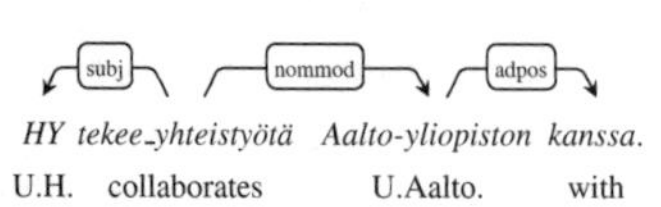

One problem of treating functional and content elements in the same way is the difficulty in reaching an actual abstract structure which contains only content words. (20) is an expansion of (19c) where, apart from the governed adposition, there is a translative case (*-ksi*), expressing purpose, which is not required by the predicate. In an abstract structure corresponding to (20), the governed adposition should not appear, unlike the non-governed case.

(20) *HY tekee yhteistyötä Aalto-yliopiston kanssa uudenlaisen digitaalisen oppimisen tukemiseksi.*
'The university of Helsinky collaborated with the University Aalto to promote a new way of digital learning.'

Another example of the difficulty of getting an appropriate mapping between syntax and semantics is the treatment of relative pronouns: in the first layer of annotation, all relative pronouns receive the same relation from the subordinate verb (i.e., *rel*), without taking into account the syntactic function of the pronoun within the subordinate clause (21).

(21) TDT treatment of relative pronouns:

a.

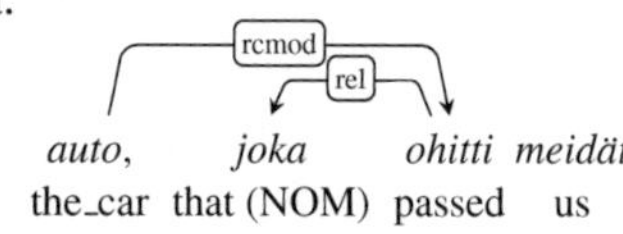

b.

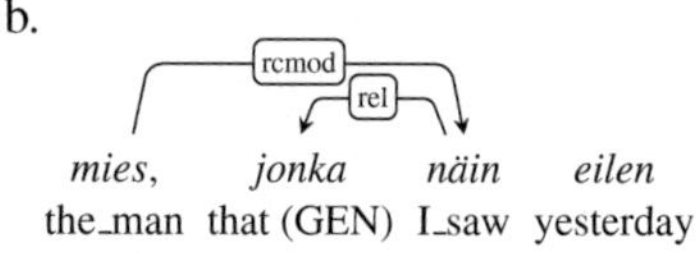

Even though a case can indicate the function occupied by the element to which it is attached, it is not enough for obtaining a direct mapping to semantics. First of all, many times, cases themselves are not enough for indicating such function, but their combinability with the involved verbs is also needed. Secondly, and more importantly, the same cases are used by elements that occupy different semantic slots. Thus, for instance, both subjects and objects accept the same set of cases (nominative, partitive and genitive), which clearly blurs a direct mapping to predicate-argument structures. In our syntactic annotation scheme, *rel* would be annotated as a subject in (21a), and as object in in (21b).

5 Conclusions

In this paper, we presented an annotation schema for Finnish that can be considered an alternative to the SD-oriented schema used in the TDT treebank. We justify and present a syntactically motivated tagset for Finnish, and the creation of a lexicon which facilitates the annotation of a deep syntactic (semantics-oriented) representation which captures lexical valency relations between content lexical items. Having two distinct levels for capturing syntactic and semantic information, has been shown to allow for developing different NLP applications in the parsing and the natural language generation fields (Ballesteros et al., 2014; Ballesteros et al., 2015).

The corpus annotated following the SSynt and DSynt annotation schemata described in this paper are made available upon request.

Acknowledgements

The work described in this paper has been carried out in the framework of the project *Personalized Environmental Service Configuration and Delivery Orchestration* (PESCaDO), supported by the European Commission under the contract number FP7-ICT-248594.

References

M. Ballesteros, B. Bohnet, S. Mille, and L. Wanner. 2014. Deep-syntactic parsing. In *Proceedings of COLING*, Dublin, Ireland.

M. Ballesteros, B. Bohnet, S. Mille, and L. Wanner. 2015. Data-driven sentence generation with non-isomorphic trees. In *Proceedings of NAACL-HLT*, Denver, CO, USA.

B. Bohnet, A. Langjahr, and L. Wanner. 2000. A development environment for an MTT-based sentence generator. In *Proceedings of INLG*.

A. Burga, S. Mille, and L. Wanner. 2014. Looking behind the scenes of syntactic dependency corpus annotation: Towards a motivated annotation schema of surface-syntax in Spanish. In *Computational Dependency Theory. Frontiers in Artificial Intelligence and Applications Series*, volume 258. Amsterdam:IOS Press.

M.C. de Marneffe and Ch. Manning. 2008. The Stanford typed dependencies representation. In *Proceedings of the workshop on Cross-Framework and Cross-Domain Parser Evaluation (COLING)*, Manchester, UK.

M.C de Marneffe, B. MacCartney, and Ch. Manning. 2006. Generating typed dependency parses from phrase structure parses. In *Proceedings of the 5th International Conference on Language Resources and Evaluation (LREC)*, pages 449–454, Genoa, Italy.

M.C. de Marneffe, T. Dozat, N. Silveira, K. Haverinen, F. Ginter, J. Nivre, and Ch. Manning. 2014. Universal Stanford dependencies: A cross-linguistic typology. In *Proceedings of the 9th International Conference on Language Resources and Evaluation (LREC)*, pages 4585–4592, Reykjavik, Iceland.

M. Gross. 1984. Lexicon-grammar and the syntactic analysis of French. In *Proceedings of the 10th International Conference on Computational Linguistics (COLING) and the 22nd Annual Meeting of the Association for Computational Linguistics (ACL)*, pages 275–282, Stanford, CA, USA.

J. Hajič, J. Panevová, E. Hajičová, P. Sgall, P. Pajas, J. Štěpánek, J. Havelka, M. Mikulová, and Z. Žabokrtský. 2006. Prague Dependency Treebank 2.0. Linguistic Data Consortium, Philadelphia.

K. Haverinen, F. Ginter, V. Laippala, S. Kohonen, T. Viljanen, J. Nyblom, and T. Salakoski. 2013. A dependency-based analysis of treebank annotation errors. In K. Gerdes, E. Hajíčova, and L. Wanner, editors, *Computational Dependency Theory*. IOS Press.

K. Haverinen, J. Nyblom, T. Viljanen, V. Laippala, S. Kohonen, A. Missilä, T. Salakoski, and F. Ginter. 2014. Building the essential resources for Finnish: the Turku Dependency Treebank. In *Proceedings of LREC*, Reykjavik, Iceland, September.

K. Haverinen. 2012. Syntax Annotation Guidelines for the Turku Dependency Treebank. *Technical Report 1034, Turku Centre for Computer Science, Turku, Finland.*

A. Ivanova, S. Oepen, L. Øvrelid, and D. Flickinger. 2012. Who did what to whom? A contrastive study of syntacto-semantic dependencies. In *Proceedings of the 6th Linguistic Annotation Workshop*, pages 2–11, Jeju, Republic of Korea.

I. Mel'čuk. 1988. Semantic description of lexical units in an explanatory combinatorial dictionary: Basic principles and heuristic criteria. *International Journal of Lexicography*, 1(3):165–188.

I. Mel'čuk. 1988. *Dependency Syntax: Theory and Practice*. State University of New York Press, Albany.

S. Mille, A. Burga, and L.Wanner. 2013. AnCora-UPF: A multi-level annotation of Spanish. In *Proceedings of DepLing*, Prague, Czech Republic.

A. Voutilainen, K. Muhonen, T. Purtonen, and K. Lindén. 2012. Specifying treebanks, outsourcing parsebanks: Finntreebank 3. In *Proceedings of LREC*, Istanbul, Turkey.

L. Wanner, H. Bosch, N. Bouayad-Agha, G. Casamayor, Th. Ertl, D. Hilbring, L. Johansson, K. Karatzas, A. Karppinen, I. Kompatsiaris, et al. 2014. Getting the environmental information across: from the web to the user. *Expert Systems*.

A Bayesian Model for Generative Transition-based Dependency Parsing

Jan Buys[1] and **Phil Blunsom**[1,2]
[1]Department of Computer Science, University of Oxford [2]Google DeepMind
{jan.buys,phil.blunsom}@cs.ox.ac.uk

Abstract

We propose a simple, scalable, fully generative model for transition-based dependency parsing with high accuracy. The model, parameterized by Hierarchical Pitman-Yor Processes, overcomes the limitations of previous generative models by allowing fast and accurate inference. We propose an efficient decoding algorithm based on particle filtering that can adapt the beam size to the uncertainty in the model while jointly predicting POS tags and parse trees. The UAS of the parser is on par with that of a greedy discriminative baseline. As a language model, it obtains better perplexity than a n-gram model by performing semi-supervised learning over a large unlabelled corpus. We show that the model is able to generate locally and syntactically coherent sentences, opening the door to further applications in language generation.

1 Introduction

Transition-based dependency parsing algorithms that perform greedy local inference have proven to be very successful at fast and accurate discriminative parsing (Nivre, 2008; Zhang and Nivre, 2011; Chen and Manning, 2014). Beam-search decoding further improves performance (Zhang and Clark, 2008; Huang and Sagae, 2010; Choi and McCallum, 2013), but increases decoding time. Graph-based parsers (McDonald et al., 2005; Koo and Collins, 2010; Lei et al., 2014) perform global inference and although they are more accurate in some cases, inference tends to be slower.

In this paper we aim to transfer the advantages of transition-based parsing to generative dependency parsing. While generative models have been used widely and successfully for constituency parsing (Collins, 1997; Petrov et al., 2006), their use in dependency parsing has been limited. Generative models offer a principled approach to semi- and unsupervised learning, and can also be applied to natural language generation tasks.

Dependency grammar induction models (Klein and Manning, 2004; Blunsom and Cohn, 2010) are generative, but not expressive enough for high-accuracy parsing. A previous generative transition-based dependency parser (Titov and Henderson, 2007) obtains competitive accuracies, but training and decoding is computationally very expensive. Syntactic language models have also been shown to improve performance in speech recognition and machine translation (Chelba and Jelinek, 2000; Charniak et al., 2003). However, the main limitation of most existing generative syntactic models is their inefficiency.

We propose a generative model for transition-based parsing (§2). The model, parameterized by Hierarchical Pitman-Yor Processes (HPYPs) (Teh, 2006), learns a distribution over derivations of parser transitions, words and POS tags (§3).

To enable efficient inference, we propose a novel algorithm for linear-time decoding in a generative transition-based parser (§4). The algorithm is based on particle filtering (Doucet et al., 2001), a method for sequential Monte Carlo sampling. This method enables the beam-size during decoding to depend on the uncertainty of the model.

Experimental results (§5) show that the model obtains 88.5% UAS on the standard WSJ parsing task, compared to 88.9% for a greedy discriminative model with similar features. The model can accurately parse up to 200 sentences per second. Although this performance is below state-of-the-art discriminative models, it exceeds existing generative dependency parsing models in either accuracy, speed or both.

As a language model, the transition-based parser offers an inexpensive way to incorporate

Proceedings of the Third International Conference on Dependency Linguistics (Depling 2015), pages 58–67,
Uppsala, Sweden, August 24–26 2015.

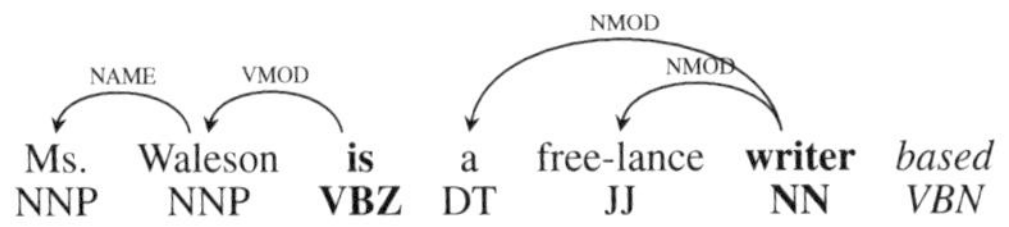

Figure 1: A partially-derived dependency tree for the sentence *Ms. Waleson is a free-lance writer based in New York.* The next word to be predicted by the generative model is *based*. Words in bold are on the stack.

syntactic structure into incremental word prediction. With supervised training the model's perplexity is comparable to that of n-gram models, although generated examples shows greater syntactic coherence. With semi-supervised learning over a large unannotated corpus its perplexity is considerably better than that of a n-gram model.

2 Generative Transition-based Parsing

Our parsing model is based on transition-based projective dependency parsing with the arc-standard parsing strategy (Nivre and Scholz, 2004). Parsing is restricted to (labelled) projective trees. An arc $(i, l, j) \in A$ encodes a dependency between two words, where i is the head node, j the dependent and l is the dependency type of j. In our generative model a word can be represented by its lexical (word) type and/or its POS tag. We add a root node to the beginning of the sentence (although it could also be added at the end of the sentence), such that the head word of the sentence is the dependent of the root node.

A parser configuration (σ, β, A) for sentence $\mathbf{s}$ consists of a stack σ of indices in $\mathbf{s}$, an index β to the next word to be generated, and a set of arcs A. The stack elements are referred to as $\sigma_1, \ldots, \sigma_{|\sigma|}$, where σ_1 is the top element. For any node a, $lc_1(a)$ refers to the leftmost child of a in A, and $rc_1(a)$ to its rightmost child.

The initial configuration is $([], 0, \emptyset)$. A terminal configuration is reached when $\beta > |\mathbf{s}|$, and σ consists only of the root. A sentence is generated left-to-right by performing a sequence of transitions. As a generative model it assigns probabilities to sentences and dependency trees: A word w (including its POS tag) is generated when it is shifted on to the stack, similar to the generative models proposed by Titov and Henderson (2007) and Cohen et al. (2011), and the joint tagging and parsing model of Bohnet and Nivre (2012).

The types of transitions in this model are shift (sh), left-arc (la) and right-arc (ra):

$$\text{sh}_w\text{: } (\sigma, i, A) \vdash (\sigma|i, i+1, A)$$

$$\text{la}_l\text{: } (\sigma|i|j, \beta, A) \vdash (\sigma|j, \beta, A \cup \{(j, l, i)\})$$

$$\text{ra}_l\text{: } (\sigma|i|j, \beta, A) \vdash (\sigma|i, \beta, A \cup \{(i, l, j)\})$$

Left-arc and right-arc (reduce) transitions add an arc between the top two words on the stack, and also generate an arc label l. The parsing strategy adds arcs bottom-up. No arc that would make the root node the dependent of another node may be added. To illustrate the generative process, the configuration of a partially generated dependency tree is given in Figure 1.

In general parses may have multiple derivations. In transition-based parsing it is common to define an oracle $o(c, G)$ that maps the current configuration c and the gold parse G to the next transition that should be performed. In our probabilistic model we are interested in performing inference over all latent structure, including spurious derivations. Therefore we propose a non-deterministic oracle which allows us to find all derivations of G. In contrast to dynamic oracles (Goldberg and Nivre, 2013), we are only interested in derivations of the correct parse tree, so the oracle can assume that given c there exists a derivation for G.

First, to enforce the bottom-up property our oracle has to ensure that an arc (i, j) in G may only be added once j has been attached to all its children – we refer to these arcs as *valid*. Most deterministic oracles add valid arcs greedily. Second, we note that if there exists a valid arc between σ_2 and σ_1 and the oracle decides to shift, the same pair will only occur on the top of the stack again after a right dependent has been attached to σ_1. Therefore right arcs have to be added greedily if they are valid, while adding a valid left arc may be delayed if σ_1 has unattached right dependents in G.

3 Probabilistic Generative Model

Our model defines a joint probability distribution over a parsed sentence with POS tags $\mathbf{t}_{1:n}$, words $\mathbf{w}_{1:n}$ and a transition sequence $\mathbf{a}_{1:2n}$ as

$$p(\mathbf{t}_{1:n}, \mathbf{w}_{1:n}, \mathbf{a}_{1:2n}) = \prod_{i=1}^{n} \left(p(t_i|\mathbf{h}^t_{m_i}) p(w_i|t_i, \mathbf{h}^w_{m_i}) \prod_{j=m_i+1}^{m_{i+1}} p(a_j|\mathbf{h}^a_j) \right),$$

where m_i is the number of transitions that have been performed when (t_i, w_i) is generated and $\mathbf{h}^t$, $\mathbf{h}^w$ and $\mathbf{h}^a$ are sequences representing the conditioning contexts for the tag, word and transition distributions, respectively.

In the generative process a shift transition is followed by a sequence of 0 or more reduce transitions. This is repeated until all the words have been generated and a terminal configuration of the parser has been reached. We shall also consider unlexicalised models, based only on POS tags.

3.1 Hierarchical Pitman-Yor processes

The probability distributions for predicting words, tags and transitions are drawn from hierarchical Pitmar-Yor Process (HPYP) priors. HPYP models were originally proposed for n-gram language modelling (Teh, 2006), and have been applied to various NLP tasks. A version of approximate inference in the HPYP model recovers interpolated Kneser-Ney smoothing (Kneser and Ney, 1995), one of the best preforming n-gram language models. The Pitman-Yor Process (PYP) is a generalization of the Dirichlet process which defines a distribution over distributions over a probability space X, with discount parameter $0 \leq d < 1$, strength parameter $\theta > -d$ and base distribution B. PYP priors encode the power-law distribution found in the distribution of words.

Sampling from the posterior is characterized by the Chinese Restaurant Process analogy, where each variable in a sequence is represented by a customer entering a restaurant and sitting at one of an infinite number of tables. Let c_k be the number of customers sitting at table k and K the number of occupied tables. The customer chooses to sit at a table according to the probability

$$P(z_i = k|\mathbf{z}_{1:i-1}) = \begin{cases} \frac{c_k - d}{i-1+\theta} & 1 \leq k \leq K \\ \frac{Kd+\theta}{i-1+\theta} & k = K+1, \end{cases}$$

where z_i is the index of the table chosen by the ith customer and $\mathbf{z}_{1:i-1}$ is the seating arrangement of the previous $i-1$ customers.

All customers at a table share the same dish, corresponding to the value assigned to the variables they represent. When a customer sits at an empty table, a dish is assigned to the table by drawing from the base distribution of the PYP.

For HPYPs, the PYP base distribution can itself be drawn from a PYP. The restaurant analogy is extended to the Chinese Restaurant Franchise, where the base distribution of a PYP corresponds to another restaurant. So when a customer sits at a new table, the dish is chosen by letting a new customer enter the base distribution restaurant. All dishes can be traced back to a uniform base distribution at the top of the hierarchy.

Inference over seating arrangements in the model is performed with Gibbs sampling, based on routines to add or remove a customer from a restaurant. In our implementation we use the efficient data structures proposed by Blunsom et al. (2009). In addition to sampling the seating arrangement, the discount and strength parameters are also sampled, using slice sampling.

In our model $T_{\mathbf{h}^t}, W_{\mathbf{h}^w}$ and $A_{\mathbf{h}^a}$ are HPYPs for the tag, word and transition distributions, respectively. The PYPs for the transition prediction distribution, with conditioning context sequence $\mathbf{h}^a_{1:L}$, are defined hierarchically as

$$\begin{aligned} A_{\mathbf{h}^a_{1:L}} &\sim \text{PYP}(d^A_L, \theta^A_L, A_{\mathbf{h}^a_{1:L-1}}) \\ A_{\mathbf{h}^a_{1:L-1}} &\sim \text{PYP}(d^A_{L-1}, \theta^A_{L-1}, A_{\mathbf{h}^a_{1:L-2}}) \\ \cdots &\quad \cdots \\ A_{\emptyset} &\sim \text{PYP}(d^A_0, \theta^A_0, \text{Uniform}), \end{aligned}$$

where d^A_k and θ^A_k are the discount and strength discount parameters for PYPs with conditioning context length k. Each back-off level drops one context element. The distribution given the empty context backs off to the uniform distribution over all predictions. The word and tag distributions are defined by similarly-structured HPYPs.

The prior specifies an ordering of the symbols in the context from most informative to least informative to the distributions being estimated. The choice and ordering of this context is crucial in the formulation of our model. The contexts that we use are given in Table 1.

4 Decoding

In the standard approach to beam search for transition-based parsing (Zhang and Clark, 2008), the beam stores partial derivations with the same number of transitions performed, and the lowest-scoring ones are removed when the size of the beam exceeds a set threshold. However, in our model we cannot compare derivations with the same number of transitions but which differ in the number of words shifted. One solution is to keep n separate beams, each containing only derivations with i words shifted, but this approach leads to

	Context elements
a_i	$\sigma_1.t, \sigma_2.t, rc_1(\sigma_1).t, lc_1(\sigma_1).t, \sigma_3.t, rc_1(\sigma_2).t, \sigma_1.w, \sigma_2.w$
t_j	$\sigma_1.t, \sigma_2.t, rc_1(\sigma_1).t, lc_1(\sigma_1).t, \sigma_3.t, rc_1(\sigma_2).t, \sigma_1.w, \sigma_2.w$
w_j	$\beta.t, \sigma_1.t, rc_1(\sigma_1).t, lc_1(\sigma_1).t, \sigma_1.w, \sigma_2.w$

Table 1: HPYP prediction contexts for the transition, tag and word distributions. The context elements are ordered from most important to least important; the last elements in the lists are dropped first in the back-off structure. The POS tag of node s is referred to as $s.t$ and the word type as $s.w$.

$O(n^2)$ decoding complexity. Another option is to prune the beam every time after the next word is shifted in all derivations – however the number of reduce transitions that can be performed between shifts is bounded by the stack size, so decoding complexity remains quadratic.

We propose a novel linear-time decoding algorithm inspired by particle filtering (see Algorithm 1). Instead of specifying a fixed limit on the size of the beam, the beam size is controlled by setting the number of particles K. Every partial derivation d_j in the beam is associated with k_j particles, such that $\sum_j k_j = K$. Each pass through the beam advances each d_j until the next word is shifted.

At each step, to predict the next transition for d_j, k_j is divided proportionally between taking a shift or reduce transition, according to $p(a|d_j.\mathbf{h}^a)$. If a non-zero number of particles are assigned to reduce, the highest scoring left-arc and right-arc transitions are chosen deterministically, and derivations that execute them are added to the beam. In practice we found that adding only the highest scoring reduce transition (left-arc or right-arc) gives very similar performance. The shift transition is performed on the current derivation, and the derivation weight is also updated with the word generation probability.

A POS tag is also generated along with a shift transition. Up to three candidate tags are assigned (more do not improve performance) and corresponding derivations are added to the beam, with particles distributed relative to the tag probability (in Algorithm 1 only one tag is predicted).

A pass is complete once the derivations in the beam, including those added by reduce transitions during the pass, have been iterated through. Then a selection step is performed to determine which

Input: Sentence $\mathbf{w}_{1:n}$, K particles.
Output: Parse tree of $\arg\max_{d \text{ in beam}} d.\theta$.
Initialize the beam with parser configuration d with weight $d.\theta = 1$ and $d.k = K$ particles;
for $i \leftarrow 1$ **to** N **do**
  Search step;
  foreach *derivation d in beam* **do**
    nShift = round($d.k \cdot p(\text{sh}|d.\mathbf{h}^a)$);
    nReduce = $d.k$ − nShift;
    if *nReduce* > 0 **then**
      $a = \arg\max_{a \neq \text{sh}} p(a|d.\mathbf{h}^a)$;
      beam.append($dd \leftarrow d$);
      $dd.k \leftarrow$ nReduce;
      $dd.\theta \leftarrow dd.\theta \cdot p(a|d.\mathbf{h}^a)$;
      dd.execute(a);
    end
    $d.k \leftarrow$ nShift;
    if *nShift* > 0 **then**
      $d.\theta \leftarrow d.\theta \cdot p(\text{sh}|d.\mathbf{h}^a) \cdot \max_{t_i} p(t_i|d.\mathbf{h}^t)p(w_i|d.\mathbf{h}^w)$;
      d.execute(sh);
    end
  end
  Selection step;
  foreach *derivation d in beam* **do**
    $d.\theta' \leftarrow \frac{d.k \cdot d.\theta}{\sum_{d'} d'.k \cdot d'.\theta}$;
  end
  foreach *derivation d in beam* **do**
    $d.k = \lfloor d.\theta' \cdot K \rfloor$;
    if $d.k = 0$ **then**
      beam.remove(d);
    end
  end
end

Algorithm 1: Beam search decoder for arc-standard generative dependency parsing.

derivations are kept. The number of particles for each derivation are reallocated based on the normalised weights of the derivations, each weighted by its current number of particles. Derivations to which zero particles are assigned are eliminated. The selection step allows the size of the beam to depend on the uncertainty of the model during decoding. The selectional branching method proposed by Choi and McCallum (2013) for discriminative beam-search parsing has a similar goal.

After the last word in the sentence has been shifted, reduce transitions are performed on each derivation until it reaches a terminal configuration. The parse tree corresponding to the highest scoring final derivation is returned.

The main differences between our algorithm and particle filtering are that we divide particles proportionally instead of sampling with replacement, and in the selection step we base the redistribution on the derivation weight instead of the importance weight (the word generation probability). Our method can be interpreted as maximizing by sampling from a peaked version of the distribution over derivations.

5 Experiments

5.1 Parsing Setup

We evaluate our model as a parser on the standard English Penn Treebank (Marcus et al., 1993) setup, training on WSJ sections 02-21, developing on section 22, and testing on section 23. We use the head-finding rules of Yamada and Matsumoto (2003) (YM)[1] for constituency-to-dependency conversion, to enable comparison with previous results. We also evaluate on the Stanford dependency representation (De Marneffe and Manning, 2008) (SD)[2].

Words that occur only once in the training data are treated as unknown words. We classify unknown words according to capitalization, numbers, punctuation and common suffixes into classes similar to those used in the implementation of generative constituency parsers such as the Stanford parser (Klein and Manning, 2003).

As a discriminative baseline we use MaltParser (Nivre et al., 2006), a discriminative, greedy transition-based parser, performing arc-standard parsing with LibLinear as classifier. Although the accuracy of this model is not state-of-the-art, it does enable us to compare our model against an optimised discriminative model with a feature-set based on the same elements as we include in our conditioning contexts.

Our HPYP dependency parser (HPYP-DP) is trained with 20 iterations of Gibbs sampling, resampling the hyper-parameters after every iteration, except when performing inference over latent structure, in which case they are only resampled every 5 iterations. Training with a deterministic oracle takes 28 seconds per iteration (excluding resampling hyper-parameters), while a non-deterministic oracle (sampling with 100 particles) takes 458 seconds.

5.2 Modelling Choices

We consider several modelling choices in the construction of our generative dependency parsing model. Development set parsing results are given in Table 2. We report unlabelled attachment score (UAS) and labelled attachment score (LAS), excluding punctuation.

[1]http://stp.lingfil.uu.se/ nivre/research/Penn2Malt.html

[2]Converted with version 3.4.1 of the Stanford parser, available at http:/nlp.stanford.edu/software/lex-parser.shtml.

Model	UAS	LAS
MaltParser Unlex	85.23	82.80
MaltParser Lex	89.17	87.81
Unlexicalised	85.64	82.93
Lexicalised, unlex context	87.95	85.04
Lexicalised, tagger POS	87.84	85.54
Lexicalised, predict POS	**89.09**	**86.78**
Lexicalised, gold POS	89.30	87.28

Table 2: HPYP parsing accuracies on the YM development set, for various lexicalised and unlexicalised setups.

Context elements	UAS	LAS
$\sigma_1.t, \sigma_2.t$	73.25	70.14
$+rc_1(\sigma_1).t$	80.21	76.64
$+lc_1(\sigma_1).t$	85.18	82.03
$+\sigma_3.t$	87.23	84.26
$+rc_1(\sigma_2).t$	87.95	85.04
$+\sigma_1.w$	88.53	86.11
$+\sigma_2.w$	88.93	86.57

Table 3: Effect of including elements in the model conditioning contexts. Results are given on the YM development set.

HPYP priors

The first modelling choice is the selection and ordering of elements in the conditioning contexts of the HPYP priors. Table 3 shows how the development set accuracy increases as more elements are added to the conditioning context. The first two words on the stack are the most important, but insufficient – second-order dependencies and further elements on the stack should also be included in the contexts. The challenge is that the back-off structure of each HPYP specifies an ordering of the elements based on their importance in the prediction. We are therefore much more restricted than classifiers with large, sparse feature-sets which are commonly used in transition-based parsers. Due to sparsity, the word types are the first elements to be dropped in the back-off structure, and elements such as third-order dependencies, which have been shown to improve parsing performance, cannot be included successfully in our model.

Sampling over parsing derivations during training further improves performance by 0.16% to

89.09 UAS. Adding the root symbol at the end of the sentence rather than at the front gives very similar parsing performance. When unknown words are not clustered according to surface features, performance drops to 88.60 UAS.

POS tags and lexicalisation

It is standard practice in transition-based parsing to obtain POS tags with a stand-alone tagger before parsing. However, as we have a generative model, we can use the model to assign POS tags in decoding, while predicting the transition sequence. We compare predicting tags against using gold standard POS tags and tags obtain using the Stanford POS tagger[3] (Toutanova et al., 2003). Even though the predicted tags are slightly less accurate than the Stanford tags on the development set (95.6%), jointly predicting tags and decoding increases the UAS by 1.1%. The jointly predicted tags are a better fit to the generative model, which can be seen by an improvement in the likelihood of the test data. Bohnet and Nivre (2012) found that joint prediction increases both POS and parsing accuracy. However, their model rescored a k-best list of tags obtained with an preprocessing tagger, while our model does not use the external tagger at all during joint prediction.

We train lexicalised and unlexicalised versions of our model. Unlexicalised parsing gives us a strong baseline (85.6 UAS) over which to consider our model's ability to predict and condition on words. Unlexicalised parsing is also considered to be robust for applications such as cross-lingual parsing (McDonald et al., 2011). Additionally, we consider a version of the model that don't include lexical elements in the conditioning context. This model performs only 1% UAS lower than the best lexicalised model, although it makes much stronger independence assumptions. The main benefit of lexicalised conditioning contexts are to make incremental decoding easier.

Speed vs accuracy trade-offs

We consider a number of trade-offs between speed and accuracy in the model. We compare using different numbers of particles during decoding, as well as jointly predicting POS tags against using pre-obtained tags (Table 4).

[3]We use the efficient "left 3 words" model, trained on the same data as the parsing model, excluding distributional features. Tagging accuracy is 95.9% on the development set and 96.5% on the test set.

Particles	Sent/sec	UAS
5000	18	89.04
1000	27	88.93
100	54	87.99
10	104	85.27
1000	108	87.59
100	198	87.46
10	333	85.86

Table 4: Speed and accuracy for different configurations of the decoding algorithm. Above the line, POS tags are predicted by the model, below pre-tagged POS are used.

Model	UAS	LAS
Eisner (1996)	80.7	-
Wallach et al. (2008)	85.7	-
Titov and Henderson (2007)	89.36	87.65
HPYP-DP	**88.47**	**86.13**
MaltParser	88.88	87.41
Zhang and Nivre (2011)	92.9	91.8
Choi and McCallum (2013)	92.96	91.93

Table 5: Parsing accuracies on the YM test set. compared against previous published results. Titov and Henderson (2007) was retrained to enable direct comparison.

The optimal number of particles is found to be 1000 - more particles only increase accuracy by about 0.1 UAS. Although jointly predicting tags is more accurate, using pre-obtained tags provides a better trade-off between speed and accuracy – 87.59 against 85.27 UAS at around 100 sentences per second. In comparison, the MaltParser parses around 500 sentences per second.

We also compare our particle filter-based algorithm against a more standard beam-search algorithm that prunes the beam to a fixed size after each word is shifted. This algorithm is much slower than the particle-based algorithm – to get similar accuracy it parses only 3 sentences per second (against 27) when predicting tags jointly, and 29 (against 108) when using pre-obtained tags.

5.3 Parsing Results

Test set results comparing our model against existing discriminative and generative dependency parsers are given in Table 5. Our HPYP model performs much better than Eisner's generative model as well as the Bayesian version of that model proposed by Wallach et al. (2008) (the result for Eisner's model is given as reported by Wallach et al. (2008) on the WSJ). The accuracy of our model is only 0.8 UAS below the generative model of Titov and Henderson (2007), despite that model being much more powerful. The Titov and Henderson model takes 3 days to train, and its decoding speed is around 1 sentence per second.

The UAS of our model is very close to that of the MaltParser. However, we do note that our model's performance is relatively worse on LAS than on UAS. An explanation for this is that as we do not include labels in the conditioning contexts, the predicted labels are independent of words that have not yet been generated.

We also test the model on the Stanford dependencies, which have a larger label set. Our model obtains 87.9/83.2 against the MaltParser's 88.9/86.2 UAS/LAS.

Despite these promising results, our model's performance still lags behind recent discriminative parsers (Zhang and Nivre, 2011; Choi and McCallum, 2013) with beam-search and richer feature sets than can be incorporated in our model. In terms of speed, Zhang and Nivre (2011) parse 29 sentences per second, against the 110 sentences per second of Choi and McCallum (2013). Recently proposed neural networks for dependency parsers have further improved performance (Dyer et al., 2015; Weiss et al., 2015), reaching up to 94.0% UAS with Stanford dependencies.

We argue that the main weakness of the HPYP parser is sparsity in the large conditioning contexts composed of tags and words. The POS tags in the parser configuration context already give a very strong signal for predicting the next transition. As a result it is challenging to construct PYP reduction lists that also include word types without making the back-off contexts too sparse.

The other limitation is that our decoding algorithm, although efficient, still prunes the search space aggressively, while not being able to take advantage of look-ahead features as discriminative models can. Interestingly, we note that a discriminative parser cannot reach high performance without look-ahead features.

5.4 Language Modelling

Next we evaluate our model as a language model. First we use the standard WSJ language modelling setup, training on sections $00 - 20$, developing on $21 - 22$ and testing on $23 - 24$. Punctuation is removed, numbers and symbols are mapped to a single symbol and the vocabulary is limited to $10,000$ words. Second we consider a semi-supervised setup where we train the model, in addition to the WSJ, on a subset of 1 million sentences (24.1 million words) from the WMT English monolingual training data[4]. This model is evaluated on `newstest2012`.

When training our models for language modelling, we first perform standard supervised training, as for parsing (although we don't predict labels). This is followed by a second training stage, where we train the model only on words, regarding the tags and parse trees as latent structure. In this unsupervised stage we train the model with particle Gibbs sampling (Andrieu et al., 2010), using a particle filter to sample parse trees. When only training on the WSJ, we perform this step on the same data, now allowing the model to learn parses that are not necessarily consistent with the annotated parse trees.

For semi-supervised training, unsupervised learning is performed on the large unannotated corpus. However, here we find the highest scoring parse trees, rather than sampling. Only the word prediction distribution is updated, not the tag and transition distributions.

Language modelling perplexity results are given in Table 6. We note that the perplexities reported are upper bounds on the true perplexity of the model, as it is intractable to sum over all possible parses of a sentence to compute the marginal probability of the words. As an approximation we sum over the final beam after decoding.

The results show that on the WSJ the model performs slightly better than a HPYP n-gram model. One disadvantage of evaluating on this dataset is that due to removing punctuation and restricting the vocabulary, the model parsing accuracy drops to 84.6 UAS. Also note that in contrast to many other evaluations, we do not interpolate with a n-gram model – this will improve perplexity further.

On the big dataset we see a larger improvement over the n-gram model. This is a promising result, as it shows that our model can successfully generalize to larger vocabularies and unannotated datasets.

[4]Available at http://www.statmt.org/wmt14/translation-task.html.

Model	Perplexity
HPYP 5-gram	147.22
Chelba and Jelinek (2000)	146.1
Emami and Jelinek (2005)	131.3
HPYP-DP	**145.54**
HPYP 5-gram	178.13
HPYP-DP	**163.96**

Table 6: Language modelling test results. Above, training and testing on WSJ. Below, training semi-supervised and testing on WMT.

5.5 Generation

To support our claim that our generative model is a good model for sentences, we generate some examples. The samples given here were obtained by generating 1000 samples, and choosing the 10 highest scoring ones with length greater or equal to 10. The models are trained on the standard WSJ training set (including punctuation).

The examples are given in Table 7. The quality of the sentences generated by the dependency model is superior to that of the n-gram model, despite the models have similar test set perplexities. The sentences generated by the dependency model tend to have more global syntactic structure (for examples having verbs where expected), while retaining the local coherence of n-gram models. The dependency model was also able to generate balanced quotation marks.

6 Related work

One of the earliest graph-based dependency parsing models (Eisner, 1996) is generative, estimating the probability of dependents given their head and previously generated siblings. To counter sparsity in the conditioning context of the distributions, backoff and smoothing are performed. Wallach et al. (2008) proposed a Bayesian HPYP parameterisation of this model.

Other generative models for dependency trees have been proposed mostly in the context of unsupervised parsing. The first successful model was the dependency model with valence (DMV) (Klein and Manning, 2004). Several extensions have been proposed for this model, for example using structural annealing (Smith and Eisner, 2006), Viterbi EM training (Spitkovsky et al., 2010) or richer contexts (Blunsom and Cohn, 2010). However, these models are not powerful enough for either accurate parsing or language modelling with rich contexts (they are usually restricted to first-order dependencies and valency).

Although any generative parsing model can be applied to language modelling by marginalising out the possible parses of a sentence, in practice the success of such models has been limited. Lexicalised PCFGs applied to language modelling (Roark, 2001; Charniak, 2001) show improvements over n-gram models, but decoding is prohibitively expensive for practical integration in language generation applications.

Chelba and Jelinek (2000) as well as Emami and Jelinek (2005) proposed incremental syntactic language models with some similarities to our model. Those models predict binarized constituency trees with a transition-based model, and are parameterized by deleted interpolation and neural networks, respectively. Rastrow et al. (2012) applies a transition-based dependency language model to speech recognition, using hierarchical interpolation and relative entropy pruning. However, the model perplexity only improves over an n-gram model when interpolated with one.

Titov and Henderson (2007) introduced a generative latent variable model for transition-based parsing. The model is based on an incremental sigmoid belief networks, using the arc-eager parsing strategy. Exact inference is intractable, so neural networks and variational mean field methods are proposed to perform approximate inference. However, this is much slower and therefore less scalable than our model.

A generative transition-based parsing model for non-projective parsing is proposed in (Cohen et al., 2011), along with a dynamic program for inference. The parser is similar to ours, but the dynamic program restricts the conditioning context to the top 2 or 3 words on the stack. No experimental results are included.

Le and Zuidema (2014) proposed a recursive neural network generative model over dependency trees. However, their model can only score trees, not perform parsing, and its perplexity (236.58 on the PTB development set) is worse than model's, despite using neural networks to combat sparsity.

Finally, incremental parsing with particle filtering has been proposed previously (Levy et al., 2009) to model human online sentence processing.

sales rose NUM to NUM million from $ NUM .
estimated volume was about $ NUM a share , .
meanwhile , annual sales rose to NUM % from $ NUM .
mr. bush 's profit climbed NUM % , to $ NUM from $ NUM million million , or NUM cents a share .
treasury securities inc. is a unit of great issues .
" he is looking out their shareholders , " says .
while he has done well , she was out .
that 's increased in the second quarter 's new conventional wisdom .
mci communications said net dropped NUM % for an investor .
association motorola inc. , offering of $ NUM and NUM cents a share .
otherwise , actual profit is compared with the 300-day estimate .
the companies are followed by at least three analysts , and had a minimum five-cent change in actual earnings per share .
bonds : shearson lehman hutton treasury index NUM , up
posted yields on NUM year mortgage commitments for delivery within NUM days .
in composite trading on the new york mercantile exchange .
the company , which has NUM million shares outstanding .
the NUM results included a one-time gain of $ NUM million .
however , operating profit fell NUM % to $ NUM billion from $ NUM billion .
merrill lynch ready assets trust : NUM % NUM days ; NUM % NUM to NUM days ; NUM % NUM to NUM days .
in new york stock exchange composite trading , one trader .

Table 7: Sentences generated, above by the generative dependency model, below by a n-gram model. In both cases, 1000 samples were generated, and the most likely sentences of length 10 or more are given.

7 Conclusion

We presented a generative dependency parsing model that, unlike previous models, retains most of the speed and accuracy of discriminative parsers. Our models can accurately estimate probabilities conditioned on long context sequences. The model is scalable to large training and test sets, and even though it defines a full probability distribution over sentences and parses, decoding speed is efficient. Additionally, the generative model gives strong performance as a language model. For future work we believe that this model can be applied successfully to natural language generation tasks such as machine translation.

References

Christophe Andrieu, Arnaud Doucet, and Roman Holenstein. 2010. Particle Markov chain Monte Carlo methods. *Journal of the Royal Statistical Society: Series B (Statistical Methodology)*, 72(3):269–342.

Phil Blunsom and Trevor Cohn. 2010. Unsupervised induction of tree substitution grammars for dependency parsing. In *EMNLP*, pages 1204–1213.

Phil Blunsom, Trevor Cohn, Sharon Goldwater, and Mark Johnson. 2009. A note on the implementation of hierarchical Dirichlet processes. In *ACL/IJCNLP (Short Papers)*, pages 337–340.

Bernd Bohnet and Joakim Nivre. 2012. A transition-based system for joint part-of-speech tagging and labeled non-projective dependency parsing. In *EMNLP-CoNLL*, pages 1455–1465.

Eugene Charniak, Kevin Knight, and Kenji Yamada. 2003. Syntax-based language models for statistical machine translation. In *Proceedings of MT Summit IX*, pages 40–46.

Eugene Charniak. 2001. Immediate-head parsing for language models. In *Proceedings of ACL*, pages 124–131.

Ciprian Chelba and Frederick Jelinek. 2000. Structured language modeling. *Computer Speech & Language*, 14(4):283–332.

Danqi Chen and Christopher D Manning. 2014. A fast and accurate dependency parser using neural networks. In *EMNLP*.

Jinho D. Choi and Andrew McCallum. 2013. Transition-based dependency parsing with selectional branching. In *ACL*.

Shay B. Cohen, Carlos Gómez-Rodríguez, and Giorgio Satta. 2011. Exact inference for generative probabilistic non-projective dependency parsing. In *EMNLP*, pages 1234–1245.

Michael Collins. 1997. Three generative, lexicalised models for statistical parsing. In *ACL*, pages 16–23.

Marie-Catherine De Marneffe and Christopher D Manning. 2008. The Stanford typed dependencies representation. In *Coling 2008: Proceedings of the workshop on Cross-Framework and Cross-Domain Parser Evaluation*, pages 1–8.

Arnaud Doucet, Nando De Freitas, and Neil Gordon. 2001. *Sequential Monte Carlo methods in practice*. Springer.

Chris Dyer, Miguel Ballesteros, Wang Ling, Austin Matthews, and Noah A. Smith. 2015. Transition-based dependency parsing with stack long short-term memory. In *Proceedings of ACL 2015*.

Jason Eisner. 1996. Three new probabilistic models for dependency parsing: An exploration. In *COLING*, pages 340–345.

Ahmad Emami and Frederick Jelinek. 2005. A neural syntactic language model. *Machine Learning*, 60(1-3):195–227.

Yoav Goldberg and Joakim Nivre. 2013. Training deterministic parsers with non-deterministic oracles. *TACL*, 1:403–414.

Liang Huang and Kenji Sagae. 2010. Dynamic programming for linear-time incremental parsing. In *ACL*, pages 1077–1086.

Dan Klein and Christopher D. Manning. 2003. Accurate unlexicalized parsing. In *ACL*, pages 423–430.

Dan Klein and Christopher D Manning. 2004. Corpus-based induction of syntactic structure: Models of dependency and constituency. In *ACL*, pages 478–586.

Reinhard Kneser and Hermann Ney. 1995. Improved backing-off for m-gram language modeling. In *ICASSP*, volume 1, pages 181–184. IEEE.

Terry Koo and Michael Collins. 2010. Efficient third-order dependency parsers. In *ACL*, pages 1–11.

Phong Le and Willem Zuidema. 2014. The inside-outside recursive neural network model for dependency parsing. In *EMNLP*, pages 729–739.

Tao Lei, Yu Xin, Yuan Zhang, Regina Barzilay, and Tommi Jaakkola. 2014. Low-rank tensors for scoring dependency structures. In *Proceedings of ACL (Volume 1: Long Papers)*, pages 1381–1391.

Roger P Levy, Florencia Reali, and Thomas L Griffiths. 2009. Modeling the effects of memory on human online sentence processing with particle filters. In *Advances in neural information processing systems*, pages 937–944.

Mitchell P. Marcus, Beatrice Santorini, and Mary Ann Marcinkiewicz. 1993. Building a large annotated corpus of English: The Penn Treebank. *Computational Linguistics*, 19(2):313–330.

Ryan T. McDonald, Koby Crammer, and Fernando C. N. Pereira. 2005. Online large-margin training of dependency parsers. In *ACL*.

Ryan McDonald, Slav Petrov, and Keith Hall. 2011. Multi-source transfer of delexicalized dependency parsers. In *EMNLP*, pages 62–72. Association for Computational Linguistics.

Joakim Nivre and Mario Scholz. 2004. Deterministic dependency parsing of English text. In *COLING*.

Joakim Nivre, Johan Hall, and Jens Nilsson. 2006. Maltparser: A data-driven parser-generator for dependency parsing. In *Proceedings of LREC*, volume 6, pages 2216–2219.

Joakim Nivre. 2008. Algorithms for deterministic incremental dependency parsing. *Computational Linguistics*, 34(4):513–553.

Slav Petrov, Leon Barrett, Romain Thibaux, and Dan Klein. 2006. Learning accurate, compact, and interpretable tree annotation. In *COLING-ACL*, pages 433–440.

Ariya Rastrow, Mark Dredze, and Sanjeev Khudanpur. 2012. Efficient structured language modeling for speech recognition. In *INTERSPEECH*.

Brian Roark. 2001. Probabilistic top-down parsing and language modeling. *Computational linguistics*, 27(2):249–276.

Noah A. Smith and Jason Eisner. 2006. Annealing structural bias in multilingual weighted grammar induction. In *Proceedings of COLING-ACL*, pages 569–576.

Valentin I. Spitkovsky, Hiyan Alshawi, Daniel Jurafsky, and Christopher D. Manning. 2010. Viterbi training improves unsupervised dependency parsing. In *CoNLL*, pages 9–17.

Yee Whye Teh. 2006. A hierarchical Bayesian language model based on Pitman-Yor processes. In *ACL*.

Ivan Titov and James Henderson. 2007. A latent variable model for generative dependency parsing. In *Proceedings of the Tenth International Conference on Parsing Technologies*, pages 144–155.

Kristina Toutanova, Dan Klein, Christopher D. Manning, and Yoram Singer. 2003. Feature-rich part-of-speech tagging with a cyclic dependency network. In *HLT-NAACL*, pages 173–180.

Hanna M Wallach, Charles Sutton, and Andrew McCallum. 2008. Bayesian modeling of dependency trees using hierarchical Pitman-Yor priors. In *ICML Workshop on Prior Knowledge for Text and Language Processing*.

David Weiss, Chris Alberti, Michael Collins, and Slav Petrov. 2015. Structured training for neural network transition-based parsing. In *Proceedings of ACL 2015*.

Hiroyasu Yamada and Yuji Matsumoto. 2003. Statistical dependency analysis with support vector machines. In *Proceedings of IWPT*.

Yue Zhang and Stephen Clark. 2008. A tale of two parsers: Investigating and combining graph-based and transition-based dependency parsing. In *EMNLP*, pages 562–571.

Yue Zhang and Joakim Nivre. 2011. Transition-based dependency parsing with rich non-local features. In *ACL-HLT short papers-Volume 2*, pages 188–193.

On the relation between verb full valency and synonymy

Radek Čech
University of Ostrava
Faculty of Arts
Department of Czech Language
Czech Republic
cechradek@gmail.com

Ján Mačutek and **Michaela Koščová**
Comenius University in Bratislava
Faculty of Mathematics, Physics and Informatics
Department of Applied Mathematic and Statistics
Slovakia
jmacutek@yahoo.com
michaela.koscova@fmph.uniba.sk

Abstract

This paper investigates the relation between the number of full valency frames (we do not distinguish between complements and optional adjuncts, both are taken into account) of a verb and the number of its synonyms. It is shown that for Czech verbs from the Prague Dependency Treebank it holds *"the greater the full valency of a verb, the more synonyms the verb has"*.

1 Introduction

Verb valency has been studied for more than fifty years in linguistics and the study of this phenomenon has enhanced knowledge about sentence functioning substantially. Although there still remain some problems (even fundamental ones) which need to be solved in this research area (see Section 2), verb valency is considered to have a decisive impact on the sentence structure. Consequently, it has become a standard part of the majority of grammar books, verb valency lexicons have appeared for many languages, and plenty of articles focused on it have been published so far. These analyses are mostly descriptive; usually valency patterns, relationship between syntax and semantics, classification criteria etc. are investigated, see, e.g., Mukherjee (2005), Herbst and Götz-Votteler (2007), and Faulhaber (2011). However, in linguistics there are also attempts to overcome the descriptive character of research and to ground the discipline on empirically testable hypotheses, see, e.g., Zipf (1935), Sampson (2001), Sampson (2005), Gries (2009), and Köhler and Altmann (2011). The goal of such a methodology is not only to describe phenomena under study but also to interpret them, i.e., to find their relations to other language properties, and, in the ideal case, to explain them within a theory of language. It is to be emphasized that, within this approach, all conclusions are based on statistically testable hypotheses, and the aim is to build a theory, i.e., a system of hypotheses and scientific laws (which are statements theoretically derived and empirically tested), see Bunge (1967) in general and Altmann (1993) more specifically for linguistics. As for verb valency, results achieved by this methodology were presented by Köhler (2005a), Liu (2009), Čech and Mačutek (2010), Čech et al. (2010), Liu (2011), Köhler (2012), Gao et al. (2014), and Vincze (2014). The authors tested hypotheses on relations between the number of valency frames and the frequency, length of verb and its polysemy; further, it was shown that the distribution of valency frames is a special case of a very general distribution which is used very often as a mathematical model in linguistics (Wimmer and Altmann, 2005).

All these studies are somewhat connected to a synergetic theory of language, see Köhler (1986) and Köhler (2005b), and they represent first steps in the endeavor to implement verb valency (or valency in general) to a synergetic model of syntax (Köhler, 2012). The paper by Gao et al. (2014) deserves a special mention, as it contains an explicit synergetic scheme of interrelations. The scheme includes the verb valency and some other verb properties (frequency, length, polysemy, polytextuality, and, in addition, two properties which are specific for the Chinese language, namely the number of strokes and the number of pinyin letters). The present study follows the same direction. Our goal is to analyse the relationship between verb valency (to be exact, its variant which is called full valency, see Section 2) and another important language property – synonymy. Specifically, we test a hypothesis on the relationship between the number of full valency frames of verb and its synonymy, namely, we suppose that it holds "the more full valency frames of a verb, the

Proceedings of the Third International Conference on Dependency Linguistics (Depling 2015), pages 68–73,
Uppsala, Sweden, August 24–26 2015.

more synonyms the verb has". The validity of this statement will be tested on data from the Czech language.

2 Full valency

The concept of full valency was introduced by Čech et al. (2010). It can be viewed as a reaction to the absence of reliable criteria for distinguishing obligatory arguments (complements) and non-obligatory arguments (optional adjuncts), see Rickheit and Sichelschmidt (2007) and Faulhaber (2011). Full valency does not distinguish between these two types of arguments; it takes into account all arguments of a verb which occur in the actual language usage (i.e., all nodes in a syntactic tree which depend directly on the verb represent its full valency frame). Following the paper by Čech et al. (2010), only formally unique full valency frames are considered. This means that if the verb occurs in two or more identical full valency frames in the corpus, only one of them is counted.

Čech et al. (2010) assumed that the distribution of the number of full valency frames is not chaotic or accidental but it is governed by fundamental principles which have an impact also on other language characteristics (such as the distribution of word frequencies, word lengths, morphological categories, etc.). Further, according to the authors, full valency of verbs should be systematically related to other language properties (e.g., to the frequency of verb, to its length, etc.) as a result of the synergetic character of language, see Köhler (2005b) and Köhler (2012).

First results – Čech et al. (2010), Gao et al. (2014) and Vincze (2014) – corroborated the reasonability of the approach. They revealed, for instance, that the distribution of full valency frames can be modelled by the same model as the distribution of valency frames based on the traditional argument classification, see Čech and Mačutek (2010) for Czech, Liu (2011) for English, Gao et al. (2014) for Chinese, and Vincze (2014) for Hungarian. Given these results, "traditional" valency and full valency seem to be governed by the same mechanism, and traditional valency can be interpreted, tentatively at least, as a special case of full valency.

3 Verb full valency a synonymy

Every hypothesis should be based on some theoretical assumption(s). Without it, one can find even strong correlation (e.g., inductively) between observed phenomena, however, it does not have to mean anything. Therefore, a crucial question is why one should expect the existence of a relationship between verb valency and synonymy. To find an answer, let us start from a wider perspective. At least since Zipf (1935), it is known that semantic properties of language are systematically related to other language characteristics (e.g., relative frequency, degree of intensity of accent, etc.). These systematic relationships can be interpreted as a consequence of the dynamic evolution of language caused by language usage (Bybee and Hopper, 2001). For an illustration, assume a development of usage of any word. Initially, it was used in a unique sense and in a specific context. Next usages of the word led both to a strengthening of the sense and to an increase of the number of contexts in which the word occurs. More generally, the word properties were formed by two opposite forces: a unification and a diversification (Zipf, 1935). As a result, fundamental characteristics of the word were established (for instance, the length of the word is a consequence of its frequency as well as the number of its derivatives, compounds in which it occurs etc.). As for the meaning of the word, a high frequency of its usage increases a chance that the word is used in different contexts. Different contexts usually modify slightly the word meaning, which leads (sometimes) to a "codification" of a new meaning of the word. Therefore, a relationship between frequency and polysemy emerges. Further, the more meanings the word has, the more semantic domains exist in which the word can occur. Obviously, different semantic domains are represented by different sets of words. Consequently, a word which occurs in more semantic domains increases its chance of having more synonyms.

As for verb valency, there is, as can be seen from any valency dictionary, a clear relationship between polysemy of the verb and its valency. Specifically, different meanings of the verb are often represented by different valency frames, see Liu (2011) for an analysis of the relation between the two properties. Consequently, it seems reasonable to hypothesize the relationship between verb valency and synonymy; to be precise, we expect that the number of synonyms of a verb tends to increase with the increasing number of its full valency frames. We thus have a deductive hypothesis which will be tested empirically in Section 5. A quantification (which necessarily precedes tests) not only enables the application of statistical methods, it also opens a way towards a mathematical model (which, in turn, makes possible more objective comparisons of different languages, language typology based on values of its parameters, etc.).

4 Language material

For the counting of full valency verb frames, the Prague Dependency Treebank 2.0 was used (Hajič et al., 2006); specifically, the data annotated on an analytical layer, which consists of 4264 documents, 68,495 sentences and 1.2 million tokens. For the determination of synonyms of a verb, we use the Czech WordNet from the EuroWordNet project (Vossen, 1997); it contains 32,116 words and collocations, 28,448 synsets, 43,958 literals, see Horák and Smrž (2004) and Hlaváčková et al. (2006).

The term "full valency" means that all verb directly dependent words (arguments) which occur in the sentence are taken into account. To determine a full valency frame of a verb, we use argument characteristics as follows: analytical functions (e.g., subject, object), morphological cases (e.g., nominative, genitive), and lemmas (only in the case of prepositions). Particular characteristics are assigned to arguments in accordance with the PDT 2.0 annotation. Specifically, from the sentence *John gave four books to Mary yesterday*, we obtain the following full valency frame of the verb *give*: GIVE [subject/nominative; object/accusative; AuxP/dative/lemma TO; Adv], see Figure 1.

This procedure is used for all predicate verbs in the corpus and, finally, we get list of verbs (lemmas) with assigned full valency frames.

The number of synonyms of a verb is determined from the database CzechWordNet which is organized as a network of basic entities called synsets, i.e., synonym sets. Each synset corresponds to one meaning of a word or a collocation. In this paper, synonymy of each verb is defined as the number of lemmas which appear with the verb in particular synsets. For instance, the verb *intend* has four synsets in English Wordnet:

1. intend: 1, mean: 4, think: 7;
2. intend: 2, destine:2 , designate: 4, specify: 6;
3. mean: 1, intend: 3;
4. mean: 3, intend: 4, signify: 1, stand for: 2;

in which nine different lemmas appear (in order to avoid confusion, it should be emphasized that, e.g., "mean: 1" and "mean: 4" express two different meanings, and hence they also represent two different lemmas) – i.e., the verb *intend* has nine synonyms. Hereby we do not claim that other possibilities of determining the number of synonyms (e.g., distinguishing among different senses of the verb) are worse; quite on the contrary, using several of them (while keeping in mind what they have in common and in what they differ) and comparing results can lead to a deeper understanding of mechanisms "behind" synonymy (and language in general).

Altogether, we work with 2120 verbs in this study.

5 Methodology and results

The validity of our hypothesis for Czech data was checked in two different (albeit related) ways.

First, one can compute the correlation coefficient between full verb valency and synonymy. There is no a priori reason to suppose the linearity of the relation; therefore, the Kendall correlation coefficient – see, e.g., Hollander and Wolfe (1999) – was used (similarly as the well-known Pearson correlation coefficient, it takes values from the interval [-1,1]; value 1 means that the relation "the greater one variable, the greater the other" is valid for all data without an exception). It is a measure of a monotonous relation (without specifying the type of a functional relation, like, e.g., linearity) between two variables (full valency and synonymy in our case). Thus it is a more general and more robust characteristic of the relation than the Pearson correlation coefficient (which is a measure of linearity of the relation).

The Kendall correlation coefficient evaluates to 0.18 for our data. It is, quite clearly, a non-zero value (if we test the hypothesis of zero value of the coefficient, we obtain the p-value lesser than 0.0001, hence, the hypothesis is rejected for all reasonable significance levels). There are, however, several minor problems associated with the test.

First, it is well-known that practically all hypotheses are rejected if sufficiently high amount of data are used. This fact was discussed specifically with respect to linguistic data by Mačutek and Wimmer (2013). Our sample size (2120 verbs)

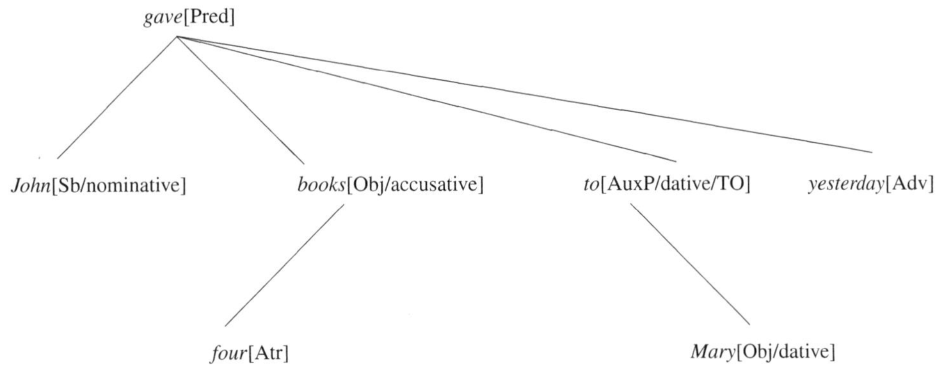

Figure 1: Syntactic tree of the sentence *John gave four books to Mary yesterday.*

is not too high yet, but studies using higher volumes of language material can appear in future (see also comments in Section 6), for which (almost) any hypothesis would be rejected in terms of the p-value. Thus, a need of a unified approach to checking the validity of the hypothesis arises.

Anyway, the p-value should be read cautiously. It can serve as a decision rule whether to reject a hypothesis or not, but p-values resulting from different tests are not directly comparable (Grendár, 2012). Applied to our problem, based on the p-value we reject the hypothesis that full valency and synonymy are (monotonously) independent, however, from the p-value we cannot deduce a strength (or a type) of their relationship.

Next, the test for the Kendall correlation coefficient supposes no ties in the data, but there are many verbs with the same full valency (especially the low values of full valency frames occur very often – which is true also for the "traditional" valency.

Finally, if an "optical criterion" is taken into account, the data fluctuate quite strongly, as can be seen in Figure 2, and the increasing trend indicated by the positive value of the Kendall correlation coefficient is not too obvious.

Therefore, in order to be able to see a clearer picture and to provide a tool applicable also to higher sample sizes, we performed also the analysis of pooled data. Groups of at least 20 verbs were created as follows. Starting from the verbs with the highest number of full valency frames, a group of the first 20 verbs was taken. Then, it

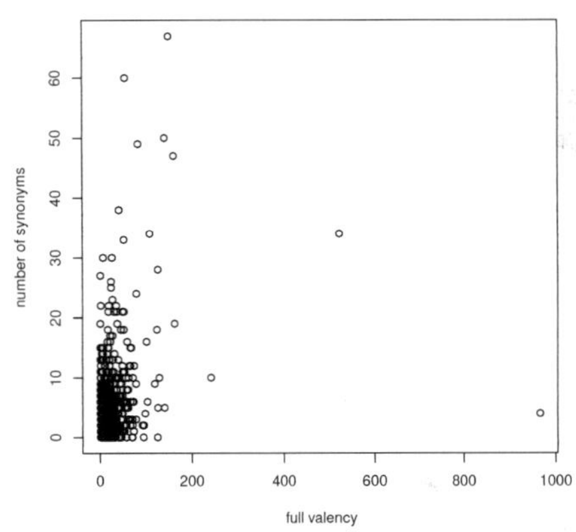

Figure 2: Number of full valency frames and number of synonyms for all verbs under study.

was checked whether the last verb in this groups has more full valency frames than the first verb in the next group – if the respective numbers of full valency frames were equal, the group was enlarged so that all verbs with the same full valency belonged to the same group. This approach was repeteadly applied, until all verbs were divided into groups. Resulting groups do not contain the same numbers of verbs, however, we prefer to keep verbs with the same number of full valency frames in one group, as there is no reasonable ordering of verbs (ones with the same full valency are either ordered alphabetically, or they appear in the chronological order as they were entered into treebanks, etc.). Then, the mean number of full valency frames and the mean number of synonyms per verb were calculated in each group. The pooling process results in much smoother data, see Figure 3. Obviously, the mean number of synonyms per group tends to increase with the increasing mean full valency.

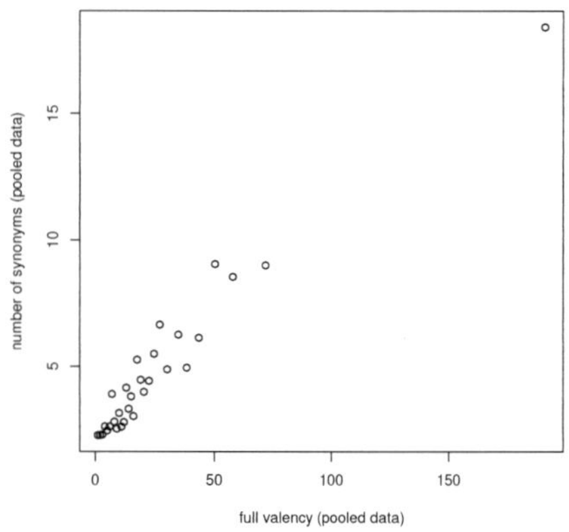

Figure 3: Number of full valency frames and number of synonyms (pooled data).

Admittedly, the minimal size of the group used (i.e., 20 in our case) is purely heuristic; however, other choices lead to very similar pooled data behaviour (an increasing, seemingly even a linear trend is observed). As we consider this paper to be a kind of a pilot study, we postpone a deeper analysis of the full valency – synonymy relation (is there really a linear dependence, or, what we see in Figure 3 is a part of a flat power law curve? are parameters of the line/curve language specific? if yes, do they correspond to an established syntax-based language typology? etc.) until results for more languages are available.

6 Conclusion

The results presented in this study can be seen as the first step in the empirical research of the relation between the number of full valency frames of verbs and the number of synonyms. It goes without saying that an analysis based on a single language cannot be interpreted as an "honest", general enough corroboration of the respective hypothesis. However, tentatively the results allow to expect that synonymy can be related to verb (full) valency, i.e., to one of fundamental syntax properties.

This paper, we hope, will serve also as an impetus for future research in this field. Some questions were already asked at the end of Section 5; in addition, our results call for substantial generalizations in (at least) two directions. First, the same phenomenon (the relation between verb valency and synonymy) should be investigated in several typologically different languages. Second, we suppose that valency of other parts of speech, see, e.g., Spevak (2014), is also related to synonymy; this topic waits for empirical approaches as well. Given the lack of a clear distinction between obligatory and non-obligatory arguments, full valency (of other parts of speech) can again be of help.

Finally, if the hypothesis on a systematic relation between (full) valency and synonymy is more generally corroborated, it should be integrated into the network of (inter)relations among linguistic units and their properties, see Köhler (2005b) and Gao et al. (2014).

Acknowledgement

Supported by the grant VEGA 2/0047/15 (J. Mačutek and M. Koščová) and by Slovak Literary Fund (J. Mačutek).

References

Gabriel Altmann. 1993. Science and linguistics. In Reinhard Köhler and Burghard B. Rieger, editors, *Contributions to Quantitative Linguistics*, pages 3–10. Kluwer, Dordrecht.

Mario Bunge. 1967. *Scientific Research I.* Springer.

Joan Bybee and Paul Hopper. 2001. *Frequency and the Emergence of Linguistic Structure*. John Benjamins, Amsterdam/Philadelphia.

Radek Čech and Ján Mačutek. 2010. On the quantitative analysis of verb valency in Czech. In Peter Grzybek, Emmerich Kelih, and Ján Mačutek, editors, *Text and Language. Structures, Functions, Interrelations, Quantitative Perspectives*, pages 21–29. Praesens, Wien.

Radek Čech, Petr Pajas, and Ján Mačutek. 2010. Full valency. verb valency without distinguishing complements and adjuncts. *Journal of Quantitative Linguistics*, 17(4):291–302.

Susen Faulhaber. 2011. *Verb Valency Patterns. A Challenge for Semantics-Based Accounts*. De Gruyter.

Song Gao, Hongxin Zhang, and Haitao Liu. 2014. Synergetic properties of Chinese verb valency. *Journal of Quantitative Linguistics*, 21(1):1–21.

Marian Grendár. 2012. Is the p-value a good measure of evidence? Asymptotic consistency criteria. *Statistics & Probability Letters*, 82(6):1116–1119.

Stefan T. Gries. 2009. *Statistics for Linguistics with R: A Practical Introduction*. De Gruyter.

Jan Hajič, Jarmila Panevová, Eva Hajičová, Petr Sgall, Petr Pajas, Jan Štěpánek, Jiří Havelka, Marie Mikulová, Zdeněk Žabokrtský, Magda Ševčíková-Razimová, and Zdenka Uresová. 2006. *Prague Dependency Treebank 2.0*. Linguistic Data Consortium, Philadelphia.

Thomas Herbst and Katrin Götz-Votteler. 2007. *Valency: Theoretical, Descriptive, and Cognitive Issues*. De Gruyter.

Dana Hlaváčková, Aleš Horák, and Vladimír Kadlec. 2006. Exploitation of the VerbaLex verb valency lexicon in the syntactic analysis of Czech. In *Proceedings of 9th International Conference on Text, Speech, and Dialogue*, pages 79–85. Springer.

Myles Hollander and Douglas A. Wolfe. 1999. *Nonparametric Statistical Methods*. Wiley, second edition.

Aleš Horák and Pavel Smrž. 2004. VisDic - WordNet browsing and editing tool. In *Proceedings of the Second International WordNet Conference - GWC 2004*, pages 136–141. Masaryk University, Brno.

Reinhard Köhler and Gabriel Altmann. 2011. Quantitative linguistics. In Patrick Colm Hogan, editor, *The Cambridge Encyclopedia of the Language Sciences*, pages 695–697. Cambridge University Press.

Reinhard Köhler. 1986. *Zur linguistische Synergetik. Struktur und Dynamik der Lexik*. Brockmeyer, Bochum.

Reinhard Köhler. 2005a. Quantitative Untersuchungen zur Valenz deutscher Verben. *Glottometrics*, 9:13–20.

Reinhard Köhler. 2005b. Synergetic linguistics. In Reinhard Köhler, Gabriel Altmann, and Rajmund G. Piotrowski, editors, *Quantitative Linguistics. An International Handbook*, pages 760–774. De Gruyter.

Reinhard Köhler. 2012. *Quantitative Syntax Analysis*. De Gruyter.

Haitao Liu. 2009. Probability distribution of dependencies basen on a Chinese dependency treebank. *Journal of Quantitative Linguistics*, 16(3):256–273.

Haitao Liu. 2011. Quantitative properties of English verb valency. *Journal of Quantitative Linguistics*, 18(3):207–233.

Ján Mačutek and Gejza Wimmer. 2013. Evaluating goodness-of-fit of discrete distribution models in quantitative linguistics. *Journal of Quantitative Linguistics*, 20(3):227–240.

Joybrato Mukherjee. 2005. *English Ditransitive Verbs: Aspects of Theory, Description and a Usage-Based Model*. Rodopi, Amsterdam/New York.

Gert Rickheit and Lorenz Sichelschmidt. 2007. Valency and cognition – a notion in transition. In Thomas Herbst and Katrin Götz-Votteler, editors, *Valency: Theoretical, Descriptive, and Cognitive Issues*, pages 163–182. De Gruyter.

Geoffrey Sampson. 2001. *Empirical Linguistics*. Continuum, London/New York.

Geoffrey Sampson. 2005. Quantifying the shift towards empirical methods. *International Journal of Corpus Linguistics*, 10(1):15–36.

Olga Spevak. 2014. *Noun Valency*. John Benjamins, Amsterdam/Philadelphia.

Veronika Vincze. 2014. Valency frames in a Hungarian corpus. *Journal of Quantitative Linguistics*, 21(2):153–176.

Piek Vossen. 1997. EuroWordNet: a multilingual database for information retrieval. In *Proceedings of the DELOS Workshop on Cross-language Information Retrieval*.

Gejza Wimmer and Gabriel Altmann. 2005. Unified derivation of some linguistic laws. In Reinhard Köhler, Gabriel Altmann, and Rajmund G. Piotrowski, editors, *Quantitative Linguistics. An International Handbook*, pages 791–807. De Gruyter.

George K. Zipf. 1935. *The Psychobiology of Language*. Houghton-Mifflin, Boston.

Classifying Syntactic Categories in the Chinese Dependency Network

Xinying Chen
Xi'an Jiaotong University
School of International Study
China
xy@yuyanxue.net

Haitao Liu
Zhejiang University
Department of Linguistics
China
lhtzju@gmail.com

Kim Gerdes
Sorbonne Nouvelle
ILPGA, LPP (CNRS)
France
kim@gerdes.fr

Abstract

This article presents a new approach of using dependency treebanks in theoretical syntactic research: The view of dependency treebanks as combined networks. This allows the usage of advanced tools for network analysis that quite easily provide novel insight into the syntactic structure of language. As an example of this approach, we will show how the network approach can provide an interesting angle to discuss the degree of connectivity of Chinese syntactic categories, which it is not so easy to detect from the original treebank.

1 Hierarchical Features inside Language

It is a widely accepted idea that language is a complex, multi-level system (Kretzschmar 2009, Beckner et al. 2009, Hudson 2006, Mel'čuk 1988, Sgall 1986, Lamb 1966). Languages can be described and analyzed on different linguistics levels, such as morphology, syntax, and semantic etc. Moreover, these different linguistics levels form a surface-deep hierarchy (Mel'čuk 1981). Besides the macro multi-level hierarchy of languages, the unequal relationships between linguistic units in sentences are also widely recognized by linguists. Such as the concept of governor in dependency grammar, head of phrase in HPSG etc. In this article, we aim to define a new kind of one-directional asymmetrical relationships between linguistic units, half-way between the macro-model of language and the syntactic analysis of single sentences.

Hierarchies have been recognized as one of the key features of any formal language description on two very different levels:

Firstly, linguistics as a whole wants to describe the relation between Saussure's signified and signifier (Saussure 2011) (or Mel'čuk's meaning and text (Mel'čuk 1981), or Chomsky's logical and phonetic structure (Chomsky 2002)). Although the theories differ widely on how the steps between the two sides of language should be described, all theories developed a hierarchy of interrelated structures that build up the language model.

Secondly, each subdomain of linguistics has developed hierarchical structures describing each utterance, for example on a semantic, communicative, phonological, and, most noteworthy, syntactic level.

It is important to reflect on the wide gap between these two types of hierarchies: One describing the language as a whole (i.e. all languages), the other just describing one utterance of one particular language by hierarchical means. This paper describes how intermediate structures can be discovered, intermediate in a sense that they describe a global feature of syntax of one language, which could then be compared to equivalent analyses of other languages.

In sections 2 to 4, we will show that syntactic categories of a language as a whole are related in complex ways, thus establishing a hierarchy among the categories. In order to proceed to the actual analysis we first have to show two points:

1. The notion of syntactic category (or part of speech, POS) has an existence in the syntactic model as a whole that goes beyond the classification of individual words.
2. A dependency treebank provides means of studying meaningful relationships between syntactic categories.

To 1: When developing a system of categorization for a given language, the syntactician already has a global view of grouping together syntactic units that have comparable distributional or morphological properties with the goal to allow for the expression of rules that generalize beyond the actual linguistic evidence. However, the analysis remains local in

Proceedings of the Third International Conference on Dependency Linguistics (Depling 2015), pages 74–81,
Uppsala, Sweden, August 24–26 2015.

a sense that the syntactician does not create relationships inside the proposed categorization, the objective of the analysis simply being to put forward distinctive features that can be tested and applied to the data. It is thus reasonable to search for ways of exploring general properties that have been implicitly encoded with the categorization.

To 2: The aforementioned distributional and morphological properties of syntactic categories make them an ideal candidate in the search for global syntactic feature of language, but the theoretical aspects and the generalizability at the basis of the categorization are difficult to study empirically. Syntactic dependency, however, describes links that represent the distributional properties of a word: Words of the same category are in general part of a paradigm of words that can hold the same syntactic position. A dependency treebank can accordingly be seen as relations between paradigms of words.

2 Networks

Over the last decade or so, driven by theoretical considerations as well as by the simple availability of large amount of connected data, network analysis has become an important factor in various domains of research ranging from sociology, biology to physics and computer science (Barabási & Bonabeau 2003, Watts & Strogatz 1998).

Equally, digital language data and the popularity of statistical approaches had the first effect that many linguists, who are mainly interested in theoretical questions as well as NLP researchers have started to quantitatively describe microscopic linguistic features in a certain level of a language system by using authentic language data. Despite the fruitful findings, one question remains unclear. That is, how can the statistical analysis of raw texts (e.g. n-gram based language models) or of treebanks (syntactic models, i.e. the statistical prediction of likely syntactic relations) provide linguistic insight? Or put differently, how does a complete empirical language system look like?

As an attempt to answer this question, the network approach, an analysis method emphasizing the macro features of linguistic structures, has been introduced into linguistic studies (Solé 2005, Ferrer-i-Cancho & Solé 2001). By analyzing different linguistics networks constructed from authentic language data, many linguistic features, such as lexical, syntactic or semantic features have been discovered and successfully applied in linguistic typological studies thus revealing the huge potential of linguistic networks research (Cong & Liu 2014).

What is particularly interesting about the recent development in this area is that researchers have been able to systematically analyze linguistic features beyond the sentence level since the network approach is not intrinsically limited by traditional linguistic feature annotations in corpora based on the lexical or the sentence level. It seems possible that linguistic network model, as the representation of the whole body of language data, is a better approach to explore the human language systems.

Moreover, just as all the networks constructed based on real data (Barabási & Bona-beau 2003, Watts & Strogatz 1998), the linguistic networks are 'small world' and 'scale free' networks too (Solé 2005, Ferrer-i-Cancho & Solé 2001, Liu 2008), which indicates that there are central nodes (Chen & Liu 2015, Chen 2013), or hubs, in language networks. And that will provide a natural hierarchy between the nodes or the units of the networks.

3 Building a Syntactic Network

When we talk about the structure of languages, the first thing that naturally comes to our mind is the syntactic structure. Both phrase structure grammar and dependency grammar have been developed and deployed in the analysis of corpora. In the past decade, dependency annotated treebanks have become the latest hype in empirical linguistics studies. Driven by the statistical NLP development and the linguist's fascination of creating a treebank following specific theoretical principles, considerable efforts have been devoted to treebank creation and analysis (among many others Marcus et al. 1993, Lacheret et al. 2014, Mille et al. 2013). Solid theoretical foundation and available well-annotated data made syntactic structural analysis the candidate of choice for most studies in linguistic network analysis just as in the present study.

In more detail, dependency treebanks, especially multi-layer dependency treebanks such as Ancora-UPF, offer interesting connections between texts and the representation of meaning, which allow us to pursue further discussion about the semantic structure more easily in the future. In addition, since our goal is finding the hierarchy between linguistic units of the same type, phrase structure, which introduces different levels of constituents, is less apt for the task than dependency structure.

Dependency treebanks commonly encode two kinds of information for each word: the word's syntactic relation with its governor and the word's syntactic category (or POS). Thus, a dependency treebank can be seen as a collection of dependency trees on words or on POS tags. We will call the first a 'word dependency tree' and the latter a 'POS dependency tree' which will be the base of the present experiment. Both trees can represent the syntactic structure of linguistic units in a sentence, while POS trees are more abstract and less detailed in a way.

Various previous research has been undertaken on the network analysis of syntactic dependency treebanks (Chen & Liu 2011, Chen et al. 2011, Čech et al. 2011, Liu 2008, Ferrer-i-Cancho 2005), some also based on the same Chinese dependency treebank used for this study (Liu 2008, Chen 2013, Chen & Liu 2011). These approaches all used word dependency trees, thus obtaining results on the network behavior of individual words. The central nodes in networks based on word dependency trees, however, are highly correlated with the frequency of the word itself and it is difficult to account for the influence of the unequal distribution of the different words. In POS dependency trees, the different classes are more evenly distributed and the role of frequency of categories may be less crucial.

Moreover, the high number of different word types makes the data exploration and explanation more complex than in networks based on POS dependency trees. Our specific goal of this present study is to find the hierarchies on Chinese categories (or POS) in the syntactic network which is constructed on empirical language data, or more specifically, the Chinese dependency treebank.

The basic idea underlying dependency networks is very simple: Instead of viewing the trees as linearly aligned on the sentences of the corpus, we fuse together each occurrence of the same POS to a unique node, thus creating a unique and connected network of POS, in which the POS are the vertices and dependency relations are the edges or arcs. This connected network is then ready to undergo common network analysis with tools like UCINET (Borgatti et al. 2002), PAJEK (Nooy et al. 2005), NETDRAW (Borgatti 2002), CYTOSCAPE (Shannon 2003), and so on. For more details, we refer to Liu (2008) for a description of multiple ways of network creation from dependency treebanks.

For the present work, we used the following treebank of Chinese, the XBSS treebank (Liu 2008): The XBSS has 37,024 tokens and is composed of 2 sections of different styles:

- "新闻联播" xin-wen-lian-bo 'news feeds' (name of a famous Chinese TV news program), is a transcription of the program. The text is usually read and the style of the language is quite formal. The section contains 17,061 words.
- "实话实说" shi-hua-shi-shuo 'straight talk' (name of a famous Chinese talk show), is of more colloquial language type, containing spontaneous speech appearing in interviews of people of various social backgrounds, ranging from farmers to successful businessmen, The section contains 19, 963 words.

Both sections have been annotated manually as described by Liu (2006). Table 1 shows the file format of this Chinese dependency treebank,

Sentence Order	Dependent			Governor			Dependency type
	Order	Character	POS	Order	Character	POS	
S1	1	*zhe*	pronoun	2	*shi*	verb	subject
S1	2	*shi*	verb	6	。	punctuation	main governor
S1	3	*yi*	numeral	4	*ge*	classifier	complement of classifier
S1	4	*ge*	classifier	5	*zuqiu*	noun	attributer
S1	5	*zuqiu*	noun	2	*shi*	verb	object
S1	6	。	punctuation				

Table 1. Annotation of a sample sentence.
这是一个足球 *zhe-shi-yi-ge-zu-qiu* 'this is a football'

which is similar to the CoNLL dependency format, although a bit more redundant (double information on the governor's POS) to allow for easy exploitation of the data in a spreadsheet and converting to language networks. The data can be represented as simple dependency graphs as shown in Figure 1: 1a is the dependency tree of the words in the sentence and 1b illustrates the dependency relationship between POS in this example. The trees both show a bottom-top hierarchy between the linguistic units in this sample sentence.

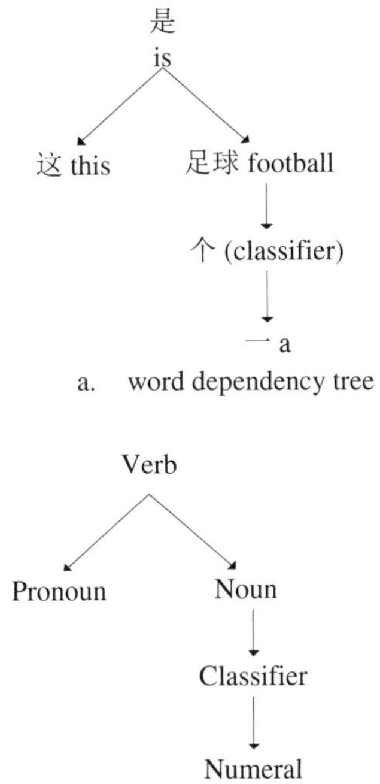

b. POS dependency tree

Figure 1. The graph of the dependency analysis of 这是一个苹果 *zhe-shi-yi-ge- zu-qiu* 'this is a football'

With POS as nodes, dependencies as arcs, and the frequency of the dependencies as the value of arcs, we can build a network. For example, our Chinese treebank can be represented as Figure 2, an image, generated by the network analysis software Pajek, which gives a broad overview of the global structure of the treebank (excluding punctuation).

The resulting network it is a fully connected network without any isolated vertices. As we set the distance between POS inversely proportional to the value of arcs (the detailed information of arcs values can be found in the table of appendix C), the graph actually can give us an intuitive idea of the 'clusters' of syntactic connections between POS already.

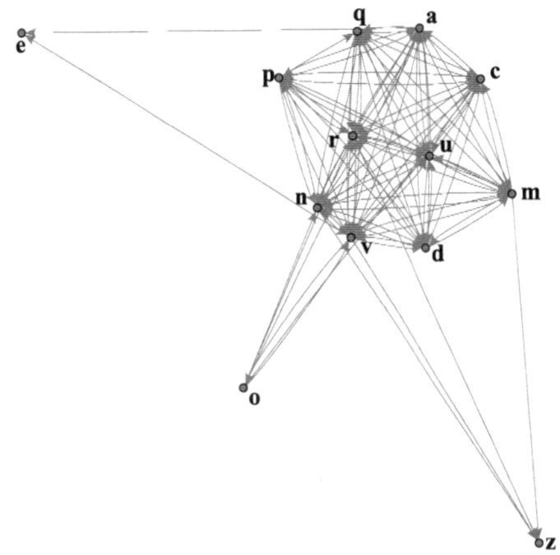

Figure 2. The POS network of the treebank. The details of all codes and symbols in tables and figures in this paper are available in Appendix A.

For minimizing the effect of genre difference to the data result, we chose to include two similar size sections of text in our treebank. However, some other factors may remain that could possibly affect the result of the study, such as the size of the treebank, the annotation schema, the language type, etc. We will leave these discussions for further work.

The reason we chose Chinese rather than other 'big' languages such as English, French or Spanish is that Chinese, as an isolating language, lacks morphological changes. Since there is no 'difference' between tokens and lemmas in Chinese dependency treebanks, Chinese syntactic networks built on dependency treebanks would only have one unique form for each treebank while every single inflectional language would have two different types of syntactic networks, word-type syntactic network and lemma syntactic network. As so, Chinese is a better choice for this study considering no ambiguity of defining a 'syntactic network'.

4 Data Analysis

There are two simple ways in a network model to detect the hierarchy of nodes. First by the degrees which represents the number of different types of links one node can have; second by the summed value of arcs which indicates, we believe, the intensity of the combination capacity of one node has. When one node can link to more nodes (or has a higher degree), as well as more connections to other nodes (or summed value of arcs), it is more likely to be the 'hub' or occupying a central position of the network structure. When we analyze or visualize a network, software such as Pajek try to optimize the positions of nodes so that they will fit the distance difference between pairs of nodes. However, for more precise result, we need to do a multi-dimensional scaling (MDS) analysis. With Ucinet (V 6.186), we did a nonmetric MDS analysis to our POS network data, and made the network data a two dimensional perceptual map as in Figure 3. The actual coordinate values of all the nodes are listed in Table 2.

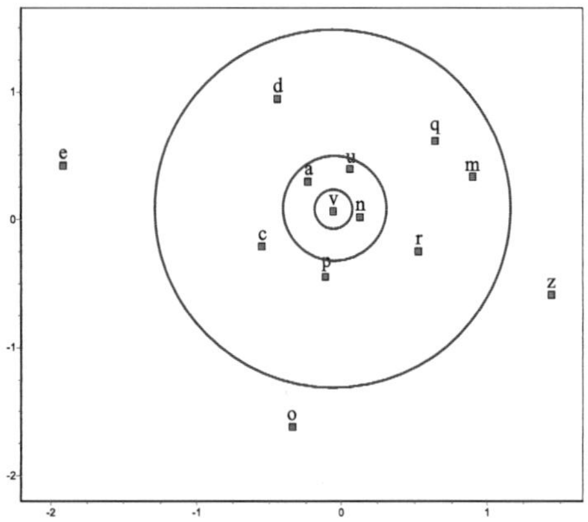

Figure 3. The perceptual map of the network.

Kruskal (1964) proposed to measure the quality of MDS result by index STRESS (the equation of STRESS can be found in appendix B). When the STRESS index is no more than 0.1, the result is acceptable for further discussion. The STRESS index of our analysis here is 0.100, which means that we are good to continue.

	POS	y	x
n	**noun**	0.021	0.127
v	**verb**	0.066	-0.059
r	**pronoun**	-0.244	0.520
q	**classifier**	0.615	0.633
m	**numeral**	0.334	0.897
p	**preposition**	-0.448	-0.115
a	**adjective**	0.297	-0.238
z	**affix**	-0.581	1.439
u	**auxiliary**	0.395	0.059
d	**adverb**	0.946	-0.447
c	**conjunction**	-0.204	-0.555
o	**mimetic word**	-1.619	-0.347
e	**interjection**	0.422	-1.913

Table 2. The coordination of POS in figure 3.

According to Figure 3, we can roughly divide the POS in to central, middle, and marginal parts. Since we are talking about the syntactic dependency structure here, verbs are expected be the very center of syntactic structures. With verb as the center, nouns, adjectives, and auxiliaries constructed scattered closely around the verb and constructed as the central part of the diagram, mimetic words, interjections, and affixes are far away from the center and they are the marginal part of the diagram. All the others POS fell between these two extremes and become the middle part of the diagram. The hierarchical structure of POS seems relatively clear according to the perceptual map already.

Yet, for more accurate result, we rely on the coordinate values of the POS in Figure 3 to do a clustering analysis, see Figure 4 (done with OriginPro, V 9.0). The result further confirmed the division we did according to Figure 3 but in greater details. Such as, we can find 'smaller groups' inside the central and middle parts of the network:

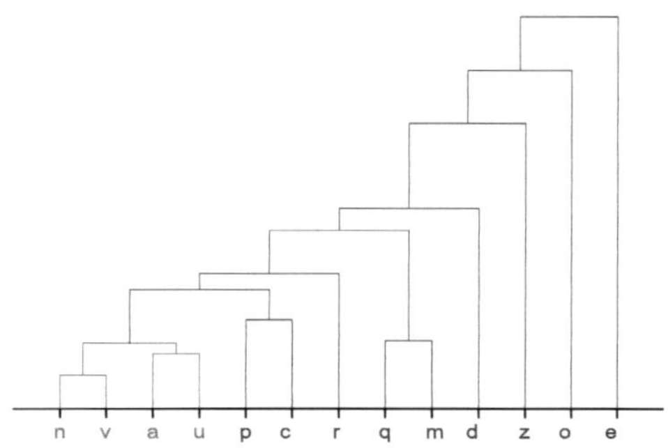

Figure 4. The clustering analysis result.

- Inside the central part, there are actually two small groups: verbs and nouns, adjectives and auxiliaries.
- Inside the middle part, there are also two closely tied small groups: propositions and coordinators, numerals and classifiers.

All these results correspond surprisingly well to our understanding of the Chinese language. For example, verbs are for sure the very center of the syntactic structure just as illustrated in Figure 3. Nouns, auxiliaries and adjectives are relatively frequent words in the treebank and hold important roles in syntactic well-formed sentences, they form the central part and are thus located in a relatively higher position in the POS hierarchy we built and showed in Figure 3 and Figure 4. Meanwhile, the infrequent mimetic words, interjections, and affixes are syntactically not very important in Chinese, therefore they have been put on a lower position, a more marginal part, of our POS hierarchy. Theoretically, the POS hierarchy may be caused by the uneven distribution of valence of POS, or more generally, by the unequal capacity of combination force of the POS. The bigger the valence a POS has, i.e. the stronger its capacity of combination it owns, the higher possibility of getting into the central part of the syntactic system.

When we look into the resulting data, it seems that the word or POS frequency played a role here. It seems that the more frequent POS in the treebank has been put in the more central part in the hierarchy, see table 3.

POS		Frequency
n	**noun**	11, 014
v	**verb**	9, 562
r	**pronoun**	3, 411
u	**auxiliary**	3, 195
d	**adverb**	2, 634
a	**adjective**	1, 976
q	**classifier**	1, 491
p	**preposition**	1, 244
m	**numeral**	1, 561
c	**conjunction**	903
z	**affix**	413
e	**interjection**	3
o	**mimetic word**	1

Table 3. The frequency distribution of POS .

As much as connections between our results and the POS frequency, they are not fully corresponding to each other, such as:

- nouns have the highest frequency in *XBSS* but they are not in the most central position in the hierarchy while verbs are.
- pronouns have the third highest frequency but only belong to the middle part of the system, meanwhile the adjectives locate on the relatively central position with a moderate frequency.
- conjunctions have relatively low frequency but they locate on a position closer to the center than numerals, classifiers, and adverbs do, and these POS all have greater frequency than conjunctions do.

We think the frequency of POS might be an explicit result of constructing sentences by following the rules of the Chinese syntactic system, which is a fully connected system that has a hierarchical feature, see Figure 2. The frequency distribution index treats the linguistic units as individuals while the network model also address the importance of the connections between linguistic units.

Although further discussion is needed for understanding the connections between the frequency distribution of POS and the positions that POS occupies in syntactic network, we speculate that the hierarchy feature may be a motive behind the POS frequency distribution or word frequency distribution, rather than, contrarily, that the central position is due to the high frequency.

5 Conclusion

For a long time, the discussion of the hierarchical features of language is mainly focusing on the hierarchical structure between different linguistic layers or inside a sentence. It seems that there is an empty gap between the very detailed sentence structures and general linguistic layers. If we find hierarchical structure inside a sentence as well as the text-meaning process, then cannot we find hierarchical structures in between, inside each linguistic layer?

The challenge of breaking the boundary of sentences while remaining reasonable syntactic structures was met by the network model. With the dependency treebank, we constructed a POS network and did several quantitative analysis to the language network data.

With empirical data support, our study found a clear hierarchical structure of POS in Chinese syntactic system. Although further study is needed for a more insightful discussion, our preliminary results made us believe that the hierarchical configuration is a natural (i.e. inborn or core) feature of language systems, which can be seen not only in the hierarchy of different linguistics levels but also inside certain linguistics layer. Moreover, such configurations probably exist inside each linguist level.

The study showed a method that not only allows us to do quantitative analysis on language data, but also empowers the theoretical discussion by offering support of concrete empirical data. We can discuss the hierarchy features of language by analyzing the authentic language data and visually present it to give us a more intuitive understanding of abstract concepts.

We believe the hierarchy we observed in this study can be seen as the result of the uneven distribution of linguistic units' valence, or more generally, linguistic units' capacity of combination. Since the valence of linguistic units is, actually a concept which closely links to semantics and syntax, we expect the hierarchical structure that we found in this study to equally be observable on the semantic level although classes in propositional semantics differ from syntactic categories. The common points and differences of hierarchical structures between syntactic and semantic layers can be a possible future direction of the methods presented in this study, as soon as comparable semantic treebanks will be available.

As we mentioned before, in future work, furthermore, we have to explore the effect of some factors such as the size of the treebank, the annotation scheme, the language type, etc.

This paper addresses the importance of developing techniques of treebank exploitation for syntactic research ranging from theorem verification to discovery of new linguistic relations invisible to the eye. We advocate in particular for the usage of network tools in this process and showed how a treebank can, and, in our view, should be seen as a unique network.

Acknowledgments

This work was supported in part by the National Social Science Fund of China (11& ZD188).

References

Barabási A L. and Bonabeau E. 2003. Scale-free networks. *Scientific American*, 288(5), 50-9.

Beckner C, Blythe R, Bybee J, Christiansen MH, Croft W, Ellis NC, Holland J, K JY, Larsen-Freeman D, Schoenemann T. 2009. Language is a complex adaptive system: Position paper. *Language learning*, 59(s1), 1-26.

Borgatti S P. 2002. *NetDraw: Graph visualization software*. Analytic Technologies, Harvard.

Borgatti S P, Everett M G, Freeman L C. 2002. *Ucinet for Windows: Software for social network analysis*. Analytic Technologies, Harvard.

Čech R, Mačutek J, Žabokrtský Z. 2011. The role of syntax in complex networks: Local and global importance of verbs in a syntactic dependency network. *Physica A*, 390(20), 3614-3623.

Chen X. 2013. Dependency Network Syntax. In *Proceedings of DepLing 2013*, 41-50.

Chen X, Liu H. 2015. Function nodes in the Chinese syntactic networks. In *Towards a Theoretical Framework for Analyzing Complex Linguistic Networks. Series on Understanding Complex Systems*, Springer.

Chen X, Liu H. 2011. Central nodes of the Chinese syntactic networks. *Chinese Science Bulletin*, 56(1): 735-740.

Chen X, Xu C, Li W. 2011. Extracting Valency Patterns of Word Classes from Syntactic Complex Networks. In *Proceedings of DepLing 2011*, 165-172.

Chomsky N. 2002. *Syntactic structures*. Walter de Gruyter.

Cong J, Liu H. 2014. Approaching human language with complex networks. *Physics of life reviews*, 11(4), 598-618.

De Saussure F. 2011. *Course in general linguistics*. Columbia University Press.

Deschenes L A, David A. 2000. Origin 6.0: Scientific Data Analysis and Graphing Software. *Journal of the American Chemical Society*, 122(39), 9567-9568.

Ferrer i Cancho R. 2005. The structure of syntactic dependency networks: insights from recent advances in network theory. Problems of quantitative linguistics, 60-75.

Ferrer-i-Cancho R, Solé R V. 2001. The small world of human language. *Proceedings of the Royal Society of London. Series B: Biological Sciences*, 268(1482), 2261-2265.

Hudson R. 2006. *Language Networks: The New Word Grammar*. Oxford University Press.

Kretzschmar W A. 2009. *The linguistics of speech*. Cambridge University Press.

Kruskal J B. 1964. Nonmetric multidimensional scaling: a numerical method. *Psychometrika*, 29(2), 115-129.

Lacheret A, Kahane S, Beliao J, Dister A, Gerdes K, Goldman J P, Obin N, Pietrandrea P, Tchobanov A. 2014. Rhapsodie: a Prosodic-Syntactic Treebank for Spoken French. In *Language Resources and Evaluation Conference*.

Lamb S. 1966. *Oueine Of Stratificational Grammar*. Washington: Georgetown University Press.

Liu H. 2008. The complexity of Chinese dependency syntactic networks. *Physica A*, 387, 3048-3058.

Liu H. 2006. Syntactic Parsing Based on Dependency Relations. *Grkg/Humankybernetik*, 47:124-135.

Mel'čuk I. 1988. *Dependency Syntax: Theory and Practice*. Albany: State University of New York Press.

Mel'čuk I. 1981. Meaning-Text Models: Arecenttrendin Sovietlinguistics. *Annual Review of Anthropology*, 10, 27-62.

Mille S, Burga A, Wanner L. 2013. AnCoraUPF: A Multi-Level Annotation of Spanish. In *Proceedings of DepLing 2013*, 217-226.

Nooy W, Mrvar A, Batagelj V. 2005. *Exploratory Network Analysis with Pajek*. Cambridge University Press, New York.

Sgall P, Hajičová E, Panevová J. 1986. *The Meaning of the Sentence in Its Semantic and Pragmatic Aspects*. Dordrecht: Reidel Publishing Company.

Shannon P, Markiel A, Ozier O, Baliga N S, Wang J T, Ramage D, Amin N, Schwikowski B, Ideker T. 2003. Cytoscape: a software environment for integrated models of biomolecular interaction networks. *Genome research*, 13(11), 2498-2504.

Solé R. 2005. Syntax for free? *Nature*, 434, 289.

Watts D. J. and Strogatz S. H. 1998. Collective dynamics of 'small-world' networks. *nature*, 393(6684), 440-442.

Appendix A. Codes meaning

code	meaning
a	adjective
c	conjunction
d	adverb
e	interjection
m	numeral
n	noun
o	mimetic word
p	preposition
q	classifier
r	pronoun
u	auxiliary
v	verb
z	affix

Appendix B. The equation of index STRESS

$$STRESS = \sqrt{\frac{\sum_{ij} (\delta_{ij} - d_{ij})^2}{\sum_{ij} d_{ij}^2}}$$

Appendix C. The value of arcs in the POS network

gov \ dep	n	v	r	q	m	p	a	z	u	d	c	o	e
n	3, 246	822	489	966	239	23	642	12	1, 417	30	115	0	0
v	5, 429	5, 707	1, 809	399	124	1, 098	705	1	1, 505	2049	632	1	1
r	71	12	67	15	1	2	3	361	11	6	7	0	0
q	31	15	471	16	1, 000	0	15	0	15	4	2	0	0
m	18	17	27	4	144	0	12	39	19	13	1	0	0
p	829	162	154	16	5	4	15	0	10	23	34	0	0
a	245	145	97	30	22	31	101	0	115	442	35	0	2
z	0	0	0	0	0	0	0	0	0	0	0	0	0
u	548	681	264	32	17	73	374	0	18	33	50	0	0
d	9	16	3	3	3	3	2	0	4	22	1	0	0
c	543	311	20	6	5	9	35	0	68	11	11	0	0
o	3	21	3	0	0	0	1	0	0	0	1	0	0
e	0	0	0	0	0	0	0	0	0	0	0	0	0

Using Parallel Texts and Lexicons for Verbal Word Sense Disambiguation

Ondřej Dušek Eva Fučíková Jan Hajič Martin Popel Jana Šindlerová Zdeňka Urešová
Charles University in Prague, Faculty of Mathematics and Physics
Institute of Formal and Applied Linguistics
Malostranské nám. 25
11800 Prague 1, Czech Republic
{odusek,fucikova,hajic,popel,sindlerova,uresova}@ufal.mff.cuni.cz

Abstract

We present a system for verbal Word Sense Disambiguation (WSD) that is able to exploit additional information from parallel texts and lexicons. It is an extension of our previous WSD method (Dušek et al., 2014), which gave promising results but used only monolingual features. In the follow-up work described here, we have explored two additional ideas: using English-Czech bilingual resources (as features only – the task itself remains a monolingual WSD task), and using a "hybrid" approach, adding features extracted both from a parallel corpus and from manually aligned bilingual valency lexicon entries, which contain subcategorization information. Albeit not all types of features proved useful, both ideas and additions have led to significant improvements for both languages explored.

1 Introduction

Using parallel data for Word Sense Disambiguation (WSD) is as old as Statistical Machine Translation (SMT): Brown et al. (1992) analyze texts in both languages before the IBM SMT models are trained and used, including WSD driven purely by translation equivalents.[1] A combination of parallel texts and lexicons also proved useful for SMT at the time (Brown et al., 1993). In our previous experiments (Dušek et al., 2014), we have shown that WSD based on a manually created valency lexicon (for verbs) can achieve encouraging results. Combining the above ideas and previous findings with parallel data and a manually created bilingual valency lexicon, we have moved to add bilingual features to improve on the previous results on the verbal WSD task. In addition, we have opted for a new machine learning system, the Vowpal Wabbit toolkit (Langford et al., 2007).[2]

In Section 2, we present the annotation framework and the lexicons used throughout this paper. Section 3 describes our experiments, Section 4 summarizes relevant previous works and Section 5 concludes the paper.

2 Verbal word senses in valency frames

2.1 Prague dependency treebanks and valency

The Prague Dependency Treebank (PDT 2.0/2.5) (Hajič et al., 2006) contains Czech texts with rich annotation.[3] Its annotation scheme is based on the formal framework called Functional Generative Description (FGD) (Sgall et al., 1986), which is dependency-based with a "stratificational" (layered) approach: The annotation contains interlinked surface dependency trees and deep syntactic/semantic (*tectogrammatical*) trees, where nodes stand for concepts rather than words. The notion of valency in the FGD is one of the core concepts on the deep layer; for the purpose of our experiments, it is important that the deep layer links each verb node (occurrence) to the corresponding valency frame in the associated valency lexicon, effectively providing verbal word sense labeling.

The parallel Prague Czech-English Dependency Treebank 2.0 (PCEDT 2.0) (Hajič et al., 2012) has been annotated using the same principles as the PDT, providing us with manually disambiguated verb senses on both the Czech and the English side. The texts are disjoint from the PDT; PCEDT contains the Wall Street Journal (WSJ) part of the Penn Treebank (Marcus et al., 1993) and its

[1] Given the "automatic" nature of the word senses so derived, no figures on the WSD accuracy within the IBM Candide SMT system had been given in the Brown et al. (1992) paper.

[2] http://hunch.net/~vw

[3] http://ufal.mff.cuni.cz/pdt2.0

Proceedings of the Third International Conference on Dependency Linguistics (Depling 2015), pages 82–90,
Uppsala, Sweden, August 24–26 2015.

radit[2] `ACT(1) PAT(4;k+3;aby) ADDR(3)`

help[1] `ACT() PAT() ADDR()`

Figure 1: Valency frame examples from PDT-Vallex and EngVallex (Czech *radit* = 'give advice, help').

translation into Czech. Sentences have been manually aligned during the human translation process, and words have been then aligned automatically using GIZA++ (Och and Ney, 2003). We have used valency frame annotation (and other features) of the PCEDT 2.0 in our previous work; however, billingual alignment information has not been used before.

2.2 Valency lexicons

PDT-Vallex[4] (Hajič et al., 2003; Urešová, 2011) is a valency lexicon of Czech verbs (and nouns), manually created during the annotation of the PDT/PCEDT 2.0.

Each entry in the lexicon contains a headword (lemma), according to which the valency frames (i.e., senses) are grouped. Each valency frame includes the valency frame members and the following information for each of them (see Fig. 1):

- its function label, such as `ACT, PAT, ADDR, EFF, ORIG, TWHEN, LOC, CAUS` (actor, patient, addressee, effect, origin, time, location, cause),[5]
- its semantic "obligatoriness" attribute,
- subcategorization: its required surface form(s) using morphosyntactic and lexical constraints.

Most valency frames are further accompanied by a note or an example which explains their meaning and usage. The version of PDT-Vallex used here contains 11,933 valency frames for 7,121 verbs.

EngVallex[6] (Cinková, 2006) is a valency lexicon of English verbs based also on the FGD framework, created by an automatic conversion from PropBank frame files (Palmer et al., 2005) and subsequent manual refinement.[7] EngVallex was used for the annotation of the English part of the

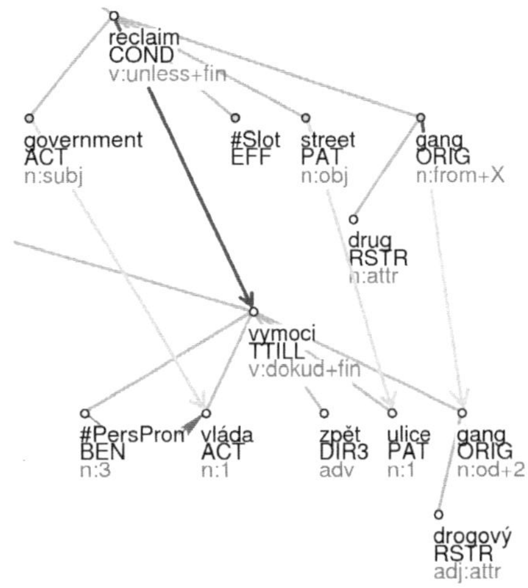

Figure 2: PCEDT trees aligned using the CzEng-Vallex mapping

PCEDT 2.0. Currently, it contains 7,148 valency frames for 4,337 verbs. EngVallex does not contain the explicitly formalized subcategorization information.

2.3 CzEngVallex: Valency lexicon mapping

CzEngVallex (Urešová et al., 2015a; Urešová et al., 2015b) is a manually annotated Czech-English valency lexicon linking the Czech and English valency lexicons, PDT-Vallex and EngVallex. It contains 19,916 frame (verb sense) pairs. CzEngVallex builds links not only between corresponding frames but also between corresponding verb arguments. This lexicon thus provides an interlinked database of argument structures for each verb and enables cross-lingual comparison of valency. As such (together with the parallel corpora to which it is linked), it aims to serve as a resource for cross-language linguistic research. Its primary purpose is linguistic and translatology research.

CzEngVallex is based on the treebank annotation of the PCEDT 2.0, covering about 86.000 aligned verbal pairs in it. Fig. 2 shows an example alignment between the English verb *reclaim* (sense: *get back by force*) and its arguments. 3,288 EngVallex and 4,192 PDT-Vallex verbs occur interlinked in the PCEDT 2.0 at least once, amounting to 4,967 and 6,776 different senses, respectively. Token-wise, over 66% of English verbs and 72% of Czech verbs in the PCEDT 2.0 have a verbal translation covered by the CzEngVallex mapping.

[4] `http://lindat.mff.cuni.cz/services/PDT-Vallex`

[5] For those familiar with PropBank, ACT and PAT typically correspond to Arg0 and Arg1, respectively.

[6] `http://lindat.mff.cuni.cz/services/EngVallex`

[7] EngVallex preserves links to PropBank and to VerbNet (Schuler, 2005) where available. Due to the refinement, the mapping is often not 1:1.

3 Verbal WSD experiments

We are focusing here on measuring the influence of parallel features on the WSD performance. In order to compare our results to our previous work, we use the same training/testing data split, i.e., PCEDT 2.0 Sections 02–21 as training data, Section 24 as development data, and Section 23 as evaluation data, and start from the same set of monolingual features. We also include Czech monolingual results on PDT 2.5 (default data split) for comparison. Unlike our previous work using LibLINEAR logistic regression (Fan et al., 2008), we apply Vowpal Wabbit (Langford et al., 2007) for classification.

Note that the input to our WSD system is plain text without any annotation, and we only use the gold verb senses from PCEDT/PDT to train the system. All required annotation for features as well as word alignment for parallel texts is performed automatically.

3.1 Monolingual experiments

We applied the one-against-all cost-sensitive setting of the Vowpal Wabbit linear classifier with label-dependent features.[8] Feature values are combined with a candidate sense label from the valency lexicon. If a verb was unseen in the training data or is sense-unambiguous, we used the first or only sense from the lexicon instead of the classifier.[9]

The training data were automatically analyzed from plain word forms up to the PDT/PCEDT-style deep layer using analysis pipelines implemented in the Treex NLP framework (Popel and Žabokrtský, 2010).[10] The gold-standard sense labels were then projected onto the automatic annotation. This emulates the real-world scenario where no gold-standard annotation is available.

The monolingual feature set of Dušek et al. (2014) includes most attributes found in the PCEDT annotation scheme:

- the surface word form of the lexical verb and all its auxiliaries,
- their part-of-speech and morphological attributes,
- formemes – compact labels capturing morphosyntactic properties of deep nodes (e.g., `v:fin` for a finite verb, `v:because+fin` for a finite verb governed by a subordinating conjunction, `v:in+ger` for a gerund governed by a preposition),[11]
- syntactic labels given by the dependency parser,
- all of the above properties found in the neighborhood of the verbal deep node (parent, children, siblings, nodes adjacent in the word order).

3.2 Using word alignment

This scenario keeps all the previous settings and includes one more feature type – the translated lemma from the other language as projected through word alignment. This feature is also concatenated with the candidate sense label from the lexicon. We reuse the automatic GIZA++ word alignment from PCEDT 2.0 and project it to the automatic deep layer annotation using rules implemented in the Treex framework.

Since GIZA++ alignment can be obtained in an unsupervised fashion, this still corresponds to a scenario where no previous word alignment is available. Our experience from the CzEngVallex project (see Section 2.3), where GIZA++ alignment links were corrected manually, suggests that the automatic alignment is quite reliable for verbs (less than 1% of alignment links leading from verbs required correction).

3.3 Combining alignment with valency lexicon mapping

This setting includes the aligned lemma features and adds a single binary feature that combines parallel data information from PCEDT 2.0 with the CzEngVallex valency lexicon mapping (see Section 2.3).

For each verbal sense from the PDT-Vallex and EngVallex lexicons, we created a list of all lemmas from the other language corresponding to senses connected to this sense through the CzEngVallex

[8] Based on preliminary experiments on development data sets, we used the following options for training: `--passes=4 -b 20 --loss_function=hinge --csoaa_ldf=mc`, i.e., 4 passes over the training data, a feature space size of 2^{20}, the hinge loss function and cost-sensitive one-against-all multiclass reduction with label-dependent features.

[9] Cf. total accuracy vs. classifier accuracy in Tables 1 and 2.

[10] The automatic deep analysis pipelines for both languages are shown on the Treex demo website at `https://lindat.mff.cuni.cz/services/treex-web/run`. They include part-of-speech taggers (Spoustová et al., 2007; Straková et al., 2014) and a dependency parser (McDonald et al., 2005), plus a rule-based conversion of the resulting dependency trees to the deep layer.

[11] See (Dušek et al., 2012) for a more detailed description of formemes.

	Unl-F1	Lab-F1	TotAcc	ClAcc
previous	94.53	80.30	84.95	80.03
Monolingual	95.84	82.39	85.97	81.38
+ aligned lemmas*	95.84	82.59	86.18	81.65
+ val. lexicon**	95.84	82.93	86.53	82.14

Table 1: Experimental results for English
All numbers are percentages. Unl-F1 and Lab-F1 stand for unlabeled and labeled sense detection F1-measure, respectively (see Section 3.4 for details). TotAcc is the total accuracy (including 1st frame from the lexicon in unambiguous verbs), ClAcc is the classifier accuracy (disregarding unambiguous verbs). "*" marks a statistically significant improvement over the Monolingual setting at 95% level, "**" at 99% level.[12]

	Unl-F1	Lab-F1	TotAcc	ClAcc
previous (PDT)	96.90	76.65	79.70	72.41
monoling./PDT	96.94	77.97	80.43	75.64
monoling./PCEDT	97.34	80.22	82.41	78.12
+ aligned lemmas	97.34	80.30	82.50	78.24
+ val. lexicon*	97.34	80.47	82.66	78.45

Table 2: Experimental results for Czech
See Table 1 for a description of labels. We include the performance of our Monolingual setting on PDT 2.5 for comparison with our previous work.

mapping, i.e., a list of "known possible translations" for this verb sense.

The new binary feature exploits the fact that the possible translation lists are typically different for different senses of the same verb: given a verb token and an aligned token from the other language, the feature is set to "true" for those candidate senses that have the aligned token's lemma on the list of their possible translations.

Since the same feature is shared for all verbs (only its value varies), it is guaranteed to occur very frequently, which should increase its usefulness to the classifier.

3.4 Results

The results of the individual settings are given in Tables 1 and 2. The figures include the sense detection F-measure in an unlabeled (just detecting a verb occurrence whose sense must be inferred) and labeled setting (also selecting the correct sense) as well as the accuracy of the sense detection alone (in total and in ambiguous verbs with two or more senses).

We can see that just using the Vowpal Wabbit classifier with the same features provides a substantial performance boost. The aligned lemma features bring a very mild improvement both in English and Czech (not statistically significant for Czech). Using the CzEngVallex mapping feature brings a significant improvement of 0.8% in English and 0.3% in Czech labeled F1 absolute.[12]

The lower gain in Czech from both aligned lemmas and the CzEngVallex mapping can be explained by a higher ambiguity on average of the equivalents used in English (cf. the number of different verbs in PCEDT used in Czech and English in Section 2.3). The aligned English verbs are thus not as helpful for the disambiguation of Czech verbs as is the case in the reversed direction. In addition, the problem itself seems to be harder for Czech on the PCEDT data, given the higher number of senses on average and the higher number of verbs, i.e., greater data sparsity.

The most probable cause for the low gain from aligned lemmas is that the aligned lemma features are relatively sparse (they are different for each lemma and the classifier is not able to connect them). On the other hand, the single binary CzEngVallex feature occurs frequently and can thus then help even in rare verbs with a low number of training examples. A more detailed analysis of the results suggests that this is indeed the case: in both languages, aligned lemma features help mostly for more common verbs whereas the CzEngVallex mapping feature also improves WSD of rarer verbs.

For each language, we examined in detail a sample of randomly selected 30 cases where our three setups gave different results. The positive effect brought about by the aligned lemma features and the CzEngVallex mapping features was evident (examples are shown in Figures 3 and 4 for English and Czech, respectively). We could also find a few cases where the setups using parallel features improved even though there was no helpful aligned translation for the verb in question: even the non-presence of information from the other language can be a hint to the classifier. We have also found cases where the parallel data information introduced noise. This was mostly caused by a translation using an ambiguous verb (see Figure 5), or a verb that would usually suggest a different sense (see Figure 6). In addition, we found in our samples one case of alignment error leading to misclassification and one probable

[12]We used paired bootstrap resampling (Koehn, 2004) with 1,000 resamples to assess statistical significance.

PCEDT annotation error. On the whole, the positive effects of using information from parallel data are prevailing.

4 Related work

Within semantic role labeling (SRL) tasks, predicate detection is often part of the task, whereas WSD is not.[13] Due to limited lexicon coverage, we have used verbs only and evaluated on the frame (sense) assigned to the occurrence of the verb in the corpus. While the best results reported for the CoNLL 2009 Shared task are 85.41% labeled F1 for Czech and 85.63% for English (Björkelund et al., 2009), they are not comparable for several reasons, the main being that SRL evaluates each argument separately, while for a frame to be counted as correct in our task, the whole frame (by means of its reference ID) must be correct, which is substantially harder (if only for verbs). Moreover, we have used a newer version of the PDT (including PDT-Vallex) and EngVallex-annotated verbs in the PCEDT, while the English CoNLL 2009 Shared Task is PropBank-based.[14]

Dependency information is also often used for WSD outside of SRL tasks (Lin, 1997; Chen et al., 2009), but remains mostly limited to surface syntax.

WSD for verbs has been tackled previously, e.g. (Edmonds and Cotton, 2001; Chen and Palmer, 2005). These experiments, however, do not consider subcategorization/valency information explicitly.

Previous work on verbal WSD using the PDT Czech data includes a rule-based tool of Honetschläger (2003) and experiments by Semecký (2007) using machine learning. However, they have used gold-standard annotation for features.

The closest approach to ours is by Tufiş et al. (2004), where both a dictionary (WordNet) and a parallel corpus is used for WSD on the Orwell's 1984 novel (achieving a relatively low 74.93% F1).

Generally, the hybrid approach combining manually created dictionaries with machine learning has been applied to other tasks as well; we have already mentioned SMT (Brown et al., 1993). Dictionaries have been used in POS tagging (Hajič, 2000). More distant is the approach of, e.g., Brown et al. (1992) and Ide et al. (2002), where parallel text is used for learning supervision, but not for feature extraction; Diab and Resnik (2002) use an unsupervised method.

We should also mention the idea of using parallel corpora as hidden features, a task first performed by (Brown et al., 1992) for WSD and subsequently in many other tasks, such as named entity recognition (Kim et al., 2012), dependency parsing (Haulrich, 2012; Rosa et al., 2012) or coreference resolution (Novák and Žabokrtský, 2014). Cross-language annotation projection is also a related method: see, for instance, (van der Plas and Apidianaki, 2014).

5 Conclusions and future work

We can conclude that the "hybrid" system combining the use of a parallel treebank and manually created bilingual valency lexicon described herein significantly outperformed the previous results, where only monolingual data and features have been used. We compared that to the case where only lemmas projected through word alignment are used (to distinguish the contribution of the parallel corpus alone vs. the manual lexicon), and the lemma features alone brought a very mild improvement (not statistically significant for Czech).

While it shows the usefulness of manually created lexical resources in this particular task,[15] we are planning to extend our WSD system in the future in two ways: first, to use automatically translated texts (instead of a manually translated parallel corpus), and second, to use automatically extracted valency alignments based on our Czech-English "manual" experience with CzEngVallex. In both cases, we would also like to test our approach on other language pairs (most likely with English as the one of the languages due to its rich resources). Both extensions are certainly possible, and they would allow a fair comparison against a truly monolingual WSD task without any additional resources at runtime, but of course it will have to be seen whether the noise introduced by these two automatic steps overrides the positive effects reported here.

[13] Predicate identification has not been part of the CoNLL 2009 shared task (Hajič et al., 2009), though.

[14] Please recall that EngVallex is a manually refined PropBank with different labeling scheme and generally $m : n$ mapping between PropBank and EngVallex frames.

[15] For POS tagging, a "hybrid" combination of a dictionary and a statistical tagger have also proved successful (Hajič, 2000).

EN: But those machines are still *considered* novelties, [...]

CS: Ale tyto stroje [...] jsou stále *považovány* ('believe to be') za novinky.

- Wrongly classified as **consider**[1] ('think about') in the monolingual setting, corrected as **consider**[2] ('believe to be') with aligned lemmas and val. lexicon.

EN: This *feels* more like a one-shot deal.

CS: Teď to *vypadá* ('looks like') spíš na jednorázovou záležitost.

- Wrongly classified as **feel**[4] ('have a feeling') in the monolingual and aligned lemma settings, corrected as **feel**[5] ('look like') with val. lexicon.

Figure 3: Examples of English WSD improved by information from Czech parallel texts (top: aligned lemma features help with a verb that is relatively frequent in the training data, bottom: the CzEngVallex mapping feature helps with a rarer verb).

CS: [...] čemu lidé z televizního průmyslu *říkají* ('call') stanice „s nejvyšší spontánní znalostí".

EN: [...] what people in the television industry *call* a "top of mind" network.

- Wrongly classified as **říkat**[7] ('say') in the monolingual setting, corrected as **říkat**[4] ('call') with aligned lemmas and val. lexicon.

CS: Jestliže investor *neposkytne* ('does not provide, give, lend') dodatečnou hotovost [...]

EN: If the investor doesn't *put up* the extra cash [...]

- Wrongly classified as **poskytnout**[2] ('light verb, give (chance, opportunity etc.)') in the monolingual and aligned lemma settings, corrected as **poskytnout**[1] ('provide, lend') with val. lexicon.

Figure 4: Examples of Czech WSD improved by information from English parallel text (top: a relatively frequent verb, bottom: less frequent verb).

EN: Laptops [...] have become the fastest-growing personal computer segment , with sales *doubling* this year .

CS: Laptopy [...] se staly, díky letošnímu *zdvojnásobení* objemu prodeje, nejrychleji rostoucím segmentem mezi osobními počítači .

- Correctly classified as **double**[3] ('become twice as large') in the monolingual setting, misclassified as **double**[2] ('make twice as large') with aligned lemmas and val. lexicon. The Czech word *zdvojnásobení* is ambiguous and allows both senses.

CS: Výrobek firmy Atari Corp . Portfolio [...] stojí pouhých 400 $ a *běží* na třech AA bateriích [...]

EN: Atari Corp. 's Portfolio [...] costs a mere $ 400 and *runs* on three AA batteries [...]

- Correctly classified as **běžet**[6] ('work, function') in the monolingual and aligned lemmas setting, misclassified as **běžet**[3] ('move on foot') with val. lexicon. The English translation *run* allows both senses.

Figure 5: Examples of translations using ambiguous verbs which did not help in WSD (top: English, bottom: Czech).

EN: "We didn't even get a chance to *do* the programs we wanted to do."

CS: „Nedali nám žádnou šanci *uskutečnit* plány, které jsme měli připravené."

- Correctly classified as **do**^{6} ('perform (a function), run (a trade)') in the monolingual and aligned lemmas setting, misclassified as **do**^{2} ('perform an act') with val. lexicon. The Czech word *uskutečnit* ('accomplish') suggests an incorrect reading.

CS: [...] například Iowa *zaznamenala* [...] nárůst populace o 11000 lidí [...]

EN: Iowa , for instance , *saw* its population grow by 11,000 people [...]

- Correctly classified as **zaznamenat**^{5} ('light verb, experience (rise, difficulty, gain etc.)') in the monolingual and val. lexicon setting, misclassified as **zaznamenat**^{1} ('notice') with aligned lemmas. The English verb *see* would usually suggest the latter sense.

Figure 6: Examples of translations using verbs that would typically suggest a different sense than the correct one.

Acknowledgments

The authors would like to thank Michal Novák for his help and ideas regarding the Vowpal Wabbit setup. The work described herein has been supported by the grant GP13-03351P of the Grant Agency of the Czech Republic, the 7th Framework Programme of the EU grant QTLeap (No. 610516), and SVV project 260 104 and GAUK grant 2058214 of the Charles University in Prague. It is using language resources hosted by the LINDAT/CLARIN Research Infrastructure, Project No. LM2010013 of the Ministry of Education, Youth and Sports.

References

A. Björkelund, L. Hafdell, and P. Nugues. 2009. Multilingual semantic role labeling. In *Proceedings of CoNLL 2009: Shared Task*, pages 43–48, Boulder, Colorado, United States.

P. F. Brown, S. A. Della Pietra, V. J. Della Pietra, J. D. Lafferty, and R. L. Mercer. 1992. Analysis, statistical transfer, and synthesis in machine translation. In *Proceedings of the Fourth International Conference on Theoretical and Methodological Issues in Machine Translation*, pages 83–100.

P. F. Brown, S. A. Della Pietra, V. J. Della Pietra, M. J. Goldsmith, J. Hajič, R. L. Mercer, and S. Mohanty. 1993. But dictionaries are data too. In *Proceedings of the Workshop on Human Language Technology*, HLT '93, pages 202–205.

J. Chen and M. Palmer. 2005. Towards robust high performance word sense disambiguation of English verbs using rich linguistic features. In *Natural Language Processing–IJCNLP 2005*, pages 933–944. Springer.

P. Chen, W. Ding, C. Bowes, and D. Brown. 2009. A fully unsupervised word sense disambiguation method using dependency knowledge. In *Proceedings of Human Language Technologies: The 2009 Annual Conference of the North American Chapter of the Association for Computational Linguistics*, pages 28–36. Association for Computational Linguistics.

S. Cinková. 2006. From PropBank to EngValLex: adapting the PropBank-Lexicon to the valency theory of the functional generative description. In *Proceedings of LREC 2006, Genova, Italy*.

M. Diab and P. Resnik. 2002. An unsupervised method for word sense tagging using parallel corpora. In *Proceedings of the 40th ACL*, pages 255–262.

O. Dušek, Z. Žabokrtský, M. Popel, M. Majliš, M. Novák, and D. Mareček. 2012. Formemes in English-Czech deep syntactic MT. In *Proceedings of the Seventh Workshop on Statistical Machine Translation*, page 267–274.

O. Dušek, J. Hajič, and Z. Urešová. 2014. Verbal valency frame detection and selection in Czech and English. In *The 2nd Workshop on EVENTS: Definition, Detection, Coreference, and Representation*, pages 6–11, Baltimore. Association for Computational Linguistics.

P. Edmonds and S. Cotton. 2001. Senseval-2: Overview. In *The Proceedings of the Second International Workshop on Evaluating Word Sense Disambiguation Systems*, SENSEVAL '01, pages 1–5.

R. E Fan, K. W Chang, C. J Hsieh, X. R Wang, and C. J Lin. 2008. LIBLINEAR: a library for large linear classification. *The Journal of Machine Learning Research*, 9:1871–1874.

J. Hajič, M. Ciaramita, R. Johansson, D. Kawahara, M. A. Martí, L. Màrquez, A. Meyers, J. Nivre, S. Padó, J. Štěpánek, P. Straňák, M. Surdeanu, N. Xue, and Y. Zhang. 2009. The CoNLL-2009 shared task: Syntactic and semantic dependencies in multiple languages. In *Proceedings of CoNLL-2009*, Boulder, Colorado, USA.

J. Hajič, E. Hajičová, J. Panevová, P. Sgall, O. Bojar, S. Cinková, E. Fučíková, M. Mikulová, P. Pajas, J. Popelka, J. Semecký, J. Šindlerová, J. Štěpánek, J. Toman, Z. Urešová, and Z. Žabokrtský. 2012. Announcing Prague Czech-English Dependency Treebank 2.0. In *Proceedings of LREC*, pages 3153–3160.

J. Hajič. 2000. Morphological tagging: Data vs. dictionaries. In *Proceedings of NAACL*, pages 94–101.

J. Hajič, J. Panevová, Z. Urešová, A. Bémová, V. Kolářová, and P. Pajas. 2003. PDT-VALLEX: creating a large-coverage valency lexicon for treebank annotation. In *Proceedings of The 2nd Workshop on Treebanks and Linguistic Theories*, volume 9, page 57–68.

J. Hajič, J. Panevová, E. Hajičová, P. Sgall, P. Pajas, J. Štěpánek, J. Havelka, M. Mikulová, Z. Žabokrtský, M. Ševčíková Razímová, and Z. Urešová. 2006. *Prague Dependency Treebank 2.0*. Number LDC2006T01. LDC, Philadelphia, PA, USA.

M. W. Haulrich. 2012. *Data-driven bitext dependency parsing and alignment*. Ph.D. thesis, Copenhagen Business School, Department of International Business Communication.

V. Honetschläger. 2003. Using a Czech valency lexicon for annotation support. In *Text, Speech and Dialogue*, pages 120–125. Springer.

N. Ide, T. Erjavec, and D. Tufiş. 2002. Sense discrimination with parallel corpora. In *Proceedings of the ACL-02 Workshop on Word Sense Disambiguation - Volume 8*, WSD '02, pages 61–66.

S. Kim, K. Toutanova, and H. Yu. 2012. Multilingual named entity recognition using parallel data and metadata from Wikipedia. In *Proceedings of the 50th Annual Meeting of the Association for Computational Linguistics: Long Papers - Volume 1*, pages 694–702, Stroudsburg, PA, USA. Association for Computational Linguistics.

P. Koehn. 2004. Statistical significance tests for machine translation evaluation. In *Empirical Methods in Natural Language Processing*, pages 388–395.

J. Langford, L. Li, and A. Strehl. 2007. Vowpal Wabbit online learning project.

D. Lin. 1997. Using syntactic dependency as local context to resolve word sense ambiguity. In *Proceedings of the 35th Annual Meeting of the Association for Computational Linguistics and Eighth Conference of the European Chapter of the Association for Computational Linguistics*, pages 64–71, Madrid, Spain. Association for Computational Linguistics.

M. P. Marcus, M. A. Marcinkiewicz, and B. Santorini. 1993. Building a large annotated corpus of English: The Penn Treebank. *COMP LING*, 19(2):330.

R. McDonald, F. Pereira, K. Ribarov, and J. Hajič. 2005. Non-projective dependency parsing using spanning tree algorithms. In *Proceedings of the conference on Human Language Technology and Empirical Methods in Natural Language Processing*, pages 523–530.

M. Novák and Z. Žabokrtský. 2014. Cross-lingual coreference resolution of pronouns. In *Proceedings of COLING 2014, the 25th International Conference on Computational Linguistics: Technical Papers*, pages 14–24, Dublin, Ireland, August. Dublin City University and Association for Computational Linguistics.

F. J. Och and H. Ney. 2003. A systematic comparison of various statistical alignment models. *Comput. Linguist.*, 29(1):19–51, March.

M. Palmer, D. Gildea, and P. Kingsbury. 2005. The proposition bank: An annotated corpus of semantic roles. *Computational Linguistics*, 31(1):71–106.

M. Popel and Z. Žabokrtský. 2010. TectoMT: modular NLP framework. *Advances in Natural Language Processing*, pages 293–304.

R. Rosa, O. Dušek, D. Mareček, and M. Popel. 2012. Using parallel features in parsing of machine-translated sentences for correction of grammatical errors. In *Proceedings of the Sixth Workshop on Syntax, Semantics and Structure in Statistical Translation*, SSST-6 '12, pages 39–48, Stroudsburg, PA, USA. Association for Computational Linguistics.

K. K. Schuler. 2005. *VerbNet: A Broad-Coverage, Comprehensive Verb Lexicon*. Ph.D. thesis, Department of Computer and Information Science, University of Pennsylvania, Philadelphia.

J. Semecký. 2007. Verb valency frames disambiguation. *The Prague Bulletin of Mathematical Linguistics*, (88):31–52.

P. Sgall, E. Hajičová, and J. Panevová. 1986. *The meaning of the sentence in its semantic and pragmatic aspects*. D. Reidel, Dordrecht.

D. J. Spoustová, J. Hajič, J. Votrubec, P. Krbec, and P. Květoň. 2007. The Best of Two Worlds: Cooperation of Statistical and Rule-based Taggers for Czech. In *Proceedings of the Workshop on Balto-Slavonic Natural Language Processing: Information Extraction and Enabling Technologies*, pages 67–74, Stroudsburg, PA, USA. Association for Computational Linguistics.

J. Straková, M. Straka, and J. Hajič. 2014. Open-Source Tools for Morphology, Lemmatization, POS Tagging and Named Entity Recognition. In *ACL 2014*, pages 13–18. Association for Computational Linguistics.

D. Tufiş, R. Ion, and N. Ide. 2004. Fine-grained word sense disambiguation based on parallel corpora, word alignment, word clustering and aligned wordnets. In *Proceedings of the 20th COLING'04*.

Z. Urešová, O. Dušek, E. Fučíková, J. Hajič, and J. Šindlerová. 2015a. Bilingual English-Czech valency lexicon linked to a parallel corpus. In *Proceedings of LAW IX - The 9th Linguistic Annotation Workshop*, pages 124–128, Denver, Colorado. Association for Computational Linguistics.

Z. Urešová, E. Fučíková, and J. Šindlerová. 2015b. CzEngVallex: Mapping Valency between Languages. Technical Report TR-2015-58, Charles University in Prague, Institute of Formal and Applied Lingustics, Prague. To appear at `http://ufal.mff.cuni.cz/techrep/tr58.pdf`.

Z. Urešová. 2011. *Valenční slovník Pražského závislostního korpusu (PDT-Vallex)*. Studies in Computational and Theoretical Linguistics. Prague.

L. van der Plas and M. Apidianaki. 2014. Cross-lingual word sense disambiguation for predicate labelling of French. In *TALN-RECITAL, 21ème Traitement Automatique des Langues Naturelles, Marseille, 2014*.

Quantifying Word Order Freedom in Dependency Corpora

Richard Futrell, Kyle Mahowald, and Edward Gibson
Department of Brain and Cognitive Sciences
Massachusetts Institute of Technology
{futrell, kylemaho, egibson}@mit.edu

Abstract

Using recently available dependency corpora, we present novel measures of a key quantitative property of language, *word order freedom*: the extent to which word order in a sentence is free to vary while conveying the same meaning. We discuss two topics. First, we discuss linguistic and statistical issues associated with our measures and with the annotation styles of available corpora. We find that we can measure reliable upper bounds on word order freedom in head direction and the ordering of certain sisters, but that more general measures of word order freedom are not currently feasible. Second, we present results of our measures in 34 languages and demonstrate a correlation between quantitative word order freedom of subjects and objects and the presence of nominative-accusative case marking. To our knowledge this is the first large-scale quantitative test of the hypothesis that languages with more word order freedom have more case marking (Sapir, 1921; Kiparsky, 1997).

1 Introduction

Comparative cross-linguistic research on the quantitative properties of natural languages has typically focused on measures that can be extracted from unannotated or shallowly annotated text. For example, probably the most intensively studied quantitative properties of language are Zipf's findings about the power law distribution of word frequencies (Zipf, 1949). However, the properties of languages that can be quantified from raw text are relatively shallow, and are not straightforwardly related to higher-level properties of languages such as their morphology and syntax. As a result, there has been relatively little large-scale comparative work on quantitative properties of natural language *syntax*.

In recent years it has become possible to bridge that gap thanks to the availability of large dependency treebanks for many languages and the development of standardized annotation schemes (de Marneffe et al., 2014; Nivre, 2015; Nivre et al., 2015). These resources make it possible to perform direct comparisons of quantitative properties of dependency trees. Previous work using dependency corpora to study crosslinguistic syntactic phenomena includes Liu (2010), who quantifies the frequency of right- and left-branching in dependency corpora, and Kuhlmann (2013), who quantifies the frequency with which natural language dependency trees deviate from projectivity. Other work has studied graph-theoretic properties of dependency trees in the context of language classification (Liu and Li, 2010; Abramov and Mehler, 2011).

Here we study a particular quantitative property of language syntax: word order freedom. We focus on developing linguistically interpretable measures, as close as possible to an intuitive, relatively theory-neutral idea of what word order freedom means. In doing so, a number of methodological issues and questions arise. What quantitative measures map most cleanly onto the concept of word order freedom? Is it feasible to estimate the proposed measure given limited corpus size? Which corpus annotation style—e.g., content-head dependencies or dependencies where function words are heads—best facilitates crosslinguistic comparison? In this work, we argue for a set of methodological decisions which we believe balance the interests of linguistic interpretability, stability with respect to corpus size, and comparability across languages.

We also present results of our measures as applied to 34 languages and discuss their linguis-

Proceedings of the Third International Conference on Dependency Linguistics (Depling 2015), pages 91–100,
Uppsala, Sweden, August 24–26 2015.

tic significance. In particular, we find that languages with quantitatively large freedom in their ordering of subject and object all have nominative/accusative case marking, but that languages with such case marking do not necessarily have much word order freedom. This asymmetric relationship has been suggested in the typological literature (Kiparsky, 1997), but this is the first work to verify it quantitatively. We also discuss some of the exceptions to this generalization in the light of recent work on information-theoretic properties of different word orders (Gibson et al., 2013).

2 Word Order and the Notion of Dependency

We define *word order freedom* as the extent to which the same word or constituent in the same form can appear in multiple positions while retaining the same propositional meaning and preserving grammaticality. For example, the sentence pair (1a-b) provides an example of word order freedom in German, while sentence pair (2a-b) provides an example of a lack of word order freedom in English. However, the sentences (2a) and (2c) do *not* provide an instance of word order freedom in English by our definition, since the agent and patient appear in different syntactic forms in (2c) compared to (2a). We provide dependency syntax analyses of these sentences below.

(1a)

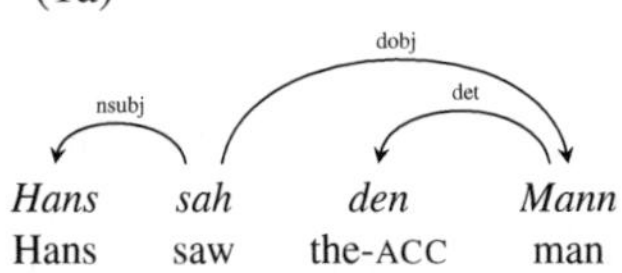

Meaning: "Hans saw the man."

(1b)

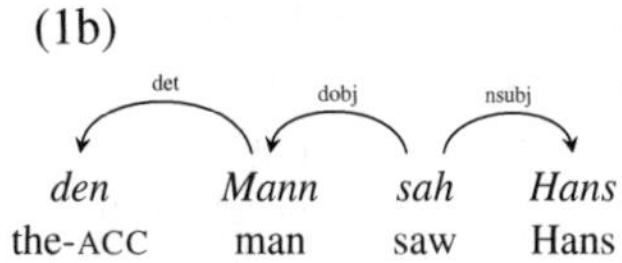

Meaning: "Hans saw the man."

(2a)

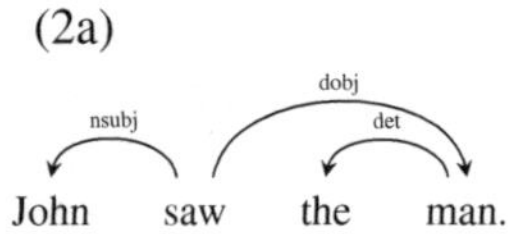

(2b)

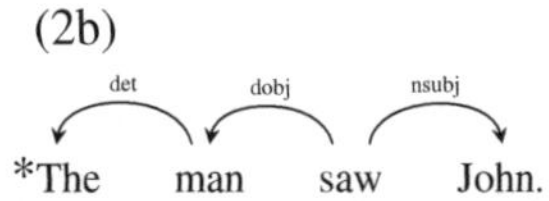

Cannot mean: "John saw the man."

(2c)

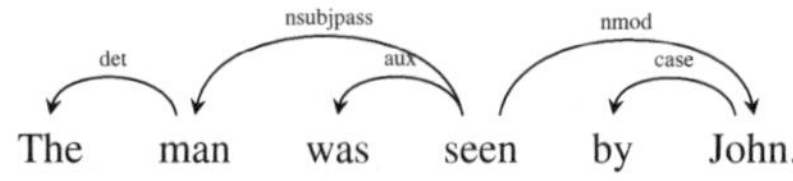

In the typological literature, this phenomenon has also been called *word order flexibility*, *pragmatic word order*, and a lack of *word order rigidity*. These last two terms reflect the fact that word order freedom does not mean that that word order is random. When word order is "free", speakers might order words to convey non-propositional aspects of their intent. For example, a speaker might place certain words earlier in a sentence in order to convey that those words refer to old information (Ferreira and Yoshita, 2003); a speaker might order words according to how accessible they are psycholinguistically (Chang, 2009); etc. Word order may be predictable given these goals, but here we are interested only in the extent to which word order is conditioned on the syntactic and compositional semantic properties of an utterance.

In a dependency grammar framework, we can conceptualize word order freedom as variability in the linear order of words given an unordered dependency graph with labelled edges. For example, both sentences (1a) and (1b) are linearizations of this unordered dependency graph:

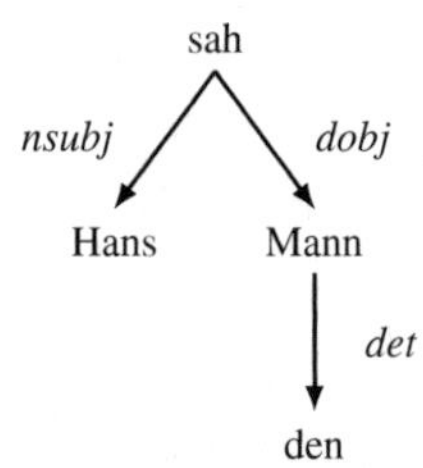

The dependency formalism also gives us a framework for a functional perspective on why word order freedom exists and under what conditions it might arise. In general, the task of understanding the propositional meaning of a sentence requires identifying which words are linked to other words, and what the relation types of those links are. The dependency formalism directly encodes a subset of these links, with the additional assumption that links are always between exactly two explicit words. Therefore, we can roughly view an utterance as an attempt by a language producer to serialize a dependency graph such that a comprehender can recover it. The producer will want to choose a serialization which is efficient to produce and which will allow the comprehender to recover the structure robustly. That is, the utterance must be informative about which pairs of words are linked in a dependency, and what the relation types of those links are.

Here we focus on the communication of relation types. In the English and German examples above, the relation types to be conveyed are *nsubj* and *dobj* in the notation of the Universal Dependencies project (Nivre et al., 2015). For the task of communicating the relation type between a head and dependent, natural languages seem to adopt two non-exclusive solutions: either the order of the head, the dependent, and the dependent's sisters is informative about relation type (a word order code), or the wordform of the head or dependent is informative about relation type (Nichols, 1986) (a case-marking code). Considerations of robustness and efficiency lead to a prediction of a tradeoff between these options. If a language uses case-marking to convey relation type, then word order can be repurposed to efficiently convey other, potentially non-propositional aspects of meaning. On the other hand, if a language uses inflexible word order to convey relation type, then it would be inefficient to also include case marking. However, some word order codes are less robust to noise than others (Gibson et al., 2013; Futrell et al., 2015), so certain rigid word orders might still require case-marking to maintain robustness. Similarly, some case-marking systems might be more or less robust, and so require rigid word order.

The idea that word order freedom is related to the prevalence of morphological marking is an old one (Sapir, 1921). A persistent generalization in the typological literature is that while word order freedom implies the existence of morphological marking, morphological marking does not imply the existence of word order freedom (Kiparsky, 1997; McFadden, 2003). These generalizations have been made primarily on the basis of native speaker intuitions and analyses of small datasets. Such data is problematic for measures such as word order freedom, since languages may vary quantitatively in how much variability they have, and it is not clear where to discretize this variability in order to form the categories "free word order" and "fixed word order". In order to test the reality of these generalizations, and to explore explanatory hypotheses for crosslinguistic variation, it is necessary to quantify the degree of word order freedom in a language.

3 Entropy Measures

Our basic idea is to measure the extent to which the linear order of words is determined by the unordered dependency graph of a sentence. A natural way to quantify this is *conditional entropy*:

$$H(X|C) = \sum_{c \in C} p_C(c) \sum_{x \in X} p_{X|C}(x|c) \log p_{X|C}(x|c), \quad (1)$$

which is the expected conditional uncertainty about a discrete random variable X, which we call the *dependent variable*, conditioned on another discrete random variable C, which we call the *conditioning variable*. In our case, the "perfect" measure of word order freedom would be the conditional entropy of sequences of words given unordered dependency graphs. Directly measuring this quantity is impractical for a number of reasons, so we will explore a number of entropy measures over partial information about dependency trees.

Using a conditional entropy measure with dependency corpora requires us to decide on three parameters: (1) the method of estimating entropy from observed joint counts of X and C, (2) the information contained in the dependent variable X, and (3) the information contained in the conditioning variable C. The two major factors in deciding these parameters are avoiding data sparsity and retaining linguistic interpretability. In this section we discuss the detailed considerations that must go into these decisions.

3.1 Estimating Entropy

The simplest way to estimate entropy given joint counts is through maximum likelihood estimation. However, maximum likelihood estimates of entropy are known to be biased and highly sensitive to sample size (Miller, 1955). The bias issues arise because the entropy of a distribution is highly sensitive to the shape of its tail, and it is difficult to estimate the tail of a distribution given a small sample size. As a result, entropy is systematically underestimated. These issues are exacerbated when applying entropy measures to natural language data, because of the especially long-tailed frequency distribution of sentences and words.

The bias issue is especially acute when doing crosslinguistic comparison with dependency corpora because the corpora available vary hugely in their sample size, from 1017 sentences of Irish to 82,451 sentences of Czech. An entropy difference between one language and another might be the result of sample size differences, rather than a real linguistic difference.

We address this issue in two ways: first, we estimate entropy using the bootstrap estimator of DeDeo et al. (2013), and apply the estimator to equally sized subcorpora across languages[1]. Second, we choose dependent and conditioning variables to minimize data sparsity and avoid long tails. In particular, we avoid entropy measures where the conditioning variable involves wordforms or lemmas. We evaluate the effects of data sparsity on our measures in Section 4.

3.2 Local Subtrees

In order to cope with data sparsity and long-tailed distributions, the dependent and conditioning variables must have manageable numbers of possible values. This means that we cannot compute something like the entropy over full sentences given full dependency graphs, as these joint counts would be incredibly sparse, even if we include only part of speech information about words.

We suggest computing conditional entropy only on *local subtrees*: just subtrees consisting of a head and its immediate dependents. We conjecture that most word order and morphological rules can be stated in terms of heads and their dependents, or in terms of sisters of the same head. For example, almost all agreement phenomena in natural language involve heads and their immediate dependents (Corbett, 2006). Prominent and successful generative models of dependency structure such as the Dependency Model with Valence (Klein and Manning, 2004) assume that dependency trees are generated recursively by generating these local subtrees.

There are two shortcomings to working only with local subtrees; here we discuss how to deal with them.

First, there are certain word order phenomena which appear variable given only local subtree structure, but which are in fact deterministic given dependency structure beyond local subtrees. The extent to which this is true depends on the specifics of the dependency formalism. For example, in German, the position of the verb depends on clause type. In a subordinate clause with a complementizer, the verb must appear after all of its dependents (V-final order). Otherwise, the verb must appear after exactly one of its dependents (V2 order). If we analyze complementizers as heading their verbs, as in (3a), then the local subtree of the verb *sah* does not include information about whether the verb is in a subordinate clause or not.

(3a)

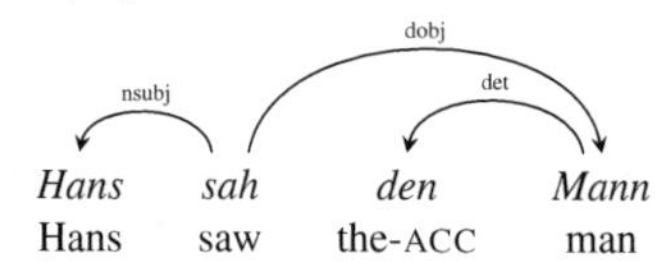

(3b)

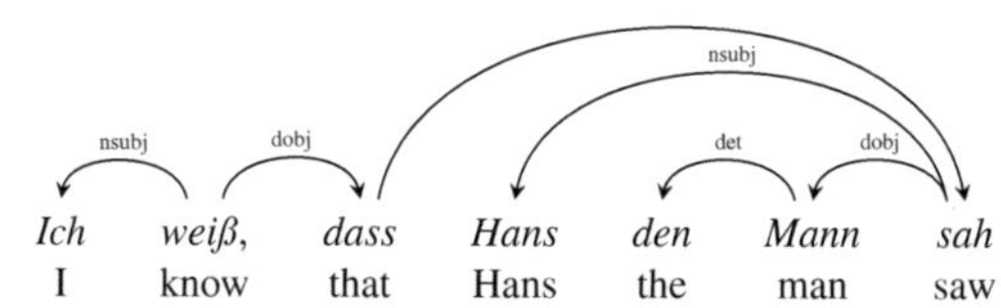

As a result, if we measure the entropy of the order of verbal dependents conditioned on the local subtree structure, then we will erroneously conclude that German is highly variable, since the order is either V2 or V-final and there is nothing in the local subtree to predict which one is appropriate. However, if we analyze complementizers as the dependent of their verb (as in the Universal Dependencies style, (3c)), then the conditional entropy of the verb position given local subtree structure is small. This is because the position of the verb is fully predicted by the presence in the local subtree of a *mark* relation whose dependent is *dass*, *weil*, etc.

(3c)

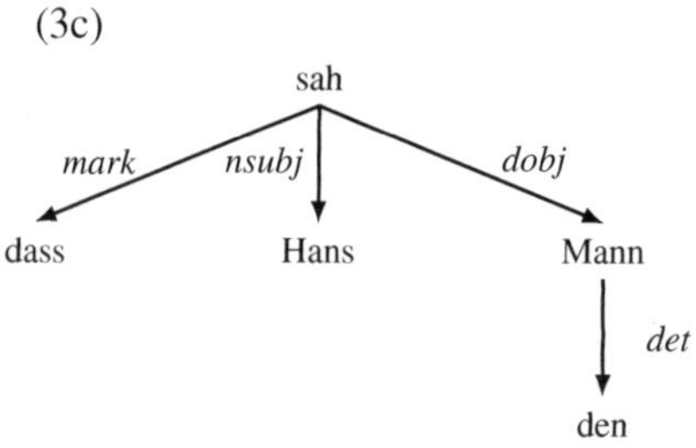

[1]At a high level, the bootstrap algorithm works by measuring entropy in the whole sample and in subsamples and uses these estimates to attempt to correct bias in the whole sample. We refer the reader to DeDeo et al. (2013) for details.

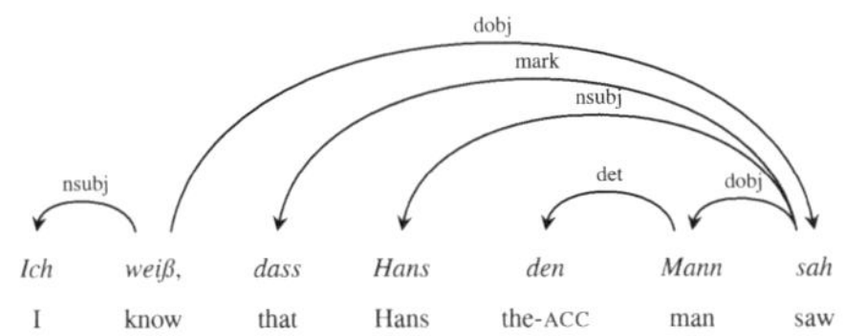

We deal with this issue by preferring annotation styles under which the determinants of the order of a local subtree are present in that subtree. This often means using the content-head dependency style, as in this example.

The second issue with looking only at local subtrees is that we miss certain word order variability associated with nonprojectivity, such as scrambling. Due to space constraints, we do not address this issue here.

When we condition on the local subtree structure and find the conditional entropy of word orders, we call this measure **Relation Order Entropy**, since we are getting the order with which relation types are expressed in a local subtree.

3.3 Dependency Direction

Another option for dealing with data sparsity is to get conditional entropy measures over even less dependency structure. In particular we consider the case of entropy measures conditioned only on a dependent, its head, and the relation type to its head, where the dependent measure is simply whether the head is to the left or right of the dependent. This measure potentially suffers much less from data sparsity issues, since the set of possible heads and dependents in a corpus is much smaller than the set of possible local subtrees. But in restricting our attention only to head direction, we miss the ability to measure any word order freedom among sister dependents. This measure also has the disadvantage that it can miss the kind of conditioning information present in local subtrees, as described in Section 3.2.

When we condition only on simple dependencies, we call this measure **Head Direction Entropy**.

3.4 Conditioning Variables

So far we have discussed our decision to use conditional entropy measures over local subtrees or single dependencies. In this setting, the conditioning variable is the unordered local subtree or dependency, and the dependent variable is the linear order of words. We now turn to the question of what information should be contained in the conditioning variable: whether it should be the full unordered tree, or just the structure of the tree, or the structure of the tree plus part-of-speech (POS) tags and relation types, etc.

In Section 3.1 we argued that we should not condition on the wordforms or lemmas due to sparsity issues. The remaining kinds of information available in corpora are the tree topology, POS tags, and relation types. Many corpora also include annotation for morphological features, but this is not reliably present.

Without conditioning on relation types, our entropy measures become much less linguistically useful. For example, if we did not condition on dependency relation types, it would be impossible to identify verbal subjects and objects or to quantify how informative word order is about these relations crosslinguistically. So we always include dependency relation type in conditioning variables.

The remaining questions are whether to include the POS tags of heads and of each dependent. Some annotation decisions in the Universal Dependencies and Stanford Dependencies argue for including POS information of heads. For example, the Universal Dependencies annotation for copular sentences has the predicate noun as the head, with the subject noun as a dependent of type *nsubj*, as in example (4):

(4)

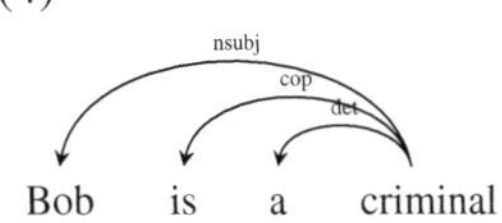

This has the effect that the linguistic meaning of the *nsubj* relation encodes one syntactic relation when its head is a verb, and another syntactic relation when its head is a noun. So we should include POS information about heads when possible.

There are also linguistic reasons for including the POS of dependents in the conditioning variable. Word order often depends on part of speech; for example, in Romance languages, the standard order in the main clause is Subject-Verb-Object if the object is a noun but Subject-Object-Verb if the object is a pronoun. Not including POS tags in the conditioning variable would lead to misleadingly high word order freedom numbers for these clauses in these languages.

Therefore, when possible, our conditioning variables include the POS tags of heads and dependents in addition to dependency relation types.

3.5 Annotation style and crosslinguistic comparability

We have discussed issues involving entropy estimation and the choice of conditioning and dependent variables. Here we discuss another dimension of choices: what dependency annotation scheme to use.

Since the informativity of dependency trees about syntax and semantics affects our word order freedom measures, it is important to ensure that dependency trees across different corpora convey the same information. Certain annotation styles might allow unordered local subtrees to convey more information in one language than in another. To ensure comparability, we should use those annotation styles which are most consistent across languages regarding how much information they give about words in local subtrees, even if this means choosing annotation schemes which are less informative overall. We give examples below.

In many cases, dependency annotation schemes where function words are heads provide more information about syntactic and semantic relations, so such annotation schemes lead to lower estimates of word order freedom. For example, consider the ordering of German verbal adjuncts. The usual order is time adjuncts followed by place adjuncts. Time is often expressed by a bare noun such as *gestern* "yesterday", while place is often expressed with an adpositional phrase.

We will consider how our measures will behave for these constructions given function-word-head dependencies, and given content-head dependencies. Given function-word-head dependencies as in (5a), these two adjuncts will appear with relations *nmod* and *adpmod* in the local subtree rooted by the verb *tanzte*; their order will be highly predictable given these relation types inasmuch as time adjuncts are usually expressed as bare nouns and place adjuncts are usually expressed as adpositional phrases. On the other hand, given content-head dependencies as in (5b), the adjuncts will appear in the local subtree as *nmod* and *nmod*, and their order will appear free.

(5a)

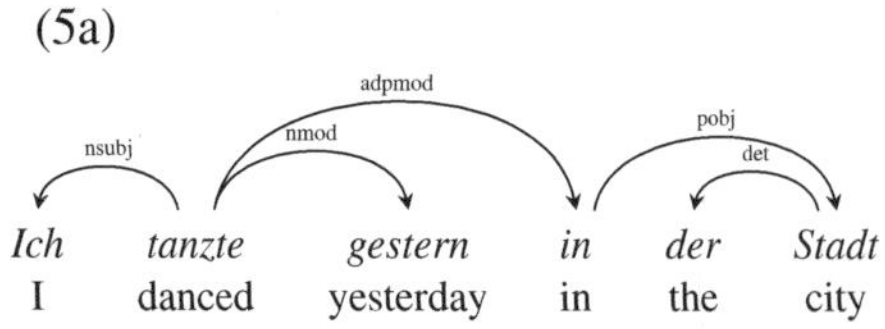

(5b)

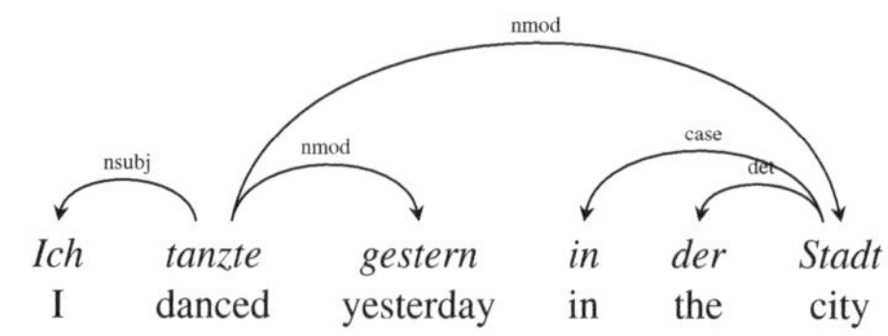

However, function-word-head dependencies do not provide the same amount of information from language to language, because languages differ in how often they use adpositions as opposed to case marking. In the German example, function-word-head dependencies allowed us to distinguish time adjuncts from place adjuncts because place adjuncts usually appear as adpositional phrases while time adjuncts often appear as noun phrases. But in a language which uses case-marked noun phrases for such adjuncts, such as Finnish, the function-word-head dependencies would not provide this information. Therefore, even if (say) Finnish and German had the same degree of freedom in their ordering of place adjuncts and time adjuncts, we would estimate more word order freedom in Finnish and less in German. However, using content-head dependencies, we get the same amount of information in both languages. Therefore, we prefer content-head dependencies for our measures.

Following similar reasoning, we decide to use only the universal POS tags and relation types in our corpora, and not finer-grained language-specific tags.

Using content-head dependencies while conditioning only on local subtrees overestimates word order freedom compared to function-word-head dependencies. At first glance, the content-head dependency annotation seems inappropriate for a typological study, because it clashes with standard linguistic analyses where function words such as adpositions and complementizers (and, in some analyses, even determiners (Abney, 1987)) are heads, rather than dependents. However, content-head dependencies provide more consistent measures across languages. Therefore we present results from our measures applied to content-head dependencies.

3.6 Summary of Parameters of Entropy Measures

We have discussed a number of parameters which go into the construction of a conditional entropy measure of word order freedom. They are:

1. Annotation style: function words as heads or content words as heads.
2. Whether we measure entropy of linearizations of local subtrees (*Relation Order Entropy*) or of simple dependencies (*Head Direction Entropy*).
3. What information we include in the conditioning variable: relation types, head and dependent POS, head and dependent wordforms, etc.
4. Whether to measure entropy over all dependents, or only over some subset of interest, such as subjects or objects.

The decisions for these parameters are dictated by balancing data sparsity and linguistic interpretability. We have argued that we should use content-head dependencies, and never include wordforms or lemmas in the conditioning variables. Furthermore, we have argued that it is generally better to include part-of-speech information in the conditioning variable, but that this may have to be relaxed to cope with data sparsity. The decisions about whether to condition on local subtrees or on simple dependencies, and whether to restrict attention to a particular subset of dependencies, depends on the particular question of interest.

3.7 Entropy Measures as Upper Bounds on Word Order Freedom

We initially defined an ideal measure, the entropy of word orders given full unordered dependency trees. We argued that we would have to back away from this measure by looking only at the conditional entropy of orders of local subtrees, and furthermore that we should only condition on the parts of speech and relation types in the local subtree. Here we argue that these steps away from the ideal measure mean that the resulting measures can only be interpreted as upper bounds on word order freedom.

With each step away from the ideal measure, we also move the *interpretation* of the measures away from the idealized notion of word order freedom. With each kind of information we remove from the independent variable, we allow instances where the word order of a phrase might in fact be fully deterministic given that missing information, but where we will erroneously measure high word order freedom. For example, in German, the order of verbal adjuncts is usually time before place. However, in a dependency treebank, these relations are all *nmod*. By considering only the ordering of dependents with respect to their relation types and parts of speech, we miss the extent to which these dependents *do* have a deterministic order determined by their semantics. Thus, we tend to overestimate true word order freedom.

On the other hand, the conditional entropy approach do not in principle *under*estimate word order freedom as we have defined it. The conditioning information present in a dependency tree represents only semantic and syntactic relations, and we are explicitly interested in word order variability beyond what can be explained by these factors. Therefore, our word order freedom measures constitute upper bounds on the true word order freedom in a language.

Underestimation can arise due to data sparsity issues and bias issues in entropy estimators. For this reason, it is important to ensure that our measures are stable with respect to sample size, lest our upper bound become a lower bound on an upper bound.

The tightness of the upper bound on word order freedom depends on the informativity of the relation types and parts of speech included in a measure. For example, if we use a system of relation types which subdivides *nmod* relations into categories like *nmod:tmod* for time phrases, then we would not overestimate the word order freedom of German verbal adjuncts. As another example, to achieve a tighter bound for a limited aspect of word order freedom at the cost of empirical coverage, we might restrict ourselves to relation types such as *nsubj* and *dobj*, which are highly informative about their meanings.

4 Applying the Measures

Here we give the results of applying some of the measures discussed in Section 3 to dependency corpora. We use the dependency corpora of the HamleDT 2.0 (Zeman et al., 2012; Rosa et al., 2014) and Universal Dependencies 1.0 (Nivre et al., 2015). All punctuation and dependencies with relation type *punct* are removed. We only examine sentences with a single root. Annotation was normalized to content-head format when necessary. Combined this gives us dependency corpora of 34 languages in a fairly standardized format.

In order to evaluate the stability of our measures with respect to sample size, we measure all en-

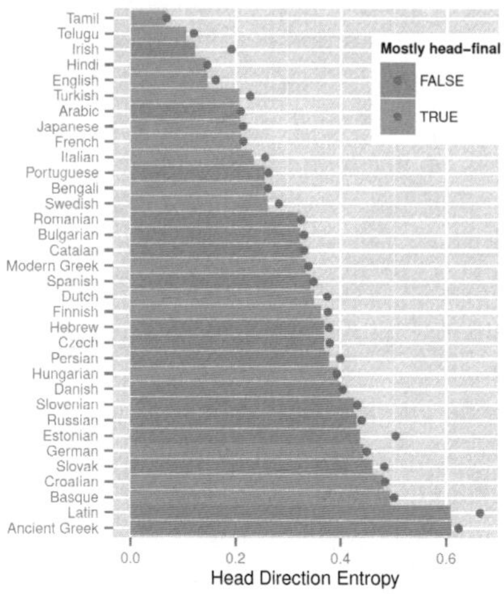

Figure 1: Head direction entropy in 34 languages. The bar represents the average magnitude of head direction entropy estimated from subcorpora of 1000 sentences; the red dot represents head direction entropy estimated from the whole corpus.

tropies using the bootstrap estimator of DeDeo et al. (2013). We report the mean results from applying our measures to subcorpora of 1000 sentences for each corpus. We also report results from applying measures to the full corpus, so that the difference between the full corpus and the subcorpora can be compared, and the effect of data sparsity evaluated.

4.1 Head Direction Entropy

Head direction entropy, defined and motivated in Section 3.3, is the conditional entropy of whether a head is to the right or left of a dependent, conditioned on relation type and part of speech of head and dependent. This measure can reflect either consistency in head direction conditioned on relation type, or consistency in head direction *overall*. Results from this measure are shown in Figure 1. As can be seen, the measure gives similar results when applied to subcorpora as when applied to full corpora, indicating that this is measure is not unduly affected by differences in sample size.

We find considerable variability in word order freedom with respect to head direction. In languages such as Korean, Telugu, Irish, and English, we find that head direction is nearly deterministic. On the other hand, in Slavic languages and in Latin and Ancient Greek we find great variability. The fact that entropy measures on subcorpora of 1000 sentences do not diverge greatly from entropy measures on full corpora indicates that this measure is stable with respect to sample size.

We find a potential relationship between predominant head direction and word order freedom in head direction. Figure 1 is coded according to whether languages have more than 50% head-final dependencies or not. The results suggest that languages which have highly predictable head direction might tend to be mostly head-final languages.

The results here also have bearing on appropriate generative models for grammar induction. Common generative models, such as DMV, use separate multinomial models for left and right dependents of a head. Our results suggest that for some languages there should be some sharing between these distributions.

4.2 Relation Order Entropy

Relation order entropy (Section 3.2) is the conditional entropy of the order of words in a local subtree, conditioned on the tree structure, relation types, and parts of speech. Figure 2 shows relation order entropy for our corpora. As can be seen, this measure is highly sensitive to sample size: for corpora with a medium sample size, such as English (16535 sentences), there is a moderate difference between the results from subcorpora and the results from the full corpus. For other languages with comparable size, such as Spanish (15906 sentences), there is a larger difference. In the case of languages with small corpora such as Bengali (1114 sentences), their true relation order entropy is almost certainly higher than measured.

While relation order entropy is the most easily interpretable and general measure of word order freedom, it does not seem to be workable given current corpora and methods. In further experiments, we found that removing POS tags from the conditioning variable does not reduce the instability of this measure.

4.3 Relation Order Entropy of Subjects and Objects

We can alleviate the data sparsity issues of relation order entropy by restricting our attention to a few relations of interest. For example, the position of subject and object in the main clause has long been of interest to typologists (Greenberg, 1963), (cf. (Dryer, 1992)). In Figure 3 we present relation order entropy of subject and object for local subtrees containing relations of type *nsubj* and *dobj* (*obj* in

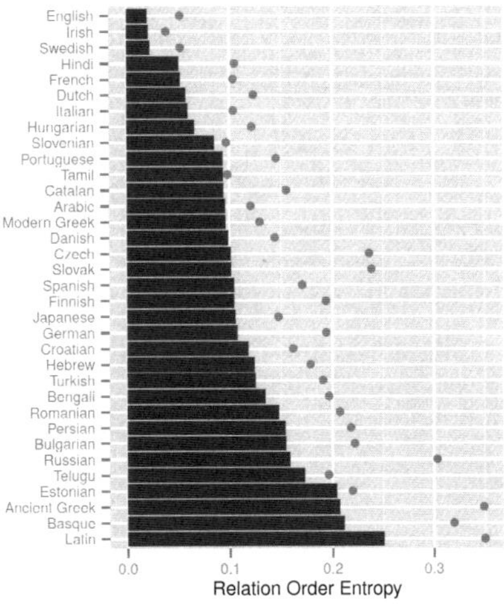

Figure 2: Relation order entropy in 34 languages. The bar represents the average magnitude of relation order entropy estimated from subcorpora of 1000 sentences; the red dot represents relation order entropy estimated from the whole corpus.

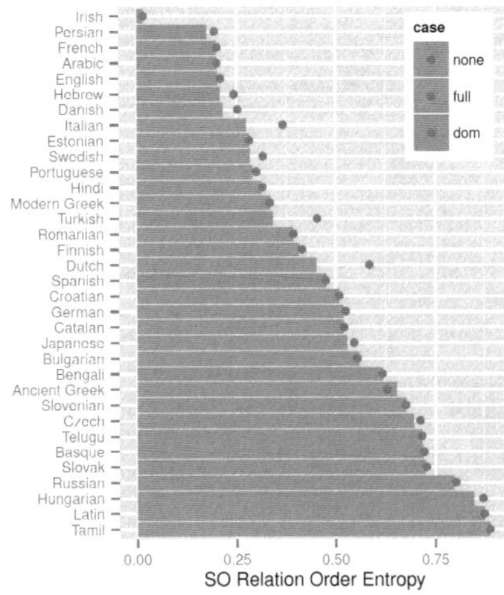

Figure 3: Relation order entropy for subject and object in 34 languages. Language names are annotated with corpus size in number of sentences. Bars are colored depending on the nominative-accusative case marking system type for each language. "Full" means fully present case marking in at least one paradigm. "dom" means Differential Object Marking.

the case of HamleDT corpora), conditioned on the parts of speech for these dependents.

The languages Figure 3 are colored according to their nominative-accusative[2] case marking on nouns. We consider a language to have full case marking if it makes a consistent morphological distinction between subject and object in at least one paradigm. If the distinction is only present conditional on animacy or definiteness, we mark the language as DOM for Differential Object Marking (Aissen, 2003).

The figure reveals a relationship between morphology and this particular aspect of word order freedom. Languages with relation order entropy above .625 all have relevant case marking, so it seems word order freedom in this domain implies the presence of case marking. However, case marking does not imply rigid word order; several languages in the sample have rigid word order while still having case marking. Our result is a quantitative sharpening of the pattern claimed in Kiparsky (1997).

Interestingly, many of the exceptional languages—those with case marking and rigid word order—are languages with verb-final or verb-initial orders. In our sample, Persian, Hindi, and Turkish are case-marking verb-final languages where we measure low levels of freedom in the order of subject and object. Modern Standard Arabic is (partly) verb-initial and case-marking (although case marking is rarely pronounced or explicitly written in modern Arabic). This finding is in line with recent work (Gibson et al., 2013; Futrell et al., 2015) which has suggested that verb-final and verb-initial orders without case marking do not allow robust communication in a noisy channel, and so should be dispreferred.

5 Conclusion

We have presented a set of interrelated methodological and linguistic issues that arise as part of quantifying word order freedom in dependency corpora. We have shown that conditional entropy measures can be used to get reliable estimates of variability in head direction and in ordering relations for certain restricted relation types. We have argued that such measures constitute upper bounds on word order freedom. Further, we have demonstrated a simple relationship between morphological case marking and word order freedom in the domain of subjects and objects, providing to our

[2]Or ergative-absolutive in the case of Basque and the Hindi past tense.

knowledge the first large-scale quantitative validation of the old intuition that languages with free word order must have case marking.

Acknowledgments

K.M. was supported by the Department of Defense through the National Defense Science & Engineering Graduate Fellowship program.

References

Steven Paul Abney. 1987. *The English noun phrase in its sentential aspect.* Ph.D. thesis, Massachusetts Institute of Technology.

Olga Abramov and Alexander Mehler. 2011. Automatic language classification by means of syntactic dependency networks. *Journal of Quantitative Linguistics*, 18(4):291–336.

Judith Aissen. 2003. Differential object marking: Iconicity vs. economy. *Natural Language & Linguistic Theory*, 21(3):435–483.

Franklin Chang. 2009. Learning to order words: A connectionist model of Heavy NP Shift and accessibility effects in Japanese and English. *Journal of Memory and Language*, 61:374–397.

Greville G Corbett. 2006. *Agreement.* Cambridge University Press.

Marie-Catherine de Marneffe, Timothy Dozat, Natalia Silveira, Katri Haverinen, Filip Ginter, Joakim Nivre, and Christopher D. Manning. 2014. Universal Stanford Dependencies: A cross-linguistic typology. In *Proceedings LREC'14*, Reykjavík, Iceland.

Simon DeDeo, Robert X. D. Hawkins, Sara Klingenstein, and Tim Hitchcock. 2013. Bootstrap methods for the empirical study of decision-making and information flows in social systems. *Entropy*, 15(6):2246–2276.

Matthew S Dryer. 1992. The Greenbergian word order correlations. *Language*, 68(1):81–138.

Victor S Ferreira and Hiromi Yoshita. 2003. Given-new ordering effects on the production of scrambled sentences in Japanese. *Journal of psycholinguistic research*, 32(6):669–692.

Richard Futrell, Tina Hickey, Aldrin Lee, Eunice Lim, Elena Luchkina, and Edward Gibson. 2015. Cross-linguistic gestures reflect typological universals: A subject-initial, verb-final bias in speakers of diverse languages. *Cognition*, 136:215–221.

Edward Gibson, Steven T Piantadosi, Kimberly Brink, Leon Bergen, Eunice Lim, and Rebecca Saxe. 2013. A noisy-channel account of crosslinguistic word-order variation. *Psychological science*, 24(7):1079–1088.

Joseph Greenberg. 1963. Some universals of grammar with particular reference to the order of meaningful elements. In Joseph Greenberg, editor, *Universals of Language*, pages 73–113. MIT Press, Cambridge, MA.

Paul Kiparsky. 1997. The rise of positional licensing. In Ans von Kemenade and Nigel Vincent, editors, *Parameters of morphosyntactic change*, pages 460–494. Cambridge University Press.

Dan Klein and Christopher D Manning. 2004. Corpus-based induction of syntactic structure: Models of dependency and constituency. In *Proceedings of the ACL*, page 478. Association for Computational Linguistics.

Marco Kuhlmann. 2013. Mildly non-projective dependency grammar. *Computational Linguistics*, 39(2):355–387.

Haitao Liu and Wenwen Li. 2010. Language clusters based on linguistic complex networks. *Chinese Science Bulletin*, 55(30):3458–3465.

Haitao Liu. 2010. Dependency direction as a means of word-order typology: A method based on dependency treebanks. *Lingua*, 120(6):1567–1578.

Thomas McFadden. 2003. On morphological case and word-order freedom. In *Proceedings of the Berkeley Linguistics Society*.

George Miller. 1955. Note on the bias of information estimates. In *Information Theory in Psychology: Problems and Methods*, pages 95–100.

Johanna Nichols. 1986. Head-marking and dependent-marking grammar. *Language*, 62.

Joakim Nivre *et al.* 2015. *Universal Dependencies 1.0.* Universal Dependencies Consortium.

Joakim Nivre. 2015. Towards a universal grammar for natural language processing. In *Computational Linguistics and Intelligent Text Processing*, pages 3–16. Springer.

Rudolf Rosa, Jan Mašek, David Mareček, Martin Popel, Daniel Zeman, and Zdeněk Žabokrtský. 2014. HamleDT 2.0: Thirty dependency treebanks Stanfordized. In *Proceedings LREC'14*, Reykjavik, Iceland.

E Sapir. 1921. *Language, an introduction to the study of speech.* Harcourt, Brace and Co., New York.

Daniel Zeman, David Marecek, Martin Popel, Loganathan Ramasamy, Jan Stepánek, Zdenek Zabokrtský, and Jan Hajič. 2012. HamleDT: To parse or not to parse? In *Proceedings LREC'12*, pages 2735–2741.

George Kingsley Zipf. 1949. *Human behavior and the principle of least effort.* Addison-Wesley Press, Oxford, UK.

Non-constituent coordination and other coordinative constructions as Dependency Graphs

Kim Gerdes
Sorbonne Nouvelle
ILPGA, LPP (CNRS)
kim@gerdes.fr

Sylvain Kahane
Université Paris Ouest Nanterre
Modyco (CNRS)
sylvain@kahane.fr

Abstract

This paper proposes a new dependency-based analysis of coordination that generalizes over existing analyses by combining symmetrical and asymmetrical analyses of coordination into a DAG structure. The new joint structure is shown to be theoretically grounded in the notion of connections between words just as the formal definition of other types of dependencies. Beside formalizations of shared dependents (including right-node raising), paradigmatic adverbs, and embedded coordinations, a completely new formalization of non-constituent coordination is proposed.

1 Introduction

Coordination is a special case of paradigmatic phenomena which extend to reformulation and disfluency. A *paradigmatic phenomenon* occurs when a segment Y of an utterance fills the same syntactic position as X.[1] For example in (1) to (3), *apply to* offers a position that has been conjointly taken by several nouns, called the *conjuncts*.

(1) A similar technique is almost impossible to apply to **cotton**, **soybeans** and **rice**.
(2) A similar technique is almost impossible to apply to **cotton**, uh **high quality cotton**.
(3) A similar technique is almost impossible to apply to **cotton**, (or) maybe **linen**.

Sentence (1) is an example of a coordination, (2) of a reformulation, (3) is an intermediate case on the continuum between the two as shown in Blanche-Benveniste et al. (1984). We consider that a formalization of coordination must be extensible to other paradigmatic phenomena in particular to cases where two elements occupy the same syntactic position without being connected by subordinating conjunctions (Gerdes & Kahane 2009). The conjuncts of such paradigmatic structures form the layers of a *paradigmatic pile* whose dependency structure will be laid out in this article.

This article proposes and justifies a new, comparably complex, dependency analysis of coordination and other paradigmatic phenomena that goes beyond the commonly assumed tree structure of dependency. We are concerned with the formal and linguistic well-foundedness of the syntactic analysis and each node and each link of the syntactic structure should be motivated exclusively and falsifiably by syntactic criteria. The goal is not to provide a minimal and computationally simple structure that simply expresses the necessary semantic distinctions. We believe that theoretical coherence of the analysis is always an advantage, including for machine learning.

In section 2, we recap the difficulties of representing coordination in dependency and other frameworks. Section 3 exposes the notions and criteria at the basis of our new analysis. Section 4 is dedicated to simple coordinations, Section 5 to shared dependents (including right-node raising), Section 6 to non-constituent coordination. We then turn to paradigmatic adverbs in Section 7 and embedded coordination in 8. Before concluding we show cases of coordinations that are not paradigmatic phenomena in Section 9.

2 Coordination and dependency

It is a well known fact that function, rather than constituent type are relevant for coordinative constraints.[2] We will provide further evidence for

[1] The term *paradigmatic* is commonly used to denote a set of elements that are of the same paradigm because they can replace one another. We prefer this term to *paratactic* used by Popel et al. (2013) following Tesnière 1959 chap. 133 who opposes *hypotaxis* (= *subordination* in modern terms) and *parataxis* (= *coordination*) because today *paratactic* commonly refers to cases of coordination without conjunction (= *juxtaposition*).

[2] *He is an architect and proud of it* is explained by the shared predicate dependency rather than the

Proceedings of the Third International Conference on Dependency Linguistics (Depling 2015), pages 101–110, Uppsala, Sweden, August 24–26 2015.

the adequateness of dependency rather than phrase structure for the description of coordination.

Nevertheless, dependency grammars (just as other syntactic theories, including categorial and phrase structure) are "head-driven" in the sense that syntax is mainly considered as the analysis of government.[3] However, paradigmatic phenomena are by definition orthogonal to government structures and their integration into dependency structures is up for debate because commonly, dependencies express head-daughter relations.

Existing dependency annotation schemes differ widely on the analysis of paradigmatic phenomena, thus reflecting important underlying syntactic choices, which often remain implicit. Ivanova et al. (2012), while comparing different dependency schemes, note that "the analysis of coordination represents a well-known area of differences" and even on a simple example like *cotton, soybeans and rice*, "none of the formats agree."

The high frequency of paradigmatic phenomena also implies that the choice of their syntactic analysis has important ramifications on the structure as a whole: Dependency distance and government-dependent relations both vary significantly with the type of representation given to paradigmatic phenomena, see Popel et al. (2013) for measures on the impact of the choices for coordination.

Syntactic analyses of coordination can generally be divided into two families of symmetrical and asymmetrical analyses (and mixed forms can be placed on a scale between these two families). *Symmetrical analyses* aim to give equal status to each conjunct. *Asymmetrical analyses* on the contrary give a special status to one, commonly the first, of the conjuncts, and iteratively place the other conjuncts below the special one.

A symmetrical analysis (Tesnière 1959, Jackendoff 1977, Hajič et al. 1999:222) constitutes a higher abstraction from the surface because the tree structure is independent of linear order of the conjuncts. However, placing the conjuncts on an equal level poses the problem of choice of the governor among the different participants in the coordination.[4]

Some work on coordination in dependency grammar, while showing the usefulness of dependency trees for the expression of the constraints, never actually propose a dependency structure for the coordination itself (Hudson 1988, Osborne 2006, 2008). Some even argue against any kind of dependency analysis of coordination on the basis that it is a different phenomenon altogether: "The only alternative to dependency analysis which is worth considering is one in terms of constituent structure, in which the conjuncts and the conjunction are PARTS of the whole coordinate structure." (Hudson 1988)

An asymmetrical analysis, in its Mel'čukian variant (Mel'čuk 1988, used in CoNLL 2008, Surdeanu et al. 2008) and in its Stanfordian variant (de Marneffe & Manning 2008), on the contrary, represents better the surface configuration: The coordinating conjunction usually forms a syntactic unit (cf. Section 3) with the following phrase (*and rice* in the above example) and only an asymmetrical analysis contains this segment as a subtree.

X-bar type phrase structures just as dependency annotations that only allow trees, therefore excluding multiple governors for the same node, have to make a choice between a symmetrical and an asymmetrical analysis. Some annotation schemes, however, do not want to make this choice. The notion of "weak head", introduced

common constituent type of *an architect* and *proud of it*.

3 We call *government* the property of words to impose constraints on other words, which can be constraints on their nature (e.g. their part of speech), their morphological and syntactic markers, or their topological (linear) position. For example, in English, a verb imposes on its direct object to be a noun phrase (or, if verbal, to be transferred into the infinitive form, Tesnière 1959), to carry the oblique case in case of pronouns, and to take a position behind the verb. A word, called *governor*, offers a syntactic position for each series of constraints it can impose on other words.

4 Under the condition that the resulting structure has to be a dependency tree, the coordinative conjunction is the only possible choice of governor. Some treebanks (Hajič et al. 1999) then go as far as using punctuation like commas as tokens that head a conjunction-less paradigmatic structure. We consider that punctuation plays a role in transcribing prosodic breaks, but certainly does not correspond to a syntactic unit and is therefore not part of the syntactic structure.

If the tree structure condition is relaxed the result can combine the conjuncts as co-heads (Tesnière 1959, Kahane 1997).

by Tseng 2002 and put forward by Abeillé 2003, to designate coordinating conjunctions, for example *and*, implies selective feature sharing between the other conjuncts and e.g. *and* as well as *rice*. Recent work by Chomsky (2013) equally assumes "that although C [the conjunction] is not a possible label [of the resulting coordinated structure], it must still be visible for determining the structure." A result, of course, is a more general "weakening" of the notion of "head" as a whole, while dodging the underlying central question about the limits of head-driven syntax.

3 Criteria for syntactic structures

In order to justify our choices of representation, it is necessary to recall the basic objectives of any syntactic structure.

Firstly, syntactic structures indicate how different words of the sentence combine. Government is one mode of combination, but not the only one – dependencies do not always correspond to government. In the case of a pile, an element Y takes the same position as an element X that precedes. Even if the two conjuncts X and Y are in a paradigmatic relation (they can commute and each conjunct alone can occupy the position), they are in a syntagmatric relation: they combine into a new unit, which must be encoded by a dependency.

Secondly, the syntactic representation is intermediate between meaning and sound. The syntactic representation thus has to allow us to compute on one hand, the semantic representation including the predicate-argument relations between lexical meanings, and on the other hand, the topological constituents observed on the surface (Gerdes & Kahane 2001).

Thirdly, the representation constrains the possible combinations of the words: A certain number of combinations are eliminated by the impossibility to associate them with a phonological or semantic representation , but equally the impossibility to associate a syntactic structure to an utterance constitutes a strong filter on the allowed combinations (from a generative point of view, this is even the primary filter). Consequently, a good syntactic representation has to be sufficiently constrained so that most badly formed utterances cannot obtain a syntactic representation (while, of course, all well-formed utterances have to obtain a syntactic representation). Recall that we propose a performance grammar and from our point of view, disfluent utterances (such as (2)) are considered well-formed. Our syntactic representation is also designed for the extraction of a grammar that holds constraints on each type of dependencies: Constraints on the orientation of the dependency (head-initial or head-final), constraints on the POS of the governor and of the dependent including sub-categorization constraints attached to the governor of the dependency relation (e.g. the constraint that a dependent object can only depend on a transitive verb). This set of constraints has to allow telling ungrammatical from well-formed utterances.

We will adopt the following principles. We consider that any part of a sentence that can stand alone with the same meaning is a *syntactic unit*. As soon as a syntactic unit can be fragmented into two units X and Y, we consider that there is a *syntactic connection* between X and Y (Gerdes & Kahane 2011). *Syntactic dependencies* are oriented connections linking a *head* with its *dependent*. The notation X → Y means that Y depends on X. Note that we distinguish the terms *head* and *governor*: if Y depends on X, then X is the governor of Y and X is the head of the unit XY. So the head of a unit U belongs to U, while the governor of U is an element outside U and connected with U.

4 Syntactic structure of coordination

In a coordination like *onions and rice*, the segment *and rice* forms a syntactic unit, because it can stand alone:

(4) I want onions. And rice.
(5) Spk1: I want onions. Spk2: And rice?

This data implies that *and* and *rice* are connected by a dependency. We can contrast this with *onions and*, which cannot stand alone. In other words, coordination is syntactically asymmetrical.

The choice of the head of the phrase *and rice* is not trivial. For instance Mazziota (2011) argues that in Old French the junctor[5] is optional,

[5] Junctor is a more general term than "coordinating conjunction", introduced by Blanche-Benveniste et al. (1990) and Ndiaye (1989), as a variant of the term "jonctif" used by Tesnière (1959). Cf. also the term "pile marker" used by Gerdes & Kahane (2009). We prefer to avoid the term *coordinating conjunction* because junctors can also appear in paradigmatic piles other than coordination, like Fr. *c'est-à-dire* 'that is'.

which is a good argument in favor of *and* as a dependent of the conjunct. Equally, the Stanford Dependency scheme (SD, de Marneffe & Manning 2008) and subsequently the Universal Dependency Treebank (McDonald et al. 2013) describe junctors as adjuncts. Nevertheless, generally, a phrase like *and rice* does not have the same distribution as *rice*, which is sufficient to consider that *and* controls the distribution of the phrase and is a head. But the distribution of the phrase depends also on the conjunct: *and rice* can combine with a noun (*onions and rice*) but it cannot combine with a verb (**Peter eats and rice*). This means that both elements bear head features (see the notion of *weak head* in section 2). In a dependency-based analysis this means that both elements should be linked to the governor of the phrase, which is not possible in a standard dependency analysis using a tree structure.

We will slightly relax the tree constraints and consider two kinds of dependencies: *pure* (or primary) *dependencies* and *secondary dependencies*. We adopt the following principles:

- Principle 1: There is exactly one pure dependency between two units that combine.
- Principle 2: As soon as X combines with Y and a subset A of Y controls the combination of X and Y, there is a dependency between X and A.

In consequence, if Y = AB and both A and B control the combination of X and Y, there will be either a pure dependency between X and A and a secondary dependency between X and B or the reverse. As A and B are also connected, the structure is no longer necessarily a tree but a DAG.

We apply our principles with X = *onions*, A = *and*, and B = *rice*. As the junctor *and* can be absent (*onions, rice, beans ...; onions, maybe rice*), we consider that B is the main head of AB and postulate a pure dependency between the two conjuncts, that we call a *paradigmatic link*. This link is doubled by a secondary link between *onions* and *and*, which is the secondary head of *and rice*. The secondary status of this link is also justified by the fact that *onions and* is not a syntactic unit. We call such a link a *bequeather*.

As *and* and *rice* are co-heads of *and rice*, we do not have clear arguments to decide which one governs the other. As soon as we suppress one of the two dependencies between *onions* and *and rice* and favor one of the two co-heads, the link is automatically oriented and we either obtain the Mel'čukian analysis (*onions* → *and* → *rice*) or Mazziotta's analysis (*onions* → *rice* → *and*). As *rice* is the semantic argument of *and* and an obligatory complement of *and*, we decide to treat *rice* as the dependent of *and*.

Let us now consider the combination between the pile and its governor:

(6) I want onions and rice.

We remark that both conjuncts can form a unit with *want*, the governor of the pile (*I want onions*; *I want rice*). This allows us to postulate that both conjuncts have head features which licenses a connection with the governor. We consider that the first conjunct opens the potential connection with the governor and is the main head. Consequently, *onions* receives a pure (object) dependency from *want*, while *rice* receives a secondary dependency, which we call an *inherited dependency* (Fig. 1).

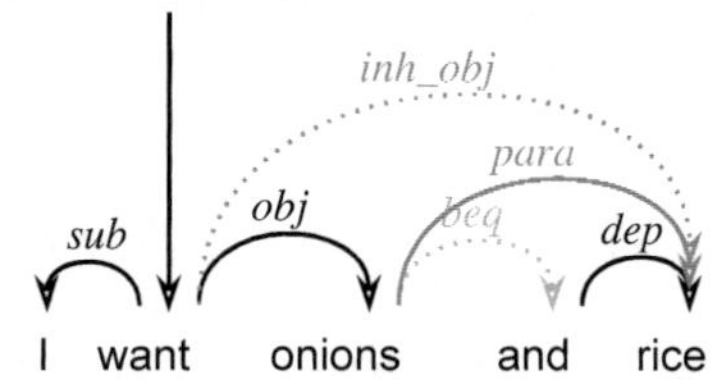

Figure 1: Analysis of a simple coordination

Secondary dependencies, represented by dotted arrows, double pure dependencies, but while a bequeather link anticipates a pure dependency, an inherited link is inherited from a pure dependency (Fig. 2).

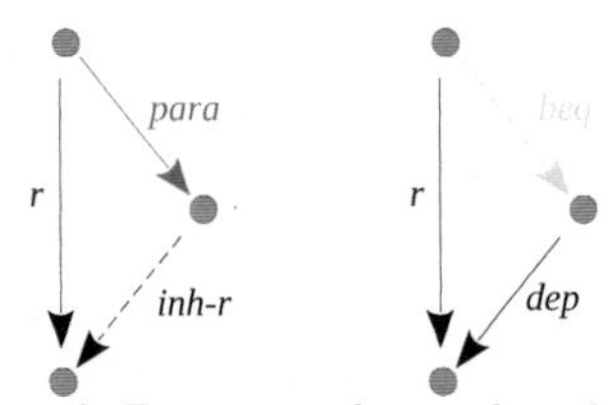

Figure 2: Two types of secondary dependencies

5 Shared dependent (including Right Node Raising)

A pile can have syntactic dependents shared by several conjuncts. In (7), *Peter* and *houses* are shared by the conjuncts *buys* and *sells* (Fig. 3).

(7) Peter buys and sells houses.

In dependency grammar, the subject and the object are encoded in a completely symmetrical way. For Generative Grammarians, the stipulation of a VP makes the case of *houses* particularly complicated, a configuration which is known as "Right Node Raising" (Postal 1974).[6]

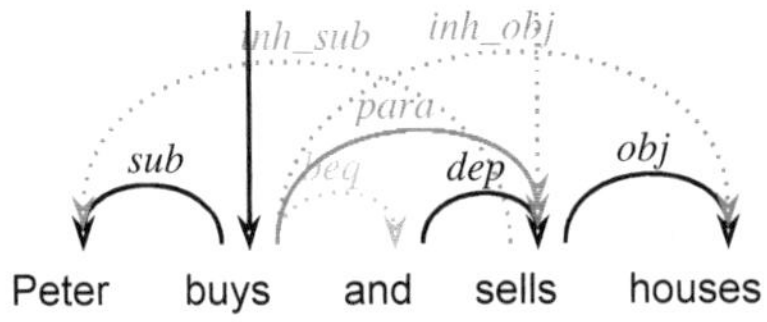

Figure 3: Shared dependents

Sharing cannot be easily modeled by a dependency tree.[7] Mel'cuk (2015:vol. 3, 493) considers different solutions for distinguishing individual from shared dependents and settles finally for "groupings" where the nodes involved in the conjunction are grouped together excluding the shared dependent: old←[men→and→women]. Tesnière (1959: ch. 143-145) analyzes sharing by multiple heads, as we propose: A dependent shared by several conjuncts is governed by each of them. We modify this analysis by considering that only one of these dependencies is a pure dependency. We consider that the shared dependent is above all the dependent of the nearest conjunct, because they can form a prosodic unit together. The dependency between a conjunct and a shared dependent is inherited by the other conjuncts and we annotate that by an inherited dependency, which allows us to disambiguate cases like (8). In both cases, *old* is a dependent of *men*,

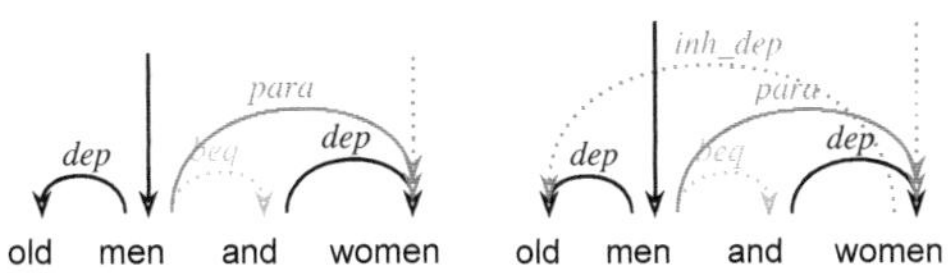

Figure 4: Optionally shared dependent

but the relation is optionally inherited by *women* (Fig. 4).

(8) old men and women

This encoding, following the asymmetrical analysis of coordination, allows us to compute the desired syntactic and prosodic units. Each word that is governed both by a pure dependency and an inherited dependency is a shared dependent. Each conjunct is the projection of the word linked by the paradigmatic links with the exclusion of shared dependents and the pile is the projection of the first conjunct without the shared dependents. We thus obtain the units:

a. ((old men) and (women))
b. old ((men) and (women))

No satisfying phrase structure representation exists for piles where the shared dependent does not modify the head of each conjunct, as for example in (9):

(9) Congratulations to Miss Fisher and to Miss Howell who are both marrying their fiancés this summer. (*www.st-peters.kent.sch.uk*)

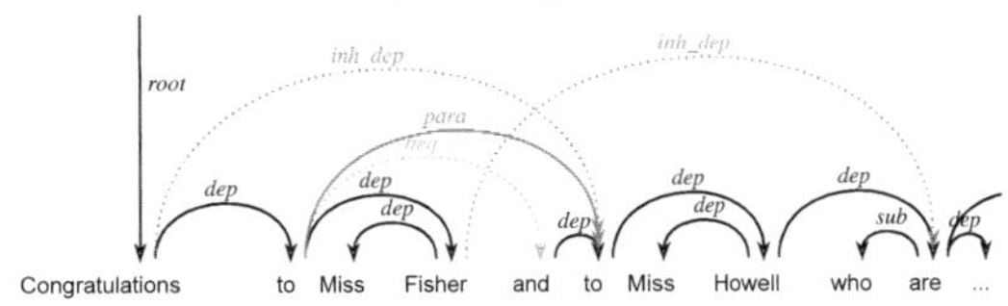

Figure 5: Shared dependent of a non-head

Here, the PPs *to Miss Fisher* and *to Miss Howell* are coordinated but only the NPs *Miss Fisher* and *Miss Howell* are modified by the relative phrase. The analysis of this example is unproblematic in our annotation scheme.

Following our principles, we have only one pure dependency between *to Miss Fisher* and *to Miss Howell*, which is a paradigmatic link between the heads of the two PPs, that is, the two *to*. We introduce a *lateral paradigmatic link*, which is a secondary dependency, between *Fisher* and *Howell*, because they share a dependent (the relative clause).[8] This link is justified for two reasons: First, we think that the piling of

[6] In English, there is nevertheless an asymmetry since the left sharing (***Peter*** *buys buildings and sells apartments*) is better than simultaneous right and left sharing (as in (7)) which again is easier than only right sharing (?*Peter sells and Mary buys* ***houses***) These preferences can be taken into account without postulating a VP, by penalizing right sharing without left sharing.

[7] Sharing can be represented in a symmetrical analysis (Hajič et al. 1999) by placing the shared dependent as a dependent of the junctor, which itself is the head of the conjuncts. Not only do we reject the symmetric analysis and the junctor as the head (in particular because a paradigmatic pile does not need a junctor), but also a link between the junctor and the shared dependent violates our principles, since these two elements do not combine to form a syntactic unit.

[8] Lateral dependencies are a third case of secondary dependencies. While an inherited dependency doubles a pure dependency with the same governor and a bequeather, a pure dependency with the same dependent, a lateral dependency doubles a pure dependency more or less parallelly. It only occurs if at least one of the elements sharing a common dependent is a non-trivial nucleus (i.e. it has more than one node).

two units is supported by parallelism and that the elements of a pile tend to forge secondary lateral links. Second, the lateral link allows us to separately state the following constraints (Fig. 6):

- Constraint 1: Governors of a shared dependent must be linked by a (eventually lateral) paradigmatic link.
- Constraint 2: Each lateral paradigmatic link has a corresponding plain paradigmatic link, and the chains from the plain to the lateral paradigmatic link form nuclei.

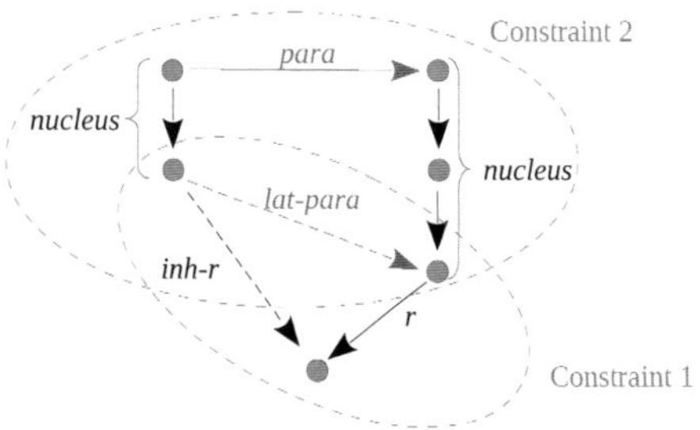

Figure 6: Configuration of shared dependents

Nuclei have been introduced in Kahane (1997, see also Osborne 2008 who calls them predicate chains). A *verbal nucleus* is a chain of words that behaves like a single verb in some constructions, such as extraction or coordination. A link in a verbal nucleus can be a complex verbal form (*is talking*), but also V-Vinf (*can talk*), V-*to*-Vinf (*want to talk*), V-Adj (*is easy*), V-N, especially in light verb constructions (*have the right*), and even V-*that*-V (*think that X talks*). A governed preposition can also form a nucleus with its governor in languages allowing preposition stranding like English (*talk to*, but not *parler à* in French, see footnote 12). A *nominal nucleus* is a chain of nouns and prepositions. A link in a nominal nucleus can be Prep-N (*to Miss Fisher*) or N-Prep-N (*the end of the movie*).

In example (10) (Osborne 2006), *admire* is conjunct of the nucleus *think* → *that* → *distrust* and the lateral paradigmatic link between *admire* and *distrusts* validates the sharing of the object *this politician*.

(10) [Some people admire], but [I think that many more people distrust] this politician

Constraint 2 excludes cases where the "path" between the head of a conjunct and a shared dependent is not a nucleus like in ???*Peter (plays on and knows the guy who owns) this piano* (*knows* → *guy* → *who* → *owns* is not a nucleus).[9]

6 Non-constituent coordination

Non-constituent coordination (NCC) can be illustrated by:

(11) Peter went to *Paris yesterday* and *London today*.

This construction is problematic for constituency-based formalisms, as well as dependency-based ones, because there is only one coordination with a unique junctor (*and*) involving two phrases with two different syntactic functions, *Paris* and *yesterday*. But while it is questionable to consider that *Paris* and *yesterday* form a syntactic unit together, it is difficult not to consider that *London* and *today* form one, because the latter words can stand alone (with the junctor):

(12) Peter went to Paris yesterday. And London today.

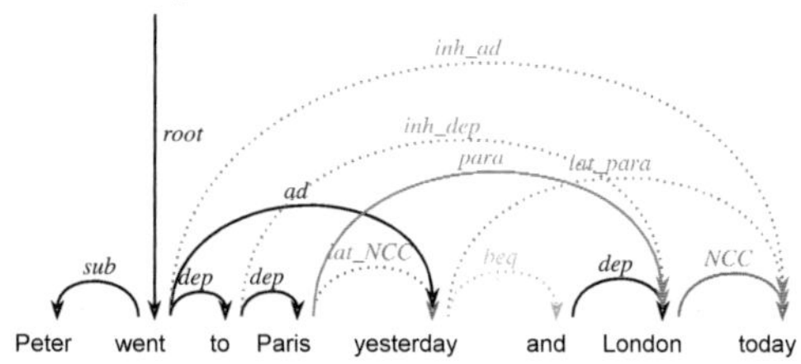

Figure 7: Non-constituent coordination

We thus consider that there is a pure dependency between *London* and *today* we call a NCC dependency. The two elements linked by a NCC dependency pile on two independent elements, here *Paris* and *yesterday*, which supposes that we have two lateral piles (Gerdes and Kahane 2009). But following our principles, we postulate only one pure dependency between *went to Paris yesterday* and *London today*, which means that we have a standard paradigmatic link between *Paris* and *London* and a lateral paradigmatic link between *yesterday* and *today*. The junctor is analyzed as a marker of the main paradigmatic link, which give us the structure of Fig. 7.

[9] RNR is rather common in reformulations, which are also paradigmatic piles. In (i) *is* is reformulated in *may appear*, which is a nucleus:
(i) { what I'm saying here is | what I'm saying here may appear } very pessimistic (translation from the Rhapsodie treebank)
We analyze (i) with a main paradigmatic link between *is* and *may* and a lateral paradigmatic link between *is* and *appear*.

We also introduce a lateral NCC dependency between *Paris* and *yesterday*. This secondary link is justified 1) by the fact that *Paris yesterday* tend to receive a prosodic shape similar to *London today*, which are linked by a NCC dependency,[10] and 2) because it allows us to express the constraints on the introduction of a NCC dependency in two steps (Fig. 8):

- Constraint 1: A NCC dependency between X' and Y' is only possible if there is a configuration with X –para→X', Y –lat-para→Y', and X –lat-NCC→X'.
- Constraint 2: X and Y can be linked by a lat-NCC dependency only if they depend on the same nucleus.[11]

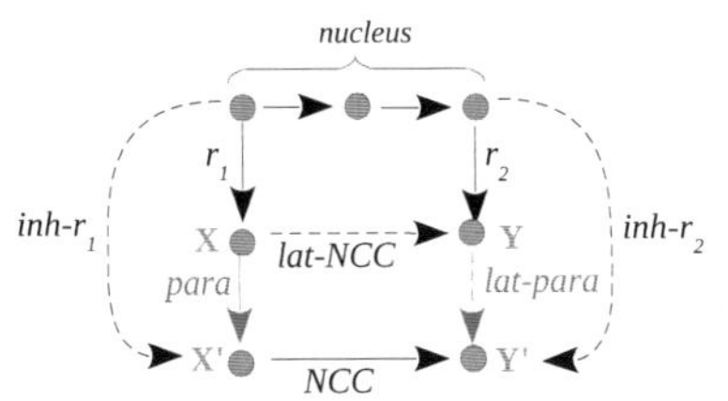

Figure 8: Configuration of NCC: X X' and Y Y' e.g. giving X to Y and X' to Y'

Constraint 2 is verified in our example, because *went to* is a verbal nucleus.[12] The following examples from Sailor and Thoms (2013) confirm that the governor must be a nucleus :

(13) a. I claimed that I was a spy to impress John and an astronaut to impress Bill
b. * I taught the guy that knows Icelandic how to dance and Faroese how to sing.
c. The witness will testify to whether John knew Icelandic tomorrow and whether he knew Faroese next week.
d. * The witness will testify to whether John knew Icelandic tomorrow and he knew Faroese next week.

In a, the governor is the nucleus *claimed → that → was*, and in b, the nucleus *will → testify → to → whether → knew*. Conversely, *taught → guy → that → knows* in b is not a nucleus due to the link *guy → that*, nor *will → testify → to → whether* in d, because a complementizer like *whether* can only be part of a nucleus with the verb it complementizes (as in c).

In the same vein, the case of gapping as in (14) can be described as a special case of NCC with two lateral piles (*Peter → Mary* and *firemen → police*) and a NCC dependency between *Mary* and *police*.

(14) Peter wants us to call the firemen and Mary the police.

The constraints are similar and (14) is possible because *Peter* and *firemen* depends on the same verbal nucleus *wants → to → call*. We see on this example that some elements of the nucleus can have dependents that are not involved in the piling (here *us*).[13] The same property holds with the object *a book* in the next example:
(15) Peter gave a book to John and Mary to Ann.

7 Junctors and paradigmatic adverbs

Next to the conjuncts, a pile can contain two kinds of elements we want to distinguish:

- *Junctors* are the elements that connect the conjuncts of a pile. Junctors have a role only inside the pile, i.e. if we only conserve one layer of a pile, junctors cannot be maintained:

(16) All I can remember is black beans, onions, **and maybe rice**. (source: web)
(17) *All I can remember is **and** rice.

- *Paradigmatic adverbs* (Nølke 1983, Masini & Pietrandrea 2010), on the contrary, can be maintained:

(18) All I can remember is **maybe** rice.

---

10 The placement of double junctors like *either ... or* shows that the coordination is indeed between the "non-constituents" (Sag et al. 1985):
(i) Il donnera soit le disque à Susanne, soit le livre à Marie 'He will give either the disk to Susanne or the book to Mary'

11 Bruening (2015) postulates that the governor of the two lateral piles (here *went to*) is a prosodic unit. We agree but go further, considering that such a segment is actually a syntactic unit, even if it is not a constituent. Kahane (1997) proposed to explicitly introduce this unit, the nucleus, in the syntactic structure by way of bubbles.

12 Note that the same construction is not possible in French, which does not accept preposition stranding:
(i) a. Pierre était à Paris hier et à Londres aujourd'hui.
b. ??Pierre était à Paris hier et Londres aujourd'hui.

13 As opposed to that, conjuncts involved in NCC cannot share a dependent, see Osborne (2006):
(i) * Susan repairs old [bicycles in winter] and [cars in summer]

Traditionally, in a sentence like (18), the adverb *maybe* is analyzed, as any common adverb, as a modifier of the verb (is → maybe), but in (16) the layer *and maybe rice* clearly forms a phrase (it can be uttered alone for instance). In fact we think that *maybe rice* forms a phrase even in (18). Paradigmatic adverbs clearly have scope over one particular element of the sentence:

(19) a. Peter will maybe give the book to Mary (unless he will only lend it)
b. Peter will give maybe the book to Mary (or maybe something else)
c. Peter will give the book maybe to Mary (or maybe to another person)

In a sentence like c, *maybe to Mary* forms a semantic and a prosodic unit, which suggest a link between the adverb and the following phrase.[14] We stipulate that such adverbs always take a phrase as argument, even if no overt second conjunct is present. Thus, the types of syntactic relations of *maybe* in (16), (18), and (19) are identical and very different from *quickly* in (20).

(20) Peter will quickly give the book to Mary.

We conclude that *maybe* and *rice* are connected in (16) and (18). Moreover, they both have head features: If the distribution of *maybe rice* is similar to the distribution of *rice*, it is nevertheless restricted by *maybe* (for instance *maybe rice* cannot be the complement of a preposition: **She spoke about maybe rice*). As for the junctor, we decide that *rice* is the dependent of *maybe* and that the dependency from the governor of *maybe rice* (here *and*) is attributed to *rice* and doubled by a bequeather link to *maybe*.

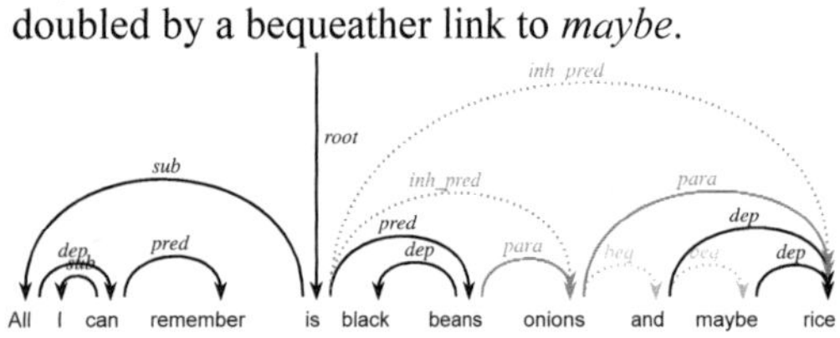

Figure 9: Paradigmatic adverbs

Even if junctors and paradigmatic adverbs have a similar representation, they restrict the distribution of their argument in a different way, which can be easily encoded by different constraints on a bequeather link governing one or the other.

[14] In a V2 language like German, *vielleicht der Maria* 'maybe to Mary' can go to the initial position, which identifies the combination of *vielleicht* and *der Maria* as a constituent.

8 Embedded Piles

It is well known that a tree-based asymmetrical dependency analysis of coordination cannot catch nested coordinations (cf. note 7). Consider a classical example like :

(21) We are looking for someone who speaks French and German or Italian.

Two interpretations are possible :

a. { French | and { German | or Italian } }
b. { { French | and German } | or Italian }

In our analysis, in both cases we have the third layer (*or Italian*) attached to the second layer (*and German*) : French → and → German → or → Italian.[15] But in case a, *Italian* inherits a dependency from *and* because it is coordinated with the dependent *German* of *and*, while in case b, *or Italian* is a shared dependent and *or* inherits a dependency from *French*, which is coordinated with *German*.

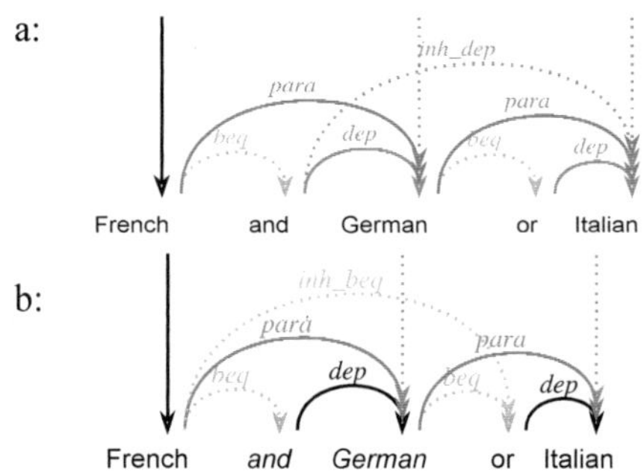

Figure 10: Embedded piles

Fig. 11 gives the two interpretations of (22) with their corresponding syntactic structures. At the semantic level, the junctor is the head of a coordination and takes the conjuncts as arguments (Mel'čuk 2015: vol. 1, 237). In the case of embedding, one junctor will be the argument of the other. We can see how the semantic dependency between the two junctors is distributed on the conjuncts at the syntactic level.

[15] Mel'čuk (1988) proposes, in case b, to attach *or Italian* to the head of the group *French and German*, that is to *French*. We disagree with this analysis because *or Italian* is a shared dependent of both *French* and *German*, and as usual it must be attached to the last conjunct it modifies, that is *German*. In any case, in the tree Mel'čuk obtains, *French* has two dependents : *German ← and ← French → or → Italian*. This tree is semantically ambiguous and correspond also to (*French or Italian*) *and German*, which is not at all equivalent to the b interpretation of our example.

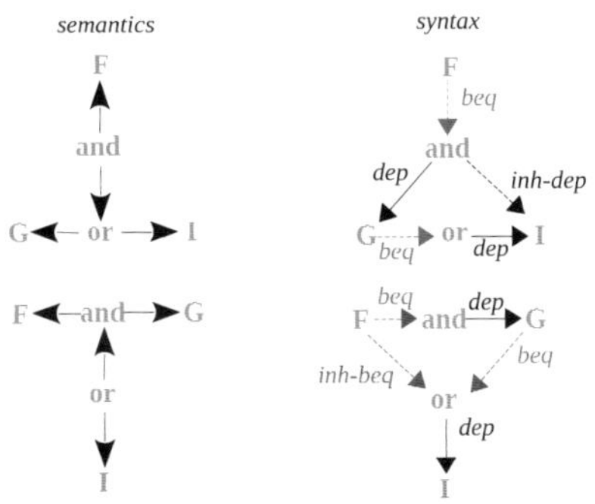

Figure 11: Semantics and syntax of embedded piles

9 Coordination without pile

Coordination is not always a paradigmatic phenomena piling two elements of the same kind.[16]

(22) Mary speaks English and well.

In cases like this, the second conjunct (*well*) does not hold the same syntactic position as the first conjunct (*Marys speaks English*). We consider that we have here a coordination between illocutionary units. In fact, the speaker makes two assertions in (22) (*Mary speaks English* and *She does it well*) in one dependency structure consisting of two illocutionary units. We model these coordinations without the use of ellipsis, only by distinguishing dependency structure spans and illocutionary units (Kahane et al. 2013). The junctor in (22) is analyzed as usual with a bequeather and a pure dependency between the junctor and the conjuncts (*speaks* → *and* → *well*). Yet, we do not consider this construction to be a pile and we analyze this sentence without paradigmatic or inherited links.

10 Conclusion

We have proposed a dependency grammar formalization of several cases of coordination, arguing for multiple governors, and thus a DAG structure. Two types of links are considered, primary and secondary links. The primary links induce a tree structure.[17] Three types of secondary links are considered: inherited, bequeather, and lateral dependencies, each of them corresponding to a different arrangement of primary links.

Following Gerdes & Kahane (2009), we argue for a paradigmatic link, which is present in all paradigmatic phenomena, involving junctors or not, ranging from simple coordination, over juxtapositions, to phenomena that are more typical for spoken language like disfluency and reformulation. Conversely, we have shown that junctors can be involved in non-paradagmatic phenomea (section 9).

We have proposed a completely new formalization of NCC. We consider that, although NCC involves two parallel paradigmatic piles filling two different syntactic positions, the second layer forms a syntactic unit. Such a unit can only be formed by the second layer of a coordination and cannot appear outside of a paradigmatic construction.[18]

We have also proposed a formalization of paradigmatic adverbs, a frequent sight in paradigmatic phenomena but rarely considered in the studies on coordination.

However, from a theoretical and practical point of view, it is important to note that we have a structure that is much more complex than a simple dependency tree. It remains to be shown that such a complex annotation scheme can be machine-learned and thus automatized. We think that doubling some links as we do allows distributing and relocalizing the constraints on smaller configurations, which could improve the model. Orféo, the ongoing follow-up project of Rhapsodie started in 2013, will have to answer that question as the new project attempts to realize these annotations on large amounts of spoken and written data.

Acknowledgements

We thank the Depling reviewers for their critical and thorough review. Nicolas Mazziotta and Tim Osborne provided valuable insight on early versions of this paper.

---

[16] In the Rhapsodie treebank (Kahane et al. 2013), a 33,000 word dependency treebank of spoken French we have a dozen of such examples such as: (i) on veut bien parler avec vous mais après le déménagement 'we are willing to talk with you but after the moving'

[17] More precisely primary dependencies governed by a bequeather link must be inverted to obtain a tree.

[18] This includes so-called partial utterances:
(i) Spk1: I go to Paris on Monday.
Spk2: And London when?
We consider that the second speech turn is governed by the first one and we have here a typical NCC. The only specificity of this NCC is to be distributed on two illocutionary units. Such a description implies that we do not have to consider the second speech turn as an elliptic utterance. It is simply an utterance that pursues the syntactic construction of the previous utterance. Such continuations are very common in our corpus of spoken French.

References

Abeillé A. (2003) A lexicon- and construction-based approach to coordination, *Proc. of the 9th International HPSG Conference*, CSLI Publication, Stanford, CA, pp. 5-25.

Blanche-Benveniste Cl., Deulofeu J., Stefanini J., van den Eynde K. (1984). *Pronom et syntaxe. L'approche pronominale et son application au français*, Paris : SELAF.

Bruening B. (2015) Non-Constituent Coordination: Prosody, Not Movement, *U. Penn Working Papers in Linguistics*, 21:1.

Chomsky N. (2013) Problems of projection. *Lingua* 130, 33-49.

de Marneffe M.-C., Manning D. (2008). Stanford typed dependencies manual. Technical report, Stanford University.

Gerdes, K., Kahane, S. (2001). Word order in German: A formal dependency grammar using a topological hierarchy. *Proceedings of ACL*.

Gerdes K., Kahane S. (2009). Speaking In Piles: Paradigmatic Annotation Of French Spoken Corpus. *Proceedings of the Fifth Corpus Linguistics Conference*, Liverpool.

Gerdes K., Kahane S. (2011). Defining dependencies (and constituents). *Proceedings of Depling*.

Hajič J. et al. (1999) *Annotation at analytical level – Instructions for annotators*. Prague Dependency web site.

Hudson R. (1988). Coordination and grammatical relations. *Journal of Linguistics*, 24(2), 303-342.

Ivanova A., Oepen S., Øvrelid L., Flickinger D. (2012), Who Did What to Whom? A Contrastive Study of Syntacto-Semantic Dependencies, *Proc. of the 6th Linguistic Annotation Workshop (LAW VI)*, ACL, Jeju, Korea.

Jackendoff R. (1977) X-bar Syntax. *A study of Phrase Structure*. MIT Press.

Kahane, S. (1997). Bubble trees and syntactic representations. *Proceedings of Mathematics of Language* (MOL5), 70-76.

Kahane S., Gerdes K., Bawden R., Pietrandrea P., Benzitoun C. (2013) Protocol for micro-syntactic coding, www.projet-rhapsodie.fr

Masini F., P. Pietrandrea. (2010) Magari, *Cognitive Linguistics, 21:1*, 75-121.

Mazziotta N. (2011) Coordination of verbal dependents in Old French: coordination as a specified juxtaposition or apposition, *Proceedings of Depling*..

McDonald, R. T. et al. (2013) Universal Dependency Annotation for Multilingual Parsing. *Proceedings of ACL*.

Mel'čuk I. (1988) *Dependency syntax: Theory and Practice*, SUNY Press.

Mel'čuk I. (2012-2015) *Semantics: From meaning to text, 3 volumes*. Benjamins.

Ndiaye M. (1989). L'analyse syntaxique par joncteurs de liste. Thèse de Doctorat, Université d'Aix-Marseille.

Nølke H. (1983). *Les adverbes paradigmatisants : fonction et analyse*. Copenhague, Akademisk Forlag.

Osborne T. (2006). Shared material and grammar: Toward a dependency grammar theory of non-gapping coordination for English and German. *Zeitschrift für Sprachwissenschaft*, 25(1), 39-93.

Osborne T. (2008). Major constituents and two dependency grammar constraints on sharing in coordination. *Linguistics*, 46(6), 1109-1165.

Popel, M., Marecek, D., Stepánek, J., Zeman, D., & Zabokrtský, Z. (2013). Coordination Structures in Dependency Treebanks. In Proceedings of ACL (pp. 517-527).

Postal P. (1974) *On Raising. One Rule of English Grammar and its Theoretical Implications*, The MIT Press: Cambridge, Mass.

Sag I. A., Gazdar G., Wasow T., Weisler S. (1985). Coordination and how to distinguish categories. *Natural Language & Linguistic Theory*, 3(2), 117-171.

Schuurman I., W. Goedertier, H. Hoekstra H., N. Oostdijk, R. Piepenbrock, M. Schouppe (2004) Linguistic annotation of the Spoken Dutch Corpus: If we had to do it all over again ..., *Proc. of LREC*, Lisbon, 57-60.

Surdeanu M., Johansson R., Meyers A., Marquez Ll., Nivre J. (2008) *The CoNLL-2008 Shared Task on Joint Parsing of Syntactic and Semantic Dependencies* (*CoNLL-2008*).

Tesnière L. (1959). *Éléments de syntaxe structurale*. Paris: Klincksieck [transl. by Osborne T., Kahane S. (2015) *Elements of structural syntax*, Benjamins].

Tseng J. (2002) Remarks on marking, *Proc. of the 8th International HPSG Conference*, CSLI Publication, Stanford, CA, pp. 267-283.

The Dependency Status of Function Words: Auxiliaries

Thomas Groß
Aichi University
tm.gross@yahoo.de

Timothy Osborne
Zhejiang University
tjo3ya@yahoo.com

Abstract

The Universal Stanford Dependencies (USD) subordinates function words to content words. Auxiliaries, adpositions and subordinators are positioned as dependents of full verbs and nouns, respectively. Such an approach to the syntax of natural languages is contrary to most work in theoretical syntax in the past 35 years, regardless of whether this work is constituency- or dependency-based. A substantial amount of evidence delivers a strong argument for the more conventional approach, which subordinates full verbs to auxiliaries and nouns to adpositions. This contribution demonstrates that the traditional approach to the dependency status of auxiliary verbs is motivated by many empirical considerations, and hence USD cannot be viewed as modeling the syntax of natural languages in a plausible way.

1 The dependency status of function words

The Universal Stanford Dependencies (USD), as presented in de Marneffe et al. (2014), advocates a scheme for parsing natural languages that categorically subordinates function words to content words. Auxiliary verbs, adpositions (prepositions and postpositions), subordinators (subordinate conjunctions), etc. are subordinated to the content words with which they co-occur. A more traditional dependency-based analysis assumes the opposite, i.e. most function words dominate the content words with which they co-occur.[1] The following diagrams illustrate both approaches:

(1)[2]

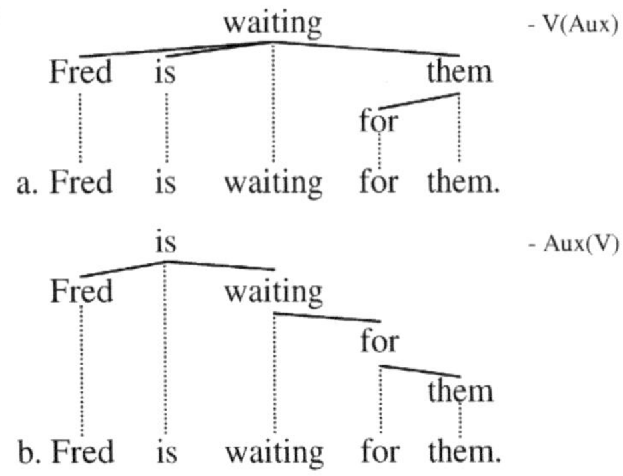

The USD analysis (1a) subordinates the auxiliary *is* to the full verb *waiting* and the preposition *for* to the pronoun *them*, whereas the traditional analysis (1b) does the opposite.

While the USD approach is still novel, it is based on the Stanford Dependencies (SD) by de Marneffe et al. (2006) and de Marneffe and Manning (2008). SD is available for English, Chinese, Finnish, and Persian.

The assumption that function words should be categorically subordinated to content words stands in stark contrast to work in theoretical syntax in the last 35 years, which has been pursuing an approach to syntactic structures that is more congruent with the analysis shown in (1b). Most phrase structure grammars – e.g. HPSG (Pollard and Sag 1994), Lexical Functional Grammar (Bresnan 2001), Categorial Grammar (Steedman 2014), Government and Binding (Chomsky 1981, 1986), Minimalist Program (Chomsky 1995) – and most dependency grammars (DGs) – Lexicase (Starosta 1988), Word Grammar (Hudson 1984, 1990, 2007), Meaning Text Theory (Mel'čuk 1988, 2003, 2009), the German schools (Kunze 1975, Engel 1994, Heringer 1996, Eroms 2000) – assume that function words are heads over content words as shown in (1b).

There are, however, also exceptions. Hays

[1] Determiners are one area of disagreement among linguists.

[2] Whenever two tree representations are contrasted, their respective preference on dependency direction is indicated at the top.

(1964: 521) assumes that non-copula auxiliaries, such as *are* in *They are flying planes*, are dependents of full verbs. Matthews (1981: 63), too, argues for subordinate auxiliaries. On the other hand, DG sources that directly motivate the status of the finite verb as the root of the clause are plentiful: Starosta (1988: 239ff.), Engel (1994: 107ff.), Jung (1995: 62f.), Eroms (2000: 129ff.), Mel'čuk (2009: 44f., 79f.).

The next section addresses the difficulty of delineating function words from content words. It looks at semi-auxiliaries, light verbs, and functional verb constructions. Section 3 produces evidence that support the view that auxiliaries are heads over their full verbs. Section 4 briefly outlines the importance of functional hierarchies, and argues for a token-based morphological account.

2 Degrees of content

The parsing scheme that USD advocates takes the division between function word and content word as its guiding principle. One major difficulty with doing this is that the dividing line between function word and content word is often not clear. The next three subsections briefly examine three problem areas for USD in this regard: semi-auxiliaries, light verb constructions, and functional verb constructions.

2.1 Semi-auxiliaries

Many constructions in natural language distribute functional meaning over varied syntactic units. Semi-auxiliaries in English – e.g. *be going to*, *be able to*, *be about to*, *ought to*, *used to*, etc. – are a case in point. The meaning contribution of these expressions is functional, yet their distribution and subcategorization traits are more like that of full content verbs. USD therefore faces the dilemma of having to value the one aspect of these expressions more than the other when deciding upon an analysis.

The point is illustrated with an example of *be going to*:

(2)

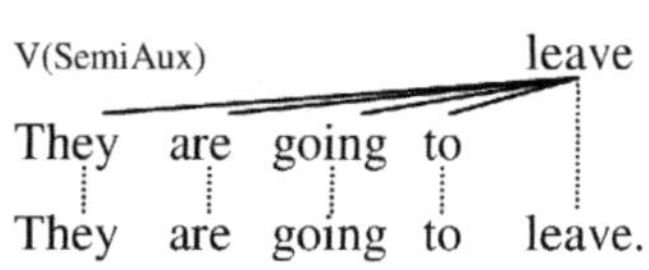

a. They are going to leave.

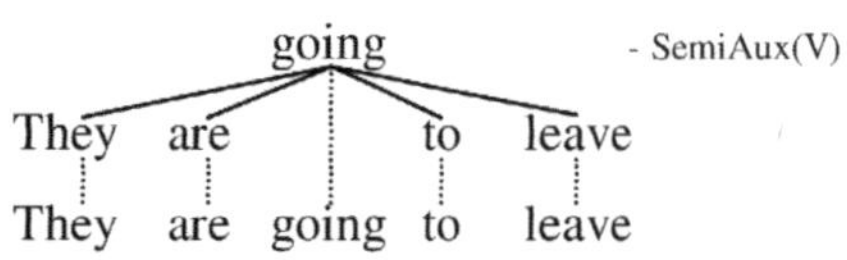

b. They are going to leave

If USD wants to be consistent, it should choose the (a)-analysis because that analysis is most in line with the distinction between function word and content word. The (b)-analysis foregoes this consistency by taking *going* as the root. It is motivated by a syntactic consideration (distribution). Either way, USD is challenged; no matter which of the two analyses it chooses, it has to ignore an important fact that speaks for the other analysis.

The traditional approach favors the following analysis:

(2)

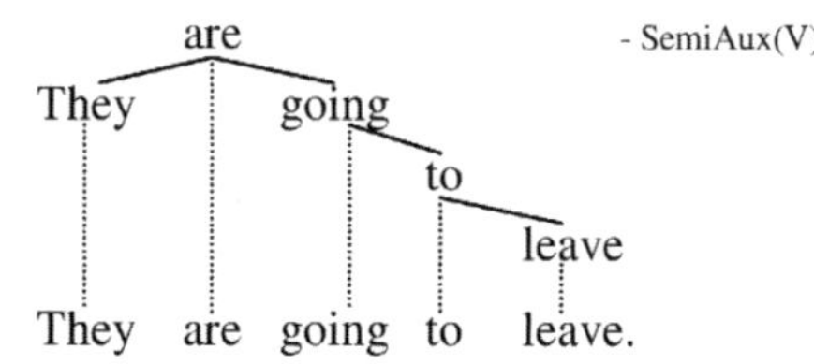

c. They are going to leave.

The hierarchy of verb forms here is motivated by various syntactic criteria, such as the ability to topicalize (e.g. *...and going to leave they are*;*...and leave they are going to*) and the ability to elide (e.g *...and they are*; *....and they are going to*).

2.2 Light verb constructions

The challenge of distinguishing function word and content word is perhaps most visible with light verb constructions. Typical light verbs in English are *do*, *give*, *have*, *make*, *take*, etc.; in German: *geben*, *haben*, *machen*, *sein*, etc.; in Japanese: *s-uru* 'do', *tor-u* 'take', *yar-u* 'do/give', etc. The defining trait of a light verb is that it co-occurs with a content noun, whereby it is the noun that is semantically loaded. Examples from English of light verb constructions are *to take a shower* (vs. *to shower*), *give a hug* (vs. *to hug*), *have a smoke* (vs. *to smoke*), etc. Many light verb constructions have a simple verb that they correspond to, as with the examples just given; other light verb constructions do not correspond to a simple verb, e.g. *make a mistake*, *have fun*, etc.

Light verbs straddle the function vs. content division. They are more like function words from a semantic point of view since they lack semantic substance, but they are more like content verbs from a syntactic point of view since their distribution is that of a full content verb.

Consider the following analyses of sentences containing the meaning 'stroll':

(3)

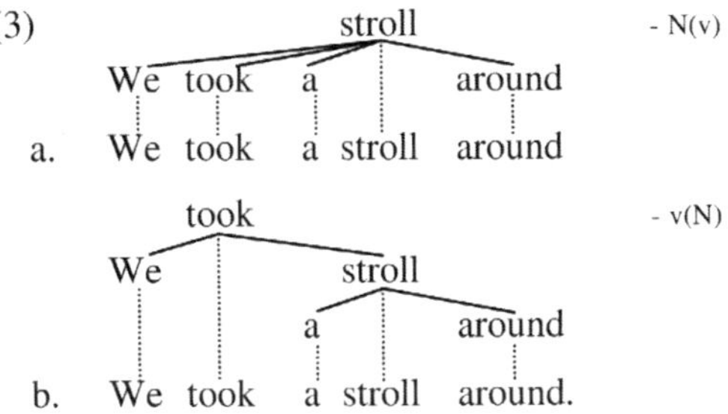

If USD chooses the analysis in (3a), then it has to ignore the fact that *took* distributes like a normal content verb, but if USD chooses the analysis in (3b), then it has to ignore the fact that *took* is largely devoid of semantic content and should therefore be treated like an auxiliary, auxiliary verbs of course lacking semantic content.

The problem just illustrated with English examples is now solidified with an example from Japanese, using the light verb construction *hanashi-o shi-ta* 'talked'.

(4)

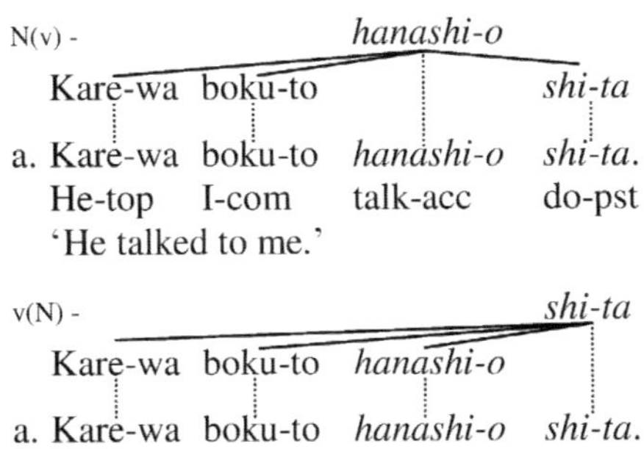

USD should choose the (4a)-analysis, since it positions the noun *hanashi-o* as the root. In so doing, it would be consistently subordinating function words to content words. The (4a)-analysis is implausible, though, mainly because Japanese is widely judged to be a strict head-final language. The traditional analysis shown in (4b) accommodates the head-final nature of Japanese syntax. Therefore the example illustrates that the traditional analysis is more in line with broad typological generalizations that have been used to characterize the syntax of the world's languages.

2.3 Functional verb constructions

German is known for its many *functional verb constructions* (*Funktionsverbgefüge*). These constructions involve a verb combined with a prepositional phrase, whereby varying degrees of semantic compositionality are involved, e.g. *in Kraft treten* 'come into force', *in Frage kommen* 'be possible', *in Kauf nehmen* 'accept', etc. Functional verb constructions differ from light verb constructions insofar as the verb in the latter is bleached but the noun is loaded with full semantic content; in the former, in contrast, the entire expression is bleached. There is no strength present in *in Kraft treten*, no question in *in Frage kommen*, and no buying in *in Kauf nehmen*.

Given the inability to identify the one or the other part of these constructions as the semantic center, the analysis that USD chooses becomes arbitrary. Consider the following possibilities:

(5)

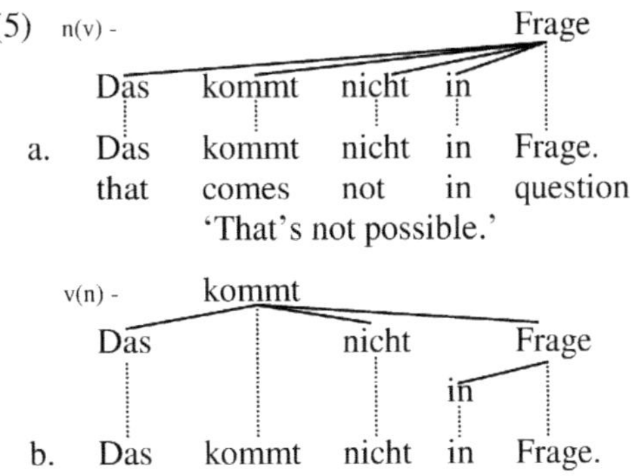

Since it is implausible to view either *kommt* or *Frage* as being semantically more loaded than the other, USD cannot provide a convincing reason why the one or the other of these two analyses should be preferred. If it chooses the (b)-analysis because *kommt* is a verb, then it is reaching to a syntactic criterion, and has thus departed from its guiding principle, this principle being that the distinction between function word and content word is decisive.

Functional verb constructions reside closer to idiomatic expressions than to light verb constructions, but both construction types are located on an *idiomaticity* cline. USD, as well as its precursors, can hardly acknowledge this idiomaticity cline; its guiding principle sees it shoehorning all complex expressions with somewhat non-compositional meaning into the multi-word-expression box. The problem with doing this is that it tends to view all structures with non-compositional meaning as fundamentally different from compositional ones. Consider in this area that, disregarding how one labels the dependency branches between nodes, the dependency structures of an idiom like *He kicked the bucket* and the similar, but non-idiomatic sentence *He kicked the car* should be isomorph. The need for such syntactic isomorphism is problem for USD, though, because it would have to depart from its guiding principle to accommodate the isomorphism.

3 Auxiliaries

The following subsections provide evidence from subcategorization, the subject-verb relation, valency change, VP-ellipsis, string coordination, and sentential negation that challenge USD's analysis of auxiliaries.

3.1 Subject-verb relation

In many languages, the finite verb enjoys a special relationship with the subject. One expression of this is agreement. The salient property is the correlation of nominative case with tense/mood markers. Tense/mood is marked only on finite verbs. Consider the following examples from German:

(6) 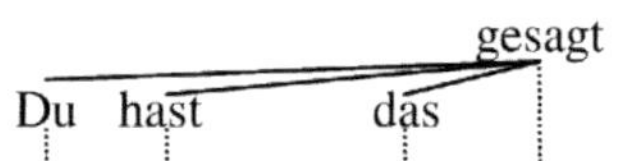

- V(Aux)

a. Du hast das gesagt.
you have.2sg that said
'You have said that.'

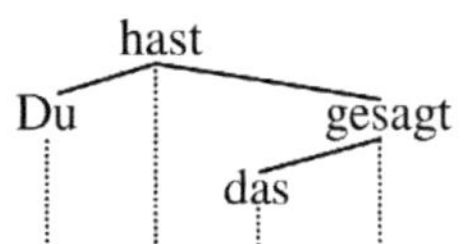

- Aux(V)

b. Du hast das gesagt.

The USD structure in (6a) does not accommodate the correlational property of tense/mood – nominative, whereas the conventional DG analysis (6b) does. The analysis in (6b) expresses this relationship by subordinating the subject directly to the finite verb. One finds the same issue in Hebrew, where agreement is present in every verb:

(7) 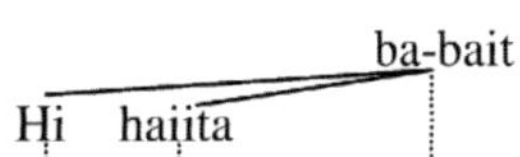

- P(Aux)

a. Hi haiita ba-bait.
she was.3sgf at.the-house
'She was at home.'

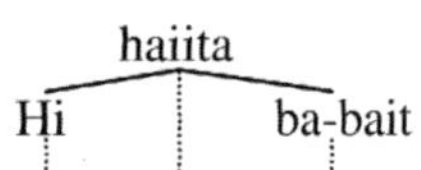

- Aux(P)

b. Hi haiita ba-bait.

Example (7a) sees the pronoun *Hi* depending on *ba-bait*, even though tense and person/number is marked on the verb. The conventional DG structure (7b) assumes again that subject and finite verb enter a special relationship.

One of the most salient reasons for assuming such a special relationship is that verbs not marked for tense/mood cannot govern the nominative. This insight is the main motivation for the assumption of IP/TP (inflection phrase/tense phrase) in Chomskian grammars. Attempts at subordinating auxiliaries fail to provide an account of the cross-linguistically salient subject-verb relationship. In particular, it fails to account for nominative case assignment to the subject.

3.2 Sentential negation

Whenever negation and auxiliation coincide, the canonical situation is that the (topmost) auxiliary is negated, rather than the lexical verb. If the lexical verb were truly the root node, then the expectation would be that the lexical verb is where negation takes place. A look across English, Hebrew, Japanese, and French shows that this expectation is not met. In English, contractions of the auxiliary and the negation are common at the top of the verb chain, but not in between:

(8) a. He won't have gone by then.
b. *He will haven't gone by then.

The full negation is marginally possible: *He will have not gone*.

In Hebrew, *lo* precedes the expression it negates, and in the case of an auxiliary, *lo* precedes it:

(9) a. ata **lo** jaxol li-sxot?
you.msg **neg** pot inf-swim
'You can't swim?'

b. *ata jaxol **lo** li-sxot?

In Japanese, negation is usually present as a suffix. Canonical negation requires that the top-most word in the verb chain to be marked with it:

(10) a. oyog-u koto-wa deki-**na**-i-no?
swim-npst that-top pot-**neg**-npst-int
'You can't swim?'

b.*oyog-**ana**-i koto-wa deki-ru-no?
swim-**neg**-npst that-top pot-npst-int

Negation in French requires two items. This two-part negation straddles the finite verb, the root of the clause, as is shown in (11):

(11) 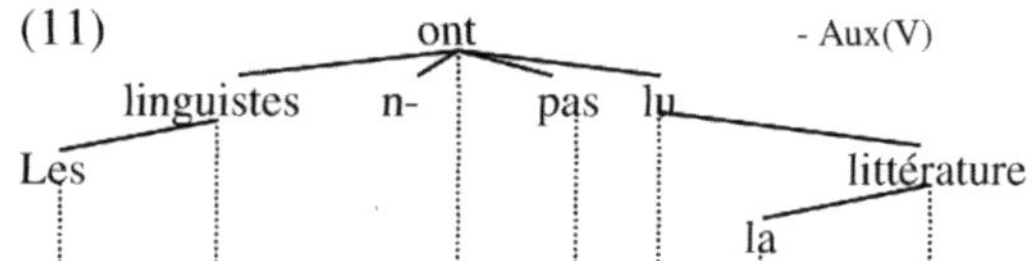

- Aux(V)

Les linguistes n'ont pas lu la littérature.
the linguists n-have not read the literature
'The linguists haven't read the literature.'

This analysis speaks to intuition, since it has the negation straddling the only hierarchically singular word, i.e. the root of the clause.

The USD analysis produces a much less intuitive analysis:

(12)

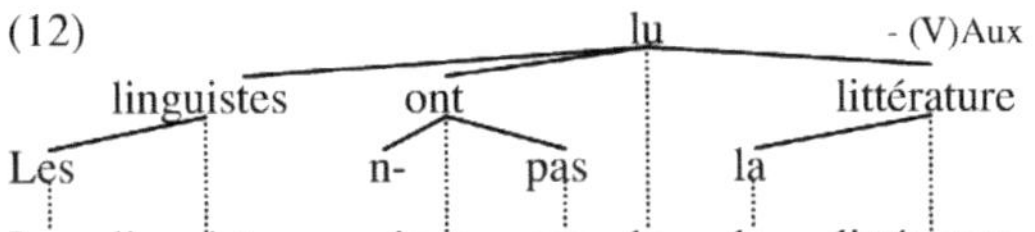

Les linguistes n'ont pas lu la littérature.
the linguists n-have not read the literature

The negation *ne…pas* is now no longer straddling the root word of the clause, a situation that would seem to complicate the account of the distribution of the negation. Note that *ne…pas* can also attach to a nonfinite verb, but when it does so, it no longer straddles the verb, e.g. *ne pas lire* 'not read'.

3.3 VP-ellipsis

The traditional approach easily accommodates core aspects of the distribution of VP-ellipsis in English. The finite auxiliary verb is the root of the clause, which means the elided VP of VP-ellipsis is (usually) a complete subtree, i.e. a constituent, e.g.

(13) Fred won't make that claim, but

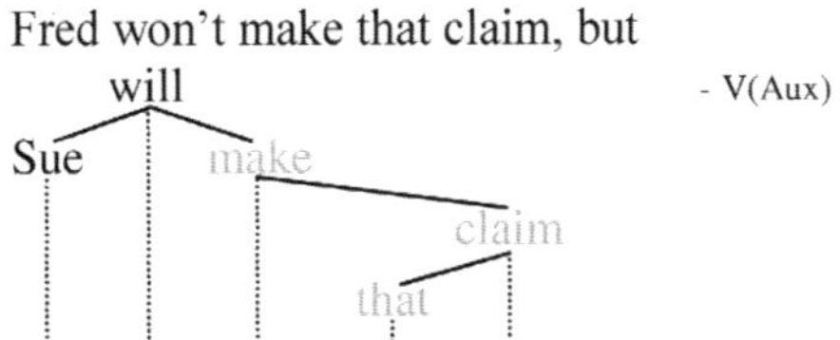

Sue will make that claim.

The elided string *make that claim* is a complete subtree. Given the treatment of function words that the USD analysis pursues, one would expect to find the following structural analysis of VP-ellipsis:

(14) Fred won't make that claim, but

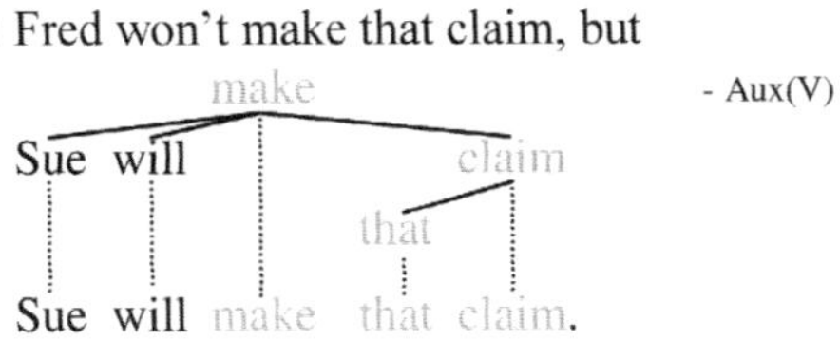

Sue will make that claim.

The elided string *make that claim* is now no longer a complete subtree, a situation that complicates the analysis and distribution of VP-ellipsis.

But in fact de Marneffe et al. (2014: 4588) do not produce an analysis of VP-ellipsis that is consistent with the principles they have laid out; they assume instead that in cases like (13-14), the auxiliary is in fact the root of the clause. In other words, they assume the analysis shown in (13), not the one in (14). Their solution is thus *ad hoc*; it reveals the difficulties they are having making their approach work.

3.4 Subcategorization

Another problem facing USD's analysis concerns subcategorization. When auxiliaries accompany a lexical verb, the lexical verb takes on a specific form that is subcategorized for by the auxiliary, e.g.

(15) The proposal was reexamined.

The lexical verb *reexamined* appears in the past participle subcategory because in this subcategory it can express the passive together with the auxiliary *BE*. The subcategory of the content word *reexamined* depends on the appearance of the function word *BE* (here *was*). Note that the opposite reasoning does not work, i.e. one cannot view the subcategory of *was*, a finite form, as reliant on the appearance of *reexamined*, because *reexamined* can appear without the specific form *was*, e.g. *The proposal has been reexamined.* This asymmetry indicates that the content verb is subordinate to the function verb. Section 4 considers multiple auxiliation with the framework of token-based morphology.

In German and Hebrew (and many other languages), modal auxiliaries govern infinitives, but infinitive verbs do not govern the form of modal auxiliaries:

(16) a. Er *(muss) komm-**en**.
he must come-**inf**
'He must come.'

b. Hu *(rotse) **li**-shon.
he wants **inf**-sleep.
'He wants to sleep.'

The brackets denote optionality, and the asterisk indicates that optionality is ungrammatical. This means that the presence of a modal auxiliary subcategorizes for the form of the content word. This is a reliable, surface-grammatical criterion.

Finally, when languages distinguish between indicative and subjunctive mood, they require an auxiliary in a complement clause to be marked for the subjunctive. The full verb is marked for the subjunctive only in the absence of an auxiliary:

(17) - A(Aux)

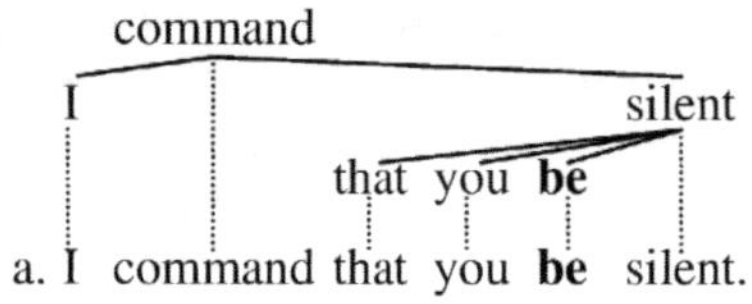

- Aux(A)

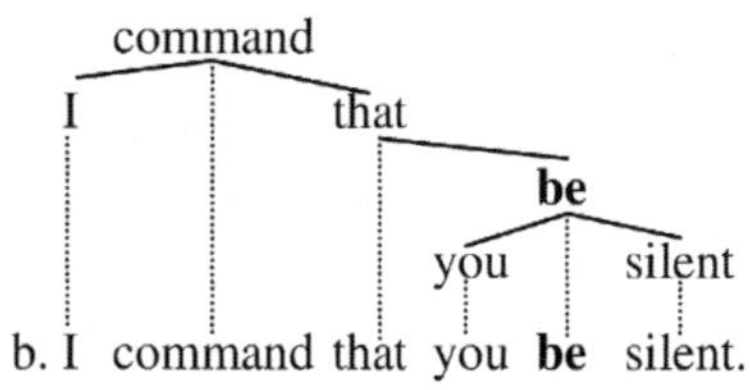

Compared with (17a), the traditional analysis in (17b) can argue for the subcategorization of the subjunctive auxiliary by demonstrating that the branch *command that* immediately above the auxiliary can elicit the subjunctive. In (17a) the subordinate conjunction and the subjunctive auxiliary are not in one another's domains, nor are they in the immediate domain of the verb *command*.

3.5 Valency change

The occurrence of auxiliaries with valency potential can override the valency potential of the full verb:

(18) - V(Aux)

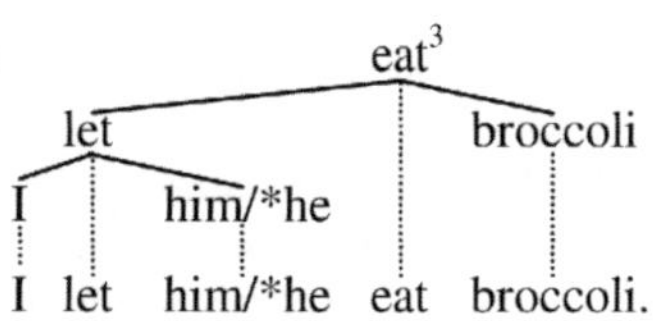

The ungrammaticality of *he*, even though it is retained as the semantic subject of *eat*, cannot be explained on the assumption that the causative auxiliary *let* is subordinate to the full verb *eat*. At the same time, *I* is clearly the matrix subject, but it should depend on the auxiliary *let*, because it is not the subject of *eat*. The causee *him* should also depend on *let*. If, however, *let* is indeed subordinate to *eat* then (18) lacks a matrix subject.

An account more in line with valency theory assumes two valency structures:

(19) a. $N1_{nom}$ *eat* $N2_{obj}$
b. $N0_{nom}$ *let* $N1_{obj}$ V_{binf}

(19a) shows the valency of *eat*. (19b) shows the valency of the causative auxiliary *let*: N0 designates a newly introduced subject. The causee N1, i.e. the demoted subject from (19a), must appear in the object case, and a bare infinitive verb must appear. Since the auxiliary overrides the lexical valency of the full verb, the expectation is that the auxiliary resides in a structurally higher position, which is associated with the potential to override grammatical functions. A tree that assumes higher position of the auxiliary is shown below:

(20) - Aux(V)

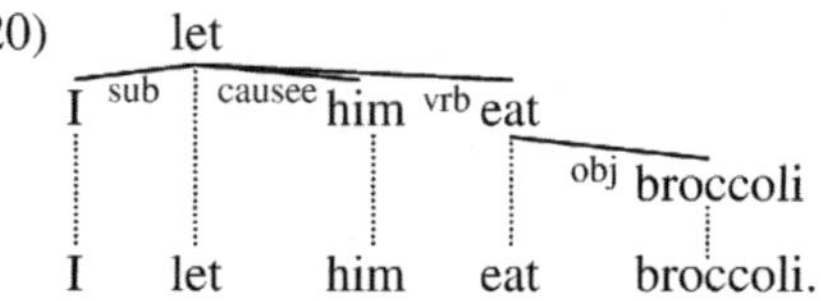

Example (20) shows the words *I*, *him*, and *eat* as dependents of the auxiliary *let*, which corresponds with (19b). The full verb *eat* in (20) continues to dominate its object, but it has relinquished its subject dependency to the auxiliary.

The assumption on the dependency structure between valency-bearing auxiliaries and full verbs is cross-linguistically valid, as the Japanese translation of (20) demonstrates:[4]

(21)

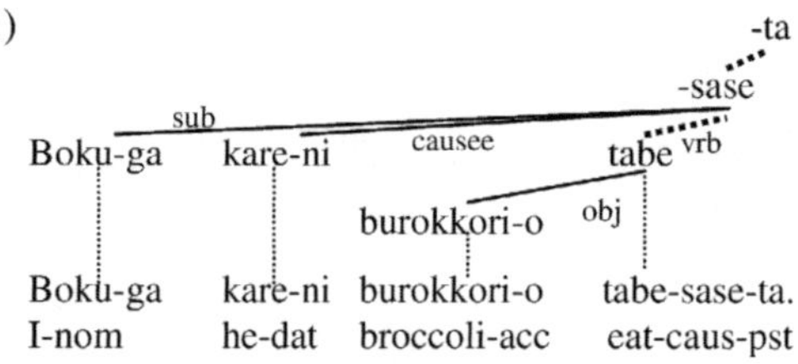

Example (21) exhibits exactly the same dependency structure of a causative auxiliary, its full verb, and their dependents. In fact, the current account has already accomplished what the USD try to achieve, namely a cross-linguistically valid representation of dependency structure.

3.6 String coordination

String coordination is constrained with respect to the material that can be shared by the conjuncts. While the exact principles that constrain sharing are at present not fully established, data are available for comparison. Material preceding the coordinate structure can be shared by both conjuncts if the conjuncts are constituents (22a), but sharing is ungrammatical if the conjuncts are non-constituents (22b):

(22) a. He treats the old [women] and [men].
b. * He treats the old [women for free], but [men for $10].

[3] It is unclear how USD would structure (18). The term causative does not appear in de Marneffe et al. (2006, 2014), or de Marneffe and Manning (2008).

[4] The verb *tabe-sase-ta* is shown as three nodes in (14), according to a dependency morphological account that is the topic of Section 4.

On the intended reading that the men are also old, (22b) is ungrammatical.

A second observation concerns the dependency status of the shared material. If material is not subordinate to the root of the first conjunct, then it can be shared (23a). However, if the material is subordinate, sharing is ungrammatical (23b):

(23) a. He met [Pete on Friday] and [Jane on Saturday].

b. * He met young [Pete on Friday] and [Jane on Saturday].

The string *He met* in (23a) can be shared. The verb *met* immediately preceding the coordinate structure is dominating every constituent inside the two conjuncts. In (23b), however, the adjective *young* cannot be shared across the conjuncts. The adjective is dependent on *Pete*. (23b) is, thus, grammatical only on the reading that Jane is not necessarily young.

Applying these observations to auxiliaries, the expectation is that auxiliaries should not be shared across non-constituent conjuncts as long as they are viewed as dependents of the full verbs. That expectation, however, is not met, as the next example demonstrates:

(24) He has had [to grade papers since March] and [to write an essay since April].

On the assumption, that *has* and *had* are dependents of the full verb *grade*, they should not be able to be shared. The auxiliaries should behave like *the old* in (22b), and *young* in (23b). The fact that the auxiliaries do not behave in the same manner, and that sharing is grammatical, supports the assumption that they are not subordinate to the full verb.

4 Functional hierarchies

De Marneffe et al. (2014: 4585) take a lexicalist, i.e. word-based, position. Such a stance comes naturally to dependency grammars, which are by their very nature word-based grammars. Regarding lexicalism, however, three issues must be considered. The first one is that lexicalism does not advocate or imply the subordination of function words to content words. The previous section produced a number of arguments that do not empirically support the proposal made by de Marneffe et al. (2014). This section adds to these arguments by addressing functional hierarchies.

Secondly, not all linguists who support the Lexical Integrity Hypothesis regard morphology as futile. Quite to the contrary, we believe that a token-based morphology can shed light on intra-word and inter-word structure. Under "token-based" morphology, we understand a morphology that acknowledges pieces, but that restricts these pieces to surface forms. Such an approach can account for functional hierarchies, while staying loyal to dependency-based approaches to linguistic structure. Below we follow the proposals made in Groß (2011, 2014), Osborne & Groß (2012), and Groß & Osborne (2013).

Finally, regarding the Lexical Integrity Hypothesis, several versions of differing strictness constrain how blind syntax is to derivational (weak hypothesis) or inflectional (strong hypothesis) suffixes (Lieber and Scalise 2007). The following Japanese data are a counterexample against the strong hypothesis:

(25)
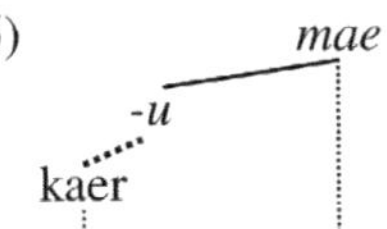

a. kaer-*u* *mae*
return-npst front
'before [he] returns'

b. *kaet-ta mae

(26)
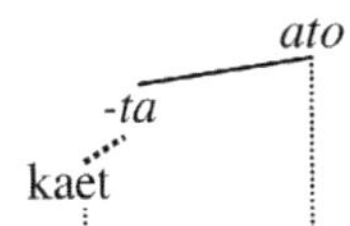

a. kaet-*ta* *ato*
return-pst rear
'after [he] returns'

b. * kaer-u ato

The nominal *mae* 'front' subcategorizes non-past tense (25a), and past tense is ungrammatical (25b). Conversely, *ato* 'rear' subcategorizes past tense (26a), while non-past tense is ungrammatical (26b). This behavior cannot be explained if the strong hypothesis were correct.

The discussion now turns to functional hierarchies. Research in morphology (Bybee 1985), on clause structure (Chomsky 1986; Rizzi 1997), on adverbs (Cinque 1999), and on verbs (Rice 2006) has produced substantial evidence that functional hierarchies must be assumed to exist above the lexical material, rather than beneath it. This necessity becomes evident when one is faced with multiple auxiliation. The earliest discussion of such a case can be found in Chomsky (1957: 39):

(27) That has been being discussed.

The complex predicate *has been being discussed* expresses 'perfective', 'progressive', and 'passive'. Chomsky realized that the functional meanings are expressed by two items, respectively:

(28) a. perfective: *has + en*
a. progressive: *be + ing*
c. passive: *be + ed*

The discontinuous surface order of these items led him to the notion of affix hopping:

(29) That (has t_1) (be-t_2)-en_1 (be-t_3)ing_2 (discuss)-ed_3.

The first bracket expresses the perfective, and the suffix *-en* dislocates and attaches to the end of the next auxiliary, i.e. the second bracket, asf.

Chomsky also realized that there is a hierarchy, i.e. perfective > progressive > passive, that may not be scrambled, e.g. **That was had being discussed*, **That was been having discussed*, etc. Bybee (1985: 196f) expands on this work when she posits the hierarchy: valency < voice < aspect < modality < tense < mood < person < number. Cinque (1999) tries to identify these categories, and possible subcategories, by looking at adverbs related to these notions. Rizzi (1997) tries to establish a phrase structure framework that can account for topic, focus, and force expressions.

Hierarchies of any type lend themselves to a dependency-based expression because hierarchies and dependencies are directed. A view that the auxiliaries in (27) are dependents of *discussed* not only forfeits the spirit of dependency, but it is also useless in explaining functional hierarchies.

(30)

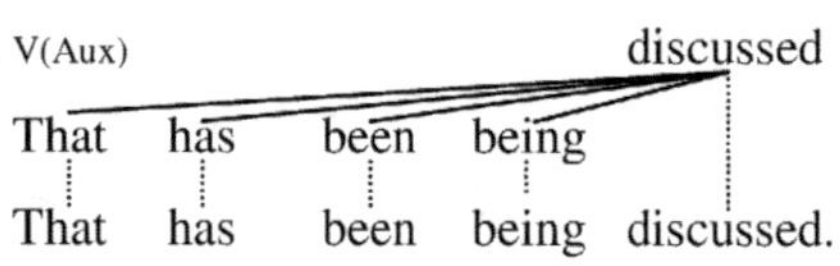

Tree (30) assumes that auxiliaries are daughters, i.e. functionally equidistant to the full verb. But the perfective always dominates the progressive, and never vice versa, and the progressive always dominates the passive, and never vice versa. An attempt to view word order, rather than dependencies, as the critical ingredient, faces problems in more synthetic languages, e.g. Hebrew *katuv* 'written", where the transfix $^{-}a^{-}u^{-}$ expresses the passive participle. Finally, it incurs the typological problem that the right-branching, i.e. head-initial, English predicate is now viewed as left-branching, i.e. head-final.

A dependency-based morphology overcomes these challenges by assuming node status for morphs, and that the relationships between morph nodes are directed, i.e. are dependencies. The result is a transparent representation of the structural relationships between morph nodes. This allows reading complex functional meaning directly off the tree structure. Finally, such an account succeeds in acknowledging functional hierarchies in spirit and form. The next example, taken from Groß (2011), illustrates these points:

(31)

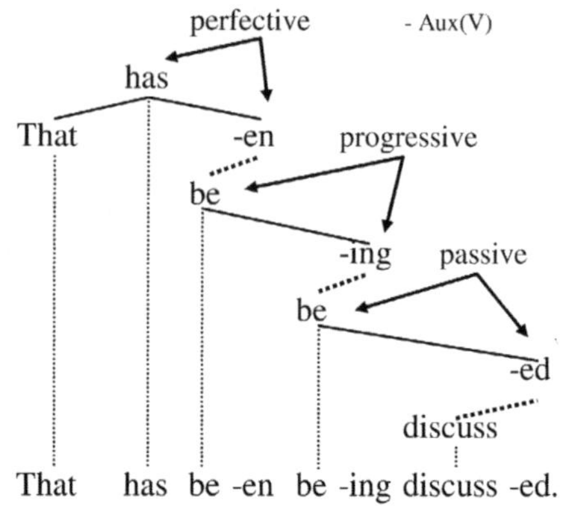

Compare (28a-c) to the meanings ascribed to the respective catenae in (31). (31) should also be compared to example (30). In (31), not only syntactic, but also morphological dependencies are accounted for, as well as the functional hierarchy.

One central motive in de Marneffe et al. (2014: 4589) is to provide "a uniform treatment of both morphologically rich and poor languages". In more synthetic languages the functional meanings tend to occur inside one word, whereas they tend to occur as distinct words in more analytic languages:

(32)

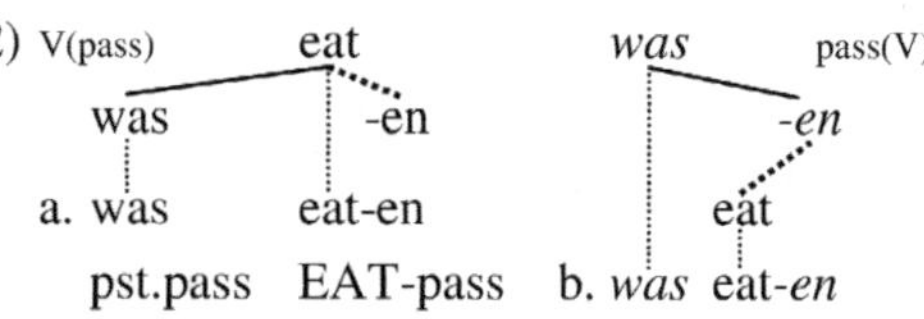

(33)

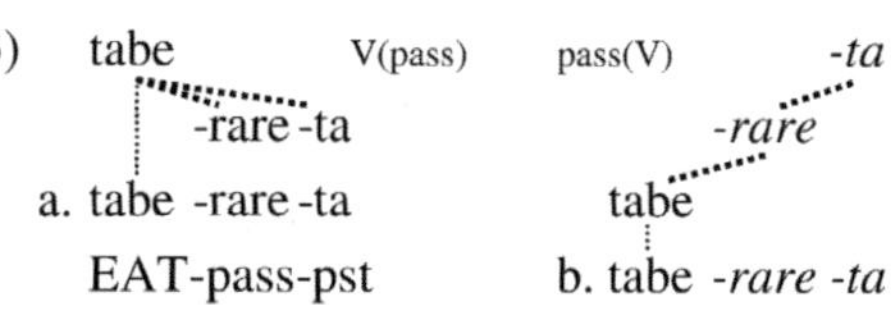

Example (32) shows the more analytic English past passive of *eat*, and (33) the corresponding synthetic construction in Japanese. The (a)-examples show an analysis that subordinates functional material to lexical material, i.e. V(pass), and the (b)-examples show the alternative approach, i.e. pass(V). Analyses similar to the (a)-examples are few in dependency grammar, with Anderson's (1980) study of Basque verbs the most famous example. Since dependency grammar tends towards granting lexical material higher priority due to valency-based considerations, analyses such as the (a)-examples naturally match preconceptions. The problem is, however, that these analyses do not offer any insights into the morphological or morpho-syntactical structure of language. Analyses such as the (a)-examples have been taken as proof against the attainability of a dependency-based morphology. As a result, dependency grammar stands apart from rival theories not only in their inability to acknowledge functional hierarchies, but also in the obvious lack of a dependency-based morphology. However, the (b)-analyses illustrate that it is not only possible to produce accurate structures, but they also account for functional hierarchies (here: content verb < voice < tense), and furthermore, they are compatible with the majority cross-theoretical research on these issues.

5 Conclusion

This paper has produced diverse observations, all of which support the conventional wisdom that lexical verbs are subordinate to auxiliaries, rather than vice versa. In Section 2, the paper argued that the distinction between function words and content words is not discrete, but rather gradient. Section 3 provided evidence from the subject-verb relation, sentential negation, VP-ellipsis, subcategorization, valency change, and string coordination supporting the assumption that auxiliaries are heads over their full verbs, which is therefore contrary to the position de Marneffe et al. (2014) adopt. Section 4 argued that a lexicalist stance does not support the assumption that function words are subordinate to content words. The Lexical Integrity Hypothesis was also shown to be less solid than it appeared. In conjunction with the possibility of a token-based approach to morphology, an account of the dependency relationships between function words and content words is attainable that not only is consistent with acknowledged research on functional hierarchies, but that also honors the dependency-based view of language.

References

John Anderson. 1980. Towards dependency morphology: The structure of the Basque verb. In John Anderson & Colin J. Ewen (eds.), *Studies in Dependency Phonology*, pp. 221–271. Ludwigsburg: R.O.U. Strauch.

Joan Bresnan. 2001. *Lexical-Functional Syntax*, Blackwell.

Joan L Bybee. 1985. *Morphology: A study of the relation between meaning and form*. John Benjamins Publishing Company, Amsterdam.

Noam Chomsky. 1957. Syntactic Structures. The Hague: Mouton & Co.

Noam Chomsky 1981. *Lectures on Government and Binding: The Pisa Lectures*. Mouton de Gruyter.

Noam Chomsky. 1986. *Barriers*. Cambridge, Mass.: MIT Press.

Noam Chomsky. 1995. *The Minimalist Program*. MIT Press, Cambridge, MA.

Guglielmo Cinque. 1999. *Adverbs and functional heads: A cross-linguistic perspective*. Oxford: Oxford University Press.

Ulrich Engel. 1994. *Syntax der deutschen Gegenwarts-sprache*, 3rd fully revised edition. Erich Schmidt, Berlin.

Hans-Werner Eroms. 2000. *Syntax der deutschen Sprache*. Walter de Gruyter, Berlin.

Thomas Groß. 2011. Catenae in morphology. In Kim Gerdes, Eva Hajičová & Leo Wanner (eds.), *Depling 2011*, pp. 47–57, Barcelona: Pompeu Fabra University.

Thomas Groß. 2014. Some Observations on the Hebrew Desiderative Construction. *SKY Journal 27*: 7-41.

Thomas Groß and Timothy Osborne. 2013. Katena und Konstruktion: Ein Vorschlag zu einer dependenziellen Konstruktionsgrammatik. *Zeitschrift für Sprachwissenschaft* 32 (1): 41–73.

David G. Hays. 1964. Dependency theory: A formalism and some observations. *Language* 40. 511-525.

Hans J. Heringer. 1996. *Deutsche Syntax Dependentiell*. Staufenberg, Tübingen.

Richard Hudson. 1984. *Word Grammar*. Basil Blackwell, New York.

Richard Hudson. 1990. *An English Word Grammar*. Oxford: Basil Blackwell.

Richard Hudson. 2007. *Language Networks: The New Word Grammar*. Oxford University Press.

Wha-Young Jung. 1995. *Syntaktische Relationen im Rahmen der Dependenzgrammatik*. Buske, Hamburg.

Jürgen Kunze. 1975. *Abhängigkeitsgrammatik. Studia Grammatica* 12. Akademie Verlag, Berlin.

Rochelle Lieber and Sergio Scalise. 2007. The Lexical Integrity Hypothesis in a New Theoretical Universe. Geert Booij et.al. (eds.), On-line Proceedings of the Fifth Mediterranean Morphology Meeting (MMM5). University of Bologna. http://mmm.lingue.unibo.it/

Marie-Catherine de Marneffe, Bill MacCartney and Christopher D. Manning. 2006. Generating Typed Dependency Parses from Phrase Structure Parses. In *LREC 2006*.

Marie-Catherine de Marneffe and Christopher Manning. 2008. The Stanford typed dependencies representation. In *Workshop on Cross-framework and Cross-domain Parser Evaluation*.

Marie-Catherine de Marneffe, Timothy Dozat, Natalia Silvaire, Katrin Haverinen, Filip Ginter, Joakim Nivre, Christopher D. Manning. 2014. Universal Stanford Dependencies: A cross-linguistic typology. LREC 14.

Peter H. Matthews. 1981. *Syntax*. Cambridge: Cambridge University Press.

Igor Mel'čuk. 1988. *Dependency Syntax: Theory and Practice*. State University of New York Press, Albany.

Igor Mel'čuk. 2003. Levels of dependency description: concepts and problems. In Vilmos Agel et al. (eds.), *Dependency and Valency: An International Handbook of Contemporary Research*, vol. 1, pp. 188-229. Walter de Gruyter, Berlin.

Igor Mel'čuk. 2009. Dependency in Natural language. In Igor Mel'čuk and Alain Polguère (eds.): *Dependency in linguistic description*, pp. 1-110. Amsterdam ; Philadelphia : John Benjamins Pub.

Timothy Osborne and Thomas Groß. 2012. Constructions are catenae: Construction Grammar meets dependency grammar. *Cognitive Linguistics* 23 (1): 163–214.

Carl Pollard and Ivan Sag. 1994. *Head-driven phrase structure grammar*. University of Chicago Press.

Keren Rice. 2006. Morpheme Order and Semantic Scope: Word Formation in the Athapaskan Verb. Cambridge et al.: Cambridge University Press.

Luigi Rizzi. 1997. The Fine Structure of the Left Periphery. L. Haegeman (ed.), *Elements of Grammar. A Handbook in Generative Syntax*, pp 281–337. Dordrecht: Kluwer.

Stanley Starosta. 1988. *The Case for Lexicase: An Outline of Lexicase Grammatical Theory*. Pinter Publishers, New York.

Mark Steedman 2014. Categorial Grammar. In Andrew Carnie, Yosuke Sato, and Daniel Siddiqi (eds.), *The Routledge Handbook of Syntax*, pp. 670-701. Routledge, London.

Diachronic Trends in Word Order Freedom and Dependency Length in Dependency-Annotated Corpora of Latin and Ancient Greek

Kristina Gulordava
University of Geneva
kristina.gulordava@unige.ch

Paola Merlo
University of Geneva
paola.merlo@unige.ch

Abstract

One easily observable aspect of language variation is the order of words. In human and machine natural language processing, it is often claimed that parsing free-order languages is more difficult than parsing fixed-order languages. In this study on Latin and Ancient Greek, two well-known and well-documented free-order languages, we propose syntactic correlates of word order freedom. We apply our indicators to a collection of dependency-annotated texts of different time periods. On the one hand, we confirm a trend towards more fixed-order patterns in time. On the other hand, we show that a dependency-based measure of the flexibility of word order is correlated with the parsing performance on these languages.

1 Introduction

Languages vary in myriad ways. One easily observable aspect of variation is the order of words. Not only do languages vary in the linear order of their phrases, they also vary in how fixed and uniform the orders are. We speak of fixed-order languages and free word order languages.

Free word order has been associated in the linguistic literature with other properties, such as richness of morphology, for example. In natural language processing, it is often claimed that parsing freer word order languages is more difficult, for instance, than parsing English, whose word order is quite fixed.

Quantitative measures of word order freedom and investigations of it on a sufficiently large scale to draw firm conclusions, however, are not common (Liu, 2010; Futrell et al., 2015b). To be able to study word order flexibility quantitatively and computationally, we need a syntactic representation that is appropriate for both fixed and flexible word order; we need languages that exhibit genuine optionality of word order, and for which large amounts of text have been carefully annotated in the chosen representation.

In the current choice of hand-annotated treebanks, these requirements are fullfilled by dependency-annotated corpora of Latin and Ancient Greek. These two languages are extensively documented, they are dead languages and are therefore studied in a tradition where careful text editing and curation is a necessity, and have the added advantage that their genealogical children, Romance languages and Modern Greek, are also grammatically well studied, so that we can add a diachronic dimension to our observations.

Both Latin and Ancient Greek allow a lot of freedom in the linearisation of sentence elements. In these languages, this also concerns the noun-phrase domain, which is otherwise typically more constrained than the verbal domain in modern European languages[1]. In this study, we propose syntactic correlates of word order freedom both in the noun phrase and at the sentence level: variability in the directionality of the head-modifier relation, adjacency of the head-modifier relation (also called non-projectivity), and degree of minimisation of dependency length.

First, we look at head directionality, that is, post-nominal versus prenominal placement, of adjectives and numerals. While the variation in adjective placement is a wide-spread and well-studied phenomenon in modern languages, such as Romance languages, for example, the variation in numeral placement is a rarer phenomenon and is particularly interesting to investigate.

Then, we analyse the discontinuity of noun-

[1]Regarding the diachronic change in word order freedom, Tily (2010) found that in the change from Old to Middle and Modern English, the verb-headed clause changed considerably in word order and dependency length, from verb-final to verb initial, while the domain of the noun phrase did not.

Proceedings of the Third International Conference on Dependency Linguistics (Depling 2015), pages 121–130,
Uppsala, Sweden, August 24–26 2015.

Language	Text	Period	#Sentences	#Words
Latin	*Caesar*, Commentarii belli Gallici	58-49 BC	1154	22408
	Cicero, Epistulae ad Atticum & De officii	68–43 BC	3830	44370
	Aetheriae, *Peregrinatio*	4th century AD	921	17554
	Jerome's *Vulgate*	4th century AD	8903	79389
Ancient Greek	*Herodotus*, Histories,	450-420 BC	5098	75032
	New Testament	4th century AD	10627	119371

Table 1: Summary of properties of the treebanks of Latin and Ancient Greek languages, including the historical period and size of each text.

phrases. Specifically, we extract the modifiers that are separated from the noun by some elements of a sentence that are not themselves noun dependents. Example (1) illustrates a non-adjacent dependency between the noun *maribus* and the adjective *reliquis*, separated by the verb *utimur*.

(1) (Caes. Gal. 5.1.2)
... quam quibus in reliquis$_a$ utimur$_v$ maribus$_n$
... than those in other we-use seas
'... than those (that) we use in (the) other seas'

We apply our two indicators to a collection of dependency-annotated texts of different time periods and show a pattern of diachronic change, demonstrating a trend towards more fixed-order patterns in time.

The different word order properties that we detect at different points in time for the same language allow us to set up a controlled experiment to ask whether greater word-order freedom causes greater parsing difficulty. We show that the dependency formalism provides us with a sentence-level measure of the flexibility of word order which we define as the distance between the actual dependency length of a sentence and its optimal dependency length (Gildea and Temperley, 2010). We demonstrate that this robust measure of the word order freedom of the languages reflects their parsing complexity.

2 Materials

Before discussing our measures in detail, we take a look at the resources that are available and that are used in our study.

2.1 Dependency-annotated corpora

The dependency treebanks of Latin and Ancient Greek used in our study come from the PROIEL project (Haug and Jøhndal, 2008). Compared to other treebanks, such as the Perseus treebanks (Bamman and Crane, 2011), previously used in the parsing literature, the PROIEL corpus contains exclusively prose and is therefore more appropriate for a word order variation study than other treebanks, which also contain poetry. Moreover, the PROIEL corpus allows us to analyze different texts and authors independently of each other. This, as we will see, provides us with interesting diachronic data. Table 1 presents the texts included in the corpus with their time periods and the size in sentences and number of words.

The texts in Latin range from the Classical Latin period (Caesar and Cicero) to the Late Latin of 4th century (Vulgate and Peregrinatio). Jerome's Vulgate is a translation from the Greek New Testament. The two Greek texts are Herodotus (4th century BC) and New Testament (4th century AD). The sizes of the texts are uneven, but include at least 17000 words or 900 sentences.

2.2 Modifier-noun dependencies in the corpus

We use the dependency and part-of-speech annotations of the PROIEL corpus to extract adjective-noun and numeral-noun dependencies and their properties.

Both Latin and Ancient Greek are annotated using the same guidelines and tagsets. We identify adjectives by their unique (fine and coarse) PoS tag "A-". The PoS annotation of the PROIEL corpora distinguishes between cardinal and ordinal numerals ("Ma" and "Mo" fine tags correspondingly). Cardinal numerals differ in their structural and functional properties from ordinal numerals; current analysis includes only cardinals to ensure the homogeneity of this class of modifiers.

For our analysis, we consider only adjectives and numerals which directly modify a noun, that is, their dependency head must be tagged as a noun ("Nb" and "Ne" fine tags). Such dependencies must also have an "atr" dependency label, for attribute.

The overall number of extracted adjective dependencies ranges from 600 (Peregrinatio) to 1700 (Herodotus and NewTestament), with an average of 1000 dependencies per text. The overall number of extracted numeral dependencies ranges from 83 (Peregrinatio) to 400 (New Testament and Vulgate), with average of 220 dependencies per text.

2.3 Measures

Our indicators of word order freedom are based on the relationship between the head and the dependent.

Head-Dependent Directionality Word order is a relative positional notion. The simplest indicator of word order is therefore the relative order of head and dependent. We say then that a language has free(r) word order if the position of the dependents relative to the head, before or after, is less uniform than for a fixed order language. In traditional linguistic studies, this is the notion that is most often used. However, it is a measure that is often too coarse to exhibit any clear patterns.

Head-Dependent Adjacency A more sensitive measure of freedom of word order will take into account adjacency to the head. Dependents can be adjacent to the head or not. Dependents that are not adjacent to the head can be separated by elements that belong to the same subtree or not. If dependents are not adjacent and are separated by a different subtree, we talk of non-projectivity.

The notion of non-projectivity encodes therefore both a notion of linear order and a notion of structural relation. It is this last notion that we consider relevant as a correlate of free word order.

The non-projectivity measure can be encoded in two ways: either as a simple indicator, a binary variable that tells us if a dependency is projective or not, or a distance measure that counts the distance of non-adjacent elements, as long as they are crossed by a non-projective dependency.

In this paper, we present an adjacency analysis for the noun phrase. More precisely, we identify modifiers which are separated from their head noun by at least one word which does not belong to the subtree headed by the noun. For instance, as can be seen from the dependency tree in Figure 1, the adjective *reliquis* is separated from its head *maribus* by the verb *utimur*, which does not be-

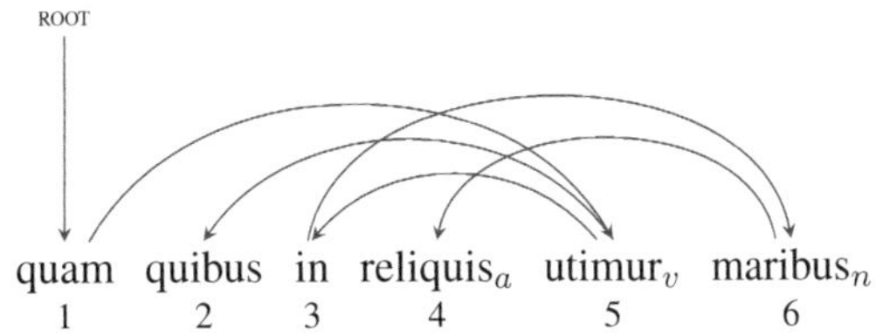

Figure 1: The dependency tree of the sentence from Example (1), extracted from the original PROIEL treebank.

long to the subtree of *maribus* (which comprises only *reliquis* and *maribus*, in this example). We calculate the proportion of such non-projective adjectives over all adjectives whose head is a noun. In addition, we report the average distance of non-projective adjectives from their head. The same values are also computed and reported for numerals.

3 NP-internal word order variation

We begin our investigation of word order variation by looking at word order in the noun phrase, a controlled setting potentially influenced by fewer factors than sentential word order.

3.1 Head-Dependent Directionality

For each of the texts in our corpus, we computed the percentage of prenominal versus post-nominal placement for two modifiers — adjectives and numerals. To avoid interference with size effects, these counts include only simple one-word modifiers.

If languages are sensitive to complexity, and tend to reduce it, our expectation for the diachronic trend is straight-forward. We expect the amount of prenominal-postnominal variation to be reduced. Also, we expect it to take the Latin grammar in the direction of the Romance-like grammar and Ancient Greek grammar in the direction of the Modern Greek grammar. Specifically, we expect adjective order to be more post-nominal in Latin in the course of time and more prenominal in Ancient Greek (Modern Greek has rigid prenominal adjective placement). For numerals, both Latin and Ancient Greek are expected to show more prenominal orders in the more recent texts (no post-nominal numerals are possible at all either in Romance languages or Modern Greek).

Table 2, left panel, shows the results. For adjectives in Latin, the observed percentages of prenominal adjectives exhibit the expected diachronic trend, moving from 73% to 36% of

		Head-Directionality				Adjacency			
		Adjective		Numeral		Adjective		Numeral	
Language	Text	#	%	#	%	%	Dist	%	Dist
Latin	Caesar	784	73	110	68	17	1.21	15	1.17
	Cicero	1064	60	104	80	11	1.14	12	1.31
	Peregrinatio	533	58	69	78	5	1.10	6	1.06
	Vulgate	1088	36	352	72	4	1.05	3	1.03
Ancient Greek	Herodotus	1409	49	282	69	27	1.38	16	1.20
	NewTestament	1257	49	400	70	9	1.10	4	1.04

Table 2: Quantitative summary of the variation in placement of two noun modifiers — adjectives and numerals in the Latin and Ancient Greek treebanks. The number of modifier-noun pairs and the percentage of prenominal order is given on the left; the percentage of non-adjacent modifiers (out of the total number) and the average distance from the noun head is given on the right.

prenominal adjectives. In terms of magnitude of the head-directionality measure, the shift from head-initial to head-final in Latin is of roughly the same size around the mean, which does not yet support strong regularisation. We know however, from statistics on modern Romance languages that this trend has converged to post-nominal patterns that range around 70% (Spanish 73%; Catalan 79%; Italian 67%; Portuguese 71%; French 74%)[2]. Adjective placement in Ancient Greek does not show any regularisation. For numerals, we do not observe a strong regularisation pattern for either language.

Since our expectations about trends of head-dependent directionality are only confirmed by adjectives in Latin, we conclude that this measure is weak and might not be sensitive to small changes in word order freedom.

3.2 Head-dependent adjacency

A more interesting diachronic observation comes from the number of non-adjacent versus adjacent modifiers (Table 2, right panel). Similar to the head-directionality patterns, our expectation is that the number of non-adjacent modifiers will decrease over time to eventually converge to the modern language situation, where such dependencies practically do not exist. The observed pattern is very sharp. This change is clear from the decline in percentage: from 17% to 4% for adjectives in Latin and 27% to 9% for adjectives in Ancient Greek. For numerals, the non-projectivity decreases from 15% to 3% in Latin and from 16% to 4% in Ancient Greek. It is important to notice that this decline can be made apparent only through a quantitative study, as it requires a full-fledged syntactic analysis of the sentence covering the non-projective dependencies. This phenomenon is relatively infrequent and the difference in percentages might not be perceived in traditional descriptive work.

Our results on head-directionality and adjacency for noun modifiers, summarised in Table 2, show that the two measures of word order freedom which we proposed do not pattern alike. While head-directionality does not show much change (with the exception of adjectives in Latin), the results on adjacency measure confirm our expectation that both languages converged with time towards a more fixed word order.

The tendency for non-projectivity and for preferences of head-adjacency of one-word modifiers are often explained as a tendency to minimise dependency-length, tendency that languages use to facilitate processing and production (Hawkins, 2004). In the next two sections, we study this more general principle of dependency length minimisation. We extend our investigation from the limited, controlled domain of the noun phrase to the more extended context of sentences. We investigate whether the dependency length measure at the sentence level correlates with our findings so far, and whether it is a good predictor of parsing complexity. We expect to see that, as languages have more and more fixed word order patterns, they become easier to parse.

4 Minimising Dependency Length

Very general, intuitive claims, both in human sentence processing and natural language processing,

[2]These counts are based on the dependency treebanks of these languages, available from Zeman et al. (2012).

state that free word order and long dependencies give rise to greater processing complexity. As such, languages should show patterns of regularisation, diachronic and synchronic, towards shorter dependencies and more homogeneous word orders. Notice, however, that these two pressures are in contradiction, as a reduction in dependency length can be obtained by placing modifiers at the two sides of the head, increasing variation in head directionality. How exactly languages develop, then, is worthy of investigation.

Experimental and theoretical language research has yielded a large and diverse body of evidence for dependency length minimisation (DLM). Gibson (1998, 2000) argues that structures with longer dependencies are more difficult to process, and shows that this principle predicts a number of phenomena in comprehension. One example is the finding that subject-extracted relative clauses are easier to process than object-extracted relative clauses.

Dependency length minimisation also concerns phenomena of syntactic choice. Hawkins (1994, 2004) shows, through a series of corpus analyses, that syntactic choices generally respect the preference for placing short elements closer to the head than long elements. This choice minimises overall dependency length in the tree. For example, in cases where a verb has two prepositional-phrase dependents, the shorter one tends to be placed closer to the verb. This preference is found both in head-first languages such as English, where PPs follow verbs and the shorter of two PPs tends to be placed first, and in head-last languages such as Japanese. Hawkins (1994, 2004) also shows that, in languages in which adjectives and relative clauses are on the same side of the head noun, the adjective, which is presumably generally shorter than the relative clause, is usually required to be closer to the noun. Temperley (2007) finds evidence for DLM in a variety of syntactic choice phenomena in written English. For example, subject NPs tend to be shorter than object NPs: as the head of an NP tends to be near its left end, a long subject NP creates a long dependency between the head of the NP and the verb, while a long object NP generally does not.

Recently, global measures of dependency length on a larger scale have been proposed, and cross-linguistic work has used these measures. Gildea and Temperley (2010) look at the overall dependency length of a sentence given its unordered structure to study whether languages tend to minimize dependency length. In particular, they observe that German tends to have longer dependencies compared to English, which they attribute to greater freedom of word order in German.

Their study, however, suffers from the shortcoming that they are comparing different annotations and different languages. From a methodological point of view, our experimental set up is more controlled because we compare several texts of the same language (Latin or Ancient Greek) and these texts belong to the same corpus and are annotated using the same annotation scheme. This means that the annotation scheme assumes the same underlying head-dependent relations in all texts for a given pair of parts-of-speech. From the linguistic point of view, the comparison of different amounts of word order freedom comes not from comparing different languages — a comparison where many other factors could come into play — but from comparing the same language over time as its word order properties were changing. The possible differences in DLM in these texts can be therefore directly attributed to the flexibility of their orders with respect to each other, since neither language nor annotation changes.

We test, then, whether a coarse dependency length measure (Gildea and Temperley, 2010) can capture the rate of the flexibility of word order in our controlled setting.

The dependency length of a sentence is simply defined as the sum of the lengths of all of its dependencies. The length of a dependency is taken to be the difference between position indices of the head and the dependent. To illustrate, for the subtree in Figure 1, the overall dependency length is equal to 14 for five dependencies. This is a particularly high value because there are two non-projective dependencies in the sentence. Dependency length is therefore conditioned both on the unordered tree structure of the sentence and the particular linearisation of this unordered graph, the order of words.

Following Gildea and Temperley (2010) and Futrell et al. (2015a) we also compute the optimal and random dependency length of a sentence, based on its unordered dependency tree available from the gold annotation. More precisely, to compute the random dependency length, we permutate the positions of the words in the sentence and cal-

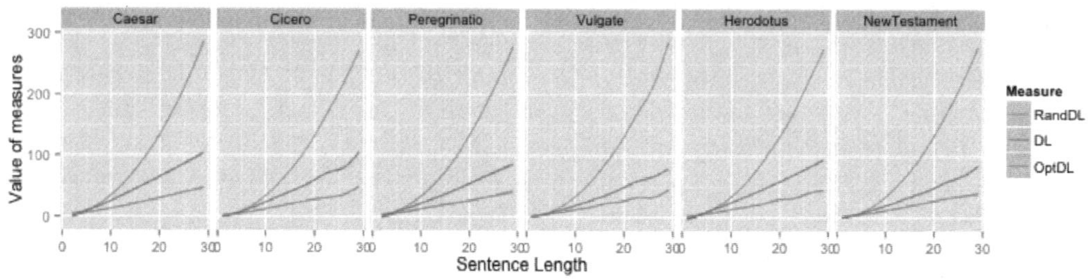

Figure 3: Average random, average optimal and actual dependency lengths of sentences by sentence length for each text.

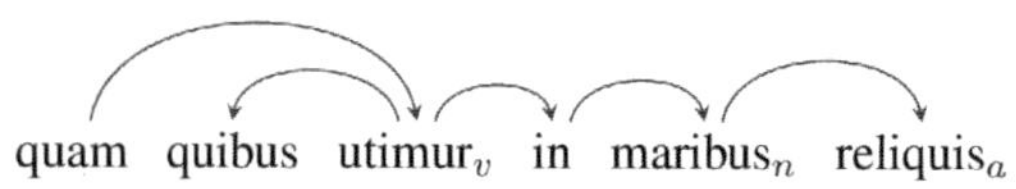

Figure 2: A word ordering of the sentence from Example (1) which yields minimal dependency length.

culate the new random dependency length preserving the original unordered tree structure.[3]

The optimal dependency length is calculated using the algorithm proposed by Gildea and Temperley (2007). Given an unordered dependency tree spanning over a sentence, the algorithm outputs the ordering of words which gives the minimal overall dependency length. Roughly, the algorithm implements the DLM tendencies widely observed in natural languages: if a head has several children, these are placed on both sides of the head; shorter children are closer to the head than longer ones; the order of the output is fully projective. Gildea and Temperley (2007) prove the optimality of the algorithm. For instance, the optimal ordering of the tree in Figure 1 would yield the dependency length of 6, as can be seen from the Figure 2.

Note that two sentences with the same unordered tree structure will have the same optimal dependency lengths.[4] If such sentences have different actual dependency lengths, this must then be directly attributed to the differences in their word order. We can generalise this observation to the structural descriptions of languages that are known to have similar grammatical structures. This similarity will be necessarily reflected by similar average values of the optimal dependency lengths in the treebanks. For such languages, systematic differences in actual dependency lengths observed across many sentences can be consequently attributed to their different word order patterns.

Our Latin and Ancient Greek texts show exactly this type of difference in their dependency lengths. Figure 3 illustrates the random, optimal and actual dependency lengths averaged for sentences of the same length.[5] First of all, we can observe that languages do optimise dependency length to some extent as their dependency lengths (indicated as DL) are lower than random. However, they are also not too close to the optimal values (indicated as $OptDL$). As can be also seen from Figure 3, the optimal dependency lengths across the texts are very similar. Their actual dependency lengths, on the contrary, are more variable. If we define the DLM score as the difference between the optimal and the actual dependency length, $DL - OptDL$, we observe a diachronic pattern aligned with the non-projectivity trends from the previous section. The patterns are shown in Figures 4 and 5, where for the sake of readability, we have plotted $DL - OptDL$ against the sentence length in log-log space.

For each language, we tested whether the pairwise differences between $DL - OptDL$ trends are significant by fitting the linear regressions $\log(DL - OptDL + 1) \sim \log(Sent)$ for two texts

[3] We do not impose any constraints on the random permutation of words. See Park and Levy (2009) for an empirical study of different randomisation strategies for the estimation of minimal dependency length with projectivity constraints.

[4] Also, two sentences with the same number of words will have the same random dependency lengths (on average).

[5] Since the optimal and random dependency length values depend (non-linearly) on the sentence length n, it is customary to analyse them as functions $DL(n)$ (and $E[DL(n)]$) and not as global averages over all sentences in a treebank (Ferrer-i-Cancho and Liu, 2014).

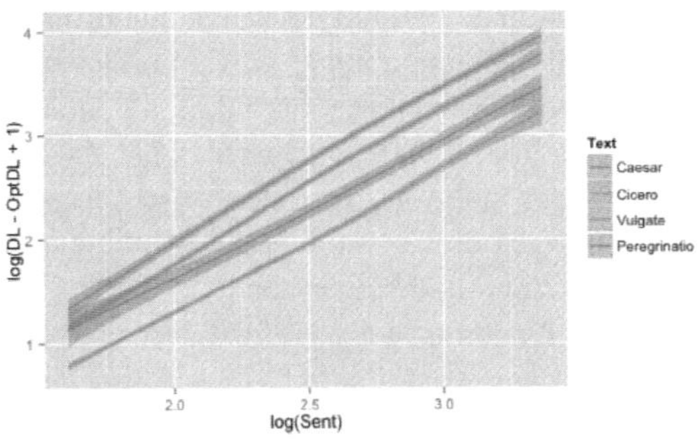

Figure 4: Rate of DLM for Latin texts, measured as $DL - OptDL$ and mapped to sentence length (in log-log space).

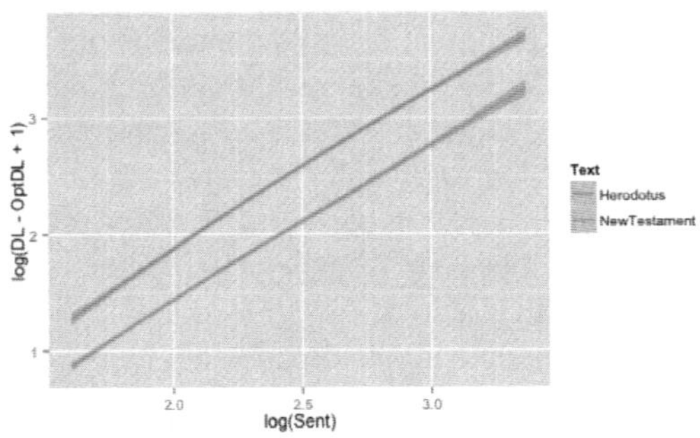

Figure 5: Rate of DLM for Greek texts, measured as $DL - OptDL$ and mapped to sentence length (in log-log space).

and comparing their intercepts[6]. These were significant at the $p < 0.001$ level for all pairs of texts.

So we can conclude that for Latin, older manuscripts of Caesar and Cicero show less minimisation of dependency length than later Latin texts of Vulgate and Peregrinatio. For Ancient Greek, Herodotus, which is the oldest test in the collection, has the smallest minimisation of dependency length. Since modern Romance languages and modern Greek have dependency lengths very close to optimal (Futrell et al., 2015a), we expect that Latin and Ancient Greek minimise the dependency length over time. Our data confirm this expectation.

We have also observed that the smaller percentage of non-projective arcs aligns with the higher rate of DLM across texts. This result confirms empirically a theoretical observation of Ferrer-i-Cancho (2006).

5 Word order flexibility and parsing performance

The previous section confirms through a globally optimised measure, what is already visible in the diachronic evolution of the adjacency measure in Table 2: older Latin and Ancient Greek texts exhibit longer dependencies and freer word order than later texts.

It is often claimed that parsing freer-order languages is harder. Specifically, parsers learn locally contained structures better and have more problems recovering long distance dependencies (Nivre et al., 2010). Handling non-projective dependencies is another long-standing problem (McDonald and Satta, 2007). We investigate the source of these difficulties, by correlating parsing performance on our texts from different time periods to our free word order measures. It is straight-forward to hypothesise that a tree with a small overall dependency length will be easier to parse than a tree with a large overall dependency length, and that a projective tree will be easier than a non-projective tree. Given our corpus, which is annotated with the same annotation scheme for all texts, we have an opportunity to test this hypothesis on texts that constitute truly controlled minimal pairs for such analysis.

The parsing results we report here are obtained using the Mate parser (Bohnet, 2010). Graph-based parsers like Mate do not have architectural constraints on handling non-projective trees and have been shown to be robust at parsing long dependencies (McDonald and Nivre, 2011). Given the high percentage of non-projective arcs and the number of long dependencies in the Latin and Ancient Greek corpora, we expect a graph-based parser to perform better than other types of dependency parsers. On a random training-testing split for all our, Mate parser shows the best performance among several of the dependency parsers we tested, including the transition-based Malt parser (Nivre et al., 2006).

We test several training and testing configurations. Since it is not clear how to evaluate a parser to compare texts with different rates of word order freedom, we used two different set-ups: training and testing within the same text and across different texts.

For the "within-text" evaluation, we apply a

[6]More precisely, we fitted a linear regression $\log(DL - OptDL+1) = \beta \cdot Text + \log(Sent)$, where $Text$ is a binary indicator variable, on the combined data for two texts. We compare this model to the null model with $\beta = 0$ by means of an ANOVA to test whether two texts are best described by linear regressions with different or equal intercepts.

Lang	Configuration	Train. Size	UAS
Latin	Caesar	18k	66.46
	Cicero	18k	63.11
	Peregr.	18k	74.35
	Vulgate	18k	83.92
	all texts	155k	78.30
Greek	Herodotus	75k	69.76
	NewTest	75k	88.01
	all texts	195k	79.94

Table 3: Parsing accuracy for random-split training (90%) and test (10%) configurations for each language and for each text independently.

Lang	Training	Test	Train. Size	UAS
Latin	BC	AD	67k	67.27
	AD	BC	106k	57.72
Greek	Herodotus	NewTest	75k	76.05
	NewTest	Herodotus	120k	61.27

Table 4: Parsing accuracy for period-based training and test configurations for Latin and Ancient Greek.

standard random split, 90% of the corpus assigned to training and 10% assigned to testing, for each text separately. We eliminated potentially confounding effects due to different training sizes by including only around 18'000 words for each text in Latin (the size of the Peregrinatio corpus), and around 100'000 in Ancient Greek. We also report a strong baseline for each language, calculated by training and testing on all texts combined and split randomly with 90%/10% proportion. We evaluate the parsing performance using Unlabelled Accuracy Scores (UAS). The use of the unlabelled, rather than labelled, accuracy scores is the appropriate choice in our case because we seek to correlate the dependency length minimisation measure, a structural measure based on unlabelled dependency trees, to the parsing performance. The results for these experiments are reported in Table 3. First, the cumulative parsing accuracy on both Latin and Ancient Greek is relatively high as seen from the 'all texts' random split configuration[7]. Importantly, we can also observe that the older varieties of both Latin and Ancient Greek have lower UAS scores than their more recent counterparts.

We also evaluate parsing performance across time periods. Our intuition is that it is harder to generalise from a more fixed-order language to a freer-order language than vice versa. In addition, this setup allows us to use larger training sets for a more robust parsing evaluation. For this experiment, for Latin, we divide the four texts into two diachronic groups, where they naturally belong, BC for Caesar and Cicero and AD for Vulgate and Peregrinatio. We then train the parser on texts from one group and test on texts from the other. For Greek, as we do not have several texts from the same period, we test a similar configuration by training on one text and testing on the other. The results of these configuration are presented in Table 4. These results confirm our hypothesis and suggest that it is better to train the parser on a freer word order language. Despite the fact that it is harder to parse freer word order languages, as shown in Table 3, they provide better generalisation ability.

To summarise, in our experiments we see that the accuracy for older texts written in Latin in the BC period is much lower than the accuracy for late Latin texts written in the AD period. This pattern correlates with the previously observed smaller degree of dependency length minimisation of BC texts compared to AD texts. Similarly, for Greek, Herodotus is much more difficult to parse than the New Testament text, which corresponds to their differences in the rate of DLM as well as the non-projectivity in the noun phrase. The presented results confirm, therefore, the postulated hypothesis that freer order languages are harder to parse. In combination with the results from the previous sections, we can conclude that this difficulty is particularly due to longer dependencies and non-projectivity.

6 Related work

Our work has both similarities and differences with traditional work on Classical languages. Much work on word order variation using traditional, scholarly methods relies on unsystematically chosen text samples. Conclusions are often made about the Latin language in general, based on relatively few examples extracted from as few as one literary work. The analyses and the conclusions could therefore be subject to both well-known kinds of sampling errors: bias error due to a skewed sample and random error due to small

[7]These performance values are especially high compared to the previous results reported on the LDT and AGDT corpora, 61.9% and 70.5% of UAS, respectively (Lee et al., 2011). This increase in accuracy is likely due to the the fact that our texts are prose and not poetry.

sample sizes.

In particular, word order variation is one of the most studied syntactic aspects of Latin. For example, much descriptive evidence is dedicated to show the change from SOV to SVO order. However, starting from the work of Panhuis (1984), the previously assumed OV/VO change has been highly debated. At present, there is no convincing quantitative evidence for the diachronic trend of this pattern of variation in Classical Latin. In general, such coarse word order variation patterns are often bad cues of diachronic change and a more accurate syntactic and pragmatic analysis is required.

Non-projectivity goes under the name of *hyperbaton* in the classical literature. Several pieces of work address this phenomenon. Some of the authors give estimations of the number of discontinuous noun phrases, based on their analysis of particular texts (see Bauer (2009, 288-290), and the references there). These estimations range from 12% to 30% and are admittedly controversial because the counting procedure is not clearly stated (Pinkster, 2005, 250).

We are aware of only very few pieces of work that make use of syntactically-annotated treebanks to study diachronic word order variation. Bamman and Crane (2008) present some statistics on SVO order and on adjective-noun order, extracted from their Perseus treebanks for several subcorpora. Their data shows very different patterns of observed SVO variation across different texts. These patterns change from author to author and are hard to analyse in a systematic way. The work described in Tily (2010) is the closest to ours. The order of Old English is analysed using the same dependency length measure proposed by Gildea and Temperley (2010). On a large sample of texts, it is shown that there is a clear decrease in overall dependency length (averaged across sentences of all lengths in a corpus) from 900 to 1500 AD.

Another very relevant piece of work by Futrell et al. (2015a) also concerns dependency length minimisation. The general results of this study over thirty-four languages is that languages minimise dependency length over a random baseline. In these results, Latin and Ancient Greek are exceptions and do not appear to show greater than random dependency length minimisation. This is in contrast to our results. We conclude that this is an effect of the corpus used in Futrell's study, which contains a lot of poetry, while our texts are prose. Our results show a more coherent picture with their general results.

Finally, in this work, we address word order variation in the noun phrase and the DLM principle applied at the sentence level independently. Gulordava et al. (2015) investigate how these two properties interact and whether DLM modulates the variation in the placement of adjectives.

7 Conclusions

This paper has presented a corpus-based, quantitative investigation of word order freedom in Latin and Ancient Greek, two well-known and well-documented free-order languages. We have proposed two syntactic correlates of word order freedom in the noun phrase: head-directionality and head-dependent adjacency, or non-projectivity. If applied to a collection of dependency-annotated texts of different time periods, the non-projectivity measure confirms an expected trend toward closer adjacency and more fixed-order patterns in time. On the contrary, the head-directionality measure is a weak indicator of the fine-grained changes in freedom of word order. We have then extended the investigation to the sentence level and applied another dependency-based indicator of free word order, the rate of dependency length minimisation. The trend toward more fixed word orders is confirmed by this measure.

Another main result of the paper correlates dependency length minimisation with parsing performances on these languages, thereby confirming the intuitive claim that free-order languages are harder to parse. As a side result, we train parsers for Latin and Ancient Greek with good performance, showing, for future directions, that it will be possible to extend the data for the analysis of these languages by automatically parsing unannotated texts.

Acknowledgements

We gratefully acknowledge the partial funding of this work by the Swiss National Science Foundation, under grant 144362. We thank Lieven Danckaert and Séverine Nasel for pointing relevant Latin and Ancient Greek references to us.

References

David Bamman and Gregory R. Crane. 2008. Building a dynamic lexicon from a digital library. In *Procs of the 8th ACM/IEEE-CS Joint Conference on Digital libraries (JCDL'08)*, 11–20, New York, NY.

David Bamman and Gregory R. Crane. 2011. The Ancient Greek and Latin Dependency Treebanks. In Caroline Sporleder, Antal Bosch, and Kalliopi Zervanou, editors, *Language Technology for Cultural Heritage*, pages 79–98. Springer, Berlin/Heidelberg.

Brigitte L. M. Bauer. 2009. Word order. In Philip Baldi and Pierluigi Cuzzolin, editors, *New Perspectives on Historical Latin Syntax. Vol. 1. Syntax of the Sentence*, 241–316, Berlin. Mouton de Gruyter.

Bernd Bohnet. 2010. Very high accuracy and fast dependency parsing is not a contradiction. In *Procs of the 23rd Int'l Conf. on Computational Linguistics*, COLING '10, 89–97, Stroudsburg, PA.

Ramon Ferrer-i-Cancho and Haitao Liu. 2014. The risks of mixing dependency lengths from sequences of different length. *Glottotheory*, 5(2):143–155.

Ramon Ferrer-i-Cancho. 2006. Why do syntactic links not cross? *EPL (Europhysics Letters)*, 76(6):12–28.

Richard Futrell, Kyle Mahowald, and Edward Gibson. 2015a. Large-Scale Evidence of Dependency Length Minimization in 37 Languages. (Submitted to Proceedings of the National Academy of Sciences of the United States of America).

Richard Futrell, Kyle Mahowald, and Edward Gibson. 2015b. Quantifying Word Order Freedom in Dependency Corpora . In *Proceedings of the Third Int'l Conf. on Dependency Linguistics (DepLing 2015)*, Uppsala, Sweden.

Edward Gibson. 1998. Linguistic complexity: Locality of syntactic dependencies. *Cognition*, 68(1):1–76.

Edward Gibson. 2000. The dependency locality theory: A distance-based theory of linguistic complexity. *Image, language, brain*, 95–126.

Daniel Gildea and David Temperley. 2007. Optimizing Grammars for Minimum Dependency Length. In *Procs of the Association for Computational Linguistics (ACL'07)*, 184–191, Prague, Czech Republic.

Daniel Gildea and David Temperley. 2010. Do Grammars Minimize Dependency Length? *Cognitive Science*, 34(2):286–310.

Kristina Gulordava, Paola Merlo, and Benoit Crabbé. 2015. Dependency length minimisation effects in short spans: a large-scale analysis of adjective placement in complex noun phrases. In *Procs of the Association for Computational Linguistics: Short Papers (ACL'15)*.

Dag T. T. Haug and Marius L. Jøhndal. 2008. Creating a Parallel Treebank of the Old Indo-European Bible Translations. In *Proc of the 2nd Workshop on Language Technology for Cultural Heritage Data*, 27–34, Marrakech, Morocco.

John A. Hawkins. 2004. *Efficiency and Complexity in Grammars*. Oxford linguistics. Oxford University Press, Oxford, UK.

John Lee, Jason Naradowsky, and David A. Smith. 2011. A Discriminative Model for Joint Morphological Disambiguation and Dependency Parsing. In *Procs of the Association for Computational Linguistics: Human Language Technologies*, 885–894, Portland, Oregon.

Haitao Liu. 2010. Dependency direction as a means of word-order typology: A method based on dependency treebanks. *Lingua*, 120(6):1567–1578.

Ryan McDonald and Joakim Nivre. 2011. Analyzing and Integrating Dependency Parsers. *Computational Linguistics*, 37(1):197–230.

Ryan McDonald and Giorgio Satta. 2007. On the complexity of non-projective data-driven dependency parsing. In *Procs of the 10th Int'l Conference on Parsing Technologies*, 121–132.

Joakim Nivre, Johan Hall, and Jens Nilsson. 2006. MaltParser: A data-driven parser-generator for dependency parsing. In *Procs of the 5th International Conference on Language Resources and Evaluation (LREC'06)*, 2216–2219.

Joakim Nivre, Laura Rimell, Ryan McDonald, and Carlos Gómez-Rodríguez. 2010. Evaluation of dependency parsers on unbounded dependencies. In *Procs of the Int'l Conference on Computational Linguistics (COLING'10)*, pages 833–841, Stroudsburg, PA.

Dirk Panhuis. 1984. Is Latin an SOV language? A diachronic perspective. *Indogermanische Forschungen*, 89:140–159.

Albert Y. Park and Roger Levy. 2009. Minimal-length linearizations for mildly context-sensitive dependency trees. In *Procs of the North American Chapter of the Association for Computational Linguistics (NAACL'09)*, 335–343.

Harm Pinkster. 2005. The language of Pliny the Elder. In *Proceedings of the British Academy*, volume 129, pages 239–256. OUP.

David Temperley. 2007. Minimization of dependency length in written English. *Cognition*, 105(2):300–333.

Harry Joel Tily. 2010. *The role of processing complexity in word order variation and change*. Ph.D. Thesis, Stanford University.

Daniel Zeman, David Mareček, Martin Popel, Loganathan Ramasamy, Jan Štěpánek, Zdeněk Žabokrtský, and Jan Hajič. 2012. HamleDT: To Parse or Not to Parse? In *Procs of the Int'l Conference on Language Resources and Evaluation (LREC'12)*, 23–25, Istanbul, Turkey.

Reconstructions of Deletions in a Dependency-based Description of Czech: Selected Issues

Eva Hajičová and **Marie Mikulová** and **Jarmila Panevová**
Charles University in Prague
Faculty of Mathematics and Physics
Institute of Formal and Applied Linguistics
Czech Republic
{hajicova,mikulova,panevova}@ufal.mff.cuni.cz

Abstract

The goal of the present contribution is to put under scrutiny the language phenomenon commonly called ellipsis or deletion, especially from the point of view of its representation in the underlying syntactic level of a dependency based syntactic description. We first give a brief account of the treatment of ellipsis in some present day dependency-based accounts of this phenomenon (Sect. 1). The core of the paper is the treatment of ellipsis within the framework of the dependency-based formal multi-level description of language called Functional Generative Description: after an attempt at a typology of ellipsis (Sect. 2) we describe in detail some selected types of grammatical ellipsis in Czech (Sect. 3). In Sect. 4 we briefly summarize the results of our analysis.

1 Treatment of ellipsis in dependency based descriptions of language

There are not many treatments of ellipsis in the framework of dependency grammar. Hudson's original conviction presented in his 'word grammar' (WG, (Hudson, 1984)) was that syntactic theory could stick firmly to the surface with dependency relations linking thoroughly concrete words. Under this assumption, such elements as those for which transformational grammar has postulated deletions, traces or unpronounced pronouns such as PRO and *pro* were part of semantics and did not appear in syntax. In his more recent work, (Hudson, 2007), pp. 267-281 revised this rather extreme position; he presents an analysis of examples of structures such as *You keep talking* (sharing of subjects), or *What do you think the others will bring* (extraction) or case agreement in predicatives (in languages such as Icelandic and Ancient Greek, where adjectives and nouns have overt case inflection and predicative adjectives agree with the subject of their clause) demonstrating that their description cannot be relegated to semantics. He concludes that covert words have the same syntactic and semantic characteristics expected from overt words and, consequently, he refers to them as to the 'unrealized' words. He proposes to use the same mechanism used in the WG theory: namely the 'realization' relation linking a word to a form, and the 'quantity' relation which shows how many instances of it are expected among the observed tokens. If the quantity of the word is zero then a word may be unrealized. Every word has the potential for being unrealized if the grammar requires this. An unrealized word is a dependent of a word which allows it to be unrealized, thus the parent word controls realization in the same way that it controls any property of the dependent.

One of the crucial issues for a formal description of ellipsis is the specification of the extent and character of the part of the sentence that is being deleted and has to be restored. Already in the papers on deletion based on the transformational type of description it has been pointed out that the deleted element need not be a constituent in the classical understanding of the notion of constituent. A natural question offers itself whether a dependency type of description provides a more adequate specification in terms of a dependency subtree. (Osborne et al., 2012) proposed a novel unit called *catena* defined as a word or a combination of words that is continuous with respect to dominance. Any dependency tree or subtree (complete or partial) of a dependency tree qualifies as a catena. The authors conclude that based on the flexibility and utility of this concept, catena may be considered as the fundamental unit of syntax and they attempt to document this view by their analysis of different kinds of ellipsis (gapping, stripping, VP ellipsis, pseudogapping, sluic-

Proceedings of the Third International Conference on Dependency Linguistics (Depling 2015), pages 131–140,
Uppsala, Sweden, August 24–26 2015.

ing and comparative deletion, see (Osborne and Liang, 2015)).

The issue of ellipsis as a mismatch between syntax and semantics is most explicitly reflected in those dependency frameworks that work with several levels of syntactic representation. This is the case of the Meaning-Text Theory (MTT) of I. Mel'čuk and the Functional Generative Description (FGD) of P. Sgall.

In the framework of the multilevel approach of MTT the rules for surface syntactic ellipsis are part of surface syntax component and they are defined as "various kinds of reductions and omissions, possible or obligatory in a given context ..." ((Mel'čuk, 1988), p. 83). For the surface syntax representation the author distinguishes between zero signs and ellipsis. Zero lexes and lexemes are covered by the term syntactic zeroes (op. c., p. 312) and due to their sign character they are reflected in the dictionary entries. On the other hand, an ellipsis is a rule, i.e. a part of the grammar, "that eliminates certain signs in certain surface contexts." (op. c., p. 326).

2 Treatment of ellipsis in the Functional Generative Description

In the dependency-based theory of the Functional Generative Description (FGD) we subscribe to (see esp. (Sgall et al., 1986)) the treatment of ellipsis is determined by the fact that this theoretical framework works with two syntactic levels of the sentence, namely with a level representing the surface shape of the sentence and the level representing the underlying, deep syntactic structure of the sentence (so-called tectogrammatical level).[1] Simplified examples of representations on these two levels for sentence (1) are presented in Fig. 1.

(1) Jan se rozhodl opustit Prahu.
John Refl. decided to_leave Prague

In the surface structure representation each element of the sentence is represented by a node of its own (more exactly, by the form given in the dictionary) and no words are added. The dependency relations have the values such as SUBJ, OBJ, ADV etc. In the tectogrammatical tree (TR in the sequel), only autosemantic lexical units are represented by a separate node of the tree; the information carried by the function words in the surface structure is represented in the tectogrammatical structure by means of complex symbols attached to the given node (e.g. the so-called grammatemes of modality, tense, etc. or the subfunctors for the meanings carried by the prepositions etc.). The semantic relation between the head and its modifier(s) is reflected by the functor(s), such as ACT, PAT, ADDR, LOC, CPR, RSTR etc., which are, if needed, supplied by more subtle syntactico-semantic distinctions reflected by the subfunctors.

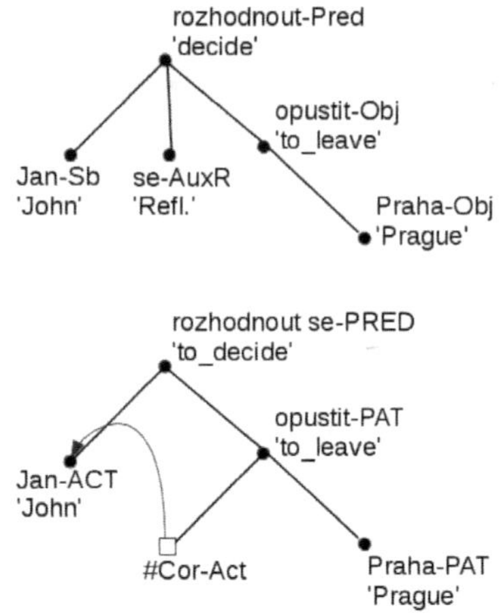

Figure 1: Simplified representations of the sentence (1) *Jan se rozhodl opustit Prahu* [John decided to leave Prague.] on the surface (above) and on the tectogrammatical (below) levels. The arrow indicates the coreferential relation.

The issue of ellipsis[2] concerns the relations between these two dependency trees. It is obvious that for an adequate representation of meaning elements of different dimensions absent on the surface need to be included in the TR. We call these elements ellipsis.

The phenomenon of ellipsis is caused by several factors:

(i) by the structure of the text (discourse),

(ii) by grammatical rules or conditions,

(iii) by an obligatory grammatically determined

[1]FGD served as a theoretical background of the annotation scheme of the Prague Dependency Treebank (PDT in the sequel; see (Bejček et al., 2013)). PDT also distinguishes an analytic syntactic level (surface) and a tectogrammatical, deep level. In the present contribution, we discuss deletions from the point of view of the theoretical approach and quote PDT only when necessary for the understanding of the point under discussion. For the treatment of deletions in the PDT see (Hajič et al., 2015).

[2]In the present discussion, we use the terms "deletion" and "ellipsis" as synonyms though we are aware that in some frameworks their meanings do not overlap.

surface deletability of an element the presence of which is required by the grammatical system.

Type (i) is called a textual ellipsis, as it is basically connected with the structure of discourse,[3] and the types (ii) and (iii) are called systemic (or grammatical) ellipsis; the type (iii) is referred to here as pseudodeletion. In the case of grammatical ellipsis the surface sentences (the "remnants") without the elliptical elements satisfy the conditions for grammatically well-formed structures; however, in order to achieve a representation of the meaning of the sentence these elements have to be filled (often using artificial nodes) in the tree even if the result of the restoration of the deletion may be stylistically awkward or even grammatically hardly acceptable in the surface shape of the sentence. On the borderline between the types (i) and (ii) there is the surface deletion of subject in Czech as a language with the property of a pro-drop language.[4]

3 The FGD treatment of selected types of systemic ellipsis in Czech

As already mentioned above, one of the crucial issues for a formal description of ellipsis is the specification of the extent of the part of the sentence that has to be restored. The extent of the restorations varies from type to type, from the more easily identifiable with the restoration of ellipsis in pro-drop cases to the least identifiable structures to be inserted in cases of deletions in coordination. In our discussion below we will concentrate on four types of systemic ellipsis in Czech with which we intend to illustrate the different possibilities and difficult points of reconstructions; we leave aside deletions in coordinated structures, which is a problem of its own and the discussion of which would go beyond the limits of this contribution.

While in 3.2 – 3.4 the problem how the items absent on the surface are to be reconstructed in TRs (as to their structure and extent), in 3.1 the reconstruction on TR is quite simple, it concerns a single node and it is manifested by the morphological categories of verb. We face here an opposite problem: how to explain the conditions where "pro-dropped" subjects are overtly expressed. In 3.1 we give only several examples with overt subjects in 1st and 2nd person without their deep analysis. By this preliminary picture of the problem we wanted to demonstrate that Czech really belongs to the "pro-drop" class of languages (see Table 1).

3.1 The pro-drop parameter in Czech

Czech belongs to languages of the pro-drop type (called sometimes zero subject or null-subject). Surprisingly, the absence of an overt subject in 1st and 2nd person was not described properly in traditional Czech grammatical handbooks (cf. (Havránek and Jedlička, 1960), p. 300 and in (Karlík et al., 1995), pp. 411–412.). The analysis of this phenomenon is given in more details in contrastive studies, esp. in those comparing Czech and Russian, because these two closely related languages differ as to their pro-drop properties.[5] Since the examples with missing pronouns of 1st and 2nd person are considered as unmarked for Czech,[6] while the overt presence of the pronouns in 1st and 2nd person as marked counterexamples, the conditions or requirements for their presence need to be listed. For the 1st person sg the following issues are mentioned in the books quoted above:

(i) the verb forms do not indicate fully the source for the agreement categories (see (2)), (ii) the contrasting position of the pronoun with regard to the other element (see (3)), (iii) the stressed position of the pronoun (often at the beginning of sentence, see (4)), (iv) the pronoun participates in a coordination chain (see (5)), and finally (v) the stylistic feature expressing pleasant or unpleasant emotions (see (6)):[7]

(2) *Já* byl vždycky tak trochu pobuda.
'*I* have always been a kind of a lounger.'

[3] So-called "textual ellipsis" typical for the spoken language and dialogues is left aside here, outside a broader context these sentences may be ungrammatical (as is the second sentence in *Have you finished your manuscript? Not yet completely.*). Their analysis is a subject of studies on discourse structure.

[4] For a detailed classification of ellipsis in Czech, see (Mikulová, 2011).

[5] A detailed analysis is given in (Isačenko, 1960), Vol 2, pp. 411f.; the author's approach seems to be too radical as to the difference between non pro-drop Russian contrary to the pro-drop Slovak; he proposed to analyse Russian constructions as *Ja splju* [*I am sleeping*] with obligatory subject pronoun *ja* [*I*] as an analytical verb form.

[6] In this section we do not pay an attention to the 3rd person; its position on the scale of deleted elements is different due to its role of anaphora.

[7] The occurrence of pronouns in marked positions in (1) through (11) is denoted by italics; these examples are taken over from the different parts of the Czech National Corpus, namely SYN2010 and SYN2013PUB.

(3) Byli bohatí, *já* jsem byl chudý.

' [They] were rich, *I* was poor.'

(4) Ten článek jsem psal *já*.

'The article *I* wrote.'

(5) Můj přítel a *já* jsme odešli z policejního úřadu.

'My friend and *I* left the police station.'

(6) *Já* jsem ti, Radku, tak šťastný, že
I am you, Radek, so happy that
už s tebou nemusím hrát.
no-longer with you need-not play.

'I am so happy, Radek, that I do not need to play with you any longer.'

The ellipsis of 1st person pl and 2nd sg and pl are not analyzed in the quoted books at all, we present here only several examples of the marked positions untypical for a pro-drop language:

(7) *My* si na něho počkáme,
We Refl. for him wait,
neuteče nám.
he will not escape us.

(8) Posekám ti zahrádku a *ty* mi za
[I] will cut you garden and *you* me for
to vyvenčíš psa.
that will take out dog.

(9) Vyrozuměli jsme, že právě *vy* jste se s ním stýkala nejčastěji ze všech.

'We have understood that exactly *you* have been meeting him most frequently from all of us.'

(10) *Ty* nevíš, kdo *já* jsem?

'*You* do not know who *I* am?'

(11) ...někdo plakal nad čerstvým hrobem a *my* šli a položili ho do hlíny.

'... somebody wept on his fresh tomb and *we* went and put him into the soil.'

In Table 1 we compare the number of sentences with an overt pronominal subject and the number of all sentences with the verb in the form corresponding to this person.[8] The degree of pro-dropness is demonstrated in the 'non-dropped' rows: e.g. in the corpus SYN2005 there are 6,8% sentences within the set of all predicates in 1st person sg where the subject *já* [I] is present (non-dropped).

corpus	SYN2005	SYN2010	SYN2013 PUB
corpus size (# of tokens)	100M	100M	935M
Verbs in 1st person sg	1 142 609	1 787 638	8 906 455
Pronoun *já* [I] is present	77 629	74 922	244 667
non-dropped	6,8%	4,2%	2,7%
Verbs in 2nd person sg	293 068	496 304	2 966 819
Pronoun *ty* [you] is present	10 265	17 328	9 779
non-dropped	3,5%	3,5%	0,3%
Verbs in 1st person pl	635 962	821 381	8 501 392
Pronoun *my* [we] is present	18 213	19 986	153 275
non-dropped	2,9%	2,4%	1,8%
Verbs in 2nd person pl	379 487	498 943	1 093 271
Pronoun *vy* [you] is present	16 596	17 344	65 707
non-dropped	4,4%	3,5%	6,0%

Table 1: Non pro-drop vs. pro-drop sentences

3.2 Coreference with raising and control verbs as "pseudo-deletions"

With regard to our aim to introduce into the deep (tectogrammatical) representation all semantically relevant information even though not expressed in the surface shape of the sentence, the coreferential units important for the interpretation of the meaning of the sentence in infinitive constructions have to be inserted. Neither speaker nor recipient are aware of any deletion in (12) and (13) (and other examples in this Section), both sentences are fully grammatical.

Thus, for the interpretation of the meaning of (12) it is necessary to know that in (12) Actor (*John*) is identical with absent subject of the infinitive clause, see Figure 1 above, while in (13) the Addressee (*girl-friend*) occupies such an empty position. These elements (indicated in PDT by the lemma #Cor) are needed for the completion of the tectogrammatical structure.

Infinitive clauses with some verbs of control are in particular contexts synonymous with the corresponding embedded clauses (12b), (13b):

[8]The number of occurrences cannot be accurate: the forms *já*, *ty*, *my*, *vy* in nominative could occur in non-subject positions in phrases introduced by *jako* [*as*]. Both meanings of the pronoun *vy* [*you*], i.e. the honorific form and the simple plural form would be difficult to distinguish in the corpus without syntactic annotation. However these occurrences are marginal, so that they do not influence the statistics substantially.

(12) a. Jan se rozhodl opustit Prahu.
'John decided to leave Prague.'
b. Jan se rozhodl, že (on) opustí Prahu.
'John decided that (he) would leave Prague.'

(13) a. Jan doporučil přítelkyni přestěhovat se.
'John recommended to his girl-friend to move.'
b. Jan doporučil přítelkyni, aby se (ona) přestěhovala.
'John recommended to his girl-friend that (she) moved.'

Another argument for the treatment of these structures as deletions is the fact that with some verbs the surface shape of the sentence is ambiguous: thus with the Czech verb *slibovat* [to promise] there are two possibilities of control (the subject of the infinitive may corefer either with the Actor or with the Addressee of the main clause) that have to be captured by the TR. Thus the sentence (14) can be understood either as (15a) with the Actor as the controller or as (15b) with the Addressee as the controller:

(14) Jirka slíbil dětem jít do divadla.
'George promised the children to go to the theatre.'

(15) a. Jirka slíbil dětem, že (on) půjde do divadla.
'George promised the children that (he) will go to the theatre.'
b. Jirka slíbil dětem, že (ony) půjdou do divadla.
'George promised the children that (they) will go to the theatre.'

The specificity of this type of deletion is caused by the fact that the deleted unit – subject (Sb) of the infinitive – cannot be expressed on the surface.

Raising and control constructions belong to the prominent topics of the studies in generative grammar, though different terminology and different solutions are used ((Růžička, 1999), (Przepiórkowski and Rosen, 2005), (Rosen, 2006), (Landau, 2013), to name just a few contributions from the last 20 years).[9] (Panevová, 1996) and (Panevová et al., 2014) base the solution on the classification of verbs of control according to their controller (examples (12) and (13) represent group 1 and 2 with *Actor (controller) – Sb (controlee)* and *Addressee (controller) – Sb (controlee)*, respectively). The other groups are represented by the Czech verbs *slibovat* [to promise] with two possibilities of control (*Actor - Sb* or *Addressee - Sb*, see (15a), (15b)) and *poslat* [to send] with the control *Patient - Sb* (see (16)).

(16) Šéf poslal asistenta roznést letáky.
'The boss sent the assistant to distribute the leaflets.'

Our discussion indicates that we have resigned on the difference between raising and control,[10] because according to the analysis of Czech data, the tests (such as passivization, identity or difference in theta-roles, the number of arguments of the head verb) prominently used in generative grammar for English do not function for our data in the same way.

In this Section we wanted to document that phenomena analyzed here and called "pseudo-deletions" are justified to be considered as a type of deletion, as the meaning of infinitive constructions can be explained only by an establishment of explicit pointers of the coreferential expressions between the argument of the governing verb and unexpressed subject of the dependent predicate.

3.3 Special types of "small clauses"

A sequence of two prepositions following one another is excluded in Czech but there are expressions in Czech[11] classified in traditional descriptions and dictionaries mostly as prepositions that can be followed by a prepositional noun group.

(17) Kromě do katedrály půjdou turisté do musea.[12]

---

[9] (Růžička, 1999), p.4: "...an infinitival S-complement creates the problem of reconstituting its empty subject"; (Landau, 2013), p. 9: "...the interpretation of the sentence [*with control*] indicates that there is an additional, invisible argument in the embedded clause, which is coreferential with (found/controlled by) the overt DP."

[10](Landau, 2013), p. 257 concludes his exhaustive analysis of the phenomena analyzed usually under the roof of raising/control by the claim that control "is neither a unitary phenomenon nor a constitutive element of grammatical theory", but rather "a heuristic label only serving to draw our attention to a certain class of linguistic facts".

[11]Equivalent expressions in other languages (e.g. in Russian), of course, exist, but as far as we know, they do not share the properties we describe for Czech in this Section.

[12]The variant *kromě* + Genitive (*kromě katedrály půjdou*

'Besides to the cathedral the tourists will go to the museum.'

(18) a. Místo do Uppsaly přijel Jan do Trondheimu.

'Instead at Uppsala John arrived at Trondheim.'

b. Místo, aby (Jan) přijel do
Instead of that (John) arrived at
Uppsaly, přijel Jan do
Uppsala, arrived John at
Trondheimu.
Trondheim.

In our proposal the double functions concentrated in "small clauses" introduced by *kromě*, *místo* [besides, instead of] are differentiated by means of the addition of the missing predicate with the lexical label repeating the lexical value of the governing predicate. The adverbials *do katedrály* (in (17)), *do Uppsaly* (in (18)) depend on the restored node with their proper function of Direction. The expanded representation for (18a) is paraphrased in (18b).

We deal here with examples (17) and (18) in detail, because they document clearly that the (lexically parallel) predicate is missing on the surface. However, there are examples where the preposition *místo* [instead of] is used with its "regular" case rection (Genitive), being sometimes synonymous with the small clause with double prepositions, e. g. (19), (20):

(19) Místo zavřeného musea(Genitive) navštíví turisté katedrálu.

'Instead of closed museum(Genitive) the tourists will attend a cathedral.'

(20) Místo manžela(Genitive) doprovodí matku na ples syn.

'Instead of her husband(Genitive) her son will accompany mother to the ball.'

There are two possible approaches how to represent (19) and (20) on TR: In the former case, the expressions *místo muzea/místo manžela* [instead of museum/instead of husband] could be represented as adjuncts of SUBST(itution) directly dependent on the predicate (*visit* or *accompany*, respectively). In the latter case, in order to achieve a symmetric representation of (18) on the one side and (19), (20) on the other, the restored version (with a repeated predicate) will be used. We preferred the latter solution which helps to eliminate an ambiguity such as in (21) paraphrased in (22a) and (22b):

(21) Místo profesorky kritizoval studenta děkan.

'Instead of the (lady)professor-*Gen-F* the dean criticized the student.'

(22) a. Místo aby kritizoval
Instead of that he-criticized
profesorku , kritizoval
the (lady)professor-*Acc-F* , criticized
děkan studenta.
the dean the student-*Acc-F*

'Instead of critizing the lady-professor, the Dean critized the student.'

b. Místo aby studenta
Instead of that the student-*Acc-F*
kritizovala profesorka ,
criticized (lady)professor-*Nom-F* ,
kritizoval ho děkan.
criticized him the dean.

'Instead of the student having been criticized by the lady-professor, he was criticized by the Dean.'

In the primary meanings of these two sentences in their restored (expanded) versions the noun *profesorka* [lady-professor] after the preposition *místo* [instead of] has the function of the subject (Actor) in (22b), while in (22a) *profesorka* [lady-professor] has the function of object (Patient).

There are additional problems connected with the expression *kromě*. This Czech expression has two meanings corresponding approximately to *besides* (inclusion) and *with exception* (exclusion). At the same time, both have the same syntactic properties. Sentences (23a) and (24a) and their proposed expansions (23b) and (24b) illustrate the two different meanings of structures with *kromě*.

... [besides the cathedral they will go ...] where the expression *kromě* can function as a proper preposition governing genitive case exists in Czech, too, but it is not applicable in all contexts. E.g. *Kromě s přítelem půjde Marie do divadla se sestrou* [lit. Besides with the boy-friend Mary will go to the theatre with her sister] cannot be changed into **Kromě přítele půjde Marie do divadla se sestrou.*[*Besides the boy-friend Mary will go to the theater with her sister.]

(23) a. (Tento přímořský hotel nabízí vynikající služby.) Kromě v moři tam můžete plavat (i) v bazénu.

'(This seaside hotel offers excellent services.) Besides in the sea you can swim there (also) in the pool.'

b. Kromě toho, že tam můžete
Besides that that there you-can
plavat v moři, můžete tam plavat
swim in sea, you-can there swim
(i) v bazénu.
(also) in pool.

For (24a) we propose the extended tectogrammatical representation as paraphrased in (24b):

(24) a. Kromě v pondělí můžete navštívit museum denně od 10 do 18 hodin.

'With the exception on Mondays you can visit the museum daily from 10 AM till 6 PM.'

b. Kromě toho, že nemůžete navštívit museum v pondělí, můžete navštívit museum denně od 10 do 18 hodin.

'With exception of the fact that you cannot visit the museum on Monday, you can visit the museum daily from 10 AM to 6 PM.'

The restored versions of the small clauses serve also as the means how to remove the ambiguities in *kromě*-phrases.[13] If in the extended version with the restored predicate both predicates are positive or both are negated, the *kromě*-phrases mean inclusion (called Addition in (Panevová et al., 2014)); if one of them is positive and the other negated, the phrases express an exclusion (called Exception in (Panevová et al., 2014)). Unfortunately, such a clear-cut criterion does not exclude all possible ambiguities. There are tricky contexts where the ambiguity could be removed only by a broader context or by the situation, see (25) and its two possible expansions in (26a) and (26b):

(25) Vydala jsem výkřik, který kromě Artura musel slyšet kdekdo.

'I have given a scream which besides Arthur must have been heard by everybody.'

[13]For a detailed analysis of these constructions including other peculiarities occurring in Czech see (Panevová et al., 2014).

(26) a. Vydala jsem výkřik, který kromě toho, že ho slyšel Artur, musel slyšet kdekdo.

'I have given a scream which in addition to that it was heard by Arthur must have been heard by everybody.'

b. Vydala jsem výkřik, který kromě toho, že ho neslyšel Artur, musel slyšet kdekdo.

'I have given a scream which in addition to that it was not heard by Arthur must have been heard by everybody.'

The restructuring proposed for the type of sentences analyzed in this Section by means of an addition of the predicate corresponding to the governing predicate seems to be helpful from two points of view: One concerns the introduction of the means for splitting two functions conflated in the small clauses and the other is reflected in a more subtle classification of the list of adverbials adding an Addition and Exception as two new semantic units (functors) on tectogrammatical level.

3.4 Deletions in structures with comparison

Comparison structures are a very well known problem for any description pretending on restoration of elements missing in the surface shape to reach a complete representation of syntax and semantics of the sentences. In FGD two types of the comparison are distinguished: one is connected with the meaning of equivalence (introduced usually by the expression *jako* [as]; the subfunctor used in PDT has the label 'basic'), the other expresses the meaning of difference (it is introduced usually by the conjunction *než* [than]; the subfunctor used is called 'than'). There are some comparison structures where the restoration of elements missing on the surface seems to be easy enough from the point of view of semantics and from the point of view of the extent of the part inserted in the TR (see (27a), and its restored version (27b)).

(27) a. Jan čte stejné knihy jako jeho kamarád.

'John reads the same books as his friend.'

b. Jan čte stejné knihy jako (čte) jeho kamarád.

'John reads the same books as his friend (reads).'

Most comparisons are, unfortunately, more complicated, see the following examples and the arguments for the necessity of their extension:

(28) a. Jan se choval na banketu jako v hospodě.

'John behaved at the reception as in the pub.'

b. Jan se choval na banketu (stejně), jako se (Jan) chová v hospodě.

'John behaved at the reception (in the same way) as (John) behaves in the pub.'

In ex. (28a) we encounter a similar problem to the one we analyzed in Sect. 3.3. when discussing the modification of substitution, addition and of exception: in the comparison structure two semantic functions are conflated (comparison-basic and locative meaning in (28a)). Thus an artificial predicate sharing in this case the same value as the governing predicate (with the syntactic label comparison-basic) must be added into the extended representation. It serves as the head for the locative adverbial, too.

For many modifications of comparison, however, even a more complex reconstruction of comparison "small clauses" is needed. For an adequate interpretation of the surface shape of (29a) not only the shortened comparison structure with locative has to be expanded but also an "operator" indicating similarity of the compared objects is missing. For the identification of the similarity the expression as *stejný/stejně* [same/identically], *podobný/podobně* [similar/similarly] are used and this operator has to be added into the corresponding TR, see ex. (29b).

(29) a. Požadavky jsou u Komerční banky jako u České spořitelny.

'The requirements are at Commercial Bank as at Czech Saving Bank.'

b. Požadavky jsou u Komerční
Requirements are at Commercial
banky (stejné) jako
Bank (same) as
(jsou požadavky) u
(are requirements) at
České spořitelny [#Some].
Czech Saving Bank [#Some].

An adequate description of the type of comparison exemplified by ex. (29) (see Figure 2) requires

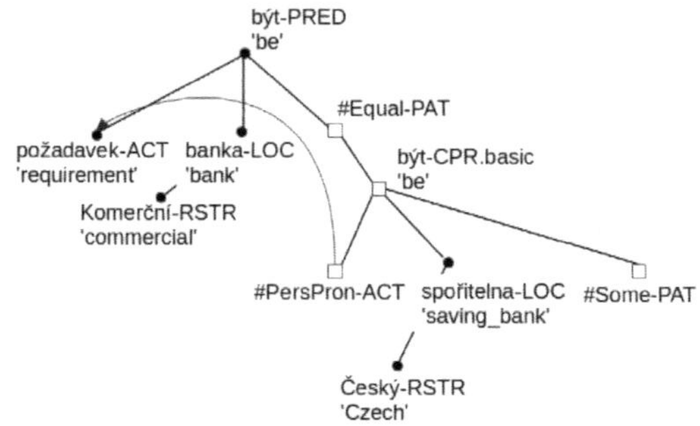

Figure 2: Deep structure of (29)

to add not only an artificial predicate the head of which copies the lemma of the main predicate, but also an operator indicating the type of comparison (#Equal, here with the meaning *stejný* [the same]). The artificial lemma #Some is used to stand for the lexically underspecified adjective/adverbial for both types of comparison, see (29b) and (30b).

While the extension of (29a) would be acceptable (at least semantically) in the form *Požadavky jsou u Komerční banky stejné jako (jsou stejné) u České spořitelny* [The requirements are at Commercial Bank the same as (are the same) at Czech Saving Bank], such type of extension is not acceptable with the comparison-than type (connected with the comparison of objects which are not similar), see (30). This sentence requires an artificial extension because the operators used for this type of comparison as *jiný/jinak* [different], *rozdílný* [different] have no semantic counterpart to be filled in the extended representation. The extension by the adjective *nějaký* [some] is given here by the fact that *jiný* has no single lexical counterpart for the expression of the Ministry situation in (30) (if the situation there is different, the appropriate adjective is actually unknown, it is underspecified).

(30) a. Situace v armádě je jiná než na ministerstvu.

'The situation in the army is different than at the Ministry.'

b. Situace v armádě je jiná než (je situace) na ministerstvu [#Some].

'The situation in the army is different than (the situation) at the Ministry is [#Some].

Our experience with the analysis of data in PDT indicates that the relations between the extension of comparison modifications and the extent of their complete structure on the deep level differ very significantly, so that a more detailed classification would be useful.

4 Summary

We have analyzed four types of elided constructions in Czech and proposed their representation on the deep (tectogrammatical) level of syntactic description within a formal dependency-based description. From the point of view of the binary relation of the governor and its dependent, either the governor or the dependent may be missing and has to be reconstructed. A reconstruction of a dependent is e.g. the case of deletions connected with the pro-drop character of Czech (*[I] came late*), or in cases of a deleted general argument (*John sells at Bata* [*what*][*to whom*]), while a governor has to be reconstructed mostly in coordinated structures (*John likes Bach and Susan* [*likes*] *Beethoven*; *We know when* [*she came*] *and why she came*). In some types of deletions, the reconstruction concerns an introduction of a rather complex structure which is, however, needed for an appropriate semantic interpretation of the surface shape of the sentence, as illustrated by the comparison phrases and structures representing Addition and Exception. Our analysis focused on several types of the so-called systemic ellipsis, i.e. such that is given by grammatical rules or conditions or by a grammatically determined surface deletability; we have left aside textual ellipsis such as coordination, which is conditioned mostly by the context or by situation.

Surface deletions reflect the openness of the language systems to compress the information. However, for the description of meaning of such compressed structures more explicit means for an adequate and unambiguous description are needed.

Acknowledgments

The authors gratefully acknowledge the detailed remarks and suggestions by the three anonymous reviewers. We are deeply indepted to Barbora Hladká for her invaluable technical assistance. The work on this contribution was supported by the grant of the Czech Grant Agency P406/12/0557 and has been using language resources developed and/or stored and/or distributed by the LINDAT/CLARIN project of the Ministry of Education of the Czech Republic (project LM2010013).

References

Eduard Bejček, Eva Hajičová, Jan Hajič, Pavlína Jínová, Václava Kettnerová, Veronika Kolářová, Marie Mikulová, Jiří Mírovský, Anna Nedoluzhko, Jarmila Panevová, Lucie Poláková, Magda Ševčíková, Jan Štěpánek, and Šárka Zikánová. 2013. Prague Dependency Treebank 3.0. `https://ufal.mff.cuni.cz/pdt3.0`.

Jan Hajič, Eva Hajičová, Marie Mikulová, Jiří Mírovský, Jarmila Panevová, and Daniel Zeman. 2015. Deletions and node reconstructions in a dependency-based mutlilevel annotation scheme. *Lecture Notes in Computer Science*, 9041:17–31.

Bohuslav Havránek and Alois Jedlička. 1960. *Česká mluvnice [Czech Grammar]*. Praha:SPN.

Richard A. Hudson. 1984. *Word Grammar*. Basil Blackwell Oxford [Oxfordshire] ; New York.

Richard A. Hudson. 2007. *Language Networks: The New Word Grammar*. Oxford University Press.

Aleksandr V. Isačenko. 1960. *Grammatičeskij stroj russkogo jazyka v sopostavlenii so slovackim*. SAV: Bratislava.

Petr Karlík, Marek Nekula, and Zdenka Rusínová, editors. 1995. *Příruční mluvnice češtiny [Handbook of Grammar of Czech]*. Nakladatelství Lidové Noviny, Praha.

Idan Landau. 2013. *Control in Generative Grammar*. Cambridge: Cambridge University Press.

Igor Mel'čuk. 1988. *Dependency Syntax: Theory and Practice*. State University of New York Press.

Marie Mikulová. 2011. *Významová reprezentace elipsy*. Studies in Computational and Theoretical Linguistics. Ústav formální a aplikované lingvistiky, Praha, Czechia.

Timothy Osborne and Junying Liang. 2015. A survey of ellipsis in chinese. In *Proceedings of the Third International Conference on Dependency Linguistics, Depling 2015*, Uppsala, Sweden. Computational Linguistics group at Uppsala University in collaboration with Akademikonferens.

Timothy Osborne, Michael Putnam, and Thomas Groß. 2012. Catenae: Introducing a novel unit of syntactic analysis. *Syntax*, 15(4):354–396.

Jarmila Panevová, Eva Hajičová, Václava Kettnerová, Markéta Lopatková, Marie Mikulová, and Magda Ševčíková. 2014. *Mluvnice současné češtiny 2, Syntax na základě anotovaného korpusu [Grammar of present-day Czech 2. Syntax of the basis of an annotated corpus]*, volume 2. Karolinum Praha, Prague.

Jarmila Panevová. 1996. More remarks on control. In Eva Hajičová, Oldřich Leška, Petr Sgall, and Zdena Skoumalová, editors, *Prague Linguistic Circle Papers*, volume 2, pages 101–120. Amsterdam/Philadelphia: John Benjamins Publ. House.

Adam Przepiórkowski and Alexandr Rosen. 2005. Czech and Polish raising/control with or without structure sharing. *Research in Language*, 3:33–66.

Alexandr Rosen. 2006. O čem vypovídá pád doplňku infinitivu [What the case of the complement of the infinitive tells us]. In František Čermák and Renata Blatná, editors, *Korpusová lingvistika: Stav a modelové přístupy*, pages 254–284. Nakladatelství Lidové Noviny, Praha.

Rudolf Růžička. 1999. *Control in Grammar and Pragmatics*. Amsterdam/Philadelphia: John Benjamins Publ. House.

Petr Sgall, Eva Hajičová, and Jarmila Panevová. 1986. *The Meaning of the Sentence in Its Semantic and Pragmatic Aspects*. Dordrecht:Reidel Publishing Company and Prague:Academia.

Non-projectivity and processing constraints: Insights from Hindi

Samar Husain
Indian Institute of Technology, Delhi
Department of Humanities and Social Sciences
India
samar@hss.iitd.ac.in

Shravan Vasishth
Universität Potsdam
Department of Linguistics
Germany
vasishth@uni-potsdam.de

Abstract

Non-projectivity is an important theoretical and computational concept that has been investigated extensively in the dependency grammar/parsing paradigms. However, from a human sentence processing perspective, non-projectivity has received very little attention. In this paper, we look at existing work and propose new factors related to processing non-projective configuration. We argue that (a) counter to the claims in the psycholinguistic literature (Levy et al, 2012), different aspects of prediction maintenance can lead to higher processing cost for a non-projective dependency, (b) parsing strategies can interact with the expectation for a non-projective dependency, and (c) memory (re)activation can explain processing cost in certain non-projective configurations.

1 Introduction

Within the dependency grammar framework, non-projectivity has received considerable attention from both the theoretical as well as the computational perspectives. Non-projective structures are assumed to be both more complex to analyze as well as more difficult to parse. Figure 1 shows a Hindi sentence involving a non-projective dependency between *abhay kaa* 'Abhay's' and *caSamaa* 'spectacles'.

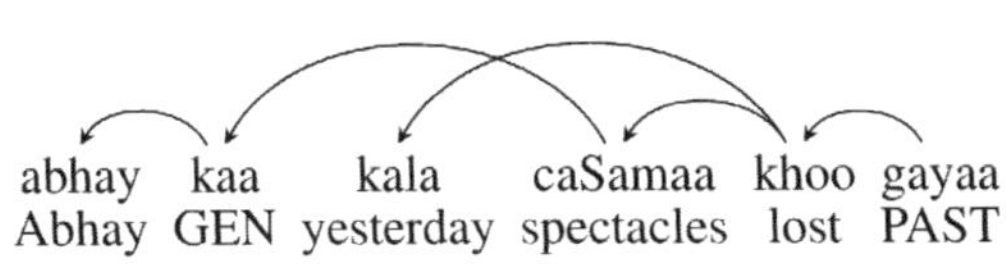

Figure 1: A Hindi sentence involving a non-projective dependency. English translation: *'Abhay's spectacles got lost yesterday.'*

Formally, an arc $i \rightarrow j$ is projective if and only if there is no word k between i and j that i does not dominate[1] (Nivre and Nilsson, 2005).

While some parsing paradigms can handle such dependencies, others either cannot or have special mechanisms to process them (e.g., Kuhlmann and Nivre (2010); Rambow and Joshi (1994)). Many theoretical approaches have special mechanisms to account for these constructions within their framework (e.g., Chomsky (1981); Pollard and Sag (1994)).

It is unclear if the complexity arising from non-projectivity has any processing cost in human language comprehension. That is, does the human sentence processing system find such sentences difficult to process, compared to projective dependencies? Previous work has addressed this question. In a classic study, Bach et al. (1986) showed that Dutch speakers find cross-serial dependencies in Dutch more acceptable compared to German speakers who read matched set of embedded constructions in German. Other work has looked at filler-gap dependencies, but these have generally focused on the question of wh movement (e.g., Traxler and Pickering (1996)). More recently, Levy et al. (2012) have directly taken up the issue of non-projectivity and sentence processing. They raised the following questions:

1. *Under what circumstances are non-projective dependency structures easier or harder to comprehend than corresponding projective-dependency structures?*

2. *How can these differences in comprehension difficulty be understood with respect to existing theories of online comprehension?*

Levy et al. (2012) try to answer the above questions using right-extraposed relative clauses in English. They show that the right-extraposed version

[1]Linearly, i could either precede j or follow it.

Proceedings of the Third International Conference on Dependency Linguistics (Depling 2015), pages 141–150,
Uppsala, Sweden, August 24–26 2015.

is more costly than the embedded relative clause (RC), hence demonstrating that non-projective structures are indeed costlier than the projective counterpart. Additionally, they argue that the expectation-based theory of surprisal (Levy, 2008) explains the experimental results better than other competing theories like the cue-based memory model of Lewis and Vasishth (2005) and the derivational theory of complexity (Miller, 1962).

In this paper, we take up Levy's questions by investigating non-projectivity in Hindi participle clauses. We confirm that non-projectivity is indeed costly. However, we show that surprisal is unable to account for the increased processing cost, and that the cue-based memory model of Lewis and Vasishth (2005) can partly account for the results. To anticipate the conclusion, we argue that while expectation (formalized as conditional probability of the head in a dependency given previous syntactic dependencies) is relevant for explaining processing of non-projective dependencies, other factors (that can be orthogonal to predictive processing) can be equally critical. In particular, the following factors are implicated in the processing of non-projective dependencies: (a) The nature of the intervening material between a head and its dependent; (b) The nature of the head-dependent relation; (c) The length/complexity of the intervening material; (d) Memory activation; and (e) Parsing strategies.

Hindi[2] is a useful language for investigating non-projectivity because its relatively free-word order allows non-projective dependencies to occur quite frequently (see Mannem et al. (2009) for a more detailed discussion).

The paper is organized as follows, we first discuss relevant processing theories and their predictions regarding non-projectivity in Section 2. Following this, in Section 3 we discuss experiments that investigate processing of non-projective structures in Hindi. In Section 4 we discuss these findings and discuss potential factors that could influence processing non-projective configurations. Section 5 concludes.

[2]Hindi is one of the official languages of India. It is the fourth most widely spoken language in the world [source: http://www.ethnologue.com/statistics/size]. It is a free-word order language and is head final. It has relatively rich morphology with verb-subject, noun-adjective agreement. See Kachru (2006) for more details on the grammatical properties of Hindi.

2 Two theories of sentence comprehension

Here, we introduce two well-established theories of sentence comprehension, surprisal and the cue-based memory model, and discuss their predictions regarding the processing of non-projective dependencies.

2.1 Surprisal

Expectation-based theories appeal to the predictive nature of the human sentence comprehension system. On this view, processing becomes difficult if the upcoming sentential material is less predictable. Surprisal (Levy, 2008) is one such account. Surprisal presupposes that sentence-comprehenders know a grammar describing the structure of the word-sequences they hear. This grammar not only says which words can combine with which other words but also assigns a probability to all well-formed combinations. Such a probabilistic grammar assigns exactly one structure to unambiguous sentences. But even before the final word, one can use the grammar to answer the question: what structures are compatible with the words that have been read (or heard) so far? This set of structures may contract more or less radically as a comprehender makes their way through a sentence. Intuitively, surprisal increases when a parser is required to build some low-probability structure. Surprisal formalises the processing difficulty of a non-projective dependency (for that matter any dependency) as the conditional probability of encountering the head of the dependency given previous context. The processing cost at word *n* can be formally represented as (1).

$$\text{surprisal}(n) = \log \frac{1}{\Pr(n|context)} \quad (1)$$

It is easy to see that surprisal can predict higher processing cost of a non-projective dependency because such dependencies are generally quite infrequent compared to their projective counterpart.

2.2 The cue-based memory model

The cue-based memory model is a working memory-based theory of human sentence processing proposed by Lewis and Vasishth (2005). Here sentence processing is modeled as skilled memory retrieval, where independently motivated principles of memory and cognitive skill play an important role in formulating the overall model. It uses the notion of decay as one determinant of memory retrieval difficulty. Elements that exists in memory without being retrieved for a long time will decay more, compared to elements that have been retrieved recently or elements that are recent. In addition to decay, the theory also incorporates the notion of interference. Memory retrievals are feature based, and feature overlap during retrieval, in addition to decay, will cause difficulty. The activation of a word i is computed using (2).

$$A_i = B_i + \left(\sum_j W_j S_{ji} \right) + \epsilon_i \qquad (2)$$

Activation is based on two separate quantities. One is the word's baseline activation B_i, which calculates activation decay due solely to the passage of time. The second variable that is used in determining a word's activation is the amount of similarity-based interference that occurs with other words that have been parsed (see Lewis and Vasishth, 2005 for a more extensive discussion).

The cue-based memory model also predicts higher processing cost for certain non-projective configurations such as the one shown in figure 2. Vasishth and Lewis (2006) have proposed that the reactivation of upcoming VPs by adjuncts, and/or reactivation of arguments by intervening adjuncts might lead to facilitation at the reactivated VP. This is because such modifications lead to an activation boost of the upcoming verb. Now assume a non-projective structure for figure 2 where *adjunct1* does not modify the non-finite verb, rather it modifies the matrix verb that follows the non-finite verb. This will make NP-gen $\leftarrow$ non-finite verb a non-projective dependency. The cue-based model will predict higher processing cost at the non-finite verb in the non-projective case as fewer pre-modifers will reactivate the critical non-finite verb compared to when all intervening phrases modify the verb in the projective configuration.

So, both surprisal (via expectation) and cue-based memory model (via memory activation) predict higher processing cost for certain non-projective configurations. The first experiment described in the next section tests this prediction using self-paced reading. The second experiment is a sentence completion study and tests the hypothesis that subjects tend to avoid producing non-projective dependencies when they can. Together,

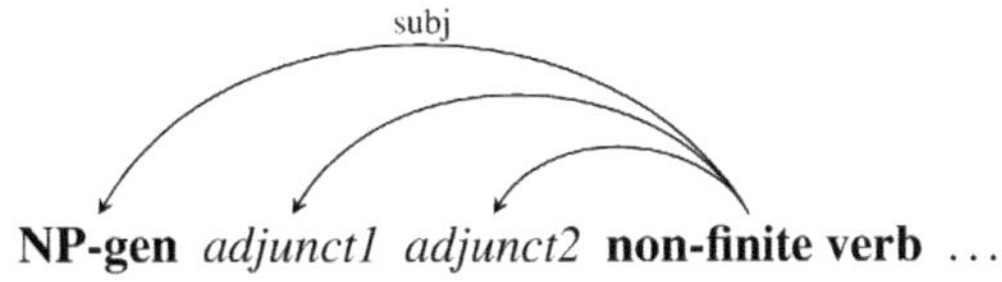

Figure 2: The base activation of a memory chunk gets a boost everytime it gets retrieved after it has been created. Above we show a schematic configuration where the non-finite verb is created/predicted at NP-gen, and it gets reactivated by its modifiers, *adjunct1* and *adjunct2*. NP-gen: Noun phrase with a genitive postposition.

these two studies suggest that reactivation can attenuate the cost of non-projective dependencies, and non-projective structures are hard (otherwise subjects would not try to avoid building them).

3 Experiments

We discuss two experiments in this section. In the first experiment, we test whether expectation and memory activation affect non-projective dependency configuration.

3.1 Experiment 1: Role of Memory Activation

The experiment has a $2 \times 2 \times 2$ factorial design, with factors Distance, Attachment, and Context. The critical region, where the dependency of interest is completed, is the non-finite verb *hasnaa* 'laughing' (see examples 1). In the context condition, the subject of the non-finite verb *raam kaa* and the non-finite verb *hasnaa* are expected, while in the no-context conditions they are not. As shown in Figure 3 and the examples 1, the attachment factor has two levels, an intervening phrase either attaches with the main verb (AttachMV) (Figure 3a), or it attaches to the non-finite verb (AttachNFV) (Figure 3b). The intervening phrase, *mere Xayaal se* 'according to me', does not modify the non-finite verb (rather it modifies the main verb); by contrast, *meri vajah se* 'because of me', modifies the non-finite verb. The Distance factor has two levels; in the short condition there is an adverbial modifying the upcoming non-finite verb (example 1a) compared to three adverbials in the long condition (example 1b). The Distance manipulation modulates the activation of the critical non-finite verb; as explained in section 2.2, in the cue-based model, more preverbal modification can lead to higher memory activation.

Note that in examples 1, some conditions are not shown due to space constraints, but they can be derived from the other conditions. In the context conditions participant first see a screen with *kyaa raam kaa haMsnaa Thiik thaa?* 'Was it ok for Ram to laugh' (literally: Was Ram's laughing ok?). Following this, they see the critical sentence (shown below) on the next screen. In the no-context condition, they see *kyaa huaa?* 'What happened?' prior to seeing the critical sentence (shown below). The dots after each sentence represent the continuation *bilkul Thiik thaa, aisaa karne meM koii buraaii nahi hai* 'was absolutely ok, there is no harm in doing that'. All experimental items can be obtained from http://web.iitd.ernet.in/~samar/data/experimental-items-depling2015.txt

(1) a. **Short, AttachMV, Context**

haan, / **[raama kaa** / mere Xayaal se
yes, Ram GEN according to me
/ zor zor se / **haMsnaa]** / ...
loudly laughing ...

'Yes, according to me it was absolutely ok for Ram to laugh loudly, there is no harm in doing that.'

b. **Long, AttachMV, Context**

haan, / **[raama kaa** / mere Xayaal se
yes, Ram GEN according to me
/ do din pehle / sabke saamne /
two days ago in front of everyone
zor zor se / **haMsnaa]** / ...
loudly laughing ...

'Yes, according to me it was absolutely ok for Ram to laugh loudly two days ago infront of every one, there is no harm in doing that.'

c. **Short, AttachNFV, Context**

haan, / **[raama kaa** / merii vajah se /
yes, Ram GEN because to me
zor zor se / **haMsnaa]** / ...
loudly laughing ...

'Yes, it was absolutely ok for Ram to laugh loudly because of me, there is no harm in doing that.'

d. **Long, AttachNFV, Context**
see above

e. **Short, AttachMV, No context**

[raama kaa / mere Xayaal se /
Ram GEN according to me
zor zor se / **haMsnaa]** / ...
loudly laughing ...

'According to me it was absolutely ok for Ram to laugh loudly, there is no harm in doing that.'

f. **Long, AttachMV, No context**
see above

g. **Short, AttachNFV, No context**
see above

h. **Long, AttachNFV, No context**
see above

3.1.1 Procedure and Participants

We used the centered self-paced reading (SPR) method (Just et al., 1982); centering was used to prevent readers from using the sentence-length cue to adapt their processing strategy. Stimulus items were presented using Douglas Rohde's Linger software, version 2.94 (http://tedlab.mit.edu/~dr/Linger/). A Latin square design ensured that each participant saw each item in only one condition. The target items and fillers were pseudo-randomized for each participant.

The experimenter (Husain) began by explaining the task to the participants. After this, six practice sentences were presented in order to familiarize participants with the task. At the beginning of each trial, the computer screen showed a single hyphen that covered the first word of the upcoming sentence; the hyphen appeared in the center of the computer screen. When the space bar was pressed, the word was unmasked. With each successive press of the space bar, the next word or phrase replaced the previous word in the center of the screen. This successive replacement continued until the participant had read the whole sentence. Reading times or RTs (in milliseconds) were taken as a measure of relative momentary processing difficulty. The f-key for was pressed for answering a question with a 'yes' response and the the j-key was pressed for answering with a 'no' response.

Eighty two native speakers of Hindi in Jawaharlal Nehru University, New Delhi, India, par-

Figure 3: Projectivity manipulation in the self-paced reading (SPR) experiment discussed in section 3.1; see examples 1. (a) shows AttachMV, the main verb attachment condition, the non-projective dependency, while (b) shows AttachNFV, the embedded verb attachment condition, the projective dependency. NP-gen: Noun phrase with a genitive postposition.

ticipated for payment. Their mean age was 23.7 years, SD 3.3 years.

3.1.2 Statistical analyses

All analyses for fixation measures were carried out using the package `lme4`, version 1.1-7, (Bates et al., 2014) for fitting linear mixed models, which is available for R, version 3.1.2 (R Development Core Team, 2006). In the `lme4` models, we fit cross varying intercepts for subjects and items, no varying slopes for subject and item were estimated, as data of this size is usually insufficient to estimate these parameters with any accuracy. The data analysis was done on log-transformed reading times to achieve approximate normality of residuals. From the `lme4` analyses, we present the t-values (z-values for response data).

3.1.3 Pretest

Before conducting the SPR study, we carried out a sentence completion study to ensure that the experimental items used in the study had the appropriate properties. Participants were asked to complete the incomplete version of the items shown in (1); for example, for 1(a) they were supposed to complete the incomplete string *haan, raama kaa mere Xayaal se zor zor se …* Twenty four sets of items, each with eight versions were presented using the centered self-paced reading method in the standard Latin square design. Items were presented using Douglas Rohde's Linger software, version 2.94 (http://tedlab.mit.edu/~dr/Linger/). The critical items were presented with 122 filler items unrelated to this study. Twenty-one Hindi native speaker in Jawaharlal Nehru University participated for payment. Their mean age was 22.7 years, SD 3.1 years.

The sentence completion confirmed that there were more exact predictions[3] in the context conditions (70.75%) compared to just 2.25% in the no-context condition; this confirms that the context condition allows us to manipulate the conditional probability of the upcoming critical non-finite verb. If considering the prediction of a non-finite verb category (i.e. any non-finite verb), then the percentage prediction in the context condition is 86.25%, and 56% in the no-context condition. This shows that in the no-context condition a non-finite verb is being predicted. Similarly, the exact prediction of the main verb was 81% and 31% respectively for the context and no-context conditions. If considering only the finite category information, i.e. any finite verb, this percentage prediction was 98% and 87% for context and no-context conditions respectively. Analysis of the binomial responses[4] using generalized linear mixed models with a logit link function also shows a significant main effect of context (z=5.76) on non-finite verb prediction accuracy.

3.2 Results

As mentioned above, the critical region in the SPR study was the non-finite verb. We find a main effect of context (t=-12.11), such that the non-finite verb was read faster in the context condition compared to the no-context condition. This is expected given the results of the sentence completion study just discussed. We also get an interaction between the three factors, distance, attachment, and context (t=-2.04). A nested contrast shows that this interaction is driven by the no-context, AttachNFV condition, such that the reading time at the non-finite verb is faster in the long condition compared to the short condition. Figure 4 shows the reading times for all the eight conditions.

[3] A response is considered as an exact prediction if it matches in type and tense/aspect features with the expected verb.

[4] Non-finite category prediction was coded as 1, while wrong category prediction was coded as 0. Data from two subjects were removed during the analysis as they did not understand the task.

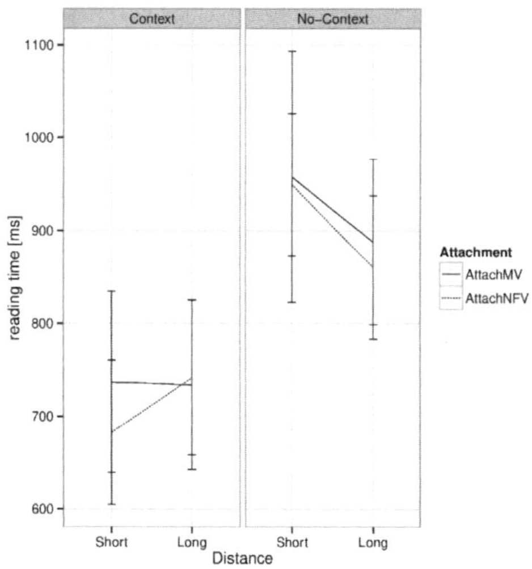

Figure 4: Reading times in ms (with 95% CIs) at the critical region (non-finite verb). The Distance × Attachment × Context interaction (t=-2.04) is driven by the No-Context condition. A nested contrast (details omitted due to lack of space) shows that RT in AttachNFV, Short, No-Context is longer than AttachNFV, Long, No-Context, this is evidence for reactivation effects as suggested by Vasishth and Lewis (2006). Note that the difference between the No-Context, AttachMV conditions is not significant.

3.2.1 Discussion

The three-way interaction is driven by a speedup in the attach non-finite verb (projective) condition when we compare the long vs short conditions in the no-context case. This is established by a nested contrast comparison. Additionally, in the attach main verb condition (the non-projective condition), when we compare long vs short conditions in the no-context case, we see no such speedup. This absence of a speedup could be due to the additional cost of non-projectivity. We suggest that the facilitation in reading time in the projective condition in long vs short cases (in the no-context condition) may be due to reactivation of the non-finite verb, and this is attenuated if the dependency is non-projective. This reactivation-based speedup is not seen in the context conditions (nested contrasts, not presented here, show that there is no significant interaction between distance and attachment in the context case). Thus, the underlying cause for the three-way interaction seems to be the reactivation-based speedup in the no-context condition. In other words, expectation in the context condition could be playing a role in eliminating any effect of reactivation between the two attachment types. These results can therefore be partly explained by Vasishth and Lewis (2006).[5]

The surprisal account cannot easily account for these results. As noted in section 3.1.3, a sentence completion study using the same items shows no significant difference in prediction type for the projective vs non-projection condition in the no-context condition. Surprisal will therefore only predict a main effect of the context condition and not predict any interactions. This does not seem to hold.

3.3 Experiment 2: The Role of Prediction Revision

Next, we investigate the role of prediction revision in processing non-projective configuration. We employ a sentence completion task with a modified design of example 1.

Similar to experiment 1, we use embedded non-finite constructions. This experiment also has a $2 \times 2 \times 2$ design: Distance × Attachment × Context. Context either generates a strong expectation for an upcoming non-finite verb or does not. The Distance factor has two levels; the short condition has one adverbial modifying the upcoming non-finite verb, while the long condition has three adverbials. The Attachment factor has two levels, AttachMV and AttachNFV. Compared to experiment 1, this manipulation has a subtle difference. While the phrase 'according to me' in the AttachMV condition of Experiment 1 was clearly an adjunct, in Experiment 2, the phrase used has an Accusative case-marker. The Accusative case marker in Hindi generally appears with arguments. In the AttachNFV condition, the phrase has the genitive case-marker, which generally appears with adjuncts. This is shown in example 2(a); the phrase *abhay ko* 'Abhay ACC[6]' is an argument of the matrix verb *lagaa thaa* 'found'. By modifying the matrix verb, *abhay ko* makes the dependency between *raama kaa* ← *haMsnaa* non-projective. In example 2(b), on the other hand, the phrase *ab-*

[5] An important caveat here is that the results are rather weakly supportive of the account we present. A stronger result would have entirely parallel lines in the context conditions, and a stronger effect size for the interaction seen in the no-context condition. We intend to try to replicate this effect in a future study.

[6] ACC: Accusative case-marker

hay par 'Abhay LOC[7]' is an adjunct of the upcoming non-finite verb *haMsnaa* 'laughing'. Example 2 shows only the attachment manipulation, we don't list all the items due to space constraints. In the context conditions participant first see a screen with *kyaa kal raam kaa haMsnaa Thiik thaa?* 'Was it ok for Ram to laugh yesterday' (literally: Was Ram's laughing yesterday ok?), following this, on the next screen, they see fragment of the critical sentence upto *zor zor se* 'loudly' (shown below). In the no-context condition, they see *kyaa huaa?* 'What happened?' prior to seeing the critical sentence. All experimental items can be obtained from http://web.iitd.ernet.in/~samar/data/experimental-items-depling2015.txt

(2) a. **Short, AttachMV, Context**

haan Thiik thaa, magar,
yes ok was, but,
mere Xayaal se **[raama kaa**
according to me Ram GEN
abhay ko do din pehle zor zor se
Abhay ACC two days ago loudly
haMsnaa] Thiik nahii lagaa thaa
laughing good not find was

'Yes it was ok, however, according to me Abhay did not find it was ok for Ram to laugh loudly two days ago.'

b. **Short, AttachNFV, Context**

haan Thiik thaa, magar, man hi man
yes ok was, but, in my heart
mujhko **[raama kaa** abhay par
I ACC Ram GEN Abhay LOC
do din pehle zor zor se **haMsnaa]**
two days ago loudly laughing
Thiik nahii lagaa thaa
good not find was

'Yes it was ok, however, in my heart I did not find it ok for Ram to laugh loudly on Abhay two days ago.'

The question here was: when the reader is given a context in which an embedded non-finite verb is highly predictable, if he encounters a phrase that requires a non-projective dependency, would the prediction for the specific non-finite verb be revised such that a projective dependency is built with a different non-finite verb?

[7]LOC: Locative case-marker

Condition	% exact predictions
AttachMV	10
AttachNFV	53

Table 1: Exact prediction (in percentage) of the non-finite verb (*haMsnaa* 'laughing') in the sentence completion study for the AttachMV and AttachNFV conditions in the context, short conditions.

3.3.1 Procedure

The same procedure as discussed in section 3.1.3 was followed. The same subjects participated in the experiment.

3.3.2 Results

The dependent measure is the proportion of exact predictions for the non-finite verb in the different conditions. There are more exact predictions of the non-finite verb in the context conditions (29%) compared to just 3% in the no-context condition. This is as expected; however, note that the proportion of exact predictions is relatively low in the context condition (cf. table 1). This is because of the AttachMV condition—the non-projective dependency causes a reduction in the proportion of exact predictions; in this condition, participants tend to use verbs that would form a projective structure (more details in the next section). We found a a significant main effect of Attachment (z=-5.05) and of context (z=5.41).[8]

3.3.3 Discussion

Together, the main effect of Attachment, Context and the percent of exact predictions shown in table 1 suggests that subjects override the prediction generated by the context in order to avoid forming a non-projective dependency. The sentence completion data show that in the AttachMV (non-projective dependency) conditions subjects used verbs that were compatible with the critical case-markers (genitive and accusative), rather than using the verb used in the context. In doing so, they form a projective structure, rather than forming a non-projective structure using the context verb. For example, subjects tend to use a transitive participle (e.g., *maarnaa* 'hitting') due to the presence of *abhay ko* 'Abhay ACC' which is

[8]Non-finite category prediction was coded as 1, while wrong category prediction was coded as 0. Data from two subjects were removed during the analysis as they did not understand the task.

not easily incorporated with the contextual prediction of intransitive *haMsnaa* 'laughing'. Using *haMsnaa* after seeing an accusative case-marker is only possible by positing a non-projective dependency shown in example 2(a), i.e. *abhay ko* $\rightarrow$ *lagaa* makes *raama kaa* $\rightarrow$ *haMsnaa* dependency non-projective. On the other hand, in the AttachNFV (projective dependency) condition, the response was *haMsnaa* 'laughing', i.e. participants did not deviate from the verb that was provided in the context. This is because the case-marker on the phrase in the AttachNFV condition *abhay par* 'Abhay LOC' can easily be incorporated with an intransitive verb like *haMsnaa* 'laughing'.

Given these results, it is reasonable to assume that, in an online study, when subjects will hear/read *haMsnaa* 'laughing' in 2(a), they would be surprised (as they are expecting *maarnaa* 'hitting') leading to additional processing cost as a result of dashed expectation. Note that, surprisal will correctly predict that reading time at *haMsnaa* in sentence 2(a) will be higher than 2(b) because P(*haMsnaa*|Noun-ACC) will be lower than P(*haMsnaa*|Noun-LOC)[9]. However, it is important to stress that this cost does not reflect prediction maintenance per se (as is argued by Levy et al. (2012)), rather it is prediction revision that eventually gets reflected as additional processing cost.

4 General Discussion

Experiment 1 shows that for a Hindi participle clause construction involving a non-projective dependency, expectation in the context condition could be playing a role in eliminating any effect of reactivation between the two attachment types; recall that in the no-context condition, reactivation effect was seen in the projective dependency conditions while non-projective processing seemed to attenuate reactivation facilitation in the non-projective conditions. This shows that a non-projective structure might not be inherently difficult to process, a claim also made in Levy et al. (2012). Levy et al. (2012) essentially cast the problem of processing a non-projective dependency as maintenance of such syntactic expectation. While such a formalization does account for the processing difficulty in their experiments, it fails to explain the results discussed in section 3.2.

[9] *haMsnaa* is an intransitive verb and in its non-finite form can only take a subject with a genitive case marker. It can easily take a locative adjunct however.

Basically, Levy et al. (2012) do not explore processes that are orthogonal to surprisal but have relevance for non-projective dependency processing. One such process is **memory activation** discussed in Experiment 1.

Another factor, **prediction revision**, was illustrated in Experiment 2 where although surprisal does correctly predict the results, it does not flesh out the source of the processing cost. As shown in figure 5, we argue that the processing cost at a head depends on the compatibility of intervening material with the predicted head. Closely related to this is the issue of **dependency type**. While certain dependencies are more inert (e.g., Adj $\leftarrow$ Noun), others are less so (e.g., Noun $\leftarrow$ Verb). This has the effect of making a prediction more immune to the influence of other dependencies in some cases. For example, once a prediction for an extraposed RC is made, following material has little influence over the validity of the prediction. On the other hand, a prediction of a verb at an argument is susceptible to revisions once additional arguments are encountered. This means that together the dependency type and the intervening material influence the longevity of a prediction.

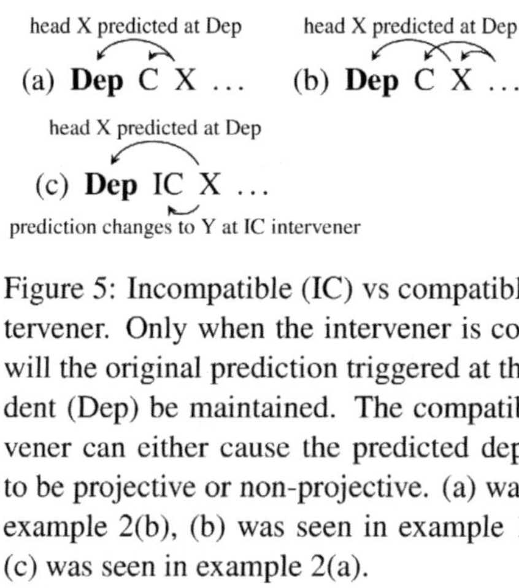

Figure 5: Incompatible (IC) vs compatible (C) intervener. Only when the intervener is compatible will the original prediction triggered at the dependent (Dep) be maintained. The compatible intervener can either cause the predicted dependency to be projective or non-projective. (a) was seen in example 2(b), (b) was seen in example 1(a), and (c) was seen in example 2(a).

We have so far discussed two factors (other than expectation strength) that can account for processing cost in non-projective structures, these are (a) memory activation, (b) prediction revision due to intervening material and dependency type. In addition to these one can posit some more factors.

One such factor is **prediction decay**. While keeping the prediction strength constant, a prediction can suffer memory decay due to the complexity of the intervening material. Such effects can arise due to limited working memory constraints. There is a large body of work that supports the role of working memory in sentence comprehension (e.g., Gibson (1998); Grodner and Gibson (2005)). Expectation-based theories such as surprisal do not make any predictions about such effects. Indeed, recent work has argued for a more unified approach to sentence processing where both expectation and working memory play a role (e.g., Vasishth and Drenhaus (2011); Levy and Keller (2012)).What concerns us here is the issue of expectation maintenance and how it interacts with working memory. Two recent results need to be mentioned here. For German, Levy and Keller (2012) show that the benefits of predictive processing can be attenuated (and be reversed) if the complexity of the phrases before the predicted head is high. Similary, Safavi et al. (2015) show that in Persian separable complex predicate, processing time at the light verb can be high in spite of it being highly predictable if the precritical phrase is a complex NP. Both works point to the possibility that even for a highly predictable non-projective dependency, processing cost can be influenced by the complexity of the intervening material. If this complexity is high, it will affect the prediction adversely and lead to higher processing cost of the non-projective dependency.

Another important factor is the **frequency of a dependency**. It is quite well known that non-projective dependencies are infrequent compared to their projective counterparts, for example, in English the right-extraposed RC is less frequent compared to the embedded RC[10] (Levy et al., 2012). Two related questions need to be asked here: (a) Will a dependency that is non-projective but highly frequent be easy to process? An interesting case in point is the relative clause in Hindi. Unlike English, the right-extraposed RC in Hindi is more frequent than the embedded RC. (b) Similarly, certain heads are always triggered due to the specific dependents, e.g., relative-correlative dependency and paired discourse connectives in Hindi. Many of these dependencies are non-projective (and are also long distance dependencies). Given their high collocational frequency, will they still be difficult to process? Surprisal will predict that, in Hindi, right-extraposed RC should be easier to process than the embedded counterpart. This needs to verified experimentally.

Finally, the processing cost of a non-projective dependency could also reflect certain **parsing heuristics/strategies**. For example, it is possible that when the expectation is weak (i.e. when the head of the dependency cannot be predicted with high certainty), cases like Figure 3(a) are costly due to incorrect dependency attachment. In particular, the phrase *according to me* is incorrectly attached to the upcoming unknown verb. After encountering the non-finite verb the attachment has to be revised leading to additional processing cost. Such a strategy implies that when expectation is weak and therefore prebuilding of structures is not possible, the parser employs a conservative projective attachment heuristic. The parser pursues and maintains a non-projective dependency only when the expectation strength is strong.

More recent developments in transition-based incremental parsing (Nivre, 2009) introduce special transitions to handle non-projectivity. Such transitions can only be employed in cases where expectation of a non-projective dependency is high, in all other cases a projective parsing algorithm could be pursued. In this context, the parsing strategies proposed by Joshi (1990)[11] to account for the results of Bach et al. (1986) are relevant. The ease of processing cross-serial dependency and the use of embedded push-down automata to process them could be understood as the parser adapting to a specific property of a language.

Processing cost of a non-projective dependency can therefore arise as a result of variety of factors. This could be either structural or non-structural. Structural factors include syntactic expectation, its revision and frequency. Non-structural factors include expectation decay, memory activation and parsing heuristics.

The factors mentioned above might interact in interesting ways and such interaction can form the focus of future investigations. In addition, as mentioned by Levy et al. (2012), information structure and grammatical weights might also have some role to play in determining processing cost in such syntactic configurations. In addition, it is an open question whether the processing patterns observed for non-projective dependency also hold true for other dependency configurations such as well-nestedness, etc. (Bodirsky et al., 2005).

[10] Table 1 in Levy et al. (2012), P(extraposedRC|context) is 0.00004, while P(RC|context) is 0.00561.

[11] Also see Rambow and Joshi (1994)

5 Conclusion

Current evidence suggests that human sentence processing is sensitive to non-projective dependencies. The increased processing cost could be a result of either structural or non-structural factors. It is unclear if these varied factors interact and if so under what circumstances. Current experimental research provides us with means to investigate these important questions along with investigating processing cost of other types of dependency configurations such as well-nestedness. Such investigations are critical and will constructively inform both theoretical work as well as parsing approaches in the dependency linguistics framework.

6 Acknowledgements

We would like to thank Dr. Ayesha Kidwai for helping with logistics to run the experiments at Jawaharlal Nehru University, Delhi.

References

E. Bach, C. Brown, and W. Marslen-Wilson. 1986. Crossed and nested dependencies in german and dutch: A psycholinguistic study. *Language and Cognitive Processes*, 1:249–262.

D. Bates, M. Maechler, B. M. Bolker, and S. Walker. 2014. lme4: Linear mixed-effects models using eigen and s4. ArXiv e-print; submitted to *Journal of Statistical Software*.

M. Bodirsky, M. Kuhlmann, and M. Möhl. 2005. Well-nested drawings as models of syntactic structure. In *In Tenth Conference on Formal Grammar and Ninth Meeting on Mathematics of Language*, pages 88–1. University Press.

N. Chomsky. 1981. *Lectures on government and binding*. Dordrecht: Foris.

E. Gibson. 1998. Linguistic complexity: Locality of syntactic dependencies. *Cognition*, 68:1–76.

D. Grodner and E. Gibson. 2005. Consequences of the serial nature of linguistic input. *Cognitive Science*, 29:261–290.

A. K. Joshi. 1990. Processing crossed and nested dependencies: An automaton perspective on the psycholinguistic results. *Language and Cognitive Processes*, 5:1–27.

M. A. Just, P. A. Carpenter, and J. D. Woolley. 1982. Paradigms and processes in reading comprehension. *Journal of Experimental Psychology: General*, 111(2):228–238.

Y. Kachru. 2006. *Hindi*. John Benjamins Publishing Company, Philadelphia.

M. Kuhlmann and J. Nivre. 2010. Transition-based techniques for non-projective dependency parsing. *Northern European Journal of Language Technology*, 2(1):1–19.

R. Levy and F. Keller. 2012. Expectation and locality effects in German verb-final structures. *Journal of Memory and Language*.

R. Levy, E. Fedorenko, M. Breen, and E. Gibson. 2012. The processing of extraposed structures in English. *Cognition*, 122(1):12–36.

R. Levy. 2008. Expectation-based syntactic comprehension. *Cognition*, 106:1126–1177.

R. L. Lewis and S. Vasishth. 2005. An activation-based model of sentence processing as skilled memory retrieval. *Cognitive Science*, 29:1–45, May.

P. Mannem, H. Chaudhry, and A. Bharati. 2009. Insights into non-projectivity in Hindi. In *ACL-IJCNLP Student Research Workshop*.

G. A. Miller. 1962. Some psychological studies of grammar. *American Psychologist*, 17:748–762.

J. Nivre and J. Nilsson. 2005. Pseudo-projective dependency parsing. In *Proceedings Of ACL 2005*.

J. Nivre. 2009. Non-Projective Dependency Parsing in Expected Linear Time. In *Proceedings of the Joint Conference of the 47th ACL and the 4th IJCNLP*, pages 351–359.

C. Pollard and I. A. Sag. 1994. *Head-Driven Phrase Structure Grammar*. The University of Chicago Press, Chicago.

R Development Core Team, 2006. *R: A language and environment for statistical computing*. R Foundation for Statistical Computing, Vienna, Austria. ISBN 3-900051-07-0.

O. Rambow and A. Joshi. 1994. A Processing Model for Free Word Order Languages. In C. Clifton Jr., L. Frazier, and K.Rayner, editors, *Perspective on Sentence Processing*, pages 267–301. Erlbaum, Hillsdale, NJ.

M. S. Safavi, S. Vasishth, and S. Husain. 2015. Locality and expectation in Persian separable complex predicates. In *Proceedings of the 28th CUNY Sentence Processing Conference*, Los Angeles, CA.

M. J. Traxler and M. J. Pickering. 1996. Plausibility and the processing of unbounded dependencies: an eye tracking study. *Journal of Memory and Language*, 35:454–475.

S. Vasishth and H. Drenhaus. 2011. Locality in German. *Dialogue and Discourse*, 1:59–82.

S. Vasishth and R. L. Lewis. 2006. Argument-head distance and processing complexity: Explaining both locality and antilocality effects. *Language*, 82(4):767–794.

From mutual dependency to multiple dimensions: remarks on the DG analysis of "functional heads" in Hungarian

András Imrényi
Jagiellonian University, Krakow
Department of Hungarian Philology
Poland
imrenyi.andras@gmail.com

Abstract

This paper addresses the question if the $Focus_0$ and Neg_0 functional heads posited by phrase structural, generative accounts of Hungarian should also be recognized in a dependency-based description of the language. It is argued that the "identificational focus" of a Hungarian clause indeed behaves like a "derived main predicate" (cf. É. Kiss 2007), as suggested by two-clause paraphrases and the fact that its assertion can be independently negated. In DG, Hudson's (2003) "mutual dependency" based analysis of *wh*-questions provides a way of capturing this intuition; however, it does so by lifting the acyclicity constraint on dependency hierarchies (Nivre 2004: 9). To avoid this potentially problematic move, I propose an alternative whereby the primacy of the finite verb and the primacy of other (focussed, interrogative or negative) expressions can be linked to separate dimensions of description. The concept of dimensions adopted in the paper is formally similar to XDG's related notion (Debusmann et al. 2004). In content, however, it is closer to Halliday's (1994, 2004) understanding of the term.

1 Introduction

Under the influence of Tesnière (1959/2015) and Valency Theory, modern Dependency Grammar (DG) has characteristically taken a highly verb-centred approach to clause structure, in which the lexical verb plays an especially prominent role. Since the lexical verb evokes the "theatrical performance" whose "actants" and "circumstants" are expressed by other elements (Tesnière 1959/2015: 97), it is naturally viewed as the root of a dependency tree. Two concessions have been made, however, in many specific versions of DG. Firstly, it is usual to regard finite auxiliaries as heads taking non-finite lexical verbs as complements (Mel'čuk 1988, Hudson 1990, Eroms 2000, Gross–Osborne 2009, etc.). Secondly, complementizers such as *that* or *if*, and even *wh*-elements, have been argued to be the roots of embedded clauses (cf. Osborne 2014, and references therein). These developments can be seen as signs of convergence toward modern phrase structure grammar (PSG), in which the functional projections IP and CP have been firmly established – in the wake of PSG's convergence toward DG with its consistent elimination of exocentric structures (S, S').

From the perspective of English grammar, no further concessions may seem necessary. For Hungarian, however, the phrase structural, generative tradition has introduced a range of functional projections beyond IP and CP, notably such phrases as FocusP and NegP (É. Kiss 2002: 86, 132). Given the "weak equivalence" between (specific kinds of) phrase structural and dependency-based representations (Gaifman 1965), this raises the question whether the functional heads $Focus_0$ and Neg_0 should be recognized in DG as well.

In the present paper, I will argue for the view that the finite verb is not invariably the highest-ranked element of a simple sentence, or at least not in every aspect of meaning and structure. More specifically, I will propose a multi-dimensional analysis whereby both the primacy of the verb and the primacy of other elements can be expressed simultaneously. The concept of dimension adopted in the paper is formally similar to XDG's related notion (cf. Debusmann et al. 2004: 2). In content, however, it is closer to Halliday's (1994, 2004) understanding of the term. In particular, the dimensions will be said to construe complementary aspects of clausal meaning such as i. the nature of the grounded process and its par-

Proceedings of the Third International Conference on Dependency Linguistics (Depling 2015), pages 151–160,
Uppsala, Sweden, August 24–26 2015.

ticipants and circumstances, and ii. illocutionary force and polarity.

The paper is structured as follows. I will first give a brief overview of the phenomena that have prompted Hungarian generative linguists to posit FocusP and NegP as functional projections on top of VP (section 2). Next I consider Hudson's (2003) unorthodox proposal within DG, according to which *wh*-elements are not only dominated by but also dominate finite verbs, with the two elements thus standing in "mutual dependency" (section 3). This will be followed in section 4 by my own analysis, which assigns the primacy of the verb and the primacy of interrogative (or other) elements to two separate dimensions. Finally, summary and conclusions follow in section 5.

2 The rationale for FocusP and NegP

In this section, I will look at some patterns of Hungarian that provide empirical support for the FocusP and NegP projections introduced by generative linguists. The presentation will proceed from basic to more complex patterns, and remain largely descriptive, glossing over many theory-internal details of generative grammar. This also applies to the evaluation of empirical evidence, which is to be as theory-neutral as possible, or to assume a DG perspective.

To begin, let us observe in (1) below a neutral positive declarative sentence which lacks both focusing and negation.[1]

(1) Mari meghívta Jánost.
Mary.NOM PV.called.3SG.DEF John.ACC
'Mary invited John.'

At the core of (1) is the predicate *meghívta*, which consists of the preverb (PV) *meg* and the inflected verb *hívta* 'called.3SG.DEF', where DEF stands for 'definite object'. The predicate as a whole has the idiomatic meaning 'invited.3SG.DEF'. Importantly, *meghívta* does not simply "evoke" an invitational event. Rather, it has all the functional ingredients of a schematic positive declarative clause expressing the occurrence of such an event. Thus, it can also be used by itself in appropriate contexts (cf. (2B)).

[1] In this context, the term "neutral" means that the clause replies to the question "What happened?" or "What is the situation?", presupposing no prior knowledge about the event denoted by the verb.

(2)A: Mari meghívta Jánost?
'Did Mary invite John?'
B: Igen, meghívta.
'Yes, she invited him.'[2]

Both participants of the event are coded morphologically by the predicate. As a special feature of Hungarian, the verb's inflection expresses not only the person and number of the subject but also the definiteness (contextual accessibility) of the object.[3] In (1), the two participants are elaborated further by the dependents *Mari* 'Mary.NOM' and *Jánost* 'John.ACC'. This is a par excellence example of micro- and macro-valency at work (cf. László 1988, Ágel–Fischer 2010: 245).

By using (1), the speaker is stating that an invitational event took place with Mary and John as participants. Clauses with a different function include the following, in which the occurrence of the invitational event is presupposed (3) or denied (4) rather than stated. In both cases, the predicate appears in inverted order (verb + preverb).

(3) JÁNOST hívta meg Mari.
'It is John who Mary invited.'

(4) Mari nem hívta meg Jánost.
Mary.NOM not called.3SG.DEF PV John.ACC
'Mary did not invite John.'

Sentence (3) expresses that out of a range of possible options, it was (none other than) John who Mary invited. Hence, a special function can be attributed to the accented preverbal element *JÁNOST*, which has been mostly referred to as "exhaustive identification" in the generative literature (É. Kiss 2002: 78). More specifically, É. Kiss (2007) suggests that this expression acts as a derived main predicate, which seems plausible given the following pseudo-cleft paraphrase:

(3') Akit Mari meghívott, az János.
whom M.NOM PV.called.3SG, that J.NOM
'Whom Mary invited is John.'

[2] The idea that the Hungarian verbal predicate has the function of a schematic clause is proposed by Imrényi (2013a), following similar suggestions by Brassai (1863/2011: 102) and Havas (2003: 17). Here, it is offered as a descriptive generalization with strong support from data like (2B). Subsequent parts of the section follow more closely the generative tradition.

[3] On the Hungarian "object conjugation", see also Tesnière (1959/2015: 136).

In generative analyses, the preverbal element performing exhaustive identification is usually assumed to occupy (move into) the Specifier of a Focus Phrase (FP), where "focus" is to be interpreted as "identificational focus" rather than "information focus", cf. É. Kiss (1998). Some theorists have argued that focus movement into Spec-FP is accompanied by the movement of V into Focus$_0$ (Bródy 1990). To keep matters simpler, however, I adopt É. Kiss's (2002: 86) proposal by which no head movement occurs, and only provide a maximally schematic representation:

(5)[$_{FP}$ JÁNOST [$_{VP}$ hívta meg Mari]].

É. Kiss (2002: 83–84) justifies the constituency [Focus [V XP*]] by coordination and deletion tests, with no separate justification for the head–complement relation between Focus$_0$ and the VP. However, given the available theoretical options, it only seems natural to handle focusing by substitution rather than adjunction,[4] given that VP-internal linear order is heavily influenced by the presence or absence of a focussed element. In addition, it seems correct to claim that (3) is a sharply different type of linguistic unit than (1), which is suitably expressed by its unique phrasal category label (FP as opposed to VP).

Although in its immediately preverbal use, the negative particle *nem* 'not' behaves very similarly to the identificational focus in Spec-FP, it is standardly assumed to project a NegP (see (6) below, cf. É. Kiss 2002: 132). One reason is that *nem* 'not' can intervene between the focus and the verb, which no other element is capable of (cf. (7)). Secondly, it may also have scope over the predication expressed by the focussed expression, as seen in (8). Theoretically, even two negations are grammatical, although patterns like (9) have a low likelihood of occurrence in real-world situations.

(6)[Mari [$_{NegP}$ nem [$_{VP}$ hívta meg Jánost]]].
'Mary didn't invite John.'
(7)[$_{FP}$ JÁNOST [$_{NegP}$ nem [$_{VP}$ hívta meg Mari]]].
'It is John who Mary didn't invite.'
(8)[$_{NegP}$ Nem [$_{FP}$ JÁNOST [$_{VP}$ hívta meg Mari]]].
'It is not John whom Mary invited.'
(9)[$_{NegP}$ Nem [$_{FP}$ JÁNOST [$_{NegP}$ nem [$_{VP}$ hívta meg Mari]]]].
'It is not John whom Mary didn't invite.'

The behaviour of *nem* 'not' and the English translations strongly suggest that the "identificational focus" of a Hungarian clause is indeed a predicate ranked higher than the verb. Note especially the fact that the English equivalents of (7), (8) and (9) include two finite verbs, and thus two clauses, either of which can host negation. Hence, it is hard to avoid the conclusion that the *nem* of (8), and the first *nem* of (9), are directly related to the identificational focus rather than the verb – not only in terms of linear order but also with regard to hierarchical structure. In (9), it would be especially awkward to link two instances of *nem* directly to the verb.

Whereas (1) is a neutral sentence answering the question "What happened?", (3) is a non-neutral one replying to "Who did Mary invite?". In Hungarian, the latter question matches the structure of its answer, and the interrogative pronoun is also in Spec-FP under the standard generative analysis (cf. (10)). In this case, the unmarked English translation does not involve two clauses, although a marked two-clause option is also available.

(10) [$_{FP}$ KIT [$_{VP}$ hívott meg Mari]]?
whom called.3SG PV Mary.NOM
'Who did Mary invite?' /
'Who is it that Mary invited?'

As additional support for the FP projection, note that it is the identificational focus and the interrogative pronoun to which their constructs can be reduced in appropriate contexts. The phenomenon illustrated in (12) is known in the literature as sluicing (Ross 1969).

(11) A: KIT hívott meg Mari?
'Who did Mary invite?'
B: JÁNOST ~~hívta meg~~.
'John.'

(12) A: Mari meghívott valakit.
Mary.NOM PV.called.3SG somebody.ACC
'Mary invited somebody.'
B: KIT ~~hívott meg~~?
'Whom?'

To conclude this section, Hungarian identificational foci do seem to act as predicates

[4] The adjunction configuration would mean that the focussed expression attaches to the VP to derive another VP: [$_{VP}$ *JÁNOST* [$_{VP}$ *hívta meg Mari*]].

ranked higher than the finite verb. Without this assumption, it is hard to see how the structure and meaning of (9) could be explained. From a DG perspective, however, it is difficult to rank the identificational focus (or the interrogative pronoun) higher than the verb, as e.g. *JÁNOST* in (3) is clearly the object of *hívta meg*, expressing the INVITEE (PATIENT) participant of the invitational event. In what follows, I consider two proposals by which certain expressions may be both higher and lower than the verb in the sentence hierarchy. First I discuss Hudson's (2003) account based on "mutual dependency" between *wh*-elements and verbs (section 3), then present my own approach relying on multiple dimensions (section 4).

3 Hudson's (2003) analysis based on mutual dependency

In his 2003 paper, Hudson makes the unorthodox proposal that English wh-elements are not only dominated by finite verbs but also dominate them, in what he calls "mutual dependency" (henceforth MD). The following illustration is taken from Hudson (2003: 632, 633).

(13)

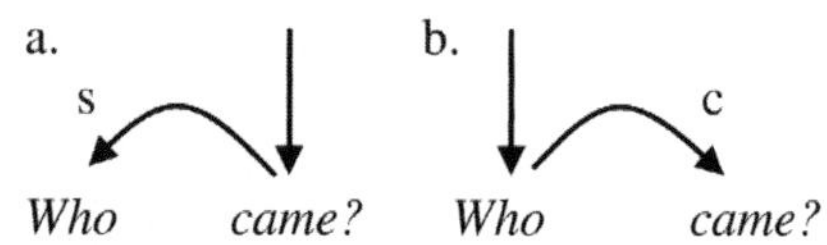

On the one hand, *who* is uncontroversially analysed as the subject of *came* (13a). On the other, Hudson also argues for a separate dependency going in the opposite direction, with *came* treated as the complement of *who* (13b). In this very specific respect, Hudson's account is somewhat similar to generative models which assume that *wh*-elements are in Spec-CP in English (or Spec-FP in Hungarian). In particular, note that the latter approach entails a (possibly empty) functional head with an interrogative feature that takes the rest of the clause as its complement.

Ever since Tesnière (1959/2015: 198), dependency grammarians have been content with analyses that subordinate *wh*-elements to verbs. This may even seem self-evident, given that *wh*-elements carry the same grammatical functions (and are marked by the same cases in morphologically rich languages) as corresponding referential expressions. One would presume, therefore, that there must be compelling reasons for any alternative, let alone one that goes far beyond the phenomenon itself, violating the acyclicity constraint of DG (cf. Nivre 2004: 9). In this section, I give an overview of Hudson's key arguments for his proposal before turning to the more problematic aspects of his MD-based account.

Hudson's first argument rests on the phenomenon of sluicing (Ross 1969), illustrated below.

(14) a. *Pat*: I know he's invited a friend. *Jo*: Oh, who [has he invited]?
b. I know he's invited a friend, but I'm not sure who [he's invited].

As Hudson remarks, "Taking the verb as the pronoun's complement allows us to explain this pattern as an example of the more general anaphoric reconstruction of optional complements" (2003: 632), as exemplified by *I wanted to see her, and I tried [to see her], but I failed [to see her].*

It is interesting to note that Osborne (2014) also employs sluicing as evidence for the root status of *wh*-elements in embedded clauses. As he puts it, "the sluiced (=elided) material of sluicing qualifies as a constituent (=a complete subtree) if the *wh*-word is taken to be the root of the embedded question" (286). At the same time, he rejects the root status of *wh*-elements in main clauses (Osborne, p.c.). One advantage of Hudson's approach is that it provides a unified account of why sluicing works the same way in both contexts, also subsuming these under a more general phenomenon.

A second argument specifically concerns subordinate clauses. As Hudson observes, "The verb must depend on the pronoun in a subordinate clause because the pronoun is what is selected by the higher verb" (2003: 633), as demonstrated by (15).

(15) a. I wonder *(who) came.
b. I am not sure *(what) happened.

One could question the force of this argument by pointing at independent differences between matrix and subordinate *wh*-clauses (e.g. with regard to word order), which may suggest that any evidence exclusive to subordinate clauses has little to no bearing on matrix ones. However, the word order difference between matrix and subordinate *wh*-clauses is far from universal (English and German attest it, but not Hungarian or Italian, for example). From an evolutionary perspective, it seems more important that dependent *wh*-clauses evolve from independent ones, which implies that there are fundamental structural similarities between the two. Hudson's account is more in line with this perspective, as it assigns analogous hierarchical structures to matrix and subordinate *wh*-questions, confining their differences to the linear axis.

Thirdly, as Hudson observes, "The pronoun selects the verb's characteristics – its finiteness (tensed, infinitive with or without *to*) and whether or not it is inverted. The characteristics selected vary lexically from pronoun to pronoun, as one would expect if the verb was the pronoun's complement" (2003: 633). The following data serve as illustrations.

(16) a. Why/When are you glum?
b. Why/*When be glum?

(17) a. Why are you so glum?
b. *Why you are so glum?
c. *How come are you so glum?
d. How come you are so glum?

(18) I'm not sure what/who/when/*why to visit.

In conclusion, Hudson uses standard assumptions to motivate his non-standard analysis. Taken individually, some of the arguments may be contested; as pieces of converging evidence, however, they make a fairly strong case for the head status of *wh*-elements. The account also makes plausible generalizations, e.g. over sluicing and other kinds of ellipsis, or over matrix and subordinate *wh*-questions. Thus, it results in simplifications in certain areas of the grammar – at the cost of lifting a ban on dependency hierarchies.

Nevertheless, it seems fair to say that the proposal has attracted few followers in the broader DG community. One trivial reason may be that it presupposes Word Grammar-style diagrams; in approaches working with straight edges and different heights for heads and dependents, MD is impossible to render visually on a single representation. More importantly, the constraint that dependency hierarchies are directed acyclic graphs is central to DG, giving it both mathematical elegance and advantages in computational processing (constraining the number of possible analyses for a sentence, and allowing for simpler parsing algorithms). As long as MD seems like an exceptional device to handle a special phenomenon, there is little incentive for DG linguists to abandon this constraint, since such a move may well create more problems than it solves.[5]

In the following section, however, I will show that the essence of Hudson's proposal can be maintained with no violation of the acyclicity constraint. Further, I will use evidence from Hungarian to demonstrate that the configuration is not so exceptional as Hudson's analysis might suggest. The proposal will also build bridges between DG and other frameworks, notably Construction Grammar and Halliday's Functional Grammar.

4 A multi-dimensional account of "focusing" and negation

As seen in the previous section, Hudson's (2003) proposal amounts to the lifting of a basic constraint on dependency structures. It implies that these structures need not take the form of directed acyclic graphs, since "loops" do occasionally occur. An alternative interpretation is also available, however. In particular, the links going in opposite directions may be assigned to two separate dimensions of description, with the result that each dimension may fully conform to the acyclicity constraint. In the present section, I first discuss the concept of dimensions on a theoretical plane, then propose a multi-dimensional account of the Hungarian phenomena reviewed in section 2. Due to space limitations, the presentation will be necessarily brief and programmatic. A detailed exposition is currently only available in Hungarian (Imrényi 2013a).

The notion that a single clause may have multiple syntactic representations (in parallel, rather than as steps of a serial derivation) is fairly common in modern grammatical theories. Perhaps the best known framework is Lexical Functional Grammar (Bresnan 2001). In the DG tradition, Functional Generative Description (Sgall et al. 1986) follows a similar path with its distinction between analytic and tectogrammatical layers of syntax. More recently, the concept has also surfaced in the form of Extensible Dependency Grammar (XDG), whose basic tenet is the following:

[5] Computational linguists may also discard MD as superfluous from a practical perspective, since full parsing can be achieved without the extra link posited by Hudson.

> An XDG grammar allows the characterisation of linguistic structure along several dimensions of description. Each dimension contains a separate graph, but all these graphs share the same set of nodes. Lexicon entries synchronise dimensions by specifying the properties of a node on all dimensions at once. (Debusmann et al. 2004: 2)

XDG adopts a componential model of language, whereby syntax and semantics are independent, albeit interfacing, modules. However, the above formulation is also compatible, at least in principle, with the view that dimensions are inherently symbolic, capturing complementary aspects of a clause's meaning and form.

Under these assumptions, link types on each dimension have both semantic and formal relevance, a familiar example being "subject", which associates semantic properties (participant roles as required by specific constructions[6]) with matching morphology or word order. More generally, dimensions may serve the purpose of separating sets of constructions (in the sense of Construction Grammar/CxG) whose workings are by and large independent. For example, CxG classifies a construct such as *What did you give Mary?* as instantiating the Ditransitive Construction (Goldberg 1995: 141) and the Nonsubject Wh-Interrogative Construction (Michaelis 2012: 35) at the same time. Under the present proposal, these constructions (accounting for different aspects of the above construct's meaning and form) belong to different dimensions, each of which takes the form of a graph.

The next issue to consider is the nature of complementary aspects of clausal meaning. At this point, it is worth recalling Halliday's approach to dimensions, which adopts a primarily semantic perspective. As Halliday (1994) puts it,

> the clause is a composite entity. It is constituted not of one dimension of structure but of three, and each of the three construes a distinctive meaning. I have labelled these 'clause as message', 'clause as exchange' and 'clause as representation' (Halliday 1994: 35).

In brief, Halliday's first dimension concerns how the clause "fits in with, and contributes to, the flow of discourse" (Halliday 2004: 64) with its theme–rheme articulation. The second dimension addresses how the clause is "organized as an interactive event involving speaker, or writer, and audience" (2004: 106), and describes the clause in terms of the speech functions offer, command, statement and question. Finally, the third dimension highlights how the clause "construes a quantum of change as a figure, or configuration of a process, participants involved in it and any attendant circumstances" (Halliday 2004: 106).

In Imrényi (2013a), I proposed a similar account of Hungarian clause structure with three dimensions of description (D1, D2, D3) more or less corresponding to Halliday's ones in reversed order. For a verb-based construct, the following basic questions are at issue in each of the dimensions:

- D1: What grounded process is evoked by the clause? What are its participants and circumstances?[7]
- D2: What is the speaker doing by using the clause? What is the illocutionary force and polarity associated with the pattern?[8]
- D3: How is the information contextualized? What reference points (cf. Langacker 2001) or mental space builders (cf. Fauconnier 1985) "situate" or "frame" the information in order to aid its processing, interpretation and evaluation?

---

[6] Langacker (e.g. 2005: 132) argues for a schematic conceptual definition of subjects across constructions. I side with Croft (2001: 170), however, and assume that the semantics of subjecthood must be defined construction-specifically. For example, the subject of a transitive verb will be the Agent or Experiencer, but that of a corresponding passive verb will be the Patient or Theme. The subjects of weather verbs and raising verbs need not be "meaningless" either (*contra* Hudson 2007: 131), as they can be seen as coding global aspects of constructional meaning (cf. Imrényi 2013b: 125).

[7] I consider finite auxiliaries to dominate non-finite lexical verbs. It is their "catena" (Osborne–Gross 2012: 174) which is at the centre of D1, evoking the grounded process (for "grounding", see Langacker 2008, Chapter 9).

[8] Although illocution and polarity may seem logically independent, Croft (1994) finds that "the positive/negative parameter (…) is comparable in typological significance to the declarative–interrogative–imperative speech act distinction" (466). One reason may be the central, prototypical status of positive declarative sentences, with respect to which both non-positive and non-declarative ones are interpreted as deviations, cf. Goldberg (2006: 179).

The three dimensions can be thought of as complementary layers of analysis with formal as well as semantic import (in Hungarian, D1 is primarily coded by morphology, while D2 and D3 by word order and prosody). Further, in contrast with Debusmann et al. (2004), the dimensions are conceived as overlapping rather than sharing precisely the same set of nodes. A given node may serve specific functions on more dimensions at once, or else its function may be restricted to just one of them. For example, as Halliday (2004: 60) suggests, interpersonal adjuncts such as *perhaps* "play no role in the clause as representation" (corresponding to my D1 dimension).

Let us now return to the data first presented in section 2, and see what a multi-dimensional approach has to offer.

(19) Mari meghívta Jánost.
'Mary invited John.'
(20) JÁNOST hívta meg Mari.
'It is John who Mary invited.'
(21) Mari nem hívta meg Jánost.
'Mary didn't invite John.'
(22) JÁNOST nem hívta meg Mari.
'It is John who Mary didn't invite.'
(23) Nem JÁNOST hívta meg Mari.
'It is not John whom Mary invited.'
(24) Nem JÁNOST nem hívta meg Mari.
'It is not John whom Mary didn't invite.'

In each example above, the proposed analysis acknowledges the primacy of the verbal predicate in the 'clause as representation' (D1), as it is this element that evokes the grounded process whose participants are elaborated by *Mari* and *János*t. Thus, they all share the following schematic structure:

(25)
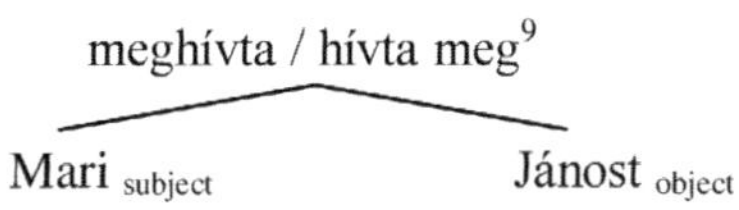

In D2, however, the verbal predicate is only central by default. As proposed above, this dimension is concerned with the clause's illocutionary force and polarity. The neutral positive declarative clause in (19) has the function of stating the occurrence of an invitational event, and the same meaning is construed schematically by *meghívta* 'he/she invited him/her'. Hence, the verbal predicate makes a key contribution to the clause not only in D1 (by evoking an invitational event) but also in D2 (by being crucial to the clause's speech function as a positive statement expressing that event's occurrence).

In (20), by contrast, the speech function of the clause is to identify a participant of an invitational event whose occurrence is presupposed. This function is an alternative to the previous one, as a single clause cannot be used to state the occurrence of an event and to identify a participant at the same time. I assume that the former function, viz. stating the occurrence of an event, is linked by default to the verbal predicate (cf. (19)). In cases like (20), this default function is overridden by a preverbal element which endows the clause with the function of identifying a participant. The overriding relation between *JÁNOST* and the verbal predicate is coded by word order (precedence, adjacency, inversion) and prosody (with the overrider receiving extra stress, and the overridden having its stress reduced or eliminated).

In the proposed representation, the links above and below the string of words belong to two different (acyclic) dimensions.

(26)
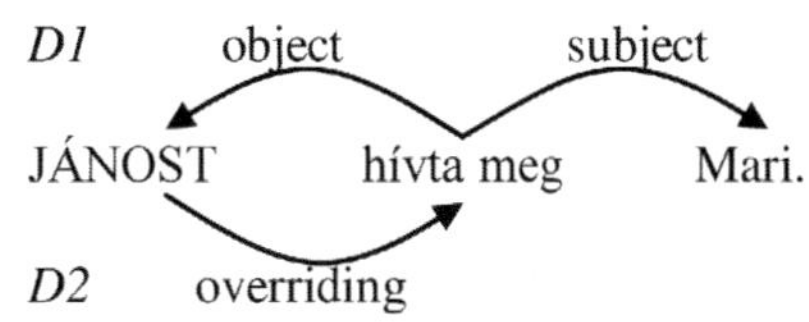

In (21), it is the negative particle *nem* 'not' which prevents the verbal predicate from determining the clause's speech function. As suggested above, the predicate functions by default as a schematic positive declarative clause expressing the occurrence of an event (*meghívta* meaning 'he/she invited him/her'). This interpretation cannot be "projected" to the clause level in the context of negation, as the negative particle overrides the default positive polarity associated with the predicate. I assume that *nem* 'not' only participates in the D2 dimension of the clause; it has no role in the 'clause as representation' (D1). In the diagrams, overriders are marked by capital letters.

(27)
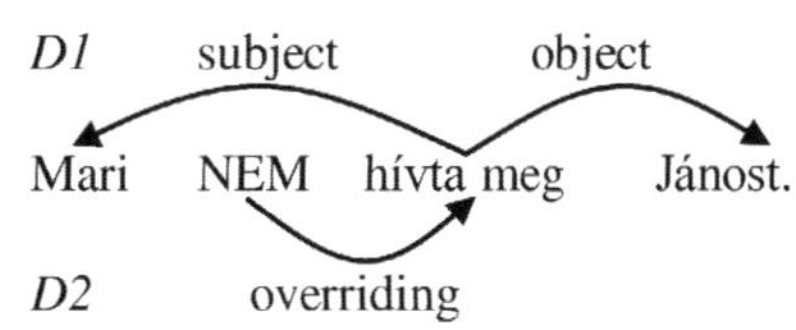

9 In a more detailed analysis, *meghívta* would be represented as two nodes linked by a dependency, forming a "catena" in the sense of Osborne–Gross (2012: 174).

Finally, (22), (23) and (24) feature chains of overriding relations.

(28)
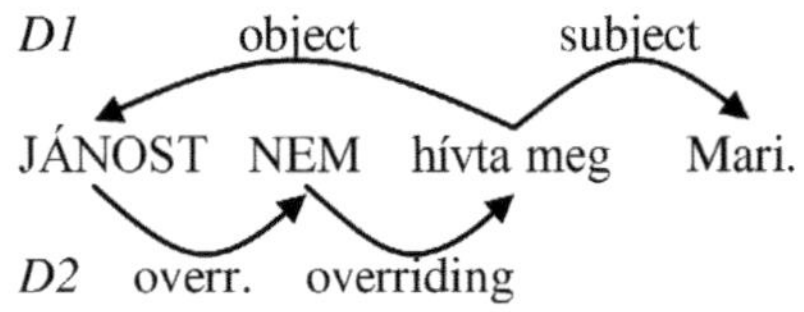

(29)
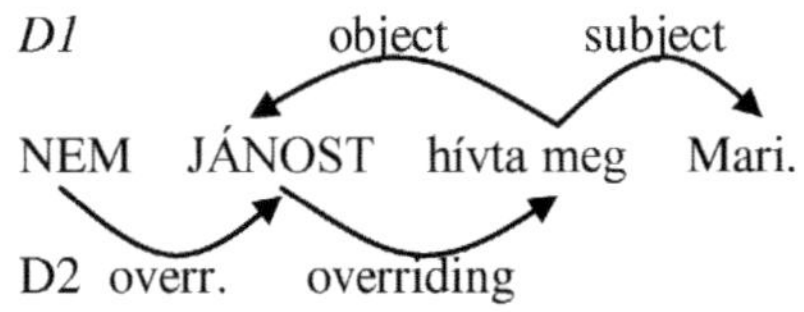

(30)
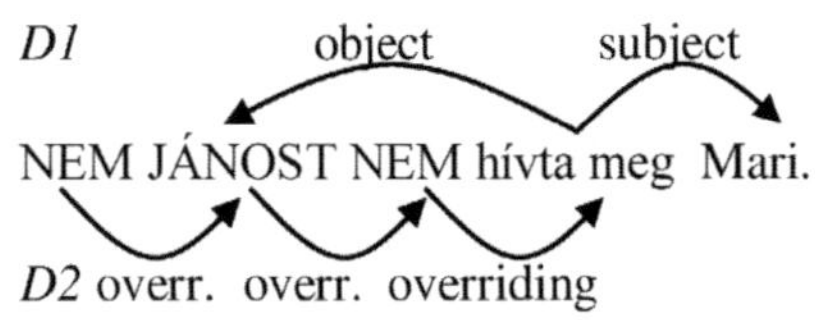

In (28), *nem* overrides the verbal predicate's default positive polarity, and derives a pattern with the function of denying an invitational event's occurrence (*nem hívta meg*). This in turn is overridden by *JÁNOST*, so that the function of the clause is not that of denying the invitational event's occurrence but rather to identify the person who was not invited. In (29), *JÁNOST* overrides the default function of the verbal predicate, and derives a pattern with the function of identifying a participant (*JÁNOST hívta meg*). This identification is in turn overridden by negation. Finally, (30) involves a chain of three overriding relations.

Elements which are not characterized on D2 are regarded as elaborators corresponding to a schematic substructure of the predicate's meaning (cf. Langacker 2008: 198). For example, *Mari* in the above examples corresponds to the schematic 3SG subject which is part of the predicate's specification. Thus, when the predicate is overridden, any elaborators are also in the scope of this operation.

In a more detailed analysis, it can be shown that the overriders and overridden elements of D2 are not necessarily single words; rather they are catenae in terms of D1.[10] For example, *JÁNOST hívta meg Mari* 'It is John who Mary invited' and *JÁNOS BARÁTJÁT hívta meg Mari* 'It is John's friend who Mary invited' have analogous structures. Whereas in the former, a single word fulfils an overriding role (cf. (26)), the latter sees a multi-word catena of D1, *János barátját* 'John's friend.ACC' correspond to a single node of D2. In the diagram below, this node is represented as a bubble (cf. Kahane 1997).

(31)
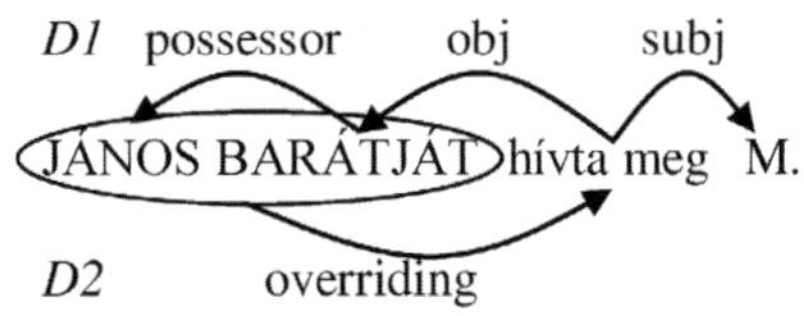

Since single words also count as catenae, the following constraint may apply to mappings between D1 and D2:

(32) A D2 node is a catena of D1.

Finally, let us take stock, and see what advantages or disadvantages the new account has. A key advantage seems to be that it captures the intuition of Hudson (2003) while respecting the acyclicity constraint on dependency structures. Secondly, it has a principled basis in clausal semantics, drawing on Halliday's (1994, 2004) insights in this area. Most importantly, though, it allows one to account for a range of complex patterns that would be difficult to handle with a single dimension. One pertinent example is (9), which contains two independent negations in the same clause, only one of which can be plausibly linked to the verbal predicate. Note also that the analysis provides a unified functional account of various inverting constructions of Hungarian. The negative particle *nem*, identificational foci and interrogative pronouns trigger inversion, overriding the verbal predicate's default linearization (preverb + verb) as they are also overriders of its default function on D2.

The price paid for all this is the addition of an extra layer of structure. However, since the dimensions are analogous and simple (each taking the form of a graph), the complexity involved is still manageable. Overall, the account supports approaches to syntax which avoid cramming all information into a single representation, opting instead for interacting dimensions of meaning and structure.

5 Summary and conclusions

This paper has considered the question if the "functional heads" Focus_0 and Neg_0 should be accommodated in a DG analysis of Hungarian.

[10] As defined by Osborne–Gross (2012: 174), "a catena is a word or a combination of words that is continuous with respect to dominance."

It has been suggested that the "identificational focus" of a Hungarian clause should indeed be analysed as a derived main predicate, as proposed by É. Kiss (2007), in view of the fact that it can be independently negated. However, this requires a DG analysis whereby the focussed expression is both higher and lower than the verb in the syntactic hierarchy.

While Hudson's (2003) mutual dependency analysis is based on a fair amount of converging evidence, it lifts a ban on "loops" in dependency structures, which may raise theoretical and practical problems. Therefore, I have offered an alternative account by which the primacy of the finite verb and the primacy of identificational foci and other (e.g. interrogative and negative) expressions can be linked to separate dimensions of description. The concept of dimensions adopted in the paper is formally similar to XDG's related notion (Debusmann et al. 2004). In content, however, it is rather different, with each dimension conceived as having symbolic (formal as well as semantic) import.

The D1 dimension is concerned with the question as to what grounded process is being evoked, and what its participants and circumstances are. Here, the central role is invariably played by the verb or a catena of verbal elements. The D2 dimension, for its part, addresses speech function (illocutionary force and polarity). Since the Hungarian verbal predicate does not merely "evoke" a process but rather functions as a schematic positive declarative clause by default, it is central to D2 as well, at least in a basic type of clauses. However, identificational foci and the negative particle *nem* 'not', among others, induce shifts in the speech function of the clause, overriding the verbal predicate's dominance in D2. The proposal accounts for a variety of patterns on the left periphery of Hungarian clauses by means of chains of overriding relations. On the semantic side, it follows Halliday (1994), who distinguishes between the 'clause as message', the 'clause as exchange' and the 'clause as representation'.

As a result of the close association between Valency Theory and Dependency Grammar, DG has traditionally focussed on the 'clause as representation', i.e. the question as to what process is being evoked by the verb, and what its participants and circumstances are. The present proposal has made the case for treating matters of speech function (illocutionary force and polarity) as an equally important facet of clausal meaning, to be addressed in a separate structural dimension. The account invites more detailed explorations along these lines, and supports convergence between DG and other theories, notably Construction Grammar and Halliday's Functional Grammar.

Acknowledgements

The research reported here was supported by the Hungarian Scientific Research Fund (OTKA), under grant number K100717.

References

Ágel, Vilmos and Klaus Fischer. 2010. Dependency Grammar and Valency Theory. In: Heine, Bernd and Heiko Narrog (eds.), *The Oxford Handbook of Linguistic Analysis.* OUP, Oxford. 223–255.

Brassai, Sámuel. 2011 [1860–1863]. *A magyar mondat.* Tinta, Budapest.

Bresnan, Joan. 2001. *Lexical Functional Syntax.* Blackwell, Oxford.

Bródy, Mihály. 1990. *Some remarks on the focus field in Hungarian. UCL Working Papers in Linguistics, Vol. 2.* University College London.

Croft, William. 1994. Speech act classification, language typology and cognition. In: Tsohatzidis, Savas L. (ed.), *Foundations of speech act theory: Philosophical and linguistic perspectives.* Routledge, London & New York. 460–77.

Croft, William. 2001. *Radical Construction Grammar: Syntactic Theory in Typological Perspective.* OUP, Oxford.

Debusmann, Ralph, D. Duchier, A. Koller, M. Kuhlmann, G. Smolka and S. Thater. 2004. A Relational Syntax-Semantics Interface Based on Dependency Grammar. *Proceedings of the 20th International Conference on Computational Linguistics.* Geneva.

É. Kiss, Katalin. 1998. Identificational Focus versus Information Focus. *Language* 74: 245–273.

É. Kiss, Katalin. 2002. *The syntax of Hungarian.* Cambridge University Press, Cambridge.

É. Kiss, Katalin. 2007. Topic and focus: two structural positions associated with logical functions in the left periphery of the Hungarian sentence. *Interdisciplinary Studies on Information Structure* 6: 69–81.

Eroms, Hans-Werner. 2000. *Syntax der deutschen Sprache*. Walter de Gruyter, Berlin & New York.

Fauconnier, Gilles. 1985. *Mental spaces: Aspects of meaning construction in natural language*. MIT Press, Cambridge MA.

Gaifman, Haim. 1965. Dependency systems and phrase-structure systems. *Information and Control* 8 (3): 304–337.

Goldberg, Adele. 1995. *Constructions: a Construction Grammar approach to argument structure*. University of Chicago Press, Chicago.

Goldberg, Adele. 2006. *Constructions at work: the nature of generalization in language*. OUP, Oxford.

Gross, Thomas and Timothy Osborne. 2009. Toward a practical Dependency Grammar theory of discontinuities. *SKY Journal of Linguistics* 22: 43–90.

Halliday, M. A. K. 1994. *An introduction to Functional Grammar*. 2nd edition. Arnold, London.

Halliday, M. A. K. 2004. *An introduction to Functional Grammar*. Third edition. Revised by Christian Matthiessen. Arnold, London.

Havas, Ferenc. 2003. A tárgy tárgyában. Mondattipológiai fontolgatások. In: Oszkó Beatrix and Sipos Mária (eds.), *Budapesti Uráli Műhely III*. MTA Nyelvtudományi Intézet, Budapest. 7–44.

Hudson, Richard. 1990. *English Word Grammar*. Blackwell, Oxford.

Hudson, Richard. 2003. Trouble on the left periphery. *Lingua* 113: 607–642.

Hudson, Richard. 2007. *Language networks. The new Word Grammar*. OUP, Oxford.

Imrényi, András. 2013a. *A magyar mondat viszonyhálózati modellje.* [A relational network model of Hungarian sentences.] Akadémiai Kiadó, Budapest.

Imrényi, András. 2013b. The syntax of Hungarian auxiliaries: a dependency grammar account. In: Hajičová, Eva, Kim Gerdes and Leo Wanner (eds.), *DepLing 2013*. Charles University in Prague, Matfyzpress, Prague. 118–127.

Kahane 1997. Bubble trees and syntactic representations. In: Becker, T. and H.-U. Krieger (eds.), *Proceedings of MOL'5*. DFKI, Saarbrücken. 70–76.

Langacker, Ronald. 2001. Topic, subject, and possessor. In: Simonsen, Hanne Gram and Rolf Theil Endresen (eds.), *A cognitive approach to the verb. Morphological and constructional perspectives*. Mouton de Gruyter, Berlin & New York. 11–48.

Langacker, Ronald. 2005. Construction grammars: cognitive, radical, and less so. In: Ruiz de Mendoza Ibáñez, Francisco J., Peña Cervel, M. Sandra (eds.), *Cognitive Linguistics: internal dynamics and interdisciplinary interaction.* Mouton de Gruyter, Berlin. 101–162.

Langacker, Ronald. 2008. *Cognitive grammar: a basic introduction*. OUP, Oxford.

László, Sarolta. 1988. Mikroebene. In: Mrazovic, Pavica and Wolfgang Teubert (eds.), *Valenzen im Kontrast.* Heidelberg. 218–233.

Mel'čuk, Igor. 1988. *Dependency Syntax: Theory and Practice.* The SUNY Press, Albany, N.Y.

Michaelis, Laura A. 2012. Making the case for Construction Grammar. In: Boas, Hans and Ivan Sag (eds.), *Sign-based Construction Grammar.* Center for the Study of Language and Information. 31–69.

Nivre, Joakim. 2004. *Dependency grammar and dependency parsing*. Vaxjo University.

Osborne, Timothy and Thomas Gross. 2012. Constructions are catenae: construction grammar meets dependency grammar. *Cognitive Linguistics* 23 (1): 165–216.

Osborne, Timothy. 2014. Type 2 rising. A contribution to a DG account of discontinuities. In: Gerdes, Kim, E. Hajičová and L. Wanner (eds.), *Dependency linguistics. Recent advances in linguistic theory using dependency structures.* John Benjamins, Amsterdam. 273–298.

Ross, John R. 1969. Guess who? In: Binnick, Robert, Alice Davison, Georgia Green and Jerry Morgan (eds.), *Papers from the 5th regional meeting of the Chicago Linguistic Society.* Chicago Linguistic Society, Chicago. 252–286.

Sgall, P., E. Hajičová and J. Panevová. 1986. *The Meaning of the Sentence in Its Semantic and Pragmatic Aspects*. Reidel, Dordrecht.

Tesnière, Lucien. 1959. *Éléments de syntaxe structurale.* Klincksieck, Paris.

Tesnière, Lucien. 1959/2015. *Elements of structural syntax.* Translated by T. Osborne and S. Kahane. John Benjamins, Amsterdam.

Mean Hierarchical Distance Augmenting Mean Dependency Distance

Yingqi Jing
Department of Linguistics
Zhejiang University
Hangzhou, China
jakenevergivesup@gmail.com

Haitao Liu
Department of Linguistics
Zhejiang University
Hangzhou, China
htliu@163.com

Abstract

With a dependency grammar, this study provides a unified method for calculating the syntactic complexity in linear and hierarchical dimensions. Two metrics, mean dependency distance (MDD) and mean hierarchical distance (MHD), one for each dimension, are adopted. Some results from the Czech-English dependency treebank are revealed: (1) Positive asymmetries in the distributions of the two metrics are observed in English and Czech, which indicates both languages prefer the minimalization of structural complexity in each dimension. (2) There are significantly positive correlations between sentence length (SL), MDD, and MHD. For longer sentences, English prefers to increase the MDD, while Czech tends to enhance the MHD. (3) A trade-off relationship of syntactic complexity in two dimensions is shown between the two languages. English tends to reduce the complexity of production in the hierarchical dimension, whereas Czech prefers to lessen the processing load in the linear dimension. (4) The threshold of the MDD_2 and MHD_2 in English and Czech is 4.

1 Introduction

The syntactic structures of human languages are generally described as two-dimensional, and many structural linguists use tree diagrams to represent them. For example, Tesnière (1959) employed tree-like dependency diagrams called *stemmas* to depict the structure of sentences. Tesnière also distinguished between linear order and structural order. In this study, we follow Tesnière's clear-cut separation of these two dimensions and investigate the relation between them by using an English and Czech dependency treebank, designing different measures to quantify the complexity of syntactic structure in each dimension.

The relationship between linear order and structural order is a crucial topic for all structural syntax. For Tesnière (1959: 19), structural order (hierarchical order) preceded linear order in the mind of a speaker. Speaking a language involves transforming structural order to linear order, whereas understanding a language involves transforming linear order to structural order. It is worth mentioning that Tesnière's stemmas do not reflect actual word order, but rather they convey only hierarchical order. This separation of the two ordering dimensions has had great influence on the development of dependency grammar and word-order typology. The ability to separate the two dimensions has been argued to be an advantage for dependency grammar, since it is more capable than constituency grammar of examining each dimension independently (Osborne, 2014).

The real connection between hierarchical order and word order is evident when the principle of projectivity or continuity is defined in dependency grammar (see, e.g., Lecerf, 1960; Hays, 1964: 519; Robinson, 1970: 260; Mel'čuk, 1988: 35; Nivre, 2006: 71). According to Hudson (1984: 98),

> "if A depends on B, and some other element C intervenes between them (in linear order of strings), then C depends directly on A or on B or on some other intervening element."

Projectivity is immediately visible in dependency trees; a projective tree, as shown in Figure 1, has no crossing lines. But it must be mentioned that projectivity is not a property of the dependency tree in itself, but only in relation to the linear string of words (Nivre, 2003: 51), and some languages with relatively free word order (e.g., German, Russian, and Czech) have more crossing lines than languages with relatively rigid word order (Liu, 2010: 1576). Here, we also use the term "pro-

Proceedings of the Third International Conference on Dependency Linguistics (Depling 2015), pages 161–170,
Uppsala, Sweden, August 24–26 2015.

jection" in linear algebra as a means of transforming a two-dimensional syntactic structure to one-dimensionality. Thus, in a projective or non-projective dependency tree, the string of words is just an image projected by the structural sentence onto the spoken chain, which extends successively on a timeline.

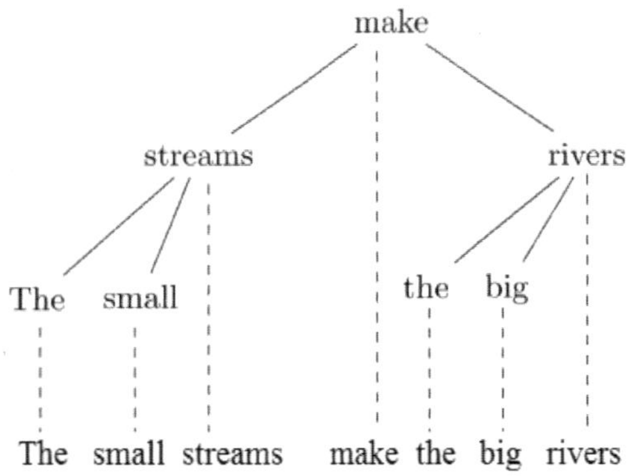

Figure 1: A dependency tree of *The small streams make the big rivers.*[1]

This study focuses on exploring the structural rules of English and Czech using two metrics, mean dependency distance (MDD), as first explored by Liu (2008), and mean hierarchical distance (MHD), as introduced and employed here for the first time. These metrics help predict language comprehension and production complexity in each dimension. The metrics are mainly based on the empirical findings in psycholinguistics and cognitive science, and we tend to bind the two dimensions of syntactic structure together. To assess the value of these metrics, we have explored the syntactic complexity of English and Czech with the help of the Prague Czech-English Dependency Treebank 2.0 (PCEDT 2.0).

The rest of this manuscript introduces the PCEDT 2.0 and data pre-processing in Section 2. The theoretical background and previous empirical studies concerned with the two metrics (MDD and MHD) are presented in Section 3, and our methods for calculating them are also given in this section. In Section 4, we present the results and findings, which are summarized in the last section.

[1]The sentence *The small streams make the big rivers* is the English translation of Tesnière's (1959: 19) example, but linear order and projection lines have been added to the stemma.

2 Czech-English dependency treebank

The material used in this study is the PCEDT 2.0, which is a manually parsed Czech-English parallel corpus, sized at over 1.2 million running words in almost 50,000 sentences for each language (Hajič et al., 2012). The English part of the PCEDT 2.0 contains the entire Penn Treebank-Wall Street Journal (WSJ) Section (Linguistic Data Consortium, 1999). The Czech part consists of Czech translations of all of the Penn Treebank-WSJ texts. The corpus is 1:1 sentence-aligned. The parallel sentences of both languages are automatically morphologically annotated and parsed into surface-syntax dependency trees according to the Prague Dependency Treebank 2.0 (PDT 2.0) annotation scheme. This scheme acknowledges an analytical layer (a-layer, surface syntax) and a tectogrammatical layer (t-layer, deep syntax) of the corpus (Hajič et al., 2012). Only the a-layer was used for the current study. More information about the treebank and its annotation scheme is available on the PCEDT 2.0 website.[2]

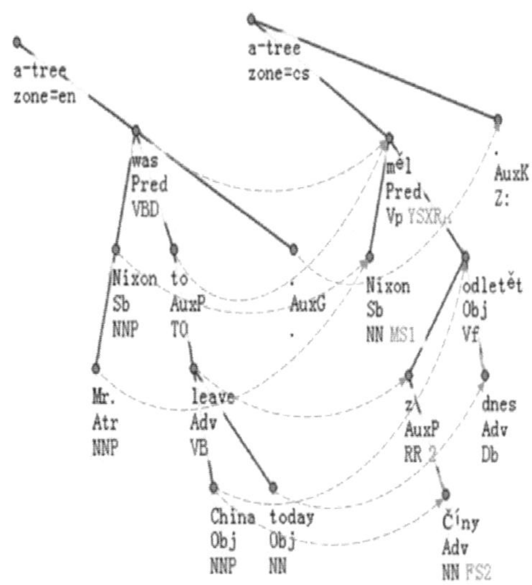

Figure 2: A sample parallel sentence at the a-layer

PCEDT 2.0 is a strictly aligned corpus, which is stored as *.treex format using the XML-based Prague Markup Language (PML). It can be easily visualized with the tree editor TrEd and displayed as the sample parallel sentence (en. *Mr. Nixon was to leave China today.* cs. *Nixon měl z Číny odletět dnes.*) in Figure 2. The word alignment is indicated by the dashed grey arrows pointing from

[2]http://ufal.mff.cuni.cz/pcedt2.0/

the English part to the Czech part.

We first extract data from the original Treex documents with R 3.0.2, supported by the XML package for parsing each node of the treebank, and restore it into a Microsoft Access database. The transformed corpus is much easier to access and analyze (Liu, 2009: 113). Table 1 shows a previous English sample sentence converted into a new format, and the header contains sentence number (sn), word number (wn), word (w), part-of-speech (POS), governor number (gn), governor (g) and dependency relations (dep). The root verb is the only word that has no governor and we indicate its lack of a governor and governor number using 0.

sn	wn	w	POS	gn	g	dep
1770	1	Mr.	NNP	2	Nixon	Atr
1770	2	Nixon	NNP	3	was	Sb
1770	3	was	VBD	0	0	Pred
1770	4	to	TO	3	was	AuxP
1770	5	leave	VB	4	to	Adv
1770	6	China	NNP	5	leave	Obj
1770	7	today	NN	5	leave	Obj
1770	8	.	.	3	was	AuxG

Table 1: A converted sample sentence in English

The a-layer of the corpus contains 1,173,766 English nodes and 1,172,626 Czech word tokens, which are combined into 49,208 parallel sentences. Sentences with less than three words (e.g., *@*, *Virginia:*, *New Jersey:*) or some special four-element sentences (e.g., *"Shocked."*, *Právníci jistě ne.*) were removed from each language (477 and 474 sentences). They are mainly specific markers in the news or incomplete sentences. Finally, the intersection of two language sets constitutes the corpus used in our study according to the sentence number. Table 2 presents an overview of our corpus with 48,647 parallel sentences (s), and the mean sentence length (msl) of English and Czech is 24.1 and 23.63, respectively. However, Czech has a much higher percentage of non-projective (n.p.) dependencies than English.

name	size	s	msl	n.p.
en	1172244	48647	24.1	0.01%
cs	1149630	48647	23.63	3.11%

Table 2: General description of the corpus

3 Mean dependency distance and mean hierarchical distance

Previous scholars have devoted a lot of effort to building a well-suited metric for measuring and predicting syntactic complexity of all human languages, for instance, Yngve's (1960; 1996) Depth Hypothesis[3] and Hawkins' (2003; 2009) principle of Domain Minimalization. The current psycholinguistics and cognitive science have also provided evidence for this issue. Gibson (1998; 2000) conducted many reading experiments and proposed a Dependency Locality Theory (DLT), which associates the increasing structural integration cost with the distance of attachment. Fiebach et al. (2002) and Phillips et al. (2005) observed a sustained negativity in the ERP signal during sentence regions with filler-gap dependencies, indicating increased syntactic integration cost. These studies have a common interest in connecting linear dependency distance with language processing difficulty.

The concept of "dependency distance (DD)" was first put forward by Heringer et al. (1980: 187) and defined by Hudson (1995: 16) as "the distance between words and their parents, measured in terms of intervening words." With the previous theoretical and empirical evidence, Liu (2008: 170) proposed the mean dependency distance (MDD) as a metric for language comprehension difficulty and gave the formula in (1) to calculate it.

$$MDD = \frac{1}{n}\sum_{i=1}^{n}|DD_i| \qquad (1)$$

In this formula, n represents the total number of dependency pairs in a sentence, and $|DD_i|$ is the absolute value of the i-th dependency distance. It must be noted that DD can be positive or negative, denoting the relative position or dependency direction between a dependent and its governor. Thus, the MDD of a sentence is the average value of all pairs of $|DD_i|$.

The present study builds on this distance-based notion of dependencies and extends the concept into the hierarchical dimension. The act of listening involves transforming a linear sentence

[3]Yngve took a constituency-based view and measured the depth of a sentence by counting the maximum number of symbols stored in the temporary memory when building a syntactic tree. Yngve's model and mertic are specifically designed for sentence production.

into a two-dimensional syntactic tree; this bottom-up process is concerned with integrating each linguistic element with its governor and forms a binary syntactic unit. Storage or processing costs occur when a node has to be retained in the listener's working memory before it forms a dependency with its governor (Gibson, 1998). This theory has laid the fundations of many comprehension-oriented metrics.

Conversely, the act of speaking involves transforming a stratified tree to a horizontal line. This top-down process is almost like a spreading activation where the activation of a concept will spread to neighboring nodes (Hudson, 2010: 74-79). Then each concept can be expressed and pronounced sequentially on a timeline. The complexity of this activation procedure is hypothesized and measured by the conceptual distance between the root of a sentence and some other nodes.

The major evidence supporting our assumption is the empirical findings of code-switching by Eppler (2010; 2011), and Wang and Liu (2013). They report that the MDD of mixed dependencies (words from distinct languages) is larger than that of monolingual ones, suggesting that increased processing complexity can actually promote code-switching. These conclusions are drawn from the studies on German-English and Chinese-English code-switching. However, Eppler, and Wang and Liu have only concentrated on investigating the phenomena from the listener's perspective in terms of MDD; they neglect the fact that one of the major motivations for code-switching is to lessen a speaker's production load.[4] For instance, appropriate words or phrases are not instantly accessible, so the speaker seeks some alternative expressions in another language to guarantee continuity in speech. This trade-off relation may provide a starting point to measure the structural complexity from the speaker's perspective.

A stratified syntactic tree can be projected horizontally, and we record the relative distance between each node and the root, as shown in Figure 3. Non-projective sentences can be represented in the same way. Here, we take the root of a syntactic tree as a reference point and designate its projection position as 0; it is the central node and provides critical information about syntactic constituency (Boland et al., 1990; Trueswell et al., 1993). The vertical distance between a node and the root, or the path length traveling from the root to a certain node along the dependency edges, is defined as "hierarchical distance (HD)". For example, the HD of the word *China* in Figure 3 is 3, which denotes the vertical distance or path length between the node and the root.

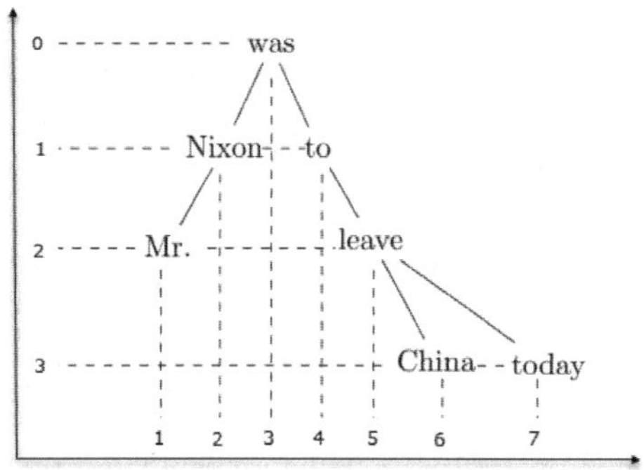

Figure 3: Projection of a dependency tree in two dimensions

The average value of all HDs in a sentence is the mean hierarchical distance (MHD). In this study we hypothesize that the MHD is a metric for predicating the structural complexity in the hierarchical dimension. It can be expressed with formula (2).

$$MHD = \frac{1}{n}\sum_{i=1}^{n} HD_i \quad (2)$$

According to the formulas (1) and (2), we can calculate MDD and MHD of the sample sentence in Figure 3. The MDD of this sentence is (1+1+1+1+1+2)/6=1.17 and the MHD is (2+1+1+2+3+3)/6=2. Note that punctuation marks are rejected when measuring the MDD and MHD.

Furthermore, these two metrics can be applied to measure a text or treebank. To do this, one need merely average the MDD and the MHD of all the sentences in the text or treebank, and in so doing the results represent the MDD and the MHD of the language at hand. In the following parts, we use MDD_2 and MHD_2 to represent the measures at the textual level. For a text with a specific number of sentences (s), its MDD_2 and MHD_2 can be calculated with (3) and (4), respectively.

[4]Some scholars may focus on the social motivations of code-switching, such as accommodating oneself to a social group, but the present study tends to emphasize its psychological property.

$$MDD_2 = \frac{1}{s}\sum_{j=1}^{s} MDD_j \quad (3)$$

$$MHD_2 = \frac{1}{s}\sum_{j=1}^{s} MHD_j \quad (4)$$

To sum up, the syntactic structure of language has two dimensions, which can be reduced to one dimension by means of orthogonal projections. Two statistical metrics (MDD and MHD), one for each dimension, are proposed. These metrics measure syntactic complexity. To be more specific, MDD is actually a comprehension-oriented metric that measures the difficulty of transforming linear sequences into layered trees, whereas MHD is a production-oriented metric that measures the complexity of transforming hierarchical structures to strings of words. These metrics are applicable at both the sentential and the textual levels. In the next section, we further investigate the relations and distributions of MDD and MHD in English and Czech sentences.

4 Results

Section 3 defined the two metrics, MDD and MHD, and gave their corresponding formulas for calculation. In this section, we first calculate the MDD and MHD of each sentence in English and Czech, and describe their distributions in nature. The correlations between sentence length (SL), MDD, and MHD are then tested. Further, we extend the two metrics to the textual level, and compare the MDD_2 and MHD_2 of English and Czech. Finally, the threshold of the two metrics in both languages is investigated.

4.1 Asymmetric distributions of MDD and MHD

Hawkins (2003: 122; 2009: 54) proposed a Performance-Grammar Correspondence Hypothesis (PGCH),

> "grammars have conventionalized syntactic structures in proportion to their degree of preference in performance, as evidenced by patterns of selection in corpora and by ease of processing in psycholinguistic experiments".

The PGCH predicts an underlying correlation between variation data in performance and the fixed conventions of grammars. In other words, the more preferred a structure X is, the more productively grammaticalized it will be, and the easier it is to process due to the frequency effect (Harley, 1995: 146-148; Hudson, 2010: 193-197).

The patterns of syntactic variation can reflect the underlying processing efficiency; hence we first focus on describing the distributions of MDD and MHD of each sentence in the treebank. Figure 4 exhibits two positively skewed distributions of MDD and MHD when the SL (no punctuations) of each English sentence equals 10. The Pearson's moment skewness coefficients (Sk) are 1.31 and 0.78.[5] The coefficients indicate that most English sentences with 10 words get MDD and MHD values below the mean.

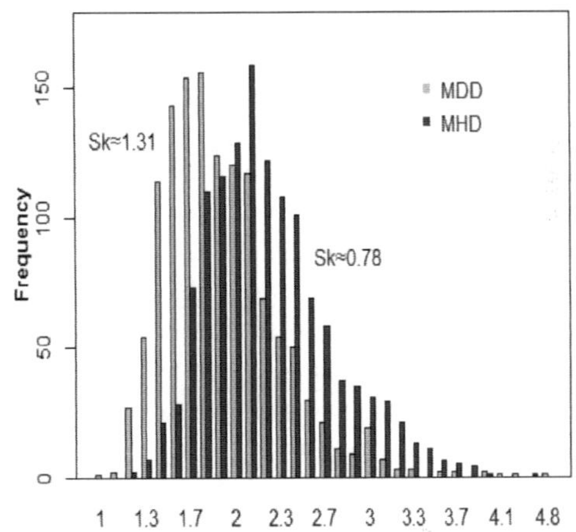

Figure 4: Asymmetric distributions of MDD and MHD for English sentences (SL=10)

Some other types of English and Czech sentences of different lengths, the frequency of which is more than 50 times in the treebank, are also positively skewed in the distribution of MDD and MHD, as shown in Figure 5. The skewness coefficients of the two metrics of both languages are all positive, fluctuating around 1, though there is no significant correlation between SL and Sk. It appears that the mass of both English and Czech sentences, of whatever length, tend to have lower

[5]The Pearson's moment coefficient of skewness is measured by the formula ($Sk = \mu_3/\mu_2^{\frac{3}{2}}$), where μ_2 and μ_3 are the second and third central moments. For a symmetric distribution, if the data set looks the same to the left and right of the center point, the skewness value is equal to zero. If $Sk > 0$, it is a positive skewing indicating more than half of the data below the mean, whereas if $Sk < 0$, it is negatively skewed with more data above the mean.

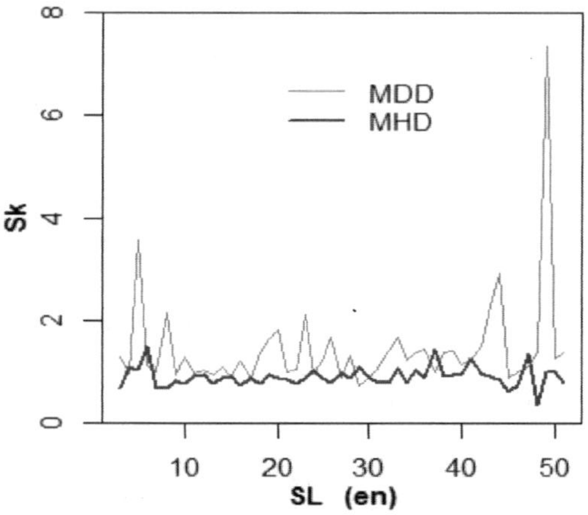

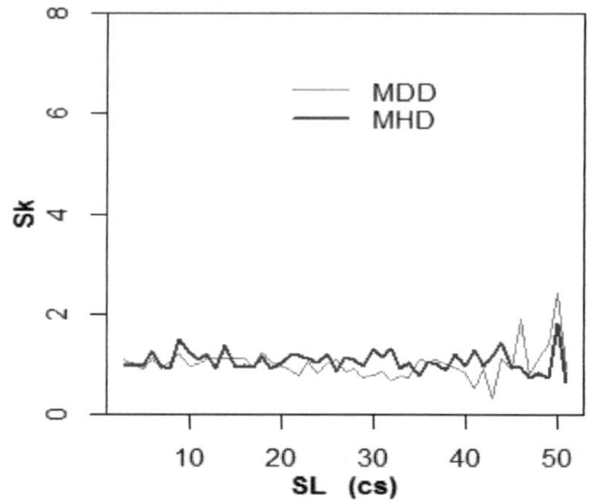

Figure 5: Relationships between SL and Sk in MDD and MHD

MDD and MHD values. Why are lower MDD and MHD preferred in both languages? If grammars are assumed to be independent of processing (Chomsky, 1969), no such consistent asymmetric distributions of the two metrics in different language types would be expected. One possibility for accounting for the skewness is that syntactic rules are direct responses to processing ease and are grammaticalizations of efficiency principles (Hawkins, 1994: 321). Hence, we can observe these preferences in two dimensions, and both English and Czech tend to minimize the MDD and MHD values. The minimalization of these two metrics reflects the efficiency principle of human language.

4.2 Correlations between SL, MDD, and MHD

Another relevant issue concerning the MDD and MHD is whether these metrics can predict the structural complexity for varying sentence lengths in different languages. Table 3 displays the positive correlations between SL, MDD and MHD in English and Czech, and they are all significantly correlated ($p<0.01$). Correlation coefficients (Cor) between SL and MHD in English and Czech are the highest (0.74 and 0.74, respectively), which is followed by moderate correlations (0.54 and 0.42) between SL and MDD in the two languages. The MDD and MHD in both languages are the least correlated with each other, but they are also significant.

More precisely, we build a linear regression model to fit the data. The goodness of fit (R^2) and slope (k) can be used to evaluate the model and predict the increase rate of the two languages. The R^2 between SL and MHD is acceptable at 0.54 and 0.54, while the other two pairs in each language get pretty low values. The slope of the SL-MHD fitting line in English (0.09) is slightly lower than that in Czech (0.12), which suggests the increase of SL will bring more gains of MHD in Czech than in English.

We also visualize the relationships between MDD and MHD of English and Czech sentences with a scatter plot in Figure 6. Although a large overlap is shown between MDD and MHD, we can still observe different extensions in each language. If the SL is taken as a moderator variable, English sentences tend to increase the MDD for longer sentences, whereas Czech sentences prefer higher MHD as the SL is increasing. This variation of preference in different languages can also be predicted by the above linear model. From the perspective of language processing, English sentences prefer to enhance the comprehension difficulty rather than the production cost as the sen-

Lang	X-Y	Cor	p	k	R^2
en	SL-MDD	0.54	<0.01	0.03	0.3
	SL-MHD	0.74	<0.01	0.09	0.54
	MDD-MHD	0.19	<0.01	0.41	0.04
cs	SL-MDD	0.42	<0.01	0.02	0.18
	SL-MHD	0.74	<0.01	0.12	0.54
	MDD-MHD	0.11	<0.01	0.36	0.01

Table 3: Correlations between SL, MDD, and MHD

tences get longer; on the contrary, Czech sentences prefer increasing the structural complexity in hierarchical dimension, which is assumed to be connected with the production load here.

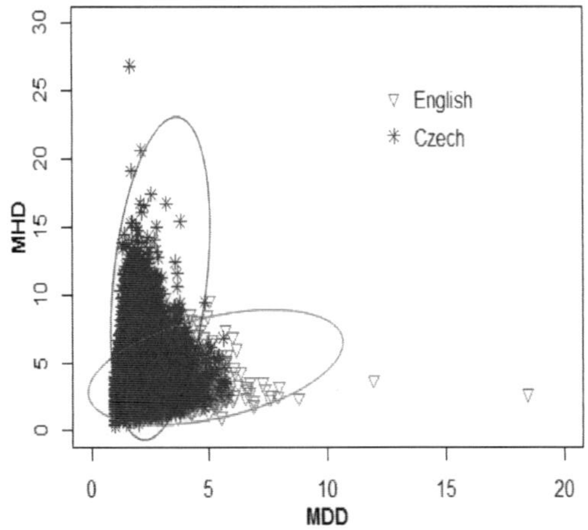

Figure 6: Relationships between MDD and MHD of English and Czech sentences

4.3 Trade-off relation between MDD_2 and MHD_2

The two metrics can be expanded to measure the MDD_2 and MHD_2 of certain languages as well, and compare the values across different language types. English and Czech are both mitigated languages with a subject-verb-object (SVO) word order, but the word order of Czech is relatively unrestricted, whereas English word order has been claimed to become rigid due to the loss of case inflections (Tesnière, 1959: 33; Vennemann, 1974; Steele, 1978; Liu, 2010). Due to this high degree of word order variation, it is almost inevitable for Czech to have more non-projective structures than English. Will the high percentage of non-projective dependency relations in Czech enlarge its MDD_2, or will the two metrics even differentiate the syntactic complexity across the two languages?

Figure 7 represents the MDD_2 and MHD_2 of English and Czech. The MDD_2 of English is 2.31 and that of Czech is 2.18. These numbers are similar to Liu's (2008) results, which were arrived at by investigating the MDD_2 of twenty languages. The MHD_2 is 3.41 for English and 3.78 for Czech. All values are below 4. English and Czech both get a lower MDD_2 than MHD_2, but the MDD_2 of Czech is slightly lower than that of English, even though Czech has a much higher percentage of non-projectivity. Projectivity is of course widely viewed as a constraint in natural language parsing, but the number of projectivity violations that actually occur does not appear to have predictive value for language processing difficulty in the linear dimension.

There seems to be a zero-sum property of the two metrics in different languages. English gains a relatively higher MDD_2 than Czech but has a lower MHD_2. Conversely, even though the MDD_2 of Czech is not as high as that of English, its MHD_2 is greater than that of English. This reciprocal relationship is given at the sentential level in Figure 6, and is also shown at the textual level in Figure 7. This trade-off relation between the structural complexity in the two dimensions partially proves the dynamic balance of code-switching from the listener's and speaker's perspectives.

This also reveals that the weights of the two metrics are not equal in varying language types. English tends to reduce the structural complexity in the hierarchical dimension, while Czech prefers to lessen the processing cost in the linear dimension.

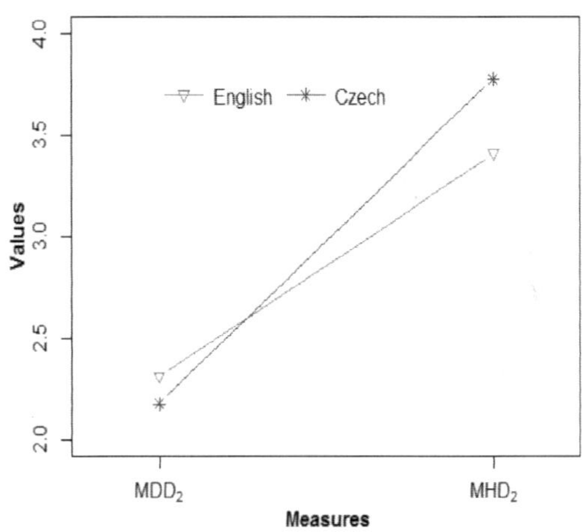

Figure 7: MDD_2 and MHD_2 of English and Czech

4.4 Threshold of MDD_2 and MHD_2

The two metrics, MDD_2 and MHD_2, can differentiate the syntactic complexity or difficulty between English and Czech in each dimension. But can they reveal any common attribute between varying languages? Cowan (2001) claimed that a more precise capacity limit of short-term memory should be about four chunks on the average, and Liu (2008) also observed a threshold of MDD_2

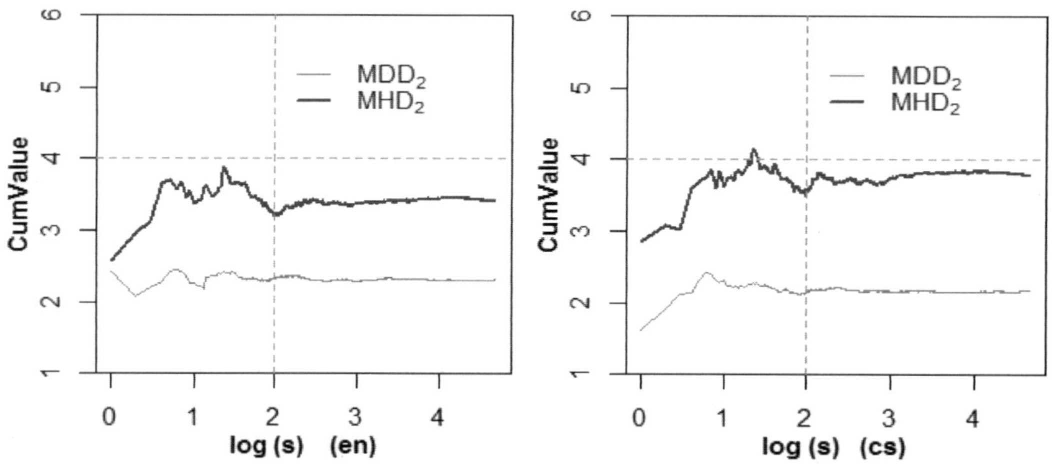

Figure 8: Cumulative average values of MDD_2 and MHD_2 in English and Czech

for twenty languages at about 4. Does there exist a universal boundary value in the hierarchical dimension?

To answer these questions, we make a time-series plot to characterize real-time variation of MDD_2 and MHD_2 in English and Czech, as shown in Figure 8. Due to a large quantity of sentences, the horizontal axis of the plot is scaled logarithmically. A high degree of variation in MDD_2 and MHD_2 is displayed at first, and when more sentences (about 10^2 sentences) are added in, the cumulative average values become stable in both languages. In this plot, we can also find that the maximum values of MDD_2 and MHD_2 in the two languages are below 4,[6] though a small part of the MHD_2 value in Czech is above 4. This minor deviation is mainly caused by fewer sentences and some extreme examples. It should be noted that the corpus used in the present study has a relatively long mean sentence length (around 24 words per sentence), and some sentences with fewer words are also removed, which will, to some extent, enlarge the MDD_2 and MHD_2 of the two languages. But a threshold of the MDD_2 and MHD_2 below 4 is shown as well, and we believe that there do exist boundary conditions for syntactic structure in the two dimensions, and the threshold is largely due to the capacity limits of short-term memory.

Thus, the capacity limit of working memory can be described in the process of both language comprehension and production, and a similar boundary value of 4 reflects their internal coherence.

5 Conclusions

We have presented a systematic study of how to measure the complexity of the syntactic structures of human languages, extending previous distance-based theories. Two statistical metrics (MDD and MHD) have been proposed for predicting the structural complexity of language, one for each dimension. The MDD is comprehension-oriented by measuring the difficulty of speaking, whereas the MHD is production-oriented, calculating the cost of listening. The two metrics are applicable at both the sentential and the textual levels.

Data from the Czech-English dependency treebank have been used to test and justify our approach. Some major findings are summarized as follows. (1) Positive asymmetries in the distributions of the MDD and MHD are observed in English and Czech. Both languages prefer to minimize the processing ease in each dimension. (2) There are significantly positive correlations between SL, MDD, and MHD. For longer sentences, English prefers to increase the MDD, while Czech tends to enhance the MHD. (3) A reciprocal relationship of syntactic complexity in the two dimensions is shown between English and Czech, which indicates an imbalance in weight of MDD_2 and MHD_2. English tends to reduce the syntactic complexity in the hierarchical dimension, whereas Czech prefers to lessen the processing load in the linear dimension. (4) The threshold of MDD_2 and MHD_2 in the two languages is 4 (even below 3 for the MDD_2), which suggests internal coherence for

[6]The MDD_2 for English and Czech is even below 3, but for another language in Liu's (2008) study, i.e. Chinese, the MDD_2 was 3.66.

the process of language comprehension and production.

More quantitative work is needed for the two metrics, especially concerning empirical validty in the arena of psycholinguistics. Furthermore, typological studies are another potentially useful direction for exploration.

Acknowledgments

We would like to thank the anonymous reviewers for their insightful suggestions and comments, Timothy Osborne for his helpful discussions and careful proofreading. This work is partly supported by the National Social Science Foundation of China (Grant No. 11&ZD188).

References

Julie E. Boland, Michael K. Tanenhaus, and Susan M. Garnsey. 1990. Evidence for the immediate use of verb control information in sentence processing. *Journal of Memory and Language*, 29(4): 413–432.

Noam Chomsky. 1969. *Aspects of the Theory of Syntax*. MIT press.

Nelson Cowan. 2001. The magical number 4 in short-term memory: A reconsideration of mental storage capacity. *Behavioral and Brain Sciences*, 24(1): 87–185.

Eva Eppler. 2010. *Emigranto: the syntax of German-English code-switching*. Vienna: Braumüller.

Eva Eppler. 2011. The Dependency Distance Hypothesis for bilingual code-switching. In *Proceedings of the International Conference on Dependency Linguistics*, pages 145–154. Barcelona, Spain, 5–7 September.

Christian J. Fiebach, Matthias Schlesewsky, and Angela D. Friederici. 2002. Separating syntactic memory costs and syntactic integration costs during parsing: The processing of German WH-questions. *Journal of Memory and Language*, 47(2): 250–272.

Edward Gibson. 1998. Linguistic complexity: locality of syntactic dependencies. *Cognition*, 68(1): 1–76.

Edward Gibson. 2000. The dependency locality theory: a distance-based theory of linguistic complexity. In Alec Marantz, Yasushi Miyashita, and Wayne O'Neil (eds.), *Image, language, brain: papers from the First Mind Articulation Project Symposium*, pages 95–126. Cambridge, MA: MIT Press.

Jan Hajič, Eva Hajičová, Jarmila Panevová, Petr Sgall, Silvie Cinková, Eva Fučíková, Marie Mikulová, Petr Pajas, Jan Popelka, Jiří Semecký, Jana Šindlerová, Jan Štěpánek, Josef Toman, Zdeňka Urešová, and Zdeněk Žabokrtský. 2012. Prague Czech-English Dependency Treebank 2.0 LDC2012T08. DVD. Philadelphia: Linguistic Data Consortium.

Jan Hajič, Eva Hajičová, Jarmila Panevová, Petr Sgall, Ondřej Bojar, Silvie Cinková, Eva Fučíková, Marie Mikulová, Petr Pajas, Jan Popelka, Jiří Semecký, Jana Šindlerová, Jan Štěpánek, Josef Toman, Zdeňka Urešová, and Zdeněk Žabokrtský. 2012. Announcing Prague Czech-English Dependency Treebank 2.0. In *Proceedings of the Eighth International Conference on Language Resources and Evaluation (LREC-2012)*, pages 3153–3160. Istanbul, Turkey, 21–27, May. European Language Resources Association (ELRA).

Linguistic Data Consortium. 1999. Penn Treebank 3. LDC99T42.

Trevor Harley. 1995. *The Psychology of Language*. Hove: Psychology Press.

John Hawkins. 1994. *A Performance Theory of Order and Constituency*. Cambridge: Cambridge University Press.

John Hawkins. 2003. Efficiency and complexity in grammars: three general principles. In John C. Moore, and Maria Polinsky (eds.), *The Nature of Explanation in Linguistic Theory*, pages 121–152. Stanford, Calif: CSLI Publications.

John Hawkins. 2009. Language universals and the performance-grammar correspondence hypothesis. In Morten H. Christiansen, Chris Collins, and Shimon Edelman (eds.), *Language Universals*, pages 54–78. Oxford: Oxford University Press.

David Hays. 1964. Dependency theory: a formalism and some observations. *Language*, 40(4): 511–525.

Hans-Jürgen Heringer, Bruno Strecker, and Rainer Wimmer. 1980. *Syntax. Fragen - Lösungen - Alternative*. München: Fink.

Richard Hudson. 1984. *Word Grammar*. Oxford: Blackwell.

Richard Hudson. 1995. Measuring syntactic difficulty. Unpublished paper. *URL www.phon.ucl.ac.uk/home/dick/papers/difficulty.htm*

Richard Hudson. 2010. *An Introduction to Word Grammar*. Cambridge: Cambridge University Press.

Yves Lecerf. 1960. Programme des Conflits, Modèle des Conflits. *Traduction Automatique*, 1(4): 11–18; 1(5): 17–36.

Haitao Liu. 2008. Dependency distance as a metric of language comprehension difficulty. *Journal of Cognitive Science*, 9(2): 159–191.

Haitao Liu. 2009. *Dependency grammar: from theory to practice*. Beijing: Science Press.

Haitao Liu. 2010. Dependency direction as a means of word-order typology: A method based on dependency treebanks. *Lingua*, 120(6): 1567–1578.

Igor Mel'čuk. 1988. *Dependency Syntax: Theory and Practice*. Albany, NY: State University of New York Press.

Joakim Nivre. 2003. An Efficient Algorithm for Projective Dependency Parsing. In *Proceedings of the 8th International Workshop on Parsing Technologies (IWPT 03)*, pages 149–160. Nancy, France, 23–25 April.

Joakim Nivre. 2006. *Inductive Dependency Parsing*. Netherlands: Springer.

Timothy Osborne. 2014. Dependency grammar. In Andrew Carnie, Yosuke Sato, and Daniel Siddiqi (eds.), *The Routledge Handbook of Syntax*, pages 604–626. London: Routledge.

Colin Phillips, Nina Kazanina, and Shani H. Abada. 2005. ERP effects of the processing of syntactic long-distance dependencies. *Cognitive Brain Research*, 22(3), 407–428.

Jane Robinson. 1970. Dependency structures and transformational rules. *Language*, 46(2): 259–285.

Susan Steele. 1978. Word order variation: A typological study. In Joseph H. Greenberg, Charles A. Ferguson, and Edith A. Moravcsik (eds.), *Universals of human language, vol. 4: Syntax*, pages 585–624. Stanford: Stanford University Press.

Lucien Tesnière. 1959. *Éléments de syntaxe structurale*. Paris: Klincksieck.

John C. Trueswell, Michael K., and Christopher Kello. 1993. Verb-specific constraints in sentence processing: separating effects of lexical preference from garden-paths. *Journal of Experimental Psychology: Learning, Memory, and Cognition*, 19(3), 528–553.

Theo Vennemann. 1974. Topics, subjects and word order: From SXV to SVX via TVX. In John M Anderson, and Charles Jones (eds.), *Historical linguistics*, pages 339–376. Amsterdam: North-Holland Pub. Co.

Lin Wang and Haitao Liu. 2013. Syntactic variations in Chinese–English code-switching. *Lingua*, 123: 58-73.

Victor Yngve. 1960. A model and an hypothesis for language structure. In *Proceedings of the American philosophical society*, pages 444–466. 17, October. Philadelphia: American Philosophical Society.

Victor Yngve. 1996. *From grammar to science: New foundations for general linguistics*. Amsterdam & Philadelphia: John Benjamins.

Towards Cross-language Application of Dependency Grammar

Timo Järvinen[*], Elisabeth Bertol[*], Septina Larasati[+], Monica-Mihaela Rizea[‡], Maria Ruiz Santabalbina[°], Milan Souček[*]

[*]Lionbridge Technologies Inc. Tampere, Finland

[+]Charles University in Prague, Czech Republic

[‡]University of Bucharest, Romania

[°]University of Valencia, Spain

{timo.jarvinen, milan.soucek}@lionbridge.com, {liz.bertol, septina.larasati, monicamihaelarizea, mrsantabalbina}@gmail.com

Abstract

This paper discusses the adaptation of the Stanford typed dependency model (de Marneffe and Manning 2008), initially designed for English, to the requirements of typologically different languages from the viewpoint of practical parsing. We argue for a framework of functional dependency grammar that is based on the idea of parallelism between syntax and semantics. There is a twofold challenge: (1) specifying the annotation scheme in order to deal with the morphological and syntactic peculiarities of each language and (2) maintaining cross-linguistically consistent annotations to ensure homogenous analysis for similar linguistic phenomena. We applied a number of modifications to the original Stanford scheme in an attempt to capture the language-specific grammatical features present in heterogeneous CoNLL-encoded data sets for German, Dutch, French, Spanish, Brazilian Portuguese, Russian, Polish, Indonesian, and Traditional Chinese. From a multilingual perspective, we discuss features such as subject and object verb complements, comparative phrases, expletives, reduplication, copula elision, clitics and adpositions.

1 Introduction

Dependency-based grammars (DG) have been used in computational linguistics since the formalization of Tesnière's (1959) structural grammar by Hays (1964). The starting point of the work presented in this paper was Stanford typed dependencies (SD) by Marneffe and Manning (2008, revised November 2012). In parallel to our work, the authors of SD have proposed an extended scheme to account for "several linguistically interesting constructions and extend the scheme to provide better coverage of modern web data" (Marneffe & al., 2013), and later, they suggested a revised cross-linguistic typology (Marneffe & al., 2014), and an online discussion forum for Universal Dependencies was opened at http://universaldependencies.github.io/docs/. However, we feel the discussion has not yet fully taken into account the important notions in dependency grammar tradition or the practical requirements of annotation and use of the syntactically annotated data. Our theoretical framework relies on the notions elaborated earlier by Järvinen and Tapanainen (1998).

2 Functional approach for dependencies

The theoretical framework adopted here applies notions inherent in dependency grammar theory to guide the descriptive decisions for particular languages with the aim of producing a universal syntactic annotation scheme that is intuitively clear and that presents the functional syntactic structure in a way that makes it most efficiently available for practical use. A more rigorous framework would help us to address the following (interrelated) deficiencies:

- English bias due to the fact that English was the starting point for the SD.
- Idiosyncracies due to various descriptive traditions as most of the languages under investigation have a long descriptive tradition not related to formal dependency theory.

Proceedings of the Third International Conference on Dependency Linguistics (Depling 2015), pages 171–180, Uppsala, Sweden, August 24–26 2015.

- Use of notions derived most notably from phrase-structure grammar, though they are not suitable as primitives in DG.
- Pure language-engineering perspective, which may lead to ad-hoc solutions.

The main features of the suggested dependency scheme are:

- The basic syntactic element is a not a word but a nucleus consisting of a semantic head and one or more optional functional words or markers.
- The dependency functions between nuclei are unique within a simple, uncoordinated clause and the inventory of these extranuclear functions is broadly universal.

As elaborated by de Marneffe & al. (2014), SD adopts the lexicalist hypothesis as its first design principle, which regards the word as the fundamental unit in syntax and posits that grammatical relations exist between whole words or lexemes. The authors acknowledge the existence of cases where this assumption fails. First, there are certain types of clitics, which they suggest be treated as independent words even when they are spelled as a single word, following a common practice in many treebanks. Second, there are multi-word lexemes, for which they suggest specific labels such as `mwe`, `name` and `compound` for annotation of the compound parts.

The existence of clitics and multi-word lexemes is not a marginal phenomenon, but it shows that the orthographic word is not suitable as a primitive in DG descriptions. In order to capture what is universal in functional dependency grammar, the notion of nucleus is crucial. It acknowledges the fact that the relations between grammatical markers and content words are different in nature from the relations between content words. The relations within the nuclei are language-specific as there is a large amount of variation in the types of grammatical markers used in different languages. Prototypical markers include adpositions, conjunctions and auxiliaries.

The latest version of SD has adopted a similar view in treating not only auxiliaries but also adpositions as dependents and marking adpositions with a label `case`, which captures the parallelism of adpositional constructions and morphological case.

We discuss the adpositional constructions in detail to illustrate the variation between languages in the choice of adpositional construction versus a specific case marker in the verb complement. In order to achieve a uniform description between languages that takes the functional parallelism fully into account a more thorough revision would be in order. The problem of tokenization is closely related to this issue.

It is a common phenomenon that an orthographic word corresponds to a multiple nucleus; for example, the subject is often incorporated into the verb. Thus, the Spanish token *dámelo* includes three syntactic functions in the verb form: subject, object and indirect object. In practical parsing it may be convenient to use an orthographic word as a primary token, but unless we specify the functional information in the morphological description of the token, the syntactic analysis is not complete.

As both the grammatical markers and syntactic nucleus may consist of several orthographic words, it is convenient to use specific intra-nuclear dependencies linking the parts within them. A common morphological process of reduplication poses problems for the lexicalist hypothesis. The nucleus analysis predicts that there is a continuum from morphological reduplication to full lexicalization.

2.1 Universal dependencies

There are obvious reservations for the universality of the functional dependencies. Presumably, an exhaustive list of functional dependencies may not exist, nor is it necessary to investigate this from the linguistic point of view. As empirical linguists, we only need to list the functions that are applicable to the languages we are analyzing, but we can not assume that all of the universal functional dependencies are applicable to all languages.

From a practical point of view, the most important choices are (i) the selection of the relevant functional categories that need to be covered and (ii) the granularity of the description.

The choice of granularity has an impact both on parsing accuracy and usability of the parsing results. Consider the inventory of adverbial functions as an example. We can use a single functional dependency, adverbial modifier (`advmod`), to annotate optional adverbial modifiers. Alternatively, we could use a more fine-graded set of adverbial functions that includes functions typically distinguished in traditional grammars, such as time, duration, frequency, quantity, manner, location, source, goal, contingency, condition. An obvious advantage of using a large inventory for adverbials is more usable output to various applications requiring even a rough semantic analysis. In fact, a larger set of adverbial roles may improve the parsing accuracy. Though the adverbial modifiers are optional and to a large extent freely combinable with any predicate (save strictly semantic restrictions), it is a commonplace in linguistics that a predicate may have only one non-coordinated adverbial of the same type – a behavior similar to the obligatory arguments or complements. This principle of uniqueness is applicable to practical parsing of adverbials (e.g. to solve the so-called PP-attachment ambiguities) only if all types of adverbial functions, in addition to the complements, are covered in the language model. Recently, Jaworski and Przepiórkowski (2014) have applied a similar idea for assigning approximate semantic roles based on grammatical functions and morphosyntactic features in syntactic-semantic parsing for Polish.

For practical parsing, the uniqueness principle is more important than the distinction of obligatory arguments. An obligatory argument is often missing (being implicit or contextually recoverable), but uniqueness cannot be violated as this would render the clause contradictory or nonsensical. Note that the principle of uniqueness is no longer applicable if several subcategories for unique functional labels are used. For example, the subcategories of subject proposed in SD (`nsubj`, `nsubjpass`, `csubj` and `csubjpass`) are mutually exclusive. As this distinction is automatically recoverable from the linguistic context, it is redundant and it would be advantageous to use only one subject label when doing practical annotation work.

3 Selected linguistic phenomena with reference to SD

3.1 Verb complementation

The grammatical form of complements of verb is governed by the verb. Traditionally, these are considered obligatory versus adjuncts that may occur freely without grammatical restrictions imposed by the verb. From the viewpoint of functional grammar the complements have a specific status. The semantic roles assigned to them are idiosyncratic, depending on the verb. For example, in English, a specific verbs may assign the role of location to a direct object, for example: *They swam a lake.*

The inventory of complement types shows a large amount of language-specific variation, but the core set of complement types is broadly universal. Which complement types are instantiated in a given language can be determined by the uniqueness test. Regarding complement types, our solution was to introduce new dependency relations in our application of the SD model as needed. The cases in point are subject complement (`scomp`) and object complement (`ocomp`), complements that refer to the subject and object, respectively.

Subject complement. The new dependency label `scomp` (subject complement) was introduced to replace `attr`, `cop` and `acomp` (McDonald et al., 2013, p. 3, Table 1; de Marneffe and Manning, 2008), which had been used inconsistently across languages and caused considerable confusion. A subject complement (`scomp`) to a verb has as its antecedent the subject of the clause. In English as well as other languages, it is a widely used grammar term covering the traditional syntactic functions of predicative noun and predicative adjective, frequently, but not exclusively, following a copular verb that links the `scomp` with the subject. `Scomp` occur not only as (pro)nouns (1) and adjectives (2), but also as adverbs (3) as well as prepositional (4) and genitive phrases (5) and in passive structures (6). In languages where `scomp` inflects, adjective `scomp` will agree with the subject in number and gender, as in Romance languages (7).

(1) *¿Qué es esto?*
"What is this?"
(2) *Gold is expensive.*
(3) *Who is there?*
(4) *Sie wurde zur ersten Astronautin Lichtensteins.*
"She became to the first astronaut of Liechtenstein."
(5) *Sie ist guter Dinge.*
"She is of good things."
(6) *Il a été nommé president.*
"He has been named president."
(7) *Quelle est la distance? Jean est petit.*
"Which is the distance? Jean is small."

Object complement (`ocomp`) is another dependency label that was introduced to capture complements to the direct object of the verb. It usually occurs in connection with verbs of creating or nominating/naming such as *make, name, elect, paint, call*, etc., which govern at least two complements. The `ocomp` relation occurs not only with nouns (8) and adjectives (9), but also in prepositional phrases (10). In languages where `ocomp` inflects, adjective `ocomp` will agree with the object in number and gender, as in Romance languages (11).

(8) *Te considero una persona inteligente.* (es)
"I consider you an intelligent person."
(9) *We painted the house green.*
(10) *Ich halte die Idee für blöd.* (de)
"I hold the idea for dumb."
(11) *Os críticos acharam o filme fabuloso.*(pt)
"Critics found the movie amazing."

Contrary to `scomp`, which replaces three previously used labels, `ocomp` is less a replacement for specific labels than an addition to the dependency relations. Only the previous label `acomp` (adjective complement) was replaced either by `scomp` or `ocomp`, depending on the functional role of the adjective. For example, Tapanainen and Järvinen (1997) include object complement, but de Marneffe and Manning, (2008), do not include anything akin to an `ocomp` in their list of complements. Prior to the introduction of `ocomp`, annotators resorted to a variety of solutions, such as `acomp` if the object complement was an adjective or `appos` if nominal. `Ocomp` has been accepted as a viable dependency label by the annotators of all languages in the scope of this project.

Expletive or Topic: The dependency relation `expl` (expletive) is defined as "a relation that captures an existential *there*". The main verb of the clause is the governor as (12) in de Marneffe and Manning, (2008).

(12) *There is a ghost in the room.*
Expl (is, There)

Also later SD adaptations use this label similarly (McDonald et al, 2013).

Although "expletive" is often defined to include non-referential *it* and equivalents in other languages as in English "*it is raining*" or German "*Es regnet*", by default we adhered to SD guidelines in that `expl` is used only for equivalents of English existential *there* or non-referential it in clauses or sentences containing a subject in addition to the expletive. Even though there is no semantic subject in structures like *It is raining*, the dummy subject is obligatory in verb-second clauses and it is tagged as `nsubj`. However in French, we used a broader definition of the notion expletive by making a distinction between the expletive value of the subject and `expl` as a dependency relation. Therefore, we were able to apply this relation to nouns as well as adverbs or even to prepositions. We needed `expl` in order to account for a particular dependency relation established by such "empty" words.

For example, we analyzed structures like (12) as expl(a,y) and decided to analyze nsubj(a,il). We also used `expl` when the subject or direct object position was already filled (for example, in co-referent expressions where we decided that the semantic subject should be analyzed as `nsubj` (14) expl(est, c'). There were also other situations such as non-negative *ne* (15), euphonic -t: ("*y a-t-il*") (13), to introduce the impersonal subject "*on*" (16), where we had to opt for `expl`. We have adapted this deprel to the specific situations of French grammar. Our use of `expl` does not contradict the initial definition. It is only a broader definition, allowing a wider range of uses.

(13) *Il y a un problème.*(fr)
"There is a problem."
(14) *C'est quoi la distance?* (fr)
[Expl]-It-is what the distance.
"What is the distance?"
(15) *Je crains qu'elle ne parte.* (fr)
"I fear she left."
(16) *La situation est bien plus grave que l'on peut imaginer.* (fr)
"The situation is well more serious than one can imagine."

We would like to point out the parallelism between the expletive in subject-prominent languages discussed here and topic in topic-prominent languages like Japanese and Korean, following the distinction by Li and Thompson (1976). From the universal dependency point of view, a single label might be appropriate for both types of languages. The difference is merely the semantically empty topic in subject-prominent languages versus the semantically indeterminate topic in topic-prominent languages.

3.2 Adpositional structures

Typically, adpositional constructions are used as adjuncts. However, in many languages some of the complements are marked with an adposition or a specific case. For example, in English a complement semantically equivalent to an indirect object (`iobj`) is marked with the preposition *to*.

3.3 Comparative constructions

Comparative sentences are those in which a comparison is established. The main clause contains the first term of the comparison, and particular words (like *que* and *como* in Spanish and Portuguese) introduce the second term of the comparison. This second term of the comparison could be a clause or a sentence.

(17) *La empresa realizó trabajos más avanzados que los pioneros de la transmisión.* (es)
"The company accomplished more advanced tasks than the pioneers of the transmission did."

(18) *La guardería no es tan cara como decían.* (es)
nsubj(es, guardería); det(guardería, La); root(es); cop(es,cara); advmod(cara, tan); mark(es,como); advcl(como,decían)
"The nursery school isn't as expensive as they said."

The difference between (17) and (18) is that the first one contains a comparative phrase with no verb in the second term of comparison whereas the latter contains a comparative clause with a verb. This formal distinction has syntactic consequences so the two cases cannot be treated in the same way.

Comparative clauses: Spanish and Portuguese grammars have pointed out that comparative and consecutive clauses are syntactically very similar.

(19) *es tan alto que no cabe por la puerta* (es)
"he's so tall he cannot get through the door"

(20) *era tão alto que batia na porta* (pt)
"he's so tall he cannot get through the door"

Sentences (19) and (20) are formally very close to (18), but the underlying meaning is different. In these cases there is not a comparison, but a cause – consequence relation. This syntactic similarity could be a good reason to consider comparative clauses as `advcl` and, consequently, consider the word that introduces the second term of the comparison as a marker (`mark`).

As shown in the example (18), since the deprel assigned to the clause is `advcl`, the head of comparative clause should be the verb of the main clause, that is, the `root`.

A final observation to be made about comparative clauses is that the preferred POS tag of these markers is CONJ: dictionaries have already pointed this out, and it is consistent with the consecutive – comparative analogy, too.

Comparative phrases: The case of comparative phrases is more complicated because they do not have a verb, and there is thus no parallelism with other kinds of clauses. While it would be possible to analyze these as clauses with omitted verbs, we still would not be able to identify the head.

The most controversial decision was to determine the most appropriate label for the word that introduces the second term of the comparison, because this decision would influence the complete analysis of these phrases.

It was pointed out that *como* could be considered as an adposition (ADP) in some contexts in Portuguese (even if in these cases the dictionaries say it should be a conjunction). In Italian, this marker even selects the oblique case of the pronoun as regular prepositions do, but that is not the case in Portuguese or in Spanish.

(21) *bella come te* (it);
bela como tu (pt);
bella como tu (es)
"beautiful like you"

In Spanish, we can find some examples where the comparative meaning is introduced by an unequivocal ADP:

(22) *es más alto de lo normal*
"he's taller than the average"

Similarly, if we say that *como* is a conjuction functioning as `prep`, the same can be applied to *que* as well:

(23) *mais bela que tu* (pt);
más bella que tu (br)
"more beautiful than you"

Since the final annotation decision was to treat these words as conjunctions with prepositional function, ADP, the complete analysis of the comparative phrase was affected. The corresponding deprel to an ADP should be `prep`, which is always the head of a `pobj`. Consequently, the most appropriate analysis for the comparative phrase is indeed `pobj` and the head would be the verb of the main clause, as in (25).

(24) *La empresa realizó trabajos más avanzados que los pioneros de la transmisión.* (es)
nsubj(realizó, empresa); det(empresa, La); root(realizó); dobj(realizó, trabajos); amod(trabajos, avanzados); advmod(avanzados, más); prep(realizó, que); pobj(que, pioneros); prep(pioneros, de); pobj(de, transmisión); det(transmisión, la)
"The company accomplished more advanced tasks than the pioneers of the transmission did."

Comparative constructions were also discussed by de Marneffe & al. (2013). We agree that their analysis to treat the word that acts as the standard of comparison as the head for the comparative clause or phrase is more adequate from a semantic point of view. This was also the intended analysis in the FDG description (Järvinen & Tapanainen 1997):

(25) *There are monkeys more intelligent than Herbert.*
modifier(more,than); pobj(than,Herbert)

This analysis is further corroborated by typological evidence. For example, in Korean the comparative particle 'more than' is a single unit that attaches to the object of comparison (Yeon & Brown, 2011):

(26) 러시아가 한국보다 더 크다.
Russia-TOPIC Korea-THAN big
"Russia is bigger than Korea."

3.4 Clitic particles

New POS tag	Description
VERBPRONACC	verb + accusative clitic
VERBPRONDAT	verb + dative clitic
VERBPRONDATACC	verb + dative clitic + accusative clitic
VERBPRT	verb + verbal morpheme (PRT)
VERBPRTPRONACC	verb + PRT + accusative clitic
AUXPRONACC	auxiliary verb + accusative clitic
AUXVPRT	auxiliary verb + PRT

Table 1. List of new POS tags created for Spanish.

Even in closely related languages such as Portuguese and Spanish, which exhibit a broadly similar behavior of clitics, the differences in orthography make the practical analysis for the latter more challenging. In Spanish, the enclitic pronouns are orthographically attached directly to the verb form and consequently, a mechanical tokenization of the complex word form is not possible as in Portuguese, which uses a hyphen in this context. Rather than attempting to tokenize the Spanish clitics separately, we used an extended set of POS labels for Spanish as illustrated in Table 1, so that there would be no loss of information as compared to the analysis of other Romance languages. This descriptive solution is made for convenience, but note that the functional description is not compromised. It is a purely technical question whether to use a single POS label or a main POS label with separate morpho-syntactic descriptors to encode the values for incorporated syntactic functions. A more complete syntactic description for the example *dámelo* would be VERB + Subj_Sg2 + Dat + Acc, thereby making the information available for conversion to a proper functional DG description showing the three nuclei as direct dependents of the verbal nucleus.

3.5 Multi-word expressions

As for mwe modifiers, we have consistently annotated idiomatic word combinations whose internal structure is not relevant for the functional analysis by using the other existing dependency relations and POS (regent–subordinate) combinations that were permitted for each language.

In de Marneffe and Manning (2008), the mwe dependency relation implies a closed set of items (restricted mainly to function words). By convention, the internal head of the mwe relation is consistently analyzed, across languages, as the rightmost element of the structure.

We kept a list of possible mwe candidates that were approved during the project for all languages. For some Romance languages (e.g. French), it was convenient to define patterns of mwe, as opposed to a plain list of these. Generally, idiomatic combinations that consisted of preposition + (preposition) + noun, pronoun, adjective, adverb or infinitive were analyzed as surface prep and pobj or/and pcomp structures; mwe was used for semantically opaque expressions that mostly included structures consisting of adverb, noun or conjunction + adposition or conjunction, for example in Spanish *mientras que* mark(*,que), mwe(que, mientras) POS: CONJ, CONJ; *para que* mark(*, que), mwe(que, para) POS: ADP, CONJ; in Brazilian Portuguese *até que* mark(*, que); mwe(que, até) POS: ADP, CONJ; and French *avant/afin de,* see (30); *pour que* mark(*,que), mwe(qu',pour) POS:ADP, CONJ.

Additionally, in deciding whether a multi-word structure is analyzable, we also had to consider the relation that needed to be established between the components of the structure and the external elements. For example, some French 'locutions prépositives' of the type preposition + noun that are followed by a nominal are analyzed as mwe since there is no acceptable interpretation for the following nominal in case we analyze the prepositional structure as prep and pobj:

(27) *Ils sont tous venus, à part Christian.*
prep (venus, part); mwe(part, à);
pobj(part,Christian).
"They are all come, except Christian."

(28) *Cet objectif peut être réalisé à travers les règles à fixer par la Commission.*
prep(réalisé,travers); mwe(travers, à);
pobj(travers, règles).
"This objective can be realized by means of the rules to fix by the commission."

It can be noticed that the governor of a multi-word expression annotated as mwe takes the head of the expression as a subordinate, using a dependency relation which describes the relation between the governor and the mwe. Examples from French:

(29) *en tant que*
prep(*,tant), mwe(tant,en), mwe(tant,que)
POS: ADP/ADV/CONJ
"as"

(30) *avant de*
mark(*,de), mwe(de,avant)
POS:ADV/ADP
"before"

(31) *beaucoup de*
det(*,de), mwe(de,beaucoup);
POS:ADV/ADP
"a lot of"

In (31) the pattern comprises of *beaucoup, plein, bien, peu, tant, assez, plus, advantage* and *sufficamment.*

Sometimes, mwe might imply a head which is morphologically different from the function of the whole structure. For example, the French mwe *peut-être* has an adverbial value. This implies that the head of the mwe, *être*, which is actually a verb, becomes subordinated by an advmod deprel to the governor of the multi-word the structure:

(32) *Criton sait que Socrate est aussi fidèle que lui et il pense que si Socrate ne se sauve pas pour lui - même , peut - être se sauvera - t - il pour ses amis.*
advmod(sauvera, être); mwe(être, peut).
"Criton knows that Socrates is as faithful as him and he thinks that if Socrates not himself saves not for himself, maybe himself will save he for his friends."

Spanish and Brazilian Portuguese also permit a noun (which was the head of a mwe functioning as a conjunction) as a subordinate in a cc deprel:

(33) *Los objetivos de los aliados , sin embargo , diferían.* (es)
cc(diferían, embargo); mwe(embargo,sin).
"However, the aims of the allies differed."

Similarly with a verb:

(34) *Es decir, un jugador puede jugar como un WHM.* (es)
cc(jugar, decir); mwe(decir, es).
"That is, a player can play as a WHM."

(35) *Denomina - se oblíquo quando não é um cone reto , ou seja , quando o eixo é oblíquo ao plano da base.* (pt)
cc(é, seja); mwe(seja, ou).
"A cone is called oblique when it's not upright, that is, when its axis is oblique to the plane of its base."

3.6 Elision

Dependency theory is inherently verb-centered. Therefore elision of a verb poses a descriptive problem that could be solved either by (a) inserting an empty node (represented as EMP in the example below), which assumes the functions of the elided element or (b) raising an existing element to the position of the elided node. The examples for solution (a) and (b) are provided in (36) and (38), respectively, for comparison.

(36) *Beliau seorang penerbit.*
PRON DET NOUN
root(*, EMP); nsubj(EMP, beliau); dobj(EMP, penerbit); det(penerbit, seorang)
"He is a publisher."

The former solution (a) is not plausible if the purpose is to provide a surface-syntactic functional description rather than an abstract deep-syntactic representation of an elliptic sentence. Positing an abstract representation by analogy, as ellipsis is often described in traditional grammar, is questionable as a syntactic analysis in the sentence level and computationally more challenging as it would mean that the parser should somehow be able to map the non-elliptic construction to the elliptic construction to produce the intended analysis. Therefore, achieving the best possible analysis between the actual elements in the sentence or sentence fragment is strongly preferred.

Elision of a copula in present tense is standard in Russian and it may appear in informal registers (speech transliterations) in Indonesian.

Our examples are from Indonesian, which uses copulas to link a subject to nouns, adjectives, or other constituents in a sentence. There are three copula constructions found in our data. These constructions are sentences with a copula, sentences with a dropped copula, and sentences with a verb that acts like a copula. For some of these constructions we use the `scomp` deprel to create the link between the constituents. These copulas are not auxiliary verbs, hence they are not annotated as AUX, but instead they are annotated as VERB.

Sentences with copulas: There are two copulas in Indonesian, *adalah* and *ialah*. They have the same function and can be used interchangeably. These copulas cannot be negated. We use the `scomp` deprel to link the subject and the other constituents that surround the copula.

(37) *Beliau adalah seorangpenerbit.*
PRON VERB DET NOUN
root(ROOT, adalah); nsubj(adalah, Beliau); scomp(adalah, penerbit); det(penerbit, seorang)
"He is a publisher."

Sentences with dropped copulas: In some cases, especially in spoken Indonesian, the copulas can be dropped. The sentence can be negated.

(38) *Beliau seorang penerbit.*
PRON DET NOUN
root(*, Beliau); scomp(Beliau, penerbit); det(penerbit, seorang)
"He is a publisher."

Sentence with copula-like verb: The verb that acts like a copula is the word *merupakan*, which links the subject to the other constituents. This verb can be negated. The sentence is annotated as a usual Subject-Verb-Object (SVO) structure in Indonesian without the `scomp` deprel.

(39) *Beliau merupakan seorang penerbit.*
PRON VERB DET NOUN
root(*, merupakan); nsubj(merupakan, Beliau); dobj(merupakan, penerbit); det(penerbit, seorang)
"He is a publisher."

3.7 Reduplication

Another common morphological process that is of interest here is reduplication. This structure is found in our data in Indonesian and traditional Chinese (Larasati, 2012, Wang, 2010). Reduplicated forms were tokenized into separated tokens.

To accommodate this phenomenon, a new dependency relation, `redup`, was introduced to link the reduplicated token. Depending on the language, a reduplicant may copy either from the right or from the left and the governing head is either to the left or to the right, respectively. We used the leftmost token as the head (Wang, 2012).

One of the uses of reduplication in Indonesian is to indicate plurality, e.g. the word *senapan-senapan* (n. 'riffles', lit. riffle-riffle). Some reduplicated nouns are lexicalized, e.g. *langit-langit* ('ceiling; palate' < langit, 'sky').

From the functional point of view, `redup` is an intranuclear link. The analysis may not distinguish fully between lexicalized and non-lexicalized instances, though in the former case a single-token analysis would be more appropriate.

For Traditional Chinese, one of the uses of reduplication is to intensify the degree to which the property denoted by the adjective holds, e.g. the word "小小"(adj. very small, lit. small small). In the data, the word is tokenized into two tokens "小"and "小".

4 Conclusion

Applying a strict linguistic theory would assist linguists in choosing between alternative annotations more consistently and efficiently.

It is not possible to achieve a consistent and descriptively adequate cross-lingual description without a consistent theoretical framework. A plain eclecticism would only lead to a proliferation of the grammatical descriptors.

Functional syntactic descriptions have gained ground in computational applications. The notions of phrase-structure grammar are tied to the form of a particular language, and as there is a need to cover more and more new languages of various types, functional descriptions that capture the implicit semantic parallelisms between languages provide an even more adequate framework for practical work and practical applications.

Acknowledgements

We wish to thank the three anonymous reviewers for their comments on the submitted version. The data annotation was conducted in a Multilingual Data Annotation Project executed for Google. This research was partially supported by SVV project No. 260 224 of the Charles University in Prague.

References

Bernard Comrie. 1989. *Language universals and linguistic typology*. 2nd edition. Chicago: University of Chicago.

David G. Hays. 1964. Dependency theory: A formalism and some observations. Language, 40:511-525.

Charles N. Li and Sandra A. Thompson . 1976. *Subject and Topic: A New Typology of Language".* In Charles N. Li. *Subject and Topic*. New York: Academic Press.

Wojziech Jaworski and Adam Przepiórkowski: Syntactic Approximation of Semantic Roles. 2014. In *Proceedings of 9th International Conference on NLP, PolTAL 2014*. Pp. 191-201.

Timo Järvinen and Pasi Tapanainen. 1997. A *Dependency Parser for English*. Technical Reports, No. TR-1. University of Helsinki.

Timo Järvinen and Pasi Tapanainen. 1998. Towards an Implementable Dependency Grammar. In: *Proceedings of Dependency-Based Grammars*, (eds.) Sylvain Kahane and Alain Polguère, Université de Montréal, Quebec, Canada.

Septina Dian Larasati. 2012. IDENTIC Corpus: Morphologically Enriched Indonesian-English Parallel Corpus. In *Proceedings of LREC 2012*, page 902-906.

Marie-Catherine de Marneffe, Miriam Connor, Natalia Silveira, Samuel R. Bowman, Timothy Dozat and Christopher D. Manning. 2013. More constructions, more genres: Extending Stanford Dependencies. In: *Proceedings of the Second International Conference on Dependency Linguistics* (Depling 2013).

Marie-Catherine de Marneffe, Timothy Dozat, Natalia Silveira, Katri Haverinen, Filip Gintner, Joakim Nivre and Christopher D. Manning. 2014. Universal Stanford Dependencies: A cross-linguistic typology. In: *Proceedings of LREC 2014*.

Marie-Catherine de Marneffe, and Christopher D. Manning. 2008 (revised Nov. 2012). *Stanford typed dependencies manual.*

Ryan McDonald, Nivre, J., Quirmbach-Brundage, Y., Goldberg, Y., Das, D., Ganchev, K., Hall, K., Petrov, S., Zhang, H., Täckström, O., Bedini, C., Bertomeu, Castelló, N., Lee, J.2013. Universal Dependency Annotation for Multilingual Parsing. In: *Proceedings of the 51st Annual Meeting of the Association for Computational Linguistics*.

Katarzyna Marszałek-Kowalewska, Anna Zaretskaya and Milan Souček. 2014. Stanford Typed Dependencies: Slavic Languages Application. In *Proceedings of 9th International Conference on NLP, PolTAL 2014*. Pp. 151-163.

Milan Souček, Timo Järvinen and Adam LaMontagne. 2013. Managing a Multilingual Treebank Project. In: Proceedings of the Second International Conference on Dependency Linguistics. (Depling 2013).

Lucien Tesnière. 1959. *Éléments de syntaxe structurale*. Librairie C. Klincksieck, Paris.

Jaehoon Yeon and Lucien Brown. 2011. Korean: A Comprehensive Grammar. Routledge.

Wang, Zhijun, 2010. The Head of the Chinese Adjectives and ABB Reduplication. NACCL.

Dependency-based analyses for function words Introducing the polygraphic approach

Sylvain Kahane
Modyco
Université Paris Ouest & CNRS
sylvain@kahane.fr

Nicolas Mazziotta
Institut für Linguistik/Romanistik
Universität Stuttgart
nicolas.mazziotta@ulg.ac.be

Abstract

This paper scrutinizes various dependency-based representations of the syntax of function words, such as prepositions. The focus is on the underlying formal object used to encode the linguistic analyses and its relation to the corresponding linguistic theory. The *polygraph* structure is introduced: it consists of a generalization of the concept of *graph* that allows edges to be vertices of other edges. Such a structure is used to encode dependency-based analyses that are founded on two kinds of morphosyntactic criteria: presence constraints and distributional constraints.

1 Introduction

The general purpose of this paper is to show that dependency-based structures can theoretically be grounded, by making explicit theoretical motivations over the data encoded by the formal structure. To a certain extent, this contradicts the following assumption by Mel'čuk (1988:12): "By its logical nature, dependency formalism cannot be "proved" or "falsified". [...] Dependency formalism is a tool proposed for representing linguistic reality, and, like any tool, it may or may not prove sufficiently useful, flexible or appropriate for the task it has been designed for; but it cannot be true or false." To achieve its goal, this paper focuses on descriptive options available in dependency-based frameworks to handle function words (especially prepositions). The choice of a particular dependency structure depends on various decisions (practical, formal, or theoretical decisions). Diverse concurrent structures can be assigned to the same sentence, depending on the semantics underlying the very concept of *dependency*, as well as the general formal constraints the linguist chooses to meet.

This study consists of two parts. The first part (sections 2-5) reviews the treatment of function words in various dependency-based models, namely Tesnière (1934, 2015), Meaning-Text Theory (henceforth MTT) (Mel'čuk 1988) and Stanford Dependency schemes (henceforth SD) (de Marneffe & Manning 2008).

The second part (sections 6 and 7) proposes an alternative approach to describing function words in a dependency-based analysis. Several theoretical motivations are chosen as the bases of the description, prior to selecting any formal constraint on the mathematical structure encoding the descriptions (except for the fact that we want to represent relations between linguistic objects by dependencies). From this stance it becomes necessary to introduce formal structures that are more general than either trees or graphs, that can be called *polygraphs*.

In the conclusion (section 8), the expressive power of polygraphs is compared with the power of the traditional structures presented in the first part.

2 Proposed representations

This section compares different dependency-based representations of constructions involving function words (mainly prepositions).

2.1 Sample data

The discussion is illustrated by the following examples (some examples are in French, when it behaves in a different way than English):

(1) Mary talked to Peter.
(2) le chien de Pierre
'Peter's dog'
(3) Marie part après Noël.
'Mary leaves after Christmas.
(4) I know Mary and Peter.

Our selection is motivated by the fact that these examples illustrate various behaviors of

Proceedings of the Third International Conference on Dependency Linguistics (Depling 2015), pages 181–190, Uppsala, Sweden, August 24–26 2015.

prepositions: in (1), *to* is an empty word, a marker of government, while in (3), *après* 'after' is a content word, part of an adjunct. Example (2) is intermediate: *de* 'of' can be analyzed as a marker of government (if it is considered that every dog has a master, and *Pierre* is an argument of the noun *chien* 'dog'), as well as a content word expressing possession. In (4), *and* is not a preposition of course, but this construction deserves to be compared with the previous ones.

Figure 1 presents the representation of the analysis of these utterances in several frameworks:

a) MTT's surface syntactic structure (SSyntS) (Mel'čuk 1988; Mel'čuk & Milićević 2014);
b) Universal Stanford Dependency scheme (USD) (de Marneffe et al. 2014);
c) Kern's representation (1883), later developped independently by Debili (1982);
d) Collapsed Stanford Dependency (CSD) (de Marneffe & Manning 2008);
e) MTT's Semantic Structure (SemS) (Mel'čuk 1988; Mel'čuk 2012-2015);
f) Tesnière's stemma (Tesnière 2015);
g) Interpretation of Tesnière's stemmas as *polygraphs* (Kahane's opinion in Kahane & Osborne 2015; Mazziotta 2014).

2.2 Modeling options

MTT considers 7 levels of representations and has even a deep-syntactic structure between the two structures we present. MTT makes a clear distinction between criteria to define surface syntax dependencies and semantic dependencies (Mel'čuk 1988; 2009).

The Stanford team also considers several kinds of representation, which mix semantic goals (to privilege relations between content words) and syntactic goals (to have a word-based structure representing phrases).

To these widely used representations, we add the representation proposed by Kern (1883) and later developed independently by Debili (1982), which prefigures CSD. Kern/Debili's aim was similar to CSD, that is, to obtain similar dependencies for *the nomination of Mary* and *to nominate Mary* (*nominate/nomination → Mary*).

Finally, we recall the structures proposed by Tesnière (1934, 2015), which, though often quoted, are not so well known. It is important to note that Tesnière's stemma was theoretically grounded but that his graphical representation remains mathematically undefined. This opens the possibility of several interpretations and *a posteriori* formalizations (an alternative interpretation of the so-called *transfer* operation is discussed in section 5).

Each of the representations in Figure 1 will now be surveyed. Section 3 describes tree-like structures in which all words are nodes in the tree. Section 4 describes tree-like structures in which function words are labels over branches. Finally, section 5 discusses Tesnière's stemma and its "retroformalization" and introduces the concept of *polygraph*.

3 Tree-based analyses

Most authors posit that the syntactic structure must be a tree, be it a dependency or a phrase structure tree. In most cases, this decision is not overtly motivated. The underlying motivations are often practical (a tree is a simple structure and many algorithms can handle it efficiently), pedagogical (a tree is easy to explain and to draw) or cultural (trees are widespread and have been used for centuries). From the theoretical point of view, it is much more difficult to motivate the choice: most of the time the principles adopted to define the syntactic structure force it to be a tree without any real justification.[1]

3.1 Tree-object

In phrase-structure grammar, one obtains a tree as soon as one considers that every unit has at most a unique possible decomposition and, for instance, that the analysis *Peter + thinks that it is possible* invalidates any other decomposition (such as *Peter thinks + that it is possible*) (Gleason 1969:130). In dependency grammar, you obtain a tree as soon as you consider that every unit has a unique governor, and thus a unique connection with the latter.

[1] SSyntS is based on the general assumption that the syntactic structure must be a tree. The recurrent justification given by Mel'čuk is: "A linguistic model must ensure the correspondence between two formal objects of a very different nature: the semantic network, a **multi**dimensional graph, and the morphological/phonological string, a **uni**dimensional graph. [...] The correspondence between the dimensionality n and the dimensionality 1 must de done through an object of dimensionality 2. The simplest bidimensional graph is what is called a dependency tree." (transl. from Mel'čuk & Milićević 2014: 31-34).

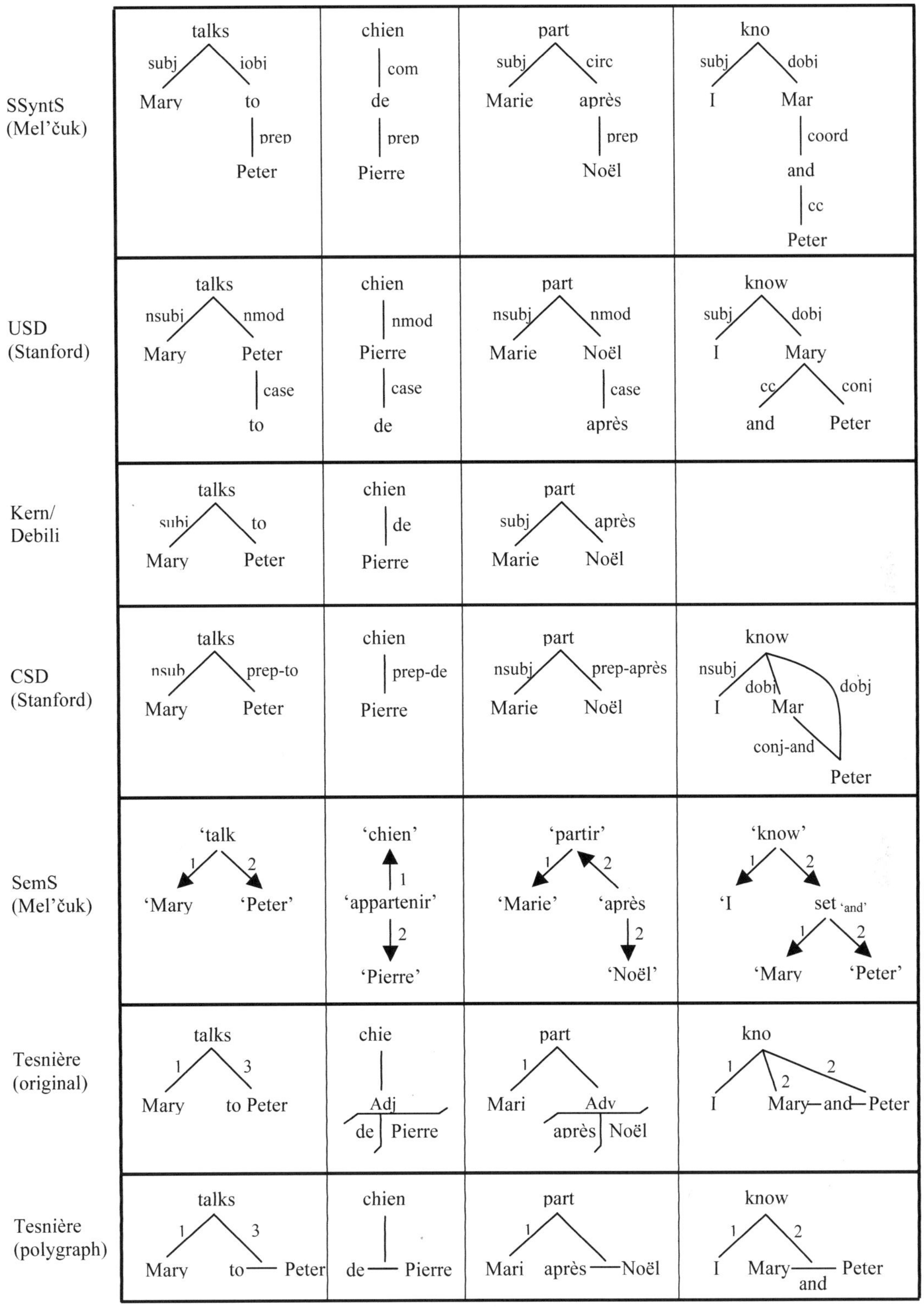

Figure 1. Dependency-based representations of function words

A tree is defined as a connected directed graph where all nodes but one appear exactly once as the second element of an ordered pair (and an indefinite number of times as the first element). The only exception, called the *root* of the tree only appears as the first element of pairs. In a labeled tree, each pair can be assigned a specific type. A tree is a formal structure, i.e. a *meaningless form.* Drawing a tree does not make it meaningful: it is the linguistic theory underlying the structure of the tree that achieves this purpose. The choice between one tree or the other is a matter of theoretical stance.

3.2 Making the tree meaningful: MTT

Defining the meaning of a tree consists in explaining what linguistic criteria are used to justify three parameters: 1) the grouping of words into a common pair; 2) the ordering of that pair;[2] 3) the labeling of that pair.

To be able to go beyond mere intuitions, one has to investigate tests that allow one to select the most appropriate hierarchy. The most explicit attempt to give a meaning to a dependency tree is Mel'čuk's linguistic criteria for SSyntS (Mel'čuk 1988).

The MTT framework posits several levels of syntactic analysis, that are part of a multidimensional modular approach involving phonological, morphological, surface-syntax and deep-syntax, as well as semantic analysis. The aforementioned criteria appear at the surface-syntax level, which encodes two-word phrases (criteria A) and identify the main word in each phrase, that is, preferably, the one constraining the syntactic distribution of the phrase (criterion B1).

A phrase is mainly defined by Mel'čuk in terms of (potential) prosody, that is the possibility for these two words to be isolated together. This is in particular the case if the two words can stand alone and form an utterance together. This use of the term *phrase* is different from the one imposed in linguistics by generativists. For instance, in *Peter reads a book*, *Peter reads* is clearly a phrase, which can form a perfect utterance. This notion of *phrase* is not far from what Saussure (1916) called a *syntagme*. Criteria B explains which of the two words of a phrase is the head of the phrase and governs the other word. For Mel'čuk, the *head* of a phrase is the word which mainly determines the passive valency of the phrase, that is, which determines in what syntactic context the phrase can be inserted. This approach consequently demotes lexical words as dependents and promotes function words as governors. The precedence of lexical words is highlighted at other levels of the linguistic description (deep-syntax and semantics).

In (1), *to Peter* forms a phrase because it can stand alone (*Who are you talking to? To Peter*). The preposition is the head because it characterizes *to Peter* as a possible complement of *talk*. The same reasoning can be applied to *de Pierre* 'of Peter' and *après Noël* 'after Christmas' in (2) and (3). In the same way, *and Peter* is a phrase of (4) because it can form a separate utterance (*I know Mary. And Peter.*) contrary to *Mary and.* Moreover *and* characterizes *and Peter* as a conjunct phrase.

While in SSyntS, relations are between words, in SemS, relations are between semantic units, that is, mainly meanings of lexical units. Empty words are eliminated. For instance, in SemS of (1), 'Mary' and 'Peter' are the two arguments of 'talk', which is indicated by arrows from the predicate to its arguments. The empty preposition *to*, which is imposed by the subcategorization of *talk*, is absent from the structure. On the contrary, in (3), 'after' is a content word, formalized as a binary predicate (X is after Y) expressing the temporal succession of two events (Mary's leaving and Christmas). The same formalization is proposed here for *de* 'of' in (2) which is analyzed as a binary predicate expressing a possessive relation between the dog and its master (*le chien* ***appartient*** *à Pierre* 'the dog **belongs** to Peter'). The case of coordination is more complex. Although *and* is treated similarly to the preposition at the syntactic level, it functions completely differently at the semantic level. The semantic role of 'and' is to form an additive set with 'Mary' and 'Peter' and it is this set that *I know*.

3.3 Making the tree meaningful: SD

Let us now compare MTT and SD. It was clearly demonstrated by Zwicky (1985) that the identification of the head in a binary rela-

[2] By definition, the elements of a pair are not hierarchized: a pair is a simple set of two elements. *Ordering* a pair means structuring it by giving precedence to one of its elements. Ordering has a meaning in a dependency-based approach: by declaring one element as the first one, one formally encodes that it is the governor of the other (which, conversely, is its dependent).

tion can rely on different criteria that can sometimes be contradictory. The major consequence of this fact is that favoring one criterion or another excludes a specific tree. The difference between MTT's analysis and SD's can be understood according to this theoretical contrast.

Nevertheless, the SD framework uses less clearly-defined criteria and does not analyze syntax in the same way, providing an analysis which, from MTT's point of view, merges several modules of description. This leads to trees where function words are governed by lexical words.

The main goal of SD schemes is to propose a universal representation, favoring the relation between content words, which is similar to SemS. While the representation proposed by USD for (1) is easily justifiable,[3] the representation for (3) becomes quite problematic because *après* 'after' is a content word and there is clearly a semantic relation between Mary's leaving and 'après'.

On the other hand, all words appear in USD and it is claimed that USD is a surface syntactic representation. Indeed syntactic arguments are sometimes used to justify certain analyses. For instance, de Marneffe et al. (2014) choose to reject the small clause analysis of *We made them leave* because "the small clause as a unit fails a considerable number of constituency tests". But if USD is supposed to represent phrases, USD's structure for (4) cannot be defended, because *Mary and* is not a possible phrase. In conclusion, the choices of SD seem to be partly arbitrary and they are not falsifiable, because they are not grounded on explicit criteria.

4 Function words as labels

Some frameworks consider function words as "markers" over a syntactic relation. The conception that grammatical markers *work as specifications over relations* is developed in Lemaréchal's work (mainly 1997). The basis of this idea is that dependencies (and syntactic relations in general) can work without the use of any grammatical marker: this is called a *minimal relation* (Fr. *relation minimale*). When one or several markers are present, they *stack* over this minimal relation. By doing so, they function as additional constraints on the distribution of the dependent, which they *specify* (hence the term *specification*). In Lemaréchal's view, specifications can be non-segmental (prosody, word order, etc.). This conception assumes that specifications are added to relations.

Such a statement corresponds very well with the syntactic representation proposed by Kern/Debili, where the preposition labels the dependency it marks. For instance, in Kern/Debili's representation of (1), *to* labels the dependency between *talked* and *Peter*. From a mathematical point of view, such a dependency is no longer a binary edge but a ternary edge: three words are linked by the same relation.[4] The representation types the three positions opened by this edge (that is, the three vertices): *talked* is the governor, *Peter* is the dependent, and *to* is a marker. (See section 7 for a third, polygraphic interpretation.)

The same graphical convention was used by Tesnière (1934) for coordination: the coordinate conjunction *and* is placed over the edge linking the two conjuncts — see our polygraphic interpretation of (4). Tesnière (1959) places the conjunction between the conjuncts, but he posits that the conjunction does not occupy a node, contrary to the conjuncts (see stemma 249 and Ch. 136, §6). Two interpretations of his stemma for (4) are possible: *and* is connected to both *Mary* and *Peter*,[5] or *Mary*, *Peter* and *and* are connected in a single ternary relation, where they assume a specific role according to their grammatical class (and the spatial position in the stemma).

Collapsed SDs operate in a similar way: the function word becomes part of the labeling of the relation it marks. But in the case of CSD the structure is declared as a tree and the function word is "dereified" (it is not a node any

[3] In fact, even the representation for (1) is problematic because due to preposition stranding, *to* can form a unit with *talk* in several constructions:
(i) the girl Peter **talked to**
(ii) Mary **talked to** Peter Monday and John Tuesday
(iii) We **talked to** and bantered with many students. (streetpastors.org)
Note that none of these constructions would be possible with Fr. *parler à* 'talk to' because French do not accept preposition stranding. Does it mean that the syntactic representation of *à* in *parler à* and *to* in *talk to* should be different?

[4] A structure with *n*-ary edges is called a *hypergraph* (Bergé 1973). A graph is a particular case of hypergraph, where all edges are binary.

[5] However, this former interpretation seems unlikely (Mazziotta 2014: 146).

longer, but a typed edge).[6] However, this implies the introduction of dozens of very specific syntactic relations, one for each function word.

5 Tesnière's transfer and polygraphic analyses

5.1 Tesnière's transfer

For Tesnière, most prepositions are *translatives*, i.e. grammatical tools that allow a unit of one syntactic category to occupy a position usually devoted to a unit of another syntactic category. The combination of a translative with a unit in order to change its category is called *transfer* (Fr. *translation*). Transfer is illustrated by (2): the preposition *de* 'of' transfers the noun *Peter* into an adjective, thus allowing *de Pierre* to modify the noun *chien* 'dog' asadjectives do (*gros chien noir* 'big black dog'). In his stemmas, Tesnière (2015) represent this operation by using a special T-like shape. This notation has three positional slots: one for the translative, one for the transferred word and the category of the phrase after the transfer on top (see figure 1).
When transfer does not change the part of speech of the main content word, but merely changes its function (Tesnière 2015: ch. 172), it may be qualified as "functional" and Tesnière no longer uses the T-like notation. Thus, the use of Fr. *à* allowing a noun to become an indirect complement expressing the recipient (*je donne une pomme à Jean* 'I give an apple to Jean') is not depicted as a classical transfer. See our representation for (1) in figure 1.

Tesnière made it clear that translatives and coordinate conjunctions do not share the same syntactic properties. From a theoretical perspective, he considered coordination to be orthogonal to subordination: the former adds elements that are at the same hierarchical level, whereas the latter creates the hierarchy. The geometric configuration of his stemmas is motivated by this theoretical choice. The conjuncts are placed equi-level and the coordinate conjunction is placed between them (see section 4). Conjuncts are treated as co-heads and are both connected to the governor of the coordinated phrase.

[6] This analysis can also compared with LFG's f-structure where function words are stored in special feature associated with the relation between the content words (Kaplan & Bresnan 1982).

5.2 Polygraphic analyses

Tesnière's stemmas lead to various interpretations. In section 4, we already discussed whether coordination involves a ternary edge or not. The T-like notation is also the source of debate (see Kahane & Osborne 2015: l-lxii). The translative combines with the transferred word in a way that is not represented with a vertical line, as subordination would be. Placing the two elements equi-level probably means that Tesnière considers this combination to be exocentric. Following Kahane (in Kahane & Osborne 2015) and Mazziotta (2014: 142), we represent transfer by a horizontal link. As a result, in figures 1 and 2a, the relation between *chien* and the transferred phrase it governs is expressed by a line between *chien* and the other line between *de* and *Pierre*. This representation is based on the idea that a two-word phrase and the connection link between these two words are in essence the same unique object. This formalizes Tesnière's well-known and insightful view of syntactic relations: they consist of objects as much as words do (Tesnière 2015: ch. 1, §5).

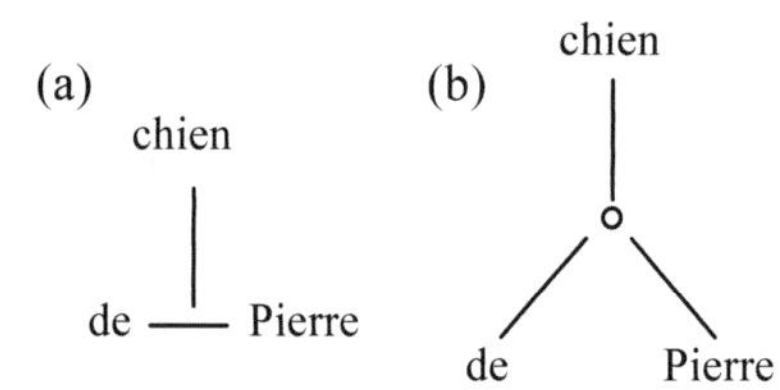

Figure 2. Interpretations of Tesnière's transfer

The formal object underlying the suggested representation of transfer can be defined from a mathematical perspective. Such an object allows some edges to have other edges as vertices in addition to nodes and will be called a *polygraph* (Kahane & Mazziotta 2015, following Burroni 1993; Bonfante & Guiraud 2008). As was already the case with the tree-object, the polygraph-object is meaningless *per se*. It is the theoretical grounding on the *transfer* concept that gives it a semiosis.

Transfer could also be encoded in a tree (Osborne in Kahane & Osborne 2015); see fig. 2b. As long as they convey the same amount of information, the depicted polygraph and its corresponding tree can be automatically converted into one another — i.e. they are formally equivalent. They have the same meaning, and the choice between one or the other can be motivated neither by formal nor by linguistic reasons. A polygraph is nevertheless more powerful because it does not need to add extra nodes to express the same amount of information. Moreover, the tree-based interpretation relies on three kinds of linguistic objects (words, phrases and relations), whereas the polygraph only needs two (words and relations). The iconic correspondence of the polygraph is direct: a node is equivalent to a word and an edge is equivalent to a relation. In the tree, one needs additional typing for the nodes to part words from phrases.

The next sections investigate how polygraphs can be used to express some properties of function words.

6 Presence constraints

When formalizing a linguistic analysis, one is deemed to provide:

1. a formal description of the mathematical object that encodes the analysis;
2. interpretation rules that govern the association between this structure as a semiotic device expressing the analysis.

The motivations underlying these choices should be expressed as well, since they are important from an epistemological perspective or to make it possible to evaluate the efficiency of the description.

In the scope of this paper, the chosen mathematical object is the aforementioned *polygraph*. How its interpretation rules help contrast function words according to their specific behaviors will be shown in this section and the next one, and is based on two theoretical motivations.

Some motivations can be stated prior to defining the phenomena at study. It is well accepted that a syntactic theory has to acknowledge the existence of *phrases*, i.e. syntactic constructions that can stand alone and be used as a speech turn under certain conditions, and thus become autonomous and form an utterance (criteria A of Mel'čuk 1988). Since the term *phrase* is widely preempted for something else by generativists, one can adopt another point of view and see these units as manifestations of presence constraints: some pairs of words must be grouped with other words to occur together, whereas others can stand alone.

Theoretical motivation 1. Presence constraints must be encoded.

6.1 Linguistic theoretical analysis

As a basis for this discussion, we will investigate the following sample material: (5) and (6) are in French, (7) is in Old French (Moignet 1988: 95), and (8) is in English.

(5) a. Marie parle à Pierre.
'Mary talks to Peter.'
b. *Marie parle à.
c. *Marie parle Pierre.

(6) a. Marie vient après Noël.
'Mary comes after Christmas.'
b. Marie vient après.
'Mary comes afterwards.'
c. *Marie vient Noël.

(7) a. le message de la roïne
'the message of the queen'
b. *le message de
c. le message la roïne
'the message of the queen'

(8) a. I know that you lie.
b. I know that.
c. I know you lie.

In (5), *Marie parle* and *à Pierre* can stand alone. It is also possible to consider that *parle à Pierre* can form a prosodic unit and stand alone when the verb is in another (non-finite) form. On the contrary neither *parle à*, nor *parle Pierre* have this kind of autonomy.

Encoding presence constraints automatically unveils their hierarchy. If one encodes presence constrains in (6), identifying the group *Marie vient après* as well as the group *après Noël* automatically identifies *après* as the governor, i.e. the word that must be present inside *après Noël.* On the contrary, in (5), since *parle à* and *parle Pierre* are not acceptable, whereas *à Pierre* is, both the preposition and the noun must be present.

It should be stressed that the preposition can also be optional. Such is the case in the so-called "absolute oblique" (Fr. *cas régime absolu*, Buridant 2000: §§59 sqq.) in Old French (7). Acknowledging the structure *le message la roïne* and *de la roïne*, but refusing **le message de* achieves the description.[7] Examples of such a structure are not seldom. Lat. *decedere (de) provinciā* 'leave (from) one's province' is similar, except that the optional expression of the preposition has a more obvious semantic value[8]. Fr. *Marie habite (à) Paris* 'Mary lives

[7] Note that the article is not compulsory in Old Fr. This issue will not be investigated here (see Mazziotta 2013).

[8] The clause usually appears with the preposition, but "verbs compounded with *ā, ab, dē*, etc., (1) take the simple ablative when used figuratively; but (2) when used literally to denote actual separation or motion, they

in Paris' displays the same feature: the locative preposition *à* is also optional.

The possibility for two words to be used independently or conjointly in the same construction is illustrated by (8). It is generally considered that *that* in *I know that* and *I know that you lie* are two different words, namely a pronoun and a conjunction. The hypothesis favored here is, on the contrary, that there exist two uses of the same lexical unit: the conjunction is described as a weakened form of the pronoun. In this sentence, *that* and *you lie* **co-occupy** the same position: they can appear alone as well as they can form a group and appear together.[9]

6.2 Encoding and representation

It is strikingly clear that the reciprocal constraints over the presence of the function word and the structure following it can be of four types, given that at least one of them is present: either both of them must be expressed (5), or only the function word (6), or only the following phrase (7), or one or the other (8). These four possibilities are theoretically predicted in Hjelmslev (1953) from a very general point of view. A formalism encoding presence constraints must therefore allow to distinguish between these possibilities.

The classical stance consists of encoding the structures by edges between nodes: for instance, *to* and *Peter* are nodes connected by a single edge between them. In (6), since *vient après* as well as *après Noël* are acceptable, the structure can be encoded by a "chain" of nodes linked by two edges, which is easily achieved in a graph.[10] The same convention can be used to encode (7). However, the graph object is not sufficient when a word or a group of words A can form a group with a group B, but no part of B can form a group with A. One needs a polygraph to encode the group B as a vertex of the edge representing the group A, which is the most direct way to achieve a formal description of such a configuration.[11] Thus, in (5), A = *talks* can form an acceptable independent construction with B = *to Peter*, but neither *to* nor *Peter* alone can be grouped with A. Therefore, there is an edge between *talks* and the edge between *to* and *Peter* (see figure 3).

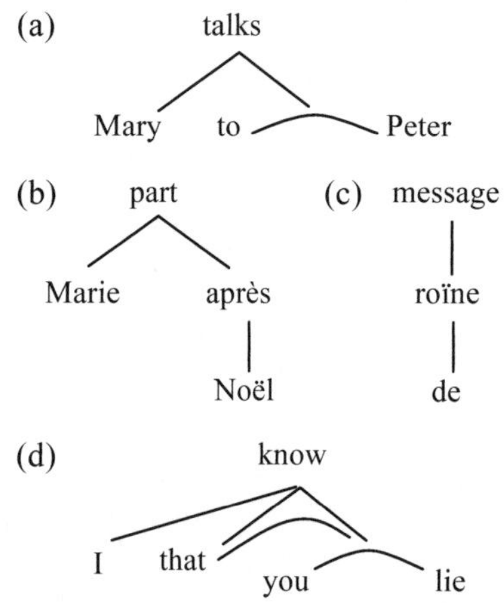

Figure 3. Presence constraints[12]

7 Distributional constraints

It also appears that the forms (lexical choice) of the function words can depend on the syntactic context of the group they appear in. I.e., their form is affected by their distribution.

Theoretical motivation 2. Form constraints affecting function words must be encoded.

7.1 Linguistic theoretical analysis

In Fr. *Marie va à Paris* 'Mary goes to Paris', the form *à* 'toward/to' is constrained by the use of the verb *va* (and expresses the destination of the movement). In Old Fr. *le message de la bone roïne* 'the message of the good

usually require a preposition". (Greenough *et al.* 1903: 302)

[9] To our knowledge, co-occupation is an overlooked phenomenon that should be investigated further. We have a quite similar situation in French where the subordinating conjunction is also a pronoun, more exactly the weak form of the interrogative pronoun *quoi*:

(i) Tu sais **quoi** ? 'You know what?'
(ii) **Que** sais-tu? 'What do you know?'
(iii) Je sais **que** tu mens. 'I know that you lie.'

However, *que* is not optional in (iii). Note that Gustave Guilleaume's followers (Moignet 1981: ch. 11 a.o.) suggest that the different uses of the forms *que* and *quoi* are instances of a unique lexical unit (Fr. *vocable* in Guilleaume's terminology).

[10] A similar structure is defined in Gerdes & Kahane (2011) and called the *connection structure*. They use an alternative mode of representation of edges based on bubbles rather than lines. (See Bergé 1973 for the equivalence between the two modes of representation.)

[11] It is possible to reify the edge as a node (as is often done in RDF), but the resulting structure contains more elements for the same amount of information.

[12] A presence-constrained structure could be called a "phrase structure". It is encoded in a non-directed polygraph. Polygraph are displayed here with the main verb on top in order to be as close as possible to a traditional dependency tree for the sake of simplicity. It must nevertheless be made clear that the hierarchization of the polygraph corresponds to other constraints that remain to be discussed.

queen', the preposition *de* 'of' is bound to the N + *de* + N construction that expresses a "genitive" relation. By contrast, the lexical choice of *bone* 'good' is not constrained by any relation or construction. Reevaluating the idea that function words may label relations or work as *specifications* over them (sec. 4), it seems reasonable to state that the form of a word can be constrained by the *relation* it is bound to at least as much as the words it connects with. In this case, function words specify the relation. For instance, in (1), the use of the preposition *to* is bound to the use of the lexical unit *talk* because only the second argument of *talk* can be introduced by such a preposition (for instance the subject cannot be: **To Mary talked to Peter*). Only one particular type of dependent can, which implies that the use of the preposition is specific to this particular relation.

This descriptive option reformulates the Mel'čukian *passive valency* criterion (see section 3 *supra*): the fact that *de* is bound to the dependency between *de la roïne* and its governor *message* is equivalent to the fact that not only *roïne* but also *de* controls the distribution of *de la roïne*. Indeed, *la roïne* and *de la roïne* do not have the same distribution: both can complement a noun, but only *la bone roïne* can be the subject of a verb.

Coordination as observed in (4) is also interesting. Any one of the conjuncts can be grouped with their common governor to form an acceptable utterance. It is a case very similar to co-occupation in (8), but for the presence of the coordinating conjunction. This conjunction is not compulsory (we consider that sentences such as *I know Mary, Peter* are acceptable), but it needs both the second conjunct and the coordination relation to be present. (See Mel'čuk 1988: 41, Gerdes & Kahane 2015 and Mazziotta 2013 for alternate theoretical stances in a dependency framework.)

7.2 Encoding and representation

With the expressing power of the polygraph structure, the relation between the function word and the relation that constrains it can be encoded as such. This introduces *specification*, a secondary dependency, between the function word and the primary dependency that binds it (figure 4). It encodes the fact that in *le message de la bone roïne*, both *de* and *bone* can group with *roïne* to form an acceptable utterance, but only *de* is bound to the relation between *message* and *roïne*. The representation proposed here contrasts a lexical dependent such as *bone* 'good' with the function word. The difference between primary dependency edges (*dependency edges* for short) and secondary dependency edges (*specification edges*) is expressed structurally by the type of the governing vertex. Specification edges are defined as having another edge as a governor.

The intricate set of relations at work with coordination structures can easily be encoded in a polygraph as well. Comparing figure 3 with figure 4 makes the similarity between coordination and co-occupation visible.

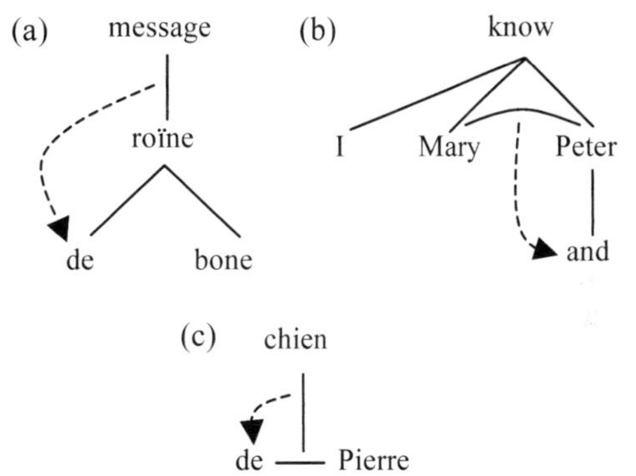

Figure 4. Distributional constraints

8 Conclusion

This paper has compared different dependency-based representations of the surface syntax organization, focusing on prepositions and function words. Several classical representations have been described (sections 2-5), as well as new representations (sections 6 and 7).

The main theoretical advantage of the stance adopted here is that it separates different primitive motivations into two sets of non-interfering linguistic relations: a relation grouping elements according to presence constraints (section 6), and a relation of co-presence between a word and another relation (section 7). Both motivations correspond to a specific set of relations, namely *dependency relations* and *specification relations*.

On the practical side, such an approach leads to much less complex structures for analyzing constructions where specification can be optional. On the computational side, it becomes possible to compute these sets separately (in a sequential or parallel process queue).

Another important feature of the present argumentation is that *a priori* formal constraints on the underlying mathematical object have been set to a minimum. Tree-based formalizations only envisage the relation of a function word in terms of stand-alone binary relations with other words. It has been shown that relations can involve secondary relations (*specifications*), i.e. relations over previously stated primary relations (*dependencies*). The networks of relations one needs to introduce when formalizing a particular property are naturally more complex than a tree.

The decision to build a dependency tree rather than a more complex structure can have practical, pedagogical or theoretical motivations. Using dependency trees because of pedagogical or practical motivations is not an issue. However, one has to admit that the theoretical arguments for a tree-based structure remain tenuous and poorly motivated in the literature.

Acknowledgements

The authors would like to thank Brigitte Antoine, Marie Steffens and Elizabeth Rowley-Jolivet for proofreading and Timothy Osborne for contents corrections and suggestions.

References

Bergé C. 1973. *Graphs and hypergraphs*. North-Holland, Amsterdam.

Bonfante G., Guiraud Y. 2008. Intensional properties of polygraphs. *Electronic Notes in Theoretical Computer Science*, 203(1), 65–77.

Buridant C. 2000. *Grammaire nouvelle de l'ancien français*. Paris: Sedes.

Burroni A. 1993. Higher-dimensional word problems with applications to equational logic. *Theoretical computer science*, 115(1), 43–62.

de Marneffe M.-C., Manning C. D. 2008. The Stanford typed dependencies representation. Proceedings of *Workshop on Cross-framework and Cross-domain Parser Evaluation*, COLING.

de Marneffe M.-C. et al. 2014. Universal Stanford Dependencies: A cross-linguistic typology. *Proceedings of LREC*.

Debili F. 1982. *Analyse syntaxico-sémantique fondée sur une acquisition automatique de relations lexicales-sémantiques*, Thèse de doctorat d'état, Université Paris Sud, Orsay.

Gerdes K., Kahane S. 2011. Defining dependencies (and constituents). *Proceedings of Depling*.

Gerdes K., Kahane S. 2015. Non-constituent coordination and other coordinative constructions as Dependency Graphs, *Proceedings of Depling*.

Gleason H. A. 1969. *An Introduction to Descriptive Linguistics*, Holt, Rinehart and Winston.

Greenough J. B. *et al.* 1903. New Latin grammar for schools and colleges, founded on comparative grammar. Boston & London: Ginn & Co.

Hjelmslev L. 1953. Prolegomena to a theory of language, transl. of *Omkring sprogteoriens grundlæggelse* (1943) Copenhagen: Munksgaard.

Kahane S., Mazziotta N. 2015. Syntactic Polygraphs - A Formalism Extending Both Constituency and Dependency, *Proceedings of MOL*.

Kahane S., Osborne T. 2015. Translators' Introduction. In Tesnière 2015, ixxx-lxxiii.

Kaplan R. M., Bresnan J. 1982. Lexical-functional grammar: A formal system for grammatical representation, in Bresnan J. (ed.), *Formal Issues in Lexical-Functional Grammar*, 29-130.

Kern, F. 1883. *Zur Methodik des deutschen Unterrichts*. Nicolai.

Lemaréchal A. 1997. *Zéro(s)*. PUF, Paris.

Mazziotta N. 2013. Grammatical markers and grammatical relations in the simple clause in Old French. *Proceedings of Depling*.

Mazziotta N. 2014. Nature et structure des relations syntaxiques dans le modèle de Lucien Tesnière. *Modèles linguistiques*, 69, 123-152.

Mel'čuk I. 1988. *Dependency syntax: theory and practice*. State University of New York, Albany.

Mel'čuk I. 2009. Dependency in natural language. In A. Polguère, I. Mel'čuk (eds.), *Dependency in linguistic description*, Benjamins, 1-110.

Mel'čuk I. 2012-2015. *Semantics: From Meaning to Text*, 3 volumes, Benjamins.

Mel'čuk I. Milićević J. 2014. *Introduction à la linguistique*, volume 2, Hermann, Paris.

Moignet G. 1981. *Systématique de la langue française*. Paris : Klincksieck.

Moignet G. 1988. *Grammaire de l'ancien français*. Paris: Klincksieck.

Saussure F. 1916. *Cours de linguistique générale*.

Tesnière L. 1934. Comment construire une syntaxe. *Bulletin de la Faculté des Lettres de Strasbourg*, 7, 219–229.

Tesnière L. 1959. *Éléments de syntaxe structurale*, Klincksieck. [transl. by Osborne T., Kahane S. 2015. *Elements of structural syntax*, Benjamins.]

Zwicky A. M. 1985. Heads. *Journal of linguistics*, 21(1), 1-29.

At the Lexicon-Grammar Interface: The Case of Complex Predicates in the Functional Generative Description

Václava Kettnerová and **Markéta Lopatková**
Charles University in Prague
Faculty of Mathematics and Physics
Czech Republic
{kettnerova,lopatkova}@ufal.mff.cuni.cz

Abstract

Complex predicates with light verbs have proven to be very challenging for syntactic theories, particularly due to the tricky distribution of valency complementations of light verbs and predicative nouns (or other predicative units) in their syntactic structure. We propose a theoretically adequate and economical representation of complex predicates with Czech light verbs based on a division of their description between the *lexicon* and the *grammar*. We demonstrate that a close interplay between these two components makes the analysis of the deep and surface syntactic structures of complex predicates reliable and efficient.

1 Introduction

Description of a language system is usually divided into two basic components – a grammar and a lexicon. The *grammar* consists of general patterns of a natural language rendered, in the form of formal rules which are applicable to whole classes of language units. The *lexicon*, on the other hand, represents an inventory of language units with their specific properties. Nevertheless, linguistic theories can substantially differ from each other in the distribution of information between the grammar and the lexicon.

Valency, which forms the core of a dependency structure of a sentence, constitutes a fundamental example of a phenomenon bridging between the grammar and the lexicon. Valency structure of verbs is so varied that it cannot be described by rules; it must be listed in lexical entries in a lexicon, see the highly elaborated lexicons, e.g., (Mel'čuk and Zholkovsky, 1984), (Apresjan, 2011). However, if a verb is a part of a complex predicate, its valency structure is involved in a complex structure the formation of which is typically regular enough to be described by rules in the grammar.

In this paper, we focus on lexicalized co-occurrence relations, namely on *complex predicates composed of light verbs and predicative nouns* (CPs) where two syntactic elements serve as a single predicate, e.g., 'to make a request', 'to give a presentation', 'to get support', 'to take a shower'.[1] We demonstrate that an adequate and economical description of CPs requires a close cooperation of the grammar and the lexicon: On the basis of the lexical representation of CPs, grammatical rules generate well-formed (both deep and surface) *dependency structures*.

The objective of this contribution is to further elaborate and modify – in light of recent investigations – the theoretical results given in (Kettnerová and Lopatková, 2013). Namely, the lexical information provided by the VALLEX lexicon (Lopatková et al., 2008) on diatheses and the grammatical rules in the grammatical component are applied to the description of CPs in *marked structures of diatheses* (e.g., passive structures) with the aim to gain all *surface syntactic manifestations* of the CPs.

The paper is structured as follows: first we discuss related work on CPs (Sect. 2); then we briefly introduce the Functional Generative Description (FGD) (Sgall et al., 1986) used as the theoretical background and the VALLEX lexicon (Sect. 3) and describe the lexical representation of CPs (Sect. 4); finally, we provide the enhancement of the grammatical component of FGD with formal rules for the generation of the syntactic structures with CPs (Sect. 5).

2 Related Work

There is a variety of approaches to *complex predicates with light verbs* (also called *light verb con-*

[1] Causative constructions of the type 'to make sb do something' are not considered here as CPs.

Proceedings of the Third International Conference on Dependency Linguistics (Depling 2015), pages 191–200,
Uppsala, Sweden, August 24–26 2015.

structions) and their characteristics, as well as to the range of issues involved in the notion of complex predicates. Despite the diversity in the treatment of complex predicates in different theoretical frameworks, there is a general agreement that the crucial issue to be resolved is that two syntactic elements function as a single predicate; this fact is corroborated by the presence of a single 'Agens'/'Bearer of action or property'/'Experiencer'. This key characteristic of complex predicates of the given type is accounted for by the mechanisms called argument fusion (Butt, 1998), argument transfer (Grimshaw and Mester, 1988), or argument composition (Hinrichs and Nakazawa, 1990) formulated within different theories.

All these mechanisms try to account for the fact that (i) light verbs, despite being depleted of semantic participants (denoting only general semantic scenario), have valency complementations, and that (ii) semantic participants (contributed to CPs primarily by predicative nouns) are usually expressed as complementations of light verbs (Alonso Ramos, 2007).

If a lexicographic representation aims at a description of syntactic behavior of CPs (not only at compiling an inventory of collocations of predicative nouns and light verbs, as e.g., (Vincze and Csirik, 2010), (Paul, 2010)), the above given mechanisms should be reflected in the lexicon. To our knowledge, the most complex representation of CPs is provided in the Explanatory Combinatorial Dictionary of Modern Russian (Mel'čuk and Zholkovsky, 1984) where the collocational potential is captured by means of lexical functions (Mel'čuk, 1996). The generation of well-formed syntactic structures with CPs is then based on the interplay of the lexical representation and grammatical rules (Alonso Ramos, 2007).

In Czech theoretical linguistics, there is only a limited number of studies devoted to CPs (Macháčková, 1994), (Cinková, 2009), (Radimský, 2010), and (Kolářová, 2010); none of them presents a mechanism aspiring to provide a thorough explanation of syntactic behavior of CPs. Moreover, the only existing lexical resource with information on syntactic properties of light verbs – PDT-Vallex – provides only partial information that does not make it possible to establish the deep and surface syntactic structures of the resulting CPs (Urešová, 2011).

3 FGD Framework

In this paper, we elaborate the representation of CPs within the Functional Generative Description, a stratificational and dependency-oriented theoretical framework (Sgall et al., 1986). One of the core concepts of FGD is that of valency (Panevová, 1994): at the layer of linguistically structured meaning (called the tectogrammatical layer), valency provides the structure of a dependency tree. The valency theory of FGD has been applied in several valency lexicons. The most elaborate one of these is the VALLEX, Valency Lexicon of Czech Verbs, which forms a solid basis for the lexical component of FGD.

VALLEX lexicon

The VALLEX lexicon[2] has resulted from an attempt to document valency behavior of Czech verbs (Lopatková et al., 2008). Over time, VALLEX has undergone many quantitative and qualitative extensions. Recent developments have focused on the linguistic phenomena that – despite representing productive grammatical processes involving changes in the valency structure of verbs – are lexically conditioned, esp. *diatheses*.

For the purposes of the representation of phenomena at the lexicon-grammar interface, VALLEX is divided into a lexical part and a grammatical part. The *lexical part* provides lexical representation of individual lexical units of verbs whereas the *grammatical part* represents formal representation of rules of the overall grammatical component of FGD that are directly connected to the valency structure of verbs.

The central organizing concept of the lexical part of VALLEX is the concept of *lexeme*. The lexeme associates a set of lexical forms representing the verb in an utterance, with a set of *lexical units* of a verb, corresponding to its senses.

Each lexical entry of a verb is described by a set of attributes (see Fig. 2 below). The core attribute `frame` contains a valency frame that is modeled as a sequence of valency slots, each corresponding to a single valency complementation of the verb; each slot consists of (i) a functor – a syntactico-semantic label reflecting the type of dependency relation of the given valency complementation, (ii) an indication of obligatoriness, and (iii) a list of possible morphemic forms specifying the usage of a lexical unit in the *active voice*.

[2] `http://ufal.mff.cuni.cz/vallex`

Of all the remaining attributes of lexical units currently employed in VALLEX, we shall further discuss the attribute `diat`, the value of which is a list of all applicable diatheses (as their applicability is lexically conditioned and thus has to be captured in the *lexical part* of VALLEX). In the *grammatical part*, grammatical rules describing individual types of diatheses are formulated. When these rules are applied to the relevant lexical units (as indicated by the attribute `diat`), all possible surface syntactic manifestations of a lexical unit in the marked structures of diatheses can be obtained (Kettnerová et al., 2012).

4 Lexical Representation of CPs

A CP, as a multiword lexical unit, is formed as a combination of a predicative noun with an appropriate light verb. It is primarily the predicative noun that contributes its *semantic participants.* Its ability to select different light verbs (and thus to create different CPs) makes it possible to embed the event expressed by the predicative noun into different *general semantic scenarios* and thus to perspectivize it from the point of view of different semantic participants. In this process, a crucial role is played by the *referential identity* of nominal and verbal valency complementations within the CP (as it is demonstrated in Sect. 4.2.1).

As a consequence, CPs can be described as a combination of the information from the *valency frames* of both the *light verb* and the *predicative noun*. Further, we propose to enhance VALLEX with three special attributes `lvc`, `map` and `caus` to capture possible combinations of these two syntactic elements into a single predicate (Sect. 4.2).

4.1 Valency Frames

It is widely acknowledged that both predicative nouns and light verbs have their own valency potentials, i.e., they have their own sets of valency complementations (Alonso Ramos, 2007), (Macháčková, 1994). As a result, both light verbs and predicative nouns should be represented by their respective valency frames in the valency lexicon.

4.1.1 Predicative Nouns

Valency frames of predicative nouns underlie their deep dependency structures, both in nominal structures and as the nominal components of CPs, see examples (2) and (6) and the valency frame of the noun *pokyn* 'instruction' in (1).[3]

(1) ***pokyn***$_{\mathrm{PN}}$ 'instruction':
$\mathrm{ACT}_{gen,pos}$ ADDR_{dat} $\mathrm{PAT}_{k+dat,inf}$

(2) ***Pokyn*** $_{\mathrm{PN}}$ *státního zástupce* $_{\mathrm{N:ACT:gen}}$ *žalobcům* $_{\mathrm{N:ADDR:dat}}$ *(posuzovat případ jako krádež)* $_{\mathrm{N:PAT:inf}}$ *přišel právě včas.*
'The **instruction**$_{\mathrm{PN}}$ of the public prosecutor$_{\mathrm{N:ACT}}$ to the prosecutors$_{\mathrm{N:ADDR}}$ (to regard the case as a theft)$_{\mathrm{N:PAT}}$ came just in time.'

Valency complementations of predicative nouns are endowed with semantic participants. For example, the noun *pokyn* 'instruction' is characterized by the participants 'Speaker', 'Recipient', and 'Information', which are mapped onto ACTor, ADDRessee, and PATient, respectively.

4.1.2 Light Verbs

Valency frames of light verbs constitute the deep dependency structure of the verbal component of CPs.

Formally, valency frames of Czech light verbs are prototypically identical to the valency frames of their full verb counterparts.[4] Hence we consider them to be inherited from the latter. The only regular difference between the valency frames of light verbs and their full verb counterparts is the functor CPHR 'Compound PHRaseme', indicating the valency position of the predicative noun.

Generally, valency complementations of a full verb correspond to its semantic participants; however, light verbs are deprived of semantic participants (Alonso Ramos, 2007).[5]

For example, the valency frame of the light verb *udělit*^{pf} 'to give, to grant' (4) is identical to the valency frame of the full verb (3), compare examples (5) and (6).

(3) ***udělit*** 'to give':
ACT_{nom} ADDR_{dat} PAT_{acc}

(4) ***udělit***$_{\mathrm{LV}}$ 'to give':
ACT_{nom} ADDR_{dat} CPHR_{acc}

(5) *Prezident* $_{\mathrm{V:ACT:nom}}$ ***udělil*** *umělcům* $_{\mathrm{V:ADDR:dat}}$ *medaile* $_{\mathrm{V:PAT:acc}}$.

[3] As the information on obligatoriness is not relevant here, we omit it from the valency frames.

[4] These findings are in line with the analysis of their morphological characteristics, which are also prototypically identical with the properties of their full counterparts (Butt, 2010).

[5] The only exception – causative light verbs – is addressed in Sect. 4.2.2.

'The President$_{V:ACT}$ **has awarded** medals$_{V:PAT}$ to the artists$_{V:ADDR}$.'

(6) *Státní zástupce* $_{V:ACT:nom}$ ***udělil*** $_{LV}$ *žalobcům* $_{V:ADDR:dat}$ ***pokyn*** $_{V:CPHR:acc}$ *posuzovat případ jako krádež.*
'The public prosecutor$_{V:ACT}$ **has given** an **instruction**$_{V:CPHR}$ to regard the case as a theft to the prosecutors$_{V:ADDR}$.'

Despite the absence of semantic participants of light verbs, their valency complementations are not semantically depleted: they acquire their semantic content from the semantic participants of predicative nouns via coreference with nominal valency complementations, as proposed, e.g., by (Butt, 1998), here Sect. 4.2.1. Then only semantically specified valency complementations are inherited from valency frames of full verb counterparts of light verbs (Kettnerová and Lopatková, 2013).[6]

4.1.3 Linking Valency Frames: Attribute `lvc`

For obtaining the deep dependency structure of a CP, the appropriate valency frames of the predicative noun and the light verb (with which the noun combines within the predicate) must be linked. In the VALLEX lexicon, the special attribute `lvc`, attached to individual valency frames of predicative nouns and (for convenience) also to those of light verbs, provides the list of references, see Fig. 1 and 2 below.

4.2 Lexical Mapping

The formation of well-formed deep and surface dependency structures with CPs requires a mechanism to account for the distribution of nominal and verbal valency complementations in the resulting syntactic structures. In this section, we show that for these purposes, additional information on the coreference of valency complementations (and thus on the mapping of semantic participants) has to be recorded as a part of lexical entries of predicative nouns and light verbs. This information is provided by two special attributes `map` (Sect. 4.2.1) and `caus` (Sect. 4.2.2).

[6]However, the cases in which the number of valency complementations in the valency frame of a light verb is reduced are rather rare in Czech (e.g., within the CP *přijmout zodpovědnost* 'to accept responsibility', the valency frame of the light verb does not inherit the ORIGin complementation as it lacks semantic specification).

4.2.1 Nominal Participants: Attribute `map`

As stated above, whereas the valency complementations of a predicative noun are semantically saturated by its semantic participants, the valency complementations of the light verb are semantically unspecified. To acquire semantic content, the verbal complementations enter in coreference relations with the nominal complementations. Pairs of nominal and verbal valency complementations within CPs thus exhibit referential identity (they refer to the same nominal semantic participant). This referential identity of verbal and nominal valency complementations represents a substantial characteristic of CPs.

For example, the CP *udělit pokyn* 'to give an instruction' can be characterized by three semantic participants given by the noun: 'Speaker', 'Recipient', and 'Information'. These participants are mapped onto the nominal valency complementations ACTor, ADDRessee, and PATient, see (1). The valency frame of the light verb in (4) comprises three complementations: one (CPHR) is occupied by the predicative noun and the remaining two (ACTor and ADDRessee) represent complementations that are not semantically specified by the light verb; however, they gain their semantic capacity via coreference with nominal ACTor and ADDRessee, see (7) specifying the referential identity.

(7) ***udělit pokyn*** 'to give an instruction':
'Speaker'$_N$ $\Rightarrow$ ACT$_N$ $\Leftrightarrow$ ACT$_V$
'Recipient'$_N$ $\Rightarrow$ ADDR$_N$ $\Leftrightarrow$ ADDR$_V$
'Information'$_N$ $\Rightarrow$ PAT$_N$

Due to the referential identity, all the valency complementations within this CP are semantically saturated. The event denoted by the predicative noun is perspectivized from the point of view of the 'Speaker', corresponding to the verbal ACTor (expressed in the active structure in the most prominent subject position, see also example (6).

Changes in the referential identity

The referential identity of the valency complementations may differ for different combinations of the same predicative noun combined with different light verbs (Kolářová, 2010), (Radimský, 2010).

For example, the referential identity within the CP *udělit pokyn* 'to give an instruction' (7) differs from that of the predicate *přijmout pokyn* 'to receive an instruction' (10). Within the latter, the same set of semantic participants are employed, i.e., 'Speaker', 'Recipient', and 'Information'. However, the verbal ACTor and ORIGin gain their semantic specification via coreference with the nominal ADDRessee and ACTor, respectively, see (1), (8) and (10).

(8) ***přijmout***$_{\mathrm{LV}}$ 'to receive':
ACT$_{\mathrm{nom}}$ CPHR$_{\mathrm{acc}}$ ORIG$_{od+\mathrm{gen}}$

(9) *Žalobci* $_{\mathrm{V:ACT:}Recip}$ ***přijali*** $_{\mathrm{LV}}$ *od státního zástupce* $_{\mathrm{V:ORIG:}Speak}$ ***pokyn*** $_{\mathrm{V:CPHR}}$ *(posuzovat případ jako krádež)* $_{\mathrm{N:PAT:}Info}$.
'The prosecutors$_{\mathrm{V:ACT:}Recip}$ **have received** the **instruction**$_{\mathrm{V:CPHR}}$ (to regard the case as a theft)$_{\mathrm{N:PAT:}Info}$ from the public prosecutor$_{\mathrm{V:ORIG:}Speak}$.'

(10) ***přijmout pokyn*** 'to receive an instruction':
'Speaker'$_{\mathrm{N}}$ $\Rightarrow$ ACT$_{\mathrm{N}}$ $\Leftrightarrow$ ORIG$_{\mathrm{V}}$
'Recipient'$_{\mathrm{N}}$ $\Rightarrow$ ADDR$_{\mathrm{N}}$ $\Leftrightarrow$ ACT$_{\mathrm{V}}$
'Information'$_{\mathrm{N}}$ $\Rightarrow$ PAT$_{\mathrm{N}}$

The referential identity of valency complementations, provided in (10), reflects changes in the semantic specifications of verbal valency complementations (see example (9) illustrating the mapping) and also the change in the perspective from which the event expressed by the noun is viewed: in this case, the event is portrayed from the perspective of the 'Recipient' as the participant corresponding to the verbal ACTor.

Attribute `map`

As referential identity has a direct influence on the syntactic structure of CPs, see Section 5, this information has to be provided in the lexical part of the language description.

As it is the predicative noun that selects an appropriate light verb, the attribute `map` – giving a list of pair(s) of referentially identical nominal and verbal valency complementations – is assigned to *valency frames of predicative nouns*. More than one attribute `map` (distinguished by numeral indexes) can appear in a lexical unit of a predicative noun to account for the possible differences in referential identity of valency complementations within several CPs with the same predicative noun. Each attribute `map` is accompanied by a set of references to light verbs provided in the attribute `lvc` that comply with the given referential identity of valency complementations. The lexical entry is exemplified on the predicative noun *pokyn* 'instruction' in Fig. 1.

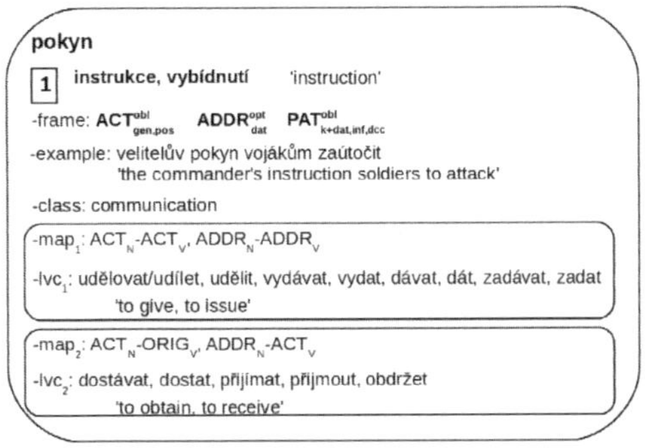

Figure 1: Simplified VALLEX lexical entry of the noun *pokyn* 'instruction'.

4.2.2 Verbal Participant 'Causator': Attribute `caus`

Typically, it is the predicative noun that determines the number and roles of semantic participants characteristic of a CP. Light verbs of causative type, which are endowed with the semantic participant 'Causator', represent the only exception. With these verbs, 'Causator' is contributed to CPs by the verb (in addition to the semantic participants provided by the predicative nouns).

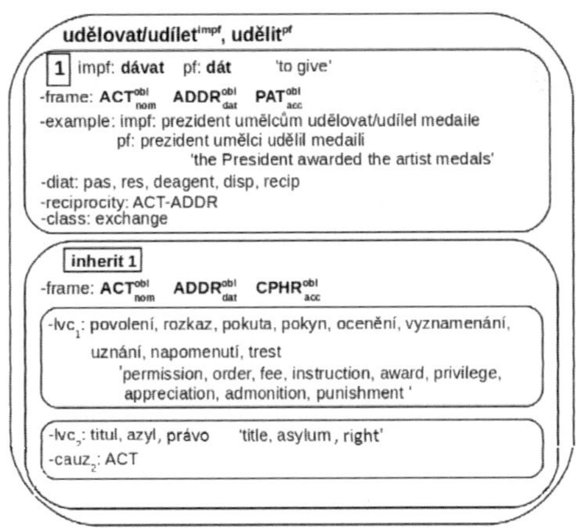

Figure 2: Simplified VALLEX lexical entry of the verb *udělovat/udílet*^{impf}, *udělit*^{pf} 'to give'.

For example, the CP *udělit právo* 'to grant a right', see example sentence (12), is characterized by three semantic participants: 'Causator', 'Bearer', and 'Theme'. 'Causator', provided by the light verb *udělit* 'to grant' (with the valency frame given in (4)), is mapped onto the verbal ACTor whereas 'Bearer' and 'Theme' given by the predicative noun *právo* 'right' correspond to the nominal ACTor and PATient, respectively, see the valency frame of the noun in (11). As the verbal ACTor is saturated by the semantic participant 'Causator', only ADDRessee is not semantically saturated; this ADDRessee acquires its semantic specification from the predicative noun via coreference with the nominal ACTor, see their referential identity in (13). As a result, all valency complementations are semantically specified.

(11) ***právo***$_{\mathrm{PN}}$ 'right':
$\mathrm{ACT}_{\mathrm{gen,pos}}$ $\mathrm{PAT}_{\mathrm{gen},na+\mathrm{acc,inf}}$

(12) ... *král Vladislav Jagellonský* $_{\mathrm{V:ACT:}Caus}$ ***udělil*** $_{\mathrm{LV}}$ *městečku* $_{\mathrm{V:ADDR:}Bearer}$ ***právo***$_{\mathrm{V:CPHR}}$ *(pořádat dva výroční trhy)* $_{\mathrm{N:PAT:}Theme}$.
'... king Ladislaus Jagiellon$_{\mathrm{V:ACT:}Caus}$ **granted** the **right**$_{\mathrm{V:CPHR}}$ (to hold two market fairs)$_{\mathrm{N:PAT:}Theme}$ to the town$_{\mathrm{V:ADDR:}Bearer}$.'

(13) ***udělit právo*** 'to grant a right':
'Causator'$_{\mathrm{V}}$ $\Rightarrow$ $\mathrm{ACT_V}$
'Bearer'$_{\mathrm{N}}$ $\Rightarrow$ $\mathrm{ACT_N}$ $\Leftrightarrow$ $\mathrm{ADDR_V}$
'Name'$_{\mathrm{N}}$ $\Rightarrow$ $\mathrm{PAT_N}$

Changes in the mapping of 'Causator'

The semantic participant 'Causator' may be mapped not only onto the verbal ACTor but also onto another valency position of a light verb. Then the change in the mapping of 'Causator' brings about further changes in the referential identity of nominal and verbal complementations.

For example, within the CP *získat právo* 'to obtain a right', see (15), the 'Causator' contributed by the light verb *získat* 'to obtain' maps onto the verbal ORIGin, see the valency frame of this light verb in (14). In this case, it is the verbal ACTor that gains semantic content from the nominal ACTor (16). As a consequence, all the valency complementations within the CP *získat práv*o 'to obtain a right' are semantically saturated.

(14) ***získat***$_{\mathrm{LV}}$ 'to obtain':
$\mathrm{ACT_{nom}}$ $\mathrm{CPHR_{acc}}$ $\mathrm{ORIG}_{od+\mathrm{gen}}$

(15) ... *od krále Vladislava Jagellonského* $_{\mathrm{V:ORIG:}Caus}$ *městečko* $_{\mathrm{N:ACT:}Bearer}$ ***získalo*** $_{\mathrm{LV}}$ ***právo*** $_{\mathrm{V:CPHR}}$ *(pořádat dva výroční trhy)* $_{\mathrm{N:PAT:}Theme}$.
'... from king Ladislaus Jagiellon$_{\mathrm{V:ORIG:}Caus}$, the town$_{\mathrm{V:ACT:}Bearer}$ **obtained** the **right**$_{\mathrm{CPHR}}$ (to hold two market fairs)$_{\mathrm{N:PAT:}Theme}$.'

(16) ***získat právo*** 'to obtain a right':
'Causator'$_{\mathrm{V}}$ $\Rightarrow$ $\mathrm{ORIG_V}$
'Bearer'$_{\mathrm{N}}$ $\Rightarrow$ $\mathrm{ACT_N}$ $\Leftrightarrow$ $\mathrm{ACT_V}$
'Name'$_{\mathrm{N}}$ $\Rightarrow$ $\mathrm{PAT_N}$

Attribute caus

The mapping of 'Causator' onto valency complementations is relevant for both deep and surface structure formation, therefore it is captured by a special attribute `caus` assigned to valency frames of light verbs of causative type. This attribute lists the verbal valency complementation onto which 'Causator' is mapped, see the light verb *udělovat/udílet*^{impf}, *udělit*^{pf} 'to give' in Fig. 2.

5 Grammatical Rules for CPs

The grammatical part of the VALLEX lexicon contains meta-rules describing the formation of deep (Sect. 5.1) and surface dependency structures of CPs (Sect. 5.2). These meta-rules are instantiated on the basis of the information stored in the lexical part of the lexicon.

5.1 Deep Syntactic Structure

The meta-rule for formation of the deep syntactic structure of a CP exploits a valency frame of a predicative noun and a valency frame of a light verb with which the noun combines (their compatibility is identified by the attribute `lvc`). Moreover, information on the referential identity of nominal and verbal valency complementations within a CP, given in the attribute `map`, as well as information on verbal 'Causator', given in the attribute `caus` (if applicable), is necessary for the identification of coreferences in the dependency tree of the CP.

For example, the deep dependency structure of the CP *udělit pokyn* 'to give an instruction' is composed of the valency frame of the predicative noun *pokyn* 'instruction' and that of the light verb *udělit* 'to give' given above in (1) and (4), respectively. Further, the deep structure of this CP is characterized by coreferential links, reflecting the referential identity of the complementations, see (7), Fig. (17) (and Tab. 1 left part).

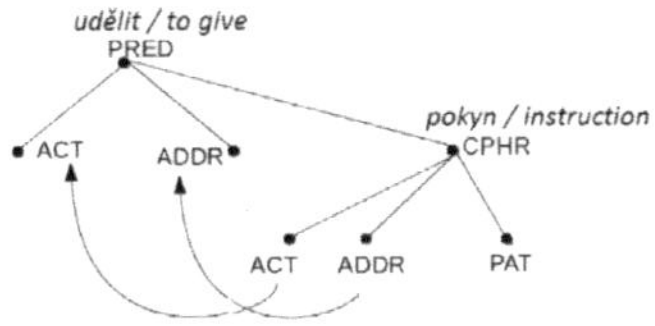

(17)

On the other hand, the valency structure of the CP *přijmout pokyn* 'to receive an instruction' results from the valency frames of the predicative noun *pokyn* 'instruction' and that of the light verb *přijmout* 'receive', given in (1) and (8), respectively, and from the referential identity provided in (10), see Fig. (18).

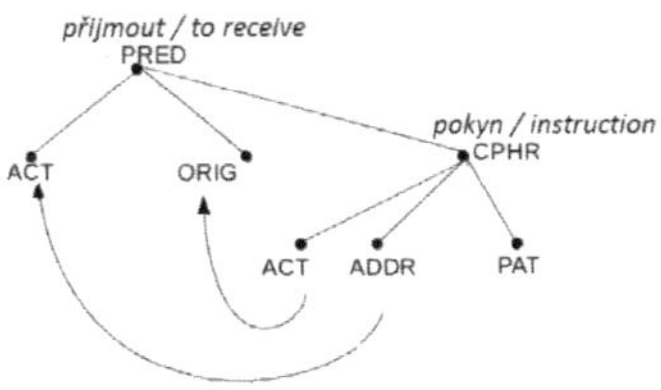

(18)

5.2 Surface Syntactic Structure

For the formation of the surface syntactic structure of a CP, its deep dependency structure is used (Sect. 5.1). In addition to the mapping of individual nominal and verbal complementations provided by the attribute `map` (Sect. 4.2.1), also the mapping of the verbal 'Causator', provided by the attribute `caus` (Sect. 4.2.2), is necessary.

Theoretical analysis has revealed that with CPs in Czech, each semantic participant is typically expressed in the surface sentence just once.[7] Despite the fact that semantic participants are contributed – with the exception of the verbal 'Causator' – by predicative nouns, Czech CPs have a strong tendency to express them in the surface structure as complementations of light verbs[8] (Macháčková, 1994). We propose the following rules for the formation of the surface syntactic structure with CPs:

All valency complementations from the *valency frame of the light verb* are expressed in the surface structure, namely:

(i) the valency complementation filled by the predicative noun (the CPHR functor);

(ii) the valency complementation corresponding to 'Causator' (the attribute `caus`);

(iii) valency complementations that are referentially identical with a nominal complementation (the attribute `map`).

Only the following valency complementations from the *valency frame of the predicative noun* are expressed in the surface structure:

(iv) valency complementations that are not referentially identical with any verbal complementation (i.e., those not listed in the attribute `map`).

For example, within the CP *udělit pokyn* 'to give an instruction' characterized by the deep dependency tree (17) the predicative noun fills the CPHR verbal position (i); two verbal valency complementations are expressed in the surface structure (iii), namely the ACT$_V$ and ADDR$_V$ (referentially identical with the ACT$_N$ and ADDR$_N$, referring to 'Speaker' and 'Recipient', respectively); from the valency frame of the noun, only the PAT$_N$ (referring to 'Information') is expressed on the surface (iv); the two remaining nominal complementations, ACT$_N$ and ADDR$_N$, are unexpressed in the surface structure (as they are referentially identical with ACT$_V$ and ADDR$_V$), see Tab. 1 column 4.

5.2.1 Unmarked (Active) Form

Morphemic forms of valency complementations of light verbs listed in the lexical part of the lexicon correspond to the *active form*. Thus the rules given above directly establish the surface syntactic structure of CPs in the active form.

For example, the surface structure of a sentence with the CP *udělit pokyn* 'to give an instruction' with the light verb in the active form can be obtained directly from morphemic forms recorded in the valency frames (1) and (4), see Tab. 1 column 5, and Fig. 3, displaying the surface syntactic tree of sentence (19) in relation to its deep dependency tree.

(19) *Státní zástupce* $_{V:ACT:Sb}$ ***udělil*** $_{LV:active}$ *žalobcům* $_{V:ADDR:Obj}$ ***pokyn*** $_{V:CPHR:Obj}$ *(posuzovat případ jako krádež)* $_{N:PAT:Atr}$.
'The public prosecutor$_{V:ACT:Sb}$ **has given** the prosecutors$_{V:ADDR:Obj}$ the **instruction**$_{V:CPHR:Obj}$ (to regard the case as a theft)$_{N:PAT:Atr}$.'

---

[7]The only exception is represented by the semantic participant mapped onto nominal ACTor; under certain conditions, this participant can be expressed twice, both as a verbal and as a nominal complementation (e.g., *Petr*$_{V:ACT:Bearer}$ *nevedl svůj*$_{N:ACT:Bearer}$ *život zrovna šťastně.* 'Peter did not lead his life very happily.').

[8]Rich morphology of Czech provides reliable clues for the identification of surface structure via morphemic cases.

CP	Deep	map & caus	Surface	active	pass	rcp-pass	deagent
Light verb	ACT_V		+	Sb:nom	Obj:instr, *od*+gen	Obj: *od*+gen	–*
	$ADDR_V$		+	Obj:dat	Obj:dat	Sb:nom	Obj:dat
	$CPHR_V$		+	Obj:acc	Sb:nom	Obj:acc	Sb:nom
Predicat. noun	ACT_N	$ACT_N \Leftrightarrow ACT_V$	–				
	$ADDR_N$	$ADDR_N \Leftrightarrow ADDR_V$	–				
	PAT_N		+	Atr:*k*+dat,inf	Atr:*k*+dat,inf	Atr:*k*+dat,inf	Atr:*k*+dat,inf

Table 1: The deep (left part) and surface (right part) structures of the CP *udělit pokyn* 'to give an instruction'. (* The surface expression is blocked by the deagentive diathesis.)

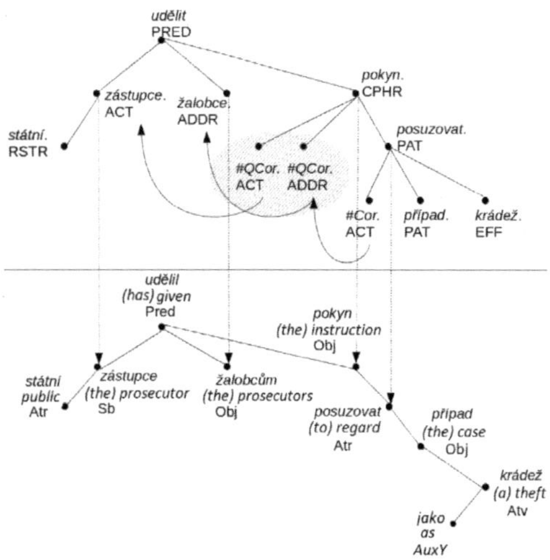

Figure 3: The simplified deep (above) and surface (below) dependency trees of sentence (19). The vertical arrows show the surface syntactic manifestations of valency complementations. The nominal valency complementations unexpressed in the surface structure (due to their referential identity with the verbal ones) are in the gray field.

5.2.2 Marked (Passive) Forms: Interplay of the Rules

The deep structure of a CP also serves as the basis for generating marked surface structures of diatheses. In this case, the rules for the formation of surface structures of CPs (Sect. 5.2 above) interplay with those for the formation of marked forms of diatheses (Vernerová et al., 2014).

In Czech, five types of diathesis (passive, resultative, recipient-passive, deagentive, and dispositional) were determined (Panevová et al., 2014). Diatheses are accompanied by changes in the morphological category of verbal voice and they are prototypically associated with shifts of valency complementations in the surface structure (while the deep structure is preserved). These shifts are indicated by changes in morphemic forms of the involved valency complementations and are regular enough to be captured by formal rules. These rules can be exemplified, e.g., by the rule for the recipient-passive diathesis:

Rcp-pass d.	
verb form	replace(active → → $AuxV_{dostat}$ + past_participle)
ACT	replace(nom → *od*+gen)
ADDR	replace(dat → nom)

The light verb and its full verb counterpart prototypically enter the same type of diatheses; the applicability of individual diatheses is provided by the attribute `diat` attached to the full verb.

For example, the light verb *udělit* 'to give, grant' can create the following marked structures (Fig. 2): passive (`pass` (20)), resultative (`res`), recipient-passive (`rcp-pass` (21)), deagentive (`deagent` (22)), and dispositional (`disp`) diathesis.

(20) *Žalobcům* $_{V:ADDR:dat}$ ***byl*** *od státního zástupce* $_{V:ACT:od+gen}$ ***udělen***$_{pass}$ ***pokyn*** $_{V:CPHR:nom}$ *(posuzovat případ jako krádež)* $_{N:PAT:inf}$.
'The **instruction**$_{V:CPHR}$ (to regard the case as a theft)$_{N:PAT}$ **was given** to the prosecutors$_{V:ADDR}$ by the public prosecutor$_{V:ACT}$.'

(21) *Žalobci* $_{V:ADDR:nom}$ ***dostali*** *od státního zástupce* $_{V:ACT:od+gen}$ ***udělen***$_{rcp\text{-}pass}$ ***pokyn*** $_{V:CPHR:acc}$ *(posuzovat případ jako krádež)* $_{N:PAT:inf}$.
'The prosecutors$_{V:ADDR}$ **have been given** the **instruction**$_{V:CPHR}$ (to regard the case as a theft)$_{N:PAT}$ by the public prosecutor$_{V:ACT}$.'

(22) *Žalobcům* $_{V:ADDR:dat}$ ***se udělil***$_{deagent}$ ***pokyn*** $_{V:CPHR:nom}$ *(posuzovat případ jako krádež)* $_{N:PAT:inf}$.
'The **instruction**$_{V:CPHR}$ (to regard the case as a theft)$_{N:PAT}$ **was given** to the prosecutors$_{V:ADDR}$.'

Valency frames describing the marked structures of diatheses of a given CP can be generated on the basis of the rules for deriving the marked structures of diatheses (stored in the grammatical part of the VALLEX lexicon), applied to the *deep and surface active structures* of the CP. The deep dependency structure of the CP (i.e., the number and the type of its verbal and nominal valency complementations) is preserved whereas the surface syntactic expression of the verb and its complementations is changed as prescribed by the rule describing the respective diathesis (the surface form of the nominal valency complementations remains unchanged).

For example, the marked structure of the recipient-passive diathesis of the CP *udělit pokyn* 'to give an instruction', as in (21), is underlain by the valency frame obtained by the application of the above given rule to the valency frame corresponding to the active form of the light verb in (4), see Tab. 1 column 7.

6 Conclusion

In this paper, we have focused on complex predicates consisting of a light verb and a predicative noun. We have proposed their theoretically adequate and economical description based on the interplay between the grammatical and the lexical components of the language description. The special attributes `lvc`, `map` and `caus`, complying with the logical structure of the VALLEX lexicon as well as with the main tenets of the Functional Generative Description, were designed. The information provided in these attributes identifies recurrent patterns of light verb collocations (similarly as lexical functions into which it can be easily transferred), while grammatical rules in the grammatical component generate their well-formed (both deep and surface) dependency structures. We have shown how the proposed rules combine with the rules describing diatheses.

At present, a large-scaled lexicographic representation of light verbs is still missing despite the fact that these phenomena are widespread in the language (Kettnerová et al., 2013). We expect that the lexicon enriched with the information on light verbs will form a solid basis for their future integration into NLP applications which can substantially contribute to verifying the results of the proposed theoretical analysis.

Acknowledgments

The work on this project was supported by the grants of GAČR No. P406/12/0557 and GA15-09979S. This work has been using language resources distributed by the LINDAT/CLARIN project of the MŠMT No. LM2010013.

References

Margarita Alonso Ramos. 2007. Towards the Synthesis of Support Verb Constructions. In L. Wanner, editor, *Selected lexical and Grammatical issues in the Meaning–Text Theory*, pages 97–137. J. Benjamins, Amsterdam.

Valentina Apresjan. 2011. Active dictionary of the Russian language: Theory and practice. In I. Boguslavsky and L. Wanner, editors, *Meaning-Text Theory 2011*, pages 13–24, Barcelona. Universitat Pompeu Fabra.

Miriam Butt. 1998. Constraining argument merger through aspect. In E. Hinrichs, A. Kathol, and T. Nakazawa, editors, *Complex Predicates in Non-derivational Syntax, Syntax and Semantics*, pages 73–113. Academic Press, San Diego.

Miriam Butt. 2010. The Light Verb Jungle: Still Hacking Away. In M. Amberber, B. Baker, and M. Harvey, editors, *Complex Predicates in Cross-Linguistic Perspective*, pages 48–78. Cambridge University Press, Cambridge.

Silvie Cinková. 2009. *Words that Matter: Towards a Swedish-Czech Colligational Dictionary of Basic Verbs*. Institute of Formal and Applied Linguistics, Prague.

Jane Grimshaw and Armin Mester. 1988. Light Verbs and Θ-Marking. *Linguistic Inquiry*, 19(2):205–232.

Erhard Hinrichs and Tsuneko Nakazawa. 1990. Subcategorization and VP structure in German. In S. Hughes and J. Salmons, editors, *Symposium on Germanic Linguistics*, Amsterdam. J. Benjamins.

Václava Kettnerová and Markéta Lopatková. 2013. The Representation of Czech Light Verb Constructions in a Valency Lexicon. In E. Hajičová, K. Gerdes, and L. Wanner, editors, *Proceedings of DepLing 2013*, pages 147–156, Praha. Matfyzpress.

Václava Kettnerová, Markéta Lopatková, and Eduard Bejček. 2012. The Syntax-Semantics Interface of Czech Verbs in the Valency Lexicon. In *Euralex International Congress 2012*, pages 434–443, Oslo. University of Oslo.

Václava Kettnerová, Markéta Lopatková, and Eduard Bejček et al. 2013. Corpus Based Identification of Czech Light Verbs. In K. Gajdošová and A. Žáková, editors, *Slovko 2013*, pages 118–128, Lüdenscheid. RAM-Verlag.

Veronika Kolářová. 2010. *Valence deverbativních substantiv v češtině (na materiálu substantiv s dativní valencí).* Karolinum Press, Prague.

Markéta Lopatková, Zdeněk Žabokrtský, and Václava Kettnerová et al. 2008. *Valenční slovník českých sloves.* Karolinum Press, Prague.

Eva Macháčková. 1994. Constructions with Verbs and Abstract Nouns in Czech (Analytical Predicates). In S. Čmejrková and Fr. Štícha, editors, *The Syntax of Sentence and Text*, pages 365–375. J. Benjamins, Amsterdam.

Igor A. Mel'čuk and Alexander K. Zholkovsky. 1984. *Explanatory Combinatorial Dictionary of Modern Russian.* Wiener Slawistischer Almanach, Vienna.

Igor A. Mel'čuk. 1996. Lexical Functions: A Tool for the description of lexical relations in a lexicon. In L. Wanner, editor, *Lexical Functions in Lexicography and Natural Language Processing*, pages 37–105. J. Benjamins, Amsterdam.

Jarmila Panevová et al. 2014. *Mluvnice současné češtiny 2, Syntax na základě anotovaného korpusu.* Karolinum Press, Prague.

Jarmila Panevová. 1994. Valency Frames and the Meaning of the Sentence. In P. A. Luelsdorff, editor, *The Prague School of Structural and Functional Linguistics*, pages 223–243. J. Benjamins, Amsterdam.

Soma Paul. 2010. Representing Compound Verbs in Indo WordNet. In *GWC-2010*, Mumbai. The Global Wordnet Association.

Jan Radimský. 2010. *Verbo-nominální predikát s kategoriálním slovesem.* Editio Universitatis Bohemiae Meridionalis, České Budějovice.

Petr Sgall, Eva Hajičová, and Jarmila Panevová. 1986. *The Meaning of the Sentence in Its Semantic and Pragmatic Aspects.* Reidel, Dordrecht.

Zdeňka Urešová. 2011. *Valence sloves v Pražském závislostním korpusu.* Ústav formální a aplikované lingvistiky, Prague.

Anna Vernerová, Václava Kettnerová, and Markéta Lopatková. 2014. To pay or to get paid: Enriching a valency lexicon with diatheses. In *LREC 2014*, pages 2452–2459, Reykjavík. ELRA.

Veronika Vincze and János Csirik. 2010. Hungarian Corpus of Light Verb Constructions. In *COLING 2010*, pages 1110–1118, Beijing.

Enhancing FreeLing Rule-Based Dependency Grammars with Subcategorization Frames

Marina Lloberes
U. de Barcelona
Barcelona, Spain
mllobesa8@alumnes.ub.edu

Irene Castellón
U. de Barcelona
Barcelona, Spain
icastellon@ub.edu

Lluís Padró
U. Politècnica de Catalunya
Barcelona, Spain
padro@cs.upc.edu

Abstract

Despite the recent advances in parsing, significant efforts are needed to improve the current parsers performance, such as the enhancement of the argument/adjunct recognition. There is evidence that verb subcategorization frames can contribute to parser accuracy, but a number of issues remain open. The main aim of this paper is to show how subcategorization frames acquired from a syntactically annotated corpus and organized into fine-grained classes can improve the performance of two rule-based dependency grammars.

1 Introduction

Statistical parsers and rule-based parsers have advanced over recent years. However, significant efforts are required to increase the performance of current parsers (Klein and Manning, 2003; Nivre et al., 2006; Ballesteros and Nivre, 2012; Marimon et al., 2014).

One of the linguistic phenomena which parsers often fail to handle correctly is the argument/adjunct distinction (Carroll et al., 1998). For this reason, the main goal of this paper is to test empirically the accuracy of rule-based dependency grammars working exclusively with syntactic rules or adding subcategorization frames to the rules.

A number of studies shows that subcategorization frames can contribute to improve parser performance (Carroll et al., 1998; Zeman, 2002; Mirroshandel et al., 2013). Particularly, these studies are mainly concerned with the integration of subcategorization information into statistical parsers.

The list of studies about rule-based parsers integrating subcategorization information is also extensive (Lin, 1998; Alsina et al., 2002; Bick, 2006; Calvo and Gelbukh, 2011). However, they do not explicitly relate the improvements in parser performance to the addition of subcategorization.

This paper analyses in detail how subcategorization frames acquired from an annotated corpus and distributed among fine-grained classes increase accuracy in rule-based dependency grammars.

The framework used is that of the FreeLing Dependency Grammars (FDGs) for Spanish and Catalan, using enriched lexical-syntactic information about the argument structure of the verb. FreeLing (Padró and Stanilovsky, 2012) is an open-source library of multilingual Natural Language Processing (NLP) tools that provide linguistic analysis for written texts. The FDGs are the core of the FreeLing dependency parser, the Txala Parser (Atserias et al., 2005).

The remainder of this paper is organized as follows. Section 2 contains an overview of previous work related to this research. Section 3 presents the rule-based dependency parser used and the Spanish and Catalan grammars. Section 4 describes the strategy followed initially to integrate subcategorization into the grammars and how this information has been redesigned. Section 5 focuses on the evaluation and the analysis of several experiments testing versions of the grammars including or discarding subcategorization frames. Finally, the main conclusions and the further research goals arisen from the results of the experiments are exposed in Section 6.

2 Related Work

There has been an extensive research on parser development, and most approaches can be classified as *statistical* or *rule-based*. In the former, a statistical model learnt from annotated or unannotated texts is applied to build the syntactic tree (Klein and Manning, 2003; Collins and Koo, 2005; Nivre et al., 2006; Ballesteros and Nivre, 2012), whereas the latter uses hand-built grammars to guide the

Proceedings of the Third International Conference on Dependency Linguistics (Depling 2015), pages 201–210,
Uppsala, Sweden, August 24–26 2015.

parser in the construction of the tree (Sleator and Temperley, 1991; Järvinen and Tapanainen, 1998; Lin, 1998).

Concerning the languages this study is based on, some research on Spanish has been performed from the perspective of Constraint Grammar (Bick, 2006), Unification Grammar (Ferrández and Moreno, 2000), Head-Driven Phrase Structure Grammar (Marimon et al., 2014), and Dependency Grammar for statistical parsing, both supervised (Carreras et al., 2006) and semi-supervised (Calvo and Gelbukh, 2011). For Catalan, a rule-based parser based on Constraint Grammar (Alsina et al., 2002) and a statistical dependency parser (Carreras, 2007) are available.

Despite the huge achievements in the area of parsing, argument/adjunct recognition is still a linguistic problem in which parsers still show low accuracy and in which there is still no generalized consensus in Theoretical Linguistics (Tesnière, 1959; Chomsky, 1965). This phenomenon refers to the subcategorization notion, which corresponds to the definition of the type and the number of arguments of a syntactic head.

The acquisition of subcategorization frames from corpora is one of the strategies for integrating information about the argument structure into a parser. Depending on the level of language analysis of the annotated corpus, two main strategies are used in automatic acquisition.

If the acquisition is performed over a *morphosyntactically annotated text*, the subcategorization frames are inferred by applying statistical techniques on morphosyntactically annotated data (Brent, 1993; Manning, 1993; Korhonen et al., 2003).

Alternatively, acquisition can be performed with *syntactically annotated texts* (Sarkar and Zeman, 2000; O'Donovan et al., 2005; Aparicio et al., 2008). Subcategorization acquisition can be performed straightforwardly because the information about the argument structure is available in the corpus. Therefore, this approach generally focuses on the methods for subcategorization frames classification.

The final classification in a lexicon of frames is a computational resource for several NLP tools. In the framework which this research focuses on, the integration of the acquired subcategorization is orientated to the contribution towards building the syntactic tree when the parser has incomplete information to make a decision (Carroll et al., 1998).

Depending on the characteristics of the parser, subcategorization assists in this task in a different way. Subcategorization information can be used to assign a probability to every possible syntactic tree and to rank them in parsers that perform the whole set of possible syntactic analysis of a particular sentence (Carroll et al., 1998; Zeman, 2002; Mirroshandel et al., 2013).

In contrast, subcategorization may help to restrict the application of certain rules. Then, when the parser detects the subcategorization frame in the input sentence, it labels the syntactic tree according to the frame discarding any other possible analysis (Lin, 1998; Calvo and Gelbukh, 2011).

3 Dependency Parsing in FreeLing

The rule-based dependency grammars presented in this article are the core of the Txala Parser (Atserias et al., 2005), the NLP module in charge of Dependency Parsing in the FreeLing library (Padró and Stanilovsky, 2012).[1]

FreeLing is an open-source project that has been developed for more than ten years. It is a complete NLP pipeline built on a chain of modules that provide a general and robust linguistic analysis. Among the available tools, FreeLing offers sentence recognition, tokenization, named entity recognition, tagging, chunking, dependency parsing, word sense disambiguation, and coreference resolution.

3.1 Txala Parser

The Txala Parser is one of the dependency parsing modules available in FreeLing. It is a rule-based, non-projective and multilingual dependency parser that provides robust syntactic analysis in three steps.

Txala receives the partial syntactic trees produced by the chunker (Civit, 2003) as input. Firstly, the head-child relations are identified using a set of heuristic rules that iteratively decide whether two adjacent trees must be merged, and in which way, until there is only one tree left. Secondly, it is converted into syntactic dependencies according to Mel'čuk (1988). Finally, each dependency arch of the tree is labelled with a syntactic function tag.

[1] `http://nlp.cs.upc.edu/freeling/`

Language	Total	Rules Linking	Labelling
English	2961	2239	722
Spanish	4042	3310	732
Catalan	2879	2099	780
Galician	178	87	91
Asturian	4438	3842	596

Table 1: Sizes of the FDGs

3.2 FreeLing Dependency Grammars

The current version of FreeLing includes rule-based dependency grammars for English, Spanish, Catalan, Galician and Asturian (see Table 1 for a brief overview of their sizes). In this paper, the Spanish and Catalan dependency grammars are described.

The FDGs follow the linguistic basis of syntactic dependencies (Tesnière, 1959; Mel'čuk, 1988). However, we propose a different analysis for prepositional phrases (preposition-headed), subordinate clauses (conjunction-headed) and coordinating structures (conjunction-headed).

A FDG is structured as a set of manually defined rules which link two adjacent syntactic partial trees (*linking rules*) and assign a syntactic function to every link of the tree (*labelling rules*), according to certain conditions and priority. They are applied based on this priority: at every step, two adjacent partial trees will be attached or will be labelled with a syntactic function tag if their rule is the highest ranked for which all the conditions are met.

Linking rules can contain four kind of conditions, regarding morphological (part-of-speech tag), lexical (word form, lemma), syntactic (syntactic context, syntactic features of lemmas) and semantic features (semantic properties predefined by the user).

For instance, the rule shown in Figure 1 has priority `911`, and states that a sub-tree marked as a subordinate clause (`subord`) whose head is a relative pronoun (`PR`) attached as a child to the noun phrase (`sn`) to its left (`top_left`) when these two consecutive sub-trees are not located to the right of a verb phrase (`!grup-verb_$$`).

Concerning the *labelling rules*, the set of conditions that the parent or the child of the dependency must meet may refer to morphological (part-of-speech tag), lexical (word form, lemma), syntactic (lower/upper sub-tree nodes, syntactic features of lemmas) and semantic properties (EuroWordNet Top Concept Ontology -TCO- features, WordNet Semantic File, WordNet Synonyms and Hypernyms and other semantic features predefined by the user).

```
911 !grup-verb_$$ - (sn,subord{^PR})
    top_left RELABEL -
```

Figure 1: Linking rule for relative clauses

```
grup-verb   dobj
            d.label=grup-sp
            p.class=trans
            d.side=right
            d.lemma=a|al
            d:sn.tonto=Human
            d:sn.tonto!=Building|Place
```

Figure 2: Labelling rule for human direct objects

In the rule illustrated in Figure 2, the direct object label (`dobj`) is assigned to the link between a verbal head (`grup-verb`) and a prepositional phrase (`grup-sp`) child when the head belongs to the transitive verbs class (`trans`) and the child is post-verbal (`right`), the preposition is `a` (or the contraction `al`), and the nominal head inside the prepositional phrase has the TCO feature `Human` but not (`!=`) the features `Building` or `Place` (to prevent organizations from being identified as a direct object).

4 CompLex-VS lexicon for Parsing

Following the hypothesis that subcategorization frames improve the parsing performance (Carroll et al., 1998), the first version of FDGs included verbal and nominal frames in order to improve argument/adjunct recognition and prepositional attachment (Lloberes et al., 2010). In this paper, only the verbal lexicon is presented because it is the resource used for the argument/adjunct recognition task in the grammars.

4.1 Initial CompLex-VS lexicon in FDGs

The initial Computational Lexicon of Verb Subcategorization (CompLex-VS) was automatically extracted from the subcategorization frames of the SenSem Corpus (Fernández and Vàzquez, 2014), which contains 30231 syntactically and semantically annotated sentences per language, and of the Volem Multilingual Lexicon (Fernández et al., 2002), which has 1700 syntactically and semantically annotated verbal lemmas per language. The patterns extracted from both resources are organized according to the linguistic-motivated classification proposed by Alonso et al. (2007).

The final lexicon applied to the FDGs has 11 subcategorization classes containing a total of 1314 Spanish verbal lemmas and 847 Catalan verbal lemmas with a different subcategorization frame.

A first experimental evaluation of the Spanish Grammar with the initial subcategorization lexicon (Lloberes et al., 2010) showed that incorporating subcategorization information is promising.

4.2 Redesign of the CompLex-VS lexicon

According to the evaluation results of the grammars with the initial CompLex-VS included, the lexicon has been redesigned, proposing a set of more fine-grained subcategorization frame classes in order to represent verb subcategorization in the dependency rules in a controlled and detailed way.

New syntactic-semantic patterns have been extracted automatically from the SenSem Corpus according to the idea that every verbal lemma with a different subcategorization frame expresses a different meaning. Therefore, a new lexicon entry is created every time an annotated verbal lemma with a different frame is detected.

The CompLex-VS contains 3102 syntactic patterns in the Spanish lexicon and 2630 patterns in the Catalan lexicon (see Section 4.3 for detailed numbers). They are organized into 15 subcategorization frames as well as into 4 subcategoriztion classes. The lexicon is distributed in XML format under the Creative Commons Attribution-ShareAlike 3.0 Unported License.[2]

Certain patterns have been discarded because they are non-prototypical in the corpus (e.g. clitic left dislocations), they alter the sentence order (e.g. relative clauses), or they involve controversial argument classes (e.g. prepositional phrases seen as arguments or adjuncts depending on the context).

As Figure 3 shows, the extracted patterns (`<verb>`) have been classified into `<frame>` classes according to the whole set of argument structures occurring in the corpus (`subj` for intransitive verbs, `subj,dobj` for transitive verbs, etc.). Simultaneously, frames have been organized in `<subcategorization>` classes (monoargumental, biargumental, triargumental and quatriargumental).

[2] http://grial.uab.es/descarregues.php

```
<subcategorization
    class="monoargumental"
    ref="1" freq="0.188480">
    <frame class="subj" ref="1"
        freq="0.188480">
        <verb lemma="pensar"
            id="2531"
            ref="1:1" fs="subj"
            cat="np" rs="exp"
            head="null"
            construction="active"
            se="no" freq="0.000070"/>
    </frame>
</subcategorization>
<subcategorization
    class="biargumental"
    ref="2" freq="0.733349">
    <frame class="subj,dobj" ref="2"
        freq="0.617452">
        <verb lemma="agradecer"
            id="454" ref="2:2" fs="subj,dobj"
            cat="np,complsc" rs="ag_exp,t"
            head="null,null"
            construction="active"
            se="no" freq="0.000140"/>
    </frame>
</subcategorization>
```

Figure 3: Example of the CompLex-VS

Every lexicon entry contains the syntactic function of every argument (`fs`), the grammatical category of the head of the argument (`cat`) and the thematic role (`rs`). The type of `construction` (e.g. active, passive, impersonal, etc.) has been inferred from the predicate and aspect annotations available in the SenSem Corpus.

Two non-annotated lexical items of the sentence have also been inserted into the subcategorization frame because the information that they provide is crucial for the argument structure configuration (e.g. the particle '`se`' and the lexical value of the prepositional phrase `head`).

In addition, meta-linguistic information has been added to every entry: a unique `id` and the relative frequency of the pattern in the corpus (`freq`). A threshold frequency has been established at $7 \cdot 10^{-5}$ (Spanish) and at $8.5 \cdot 10^{-5}$ (Catalan). Patterns below this threshold have been considered marginal in the corpus and they have been discarded.

Every pattern contains a link to the frame and subcategorization class that they belong to (`ref`). For example, if an entry has the reference `1:1`, it means that the pattern corresponds to a monoargumental verb whose unique argument is a subject.

4.3 Integration of CompLex-VS in the FDGs

From the CompLex-VS, two derived lexicons per language containing the verbal lemmas for every recorded pattern have been created to be integrated into the FDGs. The CompLex-SynF lexicon con-

Frames	Spanish	Catalan
subj	203	386
subj,att	3	7
subj,dobj	440	230
subj,iobj	37	61
subj,pobj	126	93
subj,pred	45	31
subj,attr,iobj	2	1
subj,dobj,iobj	113	72
subj,dobj,pobj	42	34
subj,dobj,pred	21	18
subj,pobj,iobj	2	1
subj,pobj,pobj	14	9
subj,pobj,pred	1	0
subj,pred,iobj	4	5
subj,dobj,pobj,iobj	1	0

Table 2: CompLex-SynF lexicon in numbers

tains the subcategorization patterns generalized by the syntactic function (Table 2). The CompLex-SynF+Cat lexicon collects the syntactic patterns combining syntactic function and grammatical category (adjective/noun/prepositional phrase, infinitive/interrogative/completive clause).

The addition of grammatical categories makes it possible to restrict the grammar rules. For example, a class of verbs containing the verb *quedarse* ('to get') whose argument is a predicative and a prepositional phrase allows the rules to identify that the prepositional phrase of the sentence *Se ha quedado de piedra* ('[He/She] got shocked') is a predicative argument. Furthermore, it allows for discarding the prepositional phrase of the sentence *Aparece de madrugada* ('[He/She] shows up at late night') being a predicative argument, although *aparecer* belongs to the class of predicative verbs but conveying a noun phrase as argument.

While in the CompLex-SynF lexicon the information is more compacted (1054 syntactic patterns classified in 15 frames), in the CompLex-SynF+Cat lexicon the classes are more granular (1356 syntactic patterns organized in 77 frames).

Only subcategorization patterns corresponding to lexicon entries referring to the active voice have been integrated in the FDGs, since they involve non-marked word order. Both lexicons also exclude information about the thematic role, although they take into account the value of the head (if the frame contains a prepositional argument) and the pronominal verbs (lexical entries that accept 'se' particle whose value neither is reflexive nor reciprocal).

Two versions of the Spanish dependency grammar and two versions of the Catalan dependency grammar have been created. One version contains the CompLex-SynF lexicon and the other one the CompLex-Synf+Cat.

Grammar	Spanish	Catalan
Bare	450	508
Baseline	732	780
SynF	872	917
SynF+Cat	869	917

Table 3: Labelling rules in the evaluated grammars

The old CompLex-VS lexicon classes have been replaced with the new ones. Specifically, this information has been inserted in the part of the labelling rules about the syntactic properties of the parent node (observe `p.class` in Figure 2).

Finally, new rules have been added for frames of CompLex-SynF and CompLex-SynF+Cat that are not present in the old CompLex-VS lexicon. Furthermore, some rules have been disabled for frames of the old CompLex-VS lexicon that do not exist in the CompLex-SynF and CompLex-SynF+Cat lexicons (see Table 3 for the detailed size of the grammars).

5 Evaluation

An evaluation task has been carried out to test empirically how the FDGs performance changes when subcategorization information is added or subtracted. Several versions of the grammars have been tested using a controlled annotated linguistic data set.

This evaluation specifically focuses on analysing the results of the experiments qualitatively. This kind of analysis makes it possible to track the decisions that the parser has made, so that it is possible to provide an explanation about the accuracy of the FDGs running with different linguistic information.

5.1 Experiments

Four versions of both Spanish and Catalan grammars are tested in order to assess the differences of the performance depending on the linguistic information added.

- Bare FDG. A version of the FDGs running without subcategorization frames.
- Baseline FDG. A version of the FDGs running with the old CompLex-VS lexicon.
- SynF FDG. A version of the FDGs running with the CompLex-SynF lexicon.

Tag	SenSem Spanish	ParTes Spanish	SenSem Catalan	ParTes Catalan
subj	42.23	34.03	43.03	28.08
dobj	35.77	29.86	34.64	34.25
pobj	16.73	13.89	16.56	17.12
iobj	4.64	6.25	4.70	2.05
pred	0.49	2.08	0.51	0.68
attr	0.14	13.89	0.56	17.81

Table 4: Comparison of the labelling tags distribution in SenSem and ParTes (%)

Tag	Description
adjt	Adjunct
attr	Attribute
dobj	Direct Object
iobj	Indirect Object
pobj	Prepositional Object
pred	Predicative
subj	Subject

Table 5: Tagset of syntactic functions related to the subcategorization

- SynF+Cat FDG. A version of the FDGs running with the CompLex-Synf+Cat lexicon.

Since this research is focused on the implementation of subcategorization information for argument/adjunct recognition, only the *labelling rules* are discussed in this paper (Table 3). However, metrics related to *linking rules* are also mentioned to provide a general description of the FDGs.

5.2 Evaluation data

To perform a qualitative evaluation, the ParTes test suite has been used (Lloberes et al., 2014). This resource is a multilingual hierarchical test suite of a representative and controlled set of syntactic phenomena which has been developed for evaluating the parsing performance as regards syntactic structure and word order.

It contains 161 syntactic phenomena in Spanish (99 referring to structure and 62 to word order) and 147 syntactic phenomena in Catalan (101 corresponding to structure phenomena and 46 to word order).

The current version of ParTes is distributed with an annotated data set in the CoNLL format. Although this data set is not initially developed for evaluating the argument/adjunct recognition, the number of arguments and adjuncts contained in ParTes is proportional to the number of arguments and adjuncts of the SenSem Corpus (Table 4). Therefore, the ParTes data set is a reduced sample of the linguistic phenomena that occur in a larger corpus, which makes ParTes an appropriate resource for this task.

5.3 Evaluation metrics

The metrics have been computed using the CoNLL-X Shared Task 2007 script (Nivre et al., 2007). The output of the FDGs (*system output*) has been compared to the ParTes annotated data set (*gold standard*).

The metrics used to evaluate the performance of the several FDGs versions are the following ones:

Accuracy[3]

$$LAS = \frac{\text{correct attachments and labellings}}{\text{total tokens}}$$

$$UAS = \frac{\text{correct attachments}}{\text{total tokens}}$$

$$LAS2 = \frac{\text{correct labellings}}{\text{total tokens}}$$

Precision

$$P = \frac{\text{system correct tokens}}{\text{system tokens}}$$

Recall

$$R = \frac{\text{system correct tokens}}{\text{gold tokens}}$$

Both quantitative and qualitative analysis detailed in Section 5.4 pay special attention to the metric LAS2, which informs about the number of heads with the correct syntactic function tag.

Precision and recall metrics of the labelling rules provide information about how the addition of verbal subcategorization information contributes to the grammar performance. For this reason, in the qualitative analysis, only labelling syntactic function tags directly related to verbal subcategorization are considered (Table 5).

5.4 Accuracy results

The global results of the FDGs evaluation (LAS) show that the whole set of evaluated grammars score over 80% accuracy in Spanish (Table 6) and around 80% in Catalan (Table 7).

In the four Spanish grammar versions (Table 6), the correct head (UAS) has been identified in 90.01% of the cases. On the other hand, the tendency changes in syntactic function labelling (LAS2). The *Baseline* establishes that 85.54% of tokens have the correct syntactic function tag.

[3]LAS: Labeled Attachment Score; UAS: Unlabeled Attachment Score; LAS2: Label Accuracy

Grammar	LAS	UAS	LAS2
Bare	81.37	90.01	82.86
Baseline	83.76	90.01	85.54
SynF	84.50	90.01	86.29
SynF+Cat	84.50	90.01	86.29

Table 6: Accuracy scores (%) in Spanish

Grammar	LAS	UAS	LAS2
Bare	78.99	86.84	81.91
Baseline	79.52	86.84	82.85
SynF	81.78	86.84	85.24
SynF+Cat	81.78	86.84	85.24

Table 7: Accuracy scores (%) in Catalan

However, *Bare* drops 2.68 scores and *SynF* and *SynF+Cat* improve 0.75 scores with respect to the baseline.

A parallel behaviour is observed in Catalan, although the scores are slightly lower than in Spanish (Table 7). The four Catalan grammars score 86.84% in attachment (UAS). The *Baseline* scores 82.85% in syntactic function assignment (LAS2). Once again FDGs perform worse without subcategorization information (0.94 points less in *Bare* grammar) and better with subcategorization information (2.39 points more in *SynF* and *SynF+Cat*).

From a general point of view, accuracy metrics show a medium-high accuracy performance of all versions of FDGs in both languages. Specifically, these first results highlight that subcategorization information helps with the syntactic function labelling. However, qualitative results will reveal how subcategorization influences the grammar performance (Sections 5.5 and 5.6).

5.5 Precision results

As observed in the quantitative analysis (Section 5.4), in both languages most of the syntactic function assignments drop in precision when subcategorization classes are blocked in the grammar (Tables 8 and 9), whereas syntactic function labelling tends to improve when subcategorization is available.

For example, the precision of the prepositional object (*pobj*) in both languages drops drastically when subcategorization is disabled (*Bare*). On the contrary, the precision improves significantly when the rules include subcategorization information (*Baseline*). Furthermore, the introduction of more fine-grained frames helps the grammars reach a precision of 94.74% in Spanish and 94.12% in Catalan (*SynF* and *SynF+Cat*). Figure 4 shows this dichotomy.

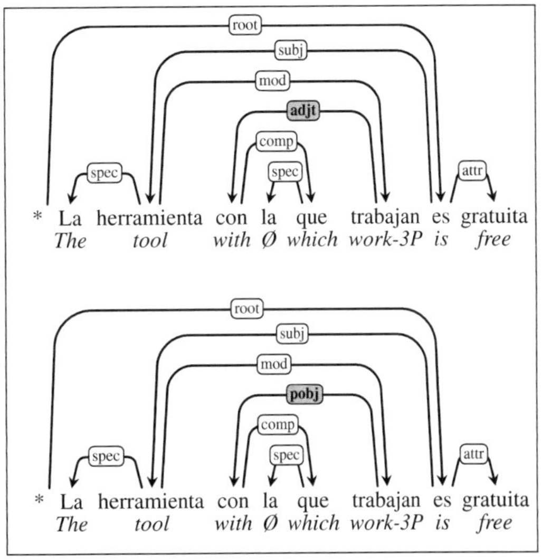

Figure 4: Example of *bare* FDGs wrongly labelling a *pobj* as *adjt* (above) and of *SynF* FDGs correctly labelling it (below)

Tag	Bare	Baseline	SynF	SynF+Cat
adjt	59.26	70.27	61.54	61.54
attr	84.21	71.43	71.43	71.43
dobj	78.26	85.71	87.80	87.80
iobj	100.00	100.00	100.00	100.00
pobj	42.50	77.27	94.74	94.74
pred	12.50	0.00	33.33	33.33
subj	90.24	90.91	91.11	91.11

Table 8: Labelling precision scores (%) in Spanish

Despite these improvements, some items differ from the general tendency.

In Spanish, the improvement of the copulative verbs (*attr*) is due to lexical information in the *Bare* FDG, while they keep stable in *SynF* and *SynF+Cat*. Precision remains the same in the indirect object (*iobj*) because morphological information is enough to detect dative clitics in singular.

The performance of predicative (*pred*) in all the grammars is related to the lack or addition of subcategorization. The *Baseline* FDG subcategorization classes do not include the same set of verbs as in the evaluation data. For this reason, a generic rule for capturing predicatives (*Bare* FDG) covers the lack of verbs in a few cases. The improvement of the coverage with new verbs (*SynF* and *SynF+Cat*) shows an increment of the precision.

Adjunct (*adjt*) recognition drops for mislabellings with predicative because of the ambiguity between the participle clause expressing time and a true predicative complement.

Tag	Bare	Baseline	SynF	SynF+Cat
adjt	60.71	61.76	62.50	62.50
attr	95.65	82.14	95.83	95.83
dobj	75.00	83.33	84.78	82.98
iobj	100.00	100.00	100.00	100.00
pobj	61.29	66.67	94.12	94.12
pred	50.00	0.00	100.00	100.00
subj	72.50	71.43	73.81	73.81

Table 9: Labelling precision scores (%) in Catalan

FDGs in Catalan show a parallel behaviour to that in Spanish, but they follow the general tendency in more cases. *SynF* and *SynF+Cat* increase the precision in all the cases, except for the direct object (*dobj*) in *SynF+Cat*. Once more the prepositional object (*pobj*) performance raises when subcategorization frames are available.

Although a drop in all the cases in the *Bare* FDG is expected, the attribute (*attr*) and the predicative (*pred*) increase the precision because of the same reasons as the Spanish grammars.

The results of *SynF* and *SynF+Cat* are almost identical. The analysis of their outputs shows that more fine-grained subcategorization classes including grammatical categories do not have a contribution to the precision improvement.

5.6 Recall results

The addition of subcategorization information in the FDGs also contributes to the improvement, almost in all the cases, in Spanish as well as in Catalan (Tables 10 and 11). The use of FDGs without subcategorization involves a decrease in the recall most of times.

In Spanish, the *Baseline* grammar contains very generic rules to capture adjuncts and more fine-grained subcategorization classes restrict these rules. For this reason, the recall slightly drops in *SynF* and *SynF+Cat*. As observed in the precision metric (Section 5.5), small populated classes related to predicative arguments make recall drop in the baseline. Consequently, generic rules for predicative labelling in the *Bare* grammar and better populated predicative classes in *SynF* and *SynF+Cat* allows a recovery in recall.

FDGs in Catalan show a similar tendency. In the *Bare* grammar, prepositional objects and predicatives are better captured than in the baseline because the lack of subcategorization information allows rules to apply in a more irrestrictive way. On the other hand, the addition of subcategorization information does not seem to help with capturing

Tag	Bare	Baseline	SynF	SynF+Cat
adjt	57.14	92.86	85.71	85.71
attr	80.00	100.00	100.00	100.00
dobj	83.72	83.72	83.72	83.72
iobj	33.33	33.33	44.44	44.44
pobj	85.00	85.00	90.00	90.00
pred	33.33	0.00	33.33	33.33
subj	75.51	81.63	83.67	83.67

Table 10: Labelling recall scores (%) in Spanish

Tag	Bare	Baseline	SynF	SynF+Cat
adjt	50.00	61.76	73.53	73.53
attr	84.62	88.46	88.46	88.46
dobj	72.00	80.00	78.00	78.00
iobj	33.33	33.33	33.33	33.33
pobj	76.00	56.00	64.00	64.00
pred	100.00	0.00	100.00	100.00
subj	70.73	73.17	75.61	75.61

Table 11: Labelling recall scores (%) in Catalan

more direct objects. Lower results are due to some verbs missing.

Once again there are no significant differences between *SynF* and *SynF+Cat*, which reinforces the idea that grammatical categories do not provide new information for capturing new argument and adjuncts.

5.7 Analysis of the results

The whole set of experiments demonstrate that subcategorization improves significantly the performance of the rule-based FDGs.

However, some arguments, such as the prepositional object and the predicative, are difficult to capture without subcategorization information. Meanwhile, there are others, such as the attribute, that do not need to be handled with subcategorization classes.

Proper subcategorization information also contributes to capture more arguments and adjuncts. The recall scores are stable among the grammars that use subcategorization information. Secondly, most of these scores are medium-high precision.

Overall, the results show that the new CompLex-VS is a suitable resource to improve the performance of rule-based dependency grammars.

The classification of frames proposed is coherent with the methodology. Furhtermore, it is an essential resource for the grammars tested since it ensures medium-high precision results (compared to medium precision results in the FDGs using the old CompLex-VS). It is important to consider the kind of information to define the subcategorization classes because it can be redundant, such as the combination of syntactic function and grammatical category.

The CompLex-VS lexicon still needs the inclusion of new verbs, since some arguments for verbs missing in the lexicon are not captured properly.

6 Conclusions

This paper presented two rule-based dependency grammars in Spanish and Catalan for the FreeLing NLP library.

Besides the grammars, a new subcategorization lexicon, CompLex-VS, has been designed using frames acquired from the SenSem Corpus. The new frames have been integrated in the argument/adjunct recognition rules of the FDGs.

A set of experiments has been carried out to test how the subcategorization information improves the performance of these grammars.

The results show that subcategorization frames ensure a high accuracy performance. In most cases, the old CompLex-VS frames and the new CompLex-VS frames show an improvement.

However, the increment is more evident in some arguments –such as the prepositional object and the predicative– than others, like the complement in attributive verbs. These results indicate that some arguments necessarily need subcategorization information to be disambiguated, while others can be disambiguated just with syntactic information.

Furthermore, the new frames of CompLex-VS provide better results than the initial ones. Therefore, more fine-grained frames (CompLex-SynF) contribute to raise the accuracy. Despite this evidence, fine-grained classes do not necessarily mean improvement of the parser performance. The most fine-grained lexicon (CompLex-SynF+Cat), which combines syntactic function and grammatical category information, neither improves nor worsens the results of the FDGs.

These conclusions are built on a small set of test data. Although it is a controlled and representative evaluation data set, these results need to be contrasted with a larger evaluation data set.

It would be interesting to evaluate how the parsing performance improves while subcategorization information is added incrementally.

Acknowledgments

This research arises from the research project SKATeR (Spanish Ministry of Economy and Competitiveness, TIN2012-38584-C06-06 and TIN2012-38584-C06-01).

References

L. Alonso, I. Castellón, and N. Tincheva. 2007. Obtaining coarse-grained classes of subcategorization patterns for Spanish. In *Proceedings of the International Conference Recent Advances in Natural Language Processing*.

À. Alsina, T. Badia, G. Boleda, S. Bott, À. Gil, M. Quixal, and O. Valentn. 2002. CATCG: Un sistema de análisis morfosintáctico para el catalán. *Procesamiento del Lenguaje Natural*, 29.

J. Aparicio, M. Taulé, and M.A. Martí. 2008. AnCora-Verb: A Lexical Resource for the Semantic Annotation of Corpora. In *Proceedings of the Sixth International Conference on Language Resources and Evaluation*.

J. Atserias, E. Comelles, and A. Mayor. 2005. TXALA un analizador libre de dependencias para el castellano. *Procesamiento del Lenguaje Natural*, 35.

M. Ballesteros and J. Nivre. 2012. MaltOptimizer: A System for MaltParser Optimization. In *Proceedings of the Eight International Conference on Language Resources and Evaluation*.

E. Bick. 2006. A Constraint Grammar-Based Parser for Spanish. In *Proceedings of TIL 2006 - 4th Workshop on Information and Human Language Technology*.

M.R. Brent. 1993. From Grammar to Lexicon: Unsupervised Learning of Lexical Syntax. *Computational Linguistics*, 19(2).

H. Calvo and A. Gelbukh. 2011. *DILUCT: Análisis Sintáctico Semisupervisado Para El Español*. Editorial Academica Espanola.

X. Carreras, M. Surdeanu, and L. Màrquez. 2006. Projective Dependency Parsing with Perceptron. In *Proceedings of the Tenth Conference on Computational Natural Language Learning*.

X. Carreras. 2007. Experiments with a Higher-Order Projective Dependency Parser. In *Proceedings of the CoNLL Shared Task Session of EMNLP-CoNLL 2007*.

J. Carroll, G. Minnen, and T. Briscoe. 1998. Can Subcategorisation Probabilities Help a Statistical Parser? In *Proceedings of the 6th ACL/SIGDAT Workshop on Very Large Corpora*.

N. Chomsky. 1965. *Aspects of the Theory of Syntax*. MIT Press.

M. Civit. 2003. Criterios de etiquetación y desambiguación morfosintáctica de corpus en español. In *Colección de Monografías de la Sociedad Española para el Procesamiento del Lenguaje Natural: 8*. Sociedad Española para el Procesamiento del Lenguaje Natural.

M. Collins and T. Koo. 2005. Discriminative Reranking for Natural Language Parsing. *Computational Linguistics*, 31(1).

A. Fernández and G. Vàzquez. 2014. The SenSem Corpus: an annotated corpus for Spanish and Catalan with information about aspectuality, modality, polarity and factuality. *Corpus Linguistics and Linguistic Theory*, 10(2).

A. Fernández, G. Vazquez, P. Saint-Dizier, F. Benamara, and M. Kamel. 2002. The VOLEM Project: A Framework for the Construction of Advanced Multilingual Lexicons. In *Proceedings of the Language Engineering Conference*.

A. Ferrández and L. Moreno. 2000. Slot Unification Grammar and Anaphora Resolution. In N. Nicolov and R. Mitkov, editors, *Recent Advances in Natural Language Processing II. Selected papers from RANLP 1997*. John Benjamins Publishing Co.

T. Järvinen and P. Tapanainen. 1998. Towards an implementable dependency grammar. In *Proceedings of Workshop on Processing of Dependence-Based Grammars, CoLing-ACL'98*.

D. Klein and C.D. Manning. 2003. Accurate Unlexicalized Parsing. In *Proceedings of the 41st Annual Meeting on Association for Computational Linguistics - Volume 1*.

A. Korhonen, Y. Krymolowski, and Z. Marx. 2003. Clustering Polysemic Subcategorization Frame Distributions Semantically. In *Proceedings of the 41st Annual Meeting of the Association for Computational Linguistics*.

D. Lin. 1998. Dependency-Based Evaluation of MINIPAR. In *Workshop on the Evaluation of Parsing Systems, First International Conference on Language Resources and Evaluation*.

M. Lloberes, I. Castellón, and L. Padró. 2010. Spanish FreeLing Dependency Grammar. In *Proceedings of the Seventh Conference on International Language Resources and Evaluation*.

M. Lloberes, I. Castellón, L. Padró, and E. Gonzàlez. 2014. ParTes. Test Suite for Parsing Evaluation. *Procesamiento del Lenguaje Natural*, 53.

C.D. Manning. 1993. Automatic Acquisition of a Large Subcategorization Dictionary from Corpora. In *Proceedings of the 31st Annual Meeting of the Association for Computational Linguistics*.

M. Marimon, N. Bel, and L. Padró. 2014. Automatic Selection of HPSG-parsed Sentences for Treebank Construction. *Computational Linguistics*, 40(3).

I.A. Mel'čuk. 1988. *Dependency Syntax: Theory and Practice*. State U. Press of NY.

S.A. Mirroshandel, A. Nasr, and B. Sagot. 2013. Enforcing Subcategorization Constraints in a Parser Using Sub-parses Recombining. In *NAACL 2013 - Conference of the North American Chapter of the Association for Computational Linguistics*.

J. Nivre, J. Hall, J. Nilsson, G. Eryiğit, and S. Marinov. 2006. Labeled Pseudo-projective Dependency Parsing with Support Vector Machines. In *Proceedings of the Tenth Conference on Computational Natural Language Learning*.

J. Nivre, J. Hall, S. Kübler, R. McDonald, J. Nilsson, S. Riedel, and D. Yuret. 2007. The CoNLL 2007 Shared Task on Dependency Parsing. In *Proceedings of the CoNLL Shared Task Session of EMNLP-CoNLL 2007*.

R. O'Donovan, M. Burke, A. Cahill, J. Van Genabith, and A. Way. 2005. Large-Scale Induction and Evaluation of Lexical Resources from the Penn-II and Penn-III Treebanks. *Computational Linguistics*, 31(3).

L. Padró and E. Stanilovsky. 2012. Freeling 3.0: Towards wider multilinguality. In *Proceedings of the Eight International Conference on Language Resources and Evaluation*.

A. Sarkar and D. Zeman. 2000. Automatic Extraction of Subcategorization Frames for Czech. In *Proceedings of the 18th Conference on Computational Linguistics - Volume 2*.

D. Sleator and D. Temperley. 1991. Parsing English with a Link Grammar. In *Third International Workshop on Parsing Technologies*.

L. Tesnière. 1959. *Eléments de syntaxe structurale*. Klincksieck.

D. Zeman. 2002. Can Subcategorization Help a Statistical Dependency Parser? In *19th International Conference on Computational Linguistics*.

Towards Universal Web Parsebanks

Juhani Luotolahti[1], **Jenna Kanerva**[1,2], **Veronika Laippala**[3,4]
Sampo Pyysalo[1], **Filip Ginter**[1]
[1]Department of Information Technology
[2]University of Turku Graduate School (UTUGS)
[3] Turku Institute for Advanced Studies, University of Turku, Finland
[4] School of Languages and Translation Studies, University of Turku, Finland
University of Turku, Finland
first.last@utu.fi

Abstract

Recently, there has been great interest both in the development of cross-linguistically applicable annotation schemes and in the application of syntactic parsers at web scale to create parsebanks of online texts. The combination of these two trends to create massive, consistently annotated parsebanks in many languages holds enormous potential for the quantitative study of many linguistic phenomena, but these opportunities have been only partially realized in previous work. In this work, we take a key step toward universal web parsebanks through a single-language case study introducing the first retrainable parser applied to the Universal Dependencies representation and its application to create a Finnish web-scale parsebank. We further integrate this data into an online dependency search system and demonstrate its applicability by showing linguistically motivated search examples and by using the dependency syntax information to analyze the language of the web corpus. We conclude with a discussion of the requirements of extending from this case study on Finnish to create consistently annotated web-scale parsebanks for a large number of languages.

1 Introduction

The enormous potential of the web as a source of material for linguistic research in a wide range of areas is well established (Kilgarriff and Grefenstette, 2003), with many new opportunities created by web-scale resources ranging from simple N-grams (Brants and Franz, 2006) to syntactically analyzed text (Goldberg and Orwant, 2013). Yet, while the use of multilingual web data to support linguistic research is well recognized (Way and Gough, 2003), cross-linguistic efforts involving syntax have so far been hampered by the lack of consistent annotation schemata and difficulties relating to coincidental differences in the syntactic analyses produced by parsers for different languages (Nivre, 2015).

The Universal Dependencies (UD) project[1] seeks to define annotation schemata and guidelines that apply consistently across languages, standardizing e.g. part-of-speech tags, morphological feature sets, dependency relation types, and structural aspects of dependency graphs. The project further aims to create dependency treebanks following these guidelines for many languages. The effort builds on many recently proposed approaches, including Google universal part-of-speech tags (Petrov et al., 2012), the Interset inventory of morphological features (Zeman, 2010) and Universal Stanford Dependencies (de Marneffe et al., 2014), and previously released datasets such as the universal dependency treebanks (McDonald et al., 2013). The first version of UD data, released in early 2015, contains annotations for 10 languages: Czech, English, Finnish, French, German, Hungarian, Irish, Italian, Spanish, and Swedish.

The availability of the UD corpora creates a wealth of new opportunities for the cross-linguistic study of morphology and dependency syntax, which are only now beginning to be explored. One particularly exiting avenue for research involves the combination of these annotated resources with fully retrainable parsers and web-scale texts to create massive, consistently annotated parsebanks for many languages. In this study, we take the first steps toward realizing these opportunities by producing a UD parsebank of Finnish comprising well over 3 billion tokens, and combining it with a scalable query system and web

[1]http://universaldependencies.github.io/docs/

Proceedings of the Third International Conference on Dependency Linguistics (Depling 2015), pages 211–220,
Uppsala, Sweden, August 24–26 2015.

interface, thus building a large-scale corpus and pairing it with the tools necessary for its efficient use. Using real-world examples, we show how the large web corpus with the syntactic annotation can be used for gathering data on rare phenomena in linguistic research.

For linguistic research web corpora, containing broad scope of text, are well suited for the search of rare linguistics constructs as well as those which do not often appear on official text, such as the use of colloquial terms and structures. Other motivations beyond linguistic research for large web-corpora alone are found in natural language processing, for example in language modeling which has uses in many areas such as information extraction and machine translation(Kilgarriff and Grefenstette, 2003).

We finish with a discussion of how to generalize our effort from one language to many, arguing that the framework and tools introduced as one of the primary contributions of this study present many opportunities and can meet the challenges for creating web parsebanks all for all existing UD treebanks.

2 Data

We next briefly introduce the manually annotated corpus used to train the machine learning-based components of our processing pipeline and the sources of unannotated data for creating the web parsebank.

2.1 Annotated data

For training the machine learning methods that form the core of the text segmentation, morphological analysis, and syntactic analysis stages of the parser, we use the Universal Dependencies (UD) release 1.0 Finnish corpus (Nivre et al., 2015). This corpus was created by converting the annotations of the Turku Dependency Treebank (TDT) corpus (Haverinen et al., 2014) from its original Stanford Dependencies (SD) scheme into the UD scheme using a combination of automatically implemented mapping heuristics and manual revisions. TDT consists of documents from 10 different domains, ranging from legal texts and EU parliamentary proceedings, through Wikipedia and online news to student magazine texts and blogs. In total, the UD Finnish data consists of 202,085 tokens in 15,136 sentences, making it a mid-sized corpus among the ten UD release 1 corpora, which range in size from 24,000 tokens (Irish) (Lynn et al., 2014) to over 1,5 million tokens (Czech) (Bejček et al., 2012).

2.2 Unannotated data

We use two web-scale sources of unannotated text data: the openly accessible Common Crawl dataset,[2] and data produced by our own large-scale web-crawl, introduced in Section 3.1. Common Crawl is a non-profit organization dedicated to producing a freely available reference web crawl dataset of the same name. As of this writing, the Common Crawl consists of several petabytes (10^{15}) of data collected over a span of 7 years, available through the Amazon web services Public Data Sets program.[3]

While web datasets such as the Common Crawl represent enormous opportunities for linguistic efforts, it should be noted that are many known challenges to extracting clean text consisting of sentences with usable syntactic structure from such data. For one, text content must primarily be extracted from HTML documents, and thus contains many lists, menus and other similar elements not (necessarily) relevant to syntactic analysis. Indeed, such text not consisting of parseable sentences represents the majority of all available text (see Section 4.1), necessitating a filtering step. Another major issue is the large prevalence of duplicate content due to advertisements often appearing on many domains, many sites hosting copied content, such as the contents of the Wikipedia, in order to generate traffic and search engine hits, and sites such as web forums containing many URLs with overlapping content (e.g. URLs which highlight a specific comment of the thread). We discuss the ways in which we address these issues in the following section.

3 Methods

In the following, we present the primary processing stages for building the parsebank, summarized in Figure 1, and the search system used to query the completed parsebank.

3.1 Dedicated web crawl

The currently existing non-UD Finnish Internet parsebank (Kanerva et al., 2014) is based on texts

[2] `http://commoncrawl.org/`

[3] `http://aws.amazon.com/public-data-sets/`

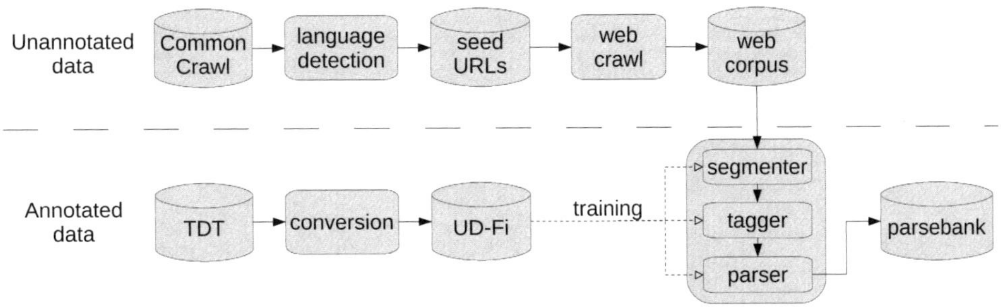

Figure 1: Processing stages. Seed URLs are first selected from Common Crawl data using language detection, and a web crawl is then performed using these seeds to identify an unannotated web corpus. To train the text segmentation, morphological tagging, and parsing stages of the analysis pipeline, UD Finnish data created by semiautomatic conversion of Turku Dependency Treebank is used. The final web parsebank is then created by applying the trained analysis pipeline on the unannotated web corpus.

extracted from the 2012 release of the Common Crawl dataset using the Compact Language Detector.[4] This 1.5 billion token corpus was assembled from approximately 4 million URLs. However, as this dataset based solely on Common Crawl data fell somewhat short of our target corpus size, we expand it as part of this study with a dedicated crawl targeting Finnish.

To seed the crawl, we obtained all public domains registered in the Finnish top level domain (`.fi`) and extracted all the URLs from the current Common Crawl-based Finnish Internet parsebank. This allows us to reach as wide a scope as possible, going beyond the Finnish top-level domain. Following the identification of the seed URLs, the final web corpus data used to build the parsebank was crawled using the open source web crawler SpiderLing (Suchomel and Pomikálek, 2012). SpiderLing is designed for collecting unilingual text corpora from the web. During the crawl, the language of each downloaded page is recognized to maintain the language focus of the crawl. The language recognition, a built-in feature of the crawler, is based on character trigrams. Similarly, the character encoding of the content is heuristically determined during the processing, and allows the content to be encoded into the standard UTF-8 encoding when storing the data for further processing.

Supporting a focus on text-rich pages, SpiderLing also keeps track of the text yield of each domain, defined as the amount of text gathered from a domain divided by the amount of bytes downloaded, and prioritizes domains from which can be obtained more usable data in less time. The crawler also makes an effort to gather only text content from the web, avoiding downloading other content such as images, javascript, etc. Further, to extract clean text consisting of sentences, as opposed to lists, menus and the like, the crawler automatically performs boilerplate removal, using the `justText` library. The usable text detection is based on various metrics such as the frequency of stop words in a given paragraph, link density, and the presence of HTML-tags. (Text deemed as boilerplate is ignored when calculating the yield.)

The crawl was performed on a single server-grade Linux computer in a series of bursts between the summer and winter of 2014, taking approximately 88 days. The crawl speed settings were kept very conservative to prevent causing false alarms to Internet security authorities. The text data from the old corpus will be merged in the corpus, but for now the result of this crawl is the source for all text in this version of the web corpus.

3.2 Text segmentation

For the segmentation of raw text into sentences and then further into tokens, we apply the machine-learning based sentence splitter and tokenizer from the Apache OpenNLP toolkit[5]. Both the sentence splitter and the tokenizer are retrainable maximum entropy-based systems, and we trained new models for both based on the data from the UD Finnish corpus.

[4] `https://code.google.com/p/cld2/`

[5] `https://opennlp.apache.org/`

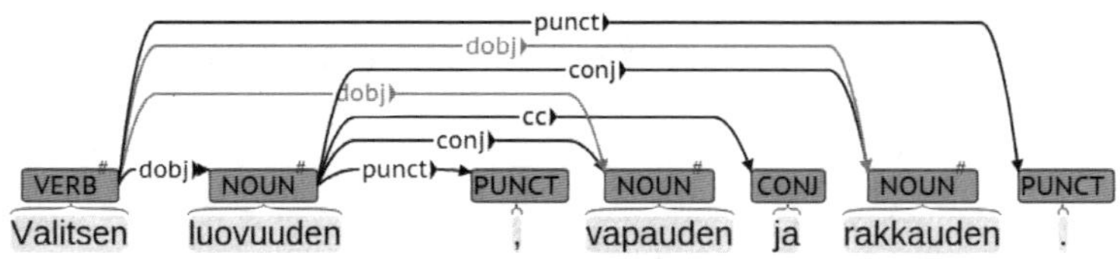

Figure 2: An example UD analysis of a Finnish sentence *Valitsen luovuuden, vapauden ja rakkauden* "I_choose creativity, freedom, and love." Extended dependencies produced by propagating the object dependency into the coordinated constituents are shown in gray. Figure created using BRAT (Stenetorp et al., 2012).

3.3 Morphological tagging

To assign the part-of-speech tags and the morphological features to words, we apply the Conditional Random Fields (CRF)-based tagger Marmot (Mueller et al., 2013), deriving lemmas and supplementing the feature set of the retrainable tagger with information derived from a pipeline combining the finite-state morphological analyzer OMorFi (Pirinen, 2011) with previously introduced heuristic rules for mapping its tags and features into UD (Pyysalo et al., 2015).

Our previous evaluation of the morphological analysis components on the UD Finnish data indicated that the best-performing combination of information derived from the finite-state analysis and the machine learning system allowed POS tags to be assigned with an accuracy of 97.0%, POS tags and the full feature representation with an accuracy of 94.0%, and the complete morphological analysis, including the lemma, with an accuracy of 90.7% (Pyysalo et al., 2015). This level of performance represents the state of the art for the analysis for Finnish and is broadly comparable to the state-of-the-art results for these tasks in other languages.

3.4 Syntactic analysis

The dependency parsing is carried out using the graph-based parser of Bohnet et al. (2010) from the Mate tools package, trained on the UD Finnish data. The parser has previously been evaluated on the test section of the TDT corpus, achieving 81.4% LAS (labeled attachment score). This approaches the best test score of 83.1% LAS reported in the study of Bohnet et al. (2013) using a parser that carries out tagging and dependency parsing jointly.[6] However, at approximately 10ms per sentence, the graph-based parser is an order of magnitude faster than the more accurate joint tagger and parser, which is a deciding factor when parsing billions of tokens of text. When re-training the graph-based parser on the UD scheme annotations, it achieved a LAS of 82.1% on the UD Finnish test set, showing that the parsing performance is not in any way degraded compared to that for the original SD scheme of the treebank.

In addition to the *basic* layer of dependencies, which constitutes dependencies that form a tree structure, the parsing pipeline also predicts the UD Finnish *extended* layer dependencies, modeled after the conjunction propagation and external subject prediction in the original SD scheme (de Marneffe and Manning, 2008). This layer anticipates the introduction of such an extended layer into the UD scheme, which allows additional, non-tree dependencies in terms of its format but only presently provides guidelines for the *basic* layer. The extended layer prediction is based on the method of Nyblom et al. (2013), originally developed on the TDT corpus SD scheme, re-trained and adapted for the current study to conform to the UD scheme. An example parse with extended layer dependencies is shown in Figure 2.

3.5 Parsebank search

A parsebank of the billion token magnitude is only useful if it can be efficiently queried, especially taking advantage of the syntactic structures, i.e. using queries which would be difficult or impossible to express in terms of the linear order of the words. We have therefore previously developed a scalable syntactic structure query system which can be applied at this scale and allows rich syntactic structure queries referring to both the basic

[6] Note that results are for the original SD annotation of the TDT corpus. While the UD Finnish treebank is created from this data (primarily) by deterministic conversion, the results are thus not fully comparable with results for the UD Finnish corpus.

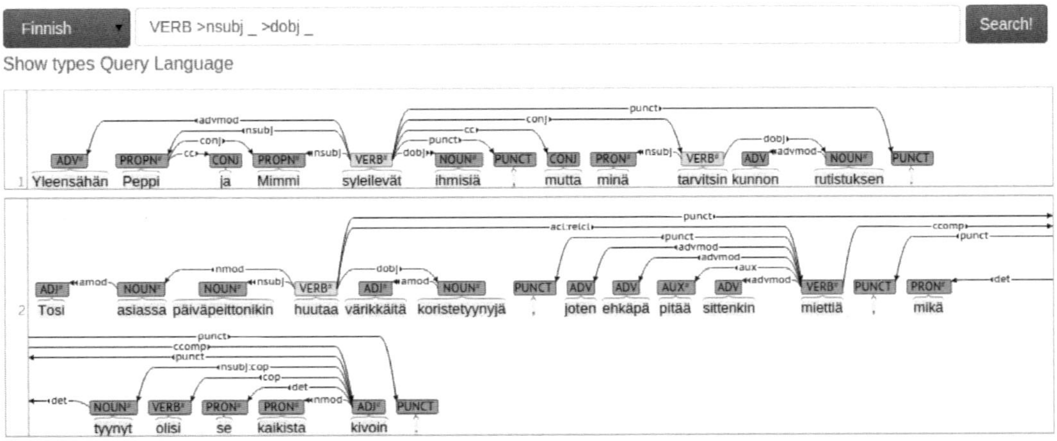

Figure 3: A screenshot of the online query interface, showing a simple query for transitive verbs.

and the extended layers of the analysis (Luotolahti et al., 2015). This detailed corpus search enables fast and easy retrieval of material for many linguistic questions that otherwise would require manual work to address.

The query system allows search for any arbitrary subtree structure, including arbitrarily nested negations. For instance, one can search for verbs which have their subject in the partitive case, unless that subject has a numeral modifier, and unless the verb is governed by the clausal complement relation. In addition to the constraints on the syntactic structure, any combination of normal and negated constraints on the morphology of the words is possible. The full description of the query system capabilities is, however, out of scope of this paper, and we refer the interested reader to the online documentation [7]. In addition to a scriptable, command-line utility meant for gathering data for further processing, the query system also has an online interface which allows the results to be visualized and inspected in real time (Figure 3).

In Section 5 we will demonstrate several real use-cases where this query system was used to obtain material for linguistic research from the parsebank.

4 Results

We next briefly present the primary quantitative results of our study, the web corpus created as the result of our custom crawl, the performance characteristics of our newly trained parsing pipeline,

Item	Number
All tokens	3,662,727,698
Lemma count	28,585,422
Sentence count	275,690,022
Unique token count	39,688,642
Unique sentence count	178,547,962
Tokens without duplicates	2,554,094,599

Table 1: Web corpus statistics.

Item	Number
All tokens	94,528,120
Lemma count	1,532,485
Sentence count	8,477,560
Unique token count	3,067,151
Unique sentence count	7,252,240
Tokens without duplicates	87,772,532

Table 2: News data statistics.

and some statistical characteristics of the web corpus. For reference, we contrast the web corpus to the *news* section of the Finnish Text Collection (*Suomen kielen tekstikokoelma*) corpus[8], below referred to as the news corpus, as these news domain texts are a typical representative of a conventional corpus used for linguistic research.

4.1 Web crawl results

The web crawl retrieved in total 1.6 terabytes of HTML pages over the 88 days it was run. From this HTML data, 170 gigabytes of plain prose text was extracted, excluding markup and boilerplate content such as menus. This body of text still con-

[7] http://bionlp.utu.fi/searchexpressions-new.html

[8] http://urn.fi/urn:nbn:fi:lb-201403268

tained a significant amount of duplication, which was eliminated on the document level in order to preserve the document context of the sentences in the parsebank. The deduplication process determined a document as a duplicate if more than 90% of its sentences were seen earlier during a sweep through the data. Following this deduplication process, the resulting final web corpus is 33 gigabytes in size, i.e. only approximately 2% of the total data downloaded by the crawler. The basic statistics of the resulting corpus are given in Table 1, and corresponding statistics for the news corpus are presented in Table 2. We note that the web corpus is an order of magnitude or more larger that the extensive newswire corpus by any metric, most notably containing nearly 40 times the number of tokens of the conventional dataset.

4.2 Parsing accuracy and speed

The syntactic parsing pipeline has previously only been evaluated on the test set of the UD Finnish dataset, which closely reflects the distribution of the training data in terms of topics, genres and styles of writing. On this test set, the parser achieved 82.1% LAS on the basic UD dependencies. To evaluate how well the parser generalizes to out-of-domain web data, we selected a random 100 sentences from the parsebank and manually annotated them for UD syntax (both basic and extended layers). In the process, we discarded two incomprehensible sentences, most likely produced by a machine translation system, for which it was not possible to arrive at a reasonable gold standard tree. We were then left with 98 sentences comprising 1,191 tokens. On this sample, the LAS of the parsing pipeline is 78.1% when we take the extended layer into account (a token is counted as correct if it is correctly attached in both the basic and extended layers), and 78.8% for the basic layer only. This about 3% point drop (from 82.1% to 78.8% LAS on UD basic layer) is quite acceptable considering that the parser has not been adapted to the general web text domain in any way. Dependency parsing errors of an earlier iteration of the same parsing-pipeline for Finnish using very related SD-scheme are analyzed in-depth by Haverinen et al.(2011).

The parsing was carried out on a cluster computer comprising thousands of compute nodes, and took approximately 8,000 CPU core hours (roughly one CPU-year), which due to the highly parallel nature of the process was completed in a little over one day. While parsing is the most computationally demanding component of the overall process of creating the parsebank, it is thus not likely to be a bottleneck for real-time work in generalizing to other languages, even if web corpora of an order of magnitude larger were considered.

4.3 Web corpus characteristics

In corpus linguistics, a standard method to provide an overview of corpus contents is offered by *keyword analysis* (Scott and Tribble, 2006). Describing statistically the most typical words of the studied corpus in relation to a reference one, keywords are typically informative on the corpus theme and style. Table 3 presents keywords extracted from the entire web corpus together with those for the news corpus used for reference. The keywords are calculated using the most significant text class features assigned to the two corpora by a linear classifier trained to distinguish short segments of the two corpora.[9] The classifier is trained using the stochastic gradient method, with a 50/50 split on testing and training data, using labeled text segments five sentences long.

The keywords presented are based on the 50 most significant tokens for the parsebank and 30 for the News corpus. Individual characters and figures are excluded from the table. As can be seen from the number of keywords presented, this is already revealing: numbers and individual characters are clearly more frequent features in the parsebank than in the news text. The actual keywords listed reflect the characteristic topics in the two corpora. The parsebank keywords include terms related to online stores, TV shows and social media. In particular the emoticon is a typical example of computer-mediated text. The news corpora keywords, in contrast, are mainly composed of the names of Finnish towns, political parties and news agencies. An interesting detail is the apparition of the former Finnish currency (*markka*, used until 2001) on the list. This is explained by the fact that the new corpus dates from the 1990s; in the more recent Finnish Internet parsebank, this old form of currency is obviously referred to considerably less frequently.

[9] Implemented using the Vowpal Wabbit machine learning package (Agarwal et al., 2014)

Parsebank keywords
euroa, lue, sosiaali-, ;), vs, tuotantokausi, työ, yms, 1990-luvun, eurolla, kommentit, kommenttia, tiivistelmä, voit, blogissa, blogi
Parsebank keywords in English
euros, read, social-. ;), vs, season (as in TV shows), work, etc, of-the-1990s, with-a-euro, comments, a-comment, summary, you-can, in-a-blog. a-blog
News Corpus keywords
karjalaisen, aamulehden, luvulla, kosovon, reuters, lieksan, tv, hhh, markalla, pohjois-karjalassa, ws, lehtikuva, n., demarin, pohjois-karjalan, joensuussa, joensuu, markan, joensuun, markkaa, demari, stt
News Corpus keywords in English
from-carelia (Finnish region), of-aamulehti (newspaper), with-the-figure, of-kosovo, reuters, of-lieksa (town), tv, hhh, with-a-mark, in-northern-carelia, ws, lehtikuva (Finland's leading photo agency), about (abbreviation), of-a-social-democrat (colloquial), of-northern-carelia, in-joensuu (town), joensuu, of-mark, of-joensuu, marks, social-democrat (colloquial), stt (abbreviation of a Finnish media outlet)

Table 3: Keywords of the parsebank texts in comparison with the news corpus.

5 Linguistic applications

We next illustrate the applicability of the web parsebank and the search system through three linguistically motivated applications based on real-world use-cases.

Web corpora with dependency syntax analyses can considerably speed-up the material collection in research of extremely rare phenomena, here exemplified by Finnish transitive sentences with a partitive subject (Huumo, 2015). Being unnormative, they cannot be easily found from edited or professionally written texts, which also makes web-crawled data a very convenient source for these constructions. In addition, gathering these examples from large corpora without the support of syntactic analyses would be extremely time-consuming. Unfortunately, the rarity of the construction also causes problems in the accuracy of their syntactic analysis. For instance, the parser training data does not have even a single example, and the parser thus tends to make errors in the analysis of this construction, often swapping the subject and the object of the verb (in Finnish, both the subject and the object can take the partitive case). In practice, when listing a random sample of candidate occurrences for manual inspection, the vast majority of these will be incorrect. Nevertheless, even though correct instances are rare in the parsebank, the speed-up in gathering real examples is enormous, considering the alternatives. To illustrate this, we consider the verb *seurata* "to follow" which is theoretized to be especially susceptible for this use. In a sample of 4 million sentences, we find 7,875 transitive occurrences of the verb, of which 111 have their subject in the partitive case, and of these 13 are correct. While this fraction is small, manually inspecting the roughly 100 occurrences took little effort and resulted in real examples being found from among a large number of occurrences of the verb.

Query	Results
koska "because" + no verb	22598
koska "because" + verb	505514

Table 4: Example queries and their results.

Conjunction	Occurrences
ja "and"	738372
mutta "but"	533683
eli "or", "in other words"	153180
tai "or"	110639
vaan "but"	9908
mut / "but" (colloquial)	25057
Total	1671041

Table 5: Sentence-initial conjunction frequencies.

Another example of a construction for which a web-based, syntactically analyzed corpus is very convenient is the new usage of the Finnish subordinating conjunction *koska* "because" (Sinnemaa, 2014; Rehn, 2014). Normatively, a subordinating conjunction should be used in an subordinate clause with a finite verb, attached to the main clause, *I ate because I was hungry*. However, Finnish has recently seen a construction where the subordinate clause is left without the finite verb, but the conjunction is still present, in particular in informal language varieties: *I ate because hungry*. Since this construction is relatively infrequent, traditional corpora without syntactic information can not be used to study the phenomenon. The syntactic analyses in the parsebank, however, enable the search for this exact construction. Table 4 shows the results of a search for *koska* "because" governed by a verb and governed by a noun. As can be seen, although the normative usage with a verb is much more frequent, the search retrieves also a useful number of occurrences where the conjunction is attached to a noun.

Finally, although the automatic analyses only concern syntax and morphology, they can also be used to retrieve material to study phenomena crossing the limits of individual sentences, such as semantic relations between text elements and discourse structure (Prasad et al., 2008; Laippala et al., 2015). As the search tool allows the restriction of the query to certain sentence elements, it can be delimited to sentence-initial elements, such as sentence-initial, individual conjunctions that instead of co-ordinating sentence-internal clauses or phrases refer to previous text elements and express relations between sentences and the discourse structure. This can provide useful information both on the frequency of different conjunctions used in this position and on discourse structure more in general. The distribution of the most frequently used conjunctions in this functions is presented in Table 5. The results conform to expectations, with *and* being the most frequent conjunction. The frequency of the colloquial form of *but* also illustrates the nature of the parsebank text.

6 Discussion

We have demonstrated the feasibility of creating a UD web parsebank at the scale of billions of words and making it searchable for complex syntactic patterns. However, our efforts in this study have a very obvious limitation, namely only involving a single language. To realize the full potential of web-scale parsebanks annotated using the cross-linguistically consistent UD scheme, this work must be extended to cover several languages, preferably at least the ten languages covered in the current, first release of UD data. We next briefly consider the technical requirements and computational costs of this extension.

First, the parsing pipeline applied here should be largely straightforwardly applicable to currently available UD languages. The core segmentation, morphological analysis, and dependency parsing components of the parser are all fully retrainable, and each implemented using approaches that achieve levels of performance broadly comparable with the state of the art for their respective tasks in the ten UD release 1 languages. A minor issue is the lack of finite-state morphological analyzers (comparable to OMorFi here) for many of the languages, but previous results suggest that the benefits of such a component may be modest for other UD languages, which are generally not as morphologically complex as Finnish (Bohnet et al., 2013). We anticipate that different strategies to tokenization will eventually become necessary to generalize the approach to languages written using systems that do not involve white-space token boundaries, such as Japanese and Chinese. However, no such language is included in the initial set of UD languages.

Second, the language considered in this case study, Finnish, is comparatively rare on the web compared to most of the UD languages. This can be considered both a positive and a negative for generalization to other languages. On the positive side, it is much easier to create corpora of comparable size (billions of tokens) for languages such as English, French, German and Spanish. Indeed, Common Crawl data will suffice, removing the need to extend the data with a custom crawl. However, it is considerably more challenging to create web corpora for such languages that would represent a substantial fraction of the web in that language, and even if such a web corpus were available, the computational cost of parsing it could become infeasible for the somewhat limited resources at our disposal. For these reasons, we will limit our near future efforts in creating the first set of universal web treebanks to similar scale as here for all considered languages (or smaller when not available for a language). We will also primarily rely on Common Crawl data, only performing additional crawls when this data fails to meet the target size for a language.

As there are no components in the processing pipeline that would scale more than linearly in their computational cost with respect to the number of sentences and we will not aim to substantially increase the size of any language-specific corpus over that created here, we expect the total computational cost of scaling from one language to ten to be simply an order of magnitude greater than that here. Thus, we estimate that the total computational cost of creating the first set of UD web parsebanks to be on the order of 100,000 CPU core hours. While this is a non-trivial cost, it is well within our resources.

7 Conclusions and future work

We have proposed to create universal web parsebanks, web-scale corpora in many languages that are automatically syntactically analyzed using the cross-linguistically consistent Universal Dependencies (UD) scheme. We have also taken a key step toward realizing this possibility in building a

UD Finnish parsebank as a case study. Seeding a web crawl from Common Crawl data, we created the largest Finnish Internet language web corpus of over 3 billion tokens, trained a state-of-the-art dependency parser on the manual UD Finnish corpus annotation, and applied the trained parser to produce the first UD parsebank. We then demonstrated the application of the parsebank to linguistically motivated tasks by integrating it into a scalable dependency corpus search system and supporting several real-world use cases focusing on the identification of relevant examples of rare phenomena.

In future work, we will extend this effort to cover all ten of the UD release 1.0 languages – Czech, English, Finnish, French, German, Hungarian, Irish, Italian, Spanish, and Swedish – to create the first set of cross-linguistically consistently annotated web treebanks, which will be made freely available under open licenses.

Acknowledgments

This work was supported by the Kone Foundation and the Emil Aaltonen Foundation. Computational resources were provided by CSC – IT Center for Science. Data from the Common Crawl foundation was used for web crawling.

References

Alekh Agarwal, Olivier Chapelle, Miroslav Dudi, and John Langford. 2014. A reliable effective terascale linear learning system. *JMLR*, 15:1111–1133.

Eduard Bejček, Jarmila Panevová, Jan Popelka, Pavel Straňák, Magda Ševčíková, Jan Štěpánek, and Zdeněk Žabokrtský. 2012. Prague dependency treebank 2.5 – a revisited version of pdt 2.0. In *Proceedings of the 24th International Conference on Computational Linguistics (Coling 2012)*, pages 231–246.

Bernd Bohnet, Joakim Nivre, Igor Boguslavsky, Richárd Farkas, Filip Ginter, and Jan Hajič. 2013. Joint morphological and syntactic analysis for richly inflected languages. *Transactions of the Association for Computational Linguistics*, 1:415–428.

Bernd Bohnet. 2010. Top accuracy and fast dependency parsing is not a contradiction. In *Proceedings of COLING'10*, pages 89–97.

Thorsten Brants and Alex Franz. 2006. Web 1T 5-gram Version 1. Linguistic Data Consortium. LDC2006T13.

Marie-Catherine de Marneffe and Christopher D Manning. 2008. Stanford typed dependencies manual. Technical report, Stanford University. http://nlp.stanford.edu/software/dependencies manual.pdf.

Marie-Catherine de Marneffe, Timothy Dozat, Natalia Silveira, Katri Haverinen, Filip Ginter, Joakim Nivre, and Christopher D Manning. 2014. Universal Stanford Dependencies: A cross-linguistic typology. In *Proceedings of the 9th International Conference on Language Resources and Evaluation (LREC)*, volume 14, pages 4585–4592.

Yoav Goldberg and Jon Orwant. 2013. A dataset of syntactic-ngrams over time from a very large corpus of english books. In *Second Joint Conference on Lexical and Computational Semantics (*SEM), Volume 1: Proceedings of the Main Conference and the Shared Task: Semantic Textual Similarity*, pages 241–247.

Katri Haverinen, Filip Ginter, Veronika Laippala, Samuel Kohonen, Timo Viljanen, Jenna Nyblom, and Tapio Salakoski. 2011. A dependency-based analysis of treebank annotation errors. In *Proceedings of International Conference on Dependency Linguistics (Depling'11), Barcelona, Spain*, pages 115–124.

Katri Haverinen, Jenna Nyblom, Timo Viljanen, Veronika Laippala, Samuel Kohonen, Anna Missilä, Stina Ojala, Tapio Salakoski, and Filip Ginter. 2014. Building the essential resources for Finnish: the Turku Dependency Treebank. *Language Resources and Evaluation*, 48(3):493–531.

Tuomas Huumo. 2015. The partitive A: On uses of the Finnish partitive subject in transitive clauses. In *Diachronic typology of differential argument marking*.

Jenna Kanerva, Juhani Luotolahti, Veronika Laippala, and Filip Ginter. 2014. Syntactic n-gram collection from a large-scale corpus of internet finnish. In *Proceedings of the Sixth International Conference Baltic HLT*, pages 184–191.

Adam Kilgarriff and Gregory Grefenstette. 2003. Introduction to the special issue on the web as corpus. *Computational linguistics*, 29(3):333–347.

Veronika Laippala, Jenna Kanerva, Anna Missilä, Katri Haverinen, Tapio Salakoski, and Filip Ginter. 2015. Towards a discourse-annotated corpus of finnish: the finnish propbank. In *Poster presented at the TextLink Cost Action seminar, Louvain-la-Neuve, Belgium, 27.1.2015.*

Juhani Luotolahti, Jenna Kanerva, Sampo Pyysalo, and Filip Ginter. 2015. Sets: Scalable and efficient tree search in dependency graphs. In *Proceedings of the 2015 Conference of the North American Chapter of the Association for Computational Linguistics: Demonstrations*, pages 51–55.

Teresa Lynn, Jennifer Foster, Mark Dras, and Lamia Tounsi. 2014. Cross-lingual transfer parsing for low-resourced languages: An Irish case study. In *Proceedings of the First Celtic Language Technology Workshop*, pages 41–49.

Ryan McDonald, Joakim Nivre, Yvonne Quirmbach-Brundage, Yoav Goldberg, Dipanjan Das, Kuzman Ganchev, Keith Hall, Slav Petrov, Hao Zhang, Oscar Täckström, Claudia Bedini, Núria Bertomeu Castelló, and Jungmee Lee. 2013. Universal dependency annotation for multilingual parsing. In *Proceedings of the 51st Annual Meeting of the Association for Computational Linguistics (ACL)*, pages 92–97.

Thomas Mueller, Helmut Schmid, and Hinrich Schütze. 2013. Efficient higher-order CRFs for morphological tagging. In *Proceedings of the 2013 Conference on Empirical Methods in Natural Language Processing*, pages 322–332.

Joakim Nivre, Cristina Bosco, Jinho Choi, Marie-Catherine de Marneffe, Timothy Dozat, Richárd Farkas, Jennifer Foster, Filip Ginter, Yoav Goldberg, Jan Hajič, Jenna Kanerva, Veronika Laippala, Alessandro Lenci, Teresa Lynn, Christopher Manning, Ryan McDonald, Anna Missilä, Simonetta Montemagni, Slav Petrov, Sampo Pyysalo, Natalia Silveira, Maria Simi, Aaron Smith, Reut Tsarfaty, Veronika Vincze, and Daniel Zeman. 2015. Universal dependencies 1.0. Available: http://hdl.handle.net/11234/1-1464.

Joakim Nivre. 2015. Towards a universal grammar for natural language processing. In *Computational Linguistics and Intelligent Text Processing*, pages 3–16. Springer.

Jenna Nyblom, Samuel Kohonen, Katri Haverinen, Tapio Salakoski, and Filip Ginter. 2013. Predicting conjunct propagation and other extended stanford dependencies. In *Proceedings of the International Conference on Dependency Linguistics (Depling 2013)*, pages 252–261.

Slav Petrov, Dipanjan Das, and Ryan McDonald. 2012. A universal part-of-speech tagset. In *Proceedings of the Eight International Conference on Language Resources and Evaluation (LREC)*, pages 2089–2096.

Tommi A Pirinen. 2011. Modularisation of Finnish finite-state language description–towards wide collaboration in open source development of a morphological analyser. In *Proceedings of the 18th Nordic Conference of Computational Linguistics (NODALIDA)*, pages 299–302.

Rashmi Prasad, Nikhil Dinesh, Alan Lee, Eleni Miltsakaki, Livio Robaldo, Aravind Joshi, and Bonnie Webber. 2008. The Penn Discourse TreeBank 2.0. In *Proceedings of the Sixth International Conference on Language Resources and Evaluation (LREC'08)*. http://www.lrec-conf.org/proceedings/lrec2008/.

Sampo Pyysalo, Jenna Kanerva, Anna Missilä, Veronika Laippala, and Filip Ginter. 2015. Universal Dependencies for Finnish. In *Proceedings of the 20th Nordic Conference of Computational Linguistics (Nodalida 2015)*, pages 163–173.

Anneliise Rehn. 2014. Because meaning: Language change through iconicity in internet speak. In *2014 SURF Conference Proceedings*.

Mike Scott and Christopher Tribble. 2006. *Textual patterns: key words and corpus analysis in language education*. John Benjamins.

Tiina Sinnemaa. 2014. Ei saa ronkkia ruokaa, koska afrikan lapset! koska np-rakenteen merkityksest ja ilmaisuvoimasta / you should not play with your food because [of] the children in africa! on the significance and expressivity of the construction 'because np'. Bachelor's thesis, Department of Finnish, University of Turku.

Pontus Stenetorp, Sampo Pyysalo, Goran Topić, Tomoko Ohta, Sophia Ananiadou, and Jun'ichi Tsujii. 2012. Brat: a web-based tool for nlp-assisted text annotation. In *Proceedings of the Demonstrations at the 13th Conference of the European Chapter of the Association for Computational Linguistics*, pages 102–107.

Vít Suchomel and Jan Pomikálek. 2012. Efficient web crawling for large text corpora. In *Proceedings of the seventh Web as Corpus Workshop (WAC7)*, pages 39–43.

Andy Way and Nano Gough. 2003. webmt: developing and validating an example-based machine translation system using the world wide web. *Computational Linguistics*, 29(3):421–457.

Daniel Zeman. 2010. Hard problems of tagset conversion. In *Proceedings of the Second International Conference on Global Interoperability for Language Resources*, pages 181–185.

Evaluation of Two-level Dependency Representations of Argument Structure in Long-Distance Dependencies

Paola Merlo
Linguistics Department
University of Geneva
1211 Geneva 4
Switzerland
Paola.Merlo@unige.ch

Abstract

Full recovery of argument structure information for question answering or information extraction requires that parsers can analyse long-distance dependencies. Previous work on statistical dependency parsing has used post-processing or additional training data to tackle this complex problem. We evaluate an alternative approach to recovering long-distance dependencies. This approach uses a two-level parsing model to recover both grammatical dependencies, such as subject and object, and full argument structure. We show that this two-level approach is competitive, while also providing useful semantic role information.

1 Introduction

One of the main motivations for adopting dependency representations in the parsing and computational linguistics community is their direct expression of the lexical-semantic properties of words and their relations. Argument structure is the representation of the argument taking properties of a predicate. It represents those semantic properties of a predicate that are expressed grammatically. It is usually defined as the specification of the arity of the predicate, its grammatical functions and the substantive labels of the arguments in the structure, what are usually called thematic or semantic roles. For example the argument structure of the verb *hit* comprises the specification that *hit* is a transitive verb and that it takes an AGENT subject and a THEME object.

Constructions involving long-distance dependencies (LDDs) — such as questions, or relative clauses — are the stress test of the ability to represent argument structure, because in these constructions argument structure information is not directly reflected in the surface order of the sentence. Despite the complexity of their representation, Rimell et al. (2009) report that these constructions cover roughly ten percent of the data in a corpus such as the PennTreebank, and therefore cannot be ignored. LDDs are illustrated in Figure 1. Representing argument structure in long-distance dependency constructions, thus, requires special mechanisms to deal with the divergence between the argument taking properties of the verb and the surface order of the sentence. The most frequently used ways to encode long-distance dependencies is either by a copy mechanism, shown in Figure 1, or by turning the tree into a directed graph, shown in Figure 2. [1]

Many current statistical dependency parsers fail to represent many long-distance dependencies and their related argument structure directly, often because the relevant information, such as traces, has been stripped from the training data. For example, most current statistical parsers do not represent directly the links drawn below the sentences in Figure 2. Moreover, there is no attempt in these representations, to encode the full argument structure directly, as the semantic role labels are usually inferred from their correlation with the grammatical function labels, but not explicitly represented. The argument structure of the verb *spread* in the first sentence in Figure 2 comprises a THEME subject in the intransitive form of the verb. This argument structure must be inferred indirectly from the graph: first the long-distance *nsubj* relation

[1] Recall that the red arcs shown in the figures are for expository purposes only, current representations do not show these direct links for long-distance dependencies.

Proceedings of the Third International Conference on Dependency Linguistics (Depling 2015), pages 221–230,
Uppsala, Sweden, August 24–26 2015.

must be inferred from a sequence of links typical of subject extraction from an embedded clause. Moreover, the notion that verbs like *spread* take THEME subjects in some, but not all cases, is not represented, and therefore the argument structure cannot be, strictly speaking, fully recovered.

These parsers can recover the long-distance dependency only through a post-processing step, which recovers the information about predicate-argument relation and the grammatical function. The semantic role label is usually not recovered even in post-processing.

We investigate here, then, the hypothesis whether current two-level syntactic-semantic parsers can fill in for the missing information, and recover the long-distance and argument structure information during parsing without need for post-processing and without loss in performance. If this were possible, we would be able to produce long-distance dependencies with more direct and perspicuous representations, and also fill in some of the semantic information currently missing from argument structure representations.

It is important to recall that the reason why predicate-argument structure is considered central for NLP applications hinges on the assumption that what needs recovering is the lexical semantics content. For example, it is likely that for information extraction, it is more useful to know which are the manner, temporal and location arguments than to know an underspecified adverbial modifier label.

In the rest of the paper, then, we will first contrast the one-level representation of long-distance dependencies to a two-level representation, where grammatical functions and argument structure are both explicitly represented. We will then briefly recall a recently proposed two-level parsing model (Henderson et al., 2013), and then present the main contribution of the paper: the evaluation of parsing models that parse these two-level syntactic-semantic dependencies on long-distance dependencies. We also compare the results to other statistical dependency parsers, investigate the usefulness and informativeness of the extracted information, discuss and conclude.

2 Single-level and Two-level Encoding of LDDs

As discussed in the introduction, traditional linguistic encodings of LDDs are integrated in the

(1) Questions

$What_i$ did William hit_i with his arrow?

(2) Relative clauses

This is the $apple_i$ that William hit_i with his arrow.

Figure 1: LDDs and their coindexed antecedent-trace representation.

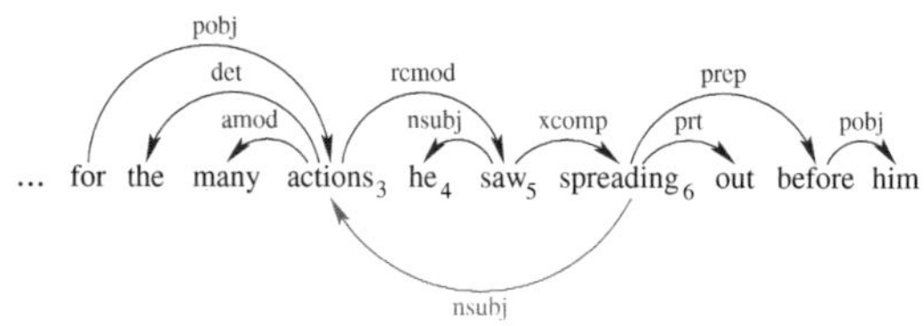

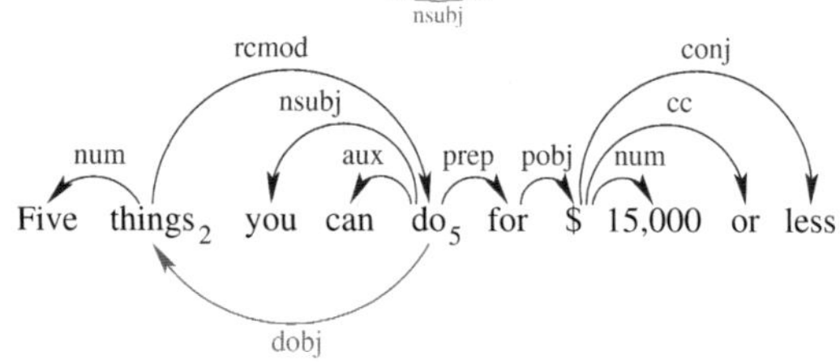

Figure 2: LDDs represented as a syntactic dependency tree labeled with grammatical relations. Recall that the LDD encoded in the arcs under the sentence are the LDD that must be recovered. They are shown for expository purpose and they are not usually part of the syntactic tree.

parse tree, either as co-indexed "traces", such as in the Penn Treebank, as illustrated in Figure 1, or as arcs as in a dependency representation. In practice, current statistical parsers do not encode LDD directly, as illustrated in Figure 2, and leave it to post-processing procedures to recover the LDD relation (Johnson, 2002; Nivre et al., 2010). These approaches exploit the very strong constraints that govern long-distance relations syntactically, and ignore the full or partial recovery of the semantic roles entirely.

Consider, for example, the representations for subject embeddings (first tree) and object reduced relatives (second tree) in Figure 2. This figure illustrates the Stanford dependency representation that was used in Rimmel et al. (2009), and Nivre et al. (2010), indicating below the sentence the long distance dependency that needs to be recovered, but that is not in the representation. The first tree encodes the subject relation between *ac-*

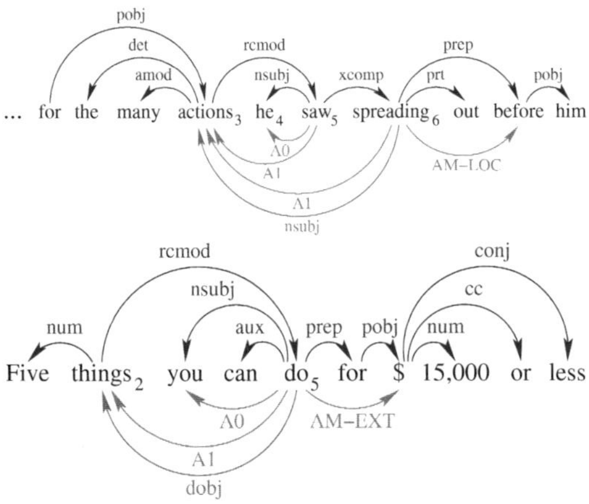

Figure 3: LDDs represented as a syntactic dependency tree above the sentence (in blue) and argument structure labels under the sentence (in green). The label A0 stands for AGENT and A1 stands for THEME. The prefix AM indicates a modifier argument. Recall that the LDDs encoded in the arcs under the sentence (in red) are the LDDs that must be recovered. They are shown for expository purpose and they are neither part of the syntactic tree nor of the semantic graph.

tions and *spreading* as a sequence of two arcs *rcmod(actions, saw)* and *xcomp(saw, spreading)*. This sequence indicates a dependency relation in the opposite direction from the one needed to correctly recover the argument structure of the verb *spread*, and does not explicitly indicate the grammatical function,SUBJECT, nor the semantic role relation, THEME. The label *rcmod* is the same label used to indicate the relationship between *do* and *things* in the second sentence, but in this case the relation is an object relation, so the distinction between subject-oriented and object-oriented relative clauses is encoded very indirectly. This kind of encoding of argument structure and long-distance dependency is indirect and potentially lacking in perspicuity.

In a dependency formalism, two-level representations have been proposed to represent the syntactic and argument structures of a sentence in terms of dependencies. Consider the representations in Figure 3. The syntactic representation is the same as in the previous figures, but LDDs and argument structures are represented directly. For example, the verb *saw* has two arguments, an AGENT and a THEME, while the verb *spread* has a long-distance dependency with the word *actions*, which is its THEME subject.[2] The verb *do* in the second sentence has a long-distance THEME object. Therefore, the overall complex graph that represents both the syntax and the underlying argument structure of the sentences comprises two half graphs, sharing all vertices, the words. They are indicated by the blue and green arcs, respectively, in Figure 3.

These representations factor the syntactic parse tree information from the argument structure information and provide, overall, more labelling information. The parse tree is needed to provide a connected graph, to provide information about constituency/dependency relations for grammatical correctness (agreement, for example, is triggered in environments defined by grammatical functions, and not by semantic relations) and grammatical functions. Argument structures are represented separately, for each predicate in the sentence and give explicit labels to the arguments. While these labels are correlated to the grammatical functions, it is a well-established fact that they are not coextensive, for instance not all subjects are Agents as shown in Figure 3, and therefore are not redundant.

From a linguistic point of view, these representations are related to many grammar formalisms that invoke the need to represent both grammatical functional level and argument structure level, such as tectogrammatical dependency representations (Hajic, 1998), or early versions of transformational grammar.

From a graph-theoretic and parsing point of view, the complete graph of both the syntax and the semantics of the sentences is composed of two half graphs, which share all their vertices, namely the words. Internally, these two half graphs exhibit different properties. The syntactic graph is a single connected tree. The semantic graph is a forest of one-level treelets, one for each proposition, which may be disconnected and may share children. In both graphs, it is not generally appropriate to assume independence across the different treelets in the structure. In the semantic graph, linguistic evidence that propositions are not independent of each other comes from constructions such

[2]This sentence also exemplifies the well-known fact, referred to in the introduction, that the mapping from grammatical function to the semantic roles useful for interpretation is not simple: the subject is not an AGENT, the most frequent mapping, but a THEME.

as coordinations where some of the arguments are shared and semantically parallel. Arcs in the semantic graph do not correspond one-to-one to arcs in the syntactic graph, indicating that a rather flexible framework is needed to capture the correlations between graphs. The challenge, then, arises in developing models of these two-level representations. These models must find an effective way of communicating the necessary information between the syntax and the argument structure representation.

From the practical point of view of existing resources, one version of these representations results from the merging of widely used and carefully annotated linguistic resources, PennTreebank (Marcus et al., 1993) and PropBank (Palmer et al., 2005). They are PennTreebank-derived dependency representations that have been stripped of long-distance dependencies, and merged with PropBank encoding of argument structures. But PropBank encodings are often based on the trace-enriched PennTreeBank representations as a starting point. Hence, these representations encode all LDDs, enriched with substantive semantic role labels, according to the PropBank labelling scheme.[3] They could also be constructed from other resources, for example by augmenting the current Universal dependency annotation scheme with extra semantic annotations (de Marneffe et al., 2014).

3 Parsing Two-level Representations

Developing models to learn these two-level analyses of syntax and argument structure raises several interesting questions regarding the design of the interface between the syntactic and the argument structure representations and how to learn these complex representations (Merlo and Musillo, 2008; Surdeanu et al., 2008).[4]

A model that can parse these two level-dependencies is proposed in Henderson et al. (2013) and we adopt it here without modifications. We choose this model for our evaluation of long-distance dependencies as the best performing among those approaches that have attempted to model jointly the relationship between argument structure and surface syntax (Lluís and Màrquez, 2008; Surdeanu et al., 2008) and developments of this model have shown good performance on several languages (Gesmundo et al., 2009), without any language-specific tailoring. These results suggest that this model can capture abstract linguistic regularities in a single parsing architecture.[5] We describe this model here very briefly. For more detail on the parser and the model, we refer the interested reader to Henderson et al. (2013) and references therein.

The crucial intuitions behind the two-level approach is that the parsing mechanism must correlate the two half-graphs, but allow them to be constructed separately as they have very different properties. The derivations for both syntactic dependency trees are based on a standard transition-based, shift-reduce style parser (Nivre et al., 2006). The derivations for argument structure dependency graphs use virtually the same set of actions, but are augmented with a *Swap* action, that swaps the two words at the top of the stack. The *Swap* action is inspired by the planarisation algorithm described in Hajicova et al.(2004), where non-planar trees are transformed into planar ones by recursively rearranging their sub-trees to find a linear order of the words for which the tree is planar.

The probability model to determine which action to pursue is a joint generative model of syntactic and argument structure dependencies. The two dependency structures are specified as the synchronised sequences of actions for a shift-reduce parser that operates on two different stacks. By synchronising parsing for both the syntactic and the argument structure representations, a probabilistic model is learnt which maximises the joint probability of the syntactic and semantic dependencies and thereby guarantees that the output structure is globally coherent, while at the same time building the two structures separately. The probabilistic estimation is based on Incremental Sigmoid Belief Networks (ISBNs). The use of latent variables allows ISBNs to induce their fea-

[3]These representations are the same, in practice, as the encoding used in some recent shared tasks (CoNLL 2008 and CoNLL 2009 (Surdeanu et al., 2008; Hajič et al., 2009)) for syntactic-semantic dependencies.

[4]Joint syntactic-semantic dependency parsing was the theme of two CoNLL shared tasks. CoNLL 2008 explored syntactic-semantic parsing for English, CoNLL 2009 extended the task to several languages. Only four truly joint models were developed, and most of the multi-lingual models were fine-tuned specifically for each language.

[5]The version of the parser, the one we use, described in Henderson et al. (2013), has a syntactic labelled accuracy of 87.5%, a semantic role F-score of 76.1%, and a syntactic-semantic F-score of 81.8%, using the data and evaluation measures of the CoNLL 2008 shared task.

(3) Each must match Wisman's pie with the fragment that they carry with him.

(4) Five things you can do for 15,000 dollars or less.

(5) They will remain on a lower-priority list that includes 17 other countries.

(6) How he felt ready for the many actions he saw spreading out before him.

(7) What you see are self-help projects.

(8) What effect does a prism have on light?

(9) The men were at first puzzled then angered by the aimless tacking.

Figure 4: Sentences exemplifying the different constructions involving LDDs, used in the test set developed by Rimell et al. (2009).

tures automatically.

4 Experiments

In this section we assess how well the two-level parser performs on constructions involving long-distance dependencies. In so doing, we verify that these two-level models of syntactic and argument structure representations can be learnt even in difficult cases, while also producing an output that is richer than what statistical parsers usually produce. To confirm this statement, we expect to see that the syntactic dependency parsing performance is not degraded, compared to more standard statistical parsing architectures on long-distance dependencies, while also producing semantic role labels on these difficult constructions.

4.1 The Test Data

To test the performance on LDDs, we use the test suites developed by Rimell et al. (2009) for English. They comprise 560 test sentences, 80 for each type of construction. Half of them are extracted from the Penn Treebank, half of them from the Brown corpus, balanced across construction types. None of these sentences is included in the training set of the parser. These sentences cover seven types of long-distance relations, illustrated in Figure 4: object extraction from relative clauses (ORC) in (3) or from reduced relative clauses (ORed) in (4), subject extraction from relative clauses (SRC) in (5) or from an embedded clause (SEmb) in (6), free relatives (Free) in (7), object-oriented questions (OQ) in (8), and right node raising constructions (RNR) in (9).

Compared to the other statistical dependency parsers, questions (OQ) are not well represented in our training data, since they do not include the additional QB data (Nivre et al., 2010) used to improve the performance of MSTParser and MaltParser.

4.2 Parsing set up

Like the dependency parser in Nivre et al. (2010), the parser was not trained on the same data or tree representations as those used in the test data. The parser is trained on the data derived by merging a dependency transformation of the Penn Treebank with Propbank and Nombank (Surdeanu et al., 2008). An illustrative example of the kind of labelled structures that we need to parse was given in Figure 3. Training and development data follow the usual partition as sections 02-21, 24 of the Penn Treebank. More details and references on the data, and the conversion of the Penn Treebank format to dependencies are given in Surdeanu et al. (2008).

Like for standard statistical and dependency parsers, the syntactic representation used by the two-level parser has been stripped of all traces. The predicates of the argument structures and their locations are not provided at testing, unlike some of the CONLL shared tasks.

Unlike Nivre et al. (2010), we did not use an external part-of-speech tagger to annotate the data of the development set. To minimize preprocessing of the data, we choose to have part-of-speech tagging as an internal part of the parsing model, which therefore, takes raw input.

In order for our results to be comparable to those reported in previous evaluations (Rimell et al., 2009; Nivre et al., 2010), we ran the parser "out of the box" directly on the test sentences, without using the development sentences to fine-tune. We were able to parse all the sentences in the test suites without any adjustments to the parser.[6]

[6]According to Rimell et al. (2009) only the C&C parser required some little adjustments to parse all sentences in the test suite. Evaluation results without these adjustments are not reported.

4.3 Evaluation Methodology

Like in previous papers (Rimell et al., 2009; Nivre et al., 2010), we evaluate the parser on its ability to recover LDDs. Two evaluations were done. The first one was semi-automatic, performed with a modified version of the evaluation script developed in Rimell et al. (2009). An independent manual evaluation was also performed.

A dependency is considered correctly recovered if a dependency in the gold data is found in the output. A dependency is a triple comprising three items: the nodes connected by the arc in the graph and the label of the arc. In principle, a dependency is considered correct if all three elements of the triple are correct. However, in this evaluation the representations vary across models and exact matches would not allow a fair assessment. Both previous evaluation exercises (Rimell et al., 2009; Nivre et al., 2010) suggest some avenues to relax the matching conditions, and define equivalence classes of representations.

4.3.1 Equivalence classes of arcs

To relax the requirement of exact match on the definition of arc, a set of equivalence classes between single arcs and paths connecting two nodes indirectly is precisely defined in the post-processing scheme of Nivre et al. (2010), which applies to the Stanford labelling scheme. In Nivre et al. (2010), the encoding of long-distance dependencies in a dependency parser is categorised as simple, complex, and indirect. In the simple case, the LDD coincides with an arc in a tree. In the complex case, the LDD is represented by a path of arcs. In the indirect case, the dependency is not directly encoded in a path in the tree, but it must be inferred from a larger portion of the tree using heuristics. The two last cases require post-processing of the tree. In Rimell et al. (2009), two dependencies are considered equivalent if they differ only in their definition of what counts as head. For example, in some dependency schemes the preposition is the head of a prepositional phrase, while in others it is the noun.

We develop a definition of equivalence classes of arcs inspired by both these approaches. Following Nivre et al. (2010), we define a long-distance dependency as simple or complex. In the simple case, the LDD coincides with an arc in a tree. A complex dependency is defined as a path of at most two simple dependencies. Unlike single-level statistical parsers, our two-level representation could create more than one path to connect two nodes, since two nodes could be connected both by a syntactic arc and by a semantic arc. Following Rimell et al. (2009), we define which path of two arcs is considered correct by allowing some flexibility in the definition of the head in very specific predefined cases, such as prepositional phrases. The head can be either the word in the position indicated in the gold annotation, or its parent. This definition applies, for example, to extraction from prepositional phrases which in our case are related to the semantic head, while in Rimell et al.'s scheme they are connected to the preposition. This relaxed definition is triggered in 31 cases of semantic matches and 40 cases of syntactic matches, over a total of 398 matches.

The evaluation script was also augmented with a construction-specific rule to capture complex dependencies with *be*-constructions. Sentence (10) is an example of a *be*-construction, where the gold dependency in (10a) corresponds to a path of two dependencies in (10b). The latter consists of the subject dependency between the copula *is*, the head, and its subject *childhood*, and the predicative dependency between the head *is* and the predicative *what*. For a complex dependency of this type to be counted correct, the end points of the path have to match the endpoints of the long-distance dependency in the gold and the labels have to be exactly as indicated, *sbj* and *prd*. This specific rule adds seven correct cases to the total.

(10) That is what childhood is , he told himself .

   a. nsubj what 2 childhood 3
   b. sbj is 1 childhood 3
      prd is 1 what 2

4.4 Equivalence classes of labels

The evaluation in Rimell et al. (2009) is largely done manually, and equivalences are decided by the authors. Different labelling schemes are considered correct, as long as they can make the distinction between subject, object, indirect object and adjunct modifier.

We establish a correspondence of labels. In our two-level representation, labels are the grammatical functions of the syntactic dependencies, and the semantic role labels, taken from PropBank. [7]

[7]The PropBank annotation was developed based on the deep structure representations of the PennTreebank and Levin

Core arguments	
nsubj	A0, A1, SBJ
obj,dobj, pobj	OBJ, A1, PMOD
passive subj	A1
obj2	A1
Other labels	
advmod	LOC,TMP,MNR
amod	MNR,NMOD
aux	MOD,VC
nn	NAME, DEP
partmod	MOD

Figure 5: Gold data and two-level output label equivalences.

Our equivalences might depend only on the labels or on the labels in the context of the sentence type. For example, the subject of a passive is an A1, that is a THEME. In some cases, direct inspection of the predicate was necessary: A1 corresponds to *subjects* for some verbs even in the active voice. A simple rule was applied to decide what verbs can exhibit an A1 subject, based on PropBank's framesets: If the frameset allowed A1 as a subject, in the appropriate sense of the verb, then the correspondence was accepted. This decision rule applied to 33 cases (the (nsubj, A1) cell in Table 2). The label equivalences are given in detail in Figure 5: the grammatical function labels of the gold data are shown on the left and labels of the two-level parser are shown on the right. The confusion matrix by labels is provided in Table 2.

Manual evaluation The evaluation was also done manually by a judge, a trained linguist, who had not developed the initial script. We used a visualisation tool (Tred) (Pajas and Štěpánek, 2008), adapted to our output, to facilitate the inspection of the two-level representations and avoid mistakes.

In the manual evaluation, a dependency is correctly recovered if an arc and its syntactic/semantic label (see Figure 4) are correct.

Three different constructions need to be mentioned, because they have special chracteristics that had to be taken into account: coordination, right node raising and small clauses.

A dependency may be found directly, as a single arc, or by coordination. Regarding coordination, we follow the Stanford scheme, according to which an argument or adjunct must be attached to the first conjunct to indicate that it belongs to both conjuncts.

Right node raising is too difficult to evaluate automatically. In Rimell et al. (2009)'s definition, right node raising is represented by two arcs. It is considered correctly recovered if one of the arcs was correct and the other was found either directly or by coordination. We evaluate right node raising by hand, in the same way: either the dependency was found directly or by coordination, either in the syntax or in the argument structure.

Small clauses are rare, complex dependencies that were evaluated by hand. Sentence (11) is an example of a small clause construction, where the *nsubj* dependency of the gold data (11a) corresponds to two dependencies (11b): one between the head *called* and its object/theme *horses*, and one between *called* and the object predicative *Dogs*. We found only five cases of this construction. However, these five dependencies do make a difference, because they all appear in SEmb, which has a low percent recall, as shown in Table 1.

(11) The sound rose on the other side of the hills , vanished and rose again and he could imagine the mad , disheveled hoofs of the Appaloosas , horses the white men once had called the Dogs of Hell .

a. nsubj Dogs 36 horses 28

b. obj called 34 horses 28
   oprd called 34 Dogs 36

5 Results and Discussion

Automatic and manual results (percent recall) are shown in Table 1, where we compare our results to the relevant ones of those reported in previous evaluations (Rimell et al., 2009; Nivre et al., 2010; Nguyen et al., 2012).[8] These papers compare several statistical parsers. Some parsers like Nguyen, the C&C parser (Clark and Curran, 2007) and Enju (Miyao and Tsujii, 2005) are based on rich grammatical formalisms, and others others are representative of statistical dependency parsers (MST, MALT, (McDonald, 2006; Nivre et al., 2006)).

(1993)'s semantic propositions of alternating verbs. PropBank propositions have been shown to be closely related to grammatical functions (Merlo and van der Plas, 2009). So we can assume that grammatical functions can also be inferred from PropBank relations in most cases.

[8] All these evaluations, like ours, can report only recall, because of the nature of the output of the parsers, which do not explicitly label a dependency with a dedicated long-distance label.

	ORC	ORed	SRC	Free	OQ	RNR	SEmb	Total
Nguyen	53	69	68	69	57	26	39	56
C&C	59	63	80	73	28	49	22	54
Enju	47	66	82	76	32	47	33	54
This paper	36/35	55/48	44/57	72/73	18/15	63	18/22	48/48
MST	34	47	79	66	14	46	38	46
Malt	41	51	84	70	16	40	24	46

Table 1: Our percent recall results, construction by construction, automatic and manual (A/M), compared to some of the results reported in Rimell et al. (2009) and Nivre et al. (2010). Abbreviations are explained in subsection 4.1. Right node raising was evaluated only manually.

	dobj	nsubj	pobj	prep
A0	0/6	37/39	0/2	
A1	146/146	12/33	6/6	3/3
A2	2/2			3/3
OBJ	16/16		1/1	
SBJ	0/7	10/10	0/4	
PMOD	5/5	0/1	13/13	2/2
TOT	167/186	75/87	20/26	25/25

Table 2: Labelled error confusion matrix of most frequent labels. Cells indicate correct labelling/total labelling. The first three rows show the results for semantic labels, and the last three rows show results for syntactic dependency labels. For reasons of space only labels with at least five occurrences are shown. The table also does not show the following perfect matches: LOC: advmod 5/5; TMP: advmod 5/5; A1: nsubjpass 14/14; NMOD: amod 7/7.

These last two parsers constitute the relevant comparison for our approach.[9]

Like the other parsers discussed in Rimell et al. (2009) and Nivre et al. (2010), the overall performance on these long-distance constructions is much lower than the overall scores for this parser. However, the parser recovers long-distance dependencies at least as well as standard statistical dependency parsers that use a post-processing step, and better than standard statistical parsers.[10]

The differences in recall between manual and automatic evaluation in Table 1 show that the automatic evaluation is sometimes too strict and sometimes too lenient. The former cases arise primarily in small clause dependencies and dependency recovery by coordination across all LDD constructions, which were taken into account in the manual evaluation, but not in the automatic evaluation, because, as indicated above, scoring coordination automatically is too difficult. This explains the recall difference between the two evaluation methods in SRC and SEmb. The latter case is due to the stricter definition of head in the manual evaluation. This is the main reason why ORed and OQ have lower recall in this evaluation.

Table 2 reports some of the labelled error counts of the most frequent labels. In general, the confusion matrix shows that the labelled correspondence is accurate, and that it corresponds to meaningful generalisations. As can also be observed, a single grammatical function label corresponds to several different semantic relations and vice versa. Full recovery of argument structure, then, requires both grammatical syntactic relations and semantic role labelling.

5.1 Error Analysis of Development Sets

We classify the errors made by our parser on the development set based on Nivre et al. (2010)'s three main error categories, Global, Arg, Link, with some more restrictive modifications that are appropriate for the two-level representation. Following Nivre et al. (2010), we define a Global error as one that applies to cases where the parser fails to build the relevant clausal structure (e.g., the relative clause and what it modifies in ORed, ORC, Free, and SRC) due to parsing/tagging errors. We split Nivre et al.'s definition of Arg errors (errors on labels) in two cases. An Arg error is

[9] Other parsers were evaluated in Rimell et al. (2009), with worse results than what reported here. However, because of differences in set up and parsing architecture, comparing results here would be misleading. For example, the Stanford parser was evaluated, reaching 38% recall. But it should be borne in mind that this result is not directly comparable, as it is likely that this parser too would have benefitted from the post-processing step used in Nivre et al. (2010) to evaluate dependency parsers.

[10] Manual inspection indicates that if we allowed more complex dependencies, such as those proposed by Nivre et al.'s evaluation, our score on subject relative clauses would increase from 57% to 69%, for a total of 49% correct. This explains in part the apparent difference between our architecture and other dependency parsers for subject relative clauses.

	Tot	G	Arg	S	SA	L	Dep
ORed	10	3	4	3	0	0	23
ORC	14	9	2	3	0	0	20
Free	8	3	5	0	0	0	22
OQ	23	14	7	1	1	0	25
RNR	15	1	2	3	0	9	28
SEm	10	4	4	2	0	0	13
SRC	16	12	0	4	0	0	43

Table 3: Distribution of error types in the development sets. (G= Global; S= Sem; SA= Sem+Arg; L= Link; Dep= number of dependencies).

	Us	MST	Malt	Dep
ORed	10	9	13	23
ORC	14	13	16	20
Free	8	5	6	22
OQ	23	17	20	25
RNR	15	14	15	28
SEm	10	9	9	13
SRC	16	10	14	43

Table 4: Comparison of the three dependency parsers based on the total number of errors in each development set.

one which occurs when the parser fails to assign the correct functional relation (e.g., subject, object), while a Sem error is one in which the parser fails to assign the correct semantic relation (e.g., A1, A2). Nivre et al's Link error is one where the parser fails to find a dependency by coordination in the case of right node raising.

Our restrictive modifications follow the constraints indicated above on what counts as a correct dependency. In particular, we only count as correct two types of dependencies: simple, in which the dependency is represented as a single arc in the parse tree; and complex, where a gold dependency corresponds to a path of only two direct dependencies, such as in the case of predicative constructions and prepositional phrases discussed above. Our definition of complex dependencies is stricter than Nivre et al.'s, and we do not count indirect dependencies. Link errors related to relative clauses (indirect dependencies) are classified as Sem errors.[11]

Table 3 shows the frequency of the error types for our parser in the seven development sets. Global errors are most frequent for OQ, ORC and SRC. Questions (OQ) are not well represented in our training data, since they do not include the additional QB data (Nivre et al., 2010) used to improve the performance of MSTParser and MaltParser (see Table 4 for comparison of number of errors for each parser). With respect to ORC and SRC, most Global errors are related to part-of-speech tagging errors and wrong head assignment of complex NPs which are modified by the relevant relative clause. In particular there seems to be a strong recency preference, which assigns the relative clause to the closest noun head in a complex NP. A closer look at Arg errors shows that, in ORed, ORC and OQ, the most frequent errors are because the parser fails to find the Arg relation between a preposition and its argument in cases of preposition stranding.

Based on the comparison of errors of other statistical dependency parsers on the development set, shown in Table 4, we can conclude that the trends of errors by constructions are the same in all three parsers.

6 Conclusions and Future Work

In this paper, we have evaluated an approach to learn two-level long-distance representations that encode argument structure information directly, as a particularly difficult test case, and shown that we can learn these difficult constructions as well as dependency parsers augmented with a dedicated long-distance dependency post-processing step. This work also shows that resources and methods to recover these richer representations already exist.

It is important to recall that the predicate-argument structure of a clause is considered central for NLP applications because it represents the grammatically relevant lexical semantic content of the clause. The two-level parser described in this paper can recover this information, while purely syntactic parsers, whether they recover long-distance dependencies or not, would still need further enhancements.

[11] Nivre et al.'s Link errors also include cases where the parser fails to find the crucial Link relations *rcmod* in ORed, ORC, SRC, and SEmb. This type of Link error is not relevant for us.

References

Stephen Clark and James Curran. 2007. Wide-coverage efficient statitstical parsing with CCG and log-linear models. *Computational Linguistics*, 33(4):493–552.

Marie-Catherine de Marneffe, Timothy Dozat, Natalia Silveira, Katri Haverinen, Filip Ginter, Joakim Nivre, and Christopher D. Manning. 2014. Universal stanford dependencies: A cross-linguistic typology. In *Proceedings of the Ninth International Conference on Language Resources and Evaluation (LREC'14)*, pages 4585–4592, Reykjavik, Iceland, May. ACL Anthology Identifier: L14-1045.

Andrea Gesmundo, James Henderson, Paola Merlo, and Ivan Titov. 2009. A latent variable model of synchronous syntactic-semantic parsing for multiple languages. In *Proceedings of the Thirteenth Conference on Computational Natural Language Learning (CoNLL 2009): Shared Task*, pages 37–42, Boulder, Colorado, June.

Jan Hajic. 1998. Building a syntactically annotated corpus: the Prague dependency treebank. In Eva Hajicova, editor, *Issues of Valency and Meaning*, pages 106–132. Karolinum, Prague.

Eva Hajičová, Jiří Havelka, Petr Sgall, Kateřina Veselá, and Daniel Zeman. 2004. Issues of Projectivity in the Prague Dependency Treebank. *Prague Bulletin of Mathematical Linguistics*, (81).

Jan Hajič, Massimiliano Ciaramita, Richard Johansson, Daisuke Kawahara, Maria Antònia Martí, Lluís Màrquez, Adam Meyers, Joakim Nivre, Sebastian Padó, Jan Štěpánek, Pavel Straňák, Mihai Surdeanu, Nianwen Xue, and Yi Zhang. 2009. The CoNLL-2009 shared task: Syntactic and semantic dependencies in multiple languages. In *Proceedings of the Thirteenth Conference on Computational Natural Language Learning (CoNLL 2009): Shared Task*, pages 1–18, Boulder, Colorado, June.

James Henderson, Paola Merlo, Ivan Titov, and Gabriele Musillo. 2013. Multilingual joint parsing of syntactic and semantic dependencies with a latent variable model. *Computational Linguistics*, 39(4):950–998.

Mark Johnson. 2002. A simple pattern-matching algorithm for recovering empty nodes and their antecedents. In *Proceedings of 40th Annual Meeting of the Association for Computational Linguistics*, pages 136–143, Philadelphia, Pennsylvania, USA, July.

Beth Levin. 1993. *English Verb Classes and Alternations*. University of Chicago Press, Chicago, IL.

Xavier Lluís and Lluís Màrquez. 2008. A joint model for parsing syntactic and semantic dependencies. In *CoNLL 2008: Proceedings of the Twelfth Conference on Computational Natural Language Learning*, pages 188–192, Manchester, England, August.

Mitch Marcus, Beatrice Santorini, and M.A. Marcinkiewicz. 1993. Building a large annotated corpus of English: the Penn Treebank. *Computational Linguistics*, 19:313–330.

Ryan McDonald. 2006. *Discriminative Learning and Spanning Tree Algorithms for Dependency Parsing*. Ph.D. thesis, University of Pennsylvania.

Paola Merlo and Gabriele Musillo. 2008. Semantic parsing for high-precision semantic role labelling. In *Proceedings of the Twelfth Conference on Computational Natural Language Learning (CONLL-08)*, pages 1–8, Manchester, UK.

Paola Merlo and Lonneke van der Plas. 2009. Abstraction and generalisation in semantic role labels: PropBank, VerbNet or both? In *Procs of ACL and AFNLP*, pages 288–296, Suntec, Singapore, August.

Yusuke Miyao and Jun'ichi Tsujii. 2005. Probabilistic disambiguation models for wide-coverage HPSG parsing. In *Proceedings of the 43th Meeting of the ACL*, pages 83–90, Ann Arbor, Michigan.

Luan Nguyen, Marten Van Schijndel, and William Schuler. 2012. Accurate unbounded dependency recovery using generalized categorial grammars. In *Proceedings of COLING 2012*, pages 2125–2140, Mumbai, India, December.

Joakim Nivre, J. Hall, and J. Nilsson. 2006. Maltparser: A data-driven parser-generator for dependency parsing. In *Proceedings of LREC*, pages 2216–2219.

Joakim Nivre, Laura Rimell, Ryan McDonald, and Carlos Gómez Rodríguez. 2010. Evaluation of dependency parsers on unbounded dependencies. In *Proceedings of the 23rd International Conference on Computational Linguistics (Coling 2010)*, pages 833–841, Beijing, China, August.

Petr Pajas and Jan Štěpánek. 2008. Recent advances in a feature-rich framework for treebank annotation. In *Proceedings of the 22nd International Conference on Computational Linguistics (Coling 2008)*, pages 673–680, Manchester, UK.

Martha Palmer, Daniel Gildea, and Paul Kingsbury. 2005. The Proposition Bank: An annotated corpus of semantic roles. *Computational Linguistics*, 31:71–105.

Laura Rimell, Stephen Clark, and Mark Steedman. 2009. Unbounded dependency recovery for parser evaluation. In *Proceedings of the 2009 Conference on Empirical Methods in Natural Language Processing*, pages 813–821, Singapore, August. Association for Computational Linguistics.

Mihai Surdeanu, Richard Johansson, Adam Meyers, Lluís Màrquez, and Joakim Nivre. 2008. The CoNLL-2008 shared task on joint parsing of syntactic and semantic dependencies. In *Proceedings of the 12th Conference on Computational Natural Language Learning (CoNLL-2008)*, pages 159–177.

The Subjectival Surface-Syntactic Relation in Serbian

Jasmina Milićević
Dalhousie University in Halifax
Department of French
Canada
jmilicev@dal.ca

Abstract

The paper focuses on the notion of (surface) syntactic subject in Serbian within the syntactic dependency framework of the Meaning-Text linguistic theory. Properties of the subject are described and its text implementations illustrated with data from a variety of contemporary texts.

1 The Problem Stated

The aim of this paper is to describe and illustrate, from a syntactic dependency viewpoint, the notion of syntactic subject as applied to Serbian. By doing so, the paper puts to test the adequacy of the conceptual and formal tools of the Meaning-Text dependency syntax, hoping to contribute to a broader understanding of the general notion of syntactic subject itself.

Syntactic subject is the dependent element of the subjectival surface-syntactic relation, a major valence-controlled syntactic-dependency relation. It is the most privileged dependent element of the clause in that it possesses properties that do not accrue to any other clause element. Understandably, the notion of syntactic subject has been vigorously investigated, especially in typological/cross-linguistic perspective, for instance, in Keenan (1976), Kibrik (1977), Foley & Van Valin (1997), Mithun & Chafe (1999), Lazard (2009), Creissels (2014) and Mel'čuk (2014), to mention just a few influential papers. Yet, a number of issues surrounding the notion remain controversial: null subjects, quirky subjects, psychological vs. grammatical subject, and so on; even the cross-linguistic nature of the notion has been questioned. For the viewpoint taken on some of these issues in this paper, see the next section.

As for the syntactic subject in Serbian, even though it has been described in studies such as Piper *et al.* (2005: 487-491), Klajn (2005: 225-227 and 256-257), and Mrazovac & Vukadinović (2009: 525-527), the latter being dependency-oriented, to the best of my knowledge, there has been no comprehensive account of this syntactic role—at any rate, not in a formalized dependency framework of the type used here. For Croatian, studies dedicated specifically to issues related to the syntactic subject include Kučanda (1998), Buljan & Kučanda (2004) and Belaj & Kučanda (2007); given the proximity of the two languages, the findings for Croatian are valid for Serbian as well.

The research reported in the paper is part of a larger project on identification and description of surface-syntactic relations in Serbian. The linguistic data used in the research comes from two contemporary novels (Žurić 2009, Arsenijević 2013), the Corpus of Serbian language, and Serbian Internet pages, accessed through Google searches; some examples are my own.

The rest of the paper is structured as follows: Section 2 presents the theoretical framework of the paper and introduces the necessary notions; Section 3 describes and illustrates the subjecthood in Serbian; Section 4 formulates a conclusion.

2 The Framework

Meaning-Text linguistic theory (Mel'čuk 1974, 1988, 2012-2013-2015; Kahane 2003) is a framework for the construction of functional models of languages, called *Meaning-Text Models*. These are dependency-based models, making use of three major dependency types: semantic, syntactic and morphological (Mel'čuk, 2009).

In a binary phrase L_1—L_2, L_1 is the syntactic governor of L_2, its dependent, if L_1 determines to a greater extent the passive syntactic valence, or distribution, of the entire phrase; we then write: L_1–**synt**→L_2. In most cases the syntactic governor also determines the dependent's linear position in the clause with respect to itself and/or its other dependents.

A Meaning-Text linguistic model has multistratal and modular organization, i.e., it presup-

Proceedings of the Third International Conference on Dependency Linguistics (Depling 2015), pages 231–240, Uppsala, Sweden, August 24–26 2015.

poses several levels of representation of utterances and consists of sets or rules, or modules, operating between adjacent representation levels. In syntax, two representational levels are foreseen: deep- and surface syntactic levels. As mentioned above, the subjectival relation is one of valence-controlled surface-syntactic relations [= SSyntRel]. Valence-controlled, or actantial, relations are opposed to circumstantial relations, this opposition being fundamental in syntax; for the Meaning-Text take on actants, see Mel'čuk (2004). Unlike deep-syntactic relations, which are language independent, SSyntRels are language specific and need to be discovered empirically. Special criteria and tests have been developed to this end within the Meaning-Text framework; for their application for distinguishing the valence-controlled SSyntRels in French, see Iordanskaja & Mel'čuk (2009). Mille (2014) follows largely the same methodology for establishing the SSyntRels for Spanish.

A given SSyntRel is described by stating the properties of its dependent element. Building upon the seminal work of Keenan (1976), Mel'čuk (2014) establishes the properties of the syntactic subject, dividing them into *defining* (= *coding*) properties and *characterizing* (= *behavioral*) properties.

Defining properties of the SyntSubj are specified along the parameters given in Table 1. For a sentence element *L* to be declared the subject (in a given language), at least some of these parameters must apply to it (i.e., have the positive value).

Characterizing properties concern the subject's specific behavior in various syntactic operations: pronominalization, ellipsis, passivization, dislocation, extraction, etc. (for a fuller list, see Table 2 below). These properties accrue only to *prototypical subjects*, i.e., they are not necessarily valid for all subjects in a language and can apply to clause elements other than the subject.

The prototypical subject is the subject that is the least constrained in its co-occurrence with the MV; in other words, the one that "passes" with the highest number of governors. Thus, the prototypical subject in Serbian is a noun in the nominative case because an N_{NOM} can function as the subject of any verb, but an infinitive, for instance, is not a prototypical subject in this language because a V_{INF} can be the subject of only a small number of verbs (copular and some modal verbs).

1.	*L* depends only on the MV
2.	*L* cannot be omitted from the SyntS
3.	*L* has a particular linear position with respect to the MV
4.	*L* controls the agreement of the MV
5.	*L*'s grammatical case is controlled by the MV
6.	*L*'s morphological links with the MV are affected by the MV's inflection
7.	*L*'s pronominalization affects its morphological links with the MV

Table 1: Defining Properties of the SyntSubj (Mel'čuk 2014: 175)

The recourse to the prototypical subject means that in our approach the subject is characterized inductively: first the prototypical subjects are identified, and than the less typical ones are determined by analogy, as those sharing at least some properties of the prototypical subjects. (This is also Keenan's 1976 legacy.)

The above inventory of subject properties—including both the defining properties and the standard characterizing properties—is universal (= sufficient to identify the subject in any language); their specific combination for a given language, however, has to be discovered empirically, as it differs from one language to the next.[1] Additionally, the subject in any given language may have some other, language-specific, characterizing properties.

<u>Definition</u>: Syntactic subject (Mel'čuk 2014: 179)

> The syntactic subject is the most privileged dependent of the Main Verb in (a clause of) a language *L*; its privileged status is determined by a list of properties elaborated specifically for *L*.

Under the postulate that there always is such a thing as the most privileged clause element, the above definition of the syntactic subject implies its existence in every language. Not everyone

[1] In the literature, there is a wide consensus as to subjecthood properties; cf., for instance, those mentioned in Creissels (2014: 3-4): marking by a special grammatical case and/or indexation on the MV (i.e., imposition of agreement on the MV) in conjunction with particular syntactic behavior: reflexivization, serialization, raising/control, topicalization, focalization, relativization, etc. It should be noted, though, that not everyone separates defining and characterizing properties as strictly as we do.

shares this point of view; thus, the universality of the syntactic subject is not recognized by a number of researches working in the typological perspective, including Kibrik (1997), Lazard (2009) and Creissels (2014). (This attitude is actually not new; already Martinet (1972) asked whether linguists should dispense with the notion.) The reluctance stems from a particular way in which these researchers approach the problem. Either they strive to isolate the core properties of the syntactic subject that are shared by all languages—which turns out to be impossible.[2] Or, while readily admitting that a universal definition of the syntactic subject is logically possible, they are not interested in finding one, focusing instead on (the limits of) cross-linguistic variation in the organization of the clause[3]. But for the proponents of Meaning-Text approach, this is exactly what is needed: a universally applicable, rigorously defined notion of subject. Because it is believed that many of the controversies surrounding the syntactic subjects arise precisely from the fact that in virtually all of the relevant linguistic literature the correspondent notion simply is not clearly defined.

This is not to deny the well-known fact that the identification of the subject is problematic in some languages: examples include syntactically ergative (or in our terminology, *deep ergative*) languages, as well as languages in which the communicative structure is the prevalent factor of clause organization. But even in such difficult cases, Meaning-Text approach does a very good job; see, for instance, Beck (2000) for the syntactic subject in Lushootseed, and case studies of subjecthood in several "problematic" languages (Amele, Archi, Lezgian, etc.) in Mel'čuk (2014).

A serious consideration in favor of maintaining the notion of syntactic subject, even though descriptions that do not make use of it are possible, is its utility for cross-linguistic comparisons.[4]

3 Subjectival SSyntRel in Serbian

In this section I will describe and illustrate the properties of the SSynt-Subject in Serbian (**3.1**), as well as its implementation in the clause (**3.2**). I will start with some basic data about the language.

Serbian has three general properties relevant for our topic:

1) It is a PRO-Drop language, i.e., it features the obligatory deletion of a communicatively unmarked pronominal subject.

2) It has a number of impersonal sentence patterns containing a semantically empty zero subject.

3) It is a flexible word-order language in which the subject can occupy any linear position in the clause as a function of specific communicative conditions. The basic, communicatively neutral, word order in a simple declarative clause is SV(O) in clauses with a Theme ~ Rheme division, and V(O)S in all-rhematic clauses.

3.1 Properties of the SSynt-Subject in Serbian

First the subject's defining properties are discussed, followed by its characterizing properties.

3.1.1 Defining Properties of the SSynt-Subject

The subject in Serbian possesses six out of seven defining subjecthood properties listed in Table 1 above.[5]

- **Exclusive Dependence on the Clause Predicate**

In a prototypical clause, whose head (= predicate) is a finite verb, the subject depends on this verb; all the examples in this paper except (1) illustrate this case. In a verbless sentence, the subject depends on the item in the role of the predicate: an interjection (1a) or a presentative (1b). Example (1b) also illustrates a non-canonical syntactic subject—in the genitive case; on genitive subjects in Serbian, see Subsection 3.2.2.

---

[2] Thus, in Lazard (2009: 152), we find (translation is mine–JM): "[...] the variations [in the inventory of the properties of the subject across languages–JM] are so great that it seems impossible to identify a single property that could be considered as defining the subject in all languages".

[3] Cf. Creissels (2014: 1-2): [...] it is not about a quest for a universal notion of subject, which, if conveniently defined, should be identifiable in any language [...].

[4] As (Beck 2000: 317) puts it succinctly: "While treatments of Lushootseed grammar which avoid the term [syntactic subject–the author] meet the criterion of language-specific descriptive adequacy, syntactic subject remains an important theoretical concept and a necessary benchmark for discourse-analysis and cross-linguistic comparison".

[5] It lacks property 7: the pronominalization of the subject does not affect in any way the MV's morphology. As an example of language where the MV is so affected, we can cite Breton, where the MV agrees with an elided subject pronoun, but does not agree with one overtly present in the clause.

(1) a. *A on*←**subj(ectival)**–*hop kroz prozor*. Lit. 'And he off through window.' = 'And off he went through the window.'

b. *Eno*–**subj**→*Jovana.* Lit. 'There of.Jovan.' 'There comes Jovan.'

- **Non-Omissibility from the Syntactic Structure**

Note that we are talking here about the non-omissibility of the subject from the syntactic structure of the clause—rather than the clause itself. Thus, a communicatively unmarked pronominal subject in a Pro-DROP language and the subject of a verb in the imperative, which do not appear on the surface, are present in the corresponding syntactic structures—if the language in question has agreement;[6] this is the case in Serbian. Sentences (2a), with an elided 1sg personal pronoun, and (2b), with this pronoun overtly present, have the SSyntSs shown in Figures 1 and 2, respectively.

(2) [Q: *Zašto?* 'Why?']

a. *Ne zna+*$m_{1,SG}$. Lit. 'Not know.'

b. *Ja*←**subj**–[*ne*]–*zna+*$m_{1,SG}$. *(Ali neko možda zna.)* Lit. 'I not know. (But someone perhaps does.)'

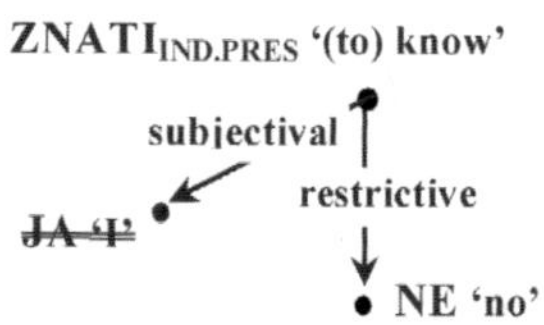

Figure 1: SSyntS of (2a)

The communicatively unmarked 1sg pronoun in the role the SSynt-Subject is earmarked for deletion (as indicated by a strikethrough of the corresponding node label) and "dropped" in the subsequent stages of text synthesis.

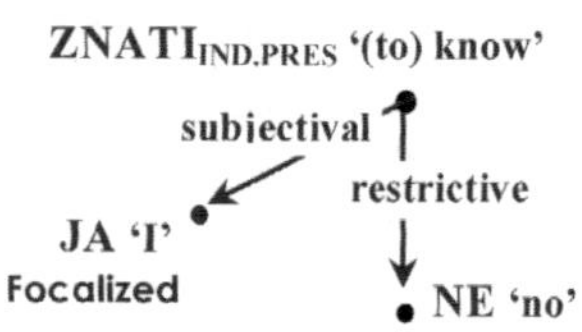

Figure 2: SSyntS of (2b)

The same pronoun in the same syntactic role, if communicatively marked as focalized, "survives" and eventually surfaces in the clause as an overt pronominal subject.

- **Specific Linear Position with Respect to the MV**

In Serbian, linear position of clause elements is determined more by communicative than syntactic factors. As mentioned at the beginning of this section, in an all-Rhematic clause, the MV is clause-initial, i.e., the Subject follows it, but in a communicatively articulated clause, a Subject expressing the Theme is clause-initial, i.e., it precedes the MV. Both of these states of affairs are illustrated in (3a). A Subject expressing the Rhematic focus is clause-final, i.e., it follows the MV, as shown (3b).

(3) a. [*Zatutnjaše*–**subj**→*bubnjevi,*]$_{\mathbf{Rh}}$ [*oglasi*–[*se*]–**subj**→*frulica,*]$_{\mathbf{Rh}}$ [*ali je oduvaše*–**subj**→*trube*]$_{\mathbf{Rh}}$. [*Trube*]$_{\mathbf{Th}}$←**subj**–[*su*$_{(MV)}$ *za sada samo otpuhivale*]$_{\mathbf{Rh}}$, *dok* ... Lit. 'Thundered drums, was.heard flute, but her blew.away trumpets. Trumpets are for now only having. blowing.in.response, while ...' = 'There was a thunder of drums, there sounded a flute, but it was blown away by trumpets. The trumpets, for the time being, were only blowing in response, while ...'

b. [*Prvu nagradu dobio je*$_{(MV)}$]$_{Th}$–**subj**→[*pesnik Z.G.*]$_{Rh}$. Lit. 'First prize.$_{ACC}$ having.gotten is poet Z.G.' = 'The first prize went to the poet Z.G.'

Given the fact that the subject's position vis-a-vis the MV can be determined, at least partially, by the communicative structure (= is not exclusively determined by the MV), does the Parameter 3 apply in Serbian (and other communicatively oriented languages)? I believe that it does because, if we exclude all-Rhematic sentences (namely, on the basis of their lesser frequency) and consider the simplest sentence possible, like [*Jovan*]$_{\mathbf{Th}}$ [*je bolestan*]$_{\mathbf{Rh}}$ 'Jovan is sick', in Serbian, the subject precedes the MV, whereas in Arabic, for example, it follows the MV.

- **Control of the Agreement of the V**

The subject controls the agreement of the MV in number and person (4a); in compound tenses, it also controls the agreement of the participle—in number and gender (4b-e). Example (4c) illustrates a more complex case of agreement, with the subject quantified by a numeral. In (4d)-(4e), we see the singular neuter agreement of the participle with a zero empty subject (see Subsection 3.2.1) and an infinitive/clausal subject, respectively.

[6] In languages that have the MV agreement with the subject, all sentences, including so-called "impersonal" sentences, necessarily have a subject, at least in their SSyntSs. But in a language without agreement, such as Lezguian, subjectless sentences—with no subject postulated in the corresponding SSyntSs—do exist (Mel'čuk 1988: 228-230).

(4) a. *Dete*$_{\text{(N, neut)NOM.SG}}$←**subj**–*spava*+∅$_{\textbf{3.SG}}$. 'The child is sleeping' ~ *Deca*$_{\text{(N)NOM.PL}}$←**subj**–*spava*+*ju*$_{\textbf{3.PL}}$. 'The children are sleeping.'

b. *Dete*$_{\text{(N, neut)NOM.SG}}$←**subj**–*je*$_{\text{(MV)3.SG}}$ *spava*+*l*$_{\text{PAST}}$+*o*$_{\textbf{NEUT.SG}}$. 'The child was sleeping.' ~ *Deca*$_{\text{(N, neut)NOM.PL}}$←**subj**–*su*$_{\text{(MV)3.PL}}$ *spava*+*l*$_{\text{PAST}}$+*a*$_{\textbf{NEUT.PL}}$. 'The children were sleeping.'

c. *Osta*+*l*$_{\text{PAST}}$+*e*$_{\textbf{FEM.PL}}$ *su*$_{\text{(MV)3,PL}}$–[*dve*]**subj**→*jabuke*$_{\text{(N, fem)GEN.SG}}$. Lit. 'Were left two apple'. ~ *Osta*+*l*+*o*$_{\textbf{NEUT.SG}}$ *je*$_{\text{(MV)3.SG}}$–[*pet*]–**subj**→*jabuka*$_{\text{(N, fem)GÉN.PL}}$. Lit. 'Was left two apples.'

d. *Bi*+*l*$_{\text{PAST}}$+*o*$_{\textbf{NEUT.SG}}$ *mi* *je*$_{\text{(MV)3.SG}}$–**subj**→∅$_{\text{(Pron, 3.SG.NEUT)}}$ *hladno*. Lit. 'Being.been to.me is cold' = 'I was cold.'

e. *Otići*$_{\text{(V)INF}}$ <[*Da se ode*]$_{\text{COMPLETIVE.CL}}$>←**subj**–*nije*$_{\text{(MV)3.SG}}$ *bi*+*l*$_{\text{PAST}}$+*o*$_{\textbf{NEUT.SG}}$ *moguće*. Lit. 'To.leave <That REFL leaves> not being.been possible' = 'To leave <Leaving> was not possible.'

- **Government for Case by the MV**

Most often, a nominal subject in Serbian receives the nominative case imposed by the MV. In some special contexts it receives the genitive case; see below, examples (12)-(15).

- **Demotion Under Passivization**

Under passivization of the MV, the subject is demoted to the role of the Agentive Complement, while the former direct object gets promoted to the subject position. This is a standard feature of the subject of a passive verb and needs not be illustrated.

3.1.2 Characterizing properties of the SSynt-Subject

Recall that characterizing properties are valid only for a prototypical subject, which in Serbian is a noun in the nominative case [= N_{NOM}]. Table 2 lists some of the characterizing properties of the Serbian subject.

1.	Target of cliticization	✖
2.	Target of relativization	✔
3.	Controller of reflexivization	✔
4.	Target of (pseudo-)clefting	✖
5.	Controller of an attributive actantial complement	✔
6.	Controller of anaphora	✔
7.	Controller of ellipsis in coordination	✔
8.	Left/right dislocation	✔
9.	Raising	✔
10.	Extraction from a completive clause	✔
11.	Reaction to negation	✖

Table 2: Characterizing Properties of the prototypical SyntSubj in Serbian

Properties 1, 4 and 11 do not apply: property 1 is not applicable because Serbian personal pronouns have no clitic forms in the nominative case, and property 4 because this language lacks the corresponding syntactic operations altogether. As for property 11, although some negated verbs can take either the genitive subject or the canonical nominative subject, this behavior cannot be tied exclusively to the negation since the same verbs in the positive polarity also allow for the genitive ~ nominative variation in the case of the subject; see example (12b) and (13a).

Illustrations for properties 3, 7-10 follow. (In the examples (5) and (6), the syntactic subject is boxed.)

- **Controller of Reflexivization**

(5) a. *Jovan*$_i$ *pije* ***svoj***$_i$ <≠ *njegov*$_j$> *čaj* Lit. 'Jovan$_i$ drinks self$_i$ <≠ his$_j$> tea' = 'Jovan drinks his (= 'his own') tea.'

vs.

b. *Jovanu*$_i$ ***se pije*** ****svoj*** <*njegov*$_{i/j}$> *čaj*. Lit. 'To.Jovan$_i$ REFL drinks *self's$_i$ <his$_{i/j}$> tea' = 'Jovan feels like drinking his tea.'

In (5a), the special form of the possessive determiner (SVOJ), is used, necessarily co-referential with the subject (JOVAN). But in (5b), with the MV in the reflexive form, within the desiderative ('feel-like') construction, where ČAJ, rather than JOVAN, is the subject, SVOJ is ungrammatical. The correct possessive form here is NJEGOV, which has an ambiguous reading ('his own' or 'that person's'), just like in English.

- **Controller of Ellipsis in Coordination**

(6) a. *Petar* ***je sreo*** *Kostu* ***i rekao*** *mu* ***(je)***... Lit. 'P. is having.met K. and having.told him (is) ...' = 'P. met K. and told him…'

vs.

b. **Petar*$_i$ ***je sreo*** *Kostu* ***i*** *on*$_i$ *mu* ***je rekao***... Lit. 'P. is having.met K. and he him is having.told …' = 'P. met K. and he told him…'

As can be concluded from the ungrammaticality of (6b), under coordination, ellipsis of the subject in the second conjunct is obligatory (and that of the auxiliary, optional).

- **Dislocation**

Left dislocation is illustrated in (7a-b), and right dislocation in (7c); the dislocated element is boxed.

(7) a. Colloq. *Jovan*$_i$ *on*$_i$←**subj**–*je super momak* Lit. 'Jovan he is super guy' = 'As for J., he is a swell guy.'

b. Colloq. *Francuzi*$_i$ *oni*$_i$←**subj**–*ručaju*$_{\text{(MV)}}$ *u podne*. 'The French they lunch at noon' = 'As for French, they have lunch at noon.'

c. *Nije*–**subj**→*on*$_i$ *naivan, taj tvoj* *drug*$_i$. Lit. 'Not.is he naïve, that your friend.' = 'He is not naïve, that friend or yours.'

Left dislocation, frowned upon by purists, is freely used in colloquial speech; its discourse function is *topic shifting* or *topic layering* (terminology taken from Delais-Roussarie *et al.* 2004). Right dislocation, not stylistically marked, serves the discourse function of *topic backgrounding.*

- **Raising**

(8) a. *Izgleda* [*da je*$_{(MV)}$–**subj**→*Jovan bolestan* <*u pravu, to zaboravio*>]. Lit. 'Seems that is J. sick/in right/this having.forgotten' = 'It seems that J. is sick/is right/has forgotten this.'

b. *Jovan*←**subj**–*izgleda*$_{(MV)}$ *bolestan* <**u pravu*, **to zaboravio*>. 'Jovan seems sick <right, to have forgotten that>.'

Raising of the subject is allowed in Serbian only out of the subordinate clause whose MV is a copula controlling an adjectival attributive complement ("N+V$_{(copula)}$+Adj"); it is thus more limited than in English or French, for instance, where the sentences corresponding to the starred Serbian examples are fully acceptable.

- **Extraction from a Completive Clause**

(9) a. ***Ko*** *misliš* [*da* ~~***ko***~~←**subj**–*dolazi*]? Lit. 'Who (you) think [that ~~who~~ comes]? = 'Who do you think is coming'?

b. ***Ko*** *kažeš* [*da* ~~***ko***~~←**subj**–*voli Petra*]? Lit. 'Who (you) say [that ~~who~~ loves P.]? = 'Who do you say loves P.?'

c. ***Šta*** *veruješ* [*da* ~~***šta***~~←**subj**–[*se*]–*desilo*]? Lit. 'What (you) believe [that what REFL having.occurred]? = 'What do you believe happened?'

Subject extraction from a completive clause seems to be unrestricted at least with communication and opinion verbs in the matrix clause; the precise conditions under which this operation is allowed remain to be determined. From a discursive viewpoint, the extraction makes the subject of the subordinate clause the rhematic focus of the entire sentence.

Discussing the prototypical subject in Croatian, Belaj & Kučanda (2007: 4) ascribe to it only the defining properties 4 and 5 from our Table 1. As one of the subject's behavioral properties, they indicate the following one: the subject is the addressee of the imperative provided it is the Agent or someone pragmatically conceived of as acting as an Agent. It is questionable, however, whether this is a purely syntactic property. Typologically, the syntactic subject of an imperative is not necessarily the Addressee: see Mel'čuk (1988: 194-196).

3.2 Implementation of the SSynt-Subject in Serbian

In addition to a prototypical implementation by an N_{NOM}, the SSynt-Subject can be implemented in Serbian by items 2-7 in Table 3 below, some of which have already been illustrated in the preceding discussion.

In what follows, I will illustrate two less usual types of subject: zero (nominative) subjects, both semantically full and empty, and subjects in the genitive case.

1.	N_{NOM}
2.	N_{GEN}
3.	$N_{(quant)NOM}$ <Adv_{-quant}> [→N_{GEN}]
4.	PREP→N_{GEN} [→Num][7]
5.	Clause (completive, interrogative, headless relative)
6.	V_{INF}
7.	Direct speech fragment

Table 3: Implementation of the SyntSubj in Serbian

3.2.1 Zero Subjects

These subjects are genuine lexemes, not to be confounded with null subjects of the generative syntax. The fact that there are lexemes that can only function as subjects speaks to the importance of this syntactic role. In Serbian, there are two such lexemes.

- **∅**$^{\text{'people'}}_{\text{(Pron, masc, 3.PL)}}$ is a semantically full zero subject. This is an **indefinite** personal (as opposed to **im**personal) pronoun, meaning, roughly, 'some unspecified people' (cf. Fr. ON and Ger. MAN).[8] It is used within the "normal" personal construction and imposes the 3pl agreement on the MV and (in compound tenses) the plural masculine agreement on the participle.

(10) a. ∅$^{\text{'people'}}_{\text{(Pron, masc, 3.PL)}}$←**subj**–*Kaž+u*$_{(MV)3PL}$ *da je to davno bilo*. Lit. 'Say that is that long.ago being.been. = 'People <They#2> say that happened long ago.'

b. *O tome* ∅$^{\text{'people'}}_{\text{(Pron, masc, 3.PL)}}$←**subj**–*su*$_{(MV)3PL}$ *pisa+l*$_{PAST}$+***i***$_{MASC, PL}$ *u novinama*. Lit. 'About that are having.written in newspapers.' = 'They#2 wrote about that in newspapers.'

[7] Some prepositions allowed in this construction: OKO/CIRKA 'around', DO 'up.to', OD 'starting.from', PREKO 'over', etc.

[8] 3pl indefinite pronouns, both zero and non-zero, are common in the world's languages (see Siewierska, 2010); they are sometimes (incorrectly) called impersonal pronouns.

This pronoun is of course not interchangeable in texts with the substitute 3pl personal pronoun form *oni* 'they' = 'entities/facts the Speaker mentioned in the previous discourse, whose referents the Addressee can identify'. (English has an overt indefinite pronoun—THEY#2 in the translation of the examples in (10)—that corresponds to Serbian $\varnothing^{\text{'people'}}_{\text{(Pron, masc. 3.PL)}}$.)

- $\boldsymbol{\varnothing}_{\textbf{(Pron, neut, 3.SG)}}$ is a semantically empty zero subject. This is an indefinite impersonal pronoun, which means that it underlies the so-called *impersonal construction*, imposing the 3sg agreement on the MV and the singular neuter agreement on the participle.

(11) a. *Kreta*+l_{PAST}+$\boldsymbol{o}_{\textbf{NEUT.3.SG}}$ *se* [*je*$_{\text{(MV)3.SG}}$–**subj**→$\varnothing_{\text{(Pron, neut, 3.SG)}}$] *u 8*. Lit. 'Being.left REFL is at 8' = 'The departure was at 8.'

b. *Vesni se* [*je*$_{\text{(MV)3.SG}}$–**subj**→$\varnothing_{\text{(Pron, neut, 3.SG)}}$][9] *spava*+$l_{\text{PAST}}$+$\boldsymbol{o}_{\textbf{NEUT.3.SG}}$. Lit. 'To.Vesna REFL is being.slept' = Vesna was sleepy.'

c. *Zuja*+l_{PAST}+$\boldsymbol{o}_{\textbf{NEUT.3.SG}}$ *mi* *je*$_{\text{(MV)3.SG}}$–**subj**→$\varnothing_{\text{(Pron, neut, 3.SG)}}$ *u ušima*. Lit. 'Being.hummed to.me is in ears' = 'It was humming in my ears'.

The impersonal construction is used in Serbian with (among other things): 1) meteorological verbs and expressions; 2) some verbal voices, such as absolute suppressive (11a); 2) some verbal derivations, such as desiderative, aka *involuntary state construction* ((11b) and (5b)), and 3) verbs and expressions denoting some sensations ((10c and (4d)) and feelings.

Impersonal constructions have received a widely varying treatment in the literature. Thus, (11a) is considered by some to be a "subjectless sentence" (Radovanović 1990, or else a "sentence with a generalized Agent" (Tanasić (2003). Sentences like those in (11b)-(11c) are sometimes described as featuring non-canonical subjects (*Vesni* 'to.Vesna' and *mi* 'to.me', respectively), variously called *dative*, *oblique*, *quirky* or *quasi* subjects (see Belaj & Kučanda, 2007 for Croatian, Rivero & Milojević-Sheppard, 2006 for Slovenian, and Moore & Perlmutter, 2000 for Russian). For us, however, the MV agreement is the key: since the MV clearly does not agree with the noun in the dative, the latter cannot be the subject; more on this at the very end of this section. For a treatment of impersonal constructions in the Meaning-Text framework, see Milićević (2013) and (2009: 107-113).

3.2.2 Subjects in the Genitive Case

In what follows, I will distinguish the genuine use of the genitive to mark the syntactic subject, i.e., such that the subject is assigned the genitive case exclusively by the main predicate, from two apparently similar but very different situations: the genitive of the subject used in semantic capacity and in the context of quantification.

- **Genuine genitive of the subject—imposed by the clause predicate**

As we have seen, verbless sentences of type (1b) have the subject in the genitive case, assigned to it by the presentative functioning as the main predicate. In full-fledged sentences, subjects in the genitive case are encountered with the existential verbs IMATI/BITI 'there.be':

(12) a. *Ima*$_{\text{(MV)}}$–[li]–**subj**→*vode*$_{\text{(N, fem)GEN.SG}}$ <**voda*$_{\text{NOM.SG}}$> *na Marsu?* Lit. 'Be INTERR of. water <*water> on Mars'? = 'Is there water on Mars?'

b. *Biće/Neće*$_{\text{(MV)}}$–**subj**→*kiše*$_{\text{(N, fem)GEN.SG}}$ <*kiša*$_{\text{NOM.SG}}$> *za vikend.* Lit. 'Will.be/Will.not.be of.rain <rain> this weekend' = 'It will rain on the weekend.'

These verbs are suppletive in the following sense: IMATI (lit. 'to have') is used in the present tense, BITI (lit. 'to be') in the past and the future. The former takes only an N_{GEN} as the subject, while the latter can also take a nominative subject—in some restricted contexts, with a slight difference in meaning (for the time being, I cannot make this statement more precise). This is a case bordering on the semantic use of genitive, to be discussed immediately below.

- **Genitive of the subject used in semantic capacity**

In some specific cases, for instance, with verbs having privative meaning, like NEDOSTAJATI '(to) lack' or FALITI '(to) lack', the subject can appear either in the canonical nominative or in the genitive, this alternation being accompanied by a semantic difference.

(13) a. *Tebi (ne) nedostaje strpljenj*+$a_{\text{SG.GEN}}$ <*strpljenje*+$\varnothing_{\text{NOM.SG}}$> Lit. To.you (not) lacks some.patience <patience>. = 'You (do not) lack patience.'

b. *Zafali*+l_{PAST}+$o_{\text{NEUT.3.SG}}$ *mi je*$_{\text{(MV)3.SG}}$–**subj**→*hleb*+$a_{\text{GEN.SG}}$ <*Zafali*+o_{PAST}+$\varnothing_{\text{MASC.3.SG}}$ *mi je*$_{\text{(MV)3.SG}}$–**subj**→*hleb*+$\varnothing_{\text{NOM.SG}}$> Lit. Being.lacked to.me is some.bread <bread>.

In (13a), with the N_{GEN} as the subject, the meaning conveyed is 'You have some patience

[9] Sentences (11a) and (11b) actually have a slightly different surface form, from which the clitic auxiliary ***je*** 'is' is deleted; the deletion happens in order to avoid the illegitimate clitic sequence **se je*. This is an interesting and rare case of deletion of the MV from the clause.

(but not enough)', while with the N_{NOM} as the subject the meaning is 'You have no patience'; the same difference is observed in (13b). Here, the structural case is overridden, as it were, for semantic reasons: the genitive expresses more than it normally does ('a part of'), and the same is true for the nominative ('the whole').[10] This is different from what we observe in Russian, where the corresponding verbs take only a genitive subject and where the partial ~ total ambiguity persists: *Mne ne xvataet bumagi <*bumaga>* Lit. 'To.me not suffice of.paper <*paper>' = 'I don't have enough paper' or 'I do not have paper at all'.

Antonić (2005) treats both (12) and (13) as impersonal constructions, on the grounds of the default, 3sg neuter, agreement of the participle in compound tenses.

- **Genitive of the subject in the context of quantification**

A subject quantified by a numeral other than 1 or ending in 1 gets automatically the genitive case. This state of affairs is illustrated in (14), as well as in (4c).

(14) a. *Trenutno se u bioskopu "Zvezda" prikazuje*$_{(MV)}$–**subj**–*[tri]*→*film+a*$_{(N)GEN.SG}$. Lit. 'Currently REFL in cinema "Zvezda" shows three movie' = 'Currently, three movies are playing in the cinema "Zvezda".

b. *Doći će*$_{(MV)}$–**subj**→*oko*$_{(Prep)}$ *deset zvanic+a*$_{(N)GEN.PL}$. Lit. 'Will.come around ten invitees' = 'Around ten invitees will come.'

The subjects FILM 'movie' and ZVANICA 'invitee' are imposed the genitive case (as well as the number) by the numerals[11]. But, while they are morphologically governed by the numerals, the nouns govern the latter syntactically.

Finally, note that quantifying nouns/adverbs, like those in (15), appear themselves in the role of syntactic subject, taking an obligatory N_{GEN} as their complement.

(15) a. *Binu zaveja*$_{(MV)}$–subj→*milion*$_{(N, Quant)}$ *šarenih konfet+a*$_{(N)GEN.PL}$. Lit. 'The scene snowed.under a million of multi-colored confetti' = 'The scene was showered by a million of multi-colored confetti.'

b. *Bez krova nad glavom ostalo je*$_{(MV)}$–subj→*mnogo*$_{(Adv, Quant)}$ *ljud+i*$_{(N)GEN.PL}$. Lit. 'Without roof above head stayed is many people' = 'Many people were left without a roof above their heads.'

I will conclude this section by illustrating the production of sentence (11c) within a Meaning-Text linguistic model of Serbian, starting from its Semantic Structure [= SemS] and "going up" to the Deep-Syntactic Structure [= DSyntS] and the Surface-Syntactic Structure [= SSyntS].

Figure 3 shows the SemS underlying the verbs of unpleasant sensations, such as ZUJATI '(to) hum' featured in (11c). The corresponding situation has two participants: the Experiencer of the sensation ('X') and the Body Part in which the sensation is localized ('Y'), representing, respectively, the verb's semantic actants (SemA) 1 and 2. (For ease of reading, the SemS is written in English although, strictly speaking, it should contain semantemes of Serbian.)

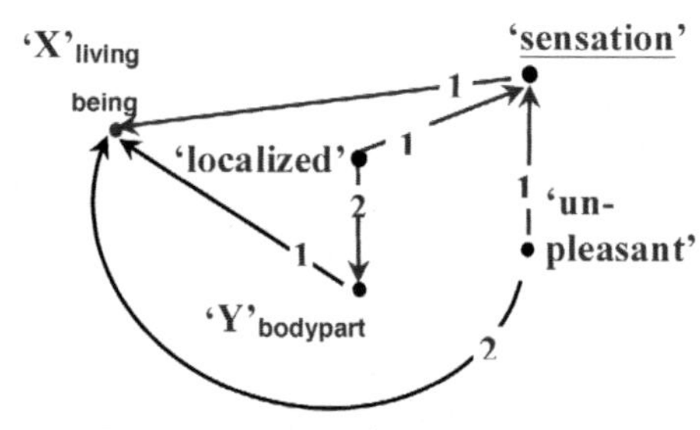

Figure 3: Incomplete SemS of (11c)

In the transition towards the DSyntS (Figure 4), the Experiencer is mapped onto the DeepSyntA II, and the Body Part, to the DSyntA **III**. At this stage, there is no DSynt-actant corresponding to the surface-syntactic subject.

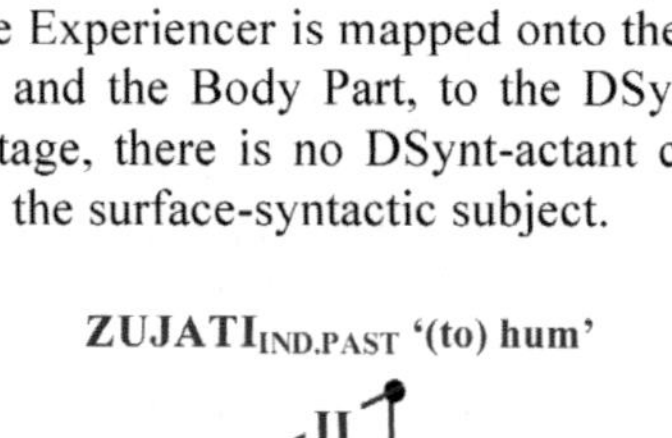

Figure 4: DSyntS of (11c)

This mapping is done using the information in the Government Pattern [= GP] of the verb ZUJATI, which is part of its dictionary entry:

$X_{Experiencer}$ ⇔ II	$Y_{Bodypart}$ ⇔ III
-indir-objectival→ *N*-DAT	**-obj.oblique→** *u* 'in' *N*-LOC

Figure 5: GP of ZUJATI '(to) hum'

[10] Cf. the same phenomenon occurring in *Imate li struj+e* $_{SG.GEN}$ *<struj+u* $_{SG.ACC}$*>?*, with the direct object in the genitive or the accusative, which mean, respectively, 'Do you have power right now?', and 'Are you on the power grid?'

[11] Strictly speaking, the subject in (14b) is the preposition, rather than the noun in the genitive, since the dependency arrow (in the corresponding SSynt-structure) enters the node labeled by the preposition. I will allow myself to ignore this fact here.

The first row in the GP indicates the verb's diathesis, i.e., the correspondence between its SemAs and its DSyntAs; this correspondence is known in other frameworks as *linking*.

The implementation of DSyntAs by concrete SSynt constructions intervenes in the transition towards the SSyntS, using the information indicated in the second row of the *GP* above: the Experiencer ends up being an indirect object, and the Body Part gets the position of an oblique object. It is at this stage that the empty zero subject is introduced (by a special syntactic rule)—for the purposes of MV agreement. The resulting SSyntS is shown in Figure 6.

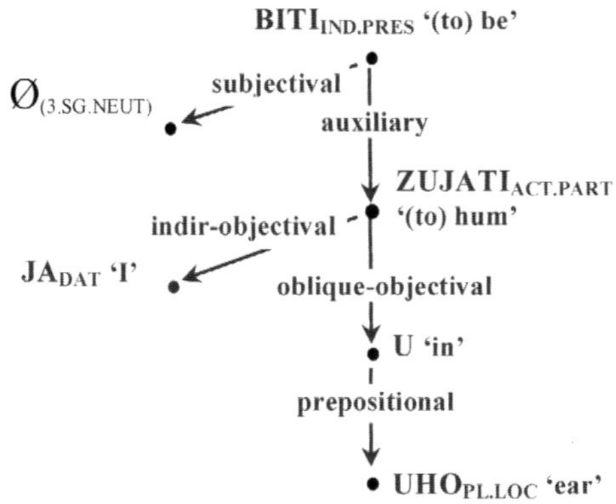

Figure 6: SSyntS of (11c)

As one can see, what is "quirky" is not the subject itself (at least not in the usual sense of the dative subject, although an empty zero subject is perhaps as deserving of the label), but the linking: the fact that in this case the Experiencer fails to correspond to DSyntA I of the verb, which itself corresponds to the SSynt subject.

4 Conclusion

The syntactic subject in Serbian is a well-behaved Indo-European subject with some more specific Slavic features. While this is obviously no news, the paper's contribution consists in a systematic overview of these features and their presentation within a coherent, formal dependency-oriented framework.

Acknowledgments

I am very grateful to Igor Mel'čuk for his comments on a pre-final version of this paper. Thanks are also due to three anonymous reviewers for their helpful suggestions. All the usual disclaimers apply.

References

Antonić, I. (2005). Subjektski genitiv u standardnom srpskom jeziku [The Subjective Genitive in Standard Serbian]. *Južnoslovenski filolog*, LXI (2005): 125-143.

Beck, D. (2000). Semantic Agents, Syntactic Subjects, and Discourse Topics: How to Locate Lushootseed Sentences in Space and Time. *Studies in Language* 24/2: 277-317.

Belaj, B. & Kučanda, D. (2007). On the Syntax, Semantics and Pragmatics of Some Subject-like NPs in Croatian. *Suvremena Lingvistika*, vol. 33, issue 63 (2007): 1-12.

Buljan G. & Kučanda, D. (2004). Semantičke funkcije subjekta, teorija prototipova i metonimija [Semantic Functions of the Subject, the Prototype Theory and Metonymy]. *Jezikoslovlje* 5.1-2 (2004): 87-101.

Creissels, D. (2014). Approche typologique de la notion du sujet. *Colloque international "Du Sujet et de son absence dans les langues"*. Université du Maine, 27-28 mars 2014; pp. 17.

Delais-Roussaire, E. Doetjes, J. & Sleeman, P. (2004). Dislocation. In Corblin, F. & Swart, H. eds, 2004, *Handbook of French Semantics*. CSLI Publications; 501-529.

Foley, W. & Van Valin, R. (1997). On the Viability of the Notion of Subject in Universal Grammar. *Proceedings of the Third Annual Meeting of the Berkeley Linguistic Society*; 293-320.

Iordanskaja, L. & Mel'čuk, I. (2009). Establishing an Inventory of Surface-Syntactic Relations: Valence-controlled Surface- syntactic Dependents of the Verb in French. In Polguère, A. & Mel'čuk, I., eds, 2009: 151-234.

Kahane, S. (2003). The Meaning-Text Theory, in Agel, V., Eichinger L. M., Eroms, H.-W., Hellwig, P. Heringer H. J., Lobin, H., eds, *Dependency and Valency. An International Handbook of Contemporary Research*, vol. 1. Berlin/New York: De Gruyter; 546-570.

Keenan, E. (1976). Towards A Universal Definition of "Subject". In Li, Ch., ed., *Subjects and Topics*. New York, etc.: Academic Press; 305-333.

Keenan, E. & Comrie, B. (1977). Noun Phrase Accessibility and Universal Grammar. *Linguistic Inquiry* 8/1: 63–99.

Kibrik, A. (1997). Beyond Subject and Object: Towards a Comprehensive Relational Typology. *Linguistic Typology*, 1: 279-346.

Klajn, I. (2005). *Gramatika srpskog jezika* [A Grammar of Serbian]. Beograd: Zavod za udžbenike i nastavna sredstva.

Kučanda, D. (1998). Rečenični subject u hrvatskom i engleskom jeziku (Clausal Subjects in Croatian and English). PhD Thesis. Zagreb: Philological Faculty, University of Zagreb.

Lazard, G. (2009). Qu'est-ce qu'un sujet ? *La linguistique*, 2009/1 Vol. 45: 151-159.

Martinet, A. (1972). Should We Drop the Notion of Subject? *La revue canadienne de linguistique*, vol. 17/2-3: 175-179.

Mel'čuk, I. (2014). Syntactic Subject: Syntactic Relations, Once Again. In Plungjan, V., ed., *Jazyk. Konstanty. Peremenye. Pamjati Aleksandra Evgen'eviča Kibrika*. Sankt-Peterburg: Aleteija; 169-216.

Mel'čuk, I. (2012-2013-2015): *Semantics: from Meaning to Text*, vols. 1-3. Amsterdam/Philadelphia: John Benjamins.

Mel'čuk, I. (2009). Dependency in Natural Language. In: Polguère, A. & Mel'čuk, I. (2009); 1-1-110.

Mel'čuk, I. (2004). Actants in Semantic and Syntax. *Linguistics*, 42/1: 1-66 and 42/2: 247-291.

Mel'čuk, I (1988). Dependency Syntax: Theory and Practice. Albany (N.-Y.): SUNY Press.

Mel'čuk, I. (1974). *Opyt teorii lingvističeskix modelej Smysl-Tekst*. Moskva: *Nauka*.

Milićević, J. (2013). Impersonal Constructions in Serbian. A Description within a Meaning-Text Linguistic Model. In: Kor-Chahine, I. ed., *Current Studies in Slavic Linguistics*. Amsterdam/Philadelphia: John Benjamins; 169-183.

Milićević, J. (2009). Schéma de régime: le pont entre le lexique et la grammaire. Blanco, X. & P.-A. Buvet, eds, *La représentation des structures prédicat-argument. Langages*, 176-4/2009 (numéro special): 94-116.

Mille, S. (2014). *Deep Stochastic Sentence Generation: Resources and Strategies*. PhD Thesis, DTIC, Universitat Pompeu Fabra, Barcelona. http://www.taln.upf.edu/system/files/biblio_files/thesis-SM-140602.pdf

Mithun, M. & Chafe, W. (1997). What are S, A, and O? *Studies in Language* 23/3: 569-596.

Moore, J. & Perlmutter, D. (2000). What Does it Take to Be a Dative Subject? *Natural Language and Linguistic Theory* 18/2: 373-416.

Mrazovac, P. & Vukadinović, Z. (2009). *Gramatika srpskog jezika za strance* [A Grammar of Serbian for Foreigners]. Sremski Karlovci/Novi Sad: Izdavačka knjižarnica Zorana Stojadonovića.

Piper, P., Antonić, I., Ružić, V., Tanasić, S., Popović, Lj. & Tošović, B. (2005). *Sintaksa savremenoga srpskog jezika: prosta rečenica* [Syntax of Contemporary Serbian: the Simple Clause]. Beograd: Beogradska knjiga & Novi Sad: Matica srpska.

Polguère, A. & Mel'čuk, I., eds (2009). *Dependency in Natural Language*. Amsterdam/Philadelphia: John Benjamins.

Radovanović, M. (1990). O bezličnoj rečenici [On the Impersonal Sentence]. In Radovanović, M., *Spisi iz sintakse i semantike*. Novi Sad: Dobra vest; 209-219.

Rivero, M.-L. & Milojević-Sheppard, M. (2006). Revisiting Involuntary State Constructions in Slovenian. In: Marušič, F. & Žaucer, R. (2006), *Studies in Formal Slavic Linguistics. Contributions from Formal Descriptions of Slavic Languages 6.5, held in Nova Gorica*. Frankfurt am Main: Peter Lang.

Siewierska, A. (2010). From Third Plural to Passive. Incipient, Emergent and Established Passives. *Diachronica* 27/1: 73-103.

Tanasić, S. (2003). Bezlične rečenice sa uopštenim agensom [Impersonal Sentences with a Generalized Agent]. *Južnoslovenski filolog*, LX (2003): 41-55.

Sources of Examples

Arsenijević, V. (2013). *Let*. Beograd: Laguna.

Žurić, V. (2009). *Narodnjakova smrt. Melo(s)drama*. Beograd: Laguna.

Korpus srpskog jezika [The Corpus of Serbian Language]: www.korpus. matf.bg.ac.rs

Serbian WWW pages

A Historical Overview of the Status of Function Words in Dependency Grammar

Timothy Osborne
Zhejiang University
Hangzhou
China
tjo3ya@yahoo.com

Daniel Maxwell
US Chess Center
Washington DC
USA
dan.maxwell@gmail.com

Abstract

This contribution provides a historical overview of the analysis of function words in surface syntactic dependency hierarchies. Starting with Tesnière (1959), the overview progresses through some prominent voices in the history of DG (Mel'čuk 1958, 1963, Hays 1964, Matthews 1981, Schubert 1987, Maxwell and Schubert 1989, Hudson 1976, 1984, etc.). The overview establishes that the analysis of prepositions has been almost unanimous: they are positioned as heads over their nouns. There has been more variation concerning the status of auxiliary verbs, although most DG grammarians have viewed them as heads over their content verbs. Concerning determiners, the dominant position is that they are dependents under their nouns, although there are a couple of prominent voices that assume the opposite stance.

1 The dependency status of function words

The distinction between function words and content words has been made by linguists of various backgrounds. A rough definition of the distinction might be that content words can be understood without any supporting context whereas function words cannot. The discussion in this article takes place in terms of specific syntactic categories which happen to be function words according to this definition.

A recent proposal for surface analyses of dependencies categorically subordinates function words to content words. Universal Stanford Dependencies (USD) (de Marneffe et al. 2014) advocate an annotation scheme that positions auxiliary verbs, adpositions, subordinators, and determiners as dependents of the content words with which they co-occur. Thus according to this scheme, the DG analysis of the sentence *The kids have eaten at school* would be as follows:

(1)

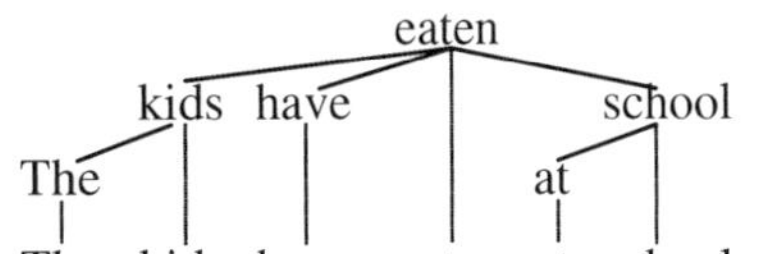

a. The kids have eaten at school.

The USD analysis shown with (1a) stands in contrast to more conventional analyses, which position auxiliaries as heads over content verbs and prepositions as heads over their nouns:

(1)

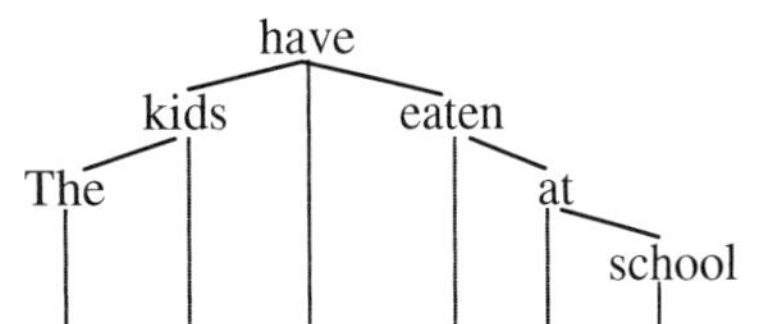

b. The kids have eaten at school.

In pursuing the analysis in (1a), USD is advocating an understanding of surface dependencies that is generally contrary to the views about function words that have crystallized over the decades in support of the analysis in (1b).

This contribution surveys some prominent voices in the DG tradition, in order to determine the extent to which the analysis in (1a) has been advocated over the decades since Tesnière (1959) and the period in which computational linguistics has become influential. Space does not allow us to try to evaluate these analyses in detail, but when the authors of these analyses attempt to justify their decisions, we occasionally make comments about their argumentation.

2 Tesnière (1959/2015)

Tesnière's analysis of function words has not survived into most modern DGs. The reason it has not done so is tied to the fact that Tesnière's subtheory of transfer has also not survived into most modern DGs. Tesnière viewed most function words as *translatives* (auxiliary verbs, prepositions, subordinators, many determiners). As such, they were not granted autonomy in the syntactic representations, but rather they appeared together with a content word, the two

Proceedings of the Third International Conference on Dependency Linguistics (Depling 2015), pages 241–250,
Uppsala, Sweden, August 24–26 2015.

forming a *dissociated nucleus*. What this means in the current context is that Tesniere's *Éléments* (1959) did not provide much direct guidance concerning the dependency analysis of function words.

While Tesnière is widely credited as the father of modern DGs, he himself was not aware of the dependency vs. constituency distinction. That distinction was first established a few years after his death. Hays (1964) is generally credited with establishing the term *dependency grammar* (as opposed to *phrase structure grammar*). Thus the fact that Tesnière's account of function words left much room for debate about the actual dependency status of function words should not be so surprising. Tesnière never intended to produce an account of function words that would be consistent with the purely dependency-based theories of syntax that followed him.

The relevant aspect of Tesnière's grammar can be seen with the sentence *Bernard est frappé par Alfred* 'Bernard is hit by Alfred', the structure of which Tesnière showed with his Stemma 95:

(2)
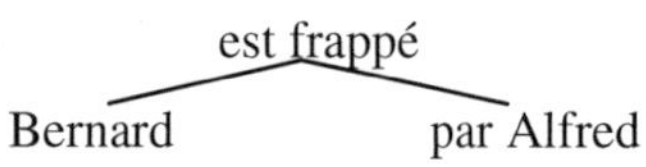

The noteworthy aspect of this stemma is the manner in which *est frappé* and *par Alfred* together occupy a single node each time. Neither can the function word be viewed as head/parent over the content word nor can the content word be viewed as head over the function word.[1] For Tesnière, the two words *est* and *frappé*, and the two words *par* and *Alfred*, formed a single nucleus together each time.

When Tesnière wanted to draw attention to the fact that a given function word forms a nucleus together with a content word, he put the two in a bubble. His stemmas of the sentences *Alfred est arrivé* 'Alfred has arrived' (Stemma 27) and *Alfred est grand* 'Alfred is big' (Stemma 28) are given here:

(3)
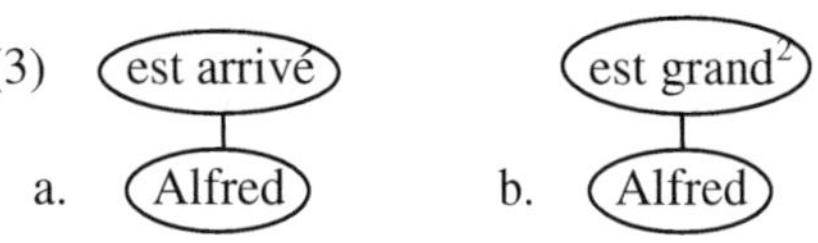

[1]One of us coauthors prefers the term *parent* to *head* in this context, reserving the latter term for one specific kind of parent, namely those which are content words rather than function words.

[2]The use of *est* 'is' in what is often considered two different ways is taken up in section 3.2.

Each of the top bubbles encloses the words of a single nucleus. Neither word in a bubble is head over the other.

This greater point established, one can nevertheless examine Tesnière's analysis of dissociated nuclei more closely. When one does so, one sees that he actually did provide some indirect guidance concerning the dependency analysis of function words. He drew a distinction between the structural and the semantic function of a nucleus (Chapter 29). In a disassociated nucleus, one of the words guarantees the structural integrity of the nucleus, and the other its semantic integrity. He also comments (Chapter 29, §18) that from an etymological point of view, the subsidiary word in a dissociated nucleus was once dependent on the constitutive word.

Tesnière later (Chapter 38, §19) states that auxiliary verbs, despite the fact that they lack semantic content, are constitutive of the nucleus in which they appear. Thus given these statements, one can extrapolate that, had Tesnière been forced to choose, he would have viewed the auxiliary verb as head over the content verb. Using his conventions, he might have produced an analysis of the sentence *Alfred est grand* 'Alfred is big' along the following lines:

(4)
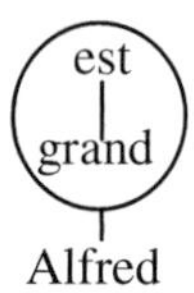

The two words *est* and *grand* together still form a single nucleus, but now the auxiliary verb is shown as head over the adjective, and at the same time, the two together form a single head over the noun *Alfred*.

One can also extend this extrapolated analysis to prepositions. Tesnière viewed a preposition as subsidiary to the noun with which it forms a dissociated nucleus (Chapter 29, §4). Thus for the phrase *livre d'Alfred*, lit. 'book of Alfred', the following analysis reflects the distinction between constitutive and subsidiary words inside the nucleus:

(5)
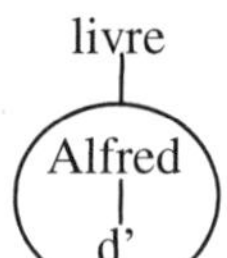

In other words, Tesnière would probably have preferred an analysis that views prepositions as dependents of their nouns, if forced to choose.

Concerning the other two relevant types of function words, i.e. subordinators and articles, Tesnière viewed subordinators as **translatives** that were essentially the same as prepositions in how they function. Translatives are part of Tesnière's theory of transfer, developed in the second half of his book. The purpose of a translative is to transfer a content word of one category to a content word of another category, e.g. a noun to an adjective, an adjective to an adverb, a verb to noun, etc. Thus he probably would have favored subordinating them to the verb with which they co-occur inside the nucleus. And concerning articles (definite and indefinite), he took a varied stance, viewing them as translatives when they perform a translative function, but as mere dependents of their noun when they do not perform a translative function.

3 Some early works

3.1 Mel'čuk (1958, 1963, 1974, etc.)

Unlike Tesnière, Igor Mel'čuk has been clear and consistent about the dependency status of function words in surface syntax. Mel'čuk and his collaborators have consistently subordinated content verbs to auxiliary verbs, nouns to adpositions, verbs to subordinators, and determiners to nouns in surface syntax in their prolific dependency-based works on syntax and grammar in the MTT (Meaning to Text Theory) framework and otherwise. Mel'čuk and his collaborators have been doing this since his earliest works, starting in 1958 (Mel'čuk 1958: 252–4, 1963: 492–3, 1974: 221–4). These early works are in Russian, but the approach is consistent with the prominent MTT works in English from the 1980s (e.g. Mel'čuk and Pertsov 1987, Mel'čuk 1988).

Judging by the dates of these early publications, it seems likely that Mel'čuk's works earn the honor of being the pathfinder in this area, since the majority of DGs that have come later have done the same, as will become increasingly clear below. Mel'čuk's position concerning the status of function words has been and is particularly firm.

3.2 Hays (1964)

Hays (1964) is considered a milestone in the development of dependency theory, in part because the article appeared in such a prominent journal, *Language*. Hays' article does not, however, say much about the dependency status of function words. The article concentrates instead on the formalization of dependency-based rewrite rules, as inspired directly by Chomsky (1957), and on the extent to which dependency and constituency formalisms are weakly or strongly equivalent. One can merely glean a sense of Hays' understanding of function words from the article.

In particular, Hays discusses the ambiguous sentence *They are flying planes*, and he captures the ambiguity with the following trees:

(6)

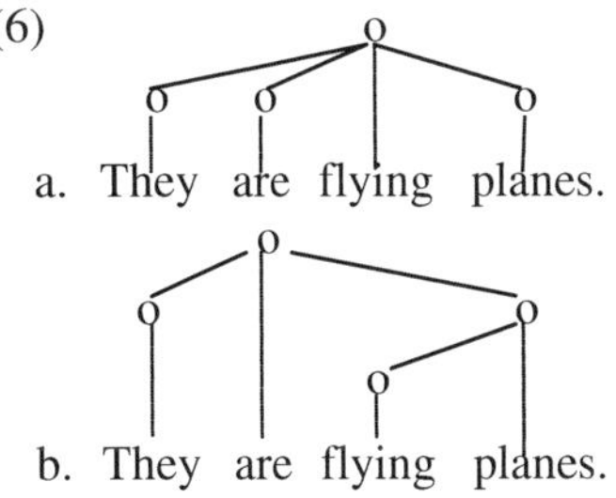

Tree (6a) reflects the meaning 'They are making the planes fly', whereas tree (6b) reflects the meaning 'They are planes that are flying'. Hays does not discuss the varying status of the auxiliary/copula *are* in these cases. But from the trees the reader can see that *are* is taken to be an auxiliary verb in tree (6a) and a copular verb in tree (6b).

Hays' interpretation of the auxiliary/copula *be* is representative of how it was widely viewed at the time. Chomsky (1957: 38f.) viewed auxiliaries as a separate class (Aux), meaning he did not classify them as verbs. Thus when a form of *be* appears with a main verb, it was deemed an auxiliary, but when it appeared in the absence of a main verb, it was deemed a copula. For Hays then, *are* in (6a) was an auxiliary, whereas *are* in (6b) was a copular verb.

From a modern perspective, the distinction Hays was building on cannot be maintained. Diagnostics for identifying auxiliary verbs reveal that the two putative types of *be* behave the same in important ways:

(7) a. Are they flying planes?
 b. They are not flying planes.
 c. They are flying planes, and they are, too.

The words *flying planes* show the same ambiguity in all three of these sentences, just as in Hays' example. Thus the putative distinction between auxiliary *be* and copular *be* lacks an empirical basis, since the two show the same syntactic behavior with respect to subject-auxiliary inversion (7a), sentence negation (7b), and VP-ellipsis (7c). The two are in fact the same type of verb; they are both auxiliary *be*.

3.3 Hudson (1976, 1984, 1990)

Richard Hudson's dependency-based framework Word Grammar (1984, 1990) has consistently taken auxiliary verbs as heads over content verbs, prepositions as heads over nouns, and subordinators as heads over verbs. And concerning determiners, Hudson has mostly preferred an analysis that positions determiners as heads over nouns (Hudson 1984: 90–2). Thus Hudson's approach concerning function words is consistent insofar as function words are heads over the content words with which they co-occur.

Concerning the latter issue, i.e. the status of determiners, the determiner phrase (DP) vs. noun phrase (NP) debate has been an ongoing dispute since the 1980s. Interestingly in this regard, Hudson's position is a minority one in the DG community in general, but it certainly finds much support among generative grammarians, the majority of whom presently pursue a DP analysis of nominal groups. This issue is not addressed here. The discussion focuses instead on auxiliary verbs.

By the time of Hudson's 1976 book, he had apparently become convinced that auxiliary verbs are heads over content verbs (p. 149–51), and in his 1984 book *Word Grammar*, Hudson writes in this regard:

> "It is now widely accepted that a main verb is syntactically subordinate to its auxiliary verb (Pullum and Wilson 1977 is particularly important collection of evidence), and I have accepted this analysis in all my dependency analyses." (p. 91)

The reference here to Pullum and Wilson (1977) is pointing to a significant debate that took place in the 1970s concerning the status of auxiliary verbs (Ross 1969, Chomsky 1972, Huddleston 1974, Pullum and Wilson 1977). The question concerned the extent to which auxiliaries should be viewed as verbs at all.

As mentioned above, Chomsky (1957) took auxiliaries to be a syntactic class that was to a large extent distinct from that of content verbs, labeling this class simply Aux (p. 39). This view of auxiliaries led to a ternary-branching analysis of basic clause structure in which an auxiliary is present, as in (8a):

(8)

a.

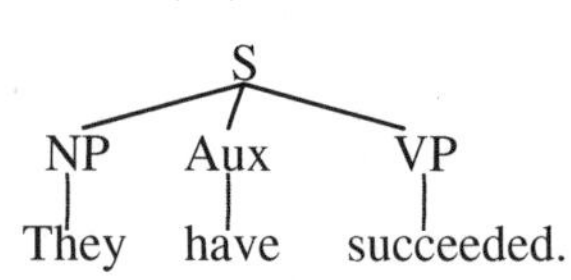

This basic constituency-based analysis is present in syntax textbooks from the 1970s (e.g. Bach 1974, Emonds 1976, Baker 1978).

Based in part on Pullum and Wilson's 1977 article, a stance took hold in the 1980s that viewed auxiliaries of every sort (aspect, voice, and modality) to be syntactically like full verbs. For example, they distinguish between present and past tense and agree with the subject. In European languages other than English, both full verbs and auxiliaries behave the same way, as already discussed in section 3.2. For this reason, auxiliaries should be granted the status of verbs in the hierarchy. This led to analyses like the following one, which shows the auxiliary as head over the content verb, e.g.

(8)

b.

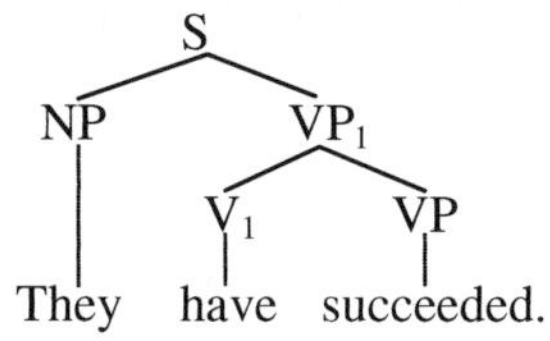

Analyses along these lines can be found in many textbooks of the era (e.g. Haegeman 1991, Napoli 1993, Ouhalla 1994), and despite the addition of numerous varied functional categories, the basic hierarchy of verbs shown with (8b) remains intact in many recent constituency grammars (e.g. Culicover 2009, Carnie 2013).

The interesting aspect of this trend in constituency grammars, i.e. the trend toward auxiliary verbs as heads over content verbs, is the fact that Hudson's dependency-based system (and Mel'čuk's) was ahead of its time. On a dependency-based analysis, there are just two basic possibilities for the hierarchical analysis of auxiliaries that must be considered: either the auxiliary is head over the content verb, or vice versa:

(9)

a.

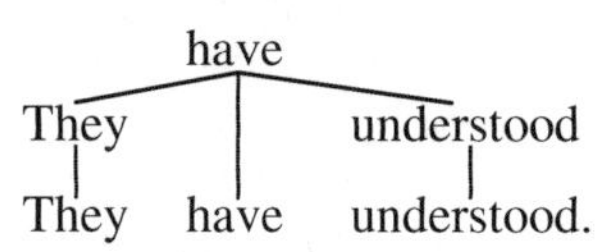

b.

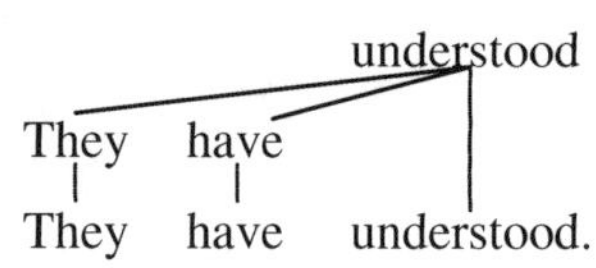

Apparently Hudson had already decided firmly in favor of the analysis in (9a) by 1976. In this regard, the trend in constituency grammars was lagging significantly behind the stance that Hudson and Mel'čuk had adopted early in the development of the Word Grammar and the Meaning-Text frameworks.

3.4 Matthews (1981)

Matthews (1981) discusses the distinction between dependency- and constituency-based syntax at length, and in this regard his book *Syntax* was a major contribution to our developing understanding of the distinction between dependency- and constituency-based systems. In the book, Matthews took content verbs to be heads over auxiliaries, prepositions to be heads over their nouns, and nouns to be heads over their determiners.

Two examples from the book illustrate Matthews' positions:

(10) a. No animal shall wear clothes.

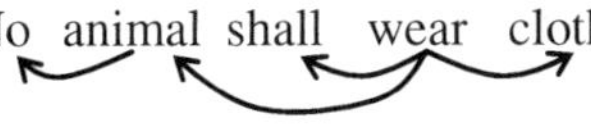

(p. 155)

b. leave the meat in the kitchen

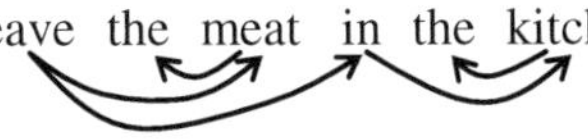

(p. 87)

The important observations here are that the modal auxiliary *shall* is dependent on the content verb *wear* in (10a), that the noun *kitchen* is dependent on the preposition *in* in (10b), and that the determiners *no*, *the*, and *the* are dependent on their nouns.

Concerning prepositions as heads over their nouns, Matthews did not motivate his position empirically, but rather appealed to traditional case government. He wrote "Grammarians also talk of prepositions having objects..., or having complements..." (p. 146). Every dependency hierarchy in Matthews' book containing a preposition shows the preposition as head over its noun.

Concerning the status of determiners, Matthews did not produce specific empirical evidence in favor of determiners as dependents of their nouns, but rather he appealed to the fact that they form a closed class. His assumption was that closed class categories are more appropriately viewed as dependents than as heads. The position Matthews was taking concerning determiners was not controversial at that time, so there would have been little reason for him to justify his decision in the area with further empirical observations.

Concerning the status of auxiliary verbs, however, Matthews had a bit more to say. He motivated their status as dependents of content verbs in two ways. The first was to point to their status as a closed class, and as a closed class, they were like determiners and thus should be viewed as dependents. He was drawing an analogy: just like determiners determine their head nouns, auxiliaries determine their head verbs. To him, this also meant that the hierarchical relationships between determiner and determined should be the same in both constructions.

The second motivation Matthews produced in favor of auxiliaries as dependents of their content verbs was subcategorization. He briefly discussed the example *has appeared* (p. 63). According to Matthews, *appeared* influences the syntactic category and semantic content of the noun with which it appears, whereas *has* lacks this ability. Matthews wrote:

> "As a form of APPEAR it can take just a subject (*He has appeared*) but not both a subject and an object (**He has appeared the speech* or **He has appeared Cicero*). For other lexemes it can be the reverse: *He has distributed the speech* or *He has visited Cicero*, but not **He has distributed* or **He has visited*. A relation is thus established between *appeared*, or the morpheme APPEAR, and a subject element. But at that level the relation of *appeared* to *has*, or of the morpheme APPEAR to the discontinuous HAVE...past participle, is quite incidental." (p. 63)

To restate Matthews' point in other words, content verbs influence their linguistic environment in a way that auxiliary verbs do not, and for this reason, auxiliary verbs should be subordinated to content verbs.

A noteworthy aspect of Matthews' reasoning in this area concerns its lexico-semantic nature. Matthews overlooked the fact that from a purely syntactic point of view, it is the finite verb (i.e. the auxiliary verb) that licenses the appearance of the subject, not the nonfinite verb, e.g. *He has gone home*, **He gone home*, *He goes home*; *She has eaten a lot*, **She eaten a lot*, *She eats a lot*. From this point of view, there should be a direct dependency linking the subject to the finite verb.

3.5 Schubert(1987)/Maxwell & Schubert(1989)

Using the dependency relations of Schubert (1987), Maxwell and Schubert (1989) gathered annotation schemes from a number of authors for machine translation of a number of languages (Bangla/Bengali, Danish, English, Esperanto, Finnish, French, German, Hungarian, Japanese, Polish). The project, based in the Netherlands, was known as *Distributed Language Translation* (DLT, 1984–1990). DG was used to provide syntactic representations of sentences in a source language, in Esperanto (the intermediate language), and in a target language. Grammars written for this project aimed to show the structural relationships to be derived by automatic parsing.

In the current context, how function words were dealt with in the various languages is the point of interest. In Schubert's analysis of Esperanto, auxiliary verbs are heads over content verbs, common nouns are heads over determiners, and subordinators are heads over verbs. Schubert (1987: 45) states that his understanding of DG was influenced by the Mannheim school of DG (Engel 1982).

These patterns were followed for all other grammars with two exceptions. In Danish, subordinators are positioned as dependents of the following finite verb rather than as the head of the subordinate clause. Here is Ingrid Schubert's (1989: 58) statement on this matter:

> "These clause introducers may under certain circumstances be omitted in Danish. I have not decided to let them be governed by a subordinating conjunction, but to consider the verb of the subordinate construction a direct dependent of the verb in the superordinate sentence."

Perhaps these cases are something like the omission of the complementizer *that* in English, which makes no contribution to meaning and accordingly can often be left out, as in *Say (that) it's true*. It is arguably the only subordinator which has this property. If so, it seems wrong to base the analysis on this one instance. The alternative of an empty node could be considered.

The other exception is in Lobin's (1989) analysis of German. The determiner rather than its noun is taken as the head of the nominal group. Lobin justifies his analysis in this area by pointing to cases like the following one:

(11) unsere Fahrt an die See und eure
our trip to the sea and yours

in die Berge
in the mountains

'our trip to the sea and yours to the mountains'

The absence of *Fahrt* in the second part of the coordinate structure forces one to view *eure* as the head of the nominal group (or to posit an empty nominal node).

While the two exceptions just noted provide insight into the difficult choices that had to be made by the authors who participated in the project, the greater point is that there was a large measure of agreement concerning the status of most function words. With the exception of determiners, most function words were taken to be heads of the content words with which they co-occur.

4 The German schools

DG has enjoyed particular favor in the German speaking world. German grammarians recognized the potential of dependency-based syntax early on. This early recognition may have been due to the particular compatibility of dependency-based syntax, which emphasizes verb centrality, with the verb second (V2) principle of German (and other Germanic languages). The finite verb is anchored in second position in German declarative clauses, thematic material tending to precede this position and rhematic material tending to follow it.

The interesting and noteworthy point about the German schools is the unanimity that one encounters among the leading voices. DG grammarians (Kunze 1975, Lobin 1993, Engel 1982, 1994, among others) are mostly unanimous in the basic hierarchical analyses of function words that they assume: auxiliary verbs are heads over content verbs; prepositions are heads over nouns; and subordinators are heads over verbs. The only area where one encounters some variation among these experts concerns determiners. The majority stance is certainly that nouns are heads over determiners, but Lobin (1993) takes the opposite stance, as he does in Lobin (1989), already mentioned in section 3.5, and Eroms (2000) has argued for interdependence between article (definite or indefinite) and noun.

Due to the large measure of agreement concerning the hierarchical status of most function words, the German-language DG world can be viewed as speaking with a single voice, and this voice is particularly loud by virtue of the fact DG enjoys a prominence at schools and universities that is not generally encountered outside of the German-speaking world. A point of interest, perhaps, is the reasoning that one finds in the German-language DG literature about the sentence root. In a two-verb combination such as *hat gelegt* 'has layed', the German schools of DG unanimously view *hat* as head over *gelegt*. It is worth considering briefly why they do so.

Engel (1994:107–109) points to facts about subcategorization. He sees the lexical stem *hab* of the auxiliary *hat* determining the form of the nonfinite verb *gelegt* as a participle. This reasoning does not work in the opposite direction, that is, one cannot view the lexical stem *leg-* as determining the syntactic form of the auxiliary *hat*. The insight can then be extended to all manner of auxiliary verbs. For instance in a combination such as *wird wollen* 'will want', the modal auxiliary *wird* subcategorizes for the infinitive form of the stem *woll-*, but not vice versa, that is, the lexical stem *woll-* does not determine the syntactic subcategory of the auxiliary *wird*.

A related issue concerns the motivation for positioning the finite verb as the root of the clause. Eroms (2000: 129ff.) motivates the hierarchical status of auxiliary verbs in another way. He appeals to the fact that when an auxiliary verb and full verb co-occur, it is the auxiliary that is finite, not the full verb. The auxiliary verb then bears the functional information of person, number, tense, and mood. The nonfinite verb typically does not express this information. Thus in the example from the previous paragraph, i.e. *hat gelegt* 'has layed', the finite auxiliary verb *hat* expresses number (singular), person (3rd person), tense (present), and mood (indicative). The participle form *gelegt*, in contrast, can be construed as helping to convey perfect aspect only. This functional load that the auxiliary verb bears motivates its status as the root of the clause, i.e. as head over the content verb.

5 The Prague school

The Prague school of DG, as associated with the Prague Dependency Treebank (PDT), agrees with most of the other DG mentioned in this contribution concerning the hierarchical status of adpositions; they are heads over their nouns. However, the annotation scheme for the PDT (Hajič 1998) began subordinating auxiliary verbs to content verbs in 1996. This aspect of the PDT remains anchored today in the analytical level (surface syntax) of the PDT. Due to the prominence of the PDT in the development of DG theory in general, the linguistic motivation for its choice to subordinate auxiliary verbs to content verbs in surface syntax is worth considering, however briefly.

There has been a difficulty in this area, though. Attempts to locate the linguistic motivation behind this aspect of the PDT annotation scheme have not turned up anything concrete in published works. For this reason, the two linguistic observations produced next are based on personal communication with Jarmila Panevová, one of the founding members of the Prague school of DG.

Worth noting first, though, is that the PDT annotation scheme subordinates only non-modal auxiliary verbs to content verbs. Modal verbs, in contrast, are heads over their content verbs. What this means is that the PDT annotation scheme for surface syntax deviates from the majority position only regarding a single auxiliary verb, namely *být* 'be' (in all its forms).

There are two linguistic motivations for subordinating the forms of *být* to the content verb. One of these concerns a general aspect of the verb 'be' in Slavic languages in general. Many Slavic languages lack or omit the finite form of this verb in certain environments. Czech omits a form of this verb in the 3rd person of the compound past, but a 1st and 2nd person form of this verb appear in such environments:

(12) a. Já jsemspal. (masculine)
I am.slept
'I slept.'

b. Já jsemspala. (feminine)
I am.slept
'I slept.'

c. John spal.
'John slept.'

If the clitic auxiliary *jsem-* is subordinated to *spal/spala*, then there is a direct dependency that connects the subject to *spal* in each of these three cases. But if *spal/spala* is subordinated to *jsem-*, then an asymmetry appears: the subject is at times (in the 1st and 2nd person) an immediate dependent of the auxiliary verb, and at other times (in the 3rd person), it is an immediate dependent of the participle. One thing that is different about this construction from others discussed earlier is that here the auxiliary and main verb form a single word. The question therefore concerns the extent to which this asymmetry should influence choices about the syntactic hierarchy.

A possible drawback of this choice is that it forces the PDT to draw a distinction between auxiliary *být* and copular *být*, since when a form of *být* is the only verb present, e.g. *Mary je velká* 'Mary is tall', the PDT positions that verb as head over the predicative expression (here *je* 'is' is head over*velká* 'tall'). Examples (7a–c) above illustrate that there is no syntactic motivation for distinguishing between an auxiliary *be* and a copular *be* in English.

Another linguistic argument for subordinating forms of the auxiliary *být* to its content verb is seen when multiple forms of *být* appear in one and the same clause:

(13) John by byl býval spal.
John be been been slept
'John would have slept.'

This sentence is an example of the past conditional. Three distinct forms of *být* appear together. By subordinating all three of them directly to *spal*, a relatively flat structure obtains, and a flat structure has the advantage of avoiding projectivity violations (cf. Mel'cuk and Pertsov 1987:181 for a discussion of such a violation in terms of the arcs used in some forms of DG), which would occur, assuming that certain other sequences of these verb forms are possible.

Gruet-Skrabalova (2012) offers a different account of the auxiliary *být* in the course of a Minimalist analysis of some kinds of ellipsis. She shows that there is a certain degree of freedom in the word order, but the only alternative order shown by her does not produce projectivity violations. In (13), *by* is the 3rd person (singular or plural) form of the conditional mood and the only one of the three which is finite. The other two are both past participles, the first in the perfect aspect and the second in the imperfect aspect. The first of them is subcategorized for by the preceding conditional verb. Gruet-Skrabovala does not discuss any sentence in which the two participles co-occur. However, sentences in this article suggest that both past tense forms of this verb subcategorize for a participial complement. From this, we judge that the first participle in (13) subcategorizes for the second, which in turn subcategorizes for the participial form of the main verb. Gruet-Skrabovala states that the final participle of the auxiliary must directly precede the main verb, although the finite conditional form can follow the main verb, just like in subordinate clauses in German.

The PDT decision to subordinate forms of *být* to the co-occurring content verb constitutes a narrow exception to the majority position concerning function words. The PDT is otherwise consistent with the majority position regarding the status of modal verbs, copular verbs, adpositions, subordinators, and determiners.

6 Concluding discussion

This survey has revealed that there is little support in the sources examined above for the Universal Stanford Dependencies' (USD) decision to categorically subordinate function words to content words. Not one of the sources surveyed clearly supports the USD analysis of adpositions, and only two of the sources provide support for the USD decision to subordinate auxiliaries to content words. The dominant position, which has crystallized through the decades, is that auxiliaries are heads over content verbs and prepositions are heads over their nouns. And concerning determiners, they are more widely viewed as dependents of their nouns – although their status has been the focus of more debate.

The survey has turned up three published arguments in support of the USD position and two unpublished arguments that partially support the USD position. The published ones are Matthews' argument concerning English auxiliaries in section 3.5, and the arguments concerning Danish subordinators and German determiners in section 3.6. The unpublished ones concerned the Czech auxiliary *být* in section 5.

De Marneffe et al. do give a few indications of the supposed linguistic superiority of USD. The choice of having nouns as heads over adpositions allows parallelism between prepositional phrases and morphological case-marking (p. 4585) and also between adpositions and adverbial clauses (p. 4587). However, it ignores the fact that adpositions assign case to their complement nouns, not vice versa. Hence what one achieves in the way of more parallelism across the structures of distinct languages, one pays for with the unorthodox stipulation that adpositions assign case up the syntactic hierarchy to their nouns.

The choice of making predicates heads over auxiliaries allows parallelism between constructions which in some languages omit the copula and those which do not (p. 4586). This is true, but alternative solutions such as an empty node should be considered. Also, if there are several linked auxiliaries, as in *might have been dreaming*, they must all have *dreaming* as their head, so the subcategorization relationship between any two consecutive auxiliaries cannot be shown by the dependency links (cf. the discussion of subcategorization by Engel in section 4).

De Marneffe et al. note that the choices discussed in their article have a negative effect on parsing:

"It is now fairly well-known that … dependency parsing numbers are higher if you make auxiliary verbs heads … and if you make prepositions the head of prepositional phrases… Under the proposed USD, SD would be making the 'wrong' choice in each case." (p. 4589)

Parsing accuracy is not the most important criteria, however, as the following statements concerning the importance of linguistic quality and downstream applications document:

"…it seems wrongheaded to choose a linguistic representation to maximize parser performance rather than based on the linguistic quality of the representation and its usefulness for applications that build further processing on top of it." (p. 4589)

For this reason, de Marneffe et al. propose transforming the USD system to provide two other results, one for **parsing** and one called **enhanced**.

Thus by de Marneffe et al.'s own admission, parsing accuracy tends to be higher if function words are heads over content words, and given the analysis and discussion above, the DG tradition agrees to a large extent that linguistic considerations support most function words as heads over the content words with which they co-occur, contrary to USD's stance.

If USD wants to claim that linguistic considerations support its unorthodox approach to surface dependencies, it of course has every right to do so in the clash of ideas. But the point we hope to have established in this contribution is that the DG tradition does not support this claim. Quite to the contrary, the DG tradition has crystallized over the decades to a position that contradicts the USD approach. Thus if USD wants to maintain its claim to "linguistic quality", the burden of proof rests firmly on its shoulders; it needs to produce the linguistic reasoning that supports its position in part by discussing and refuting the observations and reasoning that have coalesced over the decades to the opposite position.

References

Emmon Bach. 1974. *Syntactic Theory*. Holt, Rinehart and Winston, Inc., New York.

Carl Lee Baker. 1978. *Introduction to Generative Transformational Syntax*. Prentice Hall, Englewood Cliffs, NJ.

Andrew Carnie. 2013. *Syntax: A Generative Introduction*. Wiley-Blackwell, Malden, MA.

Noam Chomsky. 1957. *Syntactic Structures*. Mouton, The Hague.

Noam Chomsky. 1972. Some emperical issues in the theory of Transformational Grammar. In S. Peters (ed.), *Goals of Linguistic Thoery*, 63–130. Prentice Hall, Englewood Cliffs, NJ.

Peter Culicover. 2009. *Natural Language Syntax*. Oxford University Press, Oxford UK.

Joseph Emonds. 1976. *A Transformational Approach to English Syntax: Root, Structure-Preserving, and Local Transformations*. Academic Press, New York.

Ulrich Engel. 1982. *Syntax der deutschen Gegenwarts- sprache*, 2nd edition. Erich Schmidt, Berlin.

Ulrich Engel. 1994. *Syntax der deutschen Gegenwartssprache*, 3rd fully revised edition. Erich Schmidt, Berlin.

Hans-Werner Eroms. 2000. *Syntax der deutschen Sprache*. Walter de Gruyter, Berlin.

Hana Gruet-Skrabalova. 2012. VP-ellipsis and the Czech auxiliary *být* ('to be'). *Xlinguae*, 2012, 5, 3–15.

Liliane Haegeman. 1991. *Introduction to Government and Binding Theory*. Blackwell, Oxford, UK.

Jan Hajič. 1998. Building a syntactically annotated corpus: The Prague Dependency Treebank. In Eva Hajičcová (ed.), *Issues of Valency and Meaning: Studies in Honor of Jarmila Panevová*.106–32. Karolinum, Charles University Press, Prague.

David Hays. 1964. Dependency theory: A formalism and some observations. *Language* 40, 511–25.

Rodney Huddleston. 1974. Further remarks on the analysis of auxiliaries as main verbs. *Foundations of Language* 11, 215–29.

Richard Hudson. 1976. *Arguments for a non-Transformational Grammar*. University of Chicago Press, Chicago.

Richard Hudson. 1984. *Word Grammar*. Basil Blackwell, New York.

Richard Hudson. 1990. *An English Word Grammar*. Basil Blackwell, Oxford.

Ray Jackendoff. 1977. *X-bar Syntax: A Study of Phrase Structure*. The MIT Press, Cambridge, MA.

Jürgen Kunze.1975.*Abhängigkeitsgrammatik. Studia Grammatica* 12. Akademie Verlag, Berlin.

Henning Lobin. 1989. *A dependency syntax of German*. 17–39. In Maxwell and Schubert.

Henning Lobin. 1993. *Koordinationssyntaxalsprozedurales Phänomen. Studien zur deutschen Grammatik* 46. Gunter NarrVerlag, Tübingen.

Marie-Catherine de Marneffe, Timothy Dozat, Natalia Silveira, Katri Havarinen, Filip Ginter, Joakim Nivre, Christopher Manning. 2014. Universal Stanford Dependencies: A crosslinguistic typology. LREC, 4585–92

Peter Matthews. 1981. *Syntax*. Cambridge University Press, Cambridge, UK.

Dan Maxwell and Klaus Schubert (eds.). 1989. *Metataxis in Practice: Dependency Syntax for Multilingual Machine Translation*. Foris Publications, Dordrecht.

Igor Mel'čuk. 1958. Mašinnomperevode s vengerskogojazykanarusskij — On the automated translation of Hungarian to Russian, *Problemykibernetiki*, v. 1, 222–64.

Igor Mel'čuk. 1963. Avtomatičeskijanaliztekstov (namaterialerusskogojazyka) — Automated analysis of texts (on the basis of Russian). In *Slavjanskoejazykoznanie — Linguistique slave*. Academy of Sciences of the U.S.S.R., Moscow, 477–509.

Igor Mel'čuk. 1974. *Opytteoriilingvističeskixmodelej "Smysl - Tekst". Semantika, Sintaksis.* — Sketch of a linguistic model of the sort Meaning – Text. Semantics, Syntax. Nauka, Moscow.

Igor Mel'čuk and Nikolaj Pertsov. 1987. *Surface Syntax of English: A Formal Model within the Meaning-Text Framework*. John Benjamins, Amsterdam.

Igor Mel'čuk. 1988. *Dependency Syntax: Theory and Practice*. State University of New York Press, Albany.

Donna Jo Napoli. 1993. *Syntax: Theory and Problems*. Oxford University Press, New York.

Jamal Ouhalla. 1994. *Transformational Grammar: From rules to Principles and Parameters*. Edward Arnold, London.

Geoffrey Pullum and Deirdre Wilson. 1977. Autonomous syntax and the analysis of auxiliaries. *Language* 53, 4, 741–88.

John Robert Ross. 1969. Auxiliaries as main verbs. *Studies in Philosophical Linguistics* 1, edited by W. Todd, 77–102. Great Expectations Press, Evanston.

Ingrid Schubert. 1989. *A dependency syntax of Danish*. 39-68, in Maxwell and Schubert.

Klaus Schubert. 1987. *Metataxis: Contrastive dependency syntax for machine translation*. Foris Publications, Dordrecht.

Klaus Schubert. 1989. *A dependency syntax of Esperanto*. 207–32, in Maxwell and Schubert.

Lucien Tesnière. 1959. *Éléments de syntaxe structural*. Klincksieck, Paris.

Lucien Tesnière. 2015 (1959). *Elements of Structural Syntax*. Translated by Timothy Osborne and Sylvain Kahane. John Benjamins, Amsterdam.

Diagnostics for Constituents: Dependency, Constituency, and the Status of Function Words

Timothy Osborne
Zhejiang University
Hangzhou
China
tjo3ya@yahoo.com

Abstract

This contribution delivers two messages: 1) that the tests for constituents that are widely employed in linguistics and syntax textbooks are more congruent with dependency-based syntax than with constituency-based syntax and 2) that these same tests support the conventional analysis of function words, that is, the analysis that takes most function words (auxiliary verbs, adpositions, subordinators) to be heads over the content words with which they cooccur. The latter issue is important at present, since a recent annotation scheme is choosing to subordinate all function words to the content words with which they coocur.

1 Two messages

Most English language textbooks on syntax and linguistics rely on tests for constituents to introduce the concept of syntactic structure. Tests such as coordination, proform substitution, topicalization, answer fragments, clefting, VP-ellipsis, pseudoclefting, etc. are used to demonstrate the presence of constituents, and thus, the presence of sentence structure. The tests show that words are being grouped together into phrases, and smaller phrases are grouped into ever larger phrases, until the largest phrase, the sentence, is reached. The tests are very widely employed, so widely that they enjoy a prominent spot in the syntactician's toolbox; they are basic tools with which the syntactician works.

An interesting aspect of most tests for constituents, however, is that they identify much less syntactic structure than most constituency grammars assume. In this respect the data delivered by the tests are relatively congruent with dependency grammars (DGs), since by its very nature dependency-based syntax posits much less syntactic structure than constituency-based syntax. Interestingly, the DGs currently in existence rarely draw attention to this fact, that is, they rarely draw attention to the fact that the dependency-based understanding of syntactic structures is strongly supported by the basic tests that are, ironically, so widely employed by constituency grammars.

Tests for constituents can also be employed to shed light on debates about the best hierarchical analysis of various syntactic structures, for instance concerning the hierarchical status of function words. The tests are consistent with the traditional DG analysis of function words, namely that auxiliary verbs are heads over content verbs and prepositions are heads over their nouns.

This contribution draws attention to the two points just mentioned. It delivers two messages: 1) most commonly used tests for constituents are much more consistent with dependency-based syntax than with constituency-based syntax and DGs can and should draw attention to this fact, and 2) the tests reveal that auxiliary verbs are heads over content verbs and prepositions are heads over their nouns.

The data examined in this contribution are limited to English. This is due mainly to the fact that the most widely employed tests for constituents are employed in English language textbooks, applied to the syntactic structures of English. Section 6 below reflects on this aspect of the tests, considering the extent to which they can be employed in other languages.

2 Constituents

The term *constituent* is associated with *constituency* grammars, the morphological relatedness of the two words, *constituent* and *constituency*, being obvious. In this respect the first message delivered in this manuscript might seem contrary to basic terminology, this terminology suggesting that dependency and constituency are distinct principles of syntactic organization and that the constituent unit is not compatible with depen-

Proceedings of the Third International Conference on Dependency Linguistics (Depling 2015), pages 251–260,
Uppsala, Sweden, August 24–26 2015.

dency syntax in general. I view the terminology in this area as a historical accident, and this accident has, in m view, played out to the detriment of DG, since it has obscured the fact that dependency syntax is actually more consistent with the data delivered by diagnostics for constituents than constituency syntax.

The *dependency* vs. *constituency* terminology as it is understood and employed today is perhaps due most to Hays' (1964) seminal article *Dependency theory: A formalism and some observations*. This early article seems to be most responsible for introducing and establishing the dependency concept and for contrasting dependency with constituency. Hays employed both terms, *dependency* and *constituency*, whereby he was emphasizing that the dependency formalism was distinct from the constituency formalism. The constituent concept at that time had already been long established; it goes back at least as far as Bloomfield (1933: 160ff.), and it is associated perhaps most wi*th the immediate constituent analysis* developed by Wells (1948).

The noteworthy aspect of Hays (1964) article is the terminology that he used when describing dependency trees. It is instructive to consider exactly what he wrote in this area:

> "A SUBTREE is a connected subset of a tree. A complete subtree consists of some element of a tree, plus all others connected to it, directly or indirectly, and more remote from the origin of the tree...
>
> An IC [immediate constituent] structure and a dependency structure, both defined over the same string, correspond relationally if every constituent is coextensive with a subtree and every complete subtree is coextensive with a constituent. (Two structural entities are coextensive if they refer to the same elements of a terminal string.)" (p. 520)

The noteworthy aspect of this passage is the term *complete subtree*. Hays chose to denote a given word plus all the words that that it dominates a *complete subtree*.

Hays did not simply call the relevant unit a *constituent*. In other words, Hays was introducing a distinct terminology across dependency- and constituency-based systems. Had he employed the term *constituent* for both types of structures, the nature of the dependency vs. constituency debate might be quite different today than it is, since the terminology would have aided the comparison and evaluation of the two competing approaches to syntactic structures.

Other dependency grammarians who followed Hays realized that constituents can be acknowledged in both dependency and constituency-based systems. Hudson (1984: 92) wrote the following in this regard:

> "The general connection between dependency structure and constituent structure is that a constituent can be defined as some word plus all the words depending on it, either directly or indirectly (in other words, that word plus all the dependency chains leading up to it)."

Starosta (1988: 105) picked up on Hudson's point; Starosta wrote:

> "...and a constituent is any word plus all its direct or indirect dependents"

Hellwig (2003: 603) is more explicit with his statements in this area:

> "Contrary to other dependency grammars, the notion of constituent is endorsed in DUG [Dependency Unification Grammar]. However, it is a specific constituent structure that results from dependency analysis. Let us define a constituent as the string that corresponds to a node in the dependency tree together with all the nodes subordinated to that node (directly or mediated by other nodes). Then, any dependency tree can be dispersed into smaller trees until nodes with no dependents are reached. Each of these trees corresponds to a constituent of the sentence or phrase in question."

The three passages just cited agree that constituents can be acknowledged in dependency-based structures.

Had Hays (1964) used the term *constituent* to denote the *complete subtrees* of dependency hierarchies, the realization may have long set in by now that dependency-based syntax is much more consistent with most tests for constituents than constituency-based syntax.

3 Tests for constituents

The most widely employed tests for constituents in syntax textbooks are listed next, the order given reflecting the frequency of use:

1. Coordination
2. Topicalization

3. Proform substitution
4. Answer fragments
5. Clefting
6. VP-ellipsis
7. Pseudoclefting

Coordination is the most widely employed of these tests. There are, however, major problems with coordination as a diagnostic for constituents, since phenomena such as right node raising (RNR) (e.g. *[Fred likes], but [Sue dislikes], the Chinese beer*) and so-called non-constituent conjuncts (e.g. *Fred sent [Sue to the store] and [Jim to the post office]*) appear to involve the coordination of nonconstituent strings. Due to such problems, coordination is not employed below.

The other six diagnostics, however, are more consistent about the strings that they suggest are and are not constituents. They too are very widely employed. Just how widely is documented with the following lists of syntax and linguistics textbooks that use them:

Topicalization
Allerton 1979:114, Radford 1981:213, Burton-Roberts 1986:17, Radford 1988:95, Haegeman 1991:35, Napoli 1993: 148, Borsley 1991:24, Ouhalla 1994:20, Fabb 1994:4, Haegeman and Guéron 1999:46, Fromkin et al. 2000:151, Lasnik 2000:10, Börjars and Burridge 2001:26, van Valin 2001:11, Poole 2002:32, Adger 2003:65, Sag et al. 2003:33, Eggins 1994:72, Radford 2004:72, Kroeger 2005:31, Haegeman 2006:79, Culicover 2009:84, Müller 2010:6, Sobin 2011:31, Sportiche et al. 2014:68.
Proform substitution
Allerton 1979:113, Radford 1981:64, Radford 1988:98, Thomas 1993:10, Fabb 1994:3, Ouhalla 1994:19, Radford 1997:109, Haegeman and Guéron 1999:46, Fromkin et al. 2000:155, Lasnik 2000:9, Börjars and Burridge 2001:24, van Valin 2001:111, Poole 2002:29, Eggins 1994:131, Radford 2004:71, Tallerman 2005:142, Haegeman 2006:74, Kim and Sells 2008:21, Culicover 2009:81, Carnie 2010:20, Müller 2010:5, Sobin 2011:32, Carnie 2013:98, Sportiche et al. 2014:50
Answer fragments
Radford 1981:72, Burton-Roberts 1986:16, Radford 1988:91, Haegeman 1991:28, Radford 1997:107, Haegeman and Guéron 1999:46, Börjars and Burridge 2001:25, Eggins 1994:134, Kroeger 2005:31, Tallerman 2005:125, Haegeman 2006:82, Kim and Sells 2008:20, Carnie 2010:18, Müller 2010:6, Sobin 2011:31, Carnie 2013:98, Sportiche et al. 2014
Clefting
McCawley 1988:64, Akmajian et al. 1990:150, Borsley 1991:23, Napoli 1993:148, McCawley 1998:64, Haegeman and Guéron 1999:49, Börjars and Burridge 2001:27, Adger 2003:67, Sag et al. 2003:33, Tallerman 2005:127, Haegeman 2006:85, Kim and Sells 2008:19, Carnie 2013:98, Sportiche et al. 2014:70
VP-ellipsis
Radford 1981:67, 1988:101, Ouhalla 1994:20, Radford 1997:110, McCawley 1998: 67, Fromkin et al. 2000:158, Adger 2003:65, Kroeger 2005:82, Tallerman 2005:141, Payne 2006:163, Culicover 2009:80: Sobin 2011:58
Pseudoclefting
Borsley 1991:24, McCawley 1998: 64, Haegeman and Guéron 1999:50, Kroeger 2005:82, Haegeman 2006:88, Payne 2006:160, Culicover 2009:89, Carnie 2013:99, Sportiche et al. 2014:71

A large majority of these sources overlook DG entirely, only four of them have anything to say about DG: Borsley (1991:30f.) briefly mentions DG in passing; van Valin (2001: 86–109) grants DG more space – he devotes a chapter to it; Sag et al. (2003:535f.) grant DG less than a page; and Carnie (2010:175–8, 268f.) devotes about four pages to DG.

4 Using the tests

To illustrate what the tests reveal about syntactic structures, the following two analyses of the sentence *Larry likes to drink expensive beer* are used:

(1)

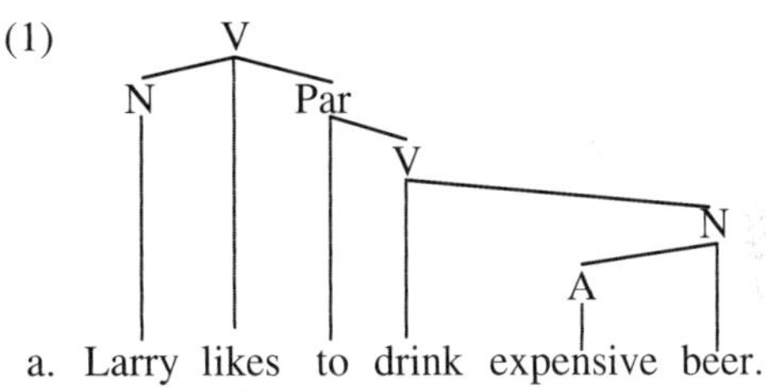

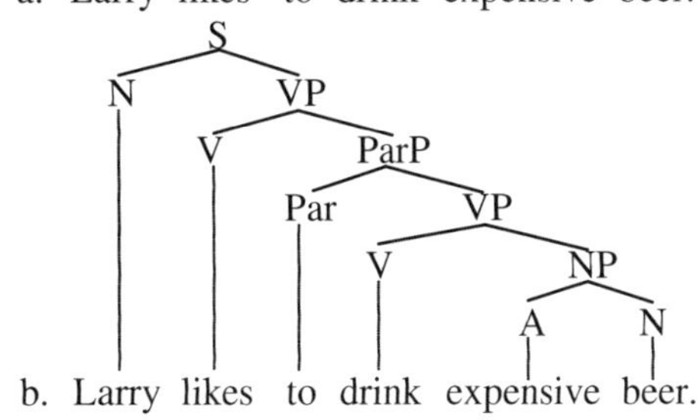

Using the concept of the constituent unit established above (i.e. a complete subtree), there are six constituents in the dependency tree (1a) (6 nodes = 6 constituents) and there are eleven constituents in tree (1b) (11 nodes = 11 constituents). These constituents are listed as follows:

6 constituents in (1a)
Larry, *expensive*, *expensive beer*, *drink expensive beer*, *to drink expensive beer*, and *Larry likes to drink expensive beer*

11 constituents in (1b)
Larry, *likes*, *to*, *drink*, *expensive*, *beer*, *expensive beer*, *drink expensive beer*, *to drink expensive beer*, *likes to drink expensive beer*, and *Larry likes to drink expensive beer*

Thus the constituency tree (1b) assumes five more constituents than the dependency tree (1a).

A pertinent observation here concerns the status of phrases in the competing analyses. The phrasal constituents in the constituency tree (1b), those labeled with ...P, are also constituents in the dependency tree (1a), the one exception being the VP *likes to drink expensive beer*, which is not a constituent in (1a). However, four of the sub-phrasal constituents shown in (1b) (*likes*, *to*, *drink*, and *beer*) are not constituents in the dependency tree (1a). These observations point to a key difference in how phrases are understood across dependency and constituency structures. Most sub-phrasal constituents in constituency structures are not constituents in dependency structures to begin with, whereas most phrasal constituents in constituency structures are also constituents in dependency structures.

Most constituency tests easily identify nouns like *Larry* and noun phrases like *expensive beer* as constituents. This point is illustrated next by focusing on *expensive beer*:

Topicalization
(2) a. ...but **expensive beer** Larry does like to drink.

Proform substitution
b. Larry likes to drink **it**. (*it = expensive beer*)

Answer fragments
c. What does Larry like to drink? – **Expensive beer**.

Clefting
d. It is **expensive beer** that Larry likes to drink.

Pseudoclefting
e. What Larry likes to drink is **expensive beer**.

The tests also converge identifying the nonfinite VP *drink expensive beer* as a constituent:

Topicalization
(3) a. ?...but **drink expensive beer** Larry does like to.

Proform substitution
b. Larry does like to **do so**. (*do so = drink expensive beer*)

Answer fragments
c. What does Larry like to do? – **Drink expensive beer**.

Clefting
d. *It is **drink expensive beer** that Larry likes to.

VP-ellipsis
e. Sam likes to drink expensive beer, and Larry also likes to drink expensive beer.

Pseudoclefting
f. What Larry likes to do is **drink expensive beer**.

Five of the six tests converge, agreeing that *drink expensive beer* should have the status of a constituent. Concerning clefting, the reason why it contradicts the other five tests is an open question.

The message currently being established is more easily arrived at if the points of agreement and disagreement are acknowledged across the two analyses. The dependency- and constituency-based analyses in trees (3a–b) agree with respect to six of the constituents shown. These six constituents are therefore not controversial, so the discussion can skip to the other five constituents, i.e. to the five constituents where the two analyses disagree. The constituency tree views *likes*, *to*, *drink*, *beer*, and *likes to drink expensive beer* as constituents, whereas the dependency tree views them as non-constituents.

The six constituency tests are almost unanimous in rejecting the status of these five strings as constituents. This point is illustrated first with the finite verb *likes*:

Topicalization
(4) a. *...and **likes** Larry to drink expensive beer.

Proform substitution
b. *Larry **does/so/does so** to drink expensive beer. (*does/so/does so = likes*)

Answer fragments
c. What does Jim feel about drinking expensive beer? – ***Likes**.

Clefting
d. *It is **likes** that Larry to drink expensive beer.

VP-ellipsis
e. *Jim likes to drink expensive beer, and Larry likes to drink expensive beer.

Pseudoclefting
e. *What Larry does concerning drinking expensive beer is **likes**.

The six tests converge; they agree that *likes* should not have the status of a constituent.

A second example solidifies the message. The tests agree that the finite VP string *likes to drink expensive beer* should not have the status of a constituent

Topicalization
(5) a. *…and **likes to drink expensive beer** Larry.

Proform substitution
b. ?Sid **does so**.
(*do so = likes to drink expensive beer*)

Answer fragments
c. What does Larry do?
– ***Likes to drink expensive beer**.

Clefting
d. *It is **likes to drink expensive beer** that Larry does.

VP-ellipsis
e. *Jim likes to drink expensive beer, and Larry likes to drink expensive beer, too.

Pseudoclefting
f. *What Larry does is **likes to drink expensive beer**.

An analysis in terms of VP-ellipsis is not available for example (5e), although one in terms of stripping is available – the star indicates badness of VP-ellipsis. The six tests mostly converge; they mostly agree that the finite VP string *likes to drink expensive beer* should not have the status of a constituent.

There is no reason to belabor the point. The reader can extend the tests for him- or herself to the other three strings for which there is disagreement (*to*, *drink*, and *beer*). The tests further support the dependency tree (1a); they agree that these strings should not be granted the status of constituents.

To summarize, the tests point to the meaningfulness of phrases: phrases can serve as topics, they can be replaced by proforms, they can be clefted and pseudoclefted, they can appear as answer fragments, and they can be elided. The tests contradict the existence of sub-phrasal constituents. Sub-phrasal constituents are an artifact of constituency-based syntax. Phrase structure grammars must posit their existence to maintain a constituency-based approach to syntactic structures. The fact that many of the most widely employed tests for constituents do not support their existence is a big problem for constituency-based syntax in general.

5 Function words

The message just delivered in the preceding section should not be controversial among DGs. The fact that dependency-based syntax is more congruent with empirical tests for syntactic structures should be a welcome insight. There are, though, points of disagreement among DGs where the tests can help. In particular, the tests can help decide points of contention when DGs disagree about the best analysis for a given structure. Indeed, the tests provide guidance concerning the status of many function words in the syntactic hierarchy. This contribution now focuses on the status of function words.

There is, namely, some disagreement concerning the best analysis of function words among DGs. Certainly the dominant position in most of the theoretically-oriented DG literature is that auxiliary verbs are heads over content verbs, adpositions are heads over their nouns, and subordinators are heads over their verbs.[1] More recently, a quite different approach to dependencies has been put forth. The Universal Stanford Dependencies (USD) (de Marneffe et al. 2014) is now advocating an annotation scheme that consistently subordinates function words to content words. Thus according to this annotation scheme, auxiliary verbs are dependents of main verbs, adpositions are dependents of nouns, and subordinators are dependents of verbs.

The USD position in this area does receive some support from Matthews (1981) and from the Prague school, both of which also subordinate auxiliary verbs to content verbs in surface syntax. Matthews and the Prague school disagree with USD concerning the status of adpositions

[1] The following linguists and sources all pursue the conventional analysis: Kunze 1975, Starosta 1988, Lobin 1993, Engel 1994, Jung 1995, Heringer 1996, Groß 1999, Eroms 2000, Hellwig 2003, Mel'čuk 1988, 2009, Hudson 1976, 1984, 1990, 2007, 2010.

and subordinators, however, since they position adpositions above their nouns and subordinators above their verbs.

In any case, the diagnostics for constituents discussed and illustrated above can shed light on the status of function words. In particular, they deliver strong support for the more traditional stance; they hence contradict the USD annotation scheme. The critique of USD presented below must be understood in a broader context, though. USD parsing actually advocates more than one annotation scheme; it advocates the unorthodox one just mentioned, which subordinates all function words to their associated content words, as well as two others, one of which is more traditional in that it positions most function words above the content words with which they co-occur. The points about function words established in the following two sections are directed at the former, more prominent annotation scheme of USD.

5.1 Auxiliary verbs

The traditional approach and the USD approach are contrasted with the following trees:

(6)

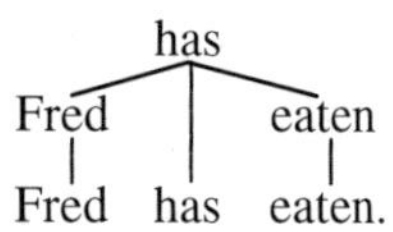

a. – Traditional analysis

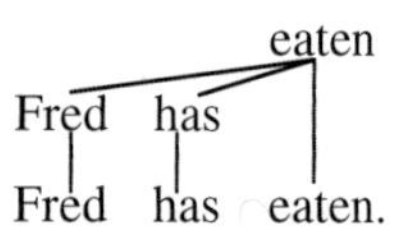

b. – USD analysis

The analysis in (6a) shows *eaten* as a constituent, whereas the analysis in (6b) shows *has* as a constituent.

The six tests mostly converge in support of the a-analysis. They mostly agree that *eaten* is a constituent:

(7) a. Topicalization
...and **eaten** Fred certainly has.

b. Proform substitution
Fred has **done so**. (*done so* = *eaten*)

c. Answer fragments
What has Fred done? – **Eaten**.

d. Clefting
*It is **eaten** that Fred has.

f. VP-ellipsis
Sue has eaten, and Fred has eaten, too.

g. Pseudoclefting
What Fred has done is **eaten**.

Five of the six tests agree that *eaten* should be viewed as a constituent. Concerning clefting, the reason why it disagrees with the other five tests is an open issue that is not addressed here.

The six tests are also unanimous in their agreement that *has* is not a constituent:

(8) a. Topicalization
*...and **has** Fred eaten.

b. Proform substitution
*Fred **does so** eaten. (*does so* = *has*)

c. Answer fragments
What concerning Fred and eating?
– ***Has**.

d. Clefting
*It is **has** that Fred eaten.

e. VP-ellipsis
*Sue has eaten, and Fred has eaten, too.

f. Pseudoclefting
*What Fred eaten is **has**.

Note that the example of topicalization should maintain the declarative force of the original sentence – the star therefore indicates that the sentence cannot be construed as a statement. Based on these results, one can conclude that the six tests for constituents provide no evidence for the status of *has* as a constituent.

5.2 Prepositions

The six tests strongly support the subordination of nouns to prepositions. This point is established with the following two competing analyses of a simple sentence containing a preposition:

(9) – Traditional analysis

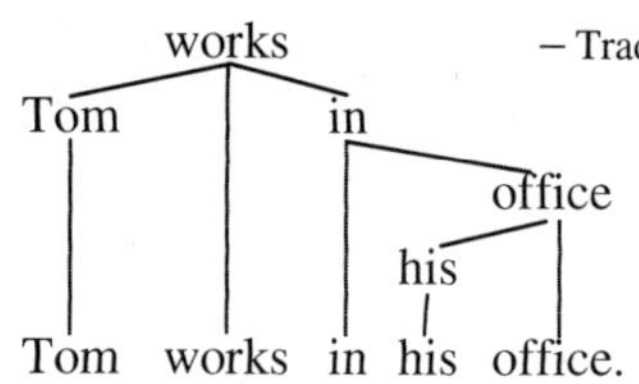

a.

– USD analysis

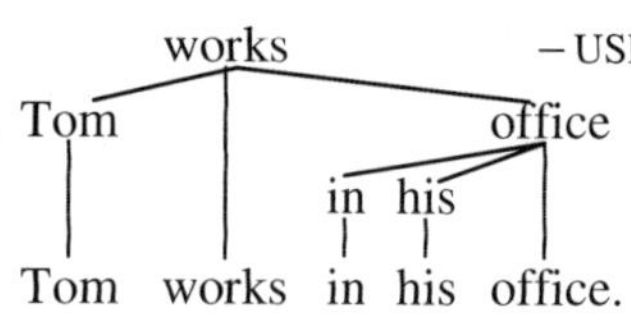

b.

The traditional analysis in (9a) takes *his office* to be a constituent, whereas the USD analysis takes *his office* to be a non-constituent.

Five of the six tests agree that *his office* is a constituent:

Topicalization

(10) a. ...but **his office** Tom does work in.

Proform substitution

b. Tom works in **there/it**.
(*there/it = his office*)

Answer fragments

c. What (room) does Tom work in?
– **His office**.

Clefting

d. It is **his office** that Tom works in.

Pseudoclefting

e. The room Tom works in is **his office**.

VP-ellipsis is not applicable in this case because no verb is involved. The other five tests agree that *his office* should be viewed as a constituent.

The USD analysis shown with (10b) takes the preposition *in* alone to be a constituent. The tests are unanimous, however, insofar as *in* alone is not a constituent:

Topicalization

(11) a. *...but **in** Tom works his office..

Proform substitution

b. *Tom works **there** his office.
(*there = in*)

Answer fragments

c. What does Tom do concerning working and his office? – ***In**.

Clefting

d. *It is **in** that Tom works his office.

Pseudoclefting

e. *Where Tom works his office is **in**. .

Based on these results, there is no motivation for granting the preposition *in* the status of a constituent.

In sum, the five applicable diagnostics clearly support the traditional analysis of prepositions: they are heads over their nouns.

5.3 Subordinators and determiners

Reaching a conclusion about the hierarchical status of subordinators and determiners using the six tests for constituents is much more difficult to do, because the tests typically do not support any analysis at all, at least not when applied to English sentences. In this respect other considerations must be accessed to help determine the hierarchical status of these two additional types of function words.

Concerning subordinators (e.g. *after*, *because*, *before*, *if*, *that*, *when*, *where*, *whether*, *why*, etc.), the fact that a couple of them also serve as prepositions is an indication that they should receive a similar analysis as prepositions; the subordinators *before*, *after*, *with*, and *for* also serve as simple prepositions. Thus since there is strong evidence supporting the status of prepositions as heads over their nouns, the same sort of analysis can be extended to these subordinators, and then by analogy to subordinators in general.

Concerning determiners, however, the debate concerning their status in the syntactic hierarchy is ongoing. This debate has split the syntax world into two camps since the 1980s: determiner phrase (DP) vs. noun phrase (NP). For the most part, the six tests for constituents do not shed much light on this debate, since they in general fail to identify either determiners or their nouns as constituents.

There are, however, a couple of limited cases that one can interpret as evidence in favor of the traditional NP analysis, a point now illustrated here using the sentence *Susan's house is beautiful*:

Proform substitution

(12) a. **Her** house is beautiful.
(*her = Susan's*)

Answer fragment

b. Whose house is beautiful? – **Susan's**.

These two examples demonstrate that proform substitution and answer fragments can be interpreted as identifying the determiner *Susan's* as a constituent. The other four tests (topicalization, clefting, VP-ellipsis, and pseudoclefting) do not support these results, however. Furthermore, the answer fragment in (12b) can be seen as involving noun ellipsis (N-ellipsis); the noun *house* has been elided, leaving just the determiner. This observation weakens any conclusion about the constituenthood of the determiner *Susan's* based on (12b).

In sum then, the hierarchical analysis of prepositions can be extended to subordinators, since there is much overlap in the forms and distributions of these two classes of function words. Concerning determiners, however, the tests deliver only rather weak evidence for the position that they are dependents of their nouns.

6. Other languages

An objection can be raised against the reasoning produced above. This objection points to the English-centered focus of the diagnostics discussed. The data produced have been from English alone. This fact raises the concern that the conclusion may not extend to other languages, and thus the diagnostics for constituents may not be very insightful from a cross-linguistic perspective. This objection is conceded here, but only in part.

There are a couple of points to keep in mind when assessing the objection. The first is that the most prominent schools of syntax internationally have been founded and are/were led primarily by native speakers of English (e.g. Noam Chomsky, Ivan Sag, Carl Pollard, Joan Bresnan, Ronald Langacker, etc.). The arguments and insights of these linguists are produced primarily in English, using examples primarily from English. Thus the syntax of English has had and continues to have a far greater influence on our understanding of syntax on the international stage in general than that of any other language. In this regard, the fact that tests for constituents developed for English sentences contradict the syntactic theories of the schools of syntax just alluded to should carry a lot of weight.

The second point to keep in mind concerns the sources that are using the tests. The textbooks that employ the tests are intended for students of linguistics. These texts are then used around the world in numerous countries by students of English in language departments at colleges and universities. Thus often the first exposure to syntactic theory that aspiring linguists receive comes in the form of textbooks written in English, using primarily English examples. This situation is suggestive of the great influence that these texts are having on the development of syntactic theory internationally. The message, then, is again that the tests as applied to English are having a disproportionate influence on the development and direction of syntactic theory in general.

The third point to consider is the extent to which the tests are in fact applicable to other languages. Some of the tests employed above should be valid for many other languages. This is particularly true of proform substitution and answer fragments. Most if not all languages have proforms, and these proforms can be used to identify syntactic structure in a manner similar to how proform substitution has been employed above. Similarly, most if not all languages allow question-answer pairs and the answer fragments that are produced can deliver important clues about syntactic structure no matter the language.

Ideally, each language needs to develop its own inventory of diagnostics for syntactic structure, based on its idiosyncrasies. Certainly some of the diagnostics above can be adopted directly into other languages (proform substitution, answer fragments), and others can perhaps be adapted in one way or another so that they can also be employed (clefting, pseudoclefting, ellipsis). When a given diagnostic does not seem to provide insights about syntactic structure, one should ask why this is so. The fact that the diagnostic is not helpful can then serve as an indicator about what is going on with the particular syntax of that language.

7. Concluding points

To conclude this contribution, two further objections that come to mind against the reasoning developed above are briefly countered. The first of these concerns the fact that diagnostics for constituents are fallible; at times the results they deliver are contradictory. This is perhaps most evident with determiners in English. Dependency- and constituency-based theories of syntax alike view determiners as constituents, yet most of the tests above fail to identify them as such. While this point must be conceded, at no time has the presentation above claimed that the diagnostics are infallible. Indeed, the tests are at times quite fallible. But what this contribution has claimed is that most diagnostics for constituents consistently fail to identify sub-phrasal strings as constituents. Since this is precisely what dependency-based models predict, the dependency models are preferable in this area. On the whole, they make much more accurate predictions about sentence structure with much less effort.

The second further objection that can be raised against the messages delivered above concerns the critique of the USD annotation scheme. No attempt has been made here to refute the main motivation for the USD scheme, this motivation being uniformity of annotation across diverse languages. Subordinating function words to content words establishes hierarchies of content words that are directly linked to each other, and these hierarchies are then relatively consistent across diverse languages. While this objection must also be conceded, this concession should not be misinterpreted, since this contribution never intended to refute this supposed strength of the USD annotation scheme.

The authors of the USD scheme claim that USD embodies "linguistic quality" (de Marneffe et al. 2014: 4589) – as opposed to accuracy of parsing. The message delivered above is that diagnostics for constituents contradict this claim to linguistic quality. Indeed, the diagnostics reveal the opposite, namely that the USD scheme cannot claim linguistic quality concerning the tests. Given the prominent role that the tests play in modeling syntactic structures, the lack of linguistic quality is in fact a major drawback of the USD approach.

References

David Adger. 2003. *Core Syntax: A Minimalist Approach*. Oxford University Press.

Adrian Akmajian, Richard Demers, Ann Farmer, and Robert Harnish. 1990. *An Introduction to Language and Communication*, 3rd edition. The MIT Press, Cambridge, MA.

David Allerton. 1979. *Essentials of Grammatical Theory: A Consensus View of Syntax and Morphology*. Routledge & Kegan Paul, London.

Carl Baker. 1978. *Introduction to Generative-Transformational Syntax*. Prentice-Hall.

Kersti Börjars and Kate Burridge. 2001. *Introducing English Grammar*. Arnold, London.

Robert Borsley. 1991. *Syntactic Theory: A Unified Approach*. Edward Arnold, London.

Noel Burton-Roberts. 1986. *Analysing Sentences: An Introduction to English Syntax*, 2nd edition. Longman, London.

Andrew Carnie. 2010. *Constituent Structure*, 2nd edition. Oxford University Press, Oxford, UK.

Andrew Carnie. 2013. *Syntax: A Generative Introduction*, 3rd edition. Wiley-Blackwell, Malden, MA.

Noam Chomsky. 1957. *Syntactic Structures*. Mouton Publishers, The Hague.

Elizabeth Cowper. 1992. *A Concise Introduction to Syntactic Theory: The Government-Binding Approach*. The University of Chicago Press, Chicago.

Peter Culicover. 2009. *Natural Language Syntax*. Oxford University Press, Oxford, UK.

Peter Culicover and Ray Jackendoff. 2005 *Simpler Syntax*. Oxford University Press, New York.

Ulrich Engel. 1994. *Syntax der deutschen Sprache*, 3rd edition. Erich Schmidt Verlag, Berlin.

Hans-Werner Eroms. 2000. *Syntax der deutschen Sprache*. de Gruyter, Berlin.

Nigel Fabb. 1994. *Sentence Structure*. Routledge, London.

Victoria Fromkin (ed.). 2000. *Linguistics: An Introduction to Linguistic Theory*. Basil-Blackwell, Malden, MA.

Thomas Groß. 1999. *Theoretical Foundations of Dependency Syntax*. Iudicium, Munich.

Liliane Haegeman. 2006. *Thinking Syntactically: A Guide to Argumentation and Analysis*. Blackwell Publishing, Malden, MA.

Liliane Haegeman and Jacqueline Guéron. 1999. *English Grammar: A Generative Perspective*. Blackwell Publishers, Oxford, UK.

Peter Hellwig. 2003. Dependency Unification Grammar. In: Vilmos Ágel et al. (eds.), *Dependency and Valency: An International Handbook of Contemporary Research*, 593–635. Walter de Gruyter, Berlin.

Hans Heringer. 1996. *Deutsche Syntax: Dependentiell*. Stauffenburg, Tübingen.

Rodney Huddleston and Geoffrey Pullum. 2002. *The Cambridge Grammar of the English Language*. Cambridge University Press.

Richard Hudson. 1984. *Word Grammar*. Basil Blackwell, Oxford, UK.

Richard Hudson. 1990. *An English Word Grammar*. Basil Blackwell, Oxford, UK.

Richard Hudson. 2007. *Language Networks: The New Word Grammar*. Oxford University Press, Oxford, UK.

Wha-Young Jung. 1995. *Syntaktische Relationen im Rahmen der Dependenzgrammatik*. Buske Verlag, Hamburg.

Samuel Keyser and Paul Postal. 1976. *Beginning English Grammar*. Harper & Row, New York.

Jong-Bok Kim and Peter Sells. 2008. *English Syntax: An Introduction*. CSLI Publications, Stanford.

Paul Kroeger. 2005. *Analyzing Grammar: An Introduction*. Cambridge University Press.

Jürgen Kunze. 1975. *Abhängigkeitsgrammatik. Studia Grammatica* 12. Akademie Verlag, Berlin.

Howard Lasnik with Marcela Depiante and Arthur Stepanov. 2000. *Syntactic Structures Revisited: Contemporary Lectures on Classic Transformational Theory*. The MIT Press, Cambridge, MA.

Henning Lobin. 1993. *Koordinationssyntax als prozedurales Phänomen. Studien zur deutschen Grammatik* 46. Gunter Narr Verlag, Tübingen.

Marie-Catherine de Marneffe, Timothy Dozat, Natalia Silvaire, Katrin Haverinen, Filip Ginter, Joakim Nivre, Christopher D. Manning. 2014. Universal Stanford Dependencies: A cross-linguistic typology. LREC 14, 4585–92.

James McCawley. 1998. *The Syntactic Phenomena of English*, 2nd edition. University of Chicago Press, Chicago.

Igor Mel'čuk. 1988. *Dependency Syntax: Theory and Practice*. State University of New York Press, Albany.

Stefan Müller. 2010. *Grammatiktheorie*. Stauffenberg Verlag, Tübingen.

Donna Napoli. 1993. *Syntax: Theory and Problems*. Oxford University Press, New York.

Jamal Ouhalla. 1994. *Transformational Grammar: From Rules to Principles and Parameters*. Edward Arnold, London.

Thomas Payne. 2006. *Exploring Language Structure: A Student's Guide*. Cambridge University Press.

Geoffrey Poole. 2002. *Syntactic Theory*. Pelgrave, New York.

Paul Postal. 1974. *On Raising: One Rule of English Grammar and its Theoretical Implications*. Cambridge University Press, Cambridge, MA.

Radford, Andrew. 1988. *Transformational Grammar: A First Course*. Cambridge University Press, Cambridge, UK.

Andrew Radford. 1997. *Syntactic Theory and the Structure of English: A Minimalist Approach*. Cambridge University Press, Cambridge, UK.

Andrew Radford. 2004. *English Syntax: An Introduction*. Cambridge University Press.

Ian Roberts. 1997. *Comparative Syntax*. Arnold, London.

Ivan Sag, Thomas Wasow, and Emily Bender. 2003. *Syntactic Theory*, 2nd edition. CSLI Publications, Stanford.

Nicholas Sobin. 2011. *Syntactic Analysis: The Basics*. Wiley-Blackwell, Malden, MA.

Dominque Sportiche, Hilda Koopman, and Edward Stabler. 2014. *An Introduction to Syntactic Analysis and Theory*. Wiley Blackwell, Malden, MA.

Stanley Starosta. 1988. *The Case for Lexicase: An Outline of Lexicase Grammatical Theory*. Pinter Publishers, London.

Maggie Tallerman. 2005. *Understanding Syntax*, 2nd edition. Hodder Education, London.

Linda Thomas. 1993. *Beginning Syntax*. Blackwell, Oxford, UK.

Robert van Valin. 2001. *An Introduction to Syntax*. Cambridge University Press, Cambridge, UK.

A DG Account of the Descriptive and Resultative *de*-Constructions in Chinese

Timothy Osborne
Zhejiang University
Hangzhou
China
tjo3ya@yahoo.com

Shudong Ma
Zhejiang University
Hangzhou
China
shudong.ma@qq.com

Abstract

This contribution examines the descriptive and resultative *de*-constructions in Mandarin Chinese, e.g. *Wǒ pǎo-de hěn kuài* 'I run very fast'. There is a longstanding debate about this construction. The primary point of dispute concerns the main predicate: Is the first predicate the root of the sentence, i.e. *pǎo-de* 'run', or is the second predicate the root, i.e. *kuài* 'fast'? We demonstrate here that from a dependency grammar (DG) perspective, the second predicate should be taken as the root. A number of diagnostics support this conclusion: 1) yes/no-questions with *ma*, 2) position of the negation *bù*, 3) omission, 4) placement of the adverb *yě* 'also', 5) *ne*-questions, and 6) modal insertion. The conclusion is important for the development of DG as applied to the syntax of Mandarin, since many basic questions about Mandarin sentence structure have not yet been examined from a DG perspective.

1 Two possibilities

There is a longstanding debate about the syntactic status of the descriptive and resultative *de*-constructions in Mandarin Chinese (henceforth jus Mandarin). The point of contention is illustrated with the following DG analyses:

(1)

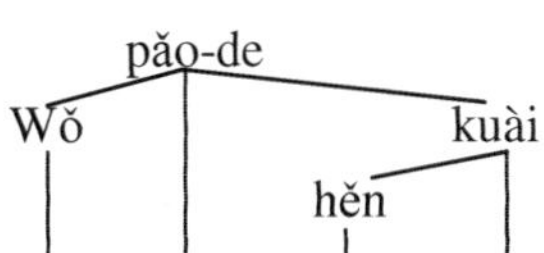

a. Wǒ pǎo-de hěn kuài. (descriptive)
I run-de very fast
'I run very fast.'

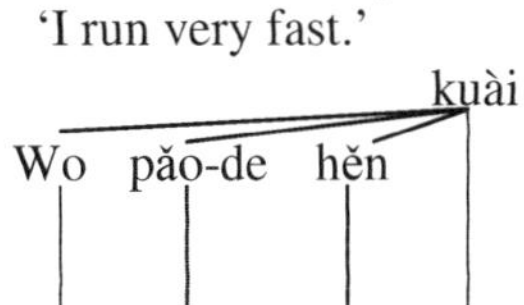

b. Wǒ pǎo-de hěn kuài.

(2)

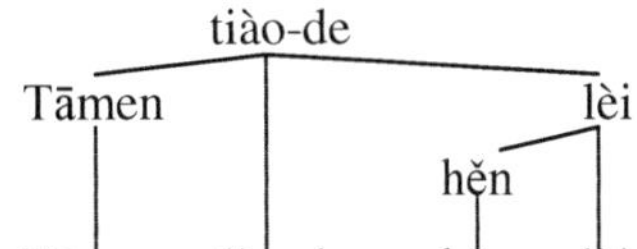

a. Tāmen tiào-de hěn lèi. (resultative)
they jump-de very tired
'They jumped till they got very tired.'

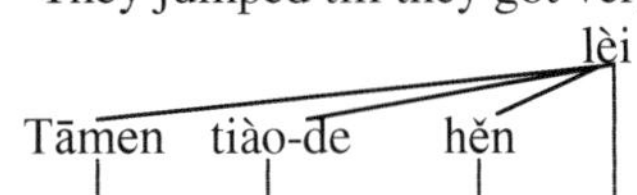

b. Tāmen tiào-de hěn lèi.

The a-analyses show the VERB-*de* as the root of the sentence, whereas the b-analyses show the adjective as the root? We argue for the b-analyses in this contribution. We will, though, also develop a somewhat more fine-grained dependency analysis of these constructions, i.e. more fine-grained than what is shown with (1b) and (2b) here.

The point of contention reaches back decades. Early accounts of the *de*-construction were more in line with the b-analyses here (e.g. Chao 1968/1979: 176-180; Li 1986: 250), but in the 1980s an alternative account closer to the a-analyses gained a number of adherents (e.g. Huang 1988; Zhu 1982: 134; Zhou and Huang 1994:47, Ding 1961/1999: 63–5; Huang et al. 2009: 84–91). Huang's (1988) article on the *de*-construction was particularly influential in establishing the validity of the a-analyses. Most of the relevant publications that have appeared more recently pursue an analysis similar to the a-analyses here (e.g. Xu and Pan 2014; Yang and Cheng 2013), though these publications diverge in the details.[1]

Most explorations of the syntactic status of the *de*-construction have been produced in the

[1] Fan (1993) proposes a tripartite demarcation: syntax, meaning, and pragmatics. The same one word can be viewed as a syntactic head but semantic dependent, or vice versa. That is, the syntactic root is different from the semantic/pragmatic root. This distinction is not observed in the DG account pursued here.

Proceedings of the Third International Conference on Dependency Linguistics (Depling 2015), pages 261–270, Uppsala, Sweden, August 24–26 2015.

tradition of constituency grammar. Thus the two competing analyses just depicted with the trees in (1–2) are casting the debate in a new light. Indeed, to our knowledge the debate concerning the status of the *de*-construction in Mandarin has not yet been examined from a DG perspective. The interesting point about this situation is that from the DG perspective, the main question is less difficult insofar as the account is confronted with just two basic possibilities (a-trees vs. b-trees), and it need merely choose between these two. Constituency grammar accounts, in contrast, have the option to posit extra functional categories and the associated structure in order to accommodate specific facts about the *de*-construction. DG, with its minimal approach to basic sentence structure, cannot entertain the same multiplicity of potential analyses.

This situation can be viewed either as a strength or weakness of the DG approach. Either the limitation on possibilities for analysis is a good thing because there is less room for disagreement, or the possibilities are too limited and thus incapable of accommodating the multiplicity of facts associated with the construction. We of course prefer the former position. In any case, achieving certainty about the basic DG analysis of the *de*-construction should be beneficial for the further development of DG as applied to Mandarin.

2 Overview of *de*-elements

The element *de* has a number of different uses in Mandarin. In general, there are at least six different *de*-elements:

1. a. *de* marking a premodifier of a noun (的)
   b. *de* functioning as a nominalizer (的)
2. *de/dì* marking premodifier of a verb (地)
3. *dé/děi* 'should' as a modal verb (得)
4. *dé* 'receive' as a content verb (得)
5. *de* 'possible' as a modal particle (得)
6. a. *de* helping to express descriptive meaning (得)
   b. *de* helping to express resultative meaning (得)

Mandarin orthography, i.e. the Hanzi characters, is a source of confusion when dealing with these *de*-elements. Hanzi distinguishes the first two *de*-elements from the other four with distinct characters, 的 and 地, whereas the latter four *de*-elements are more difficult to discern due to the use of the same one Hanzi character, i.e. 得. The third *de*-element, the modal verb *dé/děi* 'should', and the fourth *de*-element, the content verb *dé/děi* 'get, receive', have a distinct sound pattern that distinguish them from the other four, i.e. *dé* (rising tone) and *děi* (falling-rising tone), as opposed to *de* (neutral tone). The fifth *de*-element, the modal particle, is usually the second part of a three-part construction that consists of a verb, *de*, and a post-dependent on the verb. This postdependent is often a verb-like particle, e.g. *huá de xiàlái* 'can slide down', *kàn de dào* 'can see', *chēng de qǐ* 'can lift up'.

While these first five *de*-elements are certainly worthy of exploration from a DG point of view, this contribution concentrates on the sixth *de*-element, which can be split into two types depending on whether *de* helps convey descriptive or resultative meaning. This sixth *de*-element has been the focus of significant debate, since its status in the syntactic hierarchy is not immediately clear, as suggested above with the trees in (1–2). A primary characteristic of descriptive/resultative *de* is that it appears as (what we view as) a clitic on a predicate (a verb or adjective) and it precedes a second predicate (often an adjective). It is therefore often sandwiched between two predicates.

The following examples illustrate the descriptive and resultative *de*; they are taken from Li and Thompson (1981: 624ff.):

Descriptive *de*

(3) a. Tā zǒu-de hěn màn.
S/he walk-de very slow.
'S/he walks very slowly.'

b. Wǒmen shuì de hěn hǎo.
We sleep de very good
'We sleep very nicely.'

c. Tā chuān de hěn piàoliang.
he/she dress de very beautiful
'S/he dresses very beautifully.'

Resultative *de*

(4) a. Tā jiāo de lèi le.
s/he teach de tired le
'S/he taught herself tired.'

b. Wǒ kū de yǎnjing dōu hóng le.
I cry de eye all red le
'I cried my eyes all red.'

c. Wǒ è de fā huāng.
I hungry de produce panic
'I'm hungry to the point of panic.'

When it helps convey descriptive meaning, *de* is associated with an adverb in English (here *slowly*, *nicely*, *beautifully*). When it helps convey resultative meaning, *de* is often associated with a predicative adjective in English (here *tired*, *red*) or with a second verbal predicate (here *produce*).[2]

As stated in the introduction, the main source of debate for these *de*-elements concerns the two predicates with which they co-occur: Is the first predicate (the one on the left) head over the second predicate, or vice versa. These two possibilities can be rendered in the English translations as follows for example (3a):

(5) Tā zǒu-de hěn màn.
s/he walk-de very slow

a. 'S/he walks very slowly.'

b. 'S/he is very slow in walking.'

While the translation *S/he is very slow in walking* is an odd sentence in English, this manuscript now argues that it more accurately reflects the hierarchy of words in the Mandarin sentence *Tā zǒu de hěn màn*. In other words, the second predicate is in fact head over the first predicate.

3 Overview of diagnostics

To motivate the dependency analyses of descriptive and resultative *de*, we use a number of diagnostics:

1. Yes/no-questions with *ma*,
2. Position of the negation *bù*,
3. Omission,
4. Placement of the adverb *yě* 'also',
5. Questions with *ne*, and
6. Modal insertion

To illustrate these diagnostics, we first apply them to the following sentence:

(6)
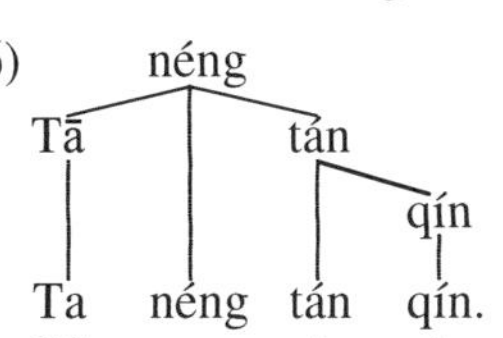

Ta néng tán qín.
S/he can play piano.

[2] Even though the elements following *de* can be viewed as an adverb or adjective, worth noting is that with no formal marker, a Chinese word often allows for a flexible categorical role.

Modal verbs such as *néng* here are widely taken to be the root of the clause in which they appear in many languages, and subordinating the subject immediately to the modal verb makes sense since doing so results in a hierarchy that corresponds exactly to the corresponding hierarchy for the English sentence, and further, it avoids the projectivity violation that would be incurred if the subject were subordinated directly to the content verb *tán*. While these aspects of the analysis in (6) can be disputed, we take the validity of (6) for granted, since doing so allows us to establish a framework that can be used to analyze *de*-constructions. The validity of (6) is then supported by the overall understanding of Mandarin sentence structure that emerges.

***Ma*-questions:** The answer to a yes/no-question that is formed with the interrogative particle *ma* is typically reduced down to just the root node, e.g.

(7) Tā néng tán qín ma?
s/he can play piano ma
'Can s/he play piano?'

a. – Néng. – 'Can.'

b. – *Tán. – 'Play.'

The answer is acceptable if it includes *néng* and unacceptable if it excludes *néng*. The assumption, then, is that the answer to a yes/no-question (expressed using the interrogative particle *ma*) should include the root of the sentence.

The negation *bù*: The negation *bù* typically precedes the root of the clause. Thus when *bù* is inserted into the test sentence, it should precede *néng*:

(8) a. Tā bù néng tán qín.
S/he not can play piano.
'She cannot play piano.'

b. Tā néng bù tán qín.
'S/he can not play piano.'
'S/he may stop playing piano.'

Sentence (8a) is natural, whereas sentence (8b) is unusual. Sentence (8b) is only possible on the unlikely reading where it means that 's/he is allowed to not play the piano (or to stop playing the piano)'. Thus the position of the negation helps identify the root of the sentence. To negate the entire sentence in a neutral manner, the negation should precede the root node.

Omission: Eliding or omitting a string is another test for identifying constituents (complete subtrees).[3] If a string can be omitted without significantly altering the meaning of the sentence, then the omitted string is potentially a constituent. In this case, *tán qín* can be omitted in terms of VP-ellipsis, whereby the meaning remains unchanged:

(9) Wǒ néng tán qín. Tā yě néng.
I can play piano. S/he also can.
'I can play the piano, and she can, too.'

The ability to omit the string *tán qín* in the same manner that one can omit a verb phrase in terms of VP-ellipsis in English suggests that *tán qín* should form a constituent. This, in turn, suggests that *néng* is head over *tán qín*, because if it were not, *tán qín* would not qualify as a constituent, and omission should then not be possible.

The adverb *yě*: The position of the adverb *yě* 'also' is another indicator that is useful for identifying the root of the sentence. This adverb must precede *néng*; it cannot follow *néng*:

(10) a. Tā yě néng tán qín.
'S/he also can play piano.'

b. *Tā néng yě tán qín.
'S/he can also play piano.'

This pattern is accounted for on the assumption that *yě* must precede the root of the clause. Inserting *yě* is therefore a simple diagnostic that can help identify which predicate is head over the other.

***Ne*-questions:** The interrogative particle *ne* 'what about' serves to form an abbreviated question of a sort. On the assumption that this particle focuses a constituent, it can be used to identify constituents in the preceding sentence and thus to identify which verb is head over the other:

(11) a. A: Tā néng tán gāngqín.
S/he can play piano.

B: Tán xiǎotíqín ne?
Play violin what about
'What about playing the violin?'

B′: *Yīnggāi ne?
'What about should?'

The acceptability of the *ne*-question *Tán xiǎotíqín ne?* is consistent with the stance that *tán gāngqín* is a constituent, which is, in turn, consistent with the position of *néng* as head over *tán gāngqín*. If *néng* were not head over *tán gāngqín* but rather a dependent of *tán*, then *tán gāngqín* would not be a constituent and we would expect the first question uttered by B to fail precisely because *tán xiǎotíqín* would not correspond to a constituent in the preceding statement. The fact that the second *ne*-question is bad is consistent with the observation that as head over *tán gāngqín*, the auxiliary *néng* is not a constituent.

Modal insertion: The final diagnostic introduced here is modal insertion. This diagnostic inserts a modal auxiliary verb into a sentence that lacks one, e.g.

(12) Tā tán qín.
S/he plays piano.

a. Tā néng tán qín. – *néng* 'can'

b. *Néng tā tán qín.

c. *Tā tán néng qín.

Given the non-controversial assumption that *tán* is the root of the sentence in (12), inserting the modal auxiliary *néng* into the sentence provides clues about the hierarchy. Since Mandarin is an SVO language,[4] the root verb of a sentence should follow the subject and precede the object. This means that when the modal auxiliary is inserted into the sentence, it becomes the root verb, and *tán qín* becomes its object in a sense. In other words, when a modal is inserted into the sentence, it should follow the subject and precede what was the root before insertion. Doing this delivers helpful clues about the hierarchical structure of the sentence, as demonstrated with (12a–c).

The six diagnostics just illustrated will now be used to identify the root word in sentences containing *de* (descriptive and resultative *de*). The tests mostly converge, identifying the second predicate, i.e. the predicate that follows *de* as head over the first predicate.

4 Descriptive and resultative *de*

4.1 Descriptive *de*

The six diagnostics just introduced will now be applied to descriptive *de*. Example (5) from above, repeated here as (13), is used as the test sentence:

[3] Following Hudson (1984: 92), Starosta (1988: 105), and Hellwig (2003: 603), we call the complete subtrees of dependency structures *constituents*.

[4] We take Chinese to be an SVO language. However, there has been some debate about this. Some have argued that Chinese is actually SOV (e.g. Sun and Givón 1985, Chen 1995).

(13) Tā zǒu-de hěn màn.
He walk-de very slow.
'He walks very slowly.'

Descriptive *de* helps express a characteristic ability or trait associated with the subject. In this case, the characteristic trait is that of walking slowly. The six diagnostics will now be applied to this sentence, each in turn.

The answer to a *ma*-question suggests that *màn* is the root:

(14) Tā zǒu-de màn ma?
S/he walk-de slow ma
'Does s/he walk slowly?

a. – Màn. – 'Slow.'

b. – *Zǒu-de. – 'Walk.'

The placement of *bù* is consistent with the assumption that *màn* is the root:

(15) a. ?Tā bú zǒu-de màn.
s/he not walk-de slow

b. Tā zǒu-de bú màn.
s/he walk not slow

The ability to omit *zǒu-de* and the inability to omit *hěn màn* indicate that *màn* is the root:

(16) a. Tā hěn màn.
s/he very slow
'S/he is very slow.'

b. *Tā zǒu-de.
s/he walk-de

The placement of *yě* is consistent with *màn* as the root, since in both of the following acceptable sentences, *yě* precedes *màn*:

(17) a. Tā yě zǒu-de hěn màn.
s/he also walk-de very slow.

b. Tā zǒu-de yě hěn màn.
s/he walk-de also very slow

The ability to form a *ne*-question corresponding to *zǒu-de* and the inability to form such a question corresponding to *màn* suggest that *màn* is the root:

(18) A: Tā zǒu-de màn. 'S/he walks slowly.'

B: Pǎo-de ne? 'What about run-de.'

B′: *Kuài ne? 'What about quickly?

And the fact that a modal verb can appear in two positions suggests that *màn* is the root, since in both cases, the modal verb follows the subject and precedes *màn*:

(19) a. Tā něng zǒu-de hěn màn.
s/he can walk-de very slow
'S/he can walk very slowly.'

b. Tā zǒu-de néng hěn màn.
s/he walk-de can very slow
'S/he can walk very slowly.'

Note that if *zǒu-de* were head over *màn* here, we would expect (19b) to be bad.

Taken together, the six diagnostics strongly support the conclusion that *màn* is the root of the sentence. The dependency-grammar analysis of the starting sentence should therefore be as follows:

(20)

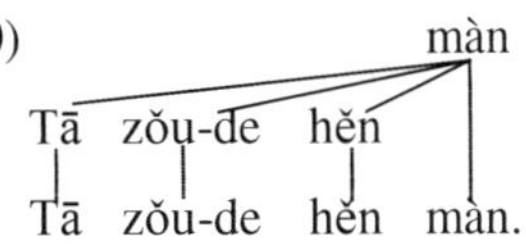

The status of *tā* as a dependent of *màn* – as opposed to as a dependent of *zǒu-de* – is motivated by the omission diagnostic (see example 16a) and the modal insertion diagnostic (see example 19a). We can therefore see what the clitic *de* is doing in such cases: it serves to subordinate *zǒu* to *màn*.

4.2 Resultative *de*

The tests also provide consistent results when applied to an example with resultative *de*. Example (4a) from above is repeated here as (21):

(21) Tā jiāo-de lèi le.
s/he taught-de tired le
'S/he taught her-/himself tired.'

This example differs from the one in the previous section insofar as the second predicate is now interpreted as the result of the action expressed by the first predicate, i.e. the teaching made her/him tired. The structure of the example, though, is similar to the structure of the example sentence from the previous section containing descriptive *de*.

The answer to a *ma*-question suggests that *lèi* is head over *jiāo-de*:

(22) Tā jiāo-de lèi le ma?
S/he teach-de tired le ma
'Did s/he teach her-/himself tired?'

a. – Lèi (le). – 'Tired.'

b. – *Jiāo-de. – 'Teach.'

The placement of *bù* (actually *mei* 'not' in this case, due to interference associated with *le*) suggests that *lèi* is the root, since in both of the following sentences, *méi* precedes *lèi*:

(23) a. Tā méi jiāo-de lèi.
s/he not teach-de tired
'S/he did not teach her-/himself tired.'

b. Tā jiāo-de méi lèi.
s/he teach-de not tired
'S/he did not teach her-/himself tired.'

If *jiāo-de* were the root in this case, we would expect (23b) to be bad because a left-branching verb chain would be present – verb chains in Mandarin are mostly right-branching.

The ability to omit *jiāo-de* and the inability to omit *lèi le* indicate that *lèi* is head over *jiào-de*:

(24) a. Tā lèi le.
s/he tired le

b. *Tā jiāo-de.
s/he teach-de

The placement of *yě* is consistent with *lèi* as the root, since in both of the following acceptable sentences, *yě* precedes *lèi*:

(25) a. Tā yě jiāo-de lèi le.
s/he also teach-de tired le
'S/he also taught her-/himself tired.'

b. Tā jiāo-de yě lèi le.
s/he teach-de also tired le.
'S/he also taughter her-/himself tired.'

The ability to form a *ne*-question corresponding to *jiāo-de* and the inability to form such a question corresponding to *lèi* suggest that *lèi* is head over *jiāo-de*:

(26) A: Tā jiāo-de lèi le.
s/he teach-de tired le

B: Xué-de ne? 'What about study?'

B′: *Fán ne? 'What about bored?'

And the fact that a modal verb can appear in two positions suggests that *lèi* is the root, since in both cases, the modal verb follows the subject and precedes *lèi*:

(27) a. Tā gāi jiāo-de lèi le.
s/he should teach-de tired le
'S/he should teach her-/himself tired.'

b. Tā jiāo-de gāi lèi le.
s/he teach-de should tired le
'S/he should teach her-/himself tired.'

Note that if *jiāo-de* were head over *lèi* here before insertion of the modal verb, we would expect (27b) to be bad because verb chains in Mandarin tend to be right-branching, not left-branching.

Taken together, the six diagnostics support the conclusion that *lèi* is head over *jiāo-de*. The DG analysis of the starting sentence should therefore be as follows:

(28)

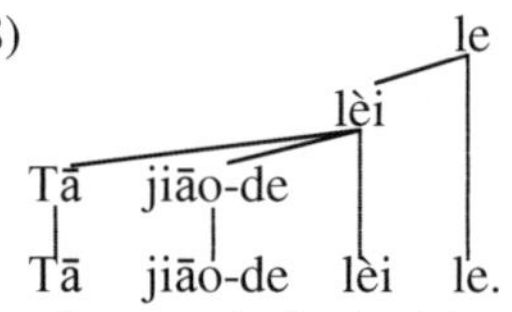

s/he teach-de tired le.

The status of *tā* as an immediate dependent of *lèi*, as opposed to as a dependent of *jiāo-de*, is supported by the omission diagnostic (see example 24a) and the modal insertion diagnostic (see example 27a). Therefore we see again what *de* is accomplishing in such cases; its appearance serves to subordinate the first predicate to the second, i.e. *jiāo* to *lèi*.

4.3 *de*-clauses

Resultative *de* also occurs in bi-clausal sentences. The following examples are unlike the examples in the previous two sections in this regard insofar as two clauses are present each time, as opposed to just one:

(29) Tā kū-de yǎnjīng hóng le.
s/he cry-de eyes red le
'Her/his crying makes her/his eyes red.'

The string *tā kū-de* can be evaluated as a clause as opposed to as a phrase because it contains the overt subject *tā*. The string *tā kū-de* is thus a clause that expresses the cause of the result expressed with the main clause *yǎnjīng hóng le*.

When yes/no questions with *ma* are applied to this sentence, the *de*-clause is most naturally omitted entirely:

(30) Tā kū-de yǎnjīng hōng le ma?
s/he cry-de eyes red le ma
'Does s/he cry her/his eyes red?'

a. – Hōng le. 'Red.'

b. – Yǎnjīng hōng le. 'Eyes red.'

c. – *Kū-de. 'Cry.'

These data are expected if *hōng* is head over *kū-de*, but unexpected if *kū-de* were head over *hōng*.

Negation should be located in front of the second predicate, not in front of the first:

(31) a. *Tā bù kū-de yǎnjīng hóng e.
s/he not cry-de eyes red le

b. Tā kū-de yǎnjīng bù hóng le.
s/he cry eyes not red le
'Crying makes her/his red eyes recover.'

The badness of (31a) is expected, since in order to negate the matrix clause, the negation should appear in the matrix clause, not in the subordinate clause.

The structural analysis predicts that the sentence should be fine if the *de*-clause is omitted entirely, and this prediction is borne out:

(32) Tā kū-de yǎnjīng hóng le.
s/he cries-de eyes red le

a. Yǎnjīng hóng le. 'Eyes red.'

b. ?Tā kū-de hóng le. 'S/he cries red.'

c. ??Tā hóng le. 'S/he is red.'

Sentence (32a), from which the *de*-clause has been removed entirely, is fine. If one attempts to remove the matrix subject *yǎnjīng* 'eyes' as in (32b), though, the result is marginal, and if one attempts to make *tā* 's/he' the matrix subject as in (32c), the meaning of the sentence changes drastically.

Interestingly, however, *yě* can appear in the subordinate clause or the matrix clause:

(33) a. Tā yě kū-de yǎnjīng hóng le.
s/he also cry-de eyes red le
'She too cried her eyes red.'

b. Tā kū-de yǎnjīng yě hóng le.
s/he cry-de eyes also red le
'S/he cried so that also her eyes were red.'

There may, however, be a slight meaning difference across these two sentences, as indicated by the translations.

The *ne*-question diagnostic identifies *Tā kū-de* as a constituent, which is expected if *hóng* is head over *kū-de*:

(34) A: Tā kū-de yǎnjīng hóng le.
S/he cry-de eyes red le
'S/he cried her/his eyes red.'

B: Nǐ kū-de ne? 'What about you crying?'

The sixth diagnostic, modal insertion, is particularly revealing. The modal verb *gāi* 'should' can be inserted into either clause:

(35) a. Tā gāi kū-de yǎnjīng hóng le.
S/he should cry-de eyes red le
'S/he should cry making her eyes red.'

b. Tā kū-de yǎnjīng gāi hóng le.
s/he cry-de eyes should red le
'By crying her/his eyes should be red.'

The English translations indicate a subtle meaning difference across the two sentences. This meaning difference is expected insofar as the modal verb scopes just over the clause in which it appears.

Taken together, the six diagnostics identify *tā kū-de* as a clausal constituent and hence as a dependent of *hóng*. The following hierarchy models the data best:

(36)

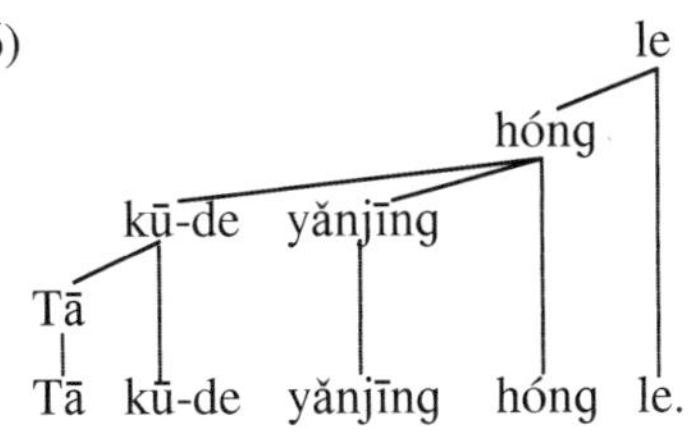

Thus if one wants to reflect the structure of this example with an English sentence, one might translate it as *By her/his crying, her/his eyes were red*. Perhaps the most important aspect of this analysis concerns the position of *tā* as a dependent of *kū-de*; *tā* is the subject *kū-de*, making *tā kū-de* a separate clause. The example is therefore bi-clausal.

5 Verb copying

The first verb in the *de*-construction, both descriptive and resultative, can, and at times must, be copied, e.g.

(37) a. *Tā shuō hànyǔ-de hǎo.
s/he speak Chinese-de good

b. *Tā shuō-de hànyǔ hǎo.[5]
s/he speak-de Chinese good

c. Tā shuō hànyǔ shuō-de hǎo.
s/he speak Chinese speak-de good
'S/he is good at speaking Chinese.'

Of these three sentences, only sentence (37c), in which the verb *shuō* is copied, is acceptable. The unacceptability of (37a) can be accounted for by the assumption that *de* must cliticize to a verb, as

[5] Example (37b) is actually acceptable in the reading where it means 'Her/his spoken Chinese is good'. On the intended reading however, i.e. 'She is good at speaking Chinese', the sentence is bad.

opposed to a noun, i.e. it cannot be a clitic on the noun *hànyǔ*. Why sentence (37b) is bad is, however, not immediately clear, although it may have something to do with the fact that *hànyǔ* is trying to be a postdependent of *shuō-de*. Perhaps the appearance of *de* blocks the verb *shuō* from taking postdependents. Verb copying would thus be a means of overcoming this block on postdependents.

The stance taken here is that verb copying as illustrated in (37c) is revealing something important about the syntactic status of *de*. Much of the literature on the *de*-constructions takes *de* to be a suffix (e.g. Li and Thompson 1981). In contrast, the observations that we now present suggest that *de* is better analyzed as a clitic. In particular, it behaves like possessive *'s* in English in an important way, which demonstrates that it is better viewed as a clitic, since possessive *'s* in English has clitic status.

First, consider (37b) again. While *shuō-de* cannot take *hànyǔ* as a postdependent, it can take *hànyǔ* as a predependent. Example (37b) is given again here as (38a) with the dependency analysis included, and sentence (38b) is added to illustrate the ability of *shuō-de* to take *hànyǔ* as a predependent:

(38)

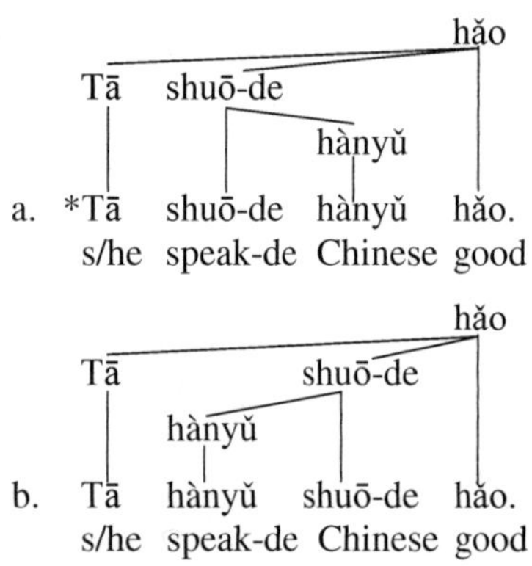

If these analyses are on the right track, they point to a partial explanation for why verb copying occurs in the *de*-construction. Copying the verb helps to overcome the block on postdependents.

Consider the following analysis of example (37c), repeated here as (39) with the dependencies added

(39)

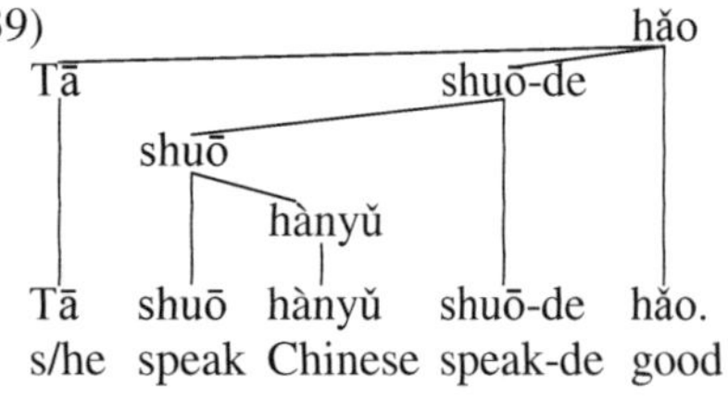

On this analysis, *shuō-de* no longer has a postdependent, but rather *hànyǔ* is a postdependent of the first *shuō*. The account might therefore simply stipulate that the appearance of *de* blocks its host from taking a postdependent. This stipulation would, however, be contradicted by other data, a point that will become evident shortly.

The analysis of descriptive and resultative *de* above has demonstrated that *de* serves to subordinate one predicate to another. It behaves like a postposition or post-subordinator. To accommodate this role of *de*, it can be positioned as the root of the entire premodifier. As the root of this modifier, it has a hierarchical status that is quite similar to the possessive clitic *'s* in English. Compare the following structures:

(40)

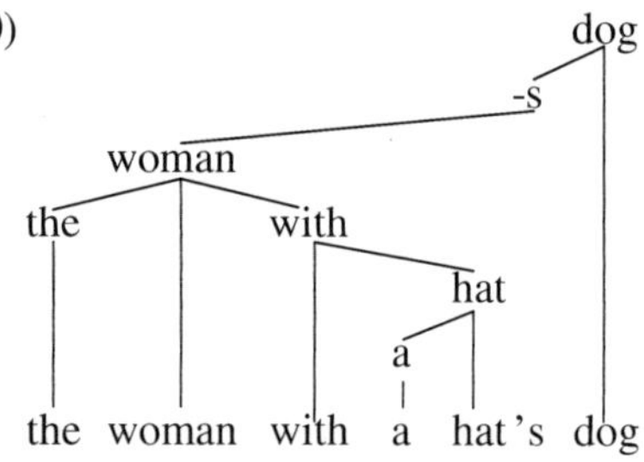

(41)

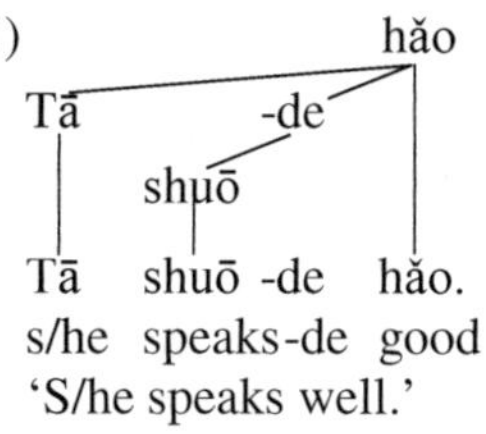

The *de* element is now shown as the root of the phrase *shuō de*, similar to the way that possessive *'s* is shown as the root of the determiner phrase *the woman with a hat's*. Both of these elements are granted the status of a clitic.

Clitics are, following Groß (2014), indicated with a hyphen and the absence of a projection line. The hyphen appears on the side of the clitic where its host is, indicating that the clitic is prosodically dependent on that host. The host of *de* must be a verb (here *shuō*), whereas the host of *'s* can be most any category (here it is the noun *hat*).

The analysis of the *de* element just sketched is supported by cases in which the verb to which it cliticizes is subordinated to a modal verb, e.g.

(42)

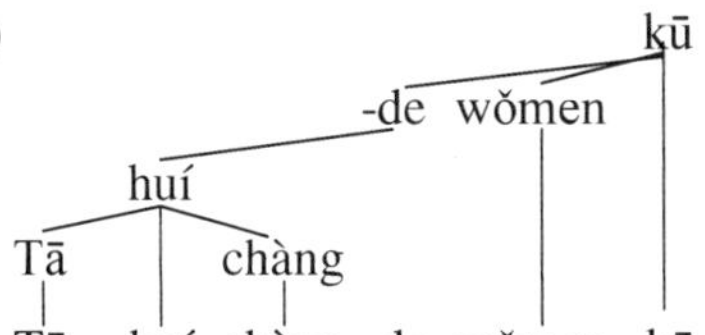

Tā huí chàng -de wǒmen kū.
S/he can sing -de we cry
'S/he can sing (so nicely that) we cry.'

The *de* cliticizes to *chàng* at the same time that *chàng* is subordinate to *huì*. This analysis grants *de* the status of a subordinator (subordinate conjunction). It serves to subordinate the immediately preceding predicate to the following predicate.

To summarize, the verb copying phenomenon has helped reveal important traits of descriptive and resultive *de*. This element is a clitic that serves to subordinate one predicate to another. It necessarily cliticizes to the preceding predicate and subordinates that predicate to a following predicate. The fact that it cliticizes to a preceding predicate blocks that predicate from taking a postdependent. This is in turn the aspect of *de* that is responsible for motivating verb copying. By copying the verb, the first instance of the verb (on the left) can take a postdependent.

6 Unification with *de* (的) and *de* (地)

Descriptive/resultative *de* (得) shares an important prosodic feature with *de* (的) and *de* (地). All three *de* receive a neutral tone – although 地 does allow an archaic falling tone at times, in which case it is pronounced as *dì*. The shared trait of a neutral tone suggests that all three *de* can be viewed as clitics. More importantly, though, all three *de* serve to subordinate what immediately precedes them to what follows them. In other words, their roles in the syntactic structure are closely similar.

The most frequently occurring *de* often subordinates material to a noun; it is written as 的, and the material that it subordinates typically corresponds to an attributive adjective, prepositional phrase, or relative clause in English, e.g.

(43)

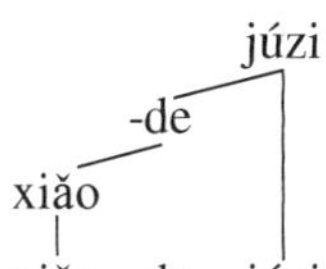

a. xiǎo -de júzi
small-de orange
'small oranges'

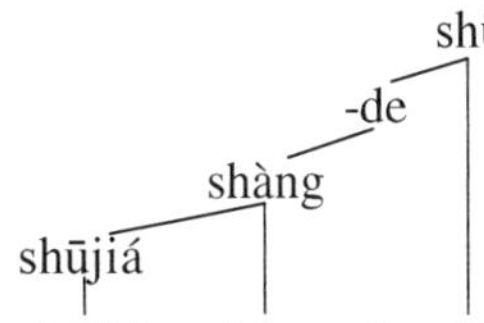

b. shūjiá shàng -de shū
shelf on -de book
'the book on the shelf'

In each case, the *de* clitic appears to subordinate the material preceding it to the noun that follows it.

The other *de* (地) performs a closely similar role, although it depends on a verb as opposed to on a noun, and the material that it subordinates is restricted to an adjective. It therefore serves to transform an adjective into an adverb; the adjective is often doubled:

(44)

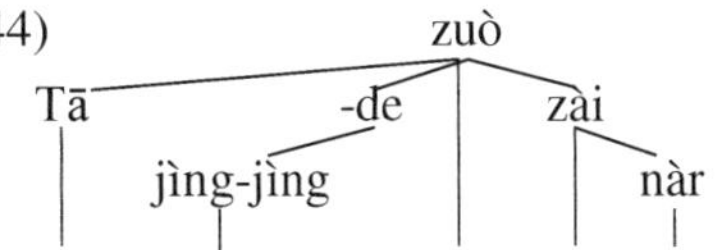

Tā jìng-jìng -de zuò zài nàr.
she quietly -de sat at there
'She quietly sat there.'

In sum, the aspect to acknowledge about all three *de* is that they are quite similar. They are clitics that subordinate what precedes them to what follows them. The point, then, is that a unified syntactic analysis of the three *de* is possible.

7 Conclusion

This manuscript has produced a DG account of the descriptive/resultative element *de* (得) in Mandarin. This element is a clitic that serves to subordinate the preceding predicate to the/a following predicate. Its role in syntax is closely similar to the roles of *de* (的) and *de* (地). All three *de* perform a translative function (Tesnière 1959: Part III).

This manuscript ends with a word of caution. The exploration of *de* elements here has focused on a particular type of *de*, namely descriptive and resultative *de* (得), and it has drawn a parallel to two other types of *de*, 的 and 地. The *de* element appears in additional constructions beyond these three, as mentioned above in the overview where six types of *de* were listed. The three types of *de* in the overview not examined in this contribution behave much differently than the three types of *de* that have been considered. Especially the modal element *de* (the fifth *de* in the list) presents challenges to syntactic theory.

Literature

Yuen-Ren Chao. 1968/1979. *A Grammar of Spoken Chinese*. Translated by Lv Shuxiang. The Commercial Press, Beijing.

Rong Chen. 1995. Communicative dynamism and word order in mandarin Chinese. *Language Sciences*, 17, 2, 201–22.

Sheng-shu Ding. 1961. *Xiàndài hànyǔ yǔfǎ jiǎnghuà* [Lectures on the modern Chinese grammar]. The Commercial Press, Beijing:

Xiao Fan. 1993. Fù dòng V-de jù [The verb-copying V-de construction]. *Yǔyánjiàoxuéyǔyánjiū* 04, 57–74.

Thomas Groß. 2014. Clitics in dependency morphology. In Kim Gerdes, Eva Hajičová, and Leo Wanner (eds.), *Dependency Linguistics: Recent Advances in Linguistic Theory Using Dependency Structures*, 229–51. John Benjamins, Amsterdam.

Peter Hellwig. 2003. Dependency Unification Grammar. In: V. Ágel, et al. (eds.), *Dependency and Valency: An International Handbook of Contemporary Research.* 593–635. Walter de Gruyter, Berlin.

James Huang. 1988. *Wǒ pǎo de kuài* and Chinese phrase structure. *Language* 64, 2, 274–311.

Richard Hudson. 1984. *Word Grammar.* Basil Blackwell, Oxford, UK.

Charles Li and Sandra Thompson. 1981. *Mandarin Chinese: A Functional Reference Grammar*. University of California Press, Berkeley.

James Huang, Audrey Li, and Yafei Li. 2009. *The Syntax of Chinese*. Cambridge University Press.

Lin-ding Li. 1986. Xiàndài hànyǔ jùxíng [The modern Chinese constructions]. The Commercial Press, Beijing.

Stanley Starosta. 1988. *The Case for Lexicase: An Outline of Lexicase Grammatical Theory*. Pinter Publishers, London:.

Chao-Fen Sun and Talmy Givón. 1985. On the so-called SOV word order in Mandarin Chinese: A quantified text study and its implications. *Language* 6, 2, 329–51.

Lucien Tesnière. 1959. *Éléments de syntaxe structurale*. Klincksieck, Paris.

Xin-yuan Xu and Haihua Pan. 2014. *Tā de lǎoshī dāng de hǎo* de shēngchéng lùjìng tànxī [An investigation into the syntactic mechanism of generating sentences like *Ta de laoshi dang–de hao*]. *Xiàndàiwàiyǔ* 04, 439–451.

Da-ran Yang and Gong Cheng. 2013. Xiànxìng duìyīng dìnglǐ yǔ hànyǔ zhòngdòng jù de cíxiàng rónghé [Linear Correspondence Axiom and Morphological Fusion in Mandarin Double-verb Constructions]. *Wàiguóyǔ* 04, 37–46.

De-xi Zhu. 1982. *Yǔfǎ jiǎngyì* [Lectures on Grammar]. The Commercial Press, Beijing.

Ming Zhou and Changning Huang. 1994. Approach to the Chinese dependency formalism for the tagging of corpus. *Journal of Chinese Information Processing*, 8, 3, 35–52.

A Survey of Ellipsis in Chinese

Timothy Osborne
Zhejiang University
Hangzhou
China
tjo3ya@yahoo.com

Junying Liang
Zhejiang University
Hangzhou
China
jyleung@iipc.zju.edu

Abstract

Much work on ellipsis has been conducted using data from English, and many widely acknowledged types of ellipsis exist in English. The extent to which the named ellipsis mechanisms exist in other languages is, though, often not clear. This manuscript surveys ellipsis in Mandarin Chinese using a dependency-based approach to syntax. It probes to see which ellipsis mechanisms exist in Mandarin. The survey demonstrates that gapping, stripping, pseudogapping, sluicing, and comparative deletion do not exist in Mandarin (or are highly restricted) and that VP-ellipsis, answer ellipsis, and N-ellipsis are all arguably present. Furthermore, zero anaphora is frequent in Mandarin, whereas it is absent from English (or highly restricted). The *catena* unit is pillar of the account, since the elided material of ellipsis is a catena.

1 An inventory of ellipsis mechanisms

The study of ellipsis recognizes numerous distinct types. The following mechanisms are among the most commonly acknowledged:

1. Gapping
2. Stripping
3. Pseudogapping
4. Sluicing
5. Comparative deletion
6. VP-ellipsis
7. Answer ellipsis
8. N-ellipsis
9. Null complement anaphora
10. Zero anaphora

Excepting zero anaphora, these mechanisms occur in English, and most of them are present in languages related to English. The extent to which they exist in languages more distant from English is often not clear, however. This contribution surveys ellipsis in Mandarin Chinese, probing to see which ellipsis mechanisms are and are not present.

The analysis of ellipsis pursued below is dependency-based, and the *catena* unit plays a central role in the account. A catena is *a word or combination of words that are linked together by dependencies* (Osborne et al. 2012). Ellipsis mechanisms in English have been shown to elide catenae. The survey seeks to determine the extent to which the catena is also the central unit for a theory of ellipsis in Mandarin.

This contribution thus pursues three goals: 1) provide an initial exploration of ellipsis in Mandarin, 2) determine the extent to which the catena unit can serve as the basis for a theory of Mandarin ellipsis, and 3) consider what can be learned about ellipsis in general from a comparison of ellipsis mechanisms across English and Mandarin.

A word of caution is appropriate concerning the dependency hierarchies assumed for Mandarin below. To our knowledge, many basic aspects of Mandarin sentence structure have not yet been worked out in theoretical detail from a DG perspective. Basic questions about the dependency status of sentence-final particles, coverbs, *de*-constructions, classifiers, etc. have not been debated from a DG perspective. Thus the validity of many of the structures posited below is taken for granted. Future explorations into the dependency structures of Mandarin may motivate corrections to the dependency hierarchies for Mandarin posited below.

2 Gapping, stripping, pseudogapping

Gapping, stripping, and pseudogapping have been thoroughly explored (e.g. Jackedoff 1971, Kuno 1976, Stump 1977, Levin 1986, McCawley 1998). The following three sentences illustrate gapping, stripping, and pseudogapping in English:

Proceedings of the Third International Conference on Dependency Linguistics (Depling 2015), pages 271–280,
Uppsala, Sweden, August 24–26 2015.

(1)

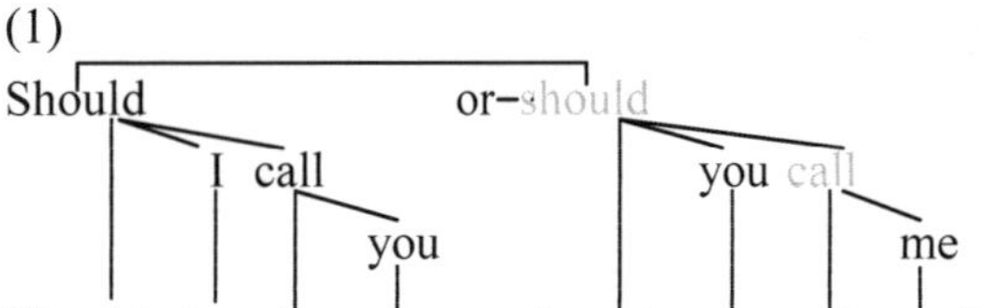

Should I call you, or should you call me?

(2)

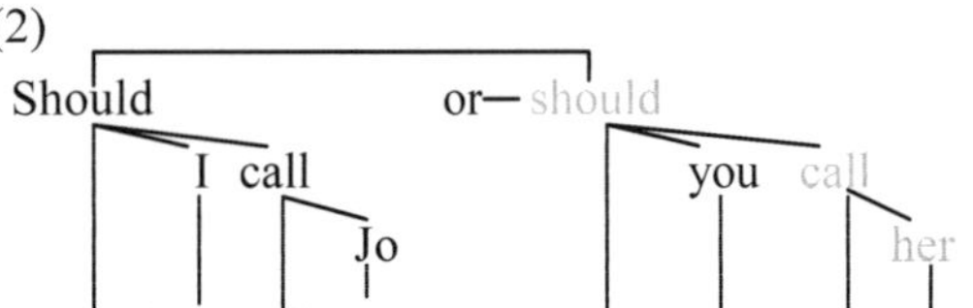

Should I call Jo, or should you call her?

(3) She should call me more than

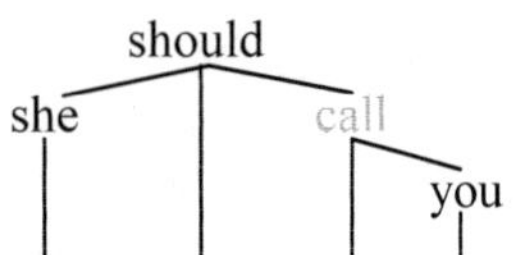

she should call you.

Example (1) illustrates gapping, example (2) stripping, and example (3) pseudogapping. Gapping and stripping occur in coordinate structures. Pseudogapping can appear in subordinate clauses in the absence of coordination, but the pseudogap must find an antecedent – it cannot take a postcedent.

The elided material *should...call* in (1) and (2) is a catena, and the word *call* in (3) is also a catena, a one-word catena. The fact that *should* immediately dominates *call* is what makes the combination *should...call* a catena. The examples therefore deliver a sense of the importance of the catena unit for the theory of ellipsis. There are, however, many details of the dependency hierarchies shown in (1–3) that can be overlooked here, since they are not important for surveying ellipsis in Mandarin.

Turning to Mandarin, we see that these ellipsis mechanisms are generally not possible. The following attempts at gapping fail:

(4)

*Tā diǎn-le kāfēi, tā diǎn-le chá.
s/he ordered coffee s/he ordered tea
Intended: 'He ordered coffee, and she tea.'

(5) *Jō xǐhuān dàngāo, Lǐ xǐhuān qiǎokèlì.
Jo likes cake. Li likes chocolate
Intended: 'Jo likes cake, and Li chocolate.'

The following attempts at stripping in Mandarin also fail:

(6)

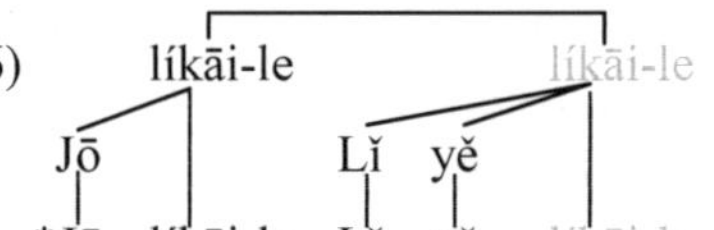

*Jō líkāi-le, Lǐ yě líkāi-le.
Jo leave-le Li also leave-le.
Intended: 'Jo left, and Li also.'

(7) *Jō bìxū gōngzuò, Lǐ ye bìxū gōnzuò.
Jo has.to work Li also has.to work.
Intended: 'Jo has to work, and Li too.'

Noteworthy about these failed attempts at gapping and stripping is the fact that Mandarin lacks a direct equivalent to *and* for coordinating clauses. Perhaps the absence of such an element is a factor limiting the distribution of gapping and stripping, since these mechanisms are widely acknowledged as occurring only in the non-initial conjuncts of coordinated clauses.

The following attempt at pseudogappng in Mandarin also fails:

(8) Nǐ yīngāi xué fǎyǔ,
you should study French

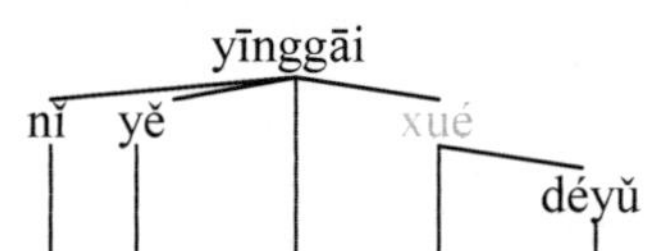

*nǐ yě yīnggāi xué déyǔ.
you also should study German

Intended: 'You should study French, and you should study German, too.'

The data just produced demonstrate that gapping, stripping, and pseudogapping are types of ellipsis that are either absent from Mandarin, or are much more restricted than in English. The fact that examples involving both gapping and stripping are bad is not surprising since the two are widely viewed as involving the same one ellipsis mechanism.

Concerning the absence of pseudogapping from Mandarin, however, the fact that it is not possible is more revealing. Pseudogapping behaves like VP-ellipsis in certain ways, and like gapping in other ways. It behaves like VP-ellipsis mainly insofar as it is licensed by an auxiliary verb just like VP-ellipsis, and it is like gapping insofar it involves a true "gap" with a remnant, whereby the remnant must stand in contrast to the parallel constituent in the antecedent clause. Thus the absence of pseudogapping verifies to an extent the insight that pseudogapping is at least somewhat related to gapping, enough so that if a language disallows gapping and stripping, then it will also disallow pseudo-gapping.

2 Sluicing

Sluicing (Ross 1969, Merchant 2001) typically elides everything from a clause except an interrogative expression (wh-element), e.g.

(9) They are hiding something, but

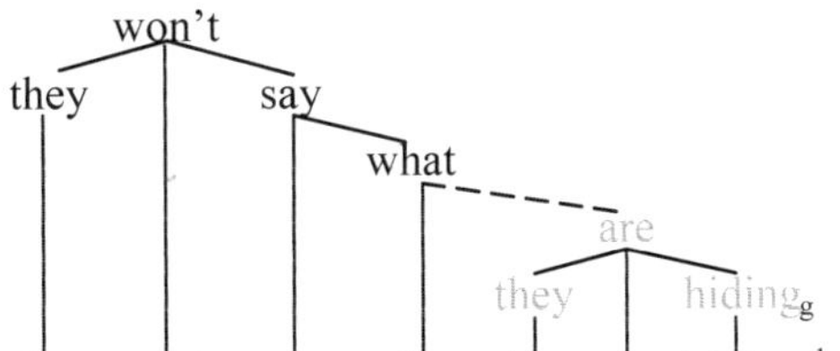

they won't say what they are hiding.[1]

The clause introduced by *what* is sluiced, that is, the string *they are hiding* is elided. Sluicing is a frequently occurring type of ellipsis mechanism, and it exists in most if not all Indo-European languages.

Checking to see if sluicing exists in Mandarin, the data are not entirely clear. Consider the following examples:

(10) Tā xǐhuān mǒu gè rén, dàn
s/he likes certain CL person, but
'S/he likes a certain person, but'

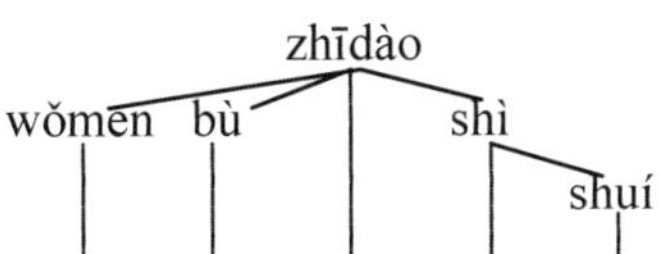

a. wǒmen bù zhīdào shì shuí.
we not know be who
'we don't know who it is.'

b. *wǒmen bù zhīdào shì shuí.
we not know be who

Example (10a), in which the verb *shì* 'be' appears, cannot, strictly speaking, be interpreted as sluicing because sluicing typically elides the dominate verb in a clause. When the dominant verb is indeed elided (here *shì*), the result is bad, as illustrated with example (10b). This fact suggests that sluicing is not present in Mandarin.

Example (10b) is an attempt at sluicing in a subordinate clause. When sluicing occurs across speakers in a main clause, the acceptability judgments are less robust:

(11) A: Jō xǐhuān mǒu gè rén.
Jo likes certain CL person
'Jo likes a certain person.'

a. B: – ?Jō xǐhuān Shuí?

b. B: – Jō Xǐhuān shuí?
Jo likes who

(12) A: Lǐ zhèng cáng zài mǒu gè dìfang.
Li now hide in certain CL place
'Li is now hiding in a certain place.'

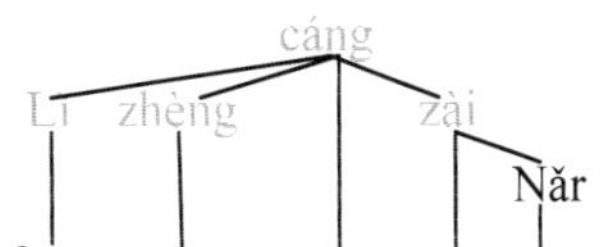

a. B: – ?Lǐ zhèng cáng zài Nǎr?
Li now hide in where

b. B: – Lǐ zhèng Cáng zài nǎr?
Li now hide in where

While there is a preference for the b-questions, in which the verb is repeated, the a-questions are not clearly bad. This situation clouds the picture, since the marginal a-questions look like the sluicing in direct questions that is frequent in those languages that have sluicing. One might, however, assume that what has actually been elided from the a-questions is the auxiliary *shì* 'be'. On such an account, such examples would, strictly speaking, not count as instances of sluicing as it is commonly understood.

Further data speak more clearly against the presence of sluicing in Mandarin. Cases of so-called *multiple sluicing* are bad in Mandarin. Multiple sluicing occurs when the sluiced clause contains two or more wh-remnants. The following example illustrates multiple sluicing in English:

(13) A: Somebody has a crush on somebody?

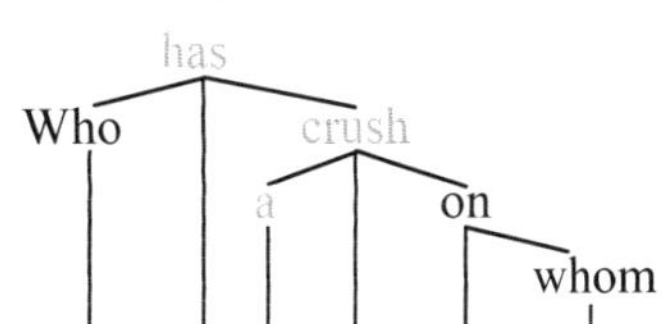

B: Who has a crush on whom?

The sluiced clause contains the two wh-remnants, *who* and *on whom*, identifying it as an instance of multiple sluicing.

[1] The hierarchical status of *what* as the root of the object clause, the dashed dependency edge, and the g subscript follow the approach to discontinuities presented by Osborne (2014). The particularities of this analysis are not relevant to the account of ellipsis.

Multiple sluicing is impossible in Mandarin:

(14) A: Yǒu rén xǐhuān mǒu gè rén.
exist person likes certain ge person
'Somebody likes somebody.'

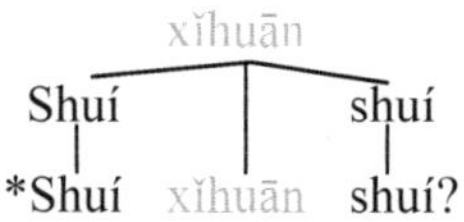

B: *Shuí xǐhuān shuí?
'Who likes whom?'

This attempt at multiple sluicing is quite bad. The example cannot be rendered in terms of the verb *shì*, unlike examples (11a) and (12a). This confirms that sluicing as it is commonly understood in English and related languages does not exist in Mandarin.

A number of accounts of sluicing-like data in Mandarin have acknowledged that what at times looks like sluicing is in fact a different mechanism, this mechanism being called *pseudosluicing* (see for instance Wei 2004, and Adams and Tamioka 2014). Pseudosluicing involves the auxiliary *shì* – but at times *shì* can be omitted. The analysis of pseudosluicing put forth in the literature (Adams and Tamioka 2014) is that it involves zero anaphora; a subject pronoun has been dropped, e.g. ...*wǒmen bù zhīdào (tā) shì shuí*, lit. 'we not know it be who' – more about zero anaphora below in Section 8.

The absence of sluicing in Mandarin is consistent with the absence of sluicing in wh-in-situ languages in general (Merchant 2001: 84f.).

3 Comparative deletion

Comparative deletion (Bresnan 1975) elides a string of words that corresponds to focused material in an antecedent clause, e.g.

(15) More men ordered beer than
a. men ordered wine.
b. *men ordered wine.

(16) We drank more beer than
a. they drank beer.
b. *they drank beer.

These examples illustrate the manner in which *men* and *beer* must be elided. They must be elided each time because their counterparts are focused by the comparative element *more* in the preceding clause. Thus comparative deletion occurs obligatorily; it is unlike most other ellipsis mechanisms in this regard, which occur optionally.

Checking to see whether comparative deletion is present in Mandarin is difficult to do. The construction used to express comparison in Mandarin is of a much different nature than in English. The elements being compared in Mandarin must be subjects, and the dimension along which they are compared must appear as the main predicate, e.g.

(17) Diǎn-le píjiǔ de rén bǐ
order-le beer de people than

diǎn-le pútáojiǔ de (rén) gèng duō.
order-le wine de people more many

'More people ordered beer than ordered wine.'

The English translation employs a type of adjunct clause (*than ordered wine*) to express the comparison, whereas its Mandarin counterpart needs relative clauses (*diǎn-le píjiǔ de* 'who ordered beer' and *diǎn-le pútáojiǔ de* 'who ordered wine') to express the comparison.

Due to the quite different syntactic means for expressing comparative meaning across the languages, it is difficult to acknowledge the presence of comparative deletion in Mandarin. Given the lack of solid evidence in favor of the existence of comparative deletion, we conclude here that it does not exist in Mandarin.

4 VP-ellipsis

VP ellipsis (Johnson 2001) occurs frequently in English. A non-finite verb phrase is elided, its content being retrieved from context, e.g.

(18)

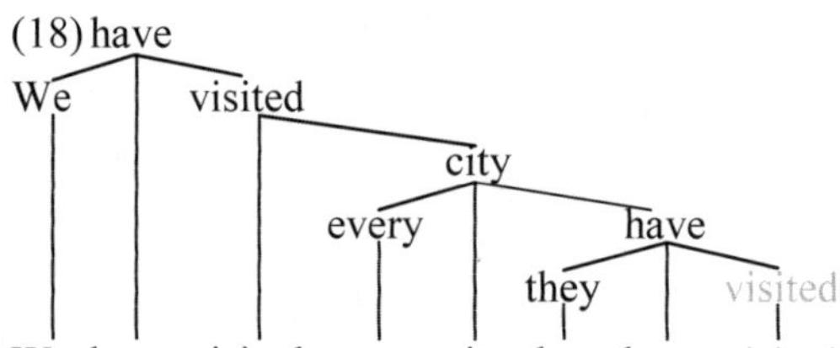

We have visited every city they have visited.

Non-finite verb phrases consist of a non-finite verb and all of its dependents. In this case here, just the nonfinite verb *visited* alone is elided because it has no dependents.

VP-ellipsis occurs frequently in Mandarin as well. As in English, it is typically introduced by a (modal) auxiliary verb. Li and Thompson (1981:182f.) classify the following verbs as auxiliaries: *yīngaī* 'should', *yīngdāng* 'should', *gāi* *'should'*, *néng* 'be able to', *nénggòu* 'be able to', *huì* 'be able to', *kěyǐ* 'be able to', *néng* 'be allowed to', *gǎn* 'dare', *kěn* 'be willing to', *děi* 'must', *bìxū* 'must', *bìyào* 'must', *huì* 'will, know how to'. The next examples illustrate VP-ellipsis in Mandarin:

(19) Wáng yīngāi fàngsōng,
Wang should relax,

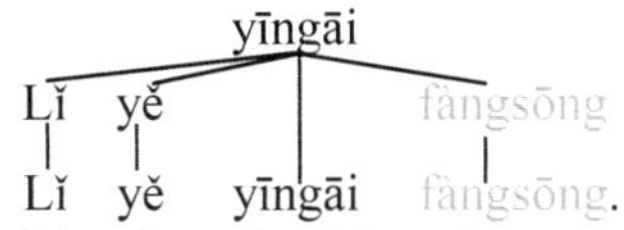

Li also should relax

'Wang should relax, and
Li should relax, too.'

(20) Zhāngsān néng dú hànyǔ,
John can read Chinese

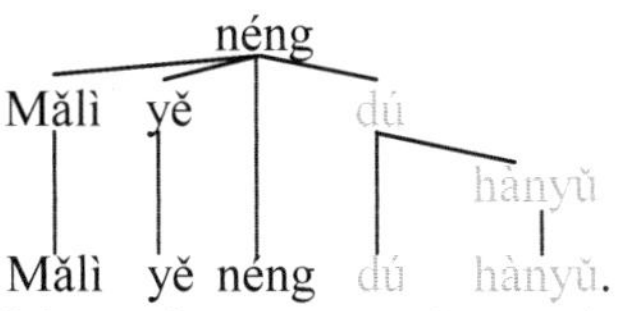

Mary also can read Mandarin

'John can read Chinese, and
Mary can read Chinese, too.'

These instances of ellipsis are closely similar to their English counterparts, as indicated with the translations. VP-ellipsis therefore appears to be quite similar across the two languages.

But while English and Mandarin both have VP-ellipsis, the two languages differ in the frequency of the mechanism. VP-ellipsis occurs frequently in English, but is licensed by a relatively limited set of verbs, i.e. by auxiliary verbs and the particle *to*. In Mandarin in contrast, VP-ellipsis occurs with auxiliary verbs as well as with (what are designated in English as) control verbs. Thus VP-ellipsis is more widely available in Mandarin than in English, e.g.

(21) Wǒ xiǎng hē jiǔ,
I intend drink wine,

tā yě xiǎng hē jiǔ.
s/he also intend drink wine

'I intend to drink some wine;
*s/he also intends to drink some wine.'

(22) Tā yào chī fàn,
s/he wants eat meal

wǒ yě yào chī fàn.
I also want eat meal

'S/he wants to eat a meal;
*I also want to eat a meal.'

Note that the English translations are unacceptable (because *intend* and *want* do not license VP-ellipsis in English).

Therefore what examples (21-22) illustrate is that the elision of verb phrases is much less restricted in Mandarin than in English. Apparently, most any verb in Mandarin that takes a VP complement can license VP-ellipsis, not just auxiliary verbs. Observe also that the elided material indicated in each of the examples is a catena.

5 Answer ellipsis

The ellipsis mechanism associated with answer fragments has been studied and debated in detail (e.g. Morgan 1973, Merchant 2004). Answer ellipsis exists in Mandarin just as it does in English, although the questions that elicit answer fragments vary significantly from the questions in English insofar as all interrogative elements remain in situ, i.e. they do not appear in clause-initial position. Mandarin is a *wh-in-situ language* in this regard. Despite this significant difference across English and Mandarin, Mandarin has answer fragments that are similar to their counterparts in English. As in English, the answer fragments in Mandarin are constituents (i.e. complete subtrees), which means that the elided material has the status of a catena.

The following examples illustrate the extent to which the elided words of answer ellipsis in English are catenae:

(23) Who are you waiting for?

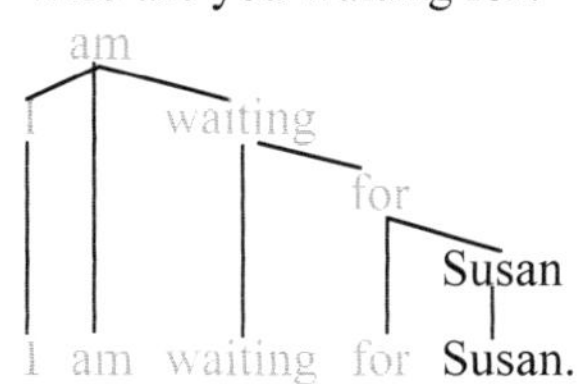

(24) Who is waiting for whom?

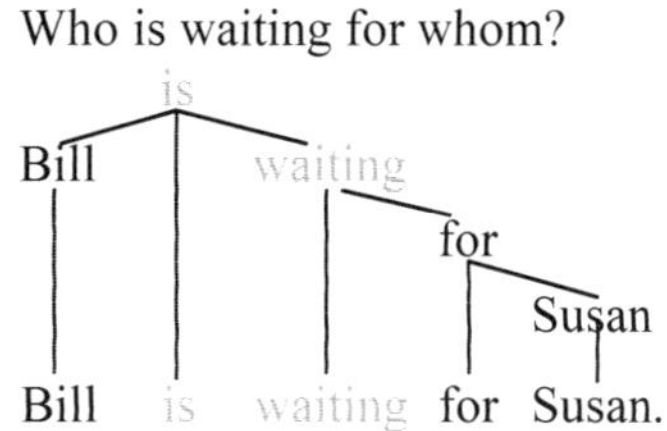

The elided material in each of these two cases has catena status, i.e. *I am waiting for* is a catena in (23), and *is waiting* is a catena in (24).

Switching to Mandarin, question-answer pairs in Mandarin also easily submit to analyses in terms of catenae:

(25) Tā shénme shíhou lái?
s/he what time come
'When is s/he coming?'

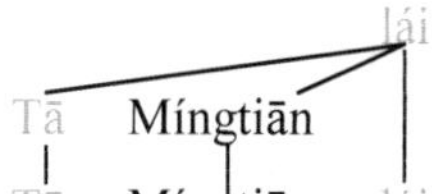

– Tā Míngtiān lái.
s/he Tomorrow come
'He is coming Tomorrow.'

(26) Nǐ bàifǎng-le shuí?
you visit-le who
'Who did you visit?

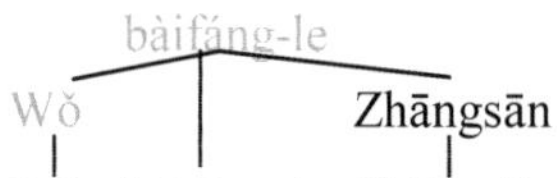

Wǒ bàifǎng-le Zhāngsān.
I visit-le John 'I visited John.'

(27) Tā bǎ wǒ de hùzhào fàng zài nǎr?
s/he ba I de passport put in where
'Where did s/he put my passport?'

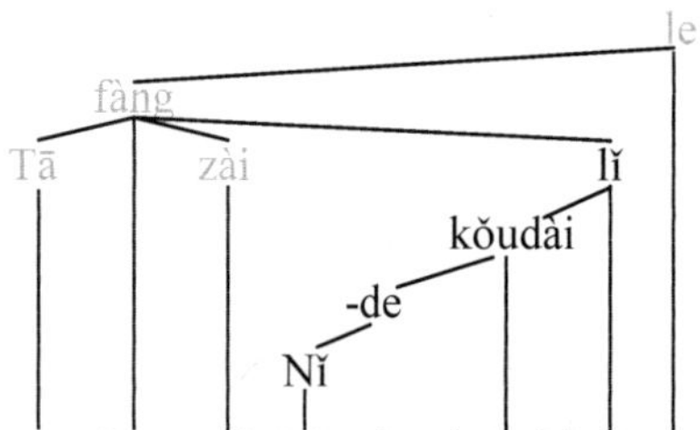

– Tā fàng zài Nǐ de kǒudài lǐ le.
s/he put in you de pocket in le
'S/he put it In your pocket.'

Examples like these illustrate best the potential of the catena concept for serving as the basis for theories of ellipsis. In each of these Mandarin examples, the elided material is discontinuous in the linear dimension, yet despite this fact, it qualifies as a catena each time. When the fragment answer is a complete subtree, the elided material is necessarily a catena. Despite the drastic differences in syntactic structures across the English and Mandarin examples, the elided material is a catena in both languages.

6 N-ellipsis

Noun ellipsis (N-ellipsis, also called NP-ellipsis or NPE) elides a noun and often additional material that is adjacent to the noun, e.g.

(28)

a. his old cat and hers old cat
b. the first talk and the third talk
c. their photos of me and ours photos of me

Interestingly, however, N-ellipsis is limited in English. It occurs mainly just with possessive determiners/pronouns (*mine*, *yours*, *his*, *hers*, *its*, *ours*, *theirs*) and cardinal and ordinal numbers (*one*, *two*, *three*, *first*, *second*, *third*, etc.). It does not occur with most adjectives, e.g. **his big cat and her small cat*.

In many languages closely related to English, however, N-ellipsis is much more productive. For instance, most adjectives can introduce N-ellipsis in German:

(29)

a. seine große Katze und ihre kleine Katze
his big cat and her small cat

b. billiges Bier und teures Bier
cheap beer and expensive beer

c. alte Lieder und neue Lieder
old songs and new songs

English has to reach to *one* in such cases. That is, when the adjective at hand cannot introduce N-ellipsis in English, the pronominal count noun *one* is employed instead to reduce redundancy, e.g. *old songs and new ones*.

Mandarin is more like those languages that more freely employ N-ellipsis (such as German). Pre-modifiers of nouns are typically immediately followed by the clitic *de* in Mandarin, this clitic serving as a marker of a pre-modifier:

(30) Wǒ xǐhuān tā de gǒu,
I like s/he de dog,

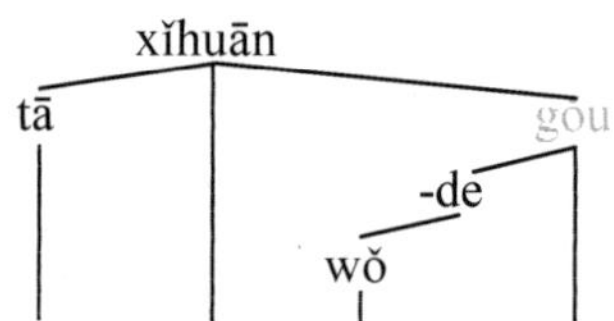

tā xǐhuān wǒ de gǒu.
s/he likes I de dog

'I like her/his dog, s/he likes mine dog.'

(31) Tā hē guì de píjiǔ, dànshì
s/he drinks expensive de beer, but

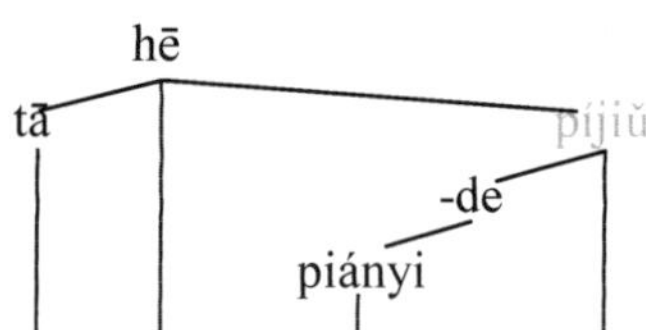

tā hē piányi de píjiǔ.
s/he drinks cheap de beer

'S/he drinks expensive beer, but s/he drinks cheap beer.'

When the noun phrase contains a classifier, the *de* clitic is usually not employed, but rather the classifier alone introduces N-ellipsis:

(32) Tā zuò-le dì yī liàng huǒchē,
s/he took-le -st one CL train

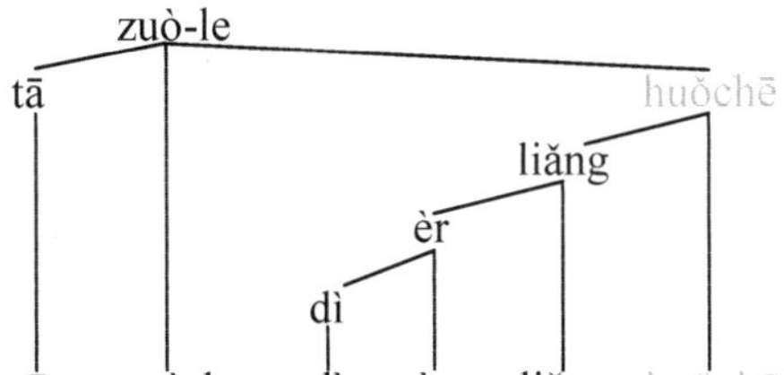

tā zuò-le dì èr liǎng huǒchē.
s/he took-le -nd two CL train

'S/he took the first train, and s/he took the second train.'

(33) Tā tīngdào-le dì yī cì tánhuà,
s/he heard-de -st one CL talk,

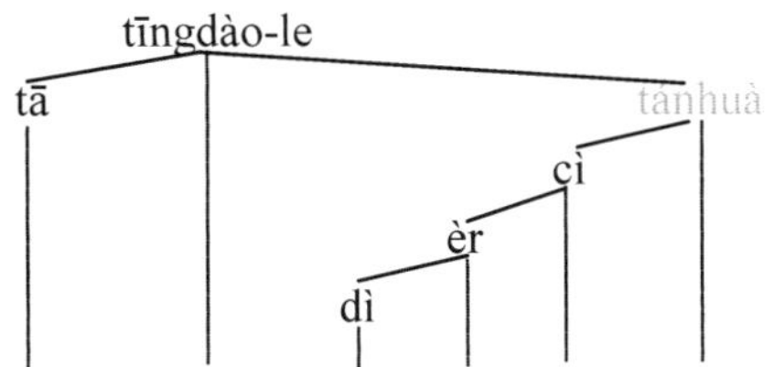

tā tīngdào-le dì èr cì tánhuà.
s/he heard-le -nd two CL talk.

'S/he listened to the first talk, and s/he listened to the second talk.'

The analysis here positions the classifier as a dependent of the noun. This analysis may be controversial, since an alternative analysis might position the classifier as head over the noun. As stated in the introduction, many aspects of Mandarin sentence structure have not yet been debated in DG circles, so the analysis assumed here is tentative.

There is, however, one consideration that supports this preliminary analysis (i.e. the classifier as a dependent of the noun). This consideration is the fact that the *de* marker can co-occur with the classifier, e.g.

(34) ?Tā zuò-le dì yī liàng de huǒchē.
s/he took-le -st one CL de train
'She took the first train.'

While the co-occurrence of *liàng* and *de* is mildly marginal, it is nevertheless good enough to support the analysis shown in (32) and (33). The *de* is serving its normal role as marker of a pre-modifier, i.e. it helps identify *dì yī liàng* as a predependent of *huǒchē*. If *huǒchē* were a post-dependent of *liàng*, we would expect (34) to be bad, because in such a case, *de* would not be marking a pre-modifier of the noun.

Otherwise, the clitic *de* occurs frequently and in numerous varied environments. At times it even serves to nominalize clauses. When it does so, the result can at times be rendered with free relative clauses in the English translation, e.g.

(35)

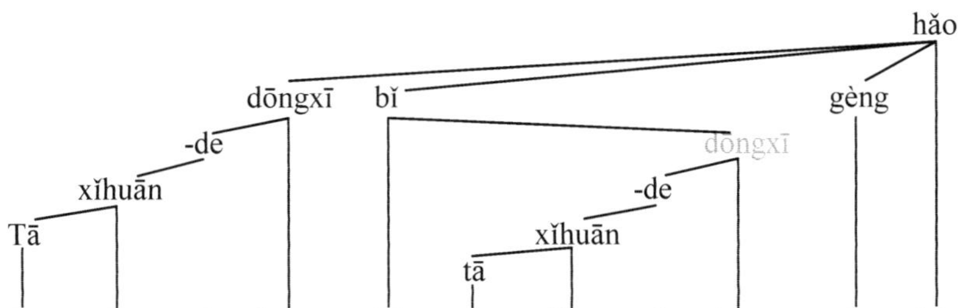

Tā xǐhuān de dōngxī bǐ tā xǐhuān de dōngxī gèng hǎo.
s/he likes de things than s/he likes de things more good
'What s/he likes is better than what s/he likes.

The two clauses *what s/he likes* in the translation are free relative clauses. The clitic *de* serves as a nominalizer in the second case, rendering the preceding clause a nominal. The noun *dōngxī* 'things' can be interpreted as having been elided, as indicated in the tree.

Many aspects of N-ellipsis in Mandarin are not clear. The examples just produced suggest, however, that N-ellipsis is a frequent occurrence in Mandarin, much more frequent than in English. The ability of *de* to serve as a nominalizer makes N-ellipsis widely available.

7 Null complement anaphora

Null complement anaphora (Hankamer and Sag 1976, Depiante 2000) is a mechanism that elides a complement clause, *to*-phrase, or prepositional phrase, e.g.

(36) Jim promised he would help, and

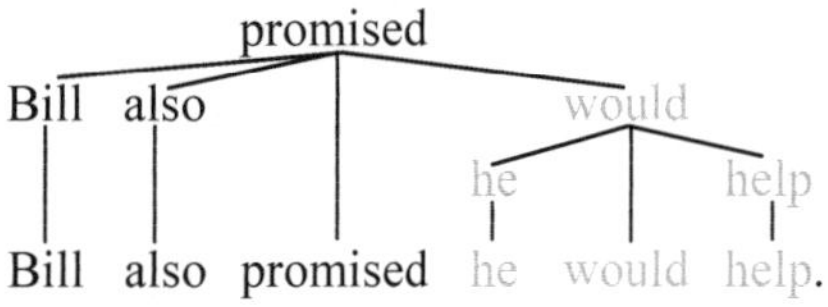

(37) Sam refuses to help, and

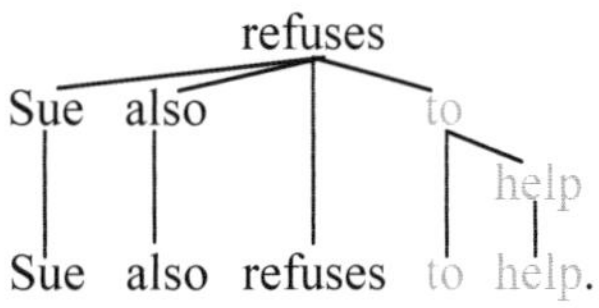

The predicates that license null complement anaphora in English (e.g. *ask*, *know*, *promise*, *refuse*, *try*) are limited. Similar predicates that one might expect to also license null complement anaphora fail to do so (e.g. *imagine*, *intend*, *pretend*, *say*, *think*, etc.).

Examples from Mandarin similar to (36-37) also allow ellipsis:

(38) A: Nǐ zhīdào fāshēng shénme le ma?
you know happened what le ma
'Do you know what happened?'

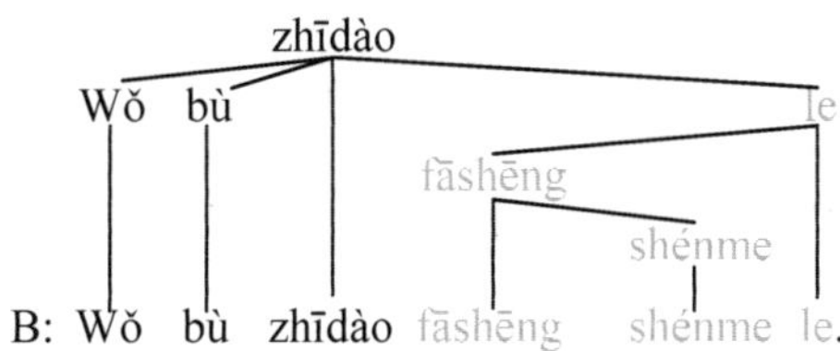

I not know happened what le
'I don't know what happened.'

(39) Tā jùjué líkāi,
s/he refuses leave

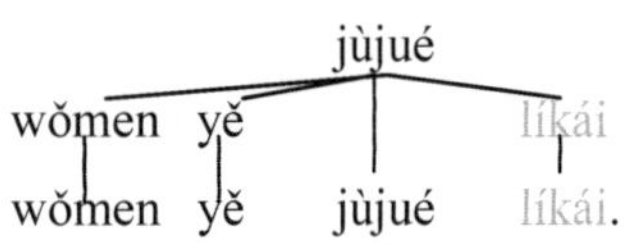

we also refuse leave

'S/he refuses to leave, and we also refuse to leave.'

These two examples suggest that the similar predicates across the languages allow for the ellipsis of a complement clause or phrase.

However, concluding that Mandarin has null complement anaphora in the same way that English does is difficult. The difficulty is due to the fact that Mandarin seems to freely allow the ellipsis of most all complements that can be easily recovered from context. When the elided complement is a verb phrase, one can acknowledge VP-ellipsis as discussed above, and when the elided complement can be interpreted as a definite or indefinite noun phrase, an analysis in terms of zero anaphora is available (see the next section). Thus the extent to which null complement anaphora is present in Mandarin is unclear.

8 Zero anaphora

Zero anaphora (Kroeger 2005: 79ff.) typically involves a null definite or indefinite pronoun or noun phrase. English and Mandarin vary significantly concerning zero anaphora; zero anahora occurs frequently in Mandarin, whereas its occurrence in English is, if it exists at all, highly restricted. The difference across the two languages is illustrated well using the answer to a yes-no question: both the subject and the object can be absent from the Mandarin answer:

(40) A: Nǐ yuèdú kèwén le ma?
you read text le ma
'Have you read the text?'

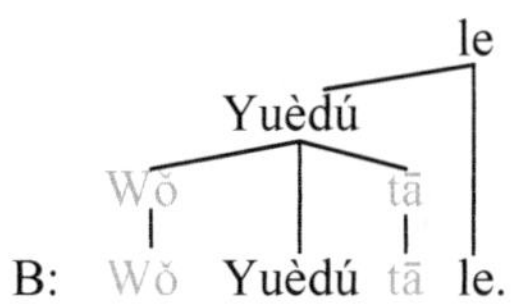

I read it le lit. 'Have read.'

In contrast, the direct English translation of this example is quite bad:

(41) A: Have you read the text?

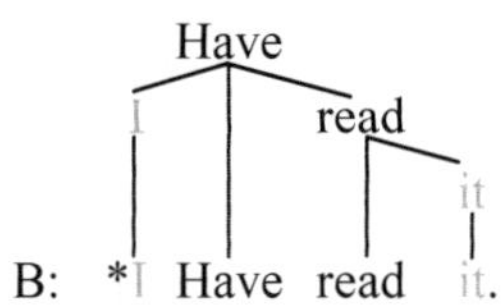

The acceptability contrast across the two languages is due to the unrestricted nature of zero anaphora in Mandarin, whereas zero anaphora may not exist in English at all.

Further examples suggesting that zero anaphora is highly restricted in, or absent from, English are given next:

(42) a. *He saw me, and she saw me, too.
b. He saw me, and she saw me, too.

(43) a. *I study Mandarin, and she studies it, too.
b. I study Mandarin, and she studies it, too.

In contrast, the Mandarin equivalents of these a-sentences are fine:

(44) Tā kàndào-le wǒ,
s/he saw-le me

tā yě kàndiào-le wǒ.
s/he also saw-le me

(45) Wǒ xuéxí hànyǔ, tā yě xuéxí tā.
I study Chinese, s/he also studies it

Furthermore, Mandarin even allows the absence of an indefinite noun phrase, i.e. what would be equivalent to *one* in English:

(46) Tā xiě-le yī gè gùshì,
s/he wrote one CL story

tā yě xiě-le yī gè gùshì.
s/he also wrote one CL story

'S/he wrote a story, and s/he also wrote one.'

The availability of zero anaphora in Mandarin means that Mandarin can omit most any subject or object pronoun, noun, or noun phrase. In fact its existence clouds the picture concerning other ellipsis mechanism. It is, for instance, difficult to acknowledge VP-ellipsis and/or null complement anaphora in Mandarin because what looks like such ellipsis mechanisms may in fact be zero anaphora instead. Finally, whether or not zero anaphora is a form of ellipsis is debatable. It seems, rather, to be the unmarked form of anaphora in Mandarin. When *tā* 'he/she/it'is or some other proform is overt, it is in fact an emphatic pronoun that serves a special discourse role, namely that of emphasis.

9 Concluding remarks

This manuscript has surveyed ellipsis in Mandarin. Gapping, stripping, pseudogapping, sluicing, and comparative deletion are either absent from Mandarin, or highly restricted. VP-ellipsis, answer ellipsis, N-ellipsis, and zero anaphora are present in Mandarin. Whether null complement anaphora is also present in Mandarin is unclear due to the overlap of the data in the area with the data of VP-ellipsis and zero anaphora. Perhaps the most noteworthy difference in ellipsis across English and Mandarin concerns the ability of Mandarin to omit complements and subjects at will, as long as they can be easily retrieved from context. In contrast, English does not elide complements (and subjects) so freely, but rather in order to do so, the requirements of VP-ellipsis, null complement anaphora, or some other ellipsis mechanism must be met.

Concerning the material that is elided, ellipsis in Mandarin is like ellipsis in English insofar as the elided material is a catena. This aspect of ellipsis is especially evident with answer ellipsis, which often elides non-string catenae.

Finally, a comment about a possible generalization is in order. Four of the five ellipsis mechanisms that are not present in Mandarin (or are highly restricted) involve the ellipsis of the matrix predicate (gapping, stripping, pseudogapping, and sluicing). Mandarin hence seems in general to be less willing than English to elide the matrix predicate. On the other hand, it is much more willing to omit the arguments of predicates (in terms of VP-ellipsis or zero anaphora). The reasons why these general differences across the languages exist is unknown, however.

References

Peter Wang Adams and Satoshi Tomioka. 2012. Sluicing in Mandarin Chinese: An instance of pseudo-sluicing. In Jason Merchant and Andrew Simpson (eds.), *Sluicing: Crosslinguistic Perspectives*, 219-47. Oxford University Press, Oxford, UK.

Ellen Barton. 1990. *Nonsentential Constituents*. John Benjamins, Philadelphia.

Joan Bresnan. 1975. Comparative deletion and constraints on transformations. *Linguistic Analysis* 1.

Johnny Cheng. 2011. Argument ellipsis in Chinese. *Proceedings of the 23rd North American Conference on Chinese Linguistics* (NACCL-23), 224–240.

Marcela Depiante 2000. *The Syntax of Deep and Surface Anaphora: A Study of Null Complement Anaphora and Stripping/Bare Argument Ellipsis*. Ph.D. thesis, University of Connecticut.

Jorge Hankamer and Ivan Sag 1976. Deep and surface anaphora. *Linguistic Inquiry* 7, 3, 391–428.

Ray Jackendoff. 1971. Gapping and related rules. *Linguistic Inquiry* 2, 21–35.

Kyle Johnson. 2001. What VP ellipsis can do, and what it can't, but not why. In Mark Baltin, M. and C. Collins, *The Handbook of Contemporary Syntactic Theory*, ed. 439–479. Blackwell Publishers, Oxford.

Paul Koreger. 2005. *Analyzing Grammar: An Introduction*. Cambridge University Press, New York.

Susumo Kuno 1976. Gapping: A functional analysis. *Linguistic Inquiry* 7, 300–18.

Nancy Levin. 1986. Main-Verb Ellipsis in Spoken English. Garland, New York.

Charles Li and Sandra Thompson. 1981. *Mandarin Chinese: A Functional Reference Grammar.* University of California Press, Berkeley.

James McCawley. 1998. *The Syntactic Phenomena of English*. The University of Chicaog Press, Chicago.

Jason Merchant. 2001. *The Syntax of Silence*. Oxford University Press, Oxford, UK.

Jason Merchant. 2004. Fragments and ellipsis. *Linguistics and Philosophy* 27, 661–38.

Jerry Morgan. 1973. Sentence fragments and the notion 'sentence'. In Braj Kachruetal. (eds.), *Issues in Linguistics*, 719-751. University of Illinois Press, Urbana.

Timothy Osborne. 2014. Type 2 rising: A contribution to a DG account of discontinuities. In Kim Gerdes, Eva Hajicová, and Leo Wanner, *Dependency Linguistics: Recent Advances in Linguistic Theory Using Dependency Structures*, 273–98. John Benjamins, Amsterdam.

Timothy Osborne, Michael Putnam, and Thomas Groß. 2012. Catenae: Introducing a novel unit of syntactic analysis. *Syntax* 15, 4, 354-396.

John Ross. 1969. Guess who? In R. Binnick, A. Davison, G. Green, and J. Morgan (eds.), *Papers from the 5th Regional Meeting of the Chicago Linguistics Society*. Chicago Linguistic Society, 252–86.

Gregory Stump. 1977. Pseudogapping. Ms., Ohio State University.

Ting-Chi Wei. 2004. *Predication and Sluicing in Mandarin Chinese*. Ph.D. dissertation, National Kaohsiung Normal University.

Multi-source Cross-lingual Delexicalized Parser Transfer: Prague or Stanford?

Rudolf Rosa
Charles University in Prague
Faculty of Mathematics and Physics
Institute of Formal and Applied Linguistics
Czech Republic
rosa@ufal.mff.cuni.cz

Abstract

We compare two annotation styles, Prague dependencies and Universal Stanford Dependencies, in their adequacy for parsing. We specifically focus on comparing the adposition attachment style, used in these two formalisms, applied in multi-source cross-lingual delexicalized dependency parser transfer performed by parse tree combination. We show that in our setting, converting the adposition annotation to Stanford style in the Prague style training treebanks leads to promising results. We find that best results can be obtained by parsing the target sentences with parsers trained on treebanks using both of the adposition annotation styles in parallel, and combining all the resulting parse trees together after having converted them to the Stanford adposition style (+0.39% UAS over Prague style baseline). The score improvements are considerably more significant when using a smaller set of diverse source treebanks (up to +2.24% UAS over the baseline).

1 Introduction

Dependency treebanks are annotated in various styles, with annotations based on Prague dependencies (Böhmová et al., 2003) and (Universal) Stanford Dependencies (De Marneffe and Manning, 2008; de Marneffe et al., 2014) being the most popular and widespread.[1] In last years, several treebank collections with unified annotation have been published. The largest of them, HamleDT, currently offers 30 treebanks, semi-automatically converted both to Prague dependencies and Universal Stanford Dependencies (Zeman et al., 2012; Rosa et al., 2014), and featuring morphological annotation using Interset (Zeman, 2008). Another collection, Google Universal Treebanks, contains 11 treebanks, generally annotated from scratch using a version of Stanford Dependencies (McDonald et al., 2013) and Universal POS (Petrov et al., 2012). Recently, these efforts have joined to produce Universal Dependencies (UD), which currently contain 18 treebanks annotated with a newly defined annotation scheme based on Universal Stanford Dependencies, Universal POS tags and Interset (Agić et al., 2015). UD are now becoming the de facto standard; however, we used the HamleDT collection for our experiments, as at the time of performing the experiments, HamleDT was much larger than UD, as well as more diverse in terms of language families represented.

[1]We use the term *annotation style* to refer to the set of annotation conventions, as applied in annotating a given treebank, typically also defined by an annotation manual.

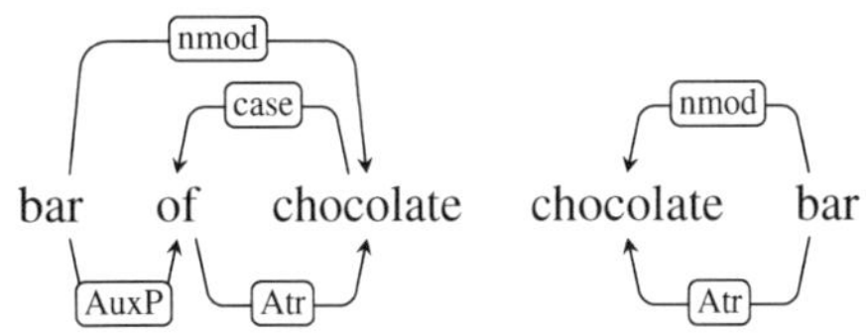

Figure 1: Stanford style (above) and Prague style (below) analysis of the phrases "bar of chocolate" and "chocolate bar". Note that in Stanford style, these phrases have a more similar structure, both featuring an *nmod* edge directly from "bar" to "chocolate". This shows the principle of constructions with a similar meaning also having a similar dependency structure.

1.1 Prague versus Stanford

One of the prominent features of Stanford style dependencies is their approach to function words. The general rule is that all function words, such

Proceedings of the Third International Conference on Dependency Linguistics (Depling 2015), pages 281–290, Uppsala, Sweden, August 24–26 2015.

as adpositions[2] or conjunctions, are attached as leaf nodes. This is a result of a standpoint which favours direct dependency relations between lexical nodes, not mediated by function words. This also makes dependency structures more similar cross-lingually, as it is very common that the same function is expressed by an adposition in one language, but by other means, such as morphology or word order, in another language – or even within the same language, as shown in Figure 1. On the other hand, Prague style dependencies annotate adpositions as heads of adpositional groups.[3]

While Stanford style trees may be more useful for further processing in NLP applications, it has been argued that Prague style trees are easier to obtain by using statistical parsers. Among other differences, adpositions provide important cues to the parser for adpositional group attachment, which is one of the most notorious parsing problems. This information becomes harder to access when the adpositions are annotated as leafs. The issue of dependency representation learnability has been studied by several authors, generally reaching similar conclusions (Schwartz et al., 2012; Søgaard, 2013; Ivanova et al., 2013). The approach suggested by de Marneffe et al. (2014) is to use a different annotation style for parsing, with Prague style adposition annotation, among other, and to convert the dependency trees to full Stanford style only after parsing for subsequent applications.

Still, while the aforementioned observations seem to hold in the general case, in multilingual parsing scenarios, the higher cross-lingual similarity of Stanford style dependency trees may be of benefit. From all of the differences between Prague and Stanford, the adposition attachment seems to be the most interesting, as adpositions are usually very frequent and diverse in languages, as well as very important in parsing. Therefore, in this work, we evaluate the influence of adposition annotation style in cross-lingual multi-source delexicalized parser transfer.

[2]Adposition is a general term for prepositions, postpositions and circumpositions.

[3]The lexical nodes are only directly connected in Prague tectogrammatical (deep-syntax) dependency trees, where function words are removed and their functions are captured via node attributes. It is worth noting that in general, there is little difference between representing information by means of node attributes or leaf nodes; thus, Stanford trees and Prague tectogrammatical trees are actually very similar in structure.

1.2 Delexicalized parser transfer

In the approach of single-source delexicalized dependency parser transfer (Zeman and Resnik, 2008), we train a parser on a treebank for a resource-rich *source language*, using non-lexical features, most notably part-of-speech (POS) tags, but not using word forms or lemmas. Then, we apply that parser to a POS-tagged corpus of an under-resourced *target language*, to obtain a dependency parse tree. Delexicalized transfer typically yields worse results than a fully supervised lexicalized parser, trained on a treebank for the target language. However, for a vast majority of languages, there are no manually devised treebanks, in which case it may be useful to obtain at least a lower-quality parse tree for tasks such as information retrieval or machine translation. Still, in this work, we do not apply delexicalized parser transfer to under-resourced languages, since there is no easy way of evaluating such experiments. Rather, we follow the usual way of using target languages for which there is a treebank available and thus the experiments can be easily evaluated, but we do not use the target treebank for training, thus simulating the under-resourcedness of the target language.

In *multi-source* delexicalized parser transfer, multiple source treebanks are used for training. McDonald et al. (2011) used simple treebank concatenation, thus obtaining one multilingual source treebank, and trained a multilingual delexicalized parser. In our work, we extend the method of Sagae and Lavie (2006), originally suggested for (monolingual) parser combination. In this approach, several independent parsers are applied to the same input sentence, and the parse trees they produce are combined into one resulting tree. The combination is performed using the idea of McDonald et al. (2005a), who formulated the problem of finding a parse tree as a problem of finding the maximum spanning tree (MST) of a weighted directed graph of potential parse tree edges. In the tree combination method, the weight of each edge is defined as the number of parsers which include that edge in their output (it can thus also be regarded as a parser voting approach). To find the MST, one can use e.g. the Chu-Liu-Edmonds algorithm (Chu and Liu, 1965; Edmonds, 1967), which was used by McDonald et al. (2005b) for non-projective parsing, and which we use in our work. The tree combination method can be easily ported from a monolingual to a multilingual setting, where the individual parsers are trained over different languages.

A possible research path which we do not follow in this work is the choice or weighting of the source languages according to their similarity to the target language, which has been successfully employed by several authors (Naseem et al., 2012; Søgaard and Wulff, 2012; Täckström et al., 2013; Rosa and Žabokrtský, 2015). This may have similar effect to our annotation style conversions, or it may be that these two approaches will behave rather orthogonally, as they might target different interlingual differences. Also, selection of a source language similar to the target may weaken the need for increasing annotation similarity, but this approach may still be useful for targets very dissimilar to the available sources. We believe these to be interesting questions that deserve further research.

1.3 This work

In this work, we use the HamleDT 2.0 collection and the MSTParser (McDonald et al., 2005b) to evaluate the potential benefit of employing Stanford style adposition attachment instead of the Prague style in parsing. We first show that in a monolingual setting, Prague style adposition annotation performs better than the Stanford style, both for lexicalized and delexicalized parsing. We also show that fully Stanfordized dependency trees perform even worse, but we further focus on adposition attachment only; the other annotation differences are of less interest for us, as they concern less frequent phenomena and/or do not seem so promising for cross-lingual experiments. We then perform extensive delexicalized parser transfer experiments, both using the full HamleDT collection as source treebanks (in a leave-one-out fashion), as well as using various smaller subsets consisting of languages with different adpositional characteristics. We also investigate a number of setups for parsing and combining the dependency trees with conversions between Prague style and Stanford style in between.

We conclude that the Stanford style of adposition attachment seems to be beneficial in multi-source cross-lingual delexicalized dependency parser transfer. Overall, best results are obtained by training parsers on source treebanks both in Prague and Stanford style, parsing the target text by all of the parsers, converting the Prague style parser outputs into Stanford style, and combining all of the parse trees. This approach achieves an average improvement of +0.39% UAS absolute over using Prague style only. When the set of source treebanks is small and the languages differ a lot in terms of adpositions, the improvements are even larger, up to +2.24% UAS absolute over the Prague style baseline.

2 Method

2.1 Dependency parser

Throughout this work, we use MSTperl (Rosa, 2015b), an implementation of the MSTParser of McDonald et al. (2005b), with first-order features and non-projective parsing. The parser is a single-best one, returning exactly one parse tree for each input sentence. It is trained using 3 iterations of MIRA (Crammer and Singer, 2003). The parser performs unlabelled parsing, returning only the dependency tree, with no dependency relation labels. We only evaluate unlabelled parsing in this work.

Our delexicalized feature set is based on (McDonald et al., 2005a), with lexical features removed, and consists of various conjunctions of the following features:

POS tags We use the coarse 12-value Universal POS Tagset (UPT) of Petrov et al. (2012).[4] For an edge, we use information about the POS tag of the head, dependent, their neighbours, and all of the nodes between them.

Token distance We use signed distance of head and dependent ($order_{head} - order_{dependent}$), bucketed into the following buckets:
$+1;\ +2;\ +3;\ +4;\ \geq +5;\ \geq +11;$
$-1;\ -2;\ -3;\ -4;\ \leq -5;\ \leq -11.$

We use exactly the same settings of the parser in all experiments. For lexicalized parsing, we also include the word form and word lemma of the head and dependent node, in various conjunctions with the POS tags and token distance as well as with each other. The configuration files that contain the feature sets and other settings, as well as the scripts we used to conduct our experiments, are available in (Rosa, 2015a).

[4] These 12 values are: NOUN, VERB, PUNCT, ADJ, ADP, PRON, CONJ, ADV, PRT, NUM, DET, X.

	Language	Size (kTokens)	
		Train	Test
ar	Arabic	250	28
bg	Bulgarian	191	6
bn	Bengali	7	1
ca	Catalan	391	54
cs	Czech	1,331	174
da	Danish	95	6
de	German	649	33
el	Greek	66	5
en	English	447	6
es	Spanish	428	51
et	Estonian	9	1
eu	Basque	138	15
fa	Persian	183	7
fi	Finnish	54	6
grc	Ancient Greek	304	6
hi	Hindi	269	27
hu	Hungarian	132	8
it	Italian	72	6
ja	Japanese	152	6
la	Latin	49	5
nl	Dutch	196	6
pt	Portuguese	207	6
ro	Romanian	34	3
ru	Russian	495	4
sk	Slovak	816	86
sl	Slovenian	29	7
sv	Swedish	192	6
ta	Tamil	8	2
te	Telugu	6	1
tr	Turkish	66	5

Table 1: List of HamleDT 2.0 treebanks.

Please note that our conclusions are only valid for the MSTperl parser, and may not hold e.g. for higher order graph based parsers or transition based parsers. In this work, we decided to focus on breadth of evaluated parsing and combination setups; we intend to evaluate a wider range of parsers in future.

2.2 Dataset and its conversions

We use the HamleDT 2.0 collection of 30 dependency treebanks, which had been semi-automatically harmonized to Prague dependencies and then Stanfordized into Universal Stanford Dependencies. We list the treebanks and their sizes in Table 1. More information about the treebanks contained in the dataset, as well as the dataset itself, can be obtained online.[5]

In most experiments, we use the Prague style version of HamleDT, as the Stanford version performs much worse for parsing (see Section 3.1). Instead of using the full Stanford version, we only focus on one of its prominent features – adposition attachment. Thus, we alternate between Prague adposition attachment as head (denoted "P"), and

[5]https://ufal.mff.cuni.cz/hamledt

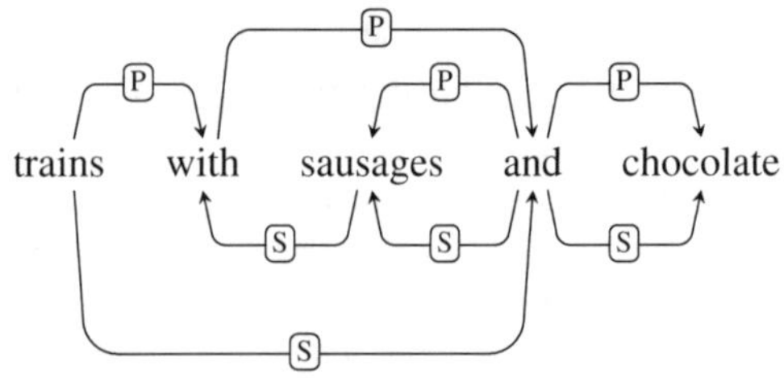

Figure 2: Original Prague style adposition analysis (above), and Stanford style adposition analysis as produced by the conversion (below). Note that the coordination stays in the Prague style. Edge labels are not shown as we do not use them in this work.

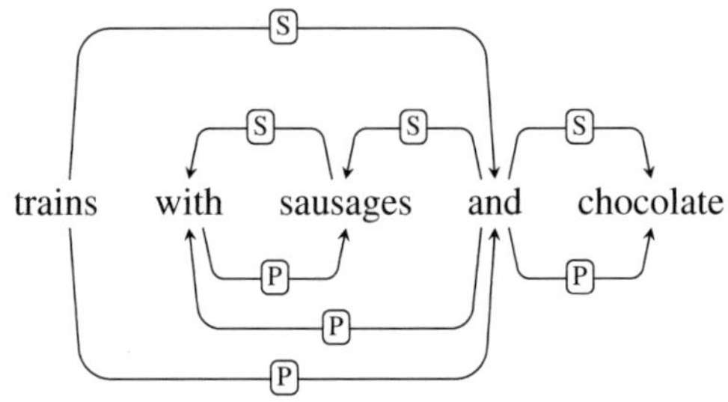

Figure 3: Stanford style adposition analysis (above), and Prague style adposition analysis as produced by the conversion (below). Together with Figure 2, this shows a case where our conversion is imperfect, as we are unable to obtain the original structure after the conversion roundtrip.

Stanford adposition attachment as leaf node (denoted "S"), using simple conversion scripts.

- The conversion from P to S takes each adposition and attaches it as a dependent of its left-most non-adpositional child, together with all of its other non-adpositional children. Thus, the adposition becomes a leaf node, unless it has adpositional dependent nodes (typically this signifies a compound adposition). Coordinating conjunctions are passed through (recursively) – if the left-most non-adpositional child is a coordinating conjunction, then its dependent leftmost non-adpositional conjunct is used instead as the new head of the adposition (see Figure 2).

- In the conversion from S to P, each adposition with a non-adpositional head is attached as a dependent of its head's head, and its original head is attached as its dependent (see Figure 3).

The roundtrip of the conversion (UAS after converting from P to S and back) is around 98% in total, and around 94% for adposition nodes alone.

2.3 Parse tree combination

The inference component of the MSTParser is also applied to perform the combination of parse trees obtained for a sentence from different parser instances. In that setting, each potential dependency edge is assigned a score equal to the number of input parse trees in which it is contained. The MST algorithm then finds and returns a dependency tree in which the edges are confirmed by the highest possible number of input trees.

The general experiment setup is as follows. One of the 30 treebanks is taken as the target treebank, and the remaining 29 treebanks become source treebanks. Then, delexicalized parsers are trained on the source treebanks, resulting in 29 trained parser models. Next, each of the parsers is applied to each sentence in the test section of the target treebank. And finally, the obtained parse trees for each sentence are combined together as has been described above, and the resulting dependency tree is evaluated using the target treebank.

Note that there are three places where a conversion from one annotation style to another may take place – conversion of the source treebank before training a parser, conversion of the parser output before the parse tree combination, and conversion of the parse tree combination output. We will denote the setups using the pattern"X/Y/Z", where "X" denotes the annotation style used for parser training and parsing, "Y" is the style into which the parser outputs are converted before being combined, and "Z" is the style into which the result of the combination is converted. Furthermore, "P,S/Y/Z" will refer to parsing both with "P" style parsers and "S" style parsers, thus resulting in 58 trees for each sentence to combine, rather than 29. In many setups, there is no conversion after the combination, or there is even no combination performed (in monolingual setups); therefore, we will often omit the last part of the pattern, using only "X/Y".

3 Experiments and Evaluation

We use the training sections of the treebanks for parser training and their testing sections for evaluation. We report the results using UAS (unlabelled attachment score).

Setup	Lex	Delex	Transfer
Prague	80.54	74.12	56.68
Stanford full	76.47	69.53	48.91
Prague non-punct	80.23	74.00	56.08
Stanford full non-punct	76.84	70.66	50.15

Table 2: Prague versus full Stanford annotation style, UAS averaged over 30 target languages.
The *Lex*icalized and *Delex*icalized parsers are monolingual. The *Transfer* parser is a combination of 29 sources parsers applied to the remaining target language.

3.1 Full Universal Stanford Dependencies

As a preliminary experiment, we compared the Prague version with its fully Stanfordized version. The results are shown in Table 2. It can be seen that the Stanford version performs much worse than the Prague one – its results are lower by around 5% UAS absolute.

Closer inspection showed that many of the errors are actually due to sentence-final punctuation attachment. In Stanford style, sentence-final punctuation is to be attached as a dependent node of the root node of the sentence (typically the main predicate). However, this is difficult for the first-order parser, as it has no knowledge of the root node when scoring the potential edges, and thus the punctuation gets often attached to some other verb. In Prague style, the sentence-final punctuation is attached to the technical root node, which is marked by special values of the node features, and thus the assignment is very easy to make. While this is an important point to keep in mind when parsing into full Stanford style, it is of little relevance to the goal of this paper – punctuation attachment is rarely important in NLP applications, and is not very likely to significantly contribute to cross-lingual dependency structure similarity either. For this reason, we also include UAS measured only on non-punctuation nodes. Still, adposition attachment, which we are mostly interested in, accounts for only a part of the score difference.

3.2 Prague versus Stanford adpositions

Further on, we only use the Prague style annotation of the treebanks, with adpositions annotated either in Prague style (P) or Stanford style (S).

3.2.1 Supervised parsers

We first evaluate supervised monolingual lexicalized and delexicalized parsers, alternating between the P and S annotation styles of adpositions. The results in Table 3 show that in the lexicalized setting, the UAS of the P style parser is +0.77%

Setup	Lexicalized	Delexicalized
P/P	**80.54**	**74.12**
S/P	78.44	72.65
S/S	79.77	73.91
P/S	80.23	73.94

Table 3: Average UAS of supervised monolingual parsers, both lexicalized and delexicalized.

Setup	P/P			S/S	
	UAS	>S/S	?	>P/P	UAS
Lexicalized	80.54	13	16	1	79.77
Delexicalized	74.12	11	16	3	73.91

Table 4: Pairs of supervised parser setups.
"UAS" = Average UAS as in Table 3
">S/S", ">P/P" = Number of languages for which the setup performed significantly better
"?" = Number of languages for which neither setup performed significantly better

P style output		S style output	
Setup	UAS	Setup	UAS
P/P/P	56.68	S/S/S	56.88
P/S/P	55.43	S/P/S	56.31
S/S/P	55.51	P/P/S	56.48
S/P/P	55.84	P/S/S	56.80
P,S/P/P	**56.81**	P,S/S/S	**57.07**
P,S/S/P	55.71	P,S/P/S	56.67

Table 5: Average UAS of various setups of delexicalized parser transfer, always using 1 language as target and the remaining 29 languages as source.

Setup A		>B	?	>A	Setup B	
	UAS				UAS	
S/S	56.88	8	13	9	56.68	P/P
P,S/P	56.81	5	22	3	56.68	P/P
P,S/S	57.07	9	19	2	56.88	S/S
P,S/S	57.07	8	17	5	56.81	P,S/P
P,S/S	57.07	7	20	3	56.68	P/P

Table 7: Pairs of delexicalized transfer setups.
"UAS" = Average UAS as in Table 5
">B", ">A" = Number of target languages for which the setup performed significantly better
"?" = Number of target languages for which neither setup performed significantly better

above the S style parser, and Table 4 confirms that the P parser is significantly better than the S parser for nearly half of the languages.[6] Actually, to obtain S style parse trees, it is better to parse the text using a parser trained on a P style treebank, and then convert the output parse trees (this yields a +0.46% higher UAS than parsing directly using an S style parser). Here, the adpositions clearly provide important information to the parser, and their annotation as heads benefits the results.

In the delexicalized setting, the P style parser scores higher than the S style one only by a small margin (+0.21% UAS), although still being significantly better for a third of the languages. Moreover, parsing directly using the S style is now comparable to parsing using P style and then converting to S style. This suggests that the most important piece of information for correctly attaching an adposition is its lemma, and delexicalizing a parser thus reduces the advantage of P style annotation for correct adposition attachment.

3.2.2 29-to-1 delexicalized parser transfer

We now move on to the main focus of our work, evaluating the effect of adposition annotation style in multilingual transfer of 29 delexicalized source parsers to a target language using parse tree combination.

Table 5 shows that using either P or S for everything leads to comparable results, with the S style now achieving a slightly better score (+0.20% UAS absolute on average). The results tend to get worse when additional conversions are performed; we thus omit such setups from further evaluation. Interestingly, slight improvements can be obtained by applying both P parsers and S parsers and combining them after conversion of the resulting trees to the S style, achieving a total average increase of +0.39 UAS absolute over the P style baseline.

Table 6 shows detailed results of the better-performing transfer setups for all target languages, together with the results of the supervised monolingual methods. Table 7 compares several pairs of the transfer setups by reporting the number of target languages (out of the total 30) for which one setup was significantly better than the other setup.

We can now see that the improvements obtained by employing S style parsers are not only low, but also usually statistically insignificant – the highest scoring P,S/S setup is significantly better than the baseline P/P setup only for 7 target languages, while also being significantly worse for other 3 target languages. Still, we believe that the sole fact that in this setting, employing the S style annotation leads to comparable or slightly better results (which is not true for the supervised monolingual parsers) indicates a potential benefit of the S style annotation in a cross-lingual setting, presumably due to the increased similarity of the dependency structures across languages.

[6] We used McNemar's test with significance level 5%.

Tgt	Lexicalized supervised			Delexicalized supervised			Delexicalized transfer			
lang	P/P	S/S	P/S	P/P	S/S	P/S	P/P	P,S/P	S/S	P,S/S
ar	**77.47**	76.32	77.17	**69.61**	69.29	69.50	44.61	**44.99**	43.16	44.13
bg	**87.95**	87.50	87.61	**83.87**	82.76	83.32	**73.17**	72.72	72.24	72.65
bn	82.27	**82.39**	82.27	77.59	**78.82**	77.59	59.98	60.34	**60.47**	60.22
ca	**86.11**	84.37	85.49	**79.71**	79.03	79.33	**66.45**	66.38	65.61	66.07
cs	**80.87**	80.31	80.63	**70.99**	70.69	70.69	64.06	**64.14**	63.62	63.93
da	**85.66**	84.42	85.12	**81.13**	80.31	80.67	**63.74**	63.53	62.82	63.09
de	**84.65**	83.57	84.53	**77.52**	76.92	77.47	52.58	55.17	**55.95**	55.32
el	**80.68**	80.20	80.18	**75.40**	75.15	74.73	67.05	67.69	67.63	**67.78**
en	**84.71**	84.37	84.05	**76.57**	76.19	76.03	46.13	**48.23**	47.65	47.09
es	**85.46**	83.55	84.74	**79.75**	78.52	79.25	**69.73**	69.61	68.85	69.17
et	85.15	**86.30**	85.46	80.96	**82.85**	80.75	71.34	72.07	74.06	**74.48**
eu	**75.28**	75.07	**75.28**	68.34	**68.41**	68.34	46.12	45.92	**46.15**	46.07
fa	**82.27**	80.21	81.70	70.44	**71.72**	70.78	54.69	54.77	56.41	**56.69**
fi	71.17	70.80	**71.21**	63.10	62.51	**63.13**	**51.48**	51.17	50.60	51.08
grc	**56.98**	56.61	56.56	48.92	**49.10**	48.80	46.24	46.38	46.48	**46.50**
hi	90.40	86.43	**90.42**	**80.55**	80.52	80.52	30.12	29.64	33.23	**33.64**
hu	**77.60**	77.07	77.40	**72.54**	71.79	72.34	59.68	59.89	60.50	**60.81**
it	**81.46**	80.57	81.22	**77.49**	76.57	76.92	64.52	**65.13**	64.44	64.50
ja	**91.17**	89.65	90.79	81.72	84.03	**84.35**	44.23	42.64	44.02	**44.88**
la	47.55	**48.72**	47.36	44.08	**44.12**	43.81	41.14	41.28	41.34	**41.47**
nl	**80.90**	80.05	80.11	**74.02**	73.70	73.57	62.47	62.04	**63.81**	63.80
pt	**83.50**	82.21	82.97	**80.14**	78.68	79.77	71.35	**71.60**	71.14	71.26
ro	**89.62**	88.79	**89.62**	85.19	**85.34**	84.85	59.66	**59.85**	58.52	58.67
ru	**83.98**	83.49	83.75	**73.08**	72.70	72.90	**63.82**	63.65	62.43	63.13
sk	**79.02**	78.70	78.63	**71.38**	70.88	70.93	63.66	**63.73**	63.36	63.62
sl	**81.19**	80.94	80.95	72.91	**72.93**	72.69	**54.40**	53.68	53.80	53.68
sv	**83.20**	81.93	82.48	**78.84**	77.97	78.18	62.08	62.18	**62.22**	61.60
ta	**72.70**	72.60	72.30	**68.17**	67.92	67.62	38.76	**39.01**	37.66	38.91
te	**87.60**	86.93	**87.60**	**85.59**	84.09	85.59	66.83	66.16	**67.00**	66.50
tr	**79.48**	79.02	79.26	**73.99**	73.72	73.72	40.39	40.82	**41.28**	41.26
Avg	**80.54**	79.77	80.23	**74.12**	73.91	73.94	56.68	56.81	56.88	**57.07**

Table 6: UAS of supervised lexicalized monolingual parsers, supervised delexicalized monolingual parsers, and delexicalized transfer parsers.

Subset	ADP freq.	Language
High	15%	Spanish
	19%	Hindi
	19%	Japanese
Med	9%	Czech
	8%	English
	9%	Swedish
Low	0%	Basque
	4%	Ancient Greek
	1%	Hungarian
Mix	15%	Spanish
	9%	Swedish
	1%	Hungarian

Table 8: Subsets of source treebanks, selected according to their frequency of adposition tokens.

Setup	High	Med	Low	Mix	All9
P/P	40.53	52.00	44.53	41.03	54.98
P,S/P	41.29	52.57	45.00	41.75	55.37
S/S	41.36	51.64	43.69	41.95	54.85
P,S/S	**42.77**	**52.67**	**46.41**	**42.66**	**55.42**

Table 9: UAS of delexicalized parser transfer, averaged over 21 target languages, with the specified subset treebanks as sources.

3.2.3 Smaller source treebank subsets

For a deeper insight and further confirmation of our findings, we also performed a set of experiments with smaller 3-member subsets of the treebank collection. We selected several treebank groups, based on the ratio of adposition tokens to all tokens. We also only chose large enough treebanks (more than 100,000 tokens). The subsets are listed in Table 8; we also used a larger "All9" set of all the 9 selected treebanks. Only these were then used for training; the remaining 21 languages were used for testing as target languages.

The summary results are to be found in Table 9; the statistical significance of the setups is evaluated in Table 10. For these datasets, the advantage of employing the S style in combination with P style becomes clearly visible, frequently leading to significantly better results than when using only the P style (however, using only S style parsers performs rather poorly). Moreover, converting the parse trees to S style before combining them is also often significantly better than converting them to P style. The improvements are large especially for the High, Low and Mix datasets. This suggests that the role of Stanford style is stronger with small and highly diverse datasets, where its benefit of making the dependency trees more similar becomes rather important.[7] For the High dataset, the best result surpasses the Prague-only baseline by as much as +2.24% UAS absolute on average, yielding a significantly better result for 19 of the 21 target languages.

Source subset	Setup A UAS	Setup A >B	?	Setup B >A	Setup B UAS
	S/S				P/P
High	41.36	12	8	1	40.53
Med	51.64	1	16	4	52.00
Low	43.69	2	8	11	44.53
Mix	41.95	9	10	2	41.03
All9	54.85	3	12	6	54.98
	P,S/P				P/P
High	41.29	9	12	0	40.53
Med	52.57	8	13	0	52.00
Low	45.00	6	14	1	44.53
Mix	41.75	8	13	0	41.03
All9	55.37	6	14	1	54.98
	P,S/S				S/S
High	42.77	15	6	0	41.36
Med	52.67	15	6	0	51.64
Low	46.41	15	5	1	43.69
Mix	42.66	11	9	1	41.95
All9	55.42	9	12	0	54.85
	P,S/S				P,S/P
High	42.77	15	6	0	41.29
Med	52.67	4	11	6	52.57
Low	46.41	15	6	0	45.00
Mix	42.66	9	10	2	41.75
All9	55.42	3	12	6	55.37
	P,S/S				P/P
High	42.77	19	2	0	40.53
Med	52.67	5	16	0	52.00
Low	46.41	15	6	0	44.53
Mix	42.66	13	8	0	41.03
All9	55.42	7	11	3	54.98

Table 10: Pairs of delexicalized transfer setups using specific source treeebank subsets.
"UAS" = Average UAS as in Table 9
">B", ">A" = Number of target languages for which the setup performed significantly better
"?" = Number of target languages for which neither setup performed significantly better

4 Conclusion

In this work, we investigated the usefulness of Stanford adposition attachment style as an alternative to the Prague style in dependency parsing, using a large set of 30 treebanks for evaluation. We especially focused on multi-source cross-lingual delexicalized parser transfer, as one of the targets behind the design of Universal Stanford Dependencies is to be more cross-lingually consistent

[7] Of course, this is only a speculation, as there are many other properties of the source treebank subsets which we were unable to factor out that may influence the results – for example, the High and Low subsets contain genealogically highly varied languages, but we were unable to find such a varied subset among the languages with a medium frequency of adpositions.

than other annotation styles.

We managed to confirm that for supervised parsing, Prague annotation style is favourable over Stanford style, as has been already stated in literature. However, in the parser transfer setting, Stanford style adposition attachment tends to perform better than the Prague style, presumably thanks to its abstraction from the high interlingual variance in adposition usage. Best results are achieved by at once combining outputs of parsers trained on treebanks of both Prague and Stanford adposition attachment style, reaching an average improvement of +0.39% UAS absolute over the Prague style baseline. Our results are further confirmed by experiments using smaller and more diverse subsets of training treebanks, where the advantage of combining Prague and Stanford adposition annotation style becomes even more pronounced, reaching average improvements of up to +2.24% UAS absolute over the Prague style baseline.

We used the first-order non-projective MSTParser in all experiments; therefore, our conclusions are valid only for that parser. The next logical research step is thus to apply other parsers in a similar setting to determine whether our findings can be further generalized, or whether using a different parser leads to different effects when comparing and combining Prague and Stanford adposition annotation styles.

Acknowledgments

This research was supported by the grants GAUK 1572314, SVV 260 224, and FP7-ICT-2013-10-610516 (QTLeap). This work has been using language resources developed, stored and distributed by the LINDAT/CLARIN project of the Ministry of Education, Youth and Sports of the Czech Republic (project LM2010013).

References

Željko Agić, Maria Jesus Aranzabe, Aitziber Atutxa, Cristina Bosco, Jinho Choi, Marie-Catherine de Marneffe, Timothy Dozat, Richárd Farkas, Jennifer Foster, Filip Ginter, Iakes Goenaga, Koldo Gojenola, Yoav Goldberg, Jan Hajič, Anders Trærup Johannsen, Jenna Kanerva, Juha Kuokkala, Veronika Laippala, Alessandro Lenci, Krister Lindén, Nikola Ljubešić, Teresa Lynn, Christopher Manning, Héctor Alonso Martínez, Ryan McDonald, Anna Missilä, Simonetta Montemagni, Joakim Nivre, Hanna Nurmi, Petya Osenova, Slav Petrov, Jussi Piitulainen, Barbara Plank, Prokopis Prokopidis, Sampo Pyysalo, Wolfgang Seeker, Mojgan Seraji, Natalia Silveira, Maria Simi, Kiril Simov, Aaron Smith, Reut Tsarfaty, Veronika Vincze, and Daniel Zeman. 2015. Universal dependencies 1.1. `http://hdl.handle.net/11234/LRT-1478`.

Alena Böhmová, Jan Hajič, Eva Hajičová, and Barbora Hladká. 2003. The Prague dependency treebank. In *Treebanks*, pages 103–127. Springer.

Yoeng-Jin Chu and Tseng-Hong Liu. 1965. On shortest arborescence of a directed graph. *Scientia Sinica*, 14(10):1396.

Koby Crammer and Yoram Singer. 2003. Ultraconservative online algorithms for multiclass problems. *The Journal of Machine Learning Research*, 3:951–991.

Marie-Catherine De Marneffe and Christopher D Manning. 2008. The Stanford typed dependencies representation. In *Coling 2008: Proceedings of the workshop on Cross-Framework and Cross-Domain Parser Evaluation*, pages 1–8. Association for Computational Linguistics.

Marie-Catherine de Marneffe, Natalia Silveira, Timothy Dozat, Katri Haverinen, Filip Ginter, Joakim Nivre, and Christopher D. Manning. 2014. Universal Stanford dependencies: A cross-linguistic typology. In *Proc. of LREC'14*, Reykjavk, Iceland. European Language Resources Association (ELRA).

Jack Edmonds. 1967. Optimum branchings. *Journal of Research of the National Bureau of Standards B*, 71(4):233–240.

Angelina Ivanova, Stephan Oepen, and Lilja Øvrelid. 2013. Survey on parsing three dependency representations for English. In *ACL (Student Research Workshop)*, pages 31–37.

Ryan McDonald, Koby Crammer, and Fernando Pereira. 2005a. Online large-margin training of dependency parsers. In *Proceedings of the 43rd annual meeting on association for computational linguistics*, pages 91–98. Association for Computational Linguistics.

Ryan McDonald, Fernando Pereira, Kiril Ribarov, and Jan Hajič. 2005b. Non-projective dependency parsing using spanning tree algorithms. In *Proceedings of the conference on Human Language Technology and Empirical Methods in Natural Language Processing*, pages 523–530. Association for Computational Linguistics.

Ryan McDonald, Slav Petrov, and Keith Hall. 2011. Multi-source transfer of delexicalized dependency parsers. In *Proceedings of the Conference on Empirical Methods in Natural Language Processing*, EMNLP '11, pages 62–72, Stroudsburg, PA, USA. Association for Computational Linguistics.

Ryan McDonald, Joakim Nivre, Yvonne Quirmbach-Brundage, Yoav Goldberg, Dipanjan Das, Kuzman Ganchev, Keith Hall, Slav Petrov, Hao Zhang, Oscar Täckström, Claudia Bedini, Núria Bertomeu Castelló, and Jungmee Lee. 2013. Universal dependency annotation for multilingual parsing. In *Proceedings of the 51st Annual Meeting of the Association for Computational Linguistics*, pages 92–97.

Tahira Naseem, Regina Barzilay, and Amir Globerson. 2012. Selective sharing for multilingual dependency parsing. In *Proceedings of the 50th Annual Meeting of the Association for Computational Linguistics: Long Papers - Volume 1*, ACL '12, pages 629–637, Stroudsburg, PA, USA. Association for Computational Linguistics.

Slav Petrov, Dipanjan Das, and Ryan McDonald. 2012. A universal part-of-speech tagset. In *Proc. of LREC-2012*, pages 2089–2096, Istanbul, Turkey. European Language Resources Association (ELRA).

Rudolf Rosa and Zdeněk Žabokrtský. 2015. KL_{cpos^3} – a language similarity measure for delexicalized parser transfer. In *Proceedings of the 51st Annual Meeting of the Association for Computational Linguistics and the 7th International Joint Conference on Natural Language Processing of the Asian Federation of Natural Language Processing, Short Papers*, Stroudsburg, PA, USA. Association for Computational Linguistics, Association for Computational Linguistics.

Rudolf Rosa, Jan Mašek, David Mareček, Martin Popel, Daniel Zeman, and Zdeněk Žabokrtský. 2014. HamleDT 2.0: Thirty dependency treebanks Stanfordized. In Nicoletta Calzolari, Khalid Choukri, Thierry Declerck, Hrafn Loftsson, Bente Maegaard, and Joseph Mariani, editors, *Proceedings of the 9th International Conference on Language Resources and Evaluation (LREC 2014)*, pages 2334–2341, Reykjavík, Iceland. European Language Resources Association.

Rudolf Rosa. 2015a. MSTperl delexicalized parser transfer scripts and configuration files. `http://hdl.handle.net/11234/1-1485`.

Rudolf Rosa. 2015b. MSTperl parser (2015-05-19). `http://hdl.handle.net/11234/1-1480`.

Kenji Sagae and Alon Lavie. 2006. Parser combination by reparsing. In *Proceedings of the Human Language Technology Conference of the NAACL, Companion Volume: Short Papers*, pages 129–132. Association for Computational Linguistics.

Roy Schwartz, Omri Abend, and Ari Rappoport. 2012. Learnability-based syntactic annotation design. In *Proceedings of COLING 2012: Technical Papers*.

Anders Søgaard and Julie Wulff. 2012. An empirical etudy of non-lexical extensions to delexicalized transfer. In *COLING (Posters)*, pages 1181–1190.

Anders Søgaard. 2013. An empirical study of differences between conversion schemes and annotation guidelines. In *Proceedings of the Second International Conference on Dependency Linguistics (DepLing 2013), Prague, Czech Republic: Charles University in Prague, Matfyzpress*, pages 298–307.

Oscar Täckström, Ryan McDonald, and Joakim Nivre. 2013. Target language adaptation of discriminative transfer parsers. *NAACL HLT 2013*, pages 1061–1071.

Daniel Zeman and Philip Resnik. 2008. Cross-language parser adaptation between related languages. In *IJCNLP 2008 Workshop on NLP for Less Privileged Languages*, pages 35–42, Hyderabad, India. Asian Federation of Natural Language Processing, International Institute of Information Technology.

Daniel Zeman, David Mareček, Martin Popel, Loganathan Ramasamy, Jan Štěpánek, Zdeněk Žabokrtský, and Jan Hajič. 2012. HamleDT: To parse or not to parse? In Nicoletta Calzolari (Conference Chair), Khalid Choukri, Thierry Declerck, Mehmet Uur Doan, Bente Maegaard, Joseph Mariani, Jan Odijk, and Stelios Piperidis, editors, *Proceedings of the Eight International Conference on Language Resources and Evaluation (LREC'12)*, Istanbul, Turkey, May. European Language Resources Association (ELRA).

Daniel Zeman. 2008. Reusable tagset conversion using tagset drivers. In *Proceedings of the 6th International Conference on Language Resources and Evaluation (LREC 2008)*, pages 213–218, Marrakech, Morocco. European Language Resources Association.

Secondary Connectives in the Prague Dependency Treebank

Magdaléna Rysová
Charles University in Prague
Faculty of Arts
Institute of Czech Language
and Theory of Communication
Czech Republic
magdalena.rysova@post.cz

Kateřina Rysová
Charles University in Prague
Faculty of Mathematics and Physics
Institute of Formal and Applied Linguistics
Czech Republic
katerina.rysova@post.cz

Abstract

The paper introduces a new annotation of discourse relations in the Prague Dependency Treebank (PDT), i.e. the annotation of the so called secondary connectives (mainly multiword phrases like *the condition is*, *that is the reason why*, *to conclude*, *this means* etc.). Firstly, the paper concentrates on theoretical introduction of these expressions (mainly with respect to primary connectives like *and*, *but*, *or*, *too* etc.) and tries to contribute to the description and definition of discourse connectives in general (both primary and secondary). Secondly, the paper demonstrates possibilities of annotations of secondary connectives in large corpora (like PDT). The paper describes general annotation principles for secondary connectives used in PDT for Czech and compares the results of this annotation with annotation of primary connectives in PDT. In this respect, the main aim of the paper is to introduce a new type of discourse annotation that could be adopted also by other languages.

1 Introduction

In the paper, we introduce a new annotation of discourse relations in the Prague Dependency Treebank (PDT) enriched by the so called secondary connectives (i.e. especially by the multiword phrases like *hlavním důvodem je* "the main reason is", *závěr zní* "the conclusion is", *to kontrastuje s tím* "this contrasts with" etc.).

We present how it is possible to annotate such variable (i.e. inflectional and modifiable) structures on big data according to general annotation principles. We believe that our methods may be used also for other languages to enrich the discourse annotations of similar corpora.

2 Theoretical Background – Discourse Connectives in General Overview

Many theoretical approaches of discourse analysis (see projects like Penn Discourse Treebank – Prasad et al., 2008 or Potsdam Commentary Corpus – Stede and Neumann, 2014) are based on detection and annotation of discourse connectives in texts. However, there is not a general agreement on definition as well as terminology concerning these expressions (called besides discourse connectives also pragmatic connectives – van Dijk, 1979, discourse particles – Fischer, 2006 etc.). In this paper, we use the term discourse connectives following the Prague tradition.

Very generally, discourse connectives may be defined as language expressions signaling discourse relations within a text. Most of the authors would agree on typical examples like *and*, *but*, *or*, *when*, *so*, *because*, *yet* etc., i.e. on the central or most frequent discourse connectives. However, the authors differ in dealing with less typical examples like *for this reason*, *this follows* etc., i.e. in (mostly) multiword phrases allowing variation and inflection (impossibility of inflection is, e.g., one of the criteria used for delimitation of connectives in Potsdam Commentary Corpus – Stede and Neumann, 2014).

From part-of-speech perspective, some authors define discourse connectives as subordinating and coordinating conjunctions, prepositional phrases and adverbs (e.g. Prasad et al., 2008, 2010, 2014; Fraser, 1999), others (like Hansen, 1998; Aijmer, 2002; Schiffrin, 1987) add also particles and nominal phrases.

In this paper, we would like to contribute to this discussion on discourse connectives, to present our definition used in PDT and to bring a

Proceedings of the Third International Conference on Dependency Linguistics (Depling 2015), pages 291–299,
Uppsala, Sweden, August 24–26 2015.

new division of discourse connectives based on a large corpus study.

2.1 Delimitation of Connectives in the Prague Dependency Treebank

During the annotation of authentic Czech texts from PDT, we have met many different possibilities of signaling discourse relations – from one-word, frozen conjunctions like *a* "and" or *ale* "but" to multiword phrases like *stručně řečeno* "simply speaking", *vzhledem k této situaci* "considering this situation", *díky této zkušenosti* "thanks to this experience" etc. All of these expressions somehow contribute to the structuring of discourse, but we felt a need to differentiate such wide group of expressions into subgroups taking into account mainly two aspects: **i) semantically, the suitability of the given expression (in its connective meaning[1]) for different contexts**, **ii) grammatically, the phase of grammaticalization of the given expression**.

i) Semantic delimitation of connectives

The suitability for different contexts divides the expressions into two groups. The first contains expressions that are (in their connective meaning) appropriate for many different contexts, the second includes expressions that are context dependent – see Examples 1, 2 and 3:

(1) *Celý den pršelo.* ***Proto*** *nepůjdu na výlet.*
"It was raining the whole day. **Therefore**, I will not go for a trip."

(2) *Chce se stát slavnou herečkou.* ***Kvůli tomu*** *udělá cokoli.*
"She wants to be a famous actress. **Because of this**, she is able to do anything."

(3) *Ředitel firmy uzavřel řadu podezřelých obchodů.* ***Kvůli této činnosti*** *byl vyšetřován policií.*
"Director of the company has entered into a series of suspicious transactions. **Because of this activity**, he was investigated by the police."

In Examples 1, 2 and 3, there are three expressions signaling a discourse relation of reason and result[2]: *proto* "therefore", *kvůli tomu* "because of this"[3] and *kvůli této činnosti* "because of this activity". However, only the first two are suitable also for the other given contexts (i.e. we may say, e.g., ***Therefore / Because of this****, he was investigated by the police.* but not *It was raining the whole day. *****Because of this activity****, I will not go for a trip.*).

In this respect, we consider *proto* "therefore" and *kvůli tomu* "because of this" suitable as connecting expressions for more contexts (i.e. more "universal") than the expression *kvůli této činnosti* "because of this activity". Generally, we call this suitability **a universality principle** according to which we define discourse connectives. In other words, the expressions like *proto* "therefore" and *kvůli tomu* "because of this" are discourse connectives in our approach, whereas expressions like *kvůli této činnosti* "because of this activity" are not, as they signal discourse relations only in a limited set of contexts (these expressions have of course also the compositional function in the text, but – unlike discourse connectives – they are very far from possible grammaticalization). We call these expressions (like *kvůli této činnosti* "because of this activity") **free connecting phrases**.

ii) Grammatical delimitation of connectives (primary vs. secondary connectives)

Within discourse connectives, we distinguish two categories (mainly in terms of grammaticalization) – primary connectives and secondary connectives (as in M. Rysová and K. Rysová, 2014).

Primary connectives are mainly grammatical (or functional) words whose primary function is to connect two units of a text (they mostly belong to conjunctions and structuring particles[4]). Thus they do not have a role of

[1] We are aware that expressions like *and*, *for*, *on the other hand* etc. have also other (non-connective) meanings. However, these other meanings are not in our interest – we evaluate only expressions in their connective function.

[2] The relation of "reason and result" is in PDT delimited as a causal relation in broader sense (i.e. including both "cause" and "consequence"). The terminology of reason and result was adopted from PDTB (see Prasad et al., 2008).

[3] We understand the whole structure *because of this* as a secondary connective, as **because of* itself is an ungrammatical structure and needs to combine with an anaphoric expression to gain a discourse connecting function. At the same time, there are some present-day primary connectives that historically arose from similar combination of a preposition and demonstrative pronoun (e.g. Czech connective *proto* "therefore" from the preposition *pro* "for" and demonstrative pronoun *to* "this").

[4] We define conjunctions (following the traditional Czech grammar) as grammatical words with primary connecting function (like *ale* "but", *nebo* "or", *a* "and" etc.), structuring

sentence elements and in this sense, they do not affect the sentence syntax. Primary connectives are mostly one-word, lexically frozen expressions. Examples of primary connectives are *ale* "but", *a* "and", *zatímco* "whereas", *protože* "because", *když* "when", *nebo* "or" etc.

Secondary connectives are mainly multiword structures functioning as connectives only in certain collocations. Most of them have a key word signaling given type of discourse relation (the cores may be nouns like *condition*, *reason*, *difference* etc., verbs like *to mean*, *to explain*, *to cause* etc., prepositions like *due to*, *because of*, *despite* etc.). Secondary connectives contain (in contrast to primary) some lexical word or words and have a role of sentence elements (*z tohoto důvodu* "for this reason"), sentence modifiers (*obecně řečeno* "generally speaking") or they may form a separate sentence (*Důvod je jednoduchý.* "The reason is simple."). Secondary connectives are not yet grammaticalized, although they exhibit several features typical for the process of grammaticalization (e.g. weakening of singular and plural distinction, gradual loss of the individual lexical meaning and gaining the primary connecting function as a whole structure etc.). Examples of secondary connectives are *podmínkou je* "the condition is", *to znamená* "this means", *to je důvod, proč* "this is the reason why", *kvůli tomu* "because of this", *z těchto důvodů* "for these reasons" etc.

The main difference between primary and secondary connectives thus lies in grammaticalization – i.e. primary connectives are grammaticalized expressions (although sometimes the grammaticalization is not fully completed, which causes discrepancy among certain parts of speech, especially conjunctions, adverbs and particles). From diachronic point of view, primary connectives arose from other parts of speech and very often from combination of several words and gradually became grammaticalized (e.g. English present-day primary connective *because* arose from *bi cause* "by cause", originally a phrase often followed by a subordinate *that*-clause; it is used as one word probably from around 1400 /see Harper, 2001/).

particles as grammatical words expressing a relation of a speaker to the structure of a text (like *jen* "only", *také* "too" etc.).

3 Discourse Annotation in the Prague Dependency Treebank

The annotation of secondary connectives was carried out on the data of the Prague Dependency Treebank (PDT). PDT contains almost 50 thousand of sentences from the Czech newspaper texts. The advantage of this corpus is that it is annotated on more language levels at once – it contains annotation on morphological, syntactical and syntactico-semantic layers, as well as the annotation of discourse phenomena (i.e. coreference and discourse relations).

Discourse relations have been annotated in two phases – firstly expressed by primary connectives, secondly by secondary connectives.

3.1 Annotation of Primary Connectives in the Prague Dependency Treebank

The annotation of primary connectives has been finished in 2012. The annotation has been carried out on the data of the Prague Dependency Treebank 2.5 (Bejček et al., 2012) and has been published as the Prague Discourse Treebank 1.0 (see Poláková et al., 2012). The annotation follows the Penn Discourse Treebank style (Prasad et al., 2008, 2014), i.e. discourse relations (both inter- and intra-sentential) are annotated between two pieces of a text called discourse arguments (defined as abstract objects according to Asher, 1993). The annotation was limited only to such primary connectives that expressed discourse relations between two verbal arguments containing predication (e.g. clauses, sentences or whole paragraphs). The annotated relation was then assigned one semantic type out of 23 types of relations.[5]

In this phase of annotation, the annotators were also asked to mark all candidates to secondary connectives. Their notes then served as a basis for creating a list of such structures used in the second phase of annotation.

3.2 Annotation of Secondary Connectives in the Prague Dependency Treebank

In the next phase, the first discourse annotation in the Prague Dependency Treebank has been extended by secondary connectives. It contains

[5]Concession, condition, confrontation, conjunction, conjunctive alternative, correction, disjunctive alternative, equivalence, exemplification, explication, pragmatic condition, pragmatic contrast, pragmatic reason, generalization, gradation, opposition, asynchronous, purpose, reason and result, restrictive opposition, specification, synchronous, other.

annotation of both inter- and intra-sentential discourse relations.

The annotation of secondary connectives in PDT was based on the list of potential secondary connectives collected during the first discourse annotation in 2012. All the key words of the collected candidates (like *důvod* "reason", *podmínka* "condition", *znamenat* "to mean" etc.) have been automatically detected in the whole PDT data and then manually sorted (as not all tokens of e.g. the word *podmínka* "condition" have a function of secondary connective) and annotated by human annotators (see Rysová and Mírovský, 2014).

The secondary connectives were annotated on the whole PDT data (i.e. almost 50 thousand of sentences).

Besides the secondary connectives, the new annotation includes also the free connecting phrases (see Section 2.1), as their annotation on big data may allow us to study discourse connectives in deeper and contrastive context. For example, we may see the ratio of universal and non-universal phrases in PDT from which we may learn whether the multiword connecting phrases have a tendency to gradually loosen the bonds to the concrete contexts and to stabilize on one, context independent form. In other words, we may learn how far from primary connectives the majority of multiword structures lies.

A significant difference between the annotations of primary and secondary connectives is that unlike the first annotation in 2012, the extended annotation of secondary connectives contains discourse relations between **both verbal and nominal arguments** (as said above, the annotation of primary connectives concentrated only on arguments expressed by verbal propositions or clauses) – see Example 4:

(4) *Koncert nezačal včas. Důvodem byl pozdní příchod houslisty.*
"The concert has not begun on time. The reason was the late arrival of the violinist."
(= because the violinist has arrived late)

In Example 4, there is a discourse relation of reason and result expressed by the secondary connective *the reason was* between two discourse arguments – the first is represented by the whole clause (*The concert has not begun on time.*), the second argument is nominal (i.e. expressed by the nominal phrase *the late arrival of the violinist*). In this case, the secondary connective cannot be replaced by the primary one – we cannot say something like **protože pozdní příchod houslisty* "*because the late arrival of the violinist". We may see that secondary connectives are not yet fully grammaticalized, which means that they may have a function of various sentence elements, including (among others) subject (*the reason*) and predicate (*was*). Therefore, some of the secondary connectives may be followed by the nominalized discourse argument.

We think that the difference between arguments expressed by a verbal or nominal phrase is purely syntactic (*the late arrival of the violinist* vs. *the violinist has arrived late*). Semantically, the meaning remains almost the same. For this reason, we have annotated all discourse arguments according to their semantics (not syntactic representation)[6].

4 Results and Evaluation

In this part of the paper, we present the main results and characteristics of secondary discourse connectives gained from the annotation in PDT with respect to their comparison with primary connectives.

4.1 Evaluation of Annotations – Inter-Annotator Agreement

The inter-annotator (I-A) agreement of secondary connectives annotation was measured on 500 sentences annotated (simultaneously) by two human annotators.[7] We have focused on two main aspects of their annotation: 1. the overall agreement on existence of the discourse relation (i.e. to which extent the annotators agreed on the fact that there is a discourse relation in the given place of a text expressed by a secondary connective); 2. the agreement on semantic types of discourse relations expressed by secondary connectives (like condition, concession etc.). At the same time, we have compared the results of the inter-annotator agreement of secondary connectives with the primary connectives (Poláková et al., 2013) – see Table 1.[8]

Table 1 demonstrates that the I-A agreement is for primary and secondary connectives comparable. The I-A agreement on the existence

[6] However, we have marked them (technically) differently for easier analysis of final results.

[7] Many thanks to Jiří Mírovský for his kind measuring of the I-A agreement.

[8] The existence of discourse relation is measured by connective-based F1-measure, types of discourse relations by simple ratio (or Cohen's κ).

of relation is higher for primary connectives (F1: 0.83 vs. 0.70). This is not so surprising due to the significantly bigger heterogeneity of secondary connectives (we deal with nominal, verbal, prepositional phrases etc.) in comparison with lexically frozen (i.e. grammaticalized) forms of primary connectives (the secondary allow a bigger degree of variation in terms of inflection, modification etc.). Therefore, the annotation of secondary connectives is for the human annotators more difficult.

Type of Inter-Annotator Agreement	Primary Con	Secondary Con
Existence of relation (F1)	0.83	0.70
Types of discourse relations	0.77	0.82
Types of discourse relations (Cohen's κ)	0.71	0.78

Table 1. Inter-Annotator Agreement.

On the other hand, the agreement on semantic types of discourse relations is slightly higher for secondary connectives – see simple ratios 0.77 (0.71 C. k.) vs. 0.82 (0.78 C. k.). This may be explained by the fact that most of the secondary connectives contain a transparent key word (like *condition*, *reason*, *result*, *concession*, *contrast* etc.) that refers directly to one of the individual semantic types of relations (although this relationship is not so straightforward in all cases).

In this respect, primary connectives seem to be more easily identifiable in authentic PDT texts and secondary connectives, on the other hand, signal more transparently the individual semantic types of discourse relations.

Altogether, the I-A agreement for the annotation of secondary connectives in PDT seems satisfactory (i.e. comparable with similar discourse annotation of primary connectives).

4.2 Primary vs. Secondary Connectives in Numbers

At the current stage, PDT data contain altogether 21,416 annotated discourse relations. Within this number, there are 20,255 tokens of primary connectives and 1,161 of secondary connectives – see Table 2 (the results are measured on the whole PDT data). In other words, primary connectives form 94.6 % and secondary connectives 5.4 % within the whole number of explicit discourse relations in PDT. Therefore, the terms primary and secondary connectives seem suitable also in terms of frequency – explicit discourse relations are signaled primarily by primary connectives. However, the number of secondary connectives in PDT is not insignificant and discourse annotation would be incomplete without them.

	Tokens in PDT	%
Primary Con	20,255	94.6
Secondary Con	1,161	5.4
Total	**21,416**	100

Table 2. Discourse Annotation in PDT.

The results of annotation also demonstrate that the majority of secondary connectives (924 within 1,161, i.e. 76 %) expresses discourse relations between two verbal (or clausal) arguments. The reason is that not all secondary connectives (e.g. prepositional phrases) allow nominalization of the second argument. Nominalization appears only with a set of similar structures like *výjimkou je* "the exception is", *důvodem je* "the reason is", *podmínkou je* "the condition is", *vysvětlením je* "the explanation is" etc. – see Example 4. Such secondary connectives contain the predicate already within their structure (mostly the verb *to be*) so they do not demand another finite verb in the argument and may be followed only by the nominal phrase. (The results of annotation also revealed that nominalization of the second argument even predominates in these structures – in 80 %. Thus the structure of the secondary connective has a direct influence on the syntactic realization of the second argument in these cases.)

As said above, the extended discourse annotation captures not only the secondary connectives but also the free connecting phrases (functioning as discourse indicators only in a limited set of contexts, like *kvůli jeho pozdnímu příchodu* "due to his late arrival", *kvůli tomuto nárůstu* "due to this increase", *kvůli tomuto rozhodnutí* "due to this decision" that may be mostly substituted by universal *kvůli tomu* "due to this" but not vice versa). Currently, PDT contains 1,161 tokens of secondary connectives and 151 of free connecting phrases (i.e. 88 % vs. 12 %). We may see that there is a strong tendency for multiword discourse phrases to gradually fix on one stable form and to gain a status of a universal connective.

4.3 Semantic Types of Discourse Relations

Distribution of the individual semantic relations (presented in Table 3) is for primary and secondary connectives similar, i.e. very numerous relations are relations of conjunction, reason and result and condition. The relations with the lowest (or very low) numbers are the pragmatic relations (i.e. pragmatic contrast, pragmatic reason and pragmatic condition).

On the other hand, primary and secondary connectives significantly differ in case of opposition and explication. The relation of opposition is the second most numerous relation expressed by primary connectives (with 3,171 tokens) whereas with secondary connectives, it occurred only in 13 cases. So the relation of opposition is almost exclusively expressed by primary connectives (in 99.6 %), which demonstrates that Czech does not have many multiword alternatives to signal this type of discourse relation.

On the other hand, the relation of explication is the fourth most numerous relation within secondary connectives (with 67 relations) whereas in case of primary connectives, it is in the middle (with rather low tokens within primary connectives).

However, the percentage of the individual relations clearly demonstrates that primary connectives prevail significantly in all cases (their percentage in comparison to secondary connectives is higher than 90 % in most of the relations).

Slightly higher percentage (within secondary connectives) occurs only in three types of relations: explication (22.7 %), exemplification (16.9 %) and generalization (16.7 %). However, generally, the primary connectives prevail in all the relations very clearly.

Type of Relation	Total	Primary Con	Primary Con %	Secondary Con	Secondary Con %
conjunction	7,730	7,386	95.5	344	4.1
opposition	3,184	3,171	99.6	13	0.4
reason and result	2,927	2,583	91.4	344	8.6
condition	1,451	1,351	93.1	100	6.9
concession	918	874	95.2	44	4.8
asynchronous	860	816	94.9	44	5.1
confrontation	666	632	94.9	34	5.1
specification	649	625	96.3	24	3.7
gradation	459	443	95.6	20	4.4
correction	456	439	97.1	13	2.9
purpose	419	412	98.3	7	1.7
explication	**295**	**261**	**77.3**	**67**	**22.7**
restrictive opposition	294	266	90.5	28	9.5
disj. alternative	271	228	96.3	10	3.7
synchronous	226	225	99.6	1	0.4
exemplification	**177**	**147**	**83.1**	**30**	**16.9**
generalization	**120**	**100**	**83.3**	**20**	**16.7**
equivalence	110	99	90	11	10
conj. alternative	90	88	97.8	2	2.2
pragmatic contrast	50	50	100	0	0
pragmatic reason	44	41	93.2	3	6.8
pragmatic condition	17	16	94.1	1	5.9
other	3	2	66.7	1	33.3
Total	**21,416**	**20,255**	**94.6**	**1,161**	**5.4**

Table 3. Primary vs. Secondary Connectives – Types of Discourse Relations in PDT.

4.4 New Semantic Types of Discourse Relations for Secondary Connectives

Another lesson we have learnt from the annotation of secondary connectives is that we cannot simply adopt the existing annotation principles created for the primary connectives. Secondary connectives are much more heterogeneous group than primary connectives (concerning lexical, syntactic as well as semantic aspects – see Rysová, 2012). Therefore, we can expect that it will project also to their annotation in large corpora and that the existing annotation principles will need to be modified and to react on all the differences.

As for types of discourse relations, we may expect that secondary connectives may express some new semantic relations (that are not in the classification of discourse relations formulated for primary connectives). Therefore, the human annotators were asked to mark all occurrences of secondary connectives expressing such "new" relations. Altogether, the remarks referred to three new relations: **a) entailment or deduction of results** (expressed, e.g., by secondary connectives *výsledkem je* "the result is"; *z toho vyplývá* "it follows"); **b) the relation of conclusion** (e.g. *závěrem je* "the conclusion is", *dojít k závěru* "to come to a conclusion"); **c) the relation of regard** (e.g. *v tomto ohledu* "in this respect", *v tomto směru* "in this regard"). The common feature of these relations is that they refer mostly to a larger piece of the text (e.g. to the whole previous paragraph etc.). In our opinion, these semantic relations cannot be included within any relation formulated for primary connectives and the existing classification should be extended.

4.5 Inter- and Intra-Sentential Discourse Relations

As said above, the PDT discourse annotation contains both inter- and intra-sentential relations (i.e. both *I would like to go on a trip.* ***But*** *it is raining.* and *I would like to go on a trip* ***but*** *it is raining.*). Therefore, we have analyzed whether primary and secondary connectives prefer one of these ways of expression. The ratio of inter- and intra-sentential relations expressed by primary and secondary connectives is presented in Table 4.

	Intra	%	**Inter**	%	**Total**
Primary Con	14,195	70 %	6,060	30 %	**20,255**
Secondary Con	432	37 %	729	63 %	**1,161**
Total	**14,627**	**68 %**	**6,789**	**32 %**	**21,416**

Table 4. Inter- and Intra-Sentential Relations

Table 4 demonstrates that primary connectives prefer intra-sentential discourse relations (in 70 %) while secondary connectives inter-sentential relations (in 63 %). Thus we may see that this is another crucial aspect in which primary and secondary connectives significantly differ.

We have carried out a further analysis and concentrated on the possible connection between the way of expressing discourse relations (i.e. inter- or intra-sentential) and the semantic types of given relations. We tried to examine whether this connection may give us some possible explanation why the authors prefer secondary connectives rather than primary connectives in certain contexts. We found out that in all the semantic types of relations (like reason and result, opposition etc.) prevail in both inter- and intra-sentential relations primary connectives except for two – **the inter-sentential relations of purpose and condition** prefer the expression by secondary connectives (in 86 % for purpose and 62 % for condition). This generally means that if the text contains either the inter-sentential relation of purpose or condition, there is a relatively high probability (at least in case of purpose) that they will be expressed by secondary (rather than primary) connectives.

5 Conclusion

In the paper, we have introduced the annotation of the so called secondary connectives (i.e. expressions like *the condition is, to conclude, for these reasons* etc.).

From theoretical point of view, we define discourse connectives as (mostly) universal indicators of discourse relations that may have different surface forms. According of their realization, we distinguish primary and secondary connectives. **Primary connectives** are expressions with universal status of discourse indicators that are grammaticalized (i.e. lexically frozen). They are functional words (i.e. mainly conjunctions and structuring particles) that are not integrated into clause structure as sentence elements like *but*, *and*, *or*, *because* etc. **Secondary connectives** are mainly multiword phrases containing a lexical word or words that are not yet fully grammaticalized; therefore, these structures are much more variable (concerning modification, inflexion etc.). The secondary connectives may be sentence elements (*because of this*), sentence modifiers (*simply speaking*) or they form a separate sentence (*The reason is simple.*).

In the paper, we demonstrated how it is possible to include secondary connectives into corpus annotations. The overall inter-annotator agreement on existence of a discourse relation is 0.70 (F1) and on the type of a discourse relation 0.82 (0.78 C. k.), which is very similar to primary connectives in PDT.

Altogether, PDT contains 1,161 tokens of secondary connectives, which is 5.4 % within all explicit discourse connectives in PDT (thus the attribute secondary seems suitable for them also in terms of frequency).

We have compared primary and secondary connectives also in terms of semantic types of discourse relations they express. The distribution of the individual semantic relations is very similar for both primary and secondary connectives (with some exceptions like the relation of opposition occurring very predominantly with primary connectives). However, the annotation has taught us that the classification of relations formulated for primary connectives cannot be simply adopted for secondary connectives – during the annotation, we have observed three "new" semantic types (that were not included into the classification for primary connectives): a) **entailment or deduction of results** (e.g. *it follows*); b) **the relation of conclusion** (e.g. *the conclusion is*); c) **the relation of regard** (e.g. *in this respect*). These three types of relation refer mostly to larger pieces of text like a whole paragraph.

The results of annotation also demonstrate that primary and secondary connectives differ in terms of inter- and intra-sentential relations. Whereas primary connectives prefer the intra-sentential relations (in 70 %), secondary connectives mostly the inter-sentential relations (in 63 %). So primary and secondary connectives do not differ only from syntactic, lexical and semantic point of view, but also in the way how they structure the text.

At the current stage, the Prague Dependency Treebank contains the most detailed annotation of secondary connectives (as far as we know, done on the largest data) that could be adopted also for other languages in other corpora focusing mostly on the annotation of primary connectives. In the paper, we tried to demonstrate that discourse annotation including secondary connectives is more complete and that similar analysis may lead to better understanding of discourse.

Acknowledgement

This paper was supported by the project "Discourse Connectives in Czech" (n. 36213) solved at the Faculty of Arts at the Charles University in Prague from the resources of the Charles University Grant Agency in 2013–2015.

The authors acknowledge support from the Czech Science Foundation (project n. P406/12/0658) and from the Ministry of Education, Youth and Sports of the Czech Republic (project n. LH14011 and LM2010013).

This work has been using language resources developed, stored and distributed by the LINDAT/CLARIN project of the Ministry of Education, Youth and Sports of the Czech Republic (project LM2010013).

The authors gratefully thank to Jiří Mírovský from the Charles University in Prague for his kind measuring the figures on the PDT data for this paper.

References

Karin Aijmer. 2002. *English Discourse Particles. Evidence from a corpus.* Studies in Corpus Linguistics 10. Amsterdam/Philadelphia: John Benjamins, ISBN 90-272-2280-0.

Nicholas Asher. 1993. *Reference to Abstract Objects in Discourse.* Dordrecht: Kluwer Academic Publishers, ISBN 0-7923-2242-8.

Eduard Bejček et al. 2012. Prague Dependency Treebank 2.5 – a revisited version of PDT 2.0. In: *Proceedings of Coling 2012*, Bombay, India, pp. 231–246.

Teuen A. van Dijk. 1979. Pragmatic Connectives. In: *Journal of Pragmatics 3*. North-Holland Publishing Company, pp. 447–456.

Kerstin Fischer, eds. 2006. *Approaches to Discourse Particles.* Studies in Pragmatics 1. Amsterdam: Elsevier, ISBN-10: 0080447376, ISBN-13: 978-0080447377.

Bruce Fraser. 1999. What are discourse markers? *Journal of Pragmatics 31 (7).* Elsevier, pp. 931–952.

Maj-Britt Mosegaard Hansen. 1998. *The Function of Discourse Particles: A study with special reference to spoken standard French*. Amsterdam: John Benjamins. ISBN 9789027250667.

Douglas Harper. 2001. Online Etymology Dictionary. <http://www.etymonline.com>.

Lucie Poláková et al. 2013. Introducing the Prague Discourse Treebank 1.0. In: *Proceedings of the 6th International Joint Conference on Natural Language Processing*, Copyright © Asian Federation of Natural Language Processing, Nagoya, Japan, ISBN 978-4-9907348-0-0, pp. 91–99.

Lucie Poláková et al. 2012. *Prague Discourse Treebank 1.0*. Data/software, ÚFAL MFF UK, Prague, Czech Republic.

Rashmi Prasad et al. 2008. The Penn Discourse Treebank 2.0. In: *Proceedings of the 6th International Conference on Language Resources and Evaluation (LREC 2008)*, Marrakech, Morocco, pp. 2961–2968.

Rashmi Prasad, Aravind Joshi, Bonnie Weber. 2010. Realization of Discourse Relations by Other Means: Alternative Lexicalizations. In: *Proceedings of Coling 2010*, Tsinghua University Press, Beijing, China, pp. 1023–1031.

Rashmi Prasad, Bonnie Webber and Aravind Joshi. 2014. Reflections on the Penn Discourse TreeBank, Comparable Corpora and Complementary Annotation. *Computational Linguistics 40 (4)*, pp. 921–950.

Magdaléna Rysová. 2012. Alternative Lexicalizations of Discourse Connectives in Czech. In: Proceedings of the 8th International Conference on Language Resources and Evaluation (LREC 2012), European Language Resources Association, Istanbul, Turkey, ISBN 978-2-9517408-7-7, pp. 2800–2807.

Magdaléna Rysová, Jiří Mírovský. 2014. Use of Coreference in Automatic Searching for Multiword Discourse Markers in the Prague Dependency Treebank. In: Proceedings of The 8th Linguistic Annotation Workshop (LAW-VIII), Copyright © Dublin City University (DCU), Dublin, Ireland, ISBN 978-1-941643-29-7, pp. 11–19.

Magdaléna Rysová, Kateřina Rysová. 2014. The Centre and Periphery of Discourse Connectives. In: Proceedings of the 28th Pacific Asia Conference on Language, Information and Computing, Copyright © Department of Linguistics, Faculty of Arts, Chulalongkorn University, Bangkok, Thailand, ISBN 978-616-551-887-1, pp. 452-459.

Deborah Schiffrin. 1987. *Discourse markers*. Cambridge: Cambridge University Press, ISBN 9780521357180.

Manfred Stede, Arne Neumann. 2014. Potsdam Commentary Corpus 2.0: Annotation for discourse research. In: N. Calzolari et al. (eds.), *Proceedings of the 9th International Conference on Language Resources and Evaluation (LREC'14)*. Reykjavík: European Language Resources Association (ELRA), pp. 925–929.

ParsPer: A Dependency Parser for Persian

Mojgan Seraji
Uppsala University
Department of Linguistics
and Philology, Sweden
mojgan.seraji@lingfil.uu.se

Bernd Bohnet
Google in London
bohnetbd@gmail.com

Joakim Nivre
Uppsala University
Department of Linguistics
and Philology, Sweden
joakim.nivre@lingfil.uu.se

Abstract

We present a dependency parser for Persian, called *ParsPer*, developed using the graph-based parser in the Mate Tools. The parser is trained on the entire *Uppsala Persian Dependency Treebank* with a specific configuration that was selected by MaltParser as the best performing parsing representation. The treebank's syntactic annotation scheme is based on Stanford Typed Dependencies with extensions for Persian. The results of the ParsPer evaluation revealed a best labeled accuracy over 82% with an unlabeled accuracy close to 87%. The parser is freely available and released as an open source tool for parsing Persian.

1 Introduction

Data-driven dependency parsing is a modern approach that has been successfully applied to develop dependency parsers for different languages (Böhmová et al., 2003; Haverinen et al., 2010; Kromann, 2003; Foth et al., 2014; Vincze et al., 2010). The approach relies solely on a syntactically annotated dataset (*treebank*). However, achieving the best results by this method relies partly on parsing algorithms and selecting the best feature settings. As data-driven dependency parsers induce the syntactic structure backbone in a treebank, they are further, to a great extent, dependent on the representation setup for part-of-speech and dependency labels. These representations are always built upon an already tokenized text. In other words, different tokenizations require different part-of-speech and dependency annotations, which in turn impact the quality of parsing analysis.

Processing and analysis of a language like Persian pose a variety of challenges on various levels, from orthography to syntactic structure (Seraji, 2015). Persian orthography does not follow a consistent standardization. The most challenging cases concern the handling of fixed expressions and various types of clitics. Different variations of writing such cases as attached or detached forms (either delimited with whitespace or zero-width non-joiner)[1] pose challenges for tokenization which in turn impacts the quality of morphological and syntactic analysis. Furthermore, the prevalence of multi-word compound verbs, functioning as a single verb in the form of so called complex predicates or light verb constructions (LVC), is another remarkable feature in the Persian syntactic structure. The situation for automatic analysis of Persian is further complicated by its high degree of free word order.

Therefore, in preparing the treebank data for Persian many difficult decisions had to be made concerning handling fixed expressions and different types of clitics such as pronominal and copula clitics (Seraji, 2015). Fixed expressions in Persian are sometimes written as one single token and sometimes as several tokens. The same happens for different types of clitics. They are sometimes segmented and sometimes unsegmented from the head words. Since the treebank data is taken from the large and open source Uppsala Persian Corpus (UPC),[2] it was impossible to manually separate fixed expressions and clitics from head words in a consistent way in a large corpus like the UPC, containing 2,703,265 tokens. On the other hand, to automatically handle such cases was also impossi-

[1] The zero-width non-joiner (ZWNJ), also known as zero-space or pseudo-space, is a non-printing character used as a boundary inside a word that keeps different affixes and/or clitics unjoined next to the head words.

[2] For a more detailed description of the *Uppsala Persian Corpus* related to the tokenization and morphological annotation see Seraji (2015, Chapter 3). The corpus is open source and freely available at http://stp.lingfil.uu.se/∼mojgan/UPC.html

Proceedings of the Third International Conference on Dependency Linguistics (Depling 2015), pages 300–309,
Uppsala, Sweden, August 24–26 2015.

ble since the process could result in many incorrect conversions by impacting orthographically similar words or endings with different part-of-speech categories.

Hence, to avoid introducing errors in the corpus, fixed expressions are handled as distinct tokens, as long as they were not written as attached forms, and clitics are not separated from the head words but analyzed with special labels at the syntactic level instead. Therefore, in the annotation scheme of the Uppsala Persian Dependency Treebank, apart from 48 dependency labels for basic relations there are 48 complex dependency labels to cover syntactic relations for words containing unsegmented clitics.

Fine-grained annotated data in treebanks normally provides a more complete grammatical analysis which in turn enhances the quality of parsing results. However, complex annotation may not always be beneficial and can impair automatic analysis (Mille et al., 2012; Jelínek, 2014). In this paper, we present different empirical studies where we systematically simplify the annotation schemes for part-of-speech tags and dependency relations within the treebank.

This paper is organized as follows: Section 2 briefly presents the *Uppsala Persian Dependency Treebank*. Section 3 introduces the experimental design. In Section 4, ParsPer is presented and evaluated. Finally, Section 5 concludes the paper.

2 The Uppsala Persian Dependency Treebank

The Uppsala Persian Dependency Treebank (UPDT)[3] (Seraji et al., 2013; Seraji, 2015)[4] is a dependency-based syntactically annotated corpus of contemporary Persian with annotation scheme based on dependency structure. The treebank consists of 6000 annotated and validated sentences, 151,671 tokens, and 15,692 word types with an average sentence length of 25 words. The data is extracted from the open source part-of-speech annotated and validated Uppsala Persian Corpus (UPC) with different genres, containing newspaper articles and texts on various topics such as culture, technology, fiction, and art.

[3]The treebank is freely available and can be downloaded from http://stp.lingfil.uu.se/~mojgan/UPDT.html

[4]For the updated version and a more comprehensive description of the *Uppsala Persian Dependency Treebank* guidelines see Seraji (2015, Chapter 5).

The treebank's syntactic annotation scheme is based on Stanford Typed Dependencies (STD) (de Marneffe and Manning, 2008) with extensions for Persian. This version of STD has a total of 96 dependency relations of which 48 (including 10 new additions to define the syntactic relations in Persian that could not be covered by the primary scheme developed for English) are used for indicating basic relations. The remaining 48 labels are complex, and are used to assign syntactic relations to words containing unsegmented clitics. The treebank is open source and freely available in CoNLL-format.[5]

3 Experimental Design

We carry out two types of experiments, experiments with different parsing representations (we define these as basic experiments henceforth) and experiments with different dependency parsers. For the experiments, the treebank is sequentially split into 10 parts, of which segments 1–8 are used for training (80%), 9 for development (10%), and 10 for test (10%). In the basic experiments, we train MaltParser on the training set and test on the development set. In the latter experiments, we train different parsers on the joint training and development sets (90%) and test on the test set.

We perform the basic experiments under four different conditions. We first experiment with all features and labels that already exist in the treebank. The results achieved by this experiment will be used as the baseline results. We then experiment with different relation sets by removing or merging various feature distinctions in the part-of-speech tagset and the syntactic annotation scheme. The experiments are designed as indicators to see if the conversions help or do not help the parser. In order to get a realistic picture of the parser performance, all these experiments will be performed using automatically generated part-of-speech tags.

All the above experiments will be carried out using MaltParser (Nivre et al., 2006). After discovering the best label set for both part-of-speech tags and dependency relations, we will experiment with other parsers such as MSTParser (McDonald et al., 2005), MateParsers (Bohnet, 2010; Bohnet and Nivre, 2012; Bohnet and Kuhn, 2012), and TurboParser (Martins et al., 2010) to find a state-of-the-art parser for Persian. We evaluate the parsers by experimenting with various feature set-

[5]http://ilk.uvt.nl/conll/#dataformat

tings when optional parameter settings for optimization are available and given by the parsers. However, only results for final settings are presented.

The selected state-of-the-art parser for Persian will be called *ParsPer*. For evaluation of ParsPer we first perform a parsing experiment on the treebank data. We then make an independent parsing evaluation by applying the parser on out-of-domain text and present the final results.

3.1 Basic Experiments with MaltParser

To evaluate the overall performance of the parser, we tune parameters to acquire the highest possible results. Thus, we experiment with different algorithms and feature settings to optimize MaltParser. To accomplish the optimization process, we apply MaltOptimizer (Ballesteros and Nivre, 2012). Parser accuracy is evaluated on automatically generated part-of-speech tags.

In order to generate automatic part-of-speech tags, we used the Persian part-of-speech tagger, *TagPer* (Seraji, 2015). However, for the treebank experiments we retrained the tagger to exclude the treebank data to avoid data overlap. The tagging evaluation performed by the new TagPer revealed an overall accuracy of 97.17%, when trained on 90% of the UPC and evaluated on the remaining 10%. The four different experiments include (1) an overall parsing evaluation on full treebank annotation (baseline), (2) an experiment without morphological features in the part-of-speech tagset, (3) an experiment without fine-grained LVC labels, and (4) an experiment without complex labels.

3.1.1 Baseline: Full Treebank Annotation

In this parsing evaluation we trained MaltParser on the UPDT with full part-of-speech tags and all existing dependency relations. The experiment resulted in a labeled attachment score of 78.84% and an unlabeled attachment score of 83.07%. The results will be used as the baseline for subsequent experiments. Labeled recall and precision for the 20 most frequently dependency relations are presented in Table 1.

The results vary greatly across the relation types, with recall ranging from 53.75% for direct object (dobj) to 97.12% for object of a preposition (pobj), and precision varying between 55.37% for clausal complement (ccomp) to 95.57% for object of a preposition (pobj). As indicated in Table 1

DepRel	*Freq. (%)*	*R (%)*	*P (%)*
pobj	16237	**97.12**	**95.57**
poss	16067	89.96	79.28
prep	15643	76.00	74.49
punct	13442	75.04	76.10
amod	9211	90.64	90.72
nsubj	8653	67.60	66.26
conj	8629	67.78	67.78
cc	7657	78.34	77.81
root	5918	81.21	79.87
cop	4427	66.22	73.51
dobj-lvc	4185	91.63	92.06
advmod	4157	70.27	65.82
ccomp	4021	63.54	**55.37**
det	3929	93.79	91.71
dobj	3723	**53.75**	57.01
nn	3339	57.28	79.73
num	2872	92.00	92.00
acc	2535	69.76	69.48
aux	2287	92.14	90.95
complm	2022	77.71	78.61

Table 1: Labeled recall and precision on the development set for the 20 most frequent dependency types in the UPDT, when *MaltParser* is trained on the full treebank annotation. DepRel = Dependency Relations, Freq. = Frequency, R = Recall, P = Precision.

the results for labeled recall and precision for core arguments such as nominal subject (nsubj) and direct object (dobj) are slightly low. This can be explained by the fact that, despite the SOV structure in Persian, subjects and objects may shift order in a sentence. As Persian is a pro-drop language, an object might be placed at the beginning of a sentence (with or without the accusative marker rā) and the subject might either be positioned next or be completely omitted in the sentence but instead be inflected as a personal ending on the verb. There are further cases when subject and object are both omitted but appear as personal endings on the verb, as Persian, syntactically, contains a vast amount of dropped subjects and objects. In all cases, it is hard for the system to identify the correct subject and object in the sentence, which may lead to the dependency relations *nsubj* and *dobj* frequently being interchanged or not being correctly identified. The dependency relation noun compound modifier (nn) is another relation with low recall. We further discovered that the parser had often selected the label possession modifier (poss) instead of *nn*. This can be explained by their usage similarities in the way that both labels are always governed by a noun and used for nouns. The possession modifier (poss) is applied to genitive complements and the compound modifier (nn) to noun compounds (and proper names). However, this difference is not marked in the part-of-speech annotation. Moreover, the number of occurrences of the label *poss* in the training data is higher than the label *nn*, therefore, it is easier for the parser to identify the structure as the dependency relation *poss* than *nn*.

3.1.2 Coarse-Grained Part-of-Speech Tags

The second empirical study was performed in order to select the best part-of-speech encoding set for parsing. In this experiment, we merged all morphological features with their main categories. In this way, feature distinctions that existed for adjective, adverb, noun, and verb were all discarded. For instance, *ADJ_CMPR, ADJ_INO, ADJ_SUP*, and *ADJ_VOC* were merged with *ADJ*, and so forth. Hence, we ran MaltParser on UPDT with 15 auto part-of-speech tags instead of 31. Parsing evaluation revealed the scores of 79.24% for labeled attachment and 83.45% for unlabeled attachment. Comparing the results to the ones obtained by the baseline experiment shows that MaltParser performs better on coarse-grained part-of-speech tags. Table 2 shows the results for labeled recall and precision for the 20 most frequent dependency labels in the UPDT. Again, object of a preposition (pobj) shows the best results with 97.07% for recall and 95.72% for precision, and direct object (dobj) shows the lowest recall and precision, with 52.55% and 55.56%, respectively.

Comparing the recall and precision results of the 20 most frequent dependency labels to the baseline, we see an improvement in many dependency relations. The highest improvement is indicated by the relation clause complement (ccomp) with 3.75% enhancement for recall and 6.3% for precision. The dependency relation clause complement (ccomp), in the treebank, is assigned for complements that are presented by verbs, nouns, or adjectives. Using coarse-grained part-of-speech tags for verbs, nouns, and adjectives leads to higher results. This further assists the relation complementizer (complm) that always introduces a clausal complement (ccomp) achieving 2.29% higher recall and 3.74% higher precision. To follow up the tables, copula (cop) is also one of the dependency relations that shows good improvements specifically for precision, resulting in 1.61% higher recall and 4.82% higher precision. As comparison goes on, results show an improvement for most of the dependency labels. However,

DepRel	*Freq. (%)*	*R (%)*	*P (%)*
pobj	16237	**97.07**	**95.72**
poss	16067	90.18	79.43
prep	15643	76.85	75.57
punct	13442	76.07	76.80
amod	9211	88.69	90.37
nsubj	8653	68.62	64.55
conj	8629	68.85	68.28
cc	7657	78.88	78.14
root	5918	81.38	80.17
cop	4427	67.83	78.33
dobj-lvc	4185	90.23	91.94
advmod	4157	73.31	66.16
ccomp	4021	67.29	61.67
det	3929	94.35	92.78
dobj	3723	**52.55**	**55.56**
nn	3339	57.04	82.46
num	2872	92.92	91.79
acc	2535	69.35	70.20
aux	2287	92.14	89.41
complm	2022	80.00	82.35

Table 2: Labeled recall and precision on the development set for the 20 most frequent dependency types in the UPDT, when *MaltParser* is trained on the UPDT with coarse-grained auto part-of-speech tags. DepRel = Dependency Relations, Freq. = Frequency, R = Recall, P = Precision.

coarse-grained part-of-speech tags have a negative impact on some dependency labels. This is more or less visible in the dependency relations object of a preposition (pobj), adjectival modifier (amod), nominal subject (nsubj), direct object in light verb construction (dobj-lvc), direct object (dobj), noun compound modifier (nn), and auxiliary (aux) which may due to the lack of various distinctions of nouns, adjectives, and verbs. For instance, plural nouns never appear in complex predicates and as seen in the tables direct object in light verb construction (dobj-lvc) has a drop with 1.40% and 0.12% for recall and precision, respectively.

3.1.3 Coarse-Grained LVC Relations

We carried out this experiment by converting all variations of light verb constructions such as *acomp-lvc*, *dobj-lvc*, *nsubj-lvc*, and *prep-lvc* to merely *lvc*. The evaluation showed that the parser achieved a labeled attachment score of 79.46% and an unlabeled attachment score of 83.52%. With respect to the fact that the labeled attachment score is based on the number of correct dependency labels and correct head, the LAS results obtained in this experiment cannot directly be compared to the baseline results, as the two experiments use different label sets. Therefore, output

DepRel	*Freq. (%)*	*R (%)*	*P (%)*
pobj	16237	**97.45**	**95.89**
poss	16067	89.91	79.65
prep	15643	75.04	73.88
punct	13442	76.22	76.72
amod	9211	89.90	90.32
nsubj	8653	70.30	66.92
conj	8629	67.66	67.90
cc	7657	78.88	78.14
root	5918	82.05	81.23
cop	4427	68.10	78.64
lvc	5427	85.92	90.54
advmod	4157	72.64	68.04
ccomp	4021	64.08	57.18
det	3929	94.07	92.76
dobj	3723	**55.26**	**56.79**
nn	3339	58.01	83.28
num	2872	92.92	92.07
acc	2535	70.97	70.97
aux	2287	92.58	92.17
complm	2022	80.57	81.50

Table 3: Labeled recall and precision on the development set for the 20 most frequent dependency types in the UPDT, when *MaltParser* is trained on the treebank with fine-grained auto part-of-speech tags only one light verb construction. DepRel = Dependency Relations, Freq. = Frequency, R = Recall, P = Precision.

differing in this regard can only be evaluated unlabeled. Thus, the unlabeled attachment score that measures the number of tokens with correct head can directly be compared with the baseline. This accordingly means that removing the LVC distinctions from the treebank helps the parser to obtain higher accuracy. As shown in Table 3, the highest recall and precision scores are shown by object of a preposition (pobj), with 97.45% and 95.89% respectively. The lowest recall and precision scores are shown by direct object (dobj) with 55.26% and 56.79%, respectively.

Compared to the baseline results, recall and precision have decreased for the dependency relations prepositional modifier (prep) and adjectival modifier (amod). This can probably be explained by the fact that merging LVC variations makes it harder for the system to select, for instance, a preposition as a prepositional modifier (prep) or an lvc, as well as an adjectival modifier (amod) or an lvc. A striking finding from the results is the outcome achieved by the conversion of different light verb constructions to *lvc*, resulting in 85.92% for recall and 90.54% for precision. Moreover Table 4 shows recall and precision for different types of LVC relations from the baseline experiment when we applied the fine-grained annotated treebank as well as recall and precision of the dependency label *lvc* from Experiment 3 when we tested the treebank with fine-grained part-of-speech tags and merged LVC relations. The entries in the table further present information about frequency of *acomp-lvc*, *dobj-lvc*, *nsubj-lvc*, and *prep-lvc* in Experiment 1[6] as well as the frequency of the label *lvc* in Experiment 3. As presented in Table 4, results for recall and precision are lower than the baseline results for direct object in light verb construction (dobj-lvc) but higher than the results obtained by the adjectival complement in light verb construction (acomp-lvc) and the prepositional modifier in light verb construction (prep-lvc). However, we should be reminded that the label *lvc* covers all types of LVC relations and, as mentioned earlier, it is harder for the system to select a proper label to tokens that sometimes participate in LVC relations and sometimes participate in similar relations to LVC labels such as prepositions that occasionally appear either as the dependency relations prepositional modifier (prep) or as the prepositional modifier in light verb construction (prep-lvc). On the other hand, recall and/or precision for the core arguments nominal subject (nsubj) and direct object (dobj) are improved. In other words, recall is improved by 2.7% and 1.51% for nominal subject (nsubj) and direct object (dobj), respectively. The dependency relation root is further improved by 0.84% for recall and 1.36% for precision. Thus, this merging might be a disadvantage for the relation prepositional modifier (prep) but favors other relations for instance the nominal subject (nsubj). Although providing recall and precision for each and every LVC distinction on a label-by-label basis is most informative, because the label *lvc* covers all types of the LVC variations, we cannot directly compare the results of each with the results obtained by the dependency relation *lvc* in Experiment 3, unless we calculate an overall recall and precision score for all the LVC types in Experiment 1. The results of such statistical calculations revealed an overall recall and precision of 85.55% and 89.16%. Hence, the overall results show that having various types of LVC distinctions in the treebank do not contribute to higher parsing performance.

[6]Given the low frequency of the LVC relations *acomp-lvc*, *nsubj-lvc*, and *prep-lvc* in the treebank, their recall and precision are not presented together with the 20 most frequent dependency types in Table 1.

DepRel	*Freq.*	*R (%)*	*P (%)*
acomp-lvc	681	80.56	78.38
dobj-lvc	4185	91.63	92.06
nsubj-lvc	7	–	–
prep-lvc	554	46.88	78.95
lvc	5427	85.92	90.54

Table 4: Recall and precision for LVC relations with fine-grained predicted part-of-speech tags in Experiments 1 and 3. DepRel = Dependency Relations, Freq. = Frequency, R = Recall, P = Precision.

3.1.4 No Complex Relations

We additionally experimented with modifying all complex syntactic relations that were used for complex unsegmented word forms (words containing unsegmented clitics). In this experiment, all complex dependency relations, containing 48 labels, were merged with basic Persian STD relations, containing 48 labels. The evaluation revealed a labeled attachment score of 79.63% and an unlabeled attachment score of 83.42%. As noted earlier, the results from labeled attachment score do not allow a direct comparison with the ones presented for baseline as the two experiments use different label sets. Hence, the comparison evaluation is considered for the unlabeled attachment score that shows an improvement in parsing performance when simplifying the complex dependency relations. This improvement is understandable as some complex relations[7] such as *ccomp\cpobj*, *ccomp\nsubj*, and so forth, occur only once in the treebank and it is almost impossible for a data-driven machine to learn such rare cases from the given data.

As presented in Table 5, there are variations in recall, ranging from 54.14% for direct object (dobj) to 97.47% for object of a preposition (pobj), and in precision, varying between 56.31% for clausal complement (ccomp) to 96.90% for object of a preposition (pobj). Compared to the baseline, recall and precision for the dependency relations adjectival modifier (amod) and complementizer (complm) have dropped in the figures. The relations *root* and noun compound modifier (nn) as well as punctuation (punct) and auxiliary (aux) further show a decline in recall and precision respectively. This can probably be explained by the way it has been annotated for the complex labels.

[7]Complex relations in the treebank are marked by backslash (\) if they precede the segment carrying the main function and a forward slash (/) if they follow it.

DepRel	*Freq. (%)*	*R (%)*	*P (%)*
pobj	16412	**97.47**	**96.90**
poss	16268	90.27	79.59
prep	15734	76.52	75.62
punct	13442	75.04	75.76
amod	9277	89.75	90.59
nsubj	8847	68.40	66.56
conj	8753	68.63	69.28
cc	7657	79.16	78.41
root	6010	81.17	80.90
cop	4427	66.76	74.55
dobj-lvc	4204	90.76	92.25
advmod	4168	71.62	67.52
ccomp	4105	64.10	**56.31**
det	3929	94.07	93.28
dobj	3862	**54.14**	57.19
nn	3340	56.31	81.98
num	2872	93.23	93.23
acc	2535	71.37	71.08
aux	2287	92.14	90.56
complm	2022	77.14	78.03

Table 5: Labeled recall and precision on the development set for the 20 most frequent dependency types in the UPDT, when *MaltParser* is trained on the treebank with fine-grained auto part-of-speech tags and only basic dependency relations. DepRel = Dependency Relations, Freq. = Frequency, R = Recall, P = Precision.

Removing the information provided by the these relations makes it harder for the parser to achieve high results when assigning these labels. However, the parser shows higher scores for the remaining dependency relations.

3.1.5 Best Parsing Representation

In the recently presented experiments we systematically simplified the annotation schemes for part-of-speech tags and dependency labels. Table 6 presents a summary of the 4 basic experiments we performed. Although the results in the table are presented with labeled and unlabeled attachment score as well as label accuracy score, figures obtained as labeled attachment in Experiments 3 and 4 are not comparable with the one presented in the baseline results, as each performed study uses different dependency relation sets. To conclude the four experiments:

- Using coarse-grained part-of-speech tags in the dependency representation improves parsing performance without losing any information. By using the part-of-speech tagger *TagPer* we can recreate and restore this information at the end once the parsing is done. Thus, fined-grained part-of-speech tags can still be in the output.

Basic Ex.	*LAS (%)*	*UAS (%)*	*LA (%)*
Baseline	78.84	83.07	88.48
CPOS	79.24	83.45	88.43
1 LVC	79.46	**83.52**	88.86
Basic DepRel	**79.63**	83.42	**89.09**

Table 6: Labeled and unlabeled attachment scores, and label accuracy in the model selection resulted from 4 empirical studies when *MaltParser* was trained on UPDT with different simplifications of annotation schemes in predicted part-of-speech tagset and dependency relations. Basic Ex. = Basic Experiments, Baseline = Experiment with a fine-grained annotated treebank, CPOS = Experiment with coarser-grained part-of-speech tags and fine-grained dependency relations, 1LVC = Experiment with fine-grained part-of-speech tags and dependency relations free from distinctive features in light verb construction, and Basic DepRel = Experiment with fine-grained part-of-speech tags and merely basic dependency relations.

- The studies additionally show that simplifying the representation of light verb constructions helps the parser to perform better without loss of important information. In other words, by using coarse LVC, the results become less specific and less informative only with respect to the LVC construction, and show better parsing performance. Furthermore, the *lvc* specification at the end can mostly be recovered from the part-of-speech tags in the output.

- Using merely basic relations might provide a marginal improvement but this is not a sufficient justification to remove them, because by eliminating the complex labels we lose essential information that cannot be recovered by the tagger and this affects the quality of parsing analysis. Applying the treebank with complex relations provides a richer grammatical analysis that boost the quality of parsing results.

These results provided us with a valuable insight about how different morphosyntactic parameters in data influence the parsing analysis. The studies also brought us to the point of how we can select the best configuration for further experiments. In other words, we will use a representation with coarse-grained part-of-speech tags, single LVC representation, and fine-grained dependency relations containing both basic and complex labels (96 labels).

3.2 Experiments with Different Parsers

This part is designed for estimating the performance of different parsers on the best performing data representations selected by MaltParser in the baseline experiments. Hence, we set up the data with the best achieved parameters which are using the automatically generated coarse-grained part-of-speech tags with a single LVC label and the fine-grained dependency relations consisting of 96 basic and complex labels. The treebank is further organized with a different split than in the basic experiments. In other words, we train the parser on the joint training and development sets (90%) and test on the test set (10%). We will experiment with MaltParser (Nivre et al., 2006), MSTParser (McDonald et al., 2005), MateParsers (Bohnet, 2010; Bohnet and Nivre, 2012), and TurboParser (Martins et al., 2010).

For evaluating MaltParser, we used *Nivre's algorithms* as the algorithms were the best parsing algorithms offered by MaltOptimizer during the previous experiments. The parser resulted in scores of 79.40% and 83.47% for labeled and unlabeled attachment, respectively.

For evaluating MSTParser, we used the second-order model with projective parsing as this setting had presented the highest results in the earlier parameter tuning experiments. The parser presented the results of 77.79% for labeled and 83.45% for unlabeled attachment scores.

For experimenting with MateParsers, we trained the graph-based and transition-based parsers on the UPDT with the best parameters selected. The results of Mate experiments showed that the graph-based parser outperformed the transition-based parser, resulting in 82.58% for labeled and 86.69% for unlabeled attachment scores.

For experimenting with TurboParser, we trained the second-order non-projective parser with features for arcs, consecutive siblings and grandparents, using the AD^3 algorithm as a decoder. We adapted the *full* setting as the setting had performed best with our earlier parameter-tuning experiments. The *full* setting enables arc-factored, consecutive sibling, grandparent, arbitrary sibling, head bigram, grand-sibling (third-order), and tri-sibling (third-order) parts. The parser showed the results of 80.57% for labeled and 85.32% for un-

Evaluations	*LAS (%)*	*UAS (%)*	*LA (%)*
MaltParser	79.40	83.47	88.72
MSTParser	77.79	83.45	87.11
MateGraph	**82.58**	**86.69**	**90.55**
MateTrans.	81.72	85.94	89.87
TurboParser	80.57	85.32	88.93

Table 7: Best results given by different parsers when trained on UPDT with auto part-of-speech tags, 1LVC, CompRel in the model assessment. MateGraph. = Mate graph-based, MateTrans. = Mate transition-based

labeled attachment scores.

As shown in Table 7 the graph-based parser in the Mate tools achieves the highest results for Persian. The developed parser will be treated as the state-of-the-art parser for the language and will be called *ParsPer*. The parser will undergo further evaluations which will be presented more in detail in the next section.

4 Dependency Parser for Persian: ParsPer

As results of the previous experiments showed, the graph-based MateParser outperformed MaltParser, MSTParser, and TurboParser obtaining scores of 82.58% and 86.69% for labeled and unlabeled attachment. This means that we need to train the graph-based MateParser, this time, on the entire UPDT with the selected configuration. The developed parser is called *ParsPer*.[8] It is released as a freely available tool for parsing of Persian and is open source under GNU General Public License. The parser will further be evaluated in the next subsection.

4.1 The Evaluation of the ParsPer

To evaluate the performance of the ParsPer we made an independent parsing evaluation by running the parser on out-of-domain text. For this, we used texts from the web-based journal *www.hamshahri.com*. We downloaded multiple texts based on different genres and then randomly picked 100 sentences containing 2778 tokens with an average sentence length of 28 tokens to develop a test set. As our experiment involved some manual work we opted for a small-sized sample to make the evaluation task more feasible. We first created a gold file by manually normalizing the internal word boundaries and character sets and then segmenting the text into sentence and token levels. We then manually annotated the file with part-of-speech and dependency information using the same part-of-speech and dependency scheme that ParsPer was built on to be served as gold.

In this task we performed three different parsing evaluations. First we applied the parser on the automatically normalized, tokenized and tagged text. This is the main experiment in the ParsPer evaluation that also indicates the performance of automatic processing of Persian texts at various levels. Next, we performed two more experiments with the 100 randomly selected sentences in order to analyze the results in a more nuanced way, by experimenting on the sentences when they are manually normalized and tokenized but automatically tagged and then, when they are manually normalized, tokenized, and tagged.

To create our test set for our first experiment, we automatically normalized the 100 sentences using the Persian normalizer *PrePer*,[9] segmented it with *SeTPer*,[10] and tagged with *TagPer*.[11] A comprehensive description of the tools *PrePer*, *SeTPer*, and *TagPer* are given in Seraji (2015, Chapter 4). Then we parsed the automatically tokenized and tagged text with ParsPer. Since the sentences were automatically tokenized, contained 10 tokens fewer than the gold file (the number of tokens in the gold file were 2788).[12] Therefore we could not directly present labeled and unlabeled attachment scores. However, instead, we present labeled recall and precision as well as unlabeled recall and precision. The parsing evaluation revealed a labeled recall and precision of 73.52% and 73.79%, and an unlabeled recall and precision of 81.99% and 82.28%, respectively. As could be expected, the results for labeled recall and precision are low. This is due to the fact that apart from incorrect tokens in the automatically tokenized file there are incorrect part-of-speech tags made by the tagger TagPer that have had a negative impact on the results.

Subsequently, we automatically parsed the manually normalized, tokenized, but automatically tagged text and compared the parsing results with the manually parsed gold text. By this ex-

[8] http://stp.lingfil.uu.se/~mojgan/parsper-mate.html

[9] http://stp.lingfil.uu.se/~mojgan/preper.html

[10] http://stp.lingfil.uu.se/~mojgan/setper.html

[11] http://stp.lingfil.uu.se/~mojgan/tagper.html

[12] In addition to the 10 fewer tokens, there were two more tokens that were not successfully been normalized by the PrePer in the normalization process and looked differently.

Evaluations	*LR* (%)	*LP* (%)	*UR* (%)	*UP* (%)
AS+AT+AP	73.52	73.79	81.99	82.28
MS+AT+AP	78.50	78.50	86.27	86.27
MS+MT+AP	78.76	78.76	86.12	86.12

Table 8: The evaluation of the *ParsPer* when tested on 100 randomly selected sentences from the web-based journal *Hamshahri*. LR = Labeled Recall, LP = Labeled Precision, UR = Unlabeled Recall, UP = Unlabeled Precision, AS = Automatically Segmented, AT = Automatically Tagged, AP = Automatically Parsed, MS = Manually Segmented, and MT = Manually Tagged.

periment, we wanted to isolate the impact of tagging errors. The evaluation resulted in labeled and unlabeled attachment scores (recall and precision) of 78.50% and 86.27% on the test set with 100 sentences and 2788 tokens. As the results indicate, the unlabeled attachment score is close to the unlabeled attachment score obtained by the parser when evaluated on in-domain text. Furthermore, the unlabeled attachment score is 7.77% higher than the labeled attachment score. This may partly be due to fact that the structural variation for the head nodes is lower than the variation for labels. Moreover, we have a firm structure for the head nodes in the syntactic annotation when invariably choosing content words as head position. This solid structure in turn makes it easier for the parser to learn that after repeatedly seeing it. Hence, the parser assigns the head nodes more accurately than the combinations of head and label. This does not mean that it does not exist a consistent structure for the dependency relations. What we mean is that the number of occurrence of certain cases for dependency relations may not be as many as the number of repeated cases for head structures. This might be perceived as a sparseness by the parser which can directly affect the labeled attachment score. Moreover, the syntactic (non)complexity in the data can have a direct impact on the parser performance.

Finally, we automatically parsed the manually normalized, tokenized, and tagged text and compared the parsing with the manually parsed gold file. The evaluation resulted in a straightforward labeled and unlabeled attachment scores of 78.76% and 86.12% on the test set with 100 sentences and 2788 tokens. The same kind of pattern as in the previous experiment was further found here. In other words, we see nearly similar gap of 7.36% between the labeled and unlabeled attachment scores. Table 8 shows results from different evaluations of the ParsPer.

The comparison of Experiments 1, 2, and 3 shows that tokenization is a greater problem than tagging for syntactic parsing. Whereas a perfectly tokenized text with tagging errors degrades parsing results by less than 1%, errors in tokenization may decrease parsing accuracy as much as 5%. To some extent, this is probably due to additional tagging errors caused by tokenization errors. It is nevertheless clear that tokenization errors disrupt the syntactic structure more than tagging errors do. Adding variations of writing styles (as mentioned earlier) on top of this triggers variations in the tokenization process, which in turn leads to the parser being unable to realize similar sentences with different tokenizations. However, this normally happens when the parser is not familiar with the tokens (or the order of how tokens are represented) in the sentence, which is due to the fact that the structure is not prevalent enough in the training data.

It might be possible to improve the parsing performance by adding to or modifying the part-of-speech tag set as well as eliminating or modifying some structures in the syntactic annotation scheme that are not properly favor the parser. Moreover, one can use joint segmentation and tagging similar to that made for Chinese (Zhang and Clark, 2010). However, this matter will remain for our future research.

5 Conclusion

In this paper, we have presented an open source dependency parser for Persian based on the graph-based parser in the Mate Tools. The dependency parser is called ParsPer and developed on the best performing data representation of the Uppsala Persian Dependency Treebank, selected by MaltParser. The parser resulted in a labeled attachment score of 82.58% and unlabeled attachment score of 86.69%

References

Ballesteros, Miguel and Joakim Nivre (2012). "MaltOptimizer: A System for MaltParser Optimization". In: *Proceedings of the 8th International Conference on Language Resources and Evaluation (LREC)*, pp. 833–841.

Böhmová, Alena, Jan Hajič, Eva Hajičocá, and Barbora Hladká (2003). "The Prague dependency treebank". In: *Treebanks*. Springer Netherlands, pp. 103–127.

Bohnet, Bernd (2010). "Top Accuracy and Fast Dependency Parsing is not a Contradiction". In: *Coling '10*, pp. 89–97.

Bohnet, Bernd and Jonas Kuhn (2012). "The Best of Both Worlds: A Graph-based Completion Model for Transition-Based Parsers". In: *EACL '12*, pp. 77–87.

Bohnet, Bernd and Joakim Nivre (2012). "A Transition-Based System for Joint Part-of-Speech Tagging and Labeled Non-Projective Dependency Parsing". In: *EMNLP-CoNLL '12*, pp. 1455–1465.

de Marneffe, Marie-Catherine and Christopher D. Manning (2008). "The Stanford Typed Dependencies Representation". In: *COLING'08*, pp. 1–8.

Foth, Kilian, Arne Köhn, Niels Beuck, and Wolfgang Menzel (2014). "Because size does matter: The Hamburg dependency treebank". In: *LREC '14*, pp. 2326–2333.

Haverinen, Katri, Timo Viljanen, Veronika Laippala, Samuel Kohonen, Filip Ginter, and Tapio Salakoski (2010). "Treebanking Finnish". In: *TLT '10*, pp. 79–90.

Jelínek, Tomáš (2014). "Improvements to Dependency Parsing Using Automatic Simplification of Data". In: *LREC'14*, pp. 73–77.

Kromann, Matthias T. (2003). "The Danish Dependency Treebank and the DTAG Treebank Tool". In: *TLT '03*. Brown University Press, pp. 217–220.

Martins, André F. T., Noah A. Smith, Eric P. Xing, Pedro M. Q. Aguiar, and Mário A. T. Figueiredo (2010). "Turbo Parsers: Dependency Parsing by Approximate Variational Inference". In: *EMNLP '10*, pp. 34–44.

McDonald, Ryan, Fernando Pereira, Kiril Ribarov, and Jan Hajič (2005). "Non-Projective Dependency Parsing Using Spanning Tree Algorithms". In: *HLT-EMNLP '05*, pp. 523–530.

Mille, Simon, Alicia Burga, Gabriela Ferraro, and Leo Wanner (2012). "How Does the Granularity of an Annotation Scheme Influence Dependency Parsing Performance?" In: *COLING '12*, pp. 839–852.

Nivre, Joakim, Johan Hall, and Jens Nilsson (2006). "MaltParser: A Data-Driven Parser-Generator for Dependency Parsing". In: *LREC '06*, pp. 2216–2219.

Seraji, Mojgan (2015). "Morphosyntactic Corpora and Tools for Persian". PhD Thesis. Studia Linguistica Upsaliensia 16.

Seraji, Mojgan, Carina Jahani, Beáta Megyesi, and Joakim Nivre (2013). *The Uppsala Persian Dependency Treebank Annotation Guidelines*. Technical Report. Department of Linguistics and Philology, Uppsala.

Vincze, Veronika, Dóra Szauter, Attila Almási, György Móra, Zoltán Alexin, and János Csirik (2010). "Hungarian Dependency Treebank". In: *LREC '10*, pp. 1855–1862.

Zhang, Yue and Stephen Clark (2010). "A fast decoder for joint word segmentation and POS-tagging using a single discriminative model". In: *EMNLP '10*, pp. 843–852.

Does Universal Dependencies need a parsing representation? An investigation of English

Natalia Silveira
Stanford University
Department of Linguistics
Stanford, CA
natalias@stanford.edu

Christopher Manning
Stanford University
Department of Linguistics and
Department of Computer Science
Stanford, CA
manning@stanford.edu

Abstract

This paper investigates the potential of defining a parsing representation for English data in Universal Dependencies, a crosslingual dependency scheme. We investigate structural transformations that change the choices of headedness in the dependency tree. The transformations make auxiliaries, copulas, subordinating conjunctions and prepositions heads, while in UD they are dependents of a lexical head. We show experimental results for the performance of MaltParser, a data-driven transition-based parser, on the product of each transformation. While some transformed representations favor performance, inverting the transformations to obtain UD for the final product propagates errors, in part due to the nature of lexical-head representations. This prevents the transformations from being profitably used to improve parser performance in that representation.

1 Introduction

There is a considerable amount of research suggesting that the choice of syntactic representation can have an impact on parsing performance, in constituency (Klein and Manning, 2003; Bikel, 2004; Petrov et al., 2006; Bengoetxea and Gojenola, 2009) as well as dependency (Nilsson et al., 2007; Nilsson et al., 2006; Schwartz et al., 2012) parsing. Recently, this has led designers of dependency representations (Marneffe et al., 2014) to suggest the use of an alternative parsing representation to support the performance of statistical learners.

While it is clear that, at the limit, trivializing a linguistic representation in order to make it easier to parse is undesirable – for example, by making each word depend on the previous one – there certainly exists a variety of choice points in which more than one type of design is defensible. In the dependency tradition, semantic and syntactic criteria have been recognized to motivate headedness, and there are well-known examples of conflicts between those criteria (Nilsson et al., 2006). Here we investigate four syntactic constructions that are *loci* of such conflicts: verb groups, prepositional phrases, copular clauses and subordinate clauses. The baseline representation is Universal Dependencies (Nivre et al., 2015), a multilingual dependency scheme that strongly prefers lexical heads. For each target construction, structural transformations are defined that demote the lexical head and make it dependent on a functional head.

We show experimental results for the performance of MaltParser, a data-driven transition-based parser, on the product of each transformation. While some transformed representations are in fact easier to learn, error propagation when inverting the transformations to obtain UD prevents them from being profitably used to improve parser performance in that representation.

2 Related work

Schwartz et al. (2012) is a systematic study of how representation choices in dependency annotation schemes affect their learnability for parsing. The choice points investigated, much like in the current paper, relate to the issue of headedness. The experiments look at functional versus content heads in six constructions: (a) coordination structures (where the head can be a conjunction or one of the conjuncts), (2) infinitives (the verb or the marker *to*), (3) nominal phrases (the determiner, if any, or the noun), (4) nominal compounds (the first noun or the last), (5) prepositional phrases (the preposition or its complement) and (6) verb groups (the main verb, or the highest modal, if any). Each combination of these binary

Proceedings of the Third International Conference on Dependency Linguistics (Depling 2015), pages 310–319,
Uppsala, Sweden, August 24–26 2015.

choices is tested with 5 different parsers, which represent different paradigms in dependency parsing.The edges in the representation are unlabeled, unlike the common practice in NLP. The results show a learnability bias towards a conjunct in (1), a noun in (3), and a preposition in (5) in all the parsers. Furthermore, a bias towards the modal heads in (6) and towards the head-initial representation in (4) is seen with some parsers. No significant results are found for (2).

In Ivanova et al. (2013), the authors run a set of experiments that provide a comparison of (1) 3 dependency schemes, (2) 3 data-driven dependency parsers and (3) 2 approaches to POS-tagging in a parsing pipeline. The comparison that is relevant here is (1). The dependency representations compared are the basic version of Stanford Dependencies (Marneffe and Manning, 2008), and two versions of the CoNLL Syntactic Dependencies (Johansson and Nugues, 2007). For all parsers and in most experiments (which explore several pipelines with different POS-tagging strategies), SD is easier to label (i.e., label accuracy scores are higher) and CoNLL is easier to structure (i.e., unlabeled attachment scores are higher). In terms of LAS, MaltParser (Nivre et al., 2007) performs best of the 3 parsers with SD, and MSTParser (McDonald et al., 2006) performs best with CoNLL.

In Nilsson et al. (2006), the authors investigate the effects of two types of input transformation on the performance of MaltParser. Those two types are: structural transformations, of the same nature of those investigated in the present paper; and projectivization transformations, that allow non-projective structures to be represented in a way that can be learned by projective-only parsing algorithms, and then transformed into the non-projective representation at the end. Of interest here are the structural transformations, which in their work target coordinated phrases and verb groups. The data and baseline representation come from the Prague Dependency Treebank (PDT) version 1.0 (Hajic et al. 2001). The PDT's representation of coordination is so different from UD's that the results cannot be expected to carry over. The verb group transformation, on the other hand, is almost identical to the auxhead transformation proposed here. In the PDT, auxiliary verbs never have dependents. Other dependents of the main verb are attached to the first verb of the verb group if they occur anywhere before the last verb; otherwise, they are attached to the left verb. In the reverse transformation, all dependents of auxiliaries go back to the main verb. All the transformations reported in the paper prove helpful for the parser. In the case of verb groups, which is of particular interest here, the labeled attachment score goes up by 0.14% (in a test set of 126k tokens).

Following up on the previous paper, (Nilsson et al., 2007) investigates the same transformations applied to different datasets and under distinct parsing algorithms, to understand if they generalize across languages and parsing strategies. The representations for the different languages studied are similar to the PDT's representation. With respect to the structural transformations, the authors find that there are, again, small gains from converting the representations of coordination and verb groups. However, in their experiments, graph-based MSTParser, unlike transition-based MaltParser, does not perform better on the transformed input.

3 Background

3.1 Universal Dependencies

The baseline representation to which transformations are applied in this set of experiments is the UD representation, which was developed to allow for parallel annotation across languages. It is based on Stanford Dependencies (Marneffe and Manning, 2008), a widely used representation for English. In order to preserve some flexibility for language-specific annotation, UD has a two-layer architecture. The universal layer is common to all languages, and it aims to capture phenomena at a level that highlights crosslinguistic commonalities. However, the need for parallelism with other languages often imposes a high level of abstraction on the annotation, which might be undesirable when working in a monolingual setting. For that reason, the representation can be extended with language-specific relations as needed, via inheritance. This makes it straightforward to informatively harmonize annotations across languages, since they already use the same dependency types at the universal level. At the same time, it allows enough expressivity for capturing detail that may be important for a specific language, but difficult to port to others.

UD inherits from SD the concern with usefulness for relation extraction, in addition to crosslinguistic parallelism. Both of those motivate a radical stance on headedness: lexical heads are adopted across the board. The idea is that, because syntax competes with morphology, grammatical functions that are performed by function words in one language may be performed by bound morphemes in another. If those function words are allowed to enter contentful relations (such as predicate-argument relations), the structures assigned in the presence of such words will be very different than the structures assigned when those words give way to bound morphemes. This has been the primary motivation for the most important change from SD to UD for English, which is the new treatment of prepositional phrases. While in SD a functional-head representation was adopted, with prepositions heading nouns, in UD a lexical representation is adopted, and the complement in the prepositional phrase depends on the preposition. This allows more parallelism with languages in which the functions of some English prepositions (such as *of*) are performed by case morphemes.

3.2 The English Web Treebank corpus

The corpus used in all of this paper's experiments is the UD-annotated English Web Treebank (EWT) corpus (Silveira et al., 2014). The EWT consists of 254,830 word tokens (16,624 sentences) of text, and was released by the Linguistic Data Consortium in 2012. The text is manually annotated for sentence- and word-level tokenization, as well as part-of-speech tags and constituency structure in the Penn Treebank scheme. The data comprises five domains of web text: blog posts, BBC newsgroup threads, emails from the Enron corpus, Amazon reviews and answers from Yahoo! answers.

This corpus was hand-annotated with dependency relations following an evolving version of Stanford Dependencies. The UD annotation was obtained from the SD annotation, partly via automatic conversions, and partly via manual revisions. The result is the first human-checked large-scale gold standard for syntactic dependency annotation of English text. The first version annotated with the UD representation was released in 2015 (Nivre et al., 2015)[1].

[1] http://universaldependencies.github.io/docs/

4 Structural transformations

All the transformations studied in this paper have the same underlying structure: they involve a content word which is a head by semantic criteria, and a functional word which is a head by syntactic criteria. They reverse those heads' roles in relation to each other, and in relation to the outer structure in which they are embedded. One head is the promoted head, and it stands in an appropriate relation with some element from outside the construction (e.g., *dobj* in the case of a noun phrase). The other (candidate) head is the demoted head, and it should be attached to the promoted counterpart. So we have:

(1) a.

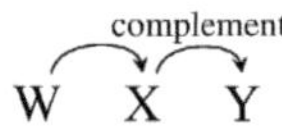

b.

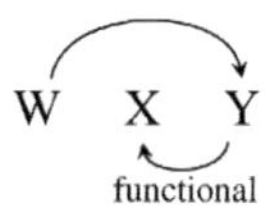

In the simplest case, transformations of this kind can be inverted with no loss, which adds interest: there is no need to allow the parser to orient design decisions. The linguistic representation can be transformed for parser training, and the parser output can go through the inverse transformation for general use. (This is the approach taken in Nilsson et al. (2006).) In other (common) cases, however, there may be important difficulties, which are discussed below. Four constructions are studied here: prepositional phrases, verb groups, copular clauses, and embedded clauses with overt complementizers.

4.1 The *casehead* transformation

To illustrate in some detail, let us examine the case of prepositional phrases. Take, for example, the sentence in 2a. The lexical-head representation, which UD adopts, chooses *life* as the promoted head and *of* as the demoted head, as shown in 2b. The functional representation, shown in 2c, swaps those roles.

(2) a. I found the love of my life

b.

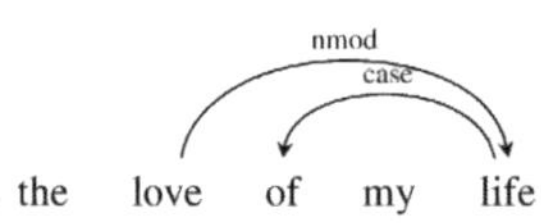

c.

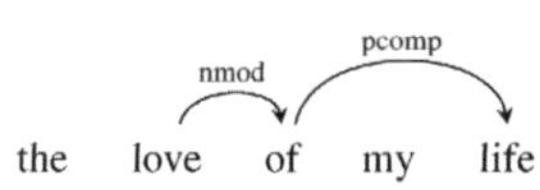

This is a particularly interesting example, because there already is evidence in the literature (Schwartz et al., 2012) that making prepositions the heads – that is, adopting the functional-head representation – can yield better parser performance. This will be called the *casehead* transformation. As mentioned above, the label *case* is used in UD for prepositions in prepositional phrases; it is also used for the genitive marker *'s*, but here the transformation is not applied to that marker. The other transformations are *auxhead*, *cophead* and *markhead*. All are named after the labels used in UD for the dependencies attaching the function word promoted by the transformation to its lexical head.

4.2 Other transformations

The sentence below exemplifies uses of the labels *aux*, *cop* and *mark*. Each transformation generates a different tree for this sentence.

It will be clear from the examples in this section that, when the functional head is promoted, the way in which the dependents of the (now demoted) lexical head are handled can have important consequences. Illustrated first are the simplest versions of each transformation, where no dependents of the lexical heads are moved. In 4.3, alternatives will be discussed. In 3a is the UD representation of a sentence that has all the target constructions for which transformations are defined.

(3) a.
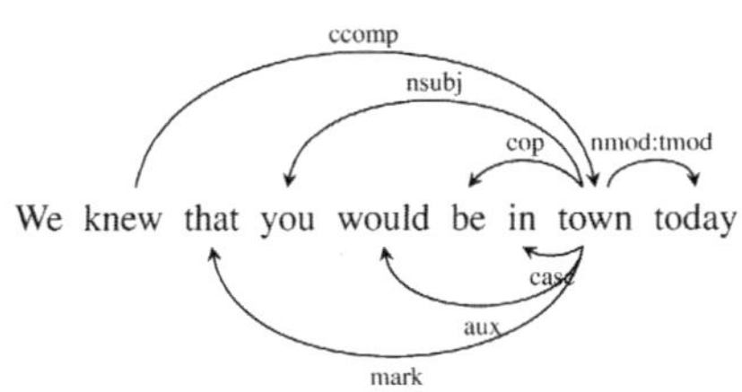

The label *cop* is used for the verb *be* in copular clauses. In relation to other dependency schemes, UD makes an unusual choice here, inherited from SD: instead of attaching the subject and other clausal dependents to the copular verb, and making the predicate itself a dependent of that verb, the representation takes the nonverbal predicate as the head and attaches the verb and clausal dependents to it. In the present example, the predicate is a prepositional phrase, but since those are also represented with lexical heads, the head of the entire copular clause is the noun *town*. In terms of crosslinguistic adequacy, it pays off, since this structure creates a parallel between English and languages where no copular verbs are used for this type of predication. Note that even the auxiliary is attached to the predicate rather than the copular verb. The simple *cophead* transformation, in which none of the dependents of the lexical head are moved to the functional head with its promotion, yields the tree in 4a.

(4) a.
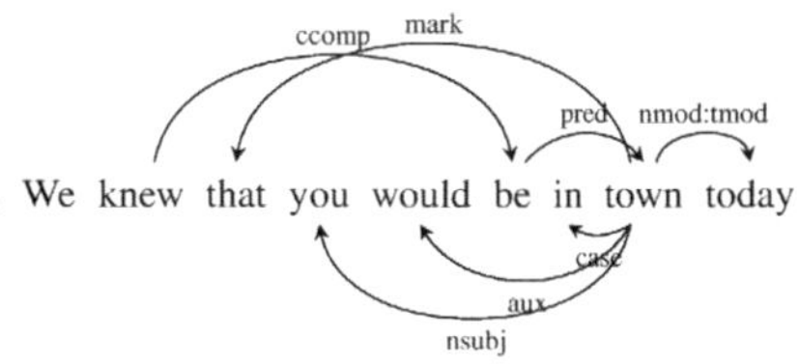

In English, the label *aux* is used to attach modals and traditional auxiliaries. In the case of auxiliary *be*, the label *auxpass* is used, to encode voice information directly in the dependency tree. These dependents are always attached to the predicate, which is why here the head of *would* is *town*. The simple *auxhead* transformation results in the tree depicted in 5a.

(5) a.
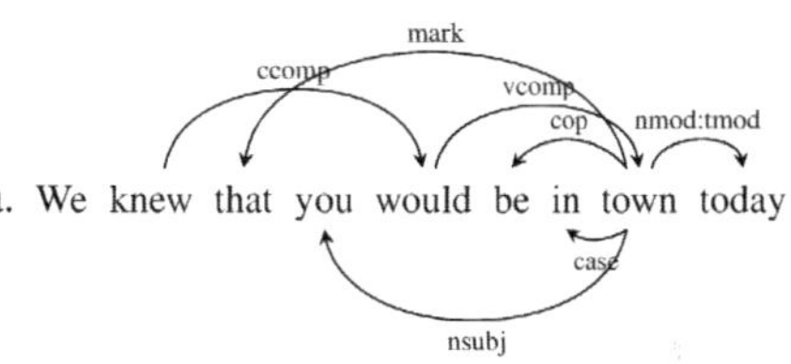

The label *mark* is used for subordinating conjunctions in embedded clauses, and additionally for the infinitive marker *to*. It is always attached to the predicate, much like *aux*. The simple *mark* transformation is illustrated in 6a.

(6) a.
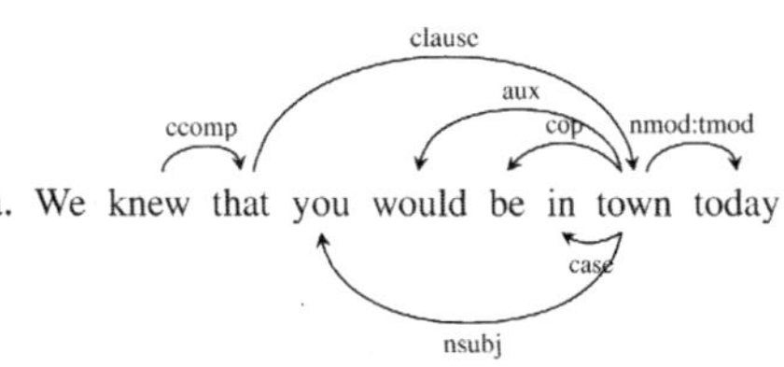

Note that in all cases, the labels used for the demoted head in the transformations are not part of the UD label set. The *auxhead* transformation is also used for *auxpass* dependencies; in those cases, the complement is called *vcomppass*. This is to avoid making the transformed representation artificially easier by eliminating the voice distinction.

4.3 Handling of dependents in transformations

The examples of simplified transformations given above make it apparent that transformations can introduce undesired nonprojectivity, and may sometimes result in representations that are linguistically objectionable. Both of those are reasons why it may be desirable to move the dependents of the lexical head when it is demoted. But exactly which dependents to move is an important question, due to the fact that modifier attachment in a dependency representation can be inevitably ambiguous, as shown below.

In UD, all the nodes in dependency graphs are words, and therefore all edges must be relations between words. However, syntactic relations can occur not only between words, but between constituents, at different levels. In UD, modifiers of constituents are indistinguishable from modifiers of the constituents head.

This has an important consequence for the distinction between functional-head and lexical-head representations. In the light of a theory of syntax in the style of Minimalist Grammar, one may argue that no two constituents share the same functional head. However, it is clear that the same lexical item can be the lexical head of multiple constituents that contain one another. Consider the example in 7a.

nsubj

(7) a. She was just a little girl at the time

amod

Here *girl* has dependents on two levels: as a nominal head, it has an adjectival dependent, *little*. As a nominal predicate, which is the lexical head of a copular clause, it has a subject dependent, 'she'. The entire clause and the noun phrase which constitutes its main predicate share a lexical head in UD. Because modifiers at both levels will be attached to that shared lexical head, it is not possible to determine from the structure alone what constituent is being modified by a dependent.

These distinctions are often very subtle and irrelevant for practical applications; but UD's radical adoption of lexical heads creates some cases where the distinctions are clear and very meaningful. Perhaps the clearest case is that of copulas with nominal predicates. In UD, we have trees like 8a and 8b.

nmod

(8) a. She was just a little girl at the time

nmod

b. She was just a little girl with red hair

In 8a, the prepositional phrase is a modifier of the predicate. In a constituent representation, its parent would not be the NP/DP node. But in 8b, clearly the modifier is in the nominal domain. In UD, the head is the noun *girl*, because it is both the head of the nominal constituent, and the head of the clausal constituent (since it is the lexical head of the copula).

If these were clausal modifiers, UD would offer an opportunity for disambiguation in the type system: clausal dependents of a noun are typed *acl* (see 9b), but clausal dependents of a predicate are typed *advcl* (as in 9a). Prepositional phrases, nonetheless, are uniformly labeled *nmod*.

advcl

(9) a. She was just a little girl when I met her parents

acl

b. She was just a little girl who loved to read

The ambiguity of the representation on this point is a consequence of the choice of representing lexical heads. Attachment would be distinct if heads were functional, because then the clausal constituent and the nominal constituent would each have its own distinct head. The functional-head representation would give us the two distinct structures in 10a and 10b.

nmod

(10) a. She was just a little girl at the time

nmod

b. She was just a little girl with red hair

This poses a problem in the context of structural transformations, because, in converting from an ambiguous representation to a non-ambiguous one (lexical-head to functional-head, in this case), it is not necessarily simple, or possible, to resolve the ambiguity in order to obtain the correct parsing representation. (The same issue arises with coordinated constituents in Nilsson et al. (2006).)

More generally, this highlights the fact that it may be harmful to blindly reattach the dependents of a lexical head to a functional head in a transformation, and careful handling of dependents may be necessary.

In an attempt to address these difficulties, 3 versions of each transformation were tested. It should be noted that dependents which are known to attach to heads rather than constituents are never moved – these are *mwe*, *compound*, *goeswith*, *name* and *foreign*. In the *simple* version, which has been illustrated above, none of the dependents of the lexical head are moved when the functional head is promoted. In the *full* version, all dependents of the lexical head are moved, except those which are known to modify nouns exclusively (in UD, these are *amod*, *acl*, *appos*, *det*, *case*, *nummod*). In the *partial* version, which is design to minimize nonprojectivity, all dependents of the lexical head which occur to the left of the functional head are moved when that head is promoted, and all other dependents are left attached to the lexical head. So now for each *Xhead* transformation, we have $Xhead_s$, $Xhead_f$ and $Xhead_p$. To provide a comparison with $cophead_s$, which was shown in 4a, $cophead_f$ and $cophead_p$ are illustrated in 11a and 11b, respectively.

(11)
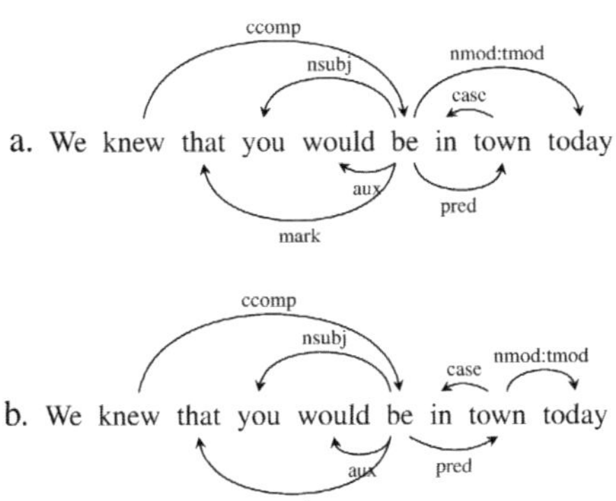

Note that, in $cophead_f$, 'today' is moved and becomes a dependent of *be*, the promoted head; in contrast, in $cophead_p$, that dependent remains attached to the lexical head *town*, since it does not occur to the left of the promoted head. If the sentence was *We knew that today you would be in town*, the two transformations would have identical results.

5 Experiments

The experiments in this paper fit the following template: a version of the training and development data from the EWT corpus was used to optimize a MaltParser model. Then that model was used to parse the test set (of 25k tokens) and evaluated on the gold standard. In the 12 experiments where the training data had undergone a transformation, the output of the parser was converted back into the original UD representation with the inverse transformation, so that it could be compared to the actual gold standard.

An important concern with this type of experiment is that the default feature sets for the algorithms may be implicitly biased towards a particular type of representation. Therefore, it was crucial to explore different hyperparameters and feature sets. This was done in two steps. The MaltParser model was obtained via an optimization heuristic: MaltOptimizer (Ballesteros and Nivre, 2012) was used on the different versions of the training set to obtain models optimized for the different transformation. This generates 13 models: one for the baseline, and one for each of the three versions of the four transformations. In a second step, all 13 representations of the dev set data were parsed with all the 13 models that MaltOptimizer produced in the previous step. Note that MaltOptimizer did not use the dev set. The model that performed best on the dev set for each transformation was chosen. Interestingly, it came out that the best-performing model for a representation was never the one recommended by MaltOptimizer for that representation. For all the representations, the models that effectively performed best on the dev set consistently used the *stackproj* algorithm, coupled with different pseudo-projectivization strategies. Throughout this procedure, the metric being maximized was the labeled attachment score (excluding punctuation), which seems to be the crucial measure of performance for most client applications.

Each *Xhead* transformation targets a different construction, and the frequency of those in the data varies. Additionally, the three versions of the transformations change the data to different extents. To give a measure of these differences, Table 1 shows the percentage of tokens in the training data that are changed by a transformation, for all 12 transformations.

These counts make it clear that, in the case of *casehead* and *markhead*, there is little difference between the *partial* and *simple* transformations. This is because in the case of these transforma-

	full	*partial*	*simple*
auxhead	21.15%	13.62%	08.37%
casehead	21.83%	19.17%	18.37%
cophead	11.62%	08.33%	04.94%
markhead	15.75%	08.04%	07.83%

Table 1: Percentage of tokens changed with relation to the gold standard by each transformation.

	full	*partial*	*simple*
auxhead	05.80%	05.49%	41.55%
casehead	06.51%	06.22%	31.57%
cophead	05.84%	05.13%	07.52%
markhead	09.71%	05.14%	10.41%
baseline		05.13%	

Table 2: Percentage of non-projective dependencies per version of the data.

tions, the lexical head is unlikely (in English) to have dependents which occur to the left of the functional head.

The transformations are also very different in terms of how much non-projectivity they introduce. Table 2 shows how that proportion changes with each transformation, which helps understand their performance.

The labeled attachment scores of the best-performing models for each representation on the test set are given in Table 3. These results were obtained by comparing the output of parsers trained on transformed representation to a transformed version of the gold-standard test set. These scores will be referred to as the *within-representation performance*. Statistical significance was assessed using Dan Bikel's parsing evaluation comparator[2], at the 0.05 significance level.

Our interest here is not to guide the design of

[2]http://pauillac.inria.fr/ seddah/compare.pl

	full	*partial*	*simple*
auxhead	84.71%	85.21%*	84.59%
casehead	84.46%	85.31%*	85.11%*
cophead	85.11%*	85.31%*	84.49%
markhead	84.29%*	84.94%	85.10%*
baseline		84.69%	

Table 3: Labeled accuracy scores for within-representation evaluations. The scores marked with * have a significant difference from the baseline.

	full	*partial*	*simple*
auxhead	84.37%	84.84%	84.43%
casehead	84.13%*	84.91%	84.86%
cophead	84.28%*	84.53%	84.03%*
markhead	84.27%*	84.89%	85.00%
baseline		84.69%	

Table 4: Labeled accuracy scores for evaluations on UD. The scores marked with * have a significant difference from the baseline.

a new representation, but rather to find strategies that will improve parser performance for the existing UD representation. For this reason, we also present results on the actual UD representation. These results are obtained by transforming the output of a parser with the inverse of the transformation applied to the training data, and comparing that to the actual gold standard annotation. The labeled accuracy scores are in Table 4.

6 Discussion

These results show that, in the case of UD, tree transformations do not seem to improve parser performance if the output needs to be converted back to UD. There are no significant positive results in Table 4, and in fact a few of the transformations have a significant negative impact on the score. Interestingly, this holds even for some representations which have better within-representation performance than the baseline.

In terms of within-representation performance, the most successful transformations were $cophead_p$ and $casehead_p$. The $cophead_p$ transformation makes the representation of copular clauses more parallel to that of other clauses in UD: it moves dependents from a nonverbal predicate to a copular verb (excluding those with labels that apply exclusively to noun modifiers or head-level modifiers). With this transformation, verbs are uniformly viewed as the heads of clauses, making the representation more predictable. The effect of this transformation is particularly notable because it is the one that affects the fewest tokens, as shown in Table 1. The results on $casehead_p$ shown in Table 3 are consistent with Schwartz et al. (2012). This transformation shortens dependency lengths, which benefits the transition-based parser. Dependency edges with $length < 5$ constitute 81.93% of the total in the $casehead_p$ data, and 81.73% in the $casehead_s$

data. These numbers are up from 80.35% in the baseline.

6.1 Inverting transformations

An obvious trend in these results is that attachment scores consistently decrease when the output of a parser trained on transformed input is inverted back to UD. On perfectly annotated data, there is no distortion: for all 12 operations proposed here, using the inverse transformation on a transformed gold standard reverts all the changes and gives back the original data. However, parser errors are not always handled well by transformations. The reason for this is that the different representations yielded in these operations reflect attachment decisions differently. The differences can skew the evaluation results.

All transformations target constructions including 2 crucial edges, as seen before: one between the promoted head and the demoted head, and another – the attachment edge – coming from the outside of the construction to the promoted head. In functional-head representations, the attachment edge can be correct even if the lexical head is wrongly identified, as in 12a, which is an actual parser error on the $cophead_f$-transformed data. The inverted version is shown in 12b.

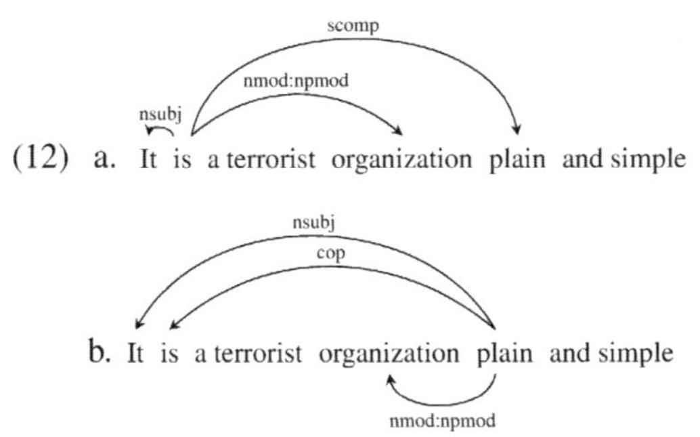

When this tree is converted back to the lexical-head representation, the attachment edge, which in this case is simply *root*, is moved to the wrongly-identified lexical head. While in 12a the root of the sentence was identified correctly, in the inverted version it is wrong; one error in the functional-head representation turns into two in its lexical-head counterpart.

Another issue that arises in inverting transformations is that, when dependents are moved from the functional head to the lexical head, errors may be amplified. This is also seen here. The phrase *plain and simple* was wrongly identified as a predicate. With the inversion of the transformation, the subject of the sentence, which was correct in 12a, is moved and made a dependent of the false predicate. This type of error propagation is the reason why the *simple* transformations have the smallest differences between the score on the transformed gold standard and the score on the inverted parsed output.

Even when the parser does correctly identify the lexical head as a dependent of the functional head, another source of complications is that it may identify additional "lexical heads" (i.e., dependents with the label reserved for the lexical head, such as *pred* in the case of *cophead*). In this implementation, we do not use any heuristics to try to identify if one of the candidates is the actual lexical head, and which. This can also lead to errors, as now the inverse transformation may erroneously move dependents.

As a counterpoint, one should note that inverting the transformations to obtain a lexical-head representation is also, in a way, forgiving: there are no distinctions between attachment to the functional or to the lexical head, because the inversion moves all dependents of the functional head to the lexical head. This eliminates a plausible source of errors – and some linguistic information, making UD the poorer representation here. Nevertheless, errors of this types seem to be outnumbered by others that are introduced or amplified by inverting these transformations.

These problems help explain why the results reported here, with respect to prepositional phrases and verb groups, and suggest different directions than those reported in Schwartz et al. (2012): in that paper, the results of different parsers are evaluated against different versions of the gold standard. Here, since the main concern is the design of a parsing representation that is meant simply as an intermediary step, all output has to be evaluated against the same gold standard. This creates an opportunity for losses that did not exist in the experiments of Schwartz et al. (2012).

7 Conclusion

Although there have been cases in the literature in which small gains in performance were obtained from invertible structural transformations on dependency trees, similar transformations do not seem to yield any significant gain for UD in English. This occurs despite the fact that these tree operations can result in performance improvements, as is evident from the within-representation scores of some of the transformed datasets. Nevertheless, because of the nature of lexical- and functional-head representations, the inversion of the transformations on the parser output can and does amplify errors. Due to these difficulties, it is not immediately possible to exploit structures transformations for the benefit of UD.

We believe that other styles of tree transformations may yield gains for parser performance on UD; specifically, ones designed in the style of the node-merging and -splitting that has been used in constituency parsing since Klein and Manning (2003). That investigation is left for future work.

References

Miguel Ballesteros and Joakim Nivre. 2012. Malt-Optimizer: An Optimization Tool for MaltParser. In *Proceedings of the Demonstrations at the 13th Conference of the European Chapter of the Association for Computational Linguistics*, EACL '12, pages 58–62, Stroudsburg, PA, USA. Association for Computational Linguistics.

Kepa Bengoetxea and Koldo Gojenola. 2009. Exploring Treebank Transformations in Dependency Parsing. In *Proceedings of the International Conference RANLP-2009*, pages 33–38, Borovets, Bulgaria. Association for Computational Linguistics.

Daniel M. Bikel. 2004. Intricacies of collins' parsing model. *Comput. Linguist.*, 30(4):479–511, December.

Angelina Ivanova, Stephan Oepen, and Lilja vrelid. 2013. Survey on parsing three dependency representations for English. *51st Annual Meeting of the Association for Computational Linguistics Proceedings of the Student Research Workshop*, pages 31–37.

Richard Johansson and Pierre Nugues. 2007. Extended constituent-to-dependency conversion for English. In Joakim Nivre, Heiki-Jaan Kalep, Kadri Muischnek, and Mare Koit, editors, *NODALIDA 2007 Proceedings*, pages 105–112, Tartu, Estonia. University of Tartu.

Dan Klein and Christopher D. Manning. 2003. Accurate Unlexicalized Parsing. In *Proceedings of the 41st Annual Meeting on Association for Computational Linguistics - Volume 1*, ACL '03, pages 423–430, Stroudsburg, PA, USA. Association for Computational Linguistics.

Marie-Catherine Marneffe and Christopher D. Manning. 2008. The Stanford Typed Dependencies Representation. *Coling 2008: Proceedings of the workshop on Cross-Framework and Cross-Domain Parser Evaluation*, pages 1–8.

Marie-Catherine de Marneffe, Timothy Dozat, Natalia Silveira, Katri Haverinen, Filip Ginter, Joakim Nivre, and Christopher D. Manning. 2014. Universal Stanford dependencies: A cross-linguistic typology. *Proceedings of the Ninth International Conference on Language Resources and Evaluation (LREC-2014)*.

Ryan McDonald, Kevin Lerman, and Fernando Pereira. 2006. Multilingual dependency analysis with a two-stage discriminative parser. In *Proceedings of the Tenth Conference on Computational Natural Language Learning*, CoNLL-X '06, pages 216–220, Stroudsburg, PA, USA. Association for Computational Linguistics.

Jens Nilsson, Joakim Nivre, and Johan Hall. 2006. Graph Transformations in Data-driven Dependency Parsing. In *Proceedings of the 21st International Conference on Computational Linguistics and the 44th Annual Meeting of the Association for Computational Linguistics*, ACL-44, pages 257–264, Stroudsburg, PA, USA. Association for Computational Linguistics.

Jens Nilsson, Joakim Nivre, and Johan Hall. 2007. Generalizing Tree Transformations for Inductive Dependency Parsing. *Proceedings of the 45th Annual Meeting of the Association of Computational Linguistics*, pages 968–975.

Joakim Nivre, Johan Hall, Jens Nilsson, Atanas Chanev, Glsen Eryigit, Sandra Kbler, Svetoslav Marinov, and Erwin Marsi. 2007. MaltParser: A language-independent system for data-driven dependency parsing. *Natural Language Engineering*, 13(02):95–135.

Joakim Nivre, Cristina Bosco, Jinho Choi, Marie-Catherine de Marneffe, Timothy Dozat, Richárd Farkas, Jennifer Foster, Filip Ginter, Yoav Goldberg, Jan Hajič, Jenna Kanerva, Veronika Laippala, Alessandro Lenci, Teresa Lynn, Christopher Manning, Ryan McDonald, Anna Missilä, Simonetta Montemagni, Slav Petrov, Sampo Pyysalo, Natalia Silveira, Maria Simi, Aaron Smith, Reut Tsarfaty, Veronika Vincze, and Daniel Zeman. 2015. Universal dependencies 1.0.

Slav Petrov, Leon Barrett, Romain Thibaux, and Dan Klein. 2006. Learning Accurate, Compact, and Interpretable Tree Annotation. In *Proceedings of the 21st International Conference on Computational Linguistics and the 44th Annual Meeting of the Association for Computational Linguistics*, ACL-44, pages 433–440, Stroudsburg, PA, USA. Association for Computational Linguistics.

Roy Schwartz, Omri Abend, and Ari Rappoport. 2012. Learnability-based syntactic annotation design. In *COLING*, volume 24, pages 2405–2422.

Natalia Silveira, Timothy Dozat, Marie-Catherine de Marneffe, Samuel Bowman, Miriam Connor, John Bauer, and Christopher D. Manning. 2014. A Gold

Standard Dependency Corpus for English. In *Proceedings of the Ninth International Conference on Language Resources and Evaluation (LREC-2014)*.

Catena Operations for Unified Dependency Analysis

Kiril Simov and **Petya Osenova**
Linguistic Modeling Department
Institute of Information and Communication Technologies
Bulgarian Academy of Sciences
Bulgaria
{kivs,petya}@bultreebank.org

Abstract

The notion of catena was introduced originally to represent the syntactic structure of multiword expressions with idiosyncratic semantics and non-constituent structure. Later on, several other phenomena (such as ellipsis, verbal complexes, etc.) were formalized as catenae. This naturally led to the suggestion that a catena can be considered a basic unit of syntax. In this paper we present a formalization of catenae and the main operations over them for modelling the combinatorial potential of units in dependency grammar.

1 Introduction

Catenae were introduced initially to handle linguistic expressions with non-constituent structure and idiosyncratic semantics. It was shown in a number of publications that this unit is appropriate for both - the analysis of syntactic (for example, ellipsis, idioms) and morphological phenomena (for example, compounds). One of the important questions in NLP is how to establish a connection between the lexicon and the text dimension in an operable way. At the moment most investigations focus on the representation and analysis of the text dimension.

We first employed catenae when modeling multiword expressions in Bulgarian within the relation lexicon - text. (Simov and Osenova, 2014). Encouraged by the promising results, we continued our research on how to exploit catenae as a unified strategy for dependency analysis. In the paper we use examples mostly from Bulgarian and to a lesser extend from English, but our approach is applicable to other languages, as well.

In this piece of research we pursue both issues mentioned above. On the one hand, we show in a formal way how the lexicon representation maps to its syntactic analysis. On the other hand, a unified strategy of dependency analysis is proposed via extending the catena to handle also phenomena as valency and other combinatorial dependencies. Thus, a two-fold analysis is achieved: handling the lexicon-grammar relation and arriving at a single means for analyzing related phenomena.

The paper is structured as follows: the next section outlines some previous work on catenae; section 3 focuses on the formal definition of the catena and of catena-based lexical entries; section 4 presents different lexical entries that demonstrate the expressive power of the catena formalism; section 5 concludes the paper.

2 Previous Work on Catenae

The notion of catena (chain) was introduced in (O'Grady, 1998) as a mechanism for representing the syntactic structure of idioms. He shows that for this task there is need for a definition of syntactic patterns that do not coincide with constituents. He defines the catena in the following way: *The words A, B, and C (order irrelevant) form a chain if and only if A immediately dominates B and C, or if and only if A immediately dominates B and B immediately dominates C.*

In recent years the notion of catena revived again and was applied also to dependency representations. Catenae have been used successfully for the modelling of problematic language phenomena. (Gross 2010) presents the problems in syntax and morphology that have led to the introduction of the subconstituent catena level. Constituency-based analysis faces non-constituent structures in ellipsis, idioms, verb complexes.

Apart from the linguistic modelling of language phenomena, catenae have been used in a number of NLP applications. (Maxwell et al., 2013), for example, presents an approach to Information Retrieval based on catenae. The authors consider the catena as a mechanism for semantic encoding

Proceedings of the Third International Conference on Dependency Linguistics (Depling 2015), pages 320–329,
Uppsala, Sweden, August 24–26 2015.

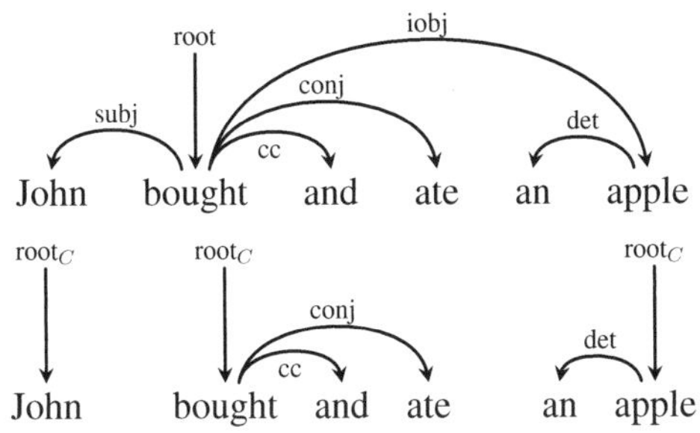

Figure 1: A complete dependency tree and some of its catenae.

which overcomes the problems of long-distance paths and elliptical sentences. The employment of catenae in NLP applications is additional motivation for us to use it in the modelling of the interface between the treebank and the lexicon.

Terminology note: an alternative term for catena is *treelet*. It has been used in the area of machine translation as a unit for translation transfer (see (Quirk et al., 2005)). Their definition is equivalent to the definition of catena. Also (Kuhlmann, 2010) uses *treelet* for a node and its children (if any). In the paper we resort to the term catena because it is closer to the spirit of the issues discussed here.

3 Formal Definition of Catena

In this section we define the formal presentation of the catena as it is used in syntax and in the lexicon. Here we follow the definition of catena provided by (O'Grady, 1998) and (Gross, 2010): a **catena** is a word or a combination of words directly connected in the dominance dimension. In reality this definition of catena for dependency trees is equivalent to a subtree definition. Fig. 1 depicts a complete dependency tree and some of its catenae. Notice that the complete tree is also a catena itself. With "root$_C$" we mark the root of the catena. It might be the same as the root of the complete tree, but also might be different as in the cases of "John" and "an apple". Following (Osborne et al., 2012) we prefer to use the notion of catena to that of dependency subtree or treelet as mentioned above. We aim to utilize the notion of catena for several purposes: representation of words and multiword expressions in the lexicon, their realization in the actual trees expressing the analysis of sentences as well as for representation of derivational structure of compounds in the lexicon.

In order to model the variety of phenomena and characteristics encoded in a dependency grammar we extend the catena with partial arc and node labels. We follow the approach taken in CoNLL shared tasks on dependency parsing representing for each node its word form, lemma, part of speech, extended part of speech, grammatical features (and later – semantics). This provides a flexible mechanism for expressing the combinatorial potential of lexical items. In the following definition all grammatical features are represented as POS tags.

Let us have the sets: LA — a set of POS tags[1], LE — a set of lemmas, WF — a set of word forms, and a set of dependency tags D ($ROOT \in D$). Let us have a sentence $x = w_1, ..., w_n$. A **tagged dependency tree** is a directed tree $T = (V, A, \pi, \lambda, \omega, \delta)$ where:

1. $V = \{0, 1, ..., n\}$ is an ordered set of nodes that corresponds to an enumeration of the words in the sentence (the root of the tree has index 0);

2. $A \subseteq V \times V$ is a set of arcs. For each node i, $1 \leq i \leq n$, there is exactly one arc in A: $\langle i, j \rangle \in A$, $0 \leq j \leq n$, $i \neq j$. There is exactly one arc $\langle i, 0 \rangle \in A$;

3. $\pi : V - \{0\} \to LA$ is a total labelling function from nodes to POS tags[2]. π is not defined for the root;

4. $\lambda : V - \{0\} \to LE$ is a total labelling function from nodes to lemmas. λ is not defined for the root;

5. $\omega : V - \{0\} \to WF$ is a total labelling function from nodes to word forms. ω is not defined for the root;

6. $\delta : A \to D$ is a total labelling function for arcs. Only the arc $\langle i, 0 \rangle$ is mapped to the label $ROOT$;

7. 0 is the root of the tree.

[1] In the formal definitions here we use tags as entities, but in practice they are sets of grammatical features

[2] In case when we are interested in part of the grammatical features encoded in a POS tag we could consider p as a set of different mappings for the different grammatical features. It is easy to extend the definition in this respect, but we do not do this here.

We will hereafter refer to this structure as a parse tree for the sentence x. The node 0 does not correspond to a word form in the sentence, but plays the role of a root of the tree.

Let $T = (V, A, \pi, \lambda, \omega, \delta)$ be a tagged dependency tree.

Let $T = (V, A, \pi, \lambda, \omega, \delta)$ be a tagged dependency tree. A directed tree $G = (V_G, A_G, \pi_G, \lambda_G, \omega_G, \delta_G)$ is called **dependency catena of** T if and only if there exists a mapping $\psi : V_G \rightarrow V^3$ such that:

1. $A_G \subseteq A$, the set of arcs of G;
2. $\pi_G \subseteq \pi$ is a partial labelling function from nodes of G to POS tags;
3. $\lambda_G \subseteq \lambda$ is a partial labelling function from nodes to lemmas;
4. $\omega_G \subseteq \omega$ is a partial labelling function from nodes to word forms;
5. $\delta_G \subseteq \delta$ is a partial labelling function for arcs.

A directed tree $G = (V_G, A_G, \pi_G, \lambda_G, \omega_G, \delta_G)$ is a **dependency catena** if and only if there exists a dependency tree T such that G is a dependency catena of T.

Having partial functions for assigning POS tags, dependency labels, word forms and lemmas allows us to construct arbitrary abstractions over the structure of a catena. Thus, the catena could be underspecified for some of the node labels, like grammatical features, lemmas and also some dependency labels. The mapping ψ parameterizes the catena with respect to different dependency trees. Using the mapping, there is a possibility to realize different word orders of the catena nodes, for instance. The omission of node 0 from the range of the mapping ψ excludes the external root of the tagged dependency tree from each catena. CatR is the root of the catena. The catena could be a word or an arbitrary subtree.

We call the mapping of a catena into a given dependency tree the **realization of the catena in the tree**. We consider the realization of the catena as a fully specified subtree including all node and arc labels. For example, the catena for "to spill the beans" will allow for any realization of the verb form like in: "they spilled the beans" and "he spills the beans". Thus, the catena in the lexicon will be underspecified with respect to the grammatical features and word form for the verb.

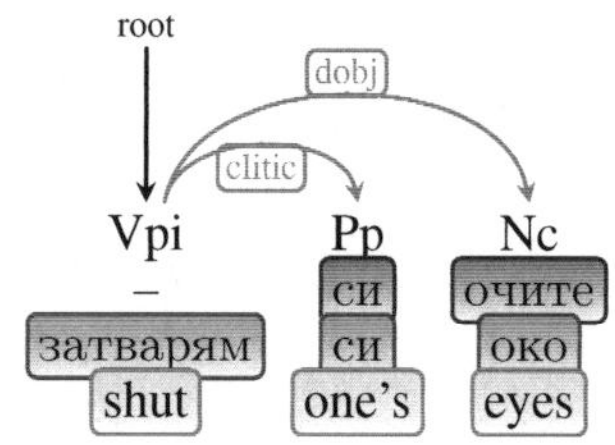

Realization 1:

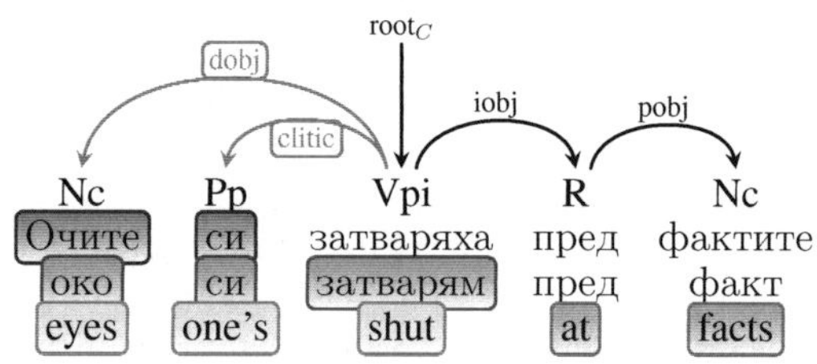

Realization 2:

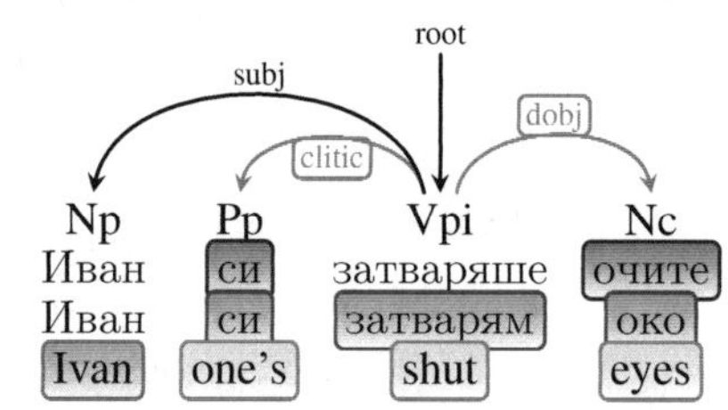

Figure 2: Catena realization

Sometimes this underspecified catena will be called a **lexicon catena** (LC), because its kind will be stored in the lexical entries. The Fig. 2 depicts two realizations (with different word orders) of the catena for the idiom затварям си очите ('zatvaryam si ochite', lit. shut one's eyes). The upper part of the image represents the lexicon catena for the idiom. It determines the fixed elements of the catena: the arcs, their labels, nodes and their labels: extended part of speech (first row), word forms (second row), lemmas (third row), and gloss in English (fourth row)[4]. The dash (–) in the word form row means that the word form is not defined

[3]This mapping allows for embedding of G in different tagged dependency trees and thus different word order realizations of the catena nodes (corresponding to word forms in T). The mapping y is specific for G and T. It allows also the image of G in T not to be a subtree of T, but several subtrees of T. A special case is discussed below — partition and extension operations.

[4]In the next examples we will present only the important information, thus, some of these rows will be missing. In other cases new rows will be used to represent additional information.

for the verbal node. In the two realizations the fixed elements of the catena are represented as in the image of the catena. The word order in the two realizations is different. Thus, using catenae with different underspecified elements defines different levels of freedom of realization of the multiword expressions.

Two catenae G_1 and G_2 could have the same set of realizations. In this case, we will say that G_1 and G_2 are **equivalent**. Representing the nodes via paths in the dependency tree from the root to the corresponding node and imposing a linear order over this representation of nodes facilitates the selection of a unique representative of each equivalent class of catenae. Thus, in the rest of the paper we assume that each catena is representative for its class of equivalence.

Let G_1 and G_2 be two catenae. A **composition** of G_1 and G_2 is a catena G_c, such that the catenae G_1 and G_2 are realized in G_e in such a way that the root node of G_2 is mapped to a node in G_c to which a node of G_1 is mapped. Each node in G_c is an image of a node from G_1 or G_2. The realizations of both catenae G_1 or G_2 share exactly one node in G_c. This node has to represent all the information from the nodes that are mapped to it. In this way we could realize the selectional restriction of a given lexical unit with respect to a catena in a sentence. For example, let us assume that the verb 'to read' requires a subject to be a human and an object to be an information object. In Fig. 3 we present how the catena for 'I read' is combined with the catena 'a book' in order to form the catena 'I read a book'. The figure represents only the level of word forms and a level of semantics (specified only for the node, on which the composition is performed). The catena for 'I read ...' specifies that the unknown direct object has the semantics of an *Information Object (InfObj)*. The catena for 'a book' represent the fact that the book is an Information Object. Thus the two catenae could be composed on the two nodes marked as InfObj. The result is represented at the bottom of the picture.[5]

Some MWEs require more complex operations over catenae in order to deal with them. Such a class of MWEs are idioms with an explicit subject, such as "the devil is in the details"; the realizations of catenae from the lexicon into syntax often are

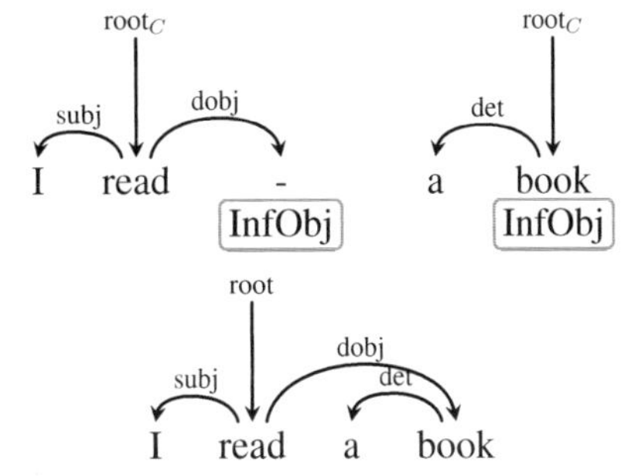

Figure 3: Composition of catenae.

accompanied by intervening material — see the discussion in (Osborne et al., 2012). For example, the idiom allows realizations such as: "the devil will be in the details", "the devil seems to be in the details", etc.

Our insight, supported by the examples, is that the intervening material forms a catena of a certain type. Such a type of catena will be called an **auxiliary catena**[6] in this paper, although it could be of different kinds (auxiliary, modal, control, etc.), depending on the verb forms. In order to implement this idea we need some additional notions.

Let $G = (V_G, A_G, \pi_G, \lambda_G, \omega_G, \delta_G)$ be a catena and $n \in V_G$, then $G_1, G_2, ..., G_n$ is a partition of G on node n if and only if for each $1 \leq i \leq n$:

1. each G_i is a catena which is a subtree of G
2. at most one subcatena G_i has n as a leaf node
3. one or more subcatenae G_i have n as a root node
4. the only common node for all subcatenae G_i is n
5. the mappings $\pi_{Gi}, \lambda_{Gi}, \omega_{Gi}, \beta_{Gi}$ are the same as for the whole catena G, except for the node n where the mappings $\pi_{Gi}, \lambda_{Gi}, \omega_{Gi}$ could be partial with respect to the original mappings.

An example of the operation **partition** of *the devil is in the details* is given in Fig. 4.

[5]In this representation many details like lemmas and grammatical features are not presented because they are not important for the example.

[6]Under auxiliary catena we understand a catena that is part of the verbal complex and contains nodes for the auxiliary verbs. In the grammars for the different languages different kinds of catena could be defined on the basis of there role in the grammar. In this respect the definition of extension here is restricted to verbal complex, but easy could be adapted for other cases when necessary.

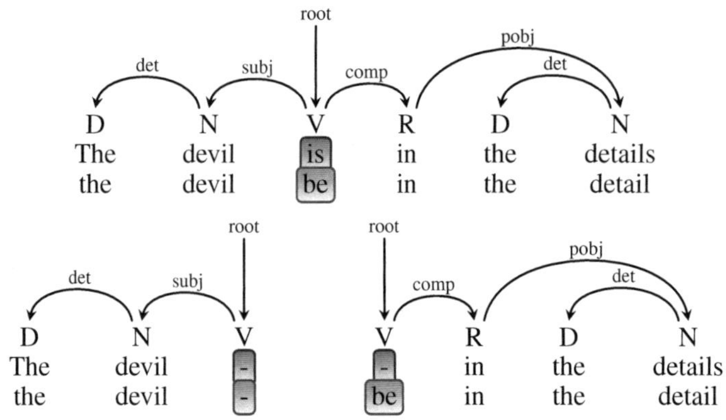

Figure 4: Partition

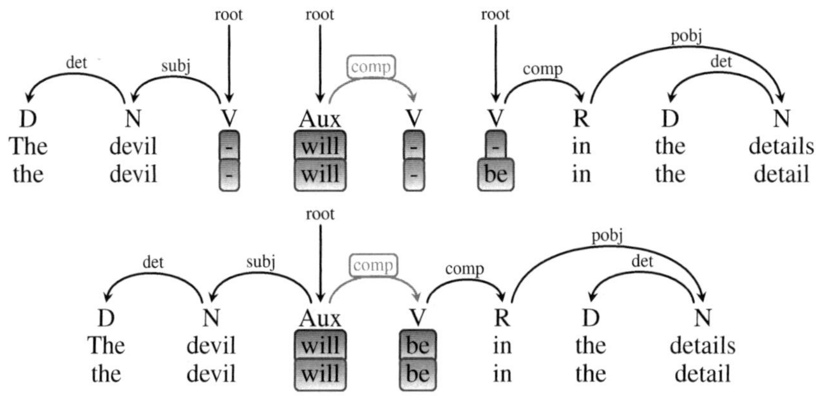

Figure 5: Extension

After the partition of a catena for an idiom we need a mechanism to connect the different catenae of the partition with the auxiliary catena.

Let G be a catena and for $n \in V_G, G_1, G, ..., G_n$ be a partition of G and G_a be an auxiliary catena. An **extension** of G on partition $G_1, G_2, ..., G_n$ with catena G_a is a catena G_e such that each catena $G_1, G_2, ..., G_n$ and the auxiliary catena G_a are realized in G_e in such a way that the node n_i in G_i (corresponding to the original node n) is mapped to a node in G_e to which a node of G_a is mapped. Each node in G_e is an image of a node from $G_1, G_2, ..., G_n$ or G_a.

An example of the operation **extention** is presented in Fig. 5[7]

Two catenae G_1 and G_2 could have the same set of realizations. In this case, we will say that G_1 and G_2 are **equivalent**. Representing the nodes via paths in the dependency tree from root to the corresponding node and imposing a linear order over this representation of nodes facilitates the selection of a unique representative of each equivalent class of catenae. Thus, in the rest of the paper we assume that each catena is representative of its class of equivalence. This representation of a catena will be called **canonical form**.

Using the notion of catena introduced in this section we define the structure of lexical items in the lexicon of a dependency grammar. Through the operations of composition, partition and extension we could define a procedure for analysis of actual sentences.

For each node in a catena or dependency tree we present the following information: POS, Grammatical Features, Word Form, Lemma, Node identifier (position of word form in a catena or a sentence). Each of the information is depicted in the node representation on a different row.

In order to model the behavior in a better way

[7]Notice that there are alternative analyses in which the auxiliary verb is not a head of the sentence, but a dependent of the copola.

we need to add semantics to the dependency representation. We will not be able to do this in full in this paper. In order to represent the interaction between lexical items and their valency frames in the lexicon, we assume a semantic analysis based on Minimal Recursion Semantics (MRS) (see (Copestake et al., 2005)). For dependency analyses, the MRS structures are constructed in a way similar to the one presented in (Simov and Osenova, 2011). In this work, the root of a subtree of a given dependency tree is associated with the MRS structure corresponding to the whole subtree. This means that for the semantic interpretation of MWEs we will use the root of the corresponding catena. In the dependency tree for the corresponding sentence the catena root will provide the interpretation of the MWE and its dependent elements, if any. In the lexicon we will provide the corresponding structure to model the idiosyncratic semantic content of MWE.

Our goal is to use catenae to represent the syntactic and morphological form of lexical units in the lexicon. The lexical units could be multiword expressions or single words. The lexical entry for a lexical unit has the following fields: **lexicon-catena** (LC) which contains a catena for the lexical item; **semantics** (SM) represents the semantic content of the lexical item; **valency frame** (Frame) contains a catena of the frame element and its semantics. The field Frame can be repeated as many times as necessary. Each valency frame corresponds to a syntactic relation of the dependent element. Alternative valencies for a given syntactic relation are represented in different Frame fields.

Here **lexicon-catena** determines the lexicon form of the lexical unit. The underspecification of the catena allows for the different realizations of the catena in the actual sentences. The **semantics** field defines the basic semantics of the lexical unit. The **valency frame** field provides selectional restriction for the lexical unit. Because the lexical unit could be a multiword expression, the semantics and selectional restrictions could be assigned to different nodes of the corresponding catena. In this way, different parts of the semantics could be provided by different nodes in the catena or from the catena related to the selectional restrictions. The selectional restrictions of a lexical unit also could be connected to different nodes of the lexical catena. In this way the lexical entry determines the possible variations of multiword expressions (MWEs). Below we will present concrete lexical entries for different types of lexical units, demonstrating selectional restrictions of verbs, nouns, multiword expressions.

4 Lexical Entry Examples

In this section we present some types of lexical entries using the structure of the lexical entry presented above. The examples are taken from the valency lexicon of Bulgarian, constructed on the basis of syntactic analyses, includes information about the main form (lemma) of the word, the valency frame with all the elements, their forms, grammatical features and semantics (Osenova et al., 2012). The lexical entry for each lexical item also includes the semantics of the main form and information on how this semantics incorporates the semantics of each frame element.

Here we first present the structure of the lexical entry for the verb ‘бягам’ (’byagam’, run) in the sense "run away from facts". The verb takes an indirect object in the form of a prepositional phrase starting with the preposition ‘от’ (’ot’, from). In the following examples we will omit the title row of the table for space reasons.

<table>
<tr><td>LC</td><td>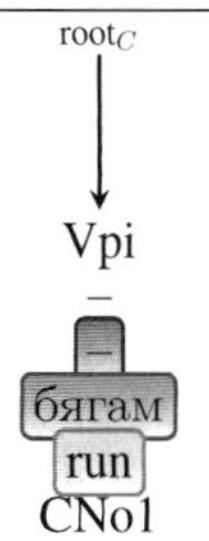
</td></tr>
<tr><td>SM</td><td>CNo1: { run-away-from_rel(e,x_0,x_1), fact(x_1), [1](x_1) }</td></tr>
<tr><td>Frame</td><td>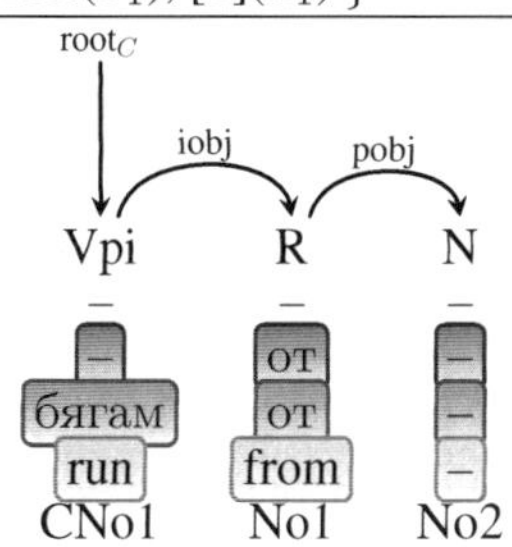

semantics:
No2: { fact(x), [1] (x) }</td></tr>
</table>

Figure 6: Lexical entry for the verb бягам "byagam", ‘run’)

In this model we use catenae for the representation of a single word and a MWE, because by definition single words are also catenae. Using the formal definition of catena from above, we might specify all grammatical features of the lexical item. The semantics in the lexical entry could be attached to each node in the lexicon-catena. In this example, there is just one node of the lexicon-catena. In the paper we present only the set of elementary predicates instead of the full MRS structures with the aim to demonstrate the principles of the representation. In the example, the verb introduces three elementary predicates: *run-away-from_rel*(e, x0, x1), *fact*(x1), [1](x1). The predicate *run-away-from_rel*(e, x0, x1) represents the event and its main participants: x0, x1. The predicate *fact*(x1) is part of the meaning of the verb in the sense that the agent represented by x0 will run away from some fact. There is also one underspecified predicate [1](x1) which has to be compatible with the predicate *fact*(x1). This predicate is used for incorporating the meaning of the indirect object. The valency frame is given as a set of valency elements. They are defined as a catena and semantic description. The catena describes the basic structure of the valency element including the necessary lexical information, grammatical features, the syntactic relation to the main lexical item. The semantic description determines the main semantic contribution of the frame element and via structural sharing it is incorporated in the semantics of the whole lexical item. In the example there is only one frame element. It is introduced via the preposition 'ot' (from). The semantics comes from the dependent noun which has to be compatible with *fact*(x) predicate and via the underspecified predicate [1](x1) which could specify a more concrete predicate. Via the structure sharing index [1] this specific predicate is copied to the semantics of the main lexical item.

The lexical entry of a MWE uses the same format: a **lexicon-catena**, **semantics** and **valency**. The lexicon-catena for the MWEs is stored in its canonical form as described above. The semantics part of a lexical entry specifies the list of elementary predicates for the MRS analysis. When the MWE allows for some modification (also adjunction) of its elements, i.e. modifiers of a noun, the lexical entry in the lexicon needs to specify the role of these modifiers. For example, the MWE from the above example 'затварям си очите' which is synonymic to the verb 'byagam' presented above, is presented in Fig. 7[8]. The lexical entry is similar to the one shown earlier. The main differences are: the lexicon-catena is for the MWE instead of a single word. The semantics is the same, because the verb and the MWE are synonyms. The valency frame contains two alternative elements for indirect object introduced by two different prepositions. The situation that the two descriptions are alternatives follows from the fact that the verb has no more than one indirect object. If there is also a direct object then the valency set will contain elements for it as well.

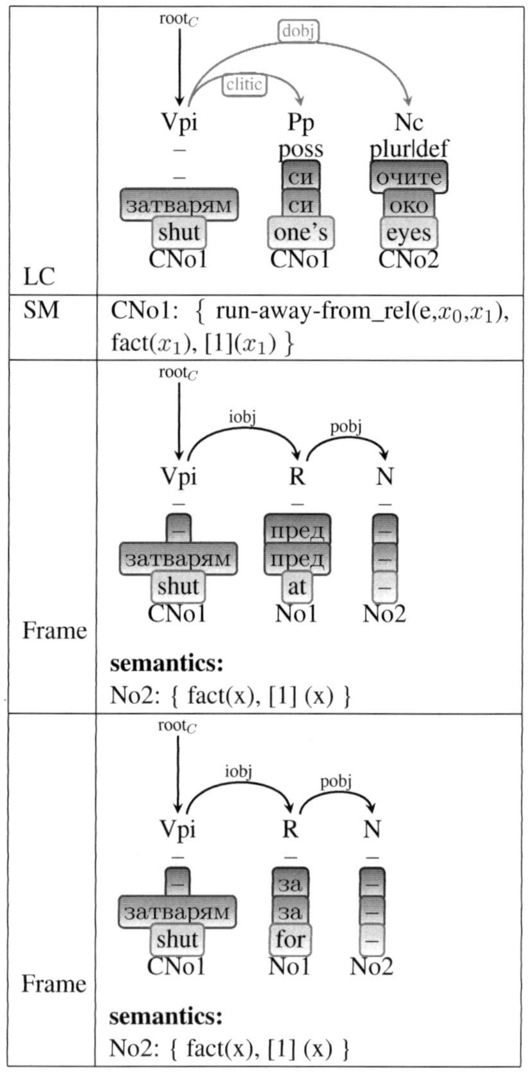

Figure 7: Lexical entry for затварям си очите "zatvaryam si ochite", 'I close my eyes'

[8]The grammatical features are: 'poss' for possessive pronoun, 'plur' for plural number and 'def' for definite noun.

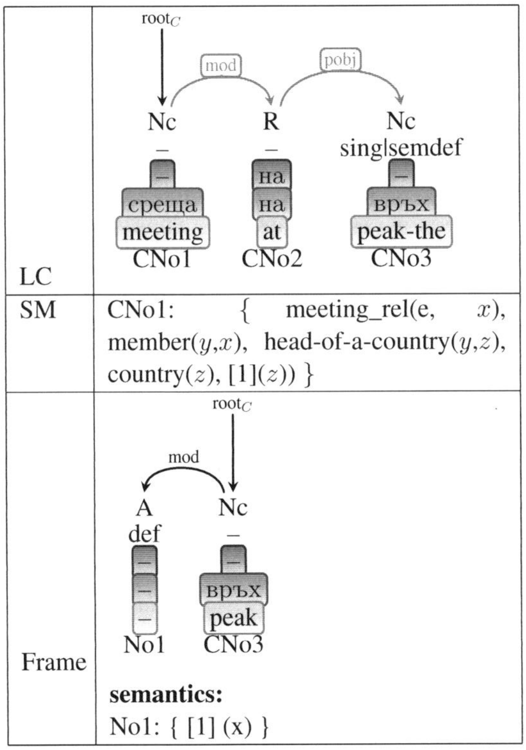

Figure 8: Lexical Entry for среща на върха "sresta na varha", 'summit'

The semantics and the valency information are attached to the corresponding nodes in the catena representation. In the example in Fig. 7 only the information for the root node of the catena is given (identifier CNo1).

In cases when other parts of the catena allow modification, the information for the corresponding nodes will be given. Here we provide examples of such cases. For example, the Multiword Expression 'среща на върха' ('sreshta na varha', summit) allows for modification not only of the whole catena, but also of the noun within the prepositional phrase. The lexical entry is given in Fig. 8[9]. This lexical entry allows modifications like 'европейски' (European) — среща на европейския връх ('sreshta na evropeyskiya vrah', meeting of the European top). This catena allows also modification of the head word.

The next example presented here is for the multiword 'снежен човек' meaning "a man-like sculpture from snow". It does not allow any modification of the dependent node 'снежен' (snowy), but it allows for modifications of the root like "large snow man" etc. The lexical entry is given in Fig. 9[10]. The grammatical features for the head noun (indef for indefinite) restricts its possible form. In this way, singular and plural forms are allowed. The empty valency ensures that the dependent adjective cannot be modified except for morphological variants like singular and plural forms, but also definite or indefinite forms depending on the usage of the phrase. The possible modifiers of the MWE are determined by the represented semantics. The relation *snowman_rel*(x) is taken from an appropriate ontology where its conceptual definition is given.

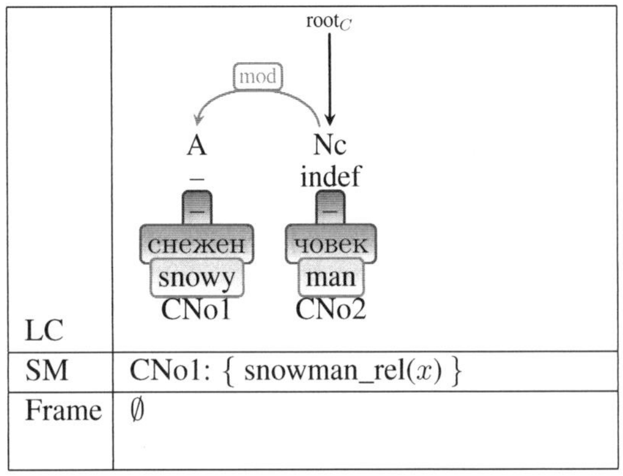

Figure 9: Lexical Entry for снежен човек "snezhen chovek", 'snowman'

Fig. 10 shows an example of non-verbal valency: the lexical entry of the relational noun 'баща [на ...]' ('bashta na...', father of ...).

In the example so far, the selectional restrictions are potential and it is possible for them not to be realized in the actual text. But in some cases they are obligatory. Here we present one such example for the verb 'състоя се' (*'sastoya se ot', consist of*). It requires an obligatory indirect object introduced by the preposition 'от' ('ot', from) as in the sentence: Системата се състои от два модула ('Sistemata se sastoi ot dva modula', The system consists of two modules.). In order to ensure that the indirect object will be always realized, we encode the preposition as an element of the lexicon catena. See the lexical entry in Fig. 11[11].

These examples demonstrate the power of the combination of catenae (as subtree units), MRS structures (as semantic units) and valency rep-

[9]The grammatical features are: 'sing' for singular number and 'semdef' for definite subtree. Features like 'semdef' are specified for root node, but can be realized on a form inside the subtree.

[10]The grammatical feature is: 'indef' for indefinite noun

[11]The grammatical feature is: 'ref' for reflexive pronoun

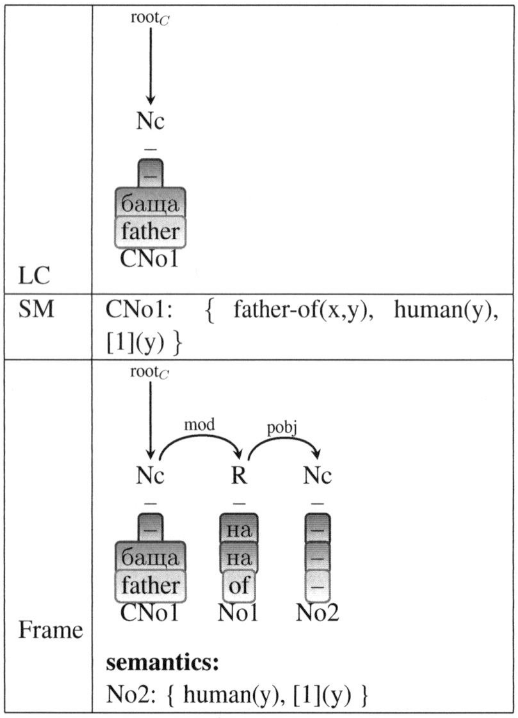

Figure 10: Lexical Entry for баща на "bashta na", 'father of'

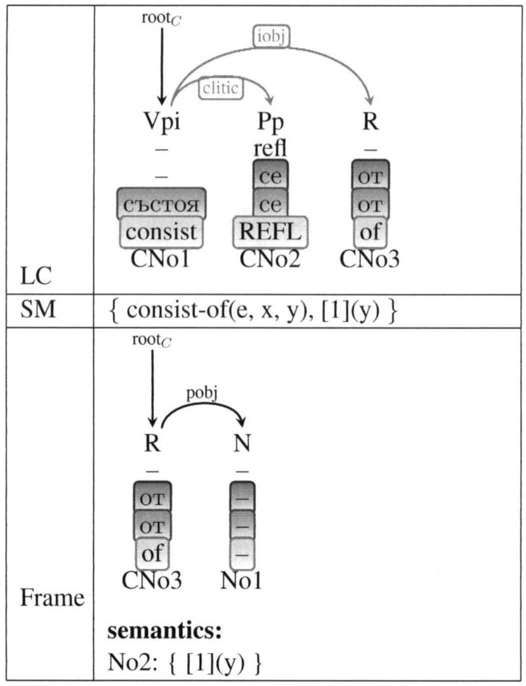

Figure 11: Lexical Entry for състоя се от "sastoya se ot", 'I consist of'

resentation (as subcategorization units) to model MWEs and valencies in the lexicon. The catena is appropriate for representation of syntactic structure; the semantic part represents the idiosyncratic semantics of the MWE and the semantics of valencies and determines the possible semantic modification, and the valency part determines the syntactic behavior of MWEs and other dependency expressions. One missing element of the lexical entry is the representation of constraints over the word order of the catena nodes. We envisage addition of such constraints as future work. The information from the lexical entries is combined by different operations on the elements of the lexical entries structure. The main operation on catenae is the realization in dependency trees. The two other operations are *extension* and *composition* of catenae. The *extension* is used when an MWE or other catena needs to be realized together with an auxiliary catena as in the case of sentence MWEs where the subject catena is detached from the verbal catena and realized as a subject of the auxiliary catena (see the example in Fig. 5). The *composition* is used when the valency catena is realized with the main lexical catena (see the example in Fig. 3).

5 Conclusion and Future Work

The paper demonstrates using Bulgarian data that the modeling at the level of catena is appropriate for encoding language units (including multiword expressions and valencies) at the lexicon-syntax interface. The catena allows for additional material to be inserted, based on the information from valence lexicons and contexts. Additionally, a semantics component is added for ensuring the correct interpretation of the language units.

The paper confirms the conclusions from previous works that catena is an appropriate means for encoding idioms and idiosyncratic language material. With respect to idioms it is very useful for cases where in addition to the figurative meaning the literal meaning also remains a possible interpretation. The paper also extends the catena mechanism to incorporate valency and semantic information.

The formalization of the catena provides definitions of operations over catenae which allow combination of catenae in complete analyses of sentences. In our work here we assume that catenae could have only one node in common — the node on which they extend or combine. This assumption is motivated by the examples of MWEs that are idioms. Idioms usually interact with other catenae in a sentence via one of their nodes. But this requirement might be relaxed for the other catenae in the lexicon. In this way, in valency one could specify more than one common node between the lexical catena and the valency catena.

We do not employ any specific dependency theory in our approach, but we believe that the proposed modeling might be incorporated in most of them, if not all.

Acknowledgements

This research has received support by the EC's FP7 (FP7/2007-2013) under grant agreement number 610516: "QTLeap: Quality Translation by Deep Language Engineering Approaches" and by European COST Action IC1207: "PARSEME: PARSing and Multi-word Expressions. Towards linguistic precision and computational efficiency in natural language processing."

We are grateful to the three anonymous reviewers, whose remarks, comments, suggestions and encouragement helped us to improve the initial variant of the paper. All errors remain our own responsibility.

References

Ann Copestake, Dan Flickinger, Carl Pollard, and Ivan Sag. 2005. Minimal recursion semantics: An introduction. *Research on Language & Computation*, 3(4):281–332.

Thomas Gross. 2010. Chains in syntax and morphology. In Ryo Otoguro, Kiyoshi Ishikawa, Hiroshi Umemoto, Kei Yoshimoto, and Yasunari Harada, editors, *PACLIC*, pages 143–152. Institute for Digital Enhancement of Cognitive Development, Waseda University.

Marco Kuhlmann. 2010. *Dependency Structures and Lexicalized Grammars: An Algebraic Approach*, volume 6270 of *Lecture Notes in Computer Science*. Springer.

K. Tamsin Maxwell, Jon Oberlander, and W. Bruce Croft. 2013. Feature-based selection of dependency paths in ad hoc information retrieval. In *Proceedings of the 51st Annual Meeting of the Association for Computational Linguistics (Volume 1: Long Papers)*, pages 507–516, Sofia, Bulgaria, August. Association for Computational Linguistics.

William O'Grady. 1998. The syntax of idioms. *Natural Language and Linguistic Theory*, 16:279–312.

Timothy Osborne, Michael Putnam, and Thomas Groß. 2012. Catenae: Introducing a novel unit of syntactic analysis. *Syntax*, 15(4):354–396.

Petya Osenova, Kiril Simov, Laska Laskova, and Stanislava Kancheva. 2012. A Treebank-driven Creation of an OntoValence Verb Lexicon for Bulgarian. In *Nicoletta Calzolari (Conference Chair) and Khalid Choukri and Thierry Declerck and Mehmet Uğur Doğan and Bente Maegaard and Joseph Mariani and Jan Odijk and Stelios Piperidis (eds. Proceedings of the Eight International Conference on Language Resources and Evaluation (LREC'12)*, pages 2636–2640.

Chris Quirk, Arul Menezes, and Colin Cherry. 2005. Dependency treelet translation: Syntactically informed phrasal smt. In *Proceedings of ACL*. Association for Computational Linguistics, June.

Kiril Simov and Petya Osenova. 2011. Towards minimal recursion semantics over bulgarian dependency parsing. In *Proceedings of the RANLP 2011*.

Kiril Simov and Petya Osenova. 2014. Formalizing multiwords as catenae in a treebank and in a lexicon. In *Verena Henrich, Erhard Hinrichs, Daniël de Kok, Petya Osenova, Adam Przepiórkowski (eds.) Proceedings of the Thirteenth International Workshop on Treebanks and Linguistic Theories (TLT13)*, pages 198–207.

Zero Alignment of Verb Arguments in a Parallel Treebank

Jana Šindlerová **Eva Fučíková** **Zdeňka Urešová**
Charles University in Prague
Faculty of Mathematics and Physics
Institute of Formal and Applied Linguistics
Czech Republic
{sindlerova,uresova,fucikova}@ufal.mff.cuni.cz

Abstract

This paper analyses several points of inter-lingual dependency mismatch on the material of a parallel Czech-English dependency treebank. Particularly, the points of alignment mismatch between the valency frame arguments of the corresponding verbs are observed and described. The attention is drawn to the question whether such mismatches stem from the inherent semantic properties of the individual languages, or from the character of the used linguistic theory. Comments are made on the possible shifts in meaning. The authors use the findings to make predictions about possible machine translation implementation of the data.

1 Introduction

In Machine translation tasks lately, paraphrases have been used and studied intensely. They basically serve to improve the evaluation metrics of MT systems. The ability to generate valid paraphrases also plays an important role in information retrieval tasks, textual entailment etc. The so-called paraphrase tables can be automatically extracted from parallel corpora (Denkowski and Lavie, 2010; Ganitkevitch et al., 2013).

So far, only lexical paraphrases have been explored for Czech (Barančíková et al., 2014), with syntactic (structural) paraphrases intended for future enhancement of the systems. For English, experiments with both lexical and syntactic paraphrases are employed (Dorr et al., 2004).

This paper presents a preliminary linguistic analysis of structural paraphrases based on valency representations. It appears that certain types of paraphrases affect the valency structure of verbs, and possibly the semantic structure of the sentence, in terms of foregrounding or backgrounding different arguments.[1]

We believe that the analysis of possible syntactic variation within paraphrases, especially such that involves a kind of "disproportion", in the parallel treebank data, would be beneficial for further MT experiments.

By a disproportion in dependencies, we mean such structural configurations that involve different number of dependencies in corresponding syntactic structures, i.e., an alignment of "something" on one side of the translation to "nothing" on the other side. For the purposes of this paper, we call it a "zero alignment".

2 Related Work

The analysis in this paper goes in a similar direction as that of (Sanguinetti et al., 2013), though our interest in what they call a "translation shift" is of a different kind. The authors claim that dependency structures are finely apt to account for the alignment of syntactically different treelets between languages, because of the subtree structures constituting similar semantic units. We take their findings as our starting point and provide a linguistic analysis of some of the well-identified categories of translation shift from their research, in order to get a better understanding of different linguistic grounds for different syntactic structures for a parallel semantic content. Also, our analysis is based on the deep syntactic layer (in contrast to the surface structure alignments used in the paper mentioned above), therefore it does not have to deal with those structural phenomena that might not have important semantic consequences, but only serve for topic-focus hierarchization purposes (such as word order variation, simple passivization etc.).

[1] Here, we use the label "argument" in a simplifying manner. Any element which is included in the valency frame is referred to as an argument.

Proceedings of the Third International Conference on Dependency Linguistics (Depling 2015), pages 330–339,
Uppsala, Sweden, August 24–26 2015.

Our research is also inspired by (Bojar et al., 2013), an attempt to generate as many possible translation paraphrases as possible, in order to enlarge the reference set of translations for MT evaluation purposes. The experiment described in the paper used mostly a flat approach, and was carried out with substantial work provided by human annotators. We believe that our research might help establish rules for automatic extraction of true syntactic paraphrases (without unnecessary noise) from parallel corpora, based on the valency patterns of words, so that most of the work could be done automatically, with minimal human control.

3 Methodology and Data

In the research, we took the advantage of the existence of Czech-English parallel data, namely the Prague Czech-English Dependency Treebank 2.5 (PCEDT 2.5) (Hajič et al., 2012).[2]

It is a collection of about 50 000 sentences, taken from the Wall Street Journal part of Penn treebank (Marcus et al., 1993),[3] translated manually to Czech, transformed into dependency trees and annotated at the level of deep syntactic relations (called tectogrammatic layer). In short, the tectogrammatic layer contains mostly content words (with several defined exceptions) connected with oriented edges and labelled with syntactico-semantic functors according to the Functional Generative Description approach (FGD), see (Sgall et al., 1986). Ellipsis and anaphora resolution is also included, as well as automatic alignment of corresponding nodes. The PCEDT 2.5 is annotated according to the the FGD valency theory (FGDVT) and two valency lexicons (one for each language) are part of the release.

PDT-Vallex[4] (Hajič et al., 2003; Urešová, 2011) has been developed as a resource for annotating argument relations in the Prague Dependency Treebank (Hajič et al., 2006). The version used here contains 11,933 valency frames for 7,121 verbs. Each valency frame in the PDT-Vallex represents a distinct verb meaning. Valency frames consist of argument slots represented by tectogrammatic functors (slots). Each slot is marked as obligatory or facultative and its typical morphological realization forms are listed. Frame entries are supplemented with illustrative sentence examples.

EngVallex[5] (Cinková, 2006) was created as an adaptation of an already existing resource of English verb argument structure characteristics, the Propbank (Palmer et al., 2005). The original Propbank argument structure frames have been adapted to the FGD scheme, so that it currently bears the structure of the PDT-Vallex, though some minor deflections from the original scheme have been allowed in order to save some important theoretical features of the original Propbank annotation. This lexicon includes 7,148 valency frames for 4,337 verbs.

PDT-Vallex and EngVallex have been interlinked together into a new resource called CzEngVallex (Urešová et al., 2015a; Urešová et al., 2015). Beside the complete data of the two lexicons, the CzEngVallex contains a database of frame-to-frame, and subsequently, argument-to-argument pairs for the purposes of machine translation experiments (Urešová et al., 2015b). PCEDT and the CzEngVallex data have already been used successfully in several MT experiments aimed at valency frame detection and selection (Dušek et al., 2014) and also for word sense disambiguation (Dušek et al., 2015).

The interlinking of CzEngVallex frames was carried out via an annotation over the PCEDT. First, an automatic alignment procedure was run over the data, which suggested translational links between nodes of the tectogrammatic layer. Corresponding verb pairs[6] and argument pairs were highlighted. Then, manual revision and correction of the alignments by two annotators was carried out. Thus, as a by-product of building the lexicon, a collection of illustrative annotated tree pairs is available for each verb pair of the CzEngVallex.

4 Zero Alignment in the Data

In the following sections, we will describe the most important, consistent and frequent points of zero alignment found in the data. For each section, we will comment on the linguistic background of the phenomena described and the possible consequences for semantic interpretation in the individual languages.

[2]https://catalog.ldc.upenn.edu/LDC2012T08

[3]https://catalog.ldc.upenn.edu/LDC99T42

[4]http://lindat.mff.cuni.cz/services/PDT-Vallex

[5]http://lindat.mff.cuni.cz/services/EngVallex

[6]As a basic stage of building the CzEngVallex, only verb-verb pairs were taken into account.

4.1 Catenative Verbs - Single vs. Double Object Interpretation

One of the prominent points of alignment disproportion in the data are sentences with catenative verbs. Catenative verbs are usually defined as those combining with non-finite verbal forms. Between the finite catenative verb and the non-finite verb form, there might appear an intervening NP that might be interpreted as the subject of the dependent verbal form. In this section, we will be concerned with exactly those verbs allowing the sequence of a finite catenative verb – NP – a non-finite catenative verb.

4.1.1 ECM Constructions, Raising to Object

Most Czech linguistic approaches do not recognize the term Exceptional Case Marking (ECM) in the sense of "raising to object", instead they generally address similar constructions under the label "accusative with infinitive". The difference between ECM and control verbs is not being taken into account in most of Czech grammars. In short, raising and ECM are generally considered a marginal phenomenon in Czech and are not being treated conceptually (Panevová, 1996), except for several attempts to describe agreement issues, e.g., the morphological behaviour of predicative complements described in a phrase structure grammar formalism (Przepiórkowski and Rosen, 2005).

The reason for this negligent approach to ECM is probably rooted in the low frequency of ECM constructions in Czech. Czech sentences corresponding to English sentences with ECM mostly do not allow catenative constructions. They usually involve a standard dependent clause with a finite verb, see Fig.1,[7] or they include a nominalization, thus keeping the structures strictly parallel.

The only exception are verbs of perception (*see, hear*), which usually allow both ways of Czech translation – with an accusative NP followed by a non-finite verb form (1a), or with a dependent clause (1b), not speaking about the third possibility involving an accusative NP followed by a dependent clause (1c).

(1) He saw Peter coming.

a. Viděl Petra přicházet.
He saw Peter.ACC to come.

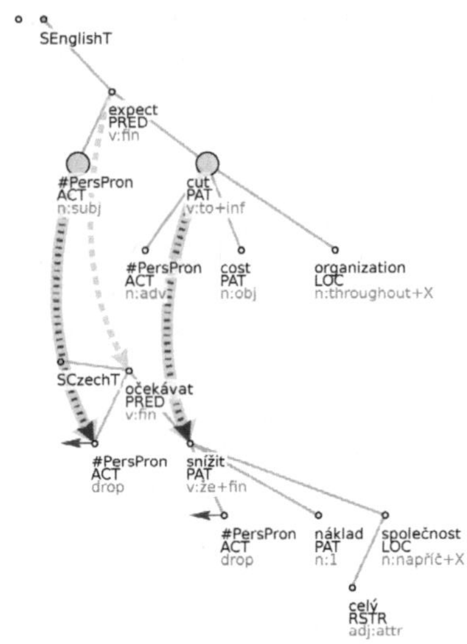

En: They expect him to cut costs...

Cz: Očekávají, že sníží náklady...

Figure 1: Alignment of the ECM construction

b. Viděl, že Petr přichází.
He saw that Peter.ACC is coming.

c. Viděl Petra, jak přichází.
He saw Peter.ACC, how is coming.

In this type of accusative-infinitive sequence, the accusative element is in FGDVT analysed consistently as the direct object of the matrix verb (the `PAT`ient argument) and the non-finite verb form then as the predicative complement of the verb (the `EFF`ect argument).

The PCEDT annotation of verbs of perception is shown in Fig. 2, with frame arguments mapped in the following way:

ACT→ACT; PAT→EFF; ---→PAT

The literature mentions two ways of ECM structural analysis, a flat one, representing the NP as dependent on the matrix verb, and a layered one, representing the intervening NP as the subject of the dependent verb. This mirrors the opinion that verbs allowing ECM usually have three syntactic, but only two semantic arguments. It is then a matter of decision between a syntactic and semantic approach to tree construction.

The English part of the PCEDT data was annotated in the layered manner,[8] thus most of the pairs in the treebank appear as strictly parallel. The consistency of structures is one of the most impor-

[7] In the examples displayed, the green dashed lines connect the annotated verb pair, the dotted lines connect verb dependents, the thick arrows mark collected verb arguments, the automatic node alignment is displayed in blue, the manually corrected alignment is marked in red. The images have been cropped or otherwise adjusted for the sake of clarity.

[8] The annotation followed the original phrasal annotation of the data in the Penn Treebank.

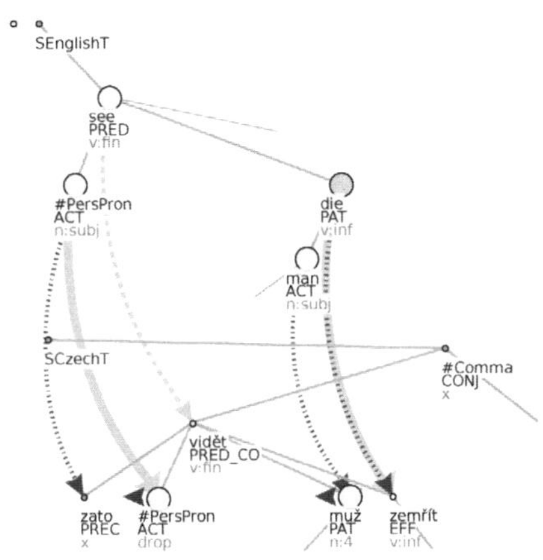

En: I have seen [one or two] men die...
Cz: Zato jsem viděla [jednoho nebo dva] muže zemřít...

Figure 2: Alignment of the perception verbs' arguments. The corresponding arguments man-muž are interpreted as belonging to verbs in different levels of the structure.

tant advantages of the layered approach; there is no need of having two distinct valency frames for the two syntactic constructions of the verb, therefore, the semantic relatedness of the verb forms is kept. Also, there are other specific constructions supporting the layered analysis for English, like the there-constructions intervening instead of the NP, see (2).

(2) We expected there to be slow growth.

On the other hand, the Czech part of the PCEDT data uses flat annotation, partly because the catenative construction with raising structure is fairly uncommon in Czech (cf. Sect. 4.1.1). The flat structure is easier to interpret, or translate in a morphologically correct way to the surface realization, but it requires multiple frames for semantically similar verb forms (the instances of the verb *to see* in *see the house fall* and *see the house* are in the FGD valency approach considered two distinct lexical units) and it also leaves alignment mismatches in the parallel data.

The treatment of ECM constructions in English and in Czech is different. It reflects both the differences internal to the languages and their consequences in theoretical thinking. Contrary to English, Czech nouns carry strong indicators of morphology – case, number and gender. The rules for the subject-verb agreement block overt realization of subjects of the infinitives. The accusative ending naturally leads to the interpretation of the presumed subject of the infinitive as the object of the matrix verb. The morphosyntactic representation is taken as a strong argument for using a flat structure in the semantic representation, and a covert co-referential element for filling the "empty" ACTor position of the infinitive. In English, in general, there is no such strong indication and therefore the layered structure is preferred in the semantic representation.

4.1.2 Object Control Verbs, Equi Verbs, Causatives

Contrary to the ECM constructions, object control verbs constructions (OCV), involving verbs such as *make, cause, or get*, are analyzed strictly as double-object in both languages, i.e., the intervening NP is dependent on the matrix verb (and licensed by it) and there is usually a co-referential empty element of some kind in the valency structure of the dependent verb form. OCV constructions are similarly frequent in Czech and English and their alignment in the PCEDT data is balanced, see Fig. 3.[9]

Interestingly, it is sometimes the case that English control verbs in the treebank are translated with non-control, non-catenative verbs on the Czech side, and the intervening NP is transformed to a dependent of the lower verb of the dependent clause (see Fig. 4), or even a more complex nominalization of the dependent structure is used.

The verb involved in this kind of translation shift may be either a more remote synonym, or a conversive verb.[10]

Such a translation shift brings about (at least a slight) semantic shift in the interpretation, usually in the sense of de-causativisation of the meaning (*prompt*→*lead to*).[11] Nevertheless, this type of semantic shift does not prevent the use of the struc-

[9] In Fig. 3, English ACT of *run* does not show the coreference link to *water* since the annotation of coreferential relations has not yet been completed on the English side of the PCEDT, as opposed to the Czech side (cf. the coreference link from ACT of *téci* to *voda*).

[10] Semantic conversion in our understanding relates different lexical units, or different meanings of the same lexical unit, which share the same situational meaning. The valency frames of conversive verbs can differ in the number and type of valency complementations, their obligatoriness or morphemic forms. Prototypically, semantic conversion involves permutation of situational participants.

[11] Note that the de-causativisation process is possible without objections whereas the reverse shift, from non-control verb to a control verb, is rare if it at all exists.

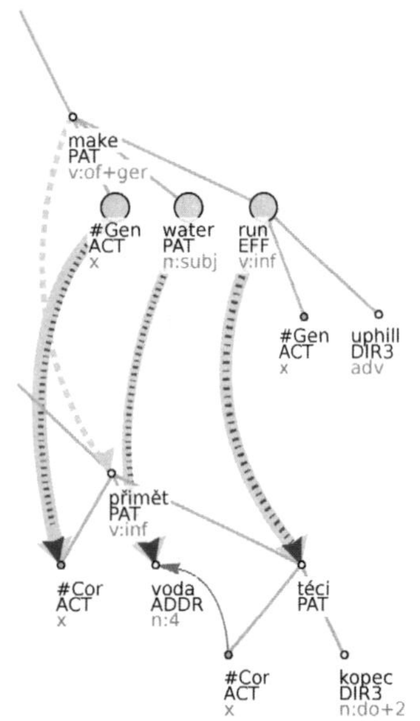

En: ...making water run...

Cz: ...přimět vodu téct...

Figure 3: Alignment of the control verbs' arguments

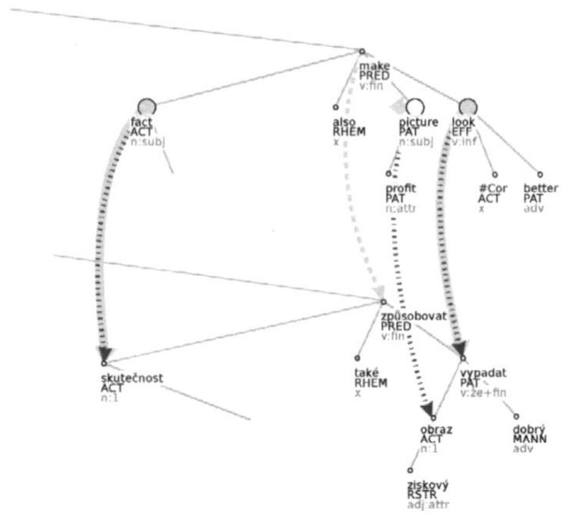

En: The fact... ...will also make the profit picture look...

Cz: Skutečnost......způsobuje, že ziskový obraz vypadá...

Figure 4: Alignment of English OCV with Czech non-OCV construction

ture as a sufficiently equivalent expression of the semantic content. We approach this as an inherent property of (any) language to suppress certain aspects of meaning without losing the general sense of synonymity.

4.2 Complex Predication

By "complex predication" we mean a combination of two lexical units, usually a (semantically empty, or "light") verb and a noun (carrying main lexical meaning and marked with `CPHR` functor in the data), forming a predicate with a single semantic reference, e.g., *to make an announcement, to undertake preparations, to get an order*. There are some direct consequences for the syntactically annotated parallel data.

First type of zero alignment is connected to the fact that a complex predication in one language can be easily translated with a one-word reference, and consequently aligned to a one-word predication, in the other language. This is quite a trivial case. In the data, then, one component of the complex predication remains unaligned. There are basically two ways of resolving such cases: either one can align the light verb with the full verb in the other language, or one can align the full verb with the dependent noun in the complex predication, based on the similarity of semantic content. In the CzEngVallex, the decision was to align the verbs, reflecting the fact that the verb and the noun phrase form a single unit from the semantic point of view.

The second type of zero alignment is connected to the presence of a "third" valency argument within the complex predication structure, e.g., En: *placed weight on retailing* - Cz: *klást důraz na prodej*, see Fig. 5.

Complex predicates have been annotated according to quite a complicated set of rules on the Czech side of the PCEDT data (for details, see (Mikulová et al., 2006)). Those rules include also the so-called dual function of a valency modification. There are two possible dependency positions for the "third" valency argument of the complex predicate: either it is modelled as the dependent of the semantically empty verb, or as a dependent of the nominal component. The decision between the two positions rely on multiple factors, such as valency structure of the semantically full use of the verb, valency structure of the noun in other contexts, behaviour of synonymous verbs etc. On the Czech side, the "third" valency argument was strongly preferred to be a dependent of the nominal component.

On the English side of the PCEDT, the preferred decision was different. The "third" argument was annotated as a direct dependent of the light verb

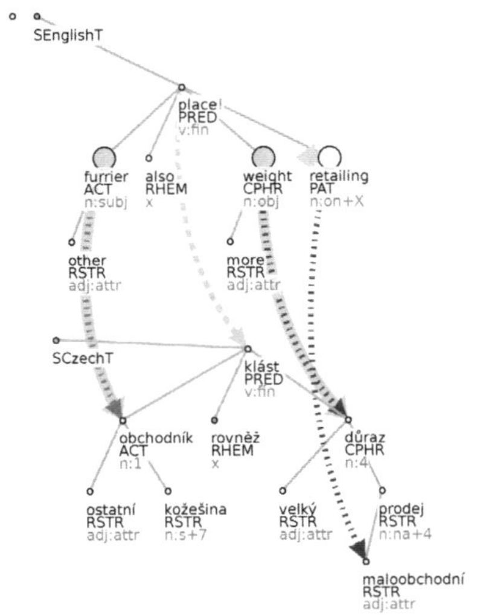

En: Other furriers have also placed more weight on retailing.

Cz: Ostatní obchodníci s kožešinami rovněž kladou větší důraz na maloobchodní prodej.

Figure 5: Mismatch due to complex predication solution

(probably due to lower confidence of non-native speaker annotators in judging verb valency issues).

There is probably no chance of dealing with the dependencies in one of the two above stated ways only. The class of complex predicates in the data is wide and heterogeneous with respect to semantic and morphosyntactic qualities. Nevertheless, the data suggest several points of interesting inconsistencies stemming from the imperfection or lack of reliability of the theoretical guidelines. For example, the dependency of the valency complementation of the complex predicate *klást důraz* 'place emphasis', as can be seen in Fig. 5, is solved as a dependency on the nominal component, whereas in the complex predicate *klást požadavek* 'place claim', the valency lexicon entry involves a direct dependency on the verb. Keeping in mind that the verb *klást* 'to place' has three arguments in its semantically full occurrences, we would expect direct dependency on the verb in both cases.

4.3 Conversive Verbs

A considerable number of unaligned arguments in the data is caused by the translator's choice of a verb in a conversive relation to the verb used in the original language. For some reason (e.g., frequency of the verbal lexical unit, topic-focus articulation etc.), the translator decides not to use the syntactically most similar lexical unit, but uses a conversive one (cf. also Sect. 4.1.2), thus causing the arguments to relocate in the deep syntactic structure, see Fig. 6.

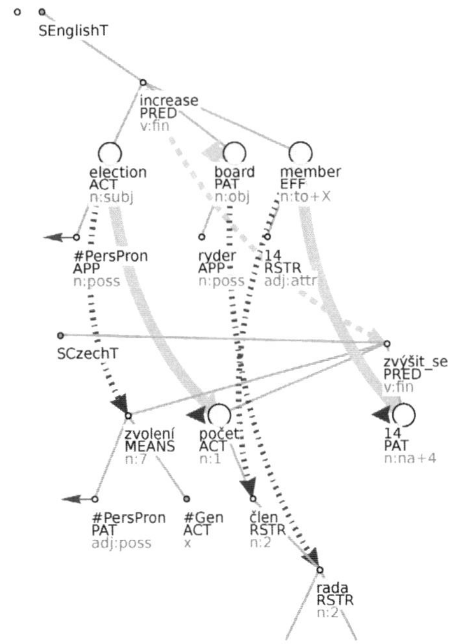

En: His election increases Ryder's board to 14 members.

Cz: Jeho zvolením se počet členů správní rady společnosti Ryder zvýšíl na 14.

Figure 6: Mismatch due to the the use of conversive verbs

The relocation of arguments frequently goes together with backgrounding of one of the arguments, which then either disappears from the translation, or is transformed into an adjunct, or into a dependent argument embedded even lower in the structure.

The first argument (actant)[12] in the FGD approach is strongly underspecified. It is mostly delimited by its position in the tectogrammatic annotation. Its prevalent morphosyntactic realization is nominative case, but certain exceptions are recognized (verbs of feeling etc.). Also, the `ACT` position (first actant) is subject to the process called "shifting of cognitive roles" (Panevová, 1974), i.e., other semantic roles can take the nominative case and the corresponding place in the structure

[12]Under the term "actant", FGDVT distinguishes five core constituting valency complementations, `ACT`, `PAT`, `ADDR`, `EFF`, and `ORIG`.

in case there is no semantic agent in the structure. Thus we get semantically quite different elements (e.g., +anim vs. -anim) in the ACT position, even with formally identical verb instances, see the English side of Figs. 7 and 8.

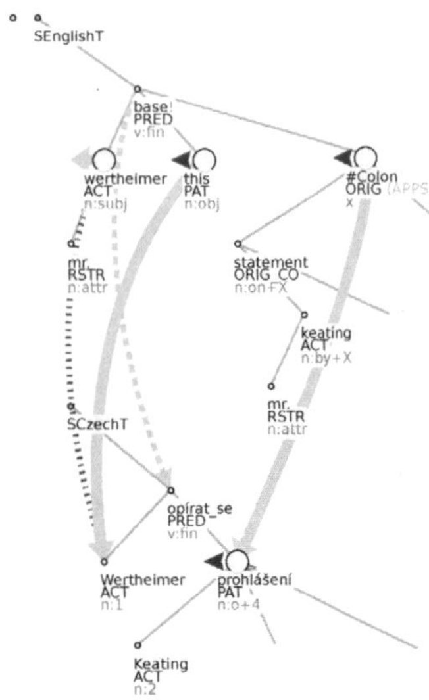

En: Mr. Wertheimer based this on a statement by Mr. Keating...

Cz: Wertheimer se opírá o prohlášení Keatinga...

Figure 7: Conflict due to the underspecification of the ACT position

This formal feature of the FGDVT gives rise to a number of conflicts in the parallel structures considering structures that undergo semantic de-agentization or (milder) de-concretization of the agent.

Here the question arises, whether such verb instances correspond to different meanings of the verb (represented by different verb frames), or whether they correspond to a single meaning (represented by a single valency frame). It is often the case, that the Czech data tend to overgeneralize the valency frames through considering the different instances as realizations of a single deep syntactic valency frame, when there is no other modification intervening in the frame. Therefore, this approach chosen for the Czech annotation sometimes shows a conflict, as in Fig. 7.

The valency structure for both instances of *base* is identical, only in the first case, the verb is used in active voice, whereas in the second case, it takes passive morphology. There are three semantic ar-

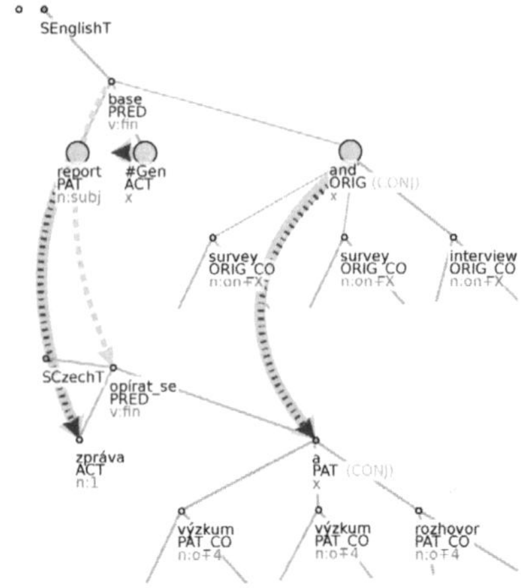

En: The report was based on a telephone survey...

Cz: Zpráva se opírá o telefonický výzkum...

Figure 8: Original collect for the verbs *base* and *opírat se*

guments in the structure. We will call them the Person that expresses an opinion, the Expressed Opinion and the Resource for the opinion. The Person bases the Expressed Opinion on the Resource. With the English verb, the Expressed Opinion always takes the PAT position and the Resource the ORIGin position in the valency structure. On the other hand, on the Czech side of the data, there is a conflict. In both cases, there are seemingly only two arguments. In the first case, the Expressed Opinion is sort of backgrounded from the semantic structure. If there were a need of overtizing it, it would probably appear with locative morphology, as an adjunct: *Wertheimer se **v tomto** opírá o prohlášení...* 'Wertheimer **in this** relies on a statement' (see also an authentic example from the data in Fig. 9). In the second case, on the other hand, the structure follows the passivized English structure in backgrounding the Person (note that the *se* morpheme does NOT stand for a passive morphology here). If there were a need for expressing the Person, it would probably appear as a specifying dependent to the ACT position: ***Jejich** zpráva se opírá o telefonický výzkum.* **'Their** report is based on a phone survey'. In the second case, the Expressed Opinion does not take the PAT position, but the ACT position in the structure, which is the cause of the conflict. We are able to reformulate the first case

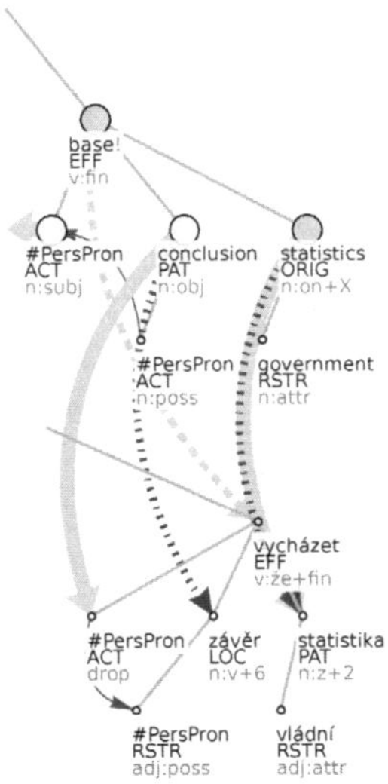

En: ...they based their conclusions on government statistics.

Cz: ...vycházejí z vládních statistik.

Figure 9: Original collect for the verbs base and vycházet with LOC argument linked to PAT

in a corresponding manner to show the Expressed Opinion argument in the ACT position and the Person backgrounded from the structure, see (3):

(3) a. Wertheimer se ve svém názoru opírá o
Wertheimer REFL in his opinion leans to
prohlášení Keatinga.
the statement by Keating

b. Wertheimerův názor se opírá o
Wertheimer's opinion REFL leans to
prohlášení Keatinga.
the statement by Keating

c. Wertheimer opírá svůj názor o
Wertheimer leans his opinion to
prohlášení Keatinga.
the statement by Keating

The problem of the status of a Czech verbal-adjoining *se*-morpheme is a complex one and there is no clear scientific consensus in this respect. The *se*-morpheme in Czech has a variety of functions, e.g., a passivization morpheme for the so-called "reflexive passive" form, a "dispositional diathesis" morpheme, a reflexive morpheme for lexical derivation of impersonal verbal variants, or an accusative reflexive pronoun.

These variants differ with respect to the way they are reflected in the data and in the lexicon. Some are treated as individual verb lemmas, some as surface variants of a common non-reflexive lemma.

The conflicts in annotation have a substantial reason – the ways in which English and Czech express backgrounding of the agent are multiple and they differ across the languages. Czech uses the *se*-morphemization often, in order to preserve the topic focus articulation (information) structure, whereas English does not have such a morpheme to work with, so it often uses simple passivization, or middle construction.

Moreover, the first valency position in Czech is often overgeneralized, allowing a multitude of semantically different arguments, which is, due to "economy of description", sometimes not reflected in the linguistic theory.

4.4 Arguments Mapped to Adjuncts

In the previous section, we have described the bilingual treebank data manifestation of the fact that languages have different means of expressing a content, and we have noted that these can also variate between argument and adjunct interpretation. This variation appears both within a single language (one language expresses a largely synonymous content with either argument or adjunct means) and across languages (a direct consequence of the former case: an argument (actant) in one language can be translated into another language using an adjunct construction). Languages may differ in the preference for either of the possibilities.

Observing such mismatches in a parallel treebank occasionally leads us to hesitate whether our interpretation of a word (or phrase) as an argument or an adjunct is proper or justifiable. There may be two possible consequences drawn from the observation of a mismatch – either there are some (rather subtle) semantic reasons for structuring a word as an argument/adjunct, or there might be some imperfection in our theoretical thinking about the internal system of a particular language.

The theoretical distinction between arguments and adjuncts is subject to serious debates in the world of linguistics (Hwang, 2011; Tutunjian and Boland, 2008), and so far there is no approach known to us that would overcome this problem easily. Still, we can see that the real data indicate some remarkable points that stand at the roots of the argument/adjunct distinction problem. Most prominently - the nature of the relation between the form of the argument and its semantics.

In the parallel treebank, we find cases (among

others) such as alignment of an actor with a temporal adjunct (4) or an actor with a causal adjunct (5), etc.

(4) Americans haven't forgiven China's leaders for the military assault of June 3-4 ***that*** killed hundreds, and perhaps thousands, of demonstrators.

a. Američané neodpustili čínským vůdcům
Americans haven't forgotten Chinese leaders
vojenský útok z 3.-4. června,
military assault from 3-4 June,
při kterém zahynuly stovky, možná i
during which died hundreds, maybe even
tisíce demonstrantů.
thousands demonstrators

(5) ***The purchase*** will make Quebecor the second-largest commercial printer in North America.

a. ***Díky této koupi*** se společnost
Thanks to this purchase REFL the company
Quebecor stane druhou největší
Quebecor will become second largest
komerční tiskárnou v Severní Americe.
commercial printer in North America

The interpretation of the argument in the above stated examples is driven mainly by its morphological form, which is a surprising finding considering that we are dealing with deep syntax, or even semantics.

It is believed that the form of the expression more or less mirrors its function in the language. The width of the paraphrasing range though, both within and across languages, leads us to questioning whether it is appropriate to lay much stress on the difference between arguments and adjuncts in the description of a language.

5 Conclusion

We have encountered several reasons for the presence of a zero alignment in the data. Though these reasons have different grounds they tend to be interconnected in the language.

1. Language is flexible in paraphrasing linguistic content with different syntactic means. Even pairs of sentences which include semantic backgrounding or foregrounding of different arguments are easily interpreted as synonymous.

2. It is possible to use predicates that are in a conversive relation, or predicates of different complexity.

3. The backgrounding and foregrounding of arguments leads to syntactic relocation of other arguments in the structure, and consequently to the shift in their morphosyntactic properties, to the shift in their valency status, or even to their complete disappearance from the structure.

4. The FGD, having been built on a morphologically rich Czech language, relies strongly on the morphosyntactic form of the individual arguments. Therefore, disproportions of the zero alignment or argument mismatch kind must appear when it is applied to other languages with different typological properties.

Points 1, 2 and 3 belong among inherent deeply rooted properties of (perhaps any) natural language. Such differences are not to be overcome by means of possible theoretical unification of description.

Point 4, on the other hand, belongs to the properties of a certain linguistic theory. We will leave it open, whether it were appropriate to change the very roots of a linguistic theory in order to make it more flexible for use across different languages. Nevertheless, it appears that it is at least possible to change those aspects that cause individual and otherwise unjustifiable conflicts in the data.

Acknowledgements

This work has been supported by the grant GP13-03351P of the Grant Agency of the Czech Rep.

References

P. Barančíková, R. Rosa, and A. Tamchyna. 2014. Improving Evaluation of English-Czech MT through Paraphrasing. In N. Calzolari, K. Choukri, T. Declerck, H. Loftsson, B. Maegaard, and J. Mariani, editors, *Proceedings of the 9th International Conference on Language Resources and Evaluation (LREC 2014)*, pages 596–601, Reykjavík, Iceland. European Language Resources Association.

O. Bojar, M. Macháček, A. Tamchyna, and D. Zeman. 2013. Scratching the surface of possible translations. In *Text, Speech, and Dialogue*, pages 465–474. Springer.

S. Cinková. 2006. From PropBank to EngValLex: adapting the PropBank-Lexicon to the valency theory of the functional generative description. In *Proceedings of the fifth International conference on Language Resources and Evaluation (LREC 2006), Genova, Italy.*

M. Denkowski and A. Lavie. 2010. Meteor-next and the meteor paraphrase tables: Improved evaluation support for five target languages. In *Proceedings of the Joint Fifth Workshop on Statistical Machine Translation and MetricsMATR*, pages 339–342. Association for Computational Linguistics.

B. J. Dorr, R. Green, L. Levin, O. Rambow, D. Farwell, N. Habash, S. Helmreich, E. Hovy, K.J. Miller, T. Mitamura, et al. 2004. Semantic annotation and lexico-syntactic paraphrase. *Proceedings of the 4th International Conference on Language Resources and Evaluation (LREC) Workshop on Building Lexical Resources from Semantically Annotated Corpora*, pages 47 – 52.

O. Dušek, J. Hajič, and Z. Urešová. 2014. Verbal valency frame detection and selection in Czech and English. In *The 2nd Workshop on EVENTS: Definition, Detection, Coreference, and Representation*, pages 6–11, Stroudsburg, PA, USA. Association for Computational Linguistics.

O. Dušek, E. Fučíková, J. Hajič, M. Popel, J. Šindlerová, and Z. Urešová. 2015. Using Parallel Texts and Lexicons for Verbal Word Sense Disambiguation. In *Proceedings of the Third International Conference on Dependency Linguistics, Depling 2015*, page this volume. Uppsala University.

J. Ganitkevitch, B. Van Durme, and Ch. Callison-Burch. 2013. PPDB: The paraphrase database. In *Proceedings of NAACL-HLT*, pages 758–764, Atlanta, Georgia, June. Association for Computational Linguistics.

J. Hajič, E. Hajičová, J. Panevová, P. Sgall, O. Bojar, S. Cinková, E. Fučíková, M. Mikulová, P. Pajas, J. Popelka, J. Semecký, J. Šindlerová, J. Štěpánek, J. Toman, Z. Urešová, and Z. Žabokrtský. 2012. Announcing Prague Czech-English Dependency Treebank 2.0. In *Proceedings of LREC*, pages 3153–3160.

J. Hajič, J. Panevová, Z. Urešová, A. Bémová, V. Kolářová, and P. Pajas. 2003. PDT-Vallex: Creating a Large-coverage Valency Lexicon for Treebank Annotation. In *Proceedings of The Second Workshop on Treebanks and Linguistic Theories*, volume 9, page 57–68.

J. Hajič, J. Panevová, E. Hajičová, P. Sgall, P. Pajas, J. Štěpánek, J. Havelka, M. Mikulová, Z. Žabokrtský, M. Ševčíková Razímová, and Z. Urešová. 2006. *Prague Dependency Treebank 2.0*. Number LDC2006T01. Linguistic Data Consortium, Philadelphia, PA, USA.

J. D. Hwang. 2011. Making verb argument adjunct distinctions in English. *Synthesis paper, University of Colorado, Boulder, Colorado.*

M. P. Marcus, B. Santorini, and M. A. Marcinkiewicz. 1993. Building a Large Annotated Corpus of English: The Penn Treebank. *COMPUTATIONAL LINGUISTICS*, 19(2):313–330.

M. Mikulová, A. Bémová, J. Hajič, E. Hajičová, J. Havelka, V. Kolářová, L. Kučová, M. Lopatková, P. Pajas, J. Panevová, M. Razímová, P. Sgall, J. Štěpánek, Z. Urešová, K. Veselá, and Z. Žabokrtský. 2006. Annotation on the tectogrammatical level in the Prague Dependency Treebank. Annotation manual. Technical Report 30, Prague, Czech Rep.

M. Palmer, D. Gildea, and P. Kingsbury. 2005. The proposition bank: An annotated corpus of semantic roles. *Computational Linguistics*, 31(1):71–106.

J. Panevová. 1974. On verbal Frames in Functional Generative Description. *Prague Bulletin of Mathematical Linguistics*, 22:3–40.

J. Panevová. 1996. More remarks on control. *Prague Linguistic Circle Papers*, 2(1):101–120.

A. Przepiórkowski and A. Rosen. 2005. Czech and Polish raising/control with or without structure sharing. 3:33–66.

M. Sanguinetti, C. Bosco, and L. Lesmo. 2013. Dependency and constituency in translation shift analysis. *DepLing 2013*, page 282.

P. Sgall, E.Hajičová, and J. Panevová. 1986. *The Meaning of the Sentence in Its Semantic and Pragmatic Aspects*. Dordrecht, Reidel, and Prague, Academia, Prague.

D. Tutunjian and J. E. Boland. 2008. Do we need a distinction between arguments and adjuncts? Evidence from psycholinguistic studies of comprehension. *Language and Linguistics Compass*, 2(4):631–646.

Z. Urešová, E. Fučíková, and J. Šindlerová. 2015. CzEngVallex: Mapping Valency between Languages. Technical Report TR-2015-58, Charles University in Prague, Institute of Formal and Applied Lingustics, Prague. To appear at `http://ufal.mff.cuni.cz/techrep/tr58.pdf`.

Z. Urešová, O. Dušek, E. Fučíková, J. Hajič, and J. Šindlerová. 2015b. Bilingual English-Czech valency lexicon linked to a parallel corpus. In *Proceedings of the The 9th Linguistic Annotation Workshop (LAW IX 2015)*, Stroudsburg, PA, USA. Association for Computational Linguistics.

Z. Urešová. 2011. *Valenční slovník Pražského závislostního korpusu (PDT-Vallex)*. Studies in Computational and Theoretical Linguistics. Ústav formální a aplikované lingvistiky, Praha, Czechia.

Z. Urešová, O. Dušek, E. Fučíková, J. Hajič, and J. Šindlerová. 2015a. Bilingual English-Czech Valency Lexicon Linked to a Parallel Corpus. In *Proceedings of The 9th Linguistic Annotation Workshop*, pages 124–128, Denver, Colorado, USA, June. Association for Computational Linguistics.

Cross-Lingual Dependency Parsing with Universal Dependencies and Predicted PoS Labels

Jörg Tiedemann
Uppsala University
Department of Linguistics and Philology
firstname.lastname@lingfil.uu.se

Abstract

This paper presents cross-lingual models for dependency parsing using the first release of the universal dependencies data set. We systematically compare annotation projection with monolingual baseline models and study the effect of predicted PoS labels in evaluation. Our results reveal the strong impact of tagging accuracy especially with models trained on noisy projected data sets. This paper quantifies the differences that can be observed when replacing gold standard labels and our results should influence application developers that rely on cross-lingual models that are not tested in realistic scenarios.

1 Introduction

Cross-lingual parsing has received considerable attention in recent years. The demand for robust NLP tools in many languages makes it necessary to port existing tools and resources to new languages in order to support low-resource languages without starting their development from scratch. Dependency parsing is one of the popular tasks in the NLP community (Kübler et al., 2009) that also found its way into commercial products and applications. Statistical parsing relies on annotated data sets, so-called treebanks. Several freely available data sets exist but still they only cover a small fraction of the linguistic variety in the world (Buchholz and Marsi, 2006; Nivre et al., 2007). Transferring linguistic information across languages is one approach to add support for new languages. There are basically two types of transfer that have been proposed in the literature: data transfer approaches and model transfer approaches. The former emphasizes the projection of data sets to new languages and it usually relies on parallel data sets and word alignment (Hwa et al., 2005; Tiedemann, 2014). Recently, machine translation was also introduced as yet another alternative to data transfer (Tiedemann et al., 2014). In model transfer, one tries to port existing parsers to new languages by (i) relying on universal features (McDonald et al., 2013; McDonald et al., 2011a; Naseem et al., 2012) and (ii) by adapting model parameters to the target language (Täckström et al., 2013). Universal features may refer to coarse part-of-speech sets that represent common word classes (Petrov et al., 2012) and may also include language-set-specific features such as cross-lingual word clusters (Täckström et al., 2012) or bilingual word embeddings (Xiao and Guo, 2014). Target language adaptation can be done using external linguistic resources such as prior knowledge about language families or lexical databases or any other existing tool for the target language.

This paper is focused on data transfer methods and especially annotation projection techniques that have been proposed in the related literature. There is an on-going effort on harmonized dependency annotations that makes it possible to transfer syntactic information across languages and to compare projected annotation and cross-lingual models even including labeled structures. The contributions of this paper include the presentation of monolingual and cross-lingual baseline models for the recently published universal dependencies data sets (UD; release 1.0)[1] and a detailed discussion of the impact of PoS labels. We systematically compare results on standard test sets with gold labels with corresponding experiments that rely on predicted labels, which reflects the typical real-world scenario.

Let us first look at baseline models before starting our discussion of cross-lingual approaches. In all our experiments, we apply the Mate tools (Bohnet, 2010; Bohnet and Kuhn, 2012) for train-

[1] http://universaldependencies.github.io/docs/

Proceedings of the Third International Conference on Dependency Linguistics (Depling 2015), pages 340–349,
Uppsala, Sweden, August 24–26 2015.

ing dependency parsers and we use standard settings throughout the paper.

2 Baseline Models

Universal Dependencies is a project that develops cross-linguistically consistent treebank annotation for many languages. The goal is to facilitate cross-lingual learning, multilingual parser development and typological research from a syntactic perspective. The annotation scheme is derived from the universal Stanford dependencies (De Marneffe et al., 2006), the Google universal part-of-speech (PoS) tags (Petrov et al., 2012) and the Interset interlingua for morphological tagsets (Zeman and Resnik, 2008). The aim of the project is to provide a universal inventory of categories and consistent annotation guidelines for similar syntactic constructions across languages. In contrast to previous attempts to create universal dependency treebanks, the project explicitly allows language-specific extensions when necessary. Current efforts involve the conversion of existing treebanks to the UD annotation scheme. The first release includes ten languages: Czech, German, English, Spanish, Finnish, French, Irish, Italian, Swedish and Hungarian. We will use ISO 639-1 language codes throughout the paper (cs, de, en, es, fi, fr, ga, it, sv and hu).

UD comes with separate data sets for training, development and testing. In our experiments, we use the provided training data subsets for inducing parser models and test their quality on the separate test sets included in UD. The data sizes vary quite a lot and the amount of language-specific information is different from language to language (see Table 1. Some languages include detailed morphological information (such as Czech, Finnish or Hungarian) whereas other languages only use coarse PoS labels besides the raw text. Some treebanks include lemmas and enhanced PoS tag sets that include some morpho-syntactic features. We will list models trained on those features under the common label "morphology" below.

The data format is a revised CoNLL-X format which is called CoNLL-U. Several extensions have been added to allow language-specific representations and special constructions. For example, dependency relations may include language-specific subtypes (separated by ":" from the main type) and multiword tokens can be represented by both, the surface form (that might be a contraction of multiple words) and a tokenized version. For multiword units, special indexing schemes are proposed that take care of the different versions.[2] For our purposes, we remove all language-specific extensions of dependency relations and special forms and rely entirely on the tokenized version of each treebank with the standard setup that is conform to the CoNLL-X format (even in the monolingual experiments). In version 1.0, language-specific relation types and CoNLL-U-specific constructions are very rare and, therefore, our simplification does not alter the data a lot.

language	size	lemma	morph.	LAS	UAS	LACC
CS	60k	X	X	85.74	90.04	91.99
DE	14k			79.39	84.38	90.28
EN	13k		(X)	85.70	87.76	93.29
ES	14k			84.05	86.77	92.90
FI	12k	X	X	84.51	86.51	93.53
FR	15k			81.03	84.39	91.02
GA	0.7k	X		72.73	78.75	84.74
HU	1k	X	X	83.19	85.28	92.73
IT	9k	X	X	89.58	91.86	95.92
SV	4k		X	82.66	85.66	91.06

Table 1: Baseline models for all languages included in release 1.0 of the universal dependencies data set. Results on the given test sets in labeled accuracy (LAS), unlabeled accuracy (UAS) and label accuracy (LACC).

After our small modifications, we are able to run standard tools for statistical parser induction and we use the Mate tools as mentioned earlier to obtain state-of-the-art models in our experiments. Table 1 summarizes the results of our baseline models in terms of labeled and unlabeled attachment scores as well as label accuracy. All models are trained with the complete information available in the given treebanks, i.e. including morphological information and lemmatized tokens if given in the data set. For morphologically rich languages such as Finnish or Hungarian these features are very important to obtain high parsing accuracies as we will see later on. In the following, we look at the impact of various labels and compare also the difference between gold annotation and predicted features in monolingual parsing performance.

3 Gold versus Predicted Labels

Parsing accuracy is often measured on test sets that include manually verified annotation of essential features such as PoS labels and morphological

[2]See http://universaldependencies.github.io/docs/format.html for more details.

LAS/ACCURACY	CS	DE	EN	ES	FI	FR	GA	HU	IT	SV
gold PoS & morphology	85.74	—	85.70	—	84.51	—	72.73	83.19	89.58	82.66
gold coarse PoS	80.75	79.39	84.81	84.05	74.62	81.03	71.39	73.39	88.25	81.02
delexicalized & gold PoS	70.36	71.29	76.04	75.47	59.54	74.19	66.97	66.57	79.07	66.95
coarse PoS tagger (accuracy)	98.28	93.19	94.89	95.13	95.69	95.99	91.97	94.69	97.63	96.79
morph. tagger (accuracy)	93.47	—	94.80	—	94.53	—	91.92	91.06	97.50	95.26
predicted PoS & morphology	82.67	—	81.36	—	80.59	—	66.74	75.78	87.16	78.76
predicted coarse PoS	79.41	74.39	80.33	80.16	70.25	78.73	65.93	68.04	85.08	76.42
delexicalized & predicted PoS	62.44	61.82	67.40	69.03	49.79	68.60	55.33	58.90	72.92	61.99

Table 2: The impact of morphology and PoS labels: Comparing gold labels with predicted labels.

properties. However, this setup is not very realistic because perfect annotation is typically not available in real-world settings in which raw text needs to be processed. In this section, we look at the impact of label accuracy and compare gold feature annotation with predicted one. Table 2 summarizes the results in terms of labeled attachment scores.

The top three rows in Table 2 refer to models tested with gold annotation. The first one corresponds to the baseline models presented in the previous section. If we leave out morphological information, we achieve the performance shown in the second row. German, Spanish and French treebanks include only the coarse universal PoS tags. English includes a slightly more fine-grained PoS set besides the universal tag set leading to a modest improvement when this feature is used. Czech, Finnish, Hungarian and Italian contain lemmas and morphological information. Irish include lemmas as well but no explicit morphology and Swedish has morphological tags but no lemmas. The impact of these extra features is as expected and mostly pronounced in Finnish and Hungarian with a drop of roughly 10 points in LAS when leaving them out. Czech also drops with about 5 points without morphology whereas Italian and Swedish do not seem to suffer much from the loss of information. The third row shows the results of delexicalized parsers. In those models, we only use the coarse universal PoS labels to train parsing models that can be applied to any of the other languages as one simple possibility of cross-lingual model transfer. As we can see, this drastic reduction leads to significant drops in attachment scores for all languages but especially for the ones that are rich in morphology and more flexible in word order.

In order to contrast these results with predicted features, we also trained taggers that provide automatic labels for PoS and morphology. We apply Marmot (Müller and Schütze, 2015), an efficient implementation for training sequence labelers that include rich morphological tag sets. The tagger performance is shown in the middle of the table.

The three rows at the bottom of Table 2 list the results of our parsing experiments. The first of them refers to the baseline model when applied to test sets with predicted coarse PoS labels and morphology (if it exists in the original treebank we train on). We can see that we loose 2-4 points in LAS with Irish and Hungarian being a bit stronger effected (showing 5-7 points drop in LAS). Irish and Hungarian treebanks are, however, very small and we cannot expect high tagging accuracies for those languages especially with the rich morphological tag set in Hungarian. In general, the performance is quite a good achievement especially considering the languages that require rich morphological information such as Finnish and Czech and this is due to the high quality of the taggers we apply. As expected, we can observe significant drops again when taking out morphology. The effect is similar to the results with gold labels when looking at absolute LAS differences.

The final row represents the LAS for delexicalized models when tested against data sets with predicted PoS labels. Here, we can see significant drops compared to the gold standard results that are much more severe than we have seen with the lexicalized counterparts. This is not surprising, of course, as these models entirely rely on these PoS tags. However, the accuracy of the taggers is quite high and it is important to stress this effect when talking about cross-lingual parsing approaches. In the next section, we will investigate this result in more detail with respect to cross-lingual models.

4 Cross-Lingual Delexicalized Models

The previous section presented delexicalized models when tested on the same language they are trained on. The primary goal of these models is,

← target (test) language →

LAS	CS	DE	EN	ES	FI	FR	GA	HU	IT	SV
CS		48.90	43.78	43.82	42.18	40.70	30.28	32.18	43.93	40.09
DE	47.27		47.80	53.63	33.45	51.60	37.63	39.41	53.63	46.14
EN	44.27	54.27		60.94	38.52	60.53	39.31	34.06	61.88	50.76
ES	48.40	52.59	50.10		32.80	65.40	43.84	34.46	69.54	46.79
FI	43.75	38.31	40.36	30.14		28.54	20.15	37.39	27.49	37.97
FR	43.63	53.04	52.55	66.42	31.44		41.82	34.53	69.62	44.98
GA	23.23	32.10	28.52	45.61	16.19	43.69		18.24	50.21	27.41
HU	31.83	38.42	29.77	31.17	36.68	30.94	17.59		30.42	25.86
IT	47.38	49.68	47.65	64.96	33.03	64.87	43.42	34.39		45.65
SV	41.20	50.48	47.16	51.93	36.46	51.07	37.76	40.48	55.65	

Table 3: Delexicalized models tested with gold PoS labels across languages.

Δ LAS	CS	DE	EN	ES	FI	FR	GA	HU	IT	SV
CS		-9.30	-7.73	-10.27	-7.17	-8.53	-8.85	-4.36	-10.59	-4.05
DE	-6.69		-6.22	-7.28	-6.62	-5.18	-7.77	-8.22	-5.26	-5.09
EN	-3.94	-5.93		-8.42	-5.37	-6.27	-6.99	-2.87	-7.96	-4.87
ES	-3.99	-7.05	-5.46		-4.58	-5.59	-7.28	-4.63	-4.86	-2.31
FI	-2.47	-7.72	-3.94	-3.80		-1.70	-5.39	-5.68	-1.59	-2.28
FR	-4.24	-7.62	-5.24	-7.68	-4.95		-9.50	-4.73	-7.61	-3.51
GA	-2.15	-2.38	-1.42	-6.91	-2.25	-3.57		-3.12	-7.13	-3.01
HU	-2.81	-5.29	-3.14	-2.50	-5.63	-1.64	-2.41		-2.05	-1.62
IT	-8.81	-7.15	-6.19	-6.98	-5.33	-5.84	-8.61	-8.08		-3.98
SV	-2.64	-10.18	-6.13	-14.78	-3.12	-13.11	-10.83	-6.68	-14.09	

Table 4: LAS differences of delexicalized models tested with **predicted** PoS labels across languages compared to gold PoS labels (shown in Table 3).

however, to be applied to other languages with the same universal features they are trained on. Figure 1 illustrates the general idea behind delexicalized parsing across languages and Table 3 lists the LAS's of applying our models across languages with the UD data set.

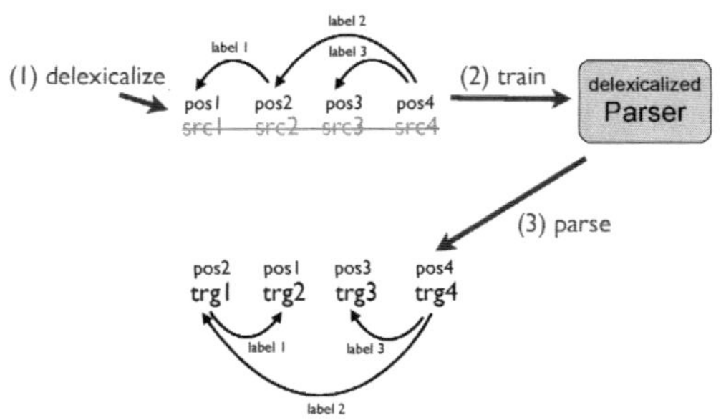

Figure 1: Delexicalized models applied across languages.

The results show that delexicalized models are quite robust across languages, at least for closely related languages like Spanish and Italian, but also for some languages from different language subfamilies such as English and French. The situation is, of course, much worse for distant languages and small training data sets such as Irish models applied to Finnish or Hungarian. Those models are essentially useless. Nevertheless, we can see the positive effect of universal annotation and harmonized annotation guidelines.

However, as argued earlier, we need to evaluate the performance of such models in real-world scenarios which require automatic annotation of PoS labels. Therefore, we used the same tagger models from the previous section to annotate the test sets in each language and parsed those data sets with our delexicalized models across languages. The LAS difference to the gold standard evaluation are listed in Table 4.

With these experiments, we can basically confirm the findings on monolingual parsing, namely that the performance drops significantly with predicted PoS labels. However, there is quite a variation among the language pairs. Models that have been quite bad to start with are in general less effected by the noise of the tagger. LAS reductions up to 14 points are certainly very serious and most models go down to way below 50% LAS. Note that we still rely on PoS taggers that are actually trained on manually verified data sets with over 90% accuracy which we cannot necessarily assume to find for low resource languages.

In the next section, we will look at annotation projection as another alternative for cross-lingual

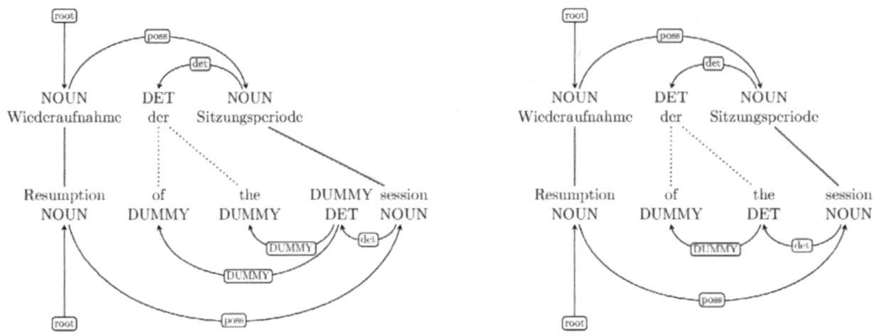

Figure 2: Reduced number of dummy labels in annotation projection as suggested by Tiedemann (2014) (bottom) compared to DCA of Hwa et al. (2005) (top).

parsing using the same setup.

5 Annotation Projection

In annotation projection, we rely on sentence aligned parallel corpora, so-called bitexts. The common setup is that source language data is parsed with a monolingually trained parser and the automatic annotation is then transfered to the target language by mapping labels through word alignment to corresponding target language sentences. The process is illustrated in Figure 3.

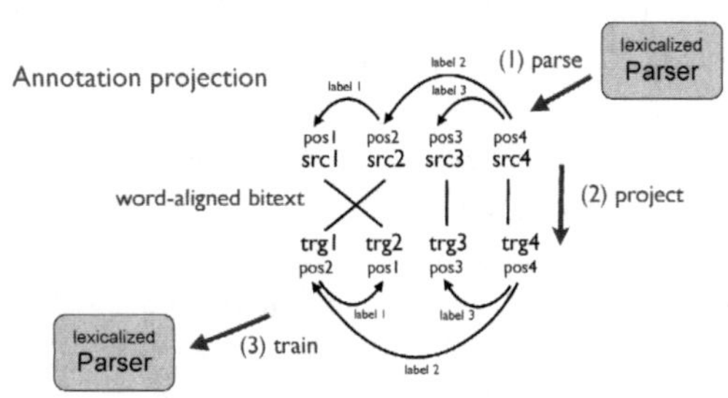

Figure 3: An illustration of annotation projection for cross-lingual dependency parsing.

There are several issues that need to be considered in this approach. First of all, we rely on noisy annotation of the source language which is usually done on out-of-domain data depending on the availability of parallel corpora. Secondly, we require accurate word alignments which are, however, often rather noisy when created automatically especially for non-literal human translations. Finally, we need to define heuristics to treat ambiguous alignments that cannot support one-to-one annotation projection. In our setup, we follow the suggested strategies of Tiedemann (2014), which are based on the projection heuristics proposed by Hwa et al. (2005). The data set that we use is a subset of the parallel Europarl corpus (version 7) which is a widely accepted data set primarily used in statistical machine translation (Koehn, 2005). We use a sample of 40,000 sentences for each language pair and annotate the data with our monolingual source language parsers presented in section 2. For the alignment, we use the symmetrized word alignments that are provided from OPUS (Tiedemann, 2012) that are created with standard statistical alignment tools such as Giza++ (Och and Ney, 2003) and Moses (Koehn et al., 2007). Our projection heuristics follow the direct correspondence assumption (DCA) algorithm of Hwa et al. (2005) but also apply the extensions proposed by Tiedemann (2014) that reduce the number of empty nodes and dummy labels. Figure 2 illustrates the effect of these extensions.

Applying the annotation projection strategy, we obtain the parsing results shown in Table 5. For each language pair, we use the same procedure and the same amount of data taken from Europarl (40,000 sentences).[3]

From the results, we can see that we beat the delexicalized models by a large margin. Some of the language pairs achieve LAS of above 70 which is quite a remarkable result. However, good results are in general only possible for closely related languages such as Spanish, Italian and French whereas more distant languages struggle more (see, for example Czech and Hungarian). For the latter, there is also a strong influence of the rich morphology which is not well supported by the projected information (we only project universal PoS tags and cross-lingually harmonized dependency relations). The results in Table 5 reflect the scores on gold

[3] Unfortunately, we have to leave out Irish as there is no data available in the same collection. The original treebank is, however, so small that the results are not very reliable for this language anyway.

LAS	CS	DE	EN	ES	FI	FR	HU	IT	SV
CS		50.20	47.96	49.17	49.58	46.48	39.34	49.24	46.38
DE	55.08		55.96	63.49	46.90	65.22	48.70	65.40	52.94
EN	57.70	63.31		65.07	48.86	67.48	49.14	68.69	54.01
ES	59.95	60.17	54.02		48.57	66.18	50.09	70.40	50.05
FI	54.67	47.06	45.69	42.37		40.56	41.72	43.06	44.03
FR	58.65	63.75	58.14	69.33	48.61		50.39	70.22	52.56
HU	46.58	48.79	41.07	48.97	40.08	48.23		51.64	38.87
IT	56.80	56.92	52.03	65.76	46.39	64.88	46.42		51.16
SV	51.71	56.37	50.46	59.06	44.51	60.39	46.86	65.15	

Table 5: Cross-lingual parsing with projected annotation (dependency relations and coarse PoS tags). Evaluation with gold PoS labels.

	CS	DE	EN	ES	FI	FR	HU	IT	SV
CS		-4.55	-2.04	-2.34	-2.48	-2.18	-3.71	-1.83	-1.87
DE	-0.71		-2.05	-2.18	-2.51	-1.74	-2.53	-2.15	-2.09
EN	-0.65	-4.43		-2.45	-2.59	-0.92	-2.57	-2.12	-2.18
ES	-1.02	-4.07	-2.08		-2.22	-1.18	-2.79	-1.75	-2.40
FI	-0.54	-3.83	-1.61	-1.41		-1.73	-3.41	-1.72	-1.85
FR	-0.84	-4.01	-2.21	-3.15	-2.70		-3.05	-1.95	-2.14
HU	-0.49	-2.63	-1.15	-1.61	-1.90	-1.67		-1.60	-1.39
IT	-0.77	-3.89	-1.96	-2.45	-3.40	-1.62	-3.78		-1.88
SV	-0.65	-3.53	-1.92	-1.63	-1.98	-2.12	-3.74	-1.43	

	CS	DE	EN	ES	FI	FR	HU	IT	SV
CS		-20.13	-14.71	-12.38	-12.73	-14.07	-14.50	-17.94	-6.37
DE	-15.20		-13.23	-10.34	-13.89	-9.25	-15.53	-9.97	-2.28
EN	-14.60	-14.53		-8.38	-10.85	-8.08	-11.75	-6.50	-0.63
ES	-16.81	-13.12	-10.53		-9.29	-7.22	-17.39	-6.78	-0.96
FI	-24.09	-23.01	-16.81	-18.87		-16.05	-16.55	-20.57	-8.55
FR	-16.13	-12.29	-11.12	-7.52	-11.55		-17.51	-5.79	-1.14
HU	-19.68	-22.76	-15.85	-22.15	-12.61	-20.71		-23.70	-12.15
IT	-17.03	-13.20	-10.18	-9.78	-11.99	-8.37	-15.48		-3.93
SV	-12.08	-10.17	-3.56	-7.00	-6.71	-6.71	-20.73	-10.13	

Table 6: Cross-lingual parsing with **predicted** PoS labels with PoS tagger models trained on verified target language treebanks (left table) and models trained on **projected** treebanks (right table). Differences in LAS compared to the results with gold PoS labels from Table 5.

standard data and the same question as before applies here: What is the drop in performance when replacing gold PoS labels with predicted ones? The answer is in Table 6 (left part). Using automatic annotation leads to substantial drops for most language pairs as expected. However, we can see that the lexicalized models trained through annotation projection are much more robust than the delexicalized transfer models presented earlier. With the drop of up to 3 LAS we are still rather close to the performance on gold annotation.

	CS	DE	EN	ES	FI	FR	HU	IT	SV
CS		70.49	67.59	71.64	79.23	71.47	67.87	72.85	80.96
DE	79.29		74.77	81.36	74.68	83.22	75.06	84.65	80.24
EN	79.22	82.24		83.04	75.08	83.49	76.81	86.97	81.52
ES	79.47	80.03	75.58		75.33	87.86	76.04	90.41	81.58
FI	72.13	62.76	63.03	57.17		58.57	64.76	57.29	69.82
FR	80.99	82.10	76.92	88.26	76.36		76.00	92.41	82.87
HU	70.08	66.48	63.64	66.24	69.45	68.04		67.83	69.43
IT	79.80	80.77	75.14	86.50	75.27	87.37	74.82		80.80
SV	81.25	77.84	74.85	83.39	77.07	83.34	67.97	83.80	

Table 7: Coarse PoS tagger accuracy on test sets from the universal dependencies data set with models trained on projected bitexts.

The experimental results in Table 6 rely on the availability of taggers trained on verified target language annotations. Low resource language may not even have resources for this purpose and, therefore, it is interesting to know if we can even learn PoS taggers from the projected data sets as well. In the following setup, we trained models on the projected data for each language pair to test this scenario. Note that we had to remove all dummy labels and tokens that may appear in the projected data. This procedure certainly corrupts the training data even further and the PoS tagging quality is effected by this noise (see Table 7). Applying cross-lingual parsers trained on the same projected data results in the scores shown in the right part of Table 6. Here, we can see that the models are seriously effected by the low quality provided by the projected PoS taggers. The LAS drops dramatically making any of these models completely useless. This result is, unfortunately, not very encouraging and shows the limitations of direct projection techniques and the importance of proper linguistic knowledge in the target language. Note that we did not spend any time on optimizing projection techniques of PoS annotation but we expect similar drops even with slightly improved cross-lingual methods.

6 Treebank Translation

The possibility of translating treebanks as another strategy for cross-lingual parsing has been proposed by Tiedemann et al. (2014). They apply

LAS	CS	DE	EN	ES	FI	FR	HU	IT	SV
CS		50.37	45.84	49.81	47.36	44.72	36.66	49.53	46.24
DE	55.06		55.89	64.88	42.29	63.95	46.68	66.17	51.76
EN	52.47	61.98		67.20	44.51	67.50	41.58	69.28	56.16
ES	60.40	57.69	54.62		42.60	68.67	30.35	72.39	51.51
FI	49.56	42.98	46.50	36.11		35.39	39.19	37.22	41.45
FR	57.35	61.33	58.12	71.15	42.60		40.33	72.84	51.58
HU	39.89	42.72	38.51	43.16	39.93	39.91		41.74	34.26
IT	58.20	55.60	53.26	68.74	41.95	68.19	39.74		50.62
SV	47.89	55.07	52.86	59.80	42.23	60.64	41.98	66.19	

Table 8: Cross-lingual parsing with translated treebanks; evaluated with gold PoS labels.

	CS	DE	EN	ES	FI	FR	HU	IT	SV
CS		-4.14	-1.72	-1.74	-2.45	-0.90	-3.38	-1.72	-2.42
DE	-0.73		-1.88	-2.54	-1.82	-1.46	-2.53	-2.22	-2.21
EN	-0.48	-4.41		-2.72	-2.85	-0.95	-1.84	-2.00	-2.77
ES	-1.03	-3.51	-2.25		-2.60	-1.22	-1.87	-2.36	-2.31
FI	-0.51	-4.37	-1.99	-1.66		-0.99	-2.68	-1.74	-1.84
FR	-0.98	-3.87	-2.25	-3.45	-2.25		-1.69	-2.11	-1.88
HU	-0.46	-2.73	-1.56	-2.09	-2.39	-0.58		-1.47	-1.57
IT	-0.90	-3.76	-2.55	-2.64	-2.58	-1.81	-2.20		-2.19
SV	-0.50	-3.51	-2.13	-2.39	-2.27	-1.68	-2.42	-1.88	

CS	DE	EN	ES	FI	FR	HU	IT	SV
	-17.74	-11.71	-9.79	-8.65	-10.65	-10.68	-13.23	-4.38
-10.57		-11.25	-11.58	-10.28	-8.55	-11.96	-10.26	-1.46
-13.68	-14.60		-11.02	-8.15	-9.75	-13.54	-10.03	-0.63
-14.91	-11.15	-9.76		-7.86	-6.03	-8.88	-5.62	-2.37
-14.57	-15.92	-14.78	-9.25		-10.88	-12.33	-10.28	-2.15
-14.23	-10.50	-8.72	-7.38	-6.79		-14.27	-4.60	-2.35
-15.29	-15.67	-14.99	-17.35	-13.51	-16.14		-16.19	-9.48
-14.21	-12.07	-8.73	-6.92	-8.24	-5.47	-14.24		-2.04
-7.62	-9.75	-4.44	-8.54	-6.86	-8.80	-19.30	-10.01	

Table 9: Cross-lingual parsing with translated treebanks and **predicted** PoS labels with PoS tagger models trained on verified target language treebanks (left table) and models trained on **projected** treebanks (right table). Differences in LAS compared to the results with gold PoS labels from Table 8.

phrase-based statistical machine translation to the universal dependency treebank (McDonald et al., 2013) and obtain encouraging results. We use a similar setup but apply it to the UD data set testing the approach on a wider range of languages. We follow the general ideas of Tiedemann (2014) and the projection heuristics described there. Our translation models apply a standard setup of a phrase-based SMT framework using the default training pipeline implemented in Moses as well as the Moses decoder with standard settings for translating the raw data sets. We consequently use Europarl data only for all models including language models and translation models. For tuning, we apply 10,000 sentences from a disjoint corpus of movie subtitles taken from OPUS (Tiedemann, 2012). We deliberately use these out-of-domain data sets to tune model parameters in order to avoid domain overfitting. A mixed-domain set would certainly have been even better for this purpose but we have to leave a closer investigation of this effect on treebank translation quality to future work. Similar to the projection approach, we have to drop Irish as there is no training data in Europarl for creating our SMT models.

Translating treebanks can be seen as creating synthetic parallel corpora and the same projection heuristics can be used again to transfer annotation to the target language. The advantage of the approach is that the source language annotation is given and manually verified and that the word alignment is an integral part of statistical machine translation. The general concept of treebank translation is illustrated in Figure 4.

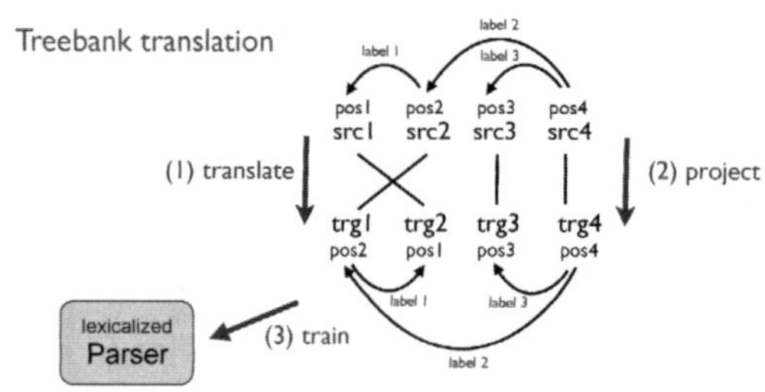

Figure 4: Translating treebanks to project syntactic information.

Applying this approach to the UD data results in the outcome summarized in Table 8. With these experiments, we can confirm the basic findings of related work, i.e. that treebank translation is a valuable alternative to annotation projection on existing parallel data with comparable results and some advantages in certain cases. In general, we can see that more distant languages are worse again mostly due to the lower quality of the basic translation model for those languages.

Similar to the previous approaches, we now test our models with predicted PoS labels. The left part in Table 9 lists the LAS differences when replacing gold annotation with automatic tags. Similar to the annotation projection approach, we can observe drops of around 2 LAS with up to over 4 LAS in some cases. This shows again, that the lexicalized models are much more robust than delexicalized ones and should be preferred when applied in real-world applications.

	CS	DE	EN	ES	FI	FR	HU	IT	SV
CS		72.17	68.80	73.81	80.28	73.72	72.02	77.36	83.27
DE	82.97		77.80	82.65	73.28	84.05	77.23	86.20	81.54
EN	78.84	83.69		83.88	77.21	84.60	74.15	87.04	84.66
ES	82.17	82.56	78.36		76.47	90.66	71.95	92.31	83.00
FI	78.25	67.09	66.70	60.67		61.05	70.80	60.06	72.11
FR	82.02	82.76	78.46	89.23	77.76		75.27	93.52	83.00
HU	71.74	67.62	63.44	65.98	69.35	66.20		68.20	67.97
IT	83.06	81.57	78.50	89.81	76.49	91.80	75.65		83.13
SV	84.62	78.53	75.98	83.97	76.80	83.66	68.74	84.20	

Table 10: Coarse PoS tagger accuracy on test sets from the universal dependencies data set with models trained on translated treebanks.

Finally, we also look at tagger models trained on projected treebanks as well (see Table 10). The parsing results on data sets that have been annotated with those taggers are shown on the right-hand side in Table 9. Not surprisingly, we observe significant drops again in LAS and, similar to annotation projection, all models are seriously damaged by the noisy annotation. Nevertheless, the difference is relatively smaller in most cases when compared to the annotation projection approach. This points to the advantage of treebank translation that makes annotation projection more straightforward due to the tendency of producing rather literal translations that are more straightforward to align than human translations. Surprising is especially the performance of the cross-lingual models from German, English and Italian to Swedish which perform better with projected PoS taggers than with monolingually trained ones. This is certainly unexpected and deserves some additional analyses. Overall, the results are still very mixed and further studies are necessary to investigate the projection quality depending on the cross-lingual parsing approach in more detail.

7 Discussion

Our results illustrate the strong impact of PoS label accuracy on dependency parsing. Our projection techniques are indeed very simple and naive. The performance of the taggers drops significantly when training models on small and noisy data sets such as the projected and translated treebanks. There are techniques that improve cross-lingual PoS tagging using a combination of projection and unsupervised learning (Das and Petrov, 2011). These techniques certainly lead to better parsing performance as shown by McDonald et al. (2011b). Another alternative would be to use the recently proposed models for joint word alignment and annotation projection (Östling, 2015). A thorough comparison with those techniques is beyond the scope of this paper but would also not contribute to the point we would like to make here. Furthermore, looking at the actual scores that we achieve with our directly projected models (see Tables 7 and 10), we can see that the PoS models seem to perform reasonably well with many of them close or above 80% accuracy, which is on par with the advanced models presented by Das and Petrov (2011).

In any case, the main conclusion from our experiments is that reliable PoS tagging is essential for the purpose of dependency parsing especially across languages. To further stress this outcome, we can look at the correlation between PoS tagging accuracy and labeled attachment scores. Figure 5 plots the scores we obtain with our naive direct projection techniques. The graph clearly shows a very strong correlation between both evaluation metrics on our data sets.

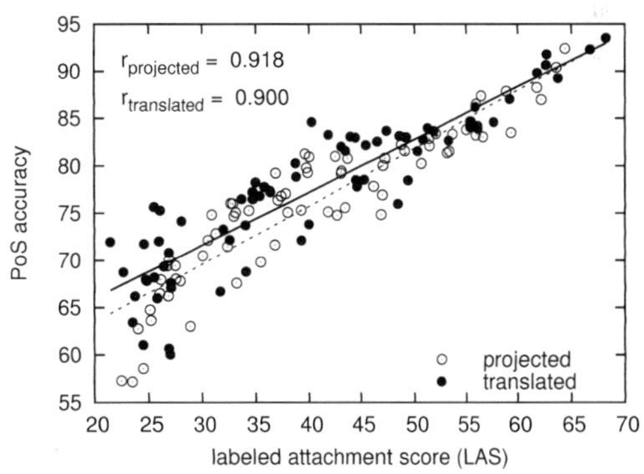

Figure 5: Correlation between PoS tagger accuracy and cross-lingual parsing performance.

Another interesting question is whether the absolute drops we observe in labeled attachment scores are also directly related to the PoS tagging performance. For this, we plot the difference between LAS on test sets with gold PoS labels and test sets with predicted labels in comparison to the PoS tagger performance used for the latter (Figure 6). As we can see, even in this case we can measure a significant (negative) correlation which is, however, not as strong as the overall correlation between PoS tagging and LAS.

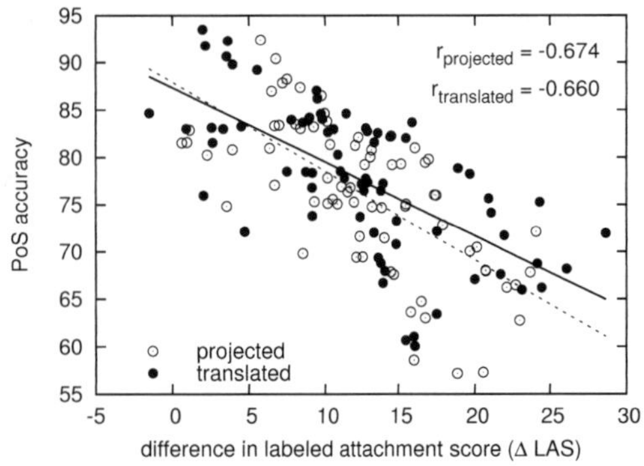

Figure 6: Correlation between PoS tagger accuracy and the **drop** in cross-lingual parsing performance.

Looking at these outcomes, it seems wise to invest some effort in improving PoS tagging performance before blindly trusting any cross-lingual approach to statistical dependency parsing. Hybrid approaches that rely on lexical information, unsupervised learning and annotation projection might be a good strategy for this purpose. Another useful framework could be active learning in which reliable annotation can be created for the induction of robust parser models. We will leave these ideas to future work.

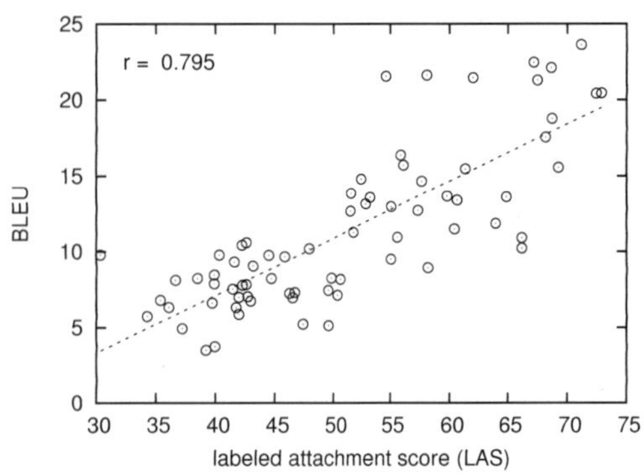

Figure 7: Correlation between translation performance (measured in BLEU) and cross-lingual parsing performance.

Finally, we can also have a look at the correlation between translation performance and cross-lingual parsing. Figure 7 plots the BLEU scores that we obtain on an out-of-domain test set (from the same subtitle corpus we used for tuning) for the phrase-based models that we have trained on Europarl data compared to the labeled attachment scores we achieve with the corresponding models trained on translated treebanks. The figure illustrates a strong correlation between the two metrics even though the results need to be taken with a grain of salt due to the domain mismatch between treebank data and SMT test data, and due to instabilities of BLEU as a general measure of translation performance. Interesting to see is that we obtain competitive results with the translation approach when compared to annotation projection even though the translation performance is really poor in terms of BLEU. Note, however, that the BLEU scores are in general very low due to the significant domain mismatch between training data and test data in the SMT setup.

8 Conclusions

This paper presents a systematic comparison of cross-lingual parsing based on delexicalization, annotation projection and treebank translation on data with harmonized annotation from the universal dependencies project. The main contributions of the paper are the presentations of cross-lingual parsing baselines for this new data set and a detailed discussion about the impact of predicted PoS labels and morphological information. With our empirical results, we demonstrate the importance of reliable features, which becomes apparent when testing models trained on noisy naively projected data. Our results also reveal the serious shortcomings of delexicalization in connection with cross-lingual parsing. Future work includes further investigations of improved annotation projection of morphosyntactic information and the use of multiple languages and prior knowledge about linguistic properties to improve the overall results of cross-lingual dependency parsing. The use of abstract cross-lingual word representations and other target language adaptations for improved model transfer are other ideas that we would like to explore. We would also like to emphasize truly under-resourced languages in further experiments that would require new data sets and manual evaluation. In connection with this we also need to focus on improved models for distant languages that exhibit significant differences in their syntax. Our experiments presented in this paper reveal already that the existing approaches to cross-lingual parsing have severe shortcomings for languages from different language families. However, we are optimistic that new techniques with stronger target language adaptation and improved transfer mechanisms will be able to support even those cases. In order to show this, we will look at downstream applications that can demonstrate the utility of cross-lingual parsing in other areas of NLP and end-user systems.

References

Bernd Bohnet and Jonas Kuhn. 2012. The Best of Both Worlds – A Graph-based Completion Model for Transition-based Parsers. In *Proceedings of EACL*, pages 77–87.

Bernd Bohnet. 2010. Top Accuracy and Fast Dependency Parsing is not a Contradiction. In *Proceedings of COLING*, pages 89–97.

Sabine Buchholz and Erwin Marsi. 2006. CoNLL-X Shared Task on Multilingual Dependency Parsing. In *Proceedings of CoNLL*, pages 149–164.

Dipanjan Das and Slav Petrov. 2011. Unsupervised part-of-speech tagging with bilingual graph-based projections. In *Proceedings of ACL*, pages 600–609.

Marie-Catherine De Marneffe, Bill MacCartney, and Christopher D. Manning. 2006. Generating Typed Dependency Parses from Phrase Structure Parses. In *Proceedings of LREC*, pages 449–454.

Rebecca Hwa, Philip Resnik, Amy Weinberg, Clara Cabezas, and Okan Kolak. 2005. Bootstrapping Parsers via Syntactic Projection across Parallel Texts. *Natural Language Engineering*, 11(3):311–325.

Philipp Koehn, Hieu Hoang, Alexandra Birch, Chris Callison-Burch, Marcello Federico, Nicola Bertoldi, Brooke Cowan, Wade Shen, Christine Moran, Richard Zens, Christopher J. Dyer, Ondřej Bojar, Alexandra Constantin, and Evan Herbst. 2007. Moses: Open Source Toolkit for Statistical Machine Translation. In *Proceedings of ACL*, pages 177–180.

Philipp Koehn. 2005. Europarl: A Parallel Corpus for Statistical Machine Translation. In *Proceedings of MT Summit*, pages 79–86.

Sandra Kübler, Ryan McDonald, and Joakim Nivre. 2009. *Dependency Parsing*. Morgan & Claypool Publishers.

Ryan McDonald, Slav Petrov, and Keith Hall. 2011a. Multi-Source Transfer of Delexicalized Dependency Parsers. In *Proceedings of EMNLP*, pages 62–72.

Ryan McDonald, Slav Petrov, and Keith Hall. 2011b. Multi-source transfer of delexicalized dependency parsers. In *Proceedings EMNLP*, pages 62–72.

Ryan McDonald, Joakim Nivre, Yvonne Quirmbach-Brundage, Yoav Goldberg, Dipanjan Das, Kuzman Ganchev, Keith Hall, Slav Petrov, Hao Zhang, Oscar Täckström, Claudia Bedini, Núria Bertomeu Castelló, and Jungmee Lee. 2013. Universal Dependency Annotation for Multilingual Parsing. In *Proceedings of ACL*, pages 92–97.

Thomas Müller and Hinrich Schütze. 2015. Robust morphological tagging with word representations. In *Proceedings of NAACL*.

Tahira Naseem, Regina Barzilay, and Amir Globerson. 2012. Selective Sharing for Multilingual Dependency Parsing. In *Proceedings of ACL*, pages 629–637.

Joakim Nivre, Johan Hall, Sandra Kübler, Ryan McDonald, Jens Nilsson, Sebastian Riedel, and Deniz Yuret. 2007. The CoNLL 2007 Shared Task on Dependency Parsing. In *Proceedings of the CoNLL Shared Task Session of EMNLP-CoNLL 2007*, pages 915–932.

Franz Josef Och and Hermann Ney. 2003. A Systematic Comparison of Various Statistical Alignment Models. *Computational Linguistics*, 29(1):19–52.

Robert Östling. 2015. *Bayesian Models for Multilingual Word Alignment*. Ph.D. thesis, Stockholm University, Department of Linguistics.

Slav Petrov, Dipanjan Das, and Ryan McDonald. 2012. A Universal Part-of-Speech Tagset. In *Proceedings of LREC*, pages 2089–2096.

Oscar Täckström, Ryan McDonald, and Jakob Uszkoreit. 2012. Cross-lingual Word Clusters for Direct Transfer of Linguistic Structure. In *Proceedings of NAACL*, pages 477–487.

Oscar Täckström, Ryan McDonald, and Joakim Nivre. 2013. Target Language Adaptation of Discriminative Transfer Parsers. In *Proceedings of NAACL*, pages 1061–1071.

Jörg Tiedemann, Željko Agić, and Joakim Nivre. 2014. Treebank Translation for Cross-Lingual Parser Induction. In *Proceedings of CoNLL*, pages 130–140.

Jörg Tiedemann. 2012. Parallel Data, Tools and Interfaces in OPUS. In *Proceedings of LREC*, pages 2214–2218.

Jörg Tiedemann. 2014. Rediscovering Annotation Projection for Cross-Lingual Parser Induction. In *Proceedings of COLING*, pages 1854–1864.

Min Xiao and Yuhong Guo. 2014. Distributed Word Representation Learning for Cross-Lingual Dependency Parsing. In *Proceedings of CoNLL*, pages 119–129.

Daniel Zeman and Philip Resnik. 2008. Cross-Language Parser Adaptation between Related Languages. In *Proceedings of IJCNLP*, pages 35–42.

Exploring Confidence-based Self-training for Multilingual Dependency Parsing in an Under-Resourced Language Scenario

Juntao Yu
University of Birmingham
Birmingham, UK
j.yu.1@cs.bham.ac.uk

Bernd Bohnet
Google
London, UK
bohnetbd@google.com

Abstract

This paper presents a novel self-training approach that we use to explore a scenario which is typical for under-resourced languages. We apply self-training on small multilingual dependency corpora of nine languages. Our approach employs a confidence-based method to gain additional training data from large unlabeled datasets. The method has been shown effective for five languages out of the nine languages of the SPMRL Shared Task 2014 datasets. We obtained the largest absolute improvement of two percentage points on Korean data. Our self-training experiments show improvements upon the best state-of-the-art systems of the SPMRL shared task that employs one parser only.

1 Introduction

The availability of the manually annotated treebanks and state-of-the-art dependency parsers (McDonald and Pereira, 2006; Nivre, 2009; Martins et al., 2010; Goldberg and Elhadad, 2010; Zhang and Nivre, 2011; Bohnet et al., 2013) leads to high accuracy on some languages such as English (Marcus et al., 1994), German (Kübler et al., 2006) and Chinese (Levy and Manning, 2003) that have large manually annotated datasets.

In contrast to resource-rich languages, languages that have less training data show a lower accuracy (Buchholz and Marsi, 2006; Nivre et al., 2007; Seddah et al., 2013; Seddah et al., 2014). Semi-supervised techniques gain popularity as they are able to improve parsing accuracy by exploiting unlabeled data which avoids the cost of labeling new data.

Self-training is one of these appealing techniques that have been successfully used for instance in constituency parsing for English texts (McClosky et al., 2006a; McClosky et al., 2006b; Reichart and Rappoport, 2007; Sagae, 2010) while for dependency parsing this approach was only effective in a few cases, in contrast to co-training which works for dependency parsing well too. In a co-training approach, at least another parser is employed to label additional training data.

McClosky et al. (2006a) used self-training for English constituency parsing. In their approaches, self-training was most effective when the parser is retrained on the combination of the initial training set and the large unlabeled dataset generated by both the generative parser and reranker. This leads to many subsequent applications on English texts via self-training for constituency parsing, cf. (McClosky et al., 2006b; Reichart and Rappoport, 2007; Sagae, 2010; Petrov and McDonald, 2012).

In contrast to English constituency parsing, self-training usually has proved to be less effective or has even shown negative results when applied to dependency parsing, cf. (Kawahara and Uchimoto, 2008; Plank, 2011; Cerisara, 2014; Björkelund et al., 2014). This paper makes the following contributions:

1. We present an effective confidence-based self-training approach.
2. We evaluate our approach on nine languages in a resource-poor parsing scenario.
3. We successfully improved the parsing performances on five languages which are Basque, German, Hungarian, Korean and Swedish.

The remainder of this paper is structured as follows: In Section 2, we discuss related work. In Section 3, we introduce our confidence-based approach to self-training and Section 4 describes the experimental set-up. Section 5 presents the results and contains a discussion of the results. Section 6 presents our conclusions.

Proceedings of the Third International Conference on Dependency Linguistics (Depling 2015), pages 350–358,
Uppsala, Sweden, August 24–26 2015.

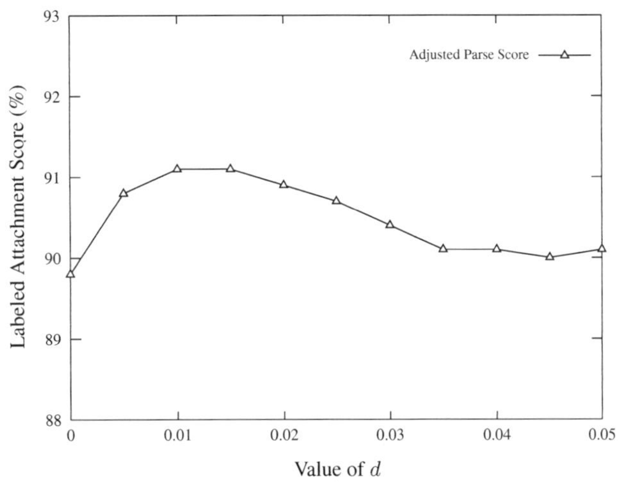

Figure 1: Accuracies of sentences which have a position number within the top 50% after ranking the auto-parsed sentences of development set by the adjusted parse scores with different values of d.

2 Related Work

Most of the reported positive results of self-training are evaluated on constituency parsing of English texts. McClosky et al. (2006a) reported strong results with an improvement of 1.1 F-score using the Charniak-parser, cf. (Charniak and Johnson, 2005). McClosky et al. (2006b) applied the method later on English out-of-domain texts which show good accuracy gains too.

Reichart and Rappoport (2007) showed that self-training can improve the performance of a constituency parser without a reranker when a small training set is used.

Sagae (2010) investigated the contribution of the reranker for a constituency parser. The results suggest that constituency parsers without a reranker can achieve significant improvements, but the results are still higher when a reranker is used.

In the SANCL 2012 shared task self-training was used by most of the constituency-based systems, cf. (Petrov and McDonald, 2012), which includes the top ranked system, this indicates that self-training is already an established technique to improve the accuracy of constituency parsing on English out-of-domain data, cf. (Le Roux et al., 2012). However, none of the dependency-based systems used self-training in the SANCL 2012 shared task.

One of the few successful approaches to self-training for dependency parsing was introduced by Chen et al. (2008). Chen et al. (2008) improved the unlabeled attachment score about one percentage point for Chinese. Chen et al. (2008) added sub-trees that span only over a few words, which means they have only short dependency edges. It is known that dependencies of short length have a higher accuracy than longer ones, cf. (McDonald and Nivre, 2007). Kawahara and Uchimoto (2008) used a separately trained binary classifier to select sentences as additional training data. Their approach improved the unlabeled accuracy of English texts in Chemical domain by about 0.5%.

Plank (2011) applied self-training with single and multiple iterations for parsing of Dutch using the Alpino parser (Malouf and Noord, 2004), which was modified to produce dependency trees. She found self-training produces only a slight improvement in some cases but worsened when more unlabeled data was added.

Cerisara (2014) and Björkelund et al. (2014) applied self-training to dependency parsing on nine languages. Cerisara (2014) found negative impacts only when they apply a basic self-training approach to a dependency parser. Similarly, Björkelund et al. (2014) observed a positive effect on Swedish only.

Recently, Dredze et al. (2008) and Crammer et al. (2009) introduced **confidence-based** learning methods that are able to measure the prediction quality. Their technique has been applied for a sequence labeling and a dependency parser which both use online-learning algorithms, cf. (Mejer

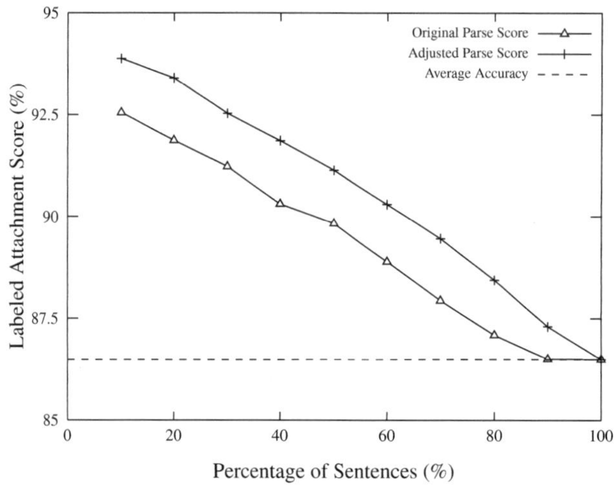

Figure 2: The accuracies when inspecting 10-100% sentences of the development set ranked by the confidence-based methods.

and Crammer, 2010; Mejer and Crammer, 2012). They evaluated several confidence-based methods and the empirical results showed that the confidence scores generated by some methods are highly relevant to the prediction accuracy, i.e. higher confidence is correlated with high accuracy scores.

The work most close to our approach is introduced by Goutam and Ambati (2011), who applied a multi-iteration self-training approach to improving Hindi in-domain parsing. In each iteration, they add 1,000 additional sentences to a small initial training set (2,972 sentences), the additional sentences are selected due to their parse scores. They improved the baseline by up to 0.7% and 0.4% for labeled and unlabeled attachment scores after 23 self-training iterations.

Our approach differs in three aspects from that of Goutam and Ambati (2011): We employ a single iteration self-training rather than multiple iterations. We add larger amounts of additional parsed unlabeled sentences to the initial training set for retraining and we applied our method in an under-resourced language scenario to nine languages.

3 Self-training

The hypotheses for our experiments is that the selection of high-quality dependency trees is a crucial precondition for the successful use of self-training in dependency parsing. Therefore, we explore a confidence-based method to select high-quality dependency trees from newly parsed sentences. Our self-training approach consists of a single iteration with the following steps:

1. A parser is trained on a (small) initial training set to generate a base model.
2. We analyze a large number of unlabeled sentences with the base model.
3. We build a new training set consisting of the initial training set and 50%[1] newly analyzed sentences parsed with a high confidence.
4. We retrain the parser on the new training set to produce a self-trained model.
5. Finally, the self-trained model is used to annotate the test set.

We use the freely available Mate tools[2] to implement the self-training approach. This tool set contains a part-of-speech (PoS) tagger, morphologic tagger, lemmatizer, graph-based parser and an arc-standard transition-based parser. The arc-standard transition-based parser has the option to use a graph-based model to rescore the beam which seems to be a sort-of reranking (Bohnet and Kuhn, 2012). The parser has further the option to use a joint tagging and parsing model with the

[1]We use 50% due to previous experiments on English that showed an optimal performance when adding 50% parsed sentences to the training set.

[2]https://code.google.com/p/mate-tools/

joint inference that improves both part-of-speech tagging and parsing accuracy.

We use the arc-standard transition-based parser employing beam search and a graph-based rescoring model. This parser computes a score for each dependency tree by summing up the scores for each transition and dividing the score by the total number of transitions, due to the swap-operation (used for non-projective parsing), the number of transition can vary, cf. (Kahane et al., 1998; Nivre, 2007).

For our self-training approach, we use the parse scores as confidence measure to select sentences. We observed that although the original parse score is the averaged value of a sequence of transitions of a parse, long sentences generally exhibit a higher score. Therefore, the score does not correlate well with the Labeled Attachment Score (LAS) as shown in Figure 2. Thus, we adjusted the score of the parser to maximize the correlation between the parse score and the labeled attachment score for each parse tree by subtracting the sentence length (L) multiplied by a fixed number d. The new parse scores are calculated as follow:

$$Score_{adjusted} = Score_{original} - L \times d \quad (1)$$

To obtain the constant d, we apply the defined formula with different values for d to all sentences of the development set and rank the sentences by their adjusted scores in a descending order. Let $No(i)$ be the position number of the i_{th} sentence after ranking them by the adjusted scores. The value of d is selected to maximize the accuracy of sentences that have a $No(i)$ within the top 50%. We evaluate stepwise different values of d from 0 to 0.05 with an increment of 0.005. The highest accuracy of the top ranked sentences is achieved when $d = 0.015$ (see Figure 1), thus d is set to 0.015 in our experiments. Figure 2 shows the accuracies when inspecting 10 -100% of sentences ranked by the adjusted and original parse scores. We found that the adjusted parse scores lead to a higher correlation with the accuracy of the parsed sentences compared to the original parse scores.

4 Experimental Set-up

We evaluate our approach on nine languages available from 2014 Shared Task at the Workshop on Statistical Parsing of Morphologically Rich Languages (SPMRL), cf. (Seddah et al., 2013; Seddah et al., 2014). We have chosen the datasets as they provide smaller data sets of 5k sentences for each language of the SPMRL shared task which are a good basis for our exploration for improving parsing accuracy of under-resourced languages and the shared task provides competitive results for these languages from the participants of the shared task that provides us strong accuracy scores against which we can compare our results.

Further, the organizers of the SPMRL shared task provided sufficient unlabeled data that are required for self-training. More precisely, for all language, we use as our initial training set the 5k datasets, we test on test sets available from the shared task and use a 100k SPMRL unlabeled data for each of the languages. We use the German development set (5,000 sentences) when tuning the fixed value d that was mentioned in Section 3. Table 1 shows statistics about the corpora that we use in our experiments.

As previously noted, the Mate transition-based dependency parser with default settings is used in our experiments, cf. (Bohnet et al., 2013). We use the parser's internal tagger to supply the part-of-speech for both unlabeled data and test data. The baselines are generated by training the parser on initial training data and testing the parser on the described test sets.

For the evaluation of the parser's accuracy, we report labeled attachment scores (LAS). In line with the SPMRL shared task evaluation, we include all punctuation marks in the evaluation.

For significance testing, we take Dan Bikel's randomized parsing evaluation comparator that was used by the CoNLL 2007 shared task with the default settings of 10,000 iterations (Nivre et al., 2007). The statistically significant results are marked due to their p-values (*) p-value<0.05, (**) p-value<0.01.

5 Results and Discussion

We evaluate our self-training approach on the test sets of nine languages. The unlabeled data was parsed and ranked by the confidence scores. Then we selected the 50k top ranked sentences and added those to the training sets.

The empirical results show that our approach worked for five languages which are Basque, German, Hungarian, Korean and Swedish. Our self-training method achieves the largest improvement on Korean with an absolute gain of 2.14 percent-

	Arabic	Basque	French	German	Hebrew
train:					
Sentences	5,000	5,000	5,000	5,000	5,000
Tokens	224,907	61,905	150,984	87,841	128,046
Avg. Length	44.98	12.38	30.19	17.56	25.60
test:					
Sentences	1,959	946	2,541	5,000	716
Tokens	73,878	11,457	75,216	92,004	16,998
Avg. Length	37.71	12.11	29.60	18.40	23.74
unlabeled:					
Sentences	100,000	100,000	100,000	100,000	100,000
Tokens	4,340,695	1,785,474	1,618,324	1,962,248	2,776,500
Avg. Length	43.41	17.85	16.18	19.62	27.77
	Hungarian	**Korean**	**Polish**	**Swedish**	
train:					
Sentences	5,000	5,000	5,000	5,000	
Tokens	109,987	68,336	52,123	76,357	
Avg. Length	21.99	13.66	10.42	15.27	
test:					
Sentences	1,009	2,287	822	666	
Tokens	19,908	33,766	8,545	10,690	
Avg. Length	19.73	14.76	10.39	16.05	
unlabeled:					
Sentences	100,000	100,000	100,000	100,000	
Tokens	1,913,154	2,147,605	2,024,323	1,575,868	
Avg. Length	19.13	21.48	20.24	15.76	

Table 1: Statistics about the corpora that we used in our experiments for the training set, test set and the unlabeled datasets for our multilingual evaluations, cf. (Seddah et al., 2014).

	Baseline	**Self-train**	**LORIA**
Arabic	82.09	**82.22**	81.65
Basque	78.35	79.22**	**81.39**
French	**81.91**	81.48	81.74
German	81.54	81.87**	**83.35**
Hebrew	78.86	**79.04**	75.55
Hungarian	83.13	**83.56***	82.88
Korean	73.31	**75.45****	74.15
Polish	**81.97**	81.35	79.95
Swedish	79.67	**80.26**	80.04
Average	80.09	**80.49**	80.08

Table 2: The table shows the results obtained for the languages of the SPMRL Shared Task 2014. The first column (Baseline) shows the results of our baseline parser (Mate), the second column shows the self-training experiments (Self-train) and the final column provides the results of the best non-ensemble system in the SPMRL Shared Task (LORIA).

age points. We also gain statistically significant improvements on Basque, German and Hungarian. Our self-training gains on these languages are 0.87%, 0.33% and 0.42% respectively.

We achieve an improvement of 0.59% on Swedish which is relatively high absolute improvement while it was not a statistically significant with a p-value of 0.067. To confirm the effectiveness of our method on Swedish, we further evaluate our method on the Swedish development set[3] (494 sentences).

Our self-training method achieves an accuracy of 76.16%*, which is 0.82 percentage points better than our baseline (75.34%). This improvement was statistically significant.

In terms of the effect of our method on other languages, our method gains moderate improvements on Arabic and Hebrew but these were not statistically significant accuracy gains. We found negative results for French and Polish. Table 2 shows a detailed evaluation of our self-training experiments.

We compare our self-training results with the best results of non- ensemble parsing system of SPMRL shared tasks (Seddah et al., 2013; Seddah et al., 2014). The average accuracy of our baseline on nine languages is same as the one achieved by the best single parser system of SPMRL 2014 shared task (Cerisara, 2014), their system employs LDA clusters (Chrupala, 2011) to exploit unlabeled data as well.

Our self-training results is on average 0.41% higher than those of Cerisara (2014). Our self-training method performs better on six languages (Arabic, Hebrew, Hungarian, Korean, Polish and Swedish) compared to the best non-ensemble system.

The confidence scores have shown to be crucial for the successful application of self-training for dependency parsing. In contrast to constituency parsing, self-training for dependency parsing does not work without this additional confidence-based selection step. The question about a possible reason for the different behavior of self-training in dependency parsing and in constituency parsing remains open and only speculative answers could be given. We plan to investigate this further in future.

Self-training behaves somewhat different from co-training in that co-training seems to be able to exploit the differences in the parse trees produced by two or more parsers. While self-training relies on a single parser due to its definition, co-training uses at least another parser what is the main difference to self-training. Co-training does not employ in its most simple form selection, but confidence helps in a co-training scenario too since selecting those dependency trees for retraining on which two or more parsers agree improves further the accuracy. Hence, confidence-based methods is a more effective for co-training, cf. (Blum and Mitchell, 1998; Sarkar, 2001; Steedman et al., 2003).

An open question remains why for some of the languages the approach did not work. In future work, we want to address this question. A first observation is that the quality of the unlabeled data

[3]We did not use the Swedish development set for tuning in our experiments.

might have an effect. For instance, the average length of unlabeled data of Polish and French is different from that of the training and test set for these languages.

6 Conclusions

In this paper, we present an effective confidence-based self-training approach for multilingual dependency parsing. We evaluated our approach on nine languages in a scenario for under-resourced languages when only a small amount of training data is available.

We apply the same setting for all language by retraining the parser on the new training set that consists of the initial training set and the top 50k ranking parse trees from the 100k parsed sentences of the unlabeled data.

As a result, our approach successfully improves the accuracies of five languages which are Basque, German, Hungarian, Korean and Swedish without tuning variables for individual language. We can report the largest accuracy gain of 2.14% on Korean, on average we improve the baselines of five languages by 0.87%. Previous work that apply self-training to dependency parsing showed often negative results (Plank, 2011; Cerisara, 2014) or was evaluated on one language only (Chen et al., 2008; Goutam and Ambati, 2011; Björkelund et al., 2014).

This is to the best of our knowledge the first time that self-training is found effective for a number of languages. In addition, our self-training results are better than the best reported results generated from a non-ensemble system that used LDA clusters, cf. Cerisara (2014).

Finally, our approach contributes a novel confidence-based self-training method that is able to access the parse quality of unlabeled data and to carry out a pre-selection of the parsed sentences. We conclude that self-training based on confidence is worth using in an under-resourced language scenario and that a confidence-based self-training approach seems to be crucial for the successful application of self-training in dependency parsing. This paper underlines the finding that the pre-selection of parsed dependency trees from unlabeled sources is probably a precondition for the effectivity of self-training and leads additionally to a higher accuracy gain.

References

Anders Björkelund, Özlem Çetinoğlu, Agnieszka Faleńska, Richárd Farkas, Thomas Mueller, Wolfgang Seeker, and Zsolt Szántó. 2014. The IMS-Wrocław-Szeged-CIS entry at the SPMRL 2014 Shared Task: Reranking and Morphosyntax meet Unlabeled Data. In *Proc. of the Shared Task on Statistical Parsing of Morphologically Rich Languages*.

Avrim Blum and Tom Mitchell. 1998. Combining labeled and unlabeled data with co-training. In *Proceedings of the Workshop on Computational Learning Theory (COLT)*, pages 92–100.

Bernd Bohnet and Jonas Kuhn. 2012. The best of both worlds – a graph-based completion model for transition-based parsers. In *Proceedings of the 13th Conference of the European Chpater of the Association for Computational Linguistics (EACL)*, pages 77–87.

Bernd Bohnet, Joakim Nivre, Igor Boguslavsky, Richárd Farkas Filip Ginter, and Jan Hajic. 2013. Joint morphological and syntactic analysis for richly inflected languages. *Transactions of the Associtation for Computational Linguistics*, 1.

Sabine Buchholz and Erwin Marsi. 2006. CoNLL-X shared task on multilingual dependency parsing. In *Proceedings of the 10th Conference on Computational Natural Language Learning (CoNLL)*, pages 149–164.

Christophe Cerisara. 2014. Semi-supervised experiments at LORIA for the SPMRL 2014 Shared Task. In *Proc. of the Shared Task on Statistical Parsing of Morphologically Rich Languages*, Dublin, Ireland, August.

Eugene Charniak and Mark Johnson. 2005. Coarse-to-fine n-best parsing and maxent discriminative reranking. In *Proceedings of the 43rd Annual Meeting on Association for Computational Linguistics*, ACL '05, pages 173–180, Stroudsburg, PA, USA. Association for Computational Linguistics.

Wenliang Chen, Youzheng Wu, and Hitoshi Isahara. 2008. Learning reliable information for dependency parsing adaptation. In *Proceedings of the 22nd International Conference on Computational Linguistics-Volume 1*, pages 113–120. Association for Computational Linguistics.

Grzegorz Chrupala. 2011. Efficient induction of probabilistic word classes with LDA. In *Proceedings of 5th International Joint Conference on Natural Language Processing*, pages 363–372. Asian Federation of Natural Language Processing.

Koby Crammer, Alex Kulesza, and Mark Dredze. 2009. Adaptive regularization of weight vectors. In *Advances in Neural Information Processing Systems*, pages 414–422.

Mark Dredze, Koby Crammer, and Fernando Pereira. 2008. Confidence-weighted linear classification. In *Proceedings of the 25th international conference on Machine learning*, pages 264–271. ACM.

Yoav Goldberg and Michael Elhadad. 2010. An efficient algorithm for easy-first non-directional dependency parsing. In *Human Language Technologies: The 2010 Annual Conference of the North American Chapter of the Association for Computational Linguistics (NAACL HLT)*, pages 742–750.

Rahul Goutam and Bharat Ram Ambati. 2011. Exploring self training for hindi dependency parsing. In *Proceedings of the 5th International Joint Conference on Natural Language Processing*, volume 2, pages 22–69.

Sylvain Kahane, Alexis Nasr, and Owen Rambow. 1998. Pseudo-projectivity: A polynomially parsable non-projective dependency grammar. In *Proceedings of the 36th Annual Meeting of the Association for Computational Linguistics (ACL) and the 17th International Conference on Computational Linguistics (COLING)*, pages 646–652.

Daisuke Kawahara and Kiyotaka Uchimoto. 2008. Learning reliability of parses for domain adaptation of dependency parsing. In *IJCNLP*, volume 8.

Sandra Kübler, Erhard W. Hinrichs, and Wolfgang Maier. 2006. Is it really that difficult to parse German? In *Proceedings of the Conference on Empirical Methods in Natural Language Processing (EMNLP)*.

Joseph Le Roux, Jennifer Foster, Joachim Wagner, Rasul Samad Zadeh Kaljahi, and Anton Bryl. 2012. Dcu-paris13 systems for the sancl 2012 shared task.

Roger Levy and Christopher Manning. 2003. Is it harder to parse Chinese, or the Chinese Treebank? In *Proceedings of the 41st Annual Meeting of the Association for Computational Linguistics (ACL)*, pages 439–446.

Robert Malouf and Gertjan Noord. 2004. Wide coverage parsing with stochastic attribute value grammars. In *In Proc. of IJCNLP-04 Workshop Beyond Shallow Analyses*.

Mitchell P. Marcus, Beatrice Santorini, Mary Ann Marcinkiewicz, Robert MacIntyre, Ann Bies, Mark Ferguson, Karen Katz, and Britta Schasberger. 1994. The Penn Treebank: Annotating predicate-argument structure. In *Proceedings of the ARPA Human Language Technology Workshop*, pages 114–119.

André FT Martins, Noah A Smith, Eric P Xing, Pedro MQ Aguiar, and Mário AT Figueiredo. 2010. Turbo parsers: Dependency parsing by approximate variational inference. In *Proceedings of the 2010 Conference on Empirical Methods in Natural Language Processing*, pages 34–44. Association for Computational Linguistics.

David McClosky, Eugene Charniak, and Mark Johnson. 2006a. Effective self-training for parsing. In *Proceedings of the Human Language Technology Conference of the NAACL, Main Conference*, pages 152–159.

David McClosky, Eugene Charniak, and Mark Johnson. 2006b. Reranking and self-training for parser adaptation. In *Proceedings of the 21st International Conference on Computational Linguistics and the 44th annual meeting of the Association for Computational Linguistics*, pages 337–344. Association for Computational Linguistics.

Ryan McDonald and Joakim Nivre. 2007. Characterizing the errors of data-driven dependency parsing models. In *Proceedings of the 2007 Joint Conference on Empirical Methods in Natural Language Processing and Computational Natural Language Learning (EMNLP-CoNLL)*, pages 122–131.

Ryan McDonald and Fernando Pereira. 2006. Online learning of approximate dependency parsing algorithms. In *Proceedings of the 11th Conference of the European Chapter of the Association for Computational Linguistics (EACL)*, pages 81–88.

Avihai Mejer and Koby Crammer. 2010. Confidence in structured-prediction using confidence-weighted models. In *Proceedings of the 2010 conference on empirical methods in natural language processing*, pages 971–981. Association for Computational Linguistics.

Avihai Mejer and Koby Crammer. 2012. Are you sure?: Confidence in prediction of dependency tree edges. In *Proceedings of the 2012 Conference of the North American Chapter of the Association for Computational Linguistics: Human Language Technologies*, NAACL HLT '12, pages 573–576, Stroudsburg, PA, USA. Association for Computational Linguistics.

Joakim Nivre, Johan Hall, Sandra Kübler, Ryan McDonald, Jens Nilsson, Sebastian Riedel, and Deniz Yuret. 2007. The CoNLL 2007 shared task on dependency parsing. In *Proceedings of the CoNLL Shared Task of EMNLP-CoNLL 2007*, pages 915–932.

Joakim Nivre. 2007. Incremental non-projective dependency parsing. In *Proceedings of Human Language Technologies: The Annual Conference of the North American Chapter of the Association for Computational Linguistics (NAACL HLT)*, pages 396–403.

Joakim Nivre. 2009. Non-projective dependency parsing in expected linear time. In *Proceedings of the Joint Conference of the 47th Annual Meeting of the ACL and the 4th International Joint Conference on Natural Language Processing of the AFNLP: Volume 1-Volume 1*, pages 351–359. Association for Computational Linguistics.

Slav Petrov and Ryan McDonald. 2012. Overview of the 2012 shared task on parsing the web. In *Notes of the First Workshop on Syntactic Analysis of Non-Canonical Language (SANCL)*, volume 59.

Barbara Plank. 2011. *Domain Adaptation for Parsing*. Ph.d. thesis, University of Groningen.

Roi Reichart and Ari Rappoport. 2007. Self-training for enhancement and domain adaptation of statistical parsers trained on small datasets. In *ACL*, volume 7, pages 616–623.

Kenji Sagae. 2010. Self-training without reranking for parser domain adaptation and its impact on semantic role labeling. In *Proceedings of the 2010 Workshop on Domain Adaptation for Natural Language Processing*, pages 37–44. Association for Computational Linguistics.

Anoop Sarkar. 2001. Applying co-training methods to statistical parsing. In *Proceedings of the Second Meeting of the North American Chapter of the Association for Computational Linguistics (NAACL)*, pages 175–182.

Djamé Seddah, Reut Tsarfaty, Sandra Kübler, Marie Candito, Jinho D. Choi, Richárd Farkas, Jennifer Foster, Iakes Goenaga, Koldo Gojenola Galletebeitia, Yoav Goldberg, Spence Green, Nizar Habash, Marco Kuhlmann, Wolfgang Maier, Joakim Nivre, Adam Przepiórkowski, Ryan Roth, Wolfgang Seeker, Yannick Versley, Veronika Vincze, Marcin Woliński, Alina Wróblewska, and Eric Villemonte de la Clergerie. 2013. Overview of the SPMRL 2013 shared task: A cross-framework evaluation of parsing morphologically rich languages. In *Proceedings of the Fourth Workshop on Statistical Parsing of Morphologically-Rich Languages*, pages 146–182, Seattle, Washington, USA, October. Association for Computational Linguistics.

Djamé Seddah, Sandra Kübler, and Reut Tsarfaty. 2014. Introducing the SPMRL 2014 shared task on parsing morphologically-rich languages. In *Proceedings of the First Joint Workshop on Statistical Parsing of Morphologically Rich Languages and Syntactic Analysis of Non-Canonical Languages*, pages 103–109, Dublin, Ireland, August. Dublin City University.

Mark Steedman, Rebecca Hwa, Miles Osborne, and Anoop Sarkar. 2003. Corrected co-training for statistical parsers. In *Proceedings of the International Conference on Machine Learning (ICML)*, pages 95–102.

Yue Zhang and Joakim Nivre. 2011. Transition-based parsing with rich non-local features. In *Proceedings of the 49th Annual Meeting of the Association for Computational Linguistics (ACL)*.

Author Index